SOCIAL PSYCHOLOGY

SOCIAL PSYCHOLOGY
A CONTEMPORARY APPROACH

LOUIS A. PENNER
Department of Psychology, University of South Florida

In collaboration with
STEPHEN L. COHEN and BETH C. STEARNS

New York   OXFORD UNIVERSITY PRESS   1978

Copyright © 1978 by Oxford University Press, Inc.

Printed in the United States of America

Library of Congress Cataloging in Publication Data

Penner, Louis, 1943–
  Social psychology.

  Bibliography: p.
  Includes index.
  1. Social psychology.   I. Title.
HM251.P413   301.1   77-28331
ISBN 0-19-502394-3

Second printing, 1979

Permission to reprint is gratefully acknowledged:

From *My Lai 4* by Seymour M. Hersh. Copyright © 1970 by Seymour M. Hersh. Reprinted by permission of Random House, Inc.

From the *Thematic Apperception Test* by Henry A. Murray, Cambridge Mass.: Harvard University Press, Copyright © by the President and Fellows of Harvard College; ©1971 by Henry A. Murray. Reprinted by permission of the publishers.

From *Motivating Economic Achievement* by David C. McClelland and David G. Winter. Copyright © 1969 by Macmillan Publishing Co., Inc. Reprinted by permission.

From *My Life in the Mafia* by Vincent Teresa. Copyright © 1975 by Vincent Teresa and Thomas C. Renner. Reprinted by permission of Doubleday & Company, Inc.

From "The Story Behind the Dirty Harry Killings" by Bob Greene. Copyright 1977 Field Enterprises, Inc. Courtesy of Field Newspaper Syndicate.

From *The Sixteenth Round* by Rubin "Hurricane" Carter. Copyright © 1974 by Rubin "Hurricane" Carter. Reprinted by permission of the Viking Press Inc.

From the *Value Survey* by Milton Rokeach. Copyright © 1967 by Milton Rokeach. Reprinted by permission of the author.

From *Serpico* by Peter Maas. Copyright © 1973 by Peter Maas and Tsampa Company, Inc. Reprinted by permission of the Viking Press Inc.

From *Alive: The Story of the Andes Survivors* by Piers Paul Read. Copyright © 1974 by Piers Paul Read. Reprinted by permission of J.B. Lippincott Company.

PREFACE

To the student

If you are reading this preface, I would be greatly surprised. In the nine years I was in college, I developed a deep fear of and suspicion about classmates who read prefaces to books. They struck me as the type of people who really believed that if they tore those tags off of pillows (the ones that say "Do not remove under penalty of law"), they would be arrested. But despite my worries, I'll try to reward you for your interest by being brief.

In writing this book, I had two goals. The first was to make the materials as understandable as possible and to provide you with a check on how well I did so. For these reasons, I decided to do the following:

1. Each chapter begins with an overview which tells what the chapter covers.

2. In each chapter, the important concepts are italicized.

3. At appropriate places in each chapter, there are self-administered quizzes designed to test your comprehension of these concepts.

4. Each quiz consists of eight to fifteen questions. If you cannot answer a question or answer it incorrectly, the correct answer can be found on the page given after each question. If you look for the italicized concepts and use the tests, you will be aided greatly in understanding the material.

My second goal was to be as interesting as possible. (Such a goal, while admirable, is hardly unique. Can you imagine a textbook whose author intended to bore you?) To this end, I attempted to relate the material to real-life events whenever possible. This resulted in a number of hypothetical examples and quotations from nonpsychological sources. These could be skipped over without any appreciable loss in understanding the material. However, I hope you will take the time to read them. At least for me, they made some seemingly dry theory and research come alive. Social psychology is an interesting, important, and challenging field. I hope I've been able to communicate that to you.

Two final points. At certain places in the text, you will find that my own beliefs, attitudes, and values may color the conclusions I draw about some social psychological phenomenon. It is difficult to avoid this in writing about social psychology. If I offend you, I apologize. If you disagree with my views, that's great. To challenge one another's ideas is the core of the educational process. Lest you think that this book is purely political propaganda, let me quickly add that as far as I am aware, my own political attitudes did not influence the choice of material. I have tried to reflect current theory and research in social psychology in an accurate and complete manner.

Second, I want to mention the use of personal pronouns. In those cases where a person's sex was not clearly specified, I tried to use feminine and masculine pronouns an equal number of times. This practice is based on the growing awareness among authors of the male-oriented nature of most textbooks. Since women comprise slightly over half the population on earth, it seems reasonable that at least half the "persons" in this book should be females.

I hope you will enjoy this book and learn from it. I'd be quite interested in your reactions. If you care to, you can write me at: Department of Psychology, University of South Florida, Tampa, Florida, 33620.

To the instructor

My goal in writing this book was to provide an overview of social psychology for students with a relatively limited background in psychology. While it would be desirable for a student to have had a prior introductory psychology course, it is not necessary. Where I felt a student with a limited background might not grasp a certain concept, I have reviewed the basic material needed. For example, in discussing the development of individual differences in aggression and pro-social behavior, I have included a brief overview of classical and operant conditioning.

An ancillary goal was to produce a book which could be used during a three- to four-month academic term without overwhelming the student. As a result, this book is not an exhaustive review of social psychology. When discussing some topic, I have used one illustrative study rather than a large number of related studies. Thus, this book is probably not appropriate for a graduate course in social psychology. At the same time, I believe that I have adequately covered the important areas of the discipline. While trying to make the material simple, I believe I have avoided the pitfalls of oversimplification.

A word about the organization and theoretical orientation of the book. In eight years of teaching social psychology, I have yet to find a book whose organization was satisfactory to me. Thus, I have few illusions about the percentage of my colleagues who will totally accept mine. (My belief is that if you put two social psychologists together, they would arrive at five perfectly valid organizational schemes.) While I feel that the first two chapters are necessary prerequisites, the balance of the book could be used in almost any sequence. For example, you might wish to present social influence before attitudes or interpersonal behavior just before small groups. To facilitate flexibility, I have tried to make each chapter stand on its own. In those instances where I used a term from another chapter, I either redefined the term or told the reader where it was presented.

With regard to my orientation to social psychology, there are two clear points of view expressed in the text. The first is based on my acceptance of Kenneth Gergen's and William McGuire's critiques of the traditional experimental, laboratory form of social psychology. Like Gergen and McGuire, I believe that the simple univariate approach to complex social phenomena has some serious weaknesses. Thus, I have attempted to provide the reader with the rudiments of a multivariate approach to social psychology, and have repeatedly stressed the complexity of the phenomena social psychologists study. This may create more ambiguity about social psychology than many would desire, but I believe it is a valid approach.

The second point of view concerns the utility of an interactionist approach to social psychology. My training, research endeavors, and a number of conversations with C. D. Spielberger have convinced me that to present social psychological theory and research adequately, the effect of *both* personality and situational variables on social behavior must be considered. As a result, I have probably included more on personality variables than is typical in a social psychology textbook.

I sincerely hope that you will find the book a useful adjunct to the teaching of social psychology.

To my Friends

Anyone who thinks that a textbook can be completed by one person without the aid of friends and colleagues is sadly mistaken. Thus, I must thank a number of people for their help. Although their contributions vary, all of the people mentioned below have been instrumental in enabling me to finish this manuscript.

Starting at the beginning, I would like to thank James H. Davis and Milton Rokeach for their guidance when I was a graduate student. They were invaluable mentors, and I have benefited greatly from knowing them. Stephen Cohen and Beth Stearns were valuable contributors to this book, in terms of both their expertise and their writing skills. Further, they were cooperative, congenial collaborators who were willing to put up with my innumerable demands on them. Don Stein, Lynn Summers, John Perrachione, and Paul Spector all read portions of the book and made extremely helpful suggestions as to how it could be improved. Len Pace, the former psychology editor at Williams and Wilkins, and Marc Boggs and Ellie Fuchs at Oxford University Press, were of great help during the writing of this book. Lynne Gardner did a superb job as the primary typist. Mary Allman, Linda Fry, and Nancy Shaw also typed later versions. Any person who has to read my handwriting and correct my grammatical errors should be given some sort of medal.

Carlos Garcia Lorenzo, John Perrachione, and Richard Taylor were extremely helpful in the selection and production of the photographs which appear in this book.

I am especially grateful to Helen Greenberg, who copy-edited the book. She is a talented, pleasant, and cooperative individual. She taught me more about writing than I taught her about social psychology.

There are two other people without whom I would never have completed this book. The first is Max Dertke, who helped me with several chapters. But his contribution extends far beyond the time he spent struggling with my prose. Max helped me to teach and write when I believed I could do neither. My wife, Rusty's, contribution cannot be adequately described. She always encouraged me. She read the manuscript, edited it, and helped me change it for the better. She tolerated almost three years of dull weekends while I worked on the book. But most of all, during a period of my life when I gave up on myself, she didn't. And, oh yes, I want to thank our son, Charlie, for making me laugh when I came home.

L.A.P.

Tampa, Florida
June 1978

CONTENTS

To Rusty, Charlie, and Max

UCTION TO SOCIAL PSYCHOLOGY

Stephen L. Cohen.

will

lems
. As you
notice
terms or
es
ing of

Carlos Garcia-Lozano

This book is probably your first exposure to social psychology. Therefore, it is important to begin by describing what social psychologists do. Then we turn to how they do it—that is, how research is conducted. After the mid-chapter quiz, the problems social psychologists encounter will be discussed. As read this and the subsequent chapters, you will words which are italicized. These are important concepts, and you should note them. The quizzes throughout the book will test your understanding these terms and concepts.

WHAT IS SOCIAL PSYCHOLOGY?

Social psychology is the scientific study of the influence process. It attempts to understand, explain, and predict how the presence of another person, a group of people, and environmental factors influence a person's thoughts and behavior (Allport, 1968). This is a rather abstract and general definition. It may let you answer the first question on a multiple-choice examination, but it doesn't really tell you what social psychology is. Here, then, is a partial listing of the kinds of phenomena social psychologists are interested in and the questions they ask about them.

Item: Rennie Davis helped found Students for a Democratic Society, a radical left-wing organization. He organized and led the anti-war protesters at the Democratic Convention held in Chicago during 1968. In 1978 Davis sold insurance in Denver and spent his spare time spreading the word for a teenage Indian guru.

A social psychologist would be interested in the dramatic changes that occurred in Davis's behavior. Did this change come from within? Was it the result of the dramatic differences between American society in 1968 and 1978, or some combination of the two? Social psychologists are interested in whether personality characteristics or situational factors are the primary causes of social behavior.

Item: Ed and Maureen decide that after five years of living in an apartment, it's time for them to buy a home. Maureen's parents hope that now she and Ed will get married. If they do, they will be going against a trend. Over the last eight years, the number of unmarried Americans who live with a person of the opposite sex has increased over 100 percent.

There are several kinds of questions social psychologists could ask about people like Ed and Maureen. First, they might be interested in the dynamics of their relationship. What attracted them to one another and what motivates them to remain together? Second, social psychologists might wonder about the reasons for this dramatic change in Americans' attitudes toward marriage. Also, they might want to find out why some people opt to live together while others prefer marriage.

Item: In New York City, a seventeen-year-old boy borrowed a friend's bicycle. When he returned the bike, it had a flat tire. The friend demanded that the boy pay $3 to have the tire repaired; he was willing to pay only $2. His friend went home, got a gun, and murdered the boy. In New York City alone, episodes of this kind happen almost five times a day.

What factors in a person's background cause him to kill another human being? Do features of his environment, such as living conditions and violence in the media, influence his behavior? Many social psychologists study questions of this kind in their research on human aggression.

Item: During the Nazi occupation of Denmark, Jews were ordered to wear yellow arm bands with the Star of David on them. On the day the order was to take effect, the King of Denmark (a non-Jew) walked from his palace wearing a yellow arm band.

Altruistic, or pro-social, behavior is of interest to many social psychologists. They attempt to determine under what conditions one person will help another and the type of people who are likely to be altruists.

Item: In central Florida a group of young black men went on a spree of murder and torture against white residents of the area. After they were caught, they were asked why. "Because I hate white folks," answered one.

Item: A judge in Wisconsin gave a young man convicted of rape a suspended sentence. According to the judge, women who wear contemporary ("sexy") clothing provoke men to rape them.

Almost from its beginnings, social psychology has been interested in prejudice. Contemporary social psychologists are interested in the causes of and cures for racism, sexism, and other forms of prejudice.

Item: During the 1977 blackout in New York City, thousands of people took part in a mass orgy of looting. Television sets, clothes, liquor, and even new cars were taken by the looters. It is estimated that they did over $156 million worth of damage.

This episode would be of interest to social psychologists for at least two reasons. First, it illustrates the effect of group influences on the behavior of an individual—an important topic in social psychology. Second, it is an example of collective behavior. Social psychologists might ask whether the looters were simply a collection of habitual criminals or people engaged in classic crowd behavior.

Item: When President John F. Kennedy came to Washington in 1960, he chose an incredibly bright and competent group of people to advise him. Some authors have called them "the best and the brightest" people who ever ran our government. In the eight years they advised President Kennedy and his successor, Lyndon B. Johnson, this group managed to devise the disastrous invasion of Cuba at the Bay of Pigs and the basic American strategy in Indochina.

How groups make decisions and attempt to solve problems is studied by many social psychologists. They are concerned with the factors that influence the dynamics of the group process and the quality of group performance.

These examples give you some idea of what social psychologists do and how diverse a field social psychology is. Remember, this is only a partial listing. Also, note that social psychologists are as interested in the behavior of individuals as they are in how groups act. This is an important point. Many people mistakenly believe that social psychologists study only group behavior. This description applies more accurately to sociology than it does to social psychology.

Speaking of mistaken impressions, we'd like to nip one in the bud. We selected socially relevant examples, but most contemporary social psychological research is not directly concerned with solving social problems. Instead, the emphasis is on basic research on social phenomena. This is not to say that this research isn't applicable to many of today's problems. It's only to stress that most social psychologists are, first and foremost, scientists. As scientists, they approach the phenomena they are interested in from some theoretical perspective.

Theories in social psychology

There is no one theory of social behavior which all social psychologists accept. In fact, explanations of social phenomena run the gamut from psychoanalytic (e.g., Sarnoff, 1960) to behavioristic ones (e.g., Parke, 1969). However, the two major theoretical approaches to social behavior are the cognitive and the behavioristic viewpoints.

Cognitive theory

The word *cognitive* refers to the thinking process. Cognitive theorists attempt to understand people's social behavior by examining how people process the information they receive from the world around them. This position is based on the premise that humans are rational, thinking beings. People do not react to the world around them in the same way a rat reacts to a bar in a "Skinner" box. Rather, they think about what is happening to them and attempt to organize their experiences into some meaningful whole.

This proposed difference between animals and humans is illustrated in a science fiction short story by noted psychologist James McConnell. The main character (a psychologist) has been captured by creatures from another planet and is being used as a subject in some classical learning experiments. He has run mazes, pressed a lever in a Skinner box to get food, and been shocked to test his ability to learn to avoid pain. Finally, he's had enough and wants to escape.

My means of escape is, therefore, obvious. He expects from me confirmation of all his pet theories. Well, He won't get it any more! I know all of His theories backwards and forwards, and this means I know how to give Him results that will tear His theories right smack in half!

I can almost predict the results. What does any learning theorist do with an animal that won't behave properly, that refuses to give the results that are predicted? One gets rid of the beast, quite naturally. For one wishes to use only healthy, normal animals in one's work, and any animal that gives "unusual" results is removed from the study but quickly. After all, if it doesn't perform as expected, it must be sick, abnormal, or aberrant in one way or another . . . . (McConnell, 1974)

Note how he has reasoned out what has happened to him and made predictions about how the experimenter will behave. Even though he is being treated like a rat, he is acting in a logical, rational manner.

The main interest of the cognitive theorist is people's cognitions. A *cognition* is any idea, opinion, belief, or bit of knowledge that a person has about himself or the world around him (Zajonc, 1960). The cognitive theorists believe that if one can understand how cognitions develop and are organized, one can explain social behavior.

Now, you cannot see or directly measure a cognition, since cognitions do not physically exist. There is no place in your brain where all your beliefs about, say, the Panama Canal Treaty are stored. Rather, cognitions are *hypothetical constructs*—entities which do not physically exist but are proposed as an explanation of a person's behavior.

For example, hate is a hypothetical construct. You cannot see, touch, or smell hate, but it can be used to explain someone's behavior. A member of the Irish Republican Army throws a bomb into a bar in Belfast which is full of Protestants. He does this because, according to a cognitive theorist, he hates them.

Behavioristic theory

According to the behaviorists, concepts such as thinking and cognition are not needed to explain social behavior. Note that we said "not needed." The behaviorists acknowledge that people think, but they believe that an analysis of cognitive (i.e., thinking) processes will not prove of much value in understanding people's behavior. They base this position on the assumption that a person's behavior is determined primarily by two things. First, what kinds of behaviors have been rewarded and/or punished in the past (this is called a reinforcement history)? Second, what are the positive and negative reinforcers for the person in his present situation? Unobservable entities such as cognitions should not be used to understand a person's behavior. Rather, the researcher should deal in observable, concrete phenomena.

A true behaviorist would not use the hypothetical construct, hate, to explain the bomb-throwing incident described above. He would explain this act by examining the past reinforcement history of the bomb thrower and those aspects of the present situation that

Carlos Garcia-Lozano

would make the death of some Protestants rewarding for him.

Thus, the difference between the cognitive and behavioristic approaches can be summarized as follows. The cognitive theorist views people as organizers and processers of information they receive from the world around them. The behaviorist views people as reactors to the events in the world around them. As a result of these different viewpoints, the cognitive theorists concentrate on what goes on within a person; the behaviorists concentrate on what goes on around him. In the chapters which follow, you will see examples of both approaches to social psychology.

RESEARCH IN SOCIAL PSYCHOLOGY

Regardless of a social psychologist's theoretical position, he approaches social behavior as a scientist. He investigates social phenomena by using the scientific method.

The scientific method requires objectivity.

A social psychologist may personally feel that neo-Nazis are sick people who should be put away. But when he studies them as a scientist, he cannot let his personal biases interfere with how he collects data about them and the conclusions he draws. Further, the scientist must show that the phenomenon he studies is a reliable one which can be studied by other scientists. To do so, he must communicate what he did to other scientists in a clear and precise fashion. Thus, a scientist attempts to define the phenomenon operationally. An *operational definition* is one that describes something in terms of the operation used to measure it. For example, a social psychologist who is studying altruism could define it operationally as the amount of money one person gives to another person. This concrete definition gives other social psychologists a clear understanding of what he meant by altruism, and they can expand his work on it.

Most of the research in social psychology is concerned with testing theories of social behavior. A *theory* consists of a set of general statements about the nature of the relationship between two or more variables.

A *variable* is a description of some quantifiable, or measurable, aspect of a person or thing. For example, your height is a variable. It describes the distance from the top of your head to the bottom of your feet. People differ in their height, and this difference can be measured.

A scientist tests a theory by making a prediction (called a *hypothesis*) about the nature of the relationship between variables. Variables can be related in two ways.

Nonfunctional relationships

A nonfunctional relationship exists between two variables, A and B, when we do not know if A causes B or B causes A. In other words, you cannot infer cause and effect from a nonfunctional relationship.

For example, a social psychologist is interested in the relationship between racial prejudice in whites and their belief that blacks are lazy, shiftless, stupid, etc. This researcher predicts that the more racially prejudiced a person is, the more strongly he will hold these opinions. He gives a group of whites a questionnaire which measures racial prejudice; then he has them rate blacks on a number of characteristics, such as lazy, shiftless, etc. The researcher's hypothesis is confirmed. People who are high in racial prejudice have negative estimates of blacks, and people who are low do not. But can the researcher conclude that racial prejudice has *caused* the negative estimates of blacks? No. On the basis of this information, he does not know if the white subjects saw negative traits in blacks because they were prejudiced or if they were prejudiced because they saw these negative traits.

When two variables are related to one another, we say that they are *correlated*. This does not mean that one causes the other; it means that if one variable changes, so does the other. The extent to which two variables are correlated is described by a statistic called the *correlation coefficient*. The largest correlation coefficient possible is 1.00, which means that two variables are perfectly correlated. Most correlations are much smaller than 1.00, but they may still describe a meaningful relationship. "Meaningful" means that knowing a person's score on one variable increases a researcher's ability to make a prediction of how he will score on the other variable. For example, the correlation between I.Q. scores and grades in college is about .50. This is less than a perfect relationship. But if we know a person's I.Q., we can make a better prediction of his grade point average than if we did not.

If the correlation between two variables is squared, it will tell you in percentages how much of the variability in one variable can be explained by the other variable (McNemar, 1969). For example, if the correlation between I.Q. and grades is .50, then I.Q. would account for 25 percent of the variance in people's grades. That is, 25 percent of the difference in people's grades can be explained by differences in their I.Q. This concept is presented in Figure 1-1. The total circle (or set) represents the variability in grades; the cross-hatched section represents the percentage of this variability which can be explained by differences in I.Q. This diagram also illustrates why a correlation cannot be larger than 1.00. It is impossible to explain more than 100 percent of the variance in a variable.

As noted above, correlation coefficients are used mainly when there is a nonfunctional relationship. But it must be strongly emphasized that correlation coefficients can also be used to describe relationships in which one variable clearly is causing the other. There are at least two instances in which this can be done. The first is when you can determine "time order" (Rosenberg, 1968). If you know

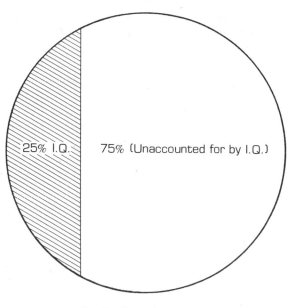

25% I.Q.   75% (Unaccounted for by I.Q.)

Total variance in grades

Figure 1-1. A +.50 correlation between IQ and grades.

that event A preceded event B in time, then you can determine causality. If, for example, you find a correlation between parental attitudes toward child rearing and homosexuality in their offspring, you can conclude that the former was at least a contributing factor in the development of the child's behavior. The second instance involves what Rosenberg called the "fixity" of the variable. Race, for example, is a fixed variable. If we go back to the 1972 presidential election, we can see how cause and effect can be inferred from a fixed variable. In that election, most blacks preferred George McGovern and most whites preferred Richard Nixon. Now, supporting one of the candidates could not *cause* a voter to be of a certain race, but being of a certain race (and, thus, being subjected to the conditions that accompany it) may cause the voter to prefer a different candidate.

Correlational research

A study which does not attempt to change or manipulate how much of a variable a person possesses is called a correlational study. Research in three areas of social psychology uses a correlational approach.

The first is research on how people are socialized and/or how past events influence a person's present behavior. The social psychologist cannot change what happened in the past. Therefore, he uses correlations to determine the relationship between the variables he is interested in. For example, Winterbottom (1958) was interested in the effect of parents' behavior on need for achievement ("a desire to compete successfully with some standard of excellence") in children. To investigate this, she questioned a number of mothers about how they had raised their children and what they expected of them. Some sample questions were: "At what age did you feel your children could choose their own friends?" "At what age did you feel your children should know their way around the city?" Afterward, Winterbottom assessed the need for achievement in the children by asking them to tell stories in response to pictures shown to them. The children's responses were correlated with the mothers' recollections of how they raised them. Winterbottom found that mothers of high-achievement-oriented children made earlier demands for independence and mastery than did mothers of low-achievement-oriented children. Thus, we see the use of correlational techniques with *retrospective* or *case history* data. Since social psychologists cannot systematically manipulate past events, they must use correlational techniques to assess adequately how these prior conditions are related to subsequent events.

Correlational techniques are also used in survey research or public opinion polling. This is because the variables of interest are as

nearly fixed as those events that have occurred in the past. Usually survey research
tries to determine how demographic variables
(e.g., age, sex, race) and attitudes, or one attitude and another, are related. In the former
case, it is obvious that the variables cannot be
systematically manipulated. For example,
unless the researcher has the funds to send all
of his subjects to Denmark (or wherever
people go) for a sex-change operation, he will
not be able systematically to manipulate the
sex of the subject and then relate that variable to the subject's attitudes toward legalized abortion. Therefore, he must rely on correlation as his means of description.

Many people believe that attitudes can be
readily changed. However, this belief is not
necessarily true. In fact, at present, we lack
the knowledge and the means necessary for
implementing immediate, large-scale attitude change outside the laboratory. Further-
more, there is some question as to whether it
is useful or ethical to produce such changes.
Therefore, in most instances, social psychologists must be satisfied with describing the
relationship between sets of attitudes via a
correlational analysis.

Studies of personality variables also use
correlational data. The reason is that a personality variable, or trait, is assumed to be a
relatively permanent part of an individual's
makeup. When we describe a person as "dogmatic," we mean that he is consistently dogmatic across situations. Thus, if personality
traits are, in fact, more or less permanent, we
must use correlations to describe their relationship with other variables.

Functional relationships

A *functional relationship* exists between two
variables, A and B, when a change in A
produces or *causes* a change in B. However,
the reverse is not true; a change in B has no
effect on A. For example, there is a functional
relationship between electric current and a
fluorescent light. It you turn on the current,
the light will go on. But if you pull a light
from its socket, this will have no effect on the
current. Functional relationships are also
called cause-and-effect relationships; most of
the research in social psychology is concerned
with identifying such relationships. This is
done via an experiment.

The experiment

An experiment attempts to determine if one
variable (A) causes another (B) by producing
changes in A and seeing if this results in
changes in B. There are two ways of doing
this. One is to create changes in a person and
see if these changes affect other aspects of the
person's behavior. The second, and more common, technique is to give groups of people
different levels of the same variable and see if
their behavior differs as a result. (This will
become clearer shortly.)

The simplest experiment in social psychology is one that uses two groups of people. The
first group is exposed to some variable; it is
called the *experimental group*. This variable
is withheld from the other group—the *control
group*. Then the two groups are compared in
terms of how much of some other variable
they possess. The variable which is given to
one group and withheld from another is called
the *independent variable*. The variable on
which the groups are compared is called the
dependent variable. This is because differences in it between the two groups depend on
differences in the independent variable.

Ideally, the social psychologist wants the
experimental and control groups to be identical in every respect except one—whether they
received the independent variable. Since it's
difficult to find a large number of identical
twins for experiment and control groups, so-

cial psychologists rely on chance to even out any important differences between these groups. That is, they *randomly assign* their subjects to the experimental and control groups. Luck determines which group a person ends up in. And thus, the two groups would probably not differ on characteristics which might themselves produce differences in the dependent variable.

An illustration of an experiment: An experiment begins with a hypothesis, or prediction, about how people will behave. Usually, but not always, this hypothesis comes from some general theory. Here's a hypothesis that several social psychologists have tested: Differences in the amount of guilt a person feels will cause differences in his willingness to help another person.

Now how could we test this hypothesis? Our first task would be to find some way of creating differences between people in terms of how much guilt they feel. One technique is to make some people feel responsible for the discomfort of another person (Carlsmith & Gross, 1969).

Carlsmith and Gross asked subjects to help them in a study. The subjects believed the study concerned the effect of negative feedback (punishment) on a person's ability to learn. They watched another person while he worked on a task; every time he made a mistake, they threw a large switch. Members of the experimental group (the ones who were supposed to feel guilty) were told that this switch would result in the other person's receiving a painful electric shock. (In fact, the other person was a confederate of the experimenters and was not shocked.) The members of the control group (who were not supposed to feel guilty) threw a switch which simply resulted in a loud buzzer's being sounded. The subjects were randomly assigned to both groups.

The dependent variable—willingness to help another person—was measured in the following manner. After the "learning" part of the experiment was over, a subject and the confederate filled out some forms so that they could be paid for their participation. At this point, the confederate turned to the subject and asked if he could talk to him for a minute. The confederate said that he belonged to a group concerned about a proposed highway which would kill a number of old and beautiful trees. He needed people to help him phone individuals who might sign a petition against the highway. He had the names of fifty people whom he wanted to call and asked the subject if he was willing to help. If the subject agreed, he was asked how many people he was willing to call. Thus, Carlsmith and Gross had a quantifiable measure of a person's willingness to help.

If the people who believed they had shocked the confederate (i.e., the people who felt guilty) agreed to make more phone calls than the control group (the group who did not shock the confederate), then the hypothesis would be confirmed. In fact, this is just what happened. The subjects who thought they had shocked the confederate were much more likely to help him than were those who had only sounded the buzzer.

Now, this is a very simple experiment. There is one independent variable (guilt) and one dependent variable (favor doing). In practice, most social psychological experiments are more complex. Usually they investigate the effect of several independent variables. In fact, Carlsmith and Gross actually looked at the effects of guilt, social status of the person making the request, and the effect of a witness when the subject was asked to help. But no matter how complex an experiment becomes, it is always asking the same basic question: Is there a functional relationship between an independent variable (or variables) and some dependent variable?

Different kinds of experiments

The experiment just described was a *laboratory experiment*. That is, it occurred in a highly structured setting, and the experimenter tightly controlled what happened to the subjects. Obviously, this has the advantage of allowing the researcher to identify clearly the reasons why subjects acted as they did. However, a laboratory in the basement of a psychology building is a very artificial setting. A person's behavior in a laboratory setting may not be the same as his behavior in the real world. One solution is to move the experiment into the real world.

This is done in the *field experiment*. Here, people are randomly assigned to experimental and control groups, and are compared on the dependent variable, just as in the laboratory experiment. However, this happens in a natural setting, and the subjects are not aware that they are in an experiment. Thus, they should behave in a more natural manner. Let's see how the relationship between guilt and helping was examined in one field experiment.

People walking in a shopping center were approached by a young man. He asked them if they would take his picture, claiming that he needed it for a class project. When a person attempted to take the picture, he discovered that the camera didn't work. In the guilt condition, the young man implied that it was the person's fault. In the no-guilt (i.e., control) condition, the young man said that the camera "acts up a lot" and it wasn't the person's fault (Regan, Williams, & Sparling, 1972).

A few minutes later, the subjects passed a woman who carried a bag which was torn with candy falling from it. The dependent variable, helping, was whether the subjects told the woman about it. A comparison of the number of experimental subjects (people who thought they were responsible for the broken camera) and the number of control subjects who told the woman provided a test of this hypothesis.

The behavior of the people in the shopping center was probably more natural than that of the people in the laboratory. But a price was paid for this naturalism. The field experimenters had less control over what happened to their subjects than did the laboratory experimenters. Since the experiment was done in a shopping center, the researchers could not ask their subjects if they felt guilty. They could not control for what happened to the subjects between the time of the camera episode and when they saw the woman; they could not even be sure that all their subjects saw the broken bag of candy. In other words, what the field experiment gave in naturalness, it took back in control. This is almost always the case.

Finally, there is the *naturally-occurring-event experiment*. This type of research can be called an experiment only in the loosest sense of the word. Since the variable of interest (the independent variable) is not systematically manipulated by the experimenter, the researcher tries to take advantage of a naturally occurring event. Consider such an experiment that could have been conducted on guilt and helping.

Germany had spent years and millions of dollars in planning the 1972 Olympics in Munich. One of the main reasons that the German government wanted to stage the Olympics was a need to remove, once and for all, the memories of the 1936 Olympics. The earlier games, as you may know, were staged by Adolf Hitler as a showcase for the superiority of the Aryan race. Munich, 1972, was intended to show the world that a new Germany existed. However, the spirit of the Olympics was shattered by the kidnapping and subsequent death of twelve Israeli athletes. As was widely reported in the press, the German people felt considerable guilt for what had occurred. The relationship between guilt

Other research techniques used by social psychologists

Although we have been concerned primarily with experiments in social psychology, other methods are used to collect data. Here are a few of them.

Content analysis

Content analysis involves the systematic observation, coding, and analysis of some written or verbal communication. These communications include such things as books, propaganda messages, magazine articles, letters to the editor, or even the content of television shows, movies, and popular songs. Let's see how content analysis has been used by social psychologists.

Ralph K. White (1970) was interested in how one country's view of another might contribute to a conflict between them. To get data on these perceptions, he analyzed the public statements United States and North Vietnamese leaders made during the war in Indochina. His analysis showed that the two countries had almost identical, negative views of one another. For example, one American leader described the war as being due to "naked aggression on the part of North Vietnam," while the President of North Vietnam declared that "It is crystal clear that the United States is the aggressor." (More recently, White [1977] has used this approach to study the Arab/Israeli conflict.)

Other researchers have used content analysis to study historical trends. In one study, the effects of the Great Depression of the 1930's on Americans' attitudes were examined by analyzing the contents of church sermons. It was found that during the prosperous 1920's, these sermons expressed an optimistic view of the world. But in the 1930's, they became much more pessimistic in content (Hamilton, 1942).

Still another use of content analysis is to examine how people and governments try to change attitudes. For example, a study done in the 1960's showed that Russian magazines intended for Americans stressed the industrial growth and high standard of living in Russia. American magazines intended for Russians stressed aesthetic and cultural aspects of America (Garver, 1961).

The interview

An *interview* involves talking to someone in order to get information from him (Cannell & Kahn, 1968). Interviews are used if a researcher wants to find out how people feel about some recent past event. For example, the residents of a city might be asked how they felt when the city was hit by a hurricane. Interviews are also used to make predictions about important events. An illustration of this is the public opinion surveys conducted during every presidential campaign. The results of these surveys are used to predict the winner.

Finally, interviews are used to determine the frequency of some behavior in the general population. For example, Kinsey's study of Americans' sexual habits used personal interviews with a large number of people (Kinsey, Pomeroy, & Martin, 1948).

Systematic observation

Systematic observation involves observing and recording people's behavior in real-world situations. Ideally, these observations are made without the awareness of the people being observed. For example, Davis, Siebert, and Breed (1966) were interested in whether residents of a Southern city were practicing racial integration in public transportation. Rather than asking people what they did, Davis et al. simply recorded where blacks and whites sat on the city buses. Similarly, Campbell, Kruskal, and Wallace (1966) observed how close black and white college students sat to one another as a measure of racial attitudes in universities.

and favor doing could have been investigated by sending letters requesting donations to a charity to a random sample of Germans and comparing their responses to those of a similar group (e.g., Austrians) who were less likely to feel guilty about what happened in Munich.

In addition to being somewhat macabre, this example of a naturally-occurring-event experiment points out the weaknesses of this approach. The experimenter assumes that the subjects (i.e., the German people) did indeed feel guilty. But he cannot be certain that the independent variable, guilt, was, in fact, manipulated. Of course, he could use a public opinion poll, but such polls are expensive and require an extremely large sample to provide representativeness. Even if he had the funds and the time for such a poll and found scientific evidence for his assumption of guilt, the experimental group (Germans)–control group (Austrians) differences, if obtained, might not be solely attributable to the independent variable. It is apparent that assignment of subjects to the experimental and control groups was not random. Germans and Austrians differ in a multitude of ways, any one of which may cause an experiment–control difference. For example, Germany is a more affluent country than Austria, and thus, the average German may have more money to contribute to charity than the average Austrian. Thus, two of the essential elements of a good social psychological experiment—random assignment to experimental and control groups and close control over the independent variable—are absent. The problems of generalizability of results that often plague the laboratory experiment have been reduced, but the tremendous loss of control over the experimental setting detracts from the value and meaning of the results. As you will see shortly, one cannot make statements about generalizability when there is no control over the variables of interest.

Naturally-occurring-event experiments are uncommon in social psychology. They are extremely costly (unfortunately, a factor which a researcher cannot ignore) and often impossible to control.

Conclusion

This introductory chapter began by telling you something about what social psychologists do. The following conclusions were drawn about contemporary theory and research in social psychology. Social psychologists are interested basically in the influence process—that is, how a person's or a group's behavior is influenced by that of other persons and groups. Most social psychologists study this influence process from a variety of theoretical positions, but almost all of them use the traditional methods of science.

The goal of science in general and social psychology in particular is to study and understand the relationships between variables. Variables can be functionally (i.e., causally) or nonfunctionally (i.e., noncausally) related. Most commonly, nonfunctional relationships are investigated by using correlational techniques, and functional relationships are investigated by using the experimental approach. Because so much of social psychology involves the experimental approach, it was described at some length. Experiments in social psychology can become quite complex. At the core of all experiments, however, is the following basic question: Do changes in one variable (the independent variable) produce changes in another variable (the dependent variable)? To answer this question, social psychologists conduct laboratory and field experiments in which one group receives the independent variable (the experimental group) and another does not (the control group). These two groups are then compared to determine if there are differences in their behavior. If there are, then it is concluded that the independent variable had a causal effect on the dependent variable.

REVIEW QUESTIONS

(Twelve out of fifteen is passing)

1. The theoretical approach which stresses the way humans process and organize information in its view of humanity is called the _____ approach. (p. 4)
2. A nonobservable variable which is proposed as an explanation of behavior is called a(n) _____ construct. (p. 5)
3. The theoretical approach which stresses external stimuli as the primary determinant of behavior is called the _____ approach. (p. 6)
4. A concept which describes an event or a thing and is quantifiable is called a(n) _____ . (p. 7)
5. A noncausal relationship is called a _____ relationship. (p. 7)
6. A noncausal relationship is most commonly described by a statistic known as the _____ _____ . (p. 7)
7. Social psychological research that uses case history data employs a correlational technique because the variables of interest cannot be _____ . (p. 8)
8. The finding that a bullet in the heart is related to death describes a(n) _____ relationship. (p. 9)
9. In a procedure called the _____ , the functional (or causal) relationship between two variables is determined by manipulating the independent variable and observing if this results in a change in the dependent variable. (p. 9)
10. In the typical experiment the _____ group receives the independent variable, but the _____ group does not. (p. 9)
11. In order to ensure that the experimental and control groups do not differ systematically on variables related to the variable of interest, the experimenter assigns the subjects _____ to each group. (p. 10)
12. The performance of the experimental and control groups is compared on the _____ variable, to determine if the independent variable had an effect. (p. 9)
13. The laboratory experiment has a good deal of control, but may suffer from a lack of _____ . (p. 11)
14. Studies which systematically manipulate variables in settings outside the laboratory are called _____ experiments. (p. 11)
15. A study of the effects of a nationwide coal-miner's strike on attitudes toward unions would be an example of a(n) _____ _____ _____ experiment. (p. 11)

ANSWERS

13. generalizability   14. field   15. naturally occurring event
9. experiment   10. experimental; control   11. randomly (by chance)   12. dependent
6. correlation coefficient   7. manipulated (i.e., they are fixed)   8. functional (causal)
1. cognitive   2. hypothetical construct   3. behavioristic   4. variable   5. nonfunctional

Carlos Garcia-Lozano

PROBLEMS IN SOCIAL PSYCHOLOGICAL RESEARCH

MURPHY'S LAW: "If anything can go wrong, it will." O'TOOLE'S COMMENTARY ON MURPHY'S LAW: "Murphy was an optimist."

We are not sure if Murphy ever talked to a social psychologist, but we are fairly confident that O'Toole did. Most people have an image of the scientist-experimenter as someone who designs a study intended to test some theory, easily conducts the study, gets perfectly clear results, and publishes the results in a prestigious journal. We wish this were the case. We could spend the rest of this book telling you about the disasters social psychologists have encountered in their experiments. (For example, Penner once spent Monday through Friday preparing tape-recorded instructions, only to discover that over the weekend a displaced pigeon had relieved itself all over the tapes.)

Entertaining as this may sound, it points to a more serious goal: the need to alert you to some problems which make it difficult for social psychologists to understand, predict, and explain social behavior. Hopefully, this will enable you to evaluate more critically and intelligently the content of the subsequent chapters. Please don't commit the error of concluding that because research problems exist, social psychology is worthless. Good research is not easy to do. Just because it runs into some difficulties, one should not "throw the baby out with the bath water."

Regardless of the type of study a social psychologist conducts, he must be able to demonstrate that it is valid. That is, the study must support the claims made about it. The first and most important type of validity is internal validity.

Internal validity

A study is *internally valid* if the independent variable was responsible for the results obtained (Campbell & Stanley, 1966). If a study does not have internal validity, it is essentially worthless. That is, if the effects observed are due to some unspecified, extraneous, or uncontrolled variable, these effects cannot be interpreted. Internal validity is often more difficult to obtain in social psychology than in other sciences. The main reason is the fact that the model upon which experimental designs are based assumes that the subject is passive. Actually, however, the typical subject is quite active. Psychology is the child of the natural or physical sciences (e.g., biology or physics). In these sciences the "subject" is usually either inert or subhuman. Beams of light or rats are not very sensitive to the world around them.

Consider the average laboratory white rat, sitting in a cage munching on its daily allotment of pellets. The rat lives in more or less a vacuum. Its environment is highly restricted, and little takes place inside the rat colony that could affect behavior in an experiment. A rat probably does not read very well and has few friends, which makes it difficult for the rat to read about the experiment in which it is participating or hear about it from other rats. Because the rat is usually exterminated after being used in an experiment, there is little opportunity for prior experience to influence its subsequent experimental performance. Finally, but perhaps most importantly, rats are not very bright. They do not form hypothesis about the true purpose of the study or worry about how the experimenter will evaluate them.

Humans, on the other hand, live in a fairly rich environment. They read and exchange information with other humans. They are generally used in more than one experiment. And, most importantly, they *do* form hypotheses about the purpose of the experiment. All of these factors may produce results which are not due to the independent variable; that is, these factors may jeopardize internal validity. In the following sections, some of these jeopardizing factors will be discussed.

History

There are usually three stages in social psychological experiments. First, there is the pretest. The subjects are given a test which measures how much of some variable they possess. Then the independent variable is administered to the subjects. Finally, the posttest is given. This is the same test as was used in the pretest. Changes from the pretest to the posttest are taken as evidence that the independent variable has had an effect. *History* refers to any event that occurs between the pretest and posttest, in addition to the independent variable, that could be responsible for a subject's performance on the posttest.

For example, Rokeach (1973) reported on a technique designed to change people's values. One test of this technique involved an attempt to increase the importance of the value of equality ("brotherhood, equal opportunity for all") among college students. His experiment was quite simple. In January, 1968, he measured the importance of equality and other values to the students, (the pretest). A month or so later, he gave them a talk designed to increase the importance of equality (the independent variable). Then in May, 1968, he retested the students' values (the posttest). He found a statistically significant increase in the importance the students placed on equality. Thus, he had shown that his technique worked. Or did he? In April, 1968, the noted civil rights leader Dr. Martin Luther King, Jr., was murdered. Could the change in the students' reactions be related to this tragic event rather than to Rokeach's talk?

Rokeach had included a control group in this study—students whose values were tested at the same time as the experimental group, but who did not receive the talk. The importance of equality in the control subjects did not change. This enabled Rokeach to rule out history, in the form of Dr. King's death, as the cause of the change in the importance placed on equality. While an experimenter cannot control history, he can determine its effect by using a control group.

Maturation

Maturation is any changes that occur within the individual as the result of the passage of time (e.g., growing older, hungrier, etc.). Sometimes maturation may produce effects similar to those of the independent variable.

Imagine that you are a woman interested in techniques for changing men's attitudes toward the Equal Rights Amendment (E.R.A.). You hypothesize that a pro-E.R.A. appeal from a male chauvinist might be quite effective. Therefore, you recruit Hugh Hefner (publisher of *Playboy*) to give a talk in favor of the E.R.A. to a group of men.

To determine if change occurs, you give the men a pretest. That is, you measure their attitudes toward the E.R.A before they hear Hefner. (This is a common procedure in attitude change research.) Then they hear Hefner extol the virtues of the E.R.A. You are about to measure their attitudes a second time (a posttest) when you notice that it is 12:30 and time for lunch. You dismiss the men with explicit instructions not to talk to one another about what they heard. (You monitor their conversations to make sure this doesn't occur.) The men return from lunch, and their attitudes are retested. When you analyze your data you find that, as a group, the men have gone from being very much against the E.R.A. to very much in favor of it. Thank you, Hugh Hefner. But wait a minute; are you sure it was Hefner's talk?

It is possible that eating lunch may have made these men feel better by alleviating their hunger. Thus, their improved mood may have made them more generous toward equal rights for women. An internal change in the subjects was responsible for the change in their attitudes. To eliminate this alternative explanation of the results, you need a control group—that is, men whose attitudes toward the E.R.A. are measured, who are given lunch, and who are then retested. If this group shows no change in its attitudes, then you can eliminate maturation as a cause of the results you obtained.

The sensitizing effect of a pretest

A pretest provides valuable information for the researcher. It tells him if the experimental and control groups were similar on the dependent variable before they received the independent variable. It also enables him to compare how much the experimental and control groups changed from the pretest to the posttest. But sometimes the pretest can interfere with internal validity.

Robert Lana discovered this, more or less by accident. He was initially interested in whether the order in which opposing viewpoints are presented affects their relative ability to change people's attitudes. For example, in a two-person debate, which debater has the advantage? Is it the first speaker, because he gets his views across first? Or is it the second speaker, because he is the last person the audience hears (Lana, 1964, 1966; Lana & Rosnow, 1963)?

To investigate this question, Lana chose the topic of censorship. He gave half his subjects a pro-censorship argument, followed by an anti-censorship one. The other half of the subjects received the arguments in the opposite order.

To measure attitude change, all the subjects' attitudes toward censorship were assessed before they heard any arguments. Some of the subjects received "open" questionnaires, which were clearly concerned with censorship. Other subjects received questionnaires in which the questions on censorship were buried or "hidden" among a number of other questions. The design of Lana's study can be diagrammed as follows.

Group	Type of Pretest	Independent Variable
1	"Open"	Pro-censorship–anti-censorship
2	"Open"	Anti-censorship–pro-censorship
3	"Hidden"	Pro-censorship–anti-censorship
4	"Hidden"	Anti-censorship–pro-censorship

After all four groups had heard the pro- and anti-censorship arguments, their attitudes were retested. Lana found no differences in attitude change as the result of the order in which the arguments were presented. What he did find was that subjects who received the "hidden" pretest showed significantly more attitude change than did subjects who received the "open" pretest. The nature of the pretest was responsible for the attitude change which occurred.

In a later study, Lana found that subjects who received no pretest changed their attitudes significantly more than subjects who received a pretest. Later research suggested an explanation of this surprising finding. A subject who takes an open pretest is, in essence, making a public statement of his attitudes. Once he has done this, it is hard for him to change these attitudes.

There is a technique that allows a researcher to determine if his pretest is affecting the subjects. It is called the *Solomon Four Group Design* (Solomon, 1949), which can be diagrammed in the following manner.

The "Yeses" and "Noes" refer to whether subjects receive the pretest, the independent variable, or the posttest.

Solomon's Four Group Design

Group	Pretest	Independent Variable?	Posttest?
1	Yes	No	Yes
2	Yes	Yes	Yes
3	No	Yes	Yes
4	No	No	Yes

Note that this technique enables a researcher to determine: (1) the effect of the pretest alone; (2) the joint effect of the pretest and the independent variable; and (3) the effect of the independent variable alone. Because pretests often cause problems in internal validity, many social psychologists will often use the Solomon Four Group Design or devise experiments that do not require a pretest measure from the subjects.

Reactive testing

Social psychologists use a large number of questionnaires in their research. These questionnaires ask people to tell how they feel about someone or something. For example, suppose a researcher was interested in your attitudes toward Puerto Ricans. How would you react to this question:

"Are you so stupid and bigoted as to hate people of Puerto Rican ancestry?"

Probably even if you hated Puerto Ricans, you would not answer "yes." To do so would be to admit that you are stupid and a bigot.

This is a *reactive* question. Rather than accurately measuring your feelings, it influences your response. Now, few social psychologists would ask such a reactive question. However, reactivity is a serious problem in social psychology. Questions which openly ask about racial prejudice, sexual practices, or illegal drug usage may elicit answers which do not reflect the person's true feelings on these topics. Rather, he may give answers that are socially desirable—that put him in a good light.

One solution to the problem of reactive testing is to use unobtrusive measures (Webb, Campbell, Schwartz, & Sechrest, 1966). An *unobtrusive measure* involves measuring some variable without making the person aware that he is being assessed. For example, in the study on values mentioned earlier, Rokeach also used an unobtrusive measure of how his subjects' feelings toward equality had changed. About three months after the talk on values, all the subjects received a letter from a black civil rights organization. This letter asked them to join the organization and send it money. Since the letter came so long after the talk, the organization was quite well known nationally, and students receive many letters like this, it is unlikely that any of the subjects realized that it was part of an experiment. Thus, their responses to the letter gave an accurate indication of their feeling toward blacks. (Reactive testing will be mentioned again in the discussion of attitude measurement in Chapter Six.)

Demand characteristics

See if you can explain this apparently bizarre behavior on the part of a group of college students.

They were given 2,000 sheets of paper. On each sheet was a series of two-digit numbers. The students were asked to add up the numbers on each page, two at a time. This required 224 additions per sheet. When someone finished a sheet, he received further instructions from a pile of cards on the table in front of him. Each card read:

You are to tear up the sheet of paper which you have just completed into a minimum of thirty two pieces and go on to the next sheet of paper and continue working as you did before; when you have completed this piece of paper, pick up the next card which will instruct you further. . . . (Orne, 1962).

Students asked to do this spent as long as 5½ hours on the task! Were they stupid? Were they stoned? The answer to both these questions is, no.

Martin Orne (1962, 1969) has suggested another explanation. He believes that the students saw the task as a test of their endurance. Thus, they persisted until the experimenter told them they could quit. Why in the world would students reach this conclusion?

Orne proposed the concept of demand char-

acteristics. According to him, a subject in an experiment is not passive. He tries to figure out what is going on: What is the purpose of the experiment? What is the experimenter "after"? In trying to answer these questions, the subject will look at the *demand characteristics* of the experiment. These consist of: rumors about the experiment, its setting, the instructions the experimenter gives, both implicitly and explicitly, how the experimenter acts, and most importantly, the experimental procedure itself (Orne, 1969). These kinds of information provide the subject with data which he uses to form hypotheses about the purpose of the experiment and what the experimenter expects from him.

A serious problem exists if demand characteristics, rather than the independent variable, are responsible for subjects' behavior. For example, it has long been assumed that if you deprive a person of any stimulation, this condition will have a very negative effect on him. A person who cannot hear, see, touch, smell, or taste anything will become anxious, think less clearly and sharply than usual, and may even hallucinate. Orne and Schiebe (1964) wondered how much of these effects might be due to demand characteristics. That is, were any of the subjects' reactions to sensory deprivation due to their expectations about its effects?

Orne and Schiebe created the following situation. Two groups of subjects were given the standard tests of intellectual performance that are used in sensory deprivation studies. Then, half the subjects were told that they would be in a sensory deprivation study. After describing the study, the experimenters showed the subjects into a furnished, well-lit room. The room contained food and water, and while it was somewhat isolated, the subjects could hear people in the hall outside the room and noises from outside the building. In short, there was no absence of stimulation in the room. The subjects were told that if they wanted to leave the room, they could push a red button on the wall. The other half of the subjects went through exactly the same procedure, but with two very important differences. First, these subjects were told that they were a *control group* for a sensory deprivation study. While they would be left alone for 4 hours, there would be no sensory deprivation. Second, no "panic button" was provided for these subjects.

After both groups had spent 4 hours in the room, they were released and retested. The subjects who thought that they were in a sensory deprivation study showed significantly more decline in intellectual performance than did the control subjects. In addition, they were judged by an interviewer to show many more of the symptoms associated with sensory deprivation (e.g., anxiety, restlessness) than did the control subjects. In other words, while there was no difference between the experimental and control subjects in terms of sensory deprivation, the experimental subjects acted as though they had been sensorily deprived. From these results, one might reasonably question the internal validity of the typical sensory deprivation study.

Demand characteristics are interesting for reasons other than the danger they present to internal validity. For example, earlier you were shown that bright, sane college students will tear up paper for 4½ hours if an experimenter asked them to. Now consider an even more bizarre behavior.

College students were asked to *pretend* they were hypnotized. Then they were told to perform the following acts: stick their hand into a beaker of acid, throw the acid in the face of another person (actually a confederate who was protected by a hidden screen), and pick up an extremely poisonous snake by the middle! Incredibly, the majority of the students did all these things (Orne & Evans, 1965). Why?

One of the "hypotheses" that a subject often has when he enters an experiment is that it is legitimate and worthwhile. There must be a good reason why the experimenter has asked him to do something, no matter how extreme. And further, the experimenter would never let him hurt himself or others. This expectation, or belief, results in many subjects doing whatever the experimenter asks them to do. Thus, demand characteristics may give an experimenter incredible control over his subjects.

Demand characteristics may also explain part of a currently popular leisure-time activity. There is evidence that a portion of the "high" one experiences on marijuana is due to something like demand characteristics. Jones (1971) gave real and placebo[1] marijuana cigarettes (the placebo "joints" smelled and tasted like marijuana but were lacking in THC, the psychoactive agent in marijuana) to a group of experienced marijuana users. Subjects were asked to rate the marijuana smoked on a scale from 0 to 100, where 100 represented "the best grass you ever smoked." Much to Jones's surprise, the placebo marijuana received an average rating of 57, while the real marijuana received a rating of only 66. Of special interest here is the fact that if a subject had a cold, and thus was unable to smell or taste the marijuana, he was much more accurate in distinguishing the placebo from the real "joints." It seems, then, that part of the marijuana "high" was due to the user's expectations of what he thought he would feel.

Let's return to the detection and control of demand characteristics. Detection is much easier than control. A researcher can never completely eliminate all the cues or prevent a subject from hypothesizing about the purpose of the experiment. An experimenter can

---

[1]A *placebo* is a substance that has no pharmacological effect but is believed by the person taking it to have this effect. For example, a "sugar pill" that a person believes will make him sleep is a placebo.

only hope that he is aware of these factors and that he can defend the statement that the independent variable provides a better explanation of the results than do the demand characteristics.

The most common method used to determine if demand characteristics were operating in an experiment is called debriefing. *Debriefing* involves asking the subjects a series of questions at the end of an experiment. These questions are usually concerned with the subjects' perceptions of the experiment, their beliefs concerning its true purpose, and their thoughts about the presence of any deception in the experiment. On the basis of this debriefing, a good questioner can determine if demand characteristics were operating during the experiment. If they were, he must revise his experimental procedure.

Evaluation apprehension

Evaluation apprehension, like demand characteristics, involves the subject's perception of the experiment. However, it is concerned with the subject's perceptions of psychological experiments *in general* and the problems they create. The typical subject enters an experiment with the assumption that part of the experimenter's purpose is to evaluate his mental health, moral character, and intellect. This causes the subject to be apprehensive or anxious and to try to put himself in the most favorable light. Thus, the results obtained in an experiment may be due to evaluation apprehension rather than to the independent variable (Rosenberg, 1965b).

Rosenberg has applied this concept to the results of some research on attitude change. Some researchers have investigated the question, How effectively can attitudes be changed by giving a person money for publicly supporting a position he does not privately agree with? Some of these studies have shown more attitude change as the result of a small re-

ward (e.g., $1) than a large reward (e.g., $20)(cf. Festinger, 1957). Rosenberg has argued that the $20 reward was so large that it made the subjects suspicious, and they came to believe that the true purpose of the experiment was to determine how much money it would take to get them to "sell out." Because the subjects did not wish to appear to be prostituting themselves, they did not change their attitudes. One dollar, on the other hand, was a reasonable amount and aroused no such suspicions. Thus, according to Rosenberg, the greater effectiveness of the small reward was due to the evaluation apprehension created by the large reward. There is good reason to believe that evaluation apprehension cannot totally explain the effectiveness of the small reward (cf. Aronson, 1969; Insko, 1967). But Rosenberg is correct in his argument that evaluation apprehension does occur among subjects in social psychological experiments.

Is evaluation apprehension a serious problem? Some researchers (e.g., Weber & Cook, 1972) believe it is. It has been argued that most subjects' principal desire in an experiment is to look good to the experimenter. When this desire comes into conflict with acting naturally, many subjects opt for behaviors that make them look good. For example, it is often difficult to get subjects in a laboratory to conform to the decisions made by other people. Weber and Cook believed that this may not be due to the weakness of the social pressure exerted on the subjects; instead, it may be caused by their desire not to appear spineless and wishy-washy.

A thoughtful examination of the study and the experimental procedure may help determine the extent to which evaluation apprehension *could* be operating. But it is difficult, if not impossible, to eliminate it. It is unreasonable to suppose that: (1) subjects will not be concerned about the experimenter's opinion of them and (2) subjects do not give a damn about this opinion. After all, no one wants to look like a fool.

How, then, can evaluation apprehension be eliminated? The best solution may be to make the experimental procedure and testing as unobtrusive or nonreactive as possible (cf. the previous section on reactive testing). This procedure would result in subjects being unaware of the fact that they are part of an experiment. Of course, we have already noted that field experiments which might accomplish this are extremely difficult to conduct. Social psychologists, for reasons of expediency, usually work in laboratory settings, and any laboratory experiment will arouse some evaluation apprehension.

Experimenter effects

So far, we have looked at how subjects view the experiment and the resultant problems. Now, let's turn to the *experimenter* as a cause of internal invalidity.

There are two types of experimenter effects that jeopardize internal validity: (1) those that do not affect the subjects' behavior in the experiment and (2) those that do. In the first category are factors such as recording errors, computational errors, and interpretation errors (Rosenthal, 1966). These are usually mistakes (the vast majority of which are unintentional) that the researcher makes in observing subjects' behavior, transcribing data, and analyzing the results. Psychologists, after all, are human and do make mistakes. If these mistakes are random (i.e., follow no clear pattern), then they tend to cancel one another out and present no real problem. If, however, there is a consistent (though unintentional) bias in the mistakes, especially in the direction of confirming the hypothesis, there may be potential problems. Rosenthal (1969) presented data which suggested that a good proportion of experimenters make errors in the direction of confirming their hypothesis.

However, Rosenthal quickly added that such errors are generally trivial and can be taken care of fairly easily by cross-checking the observations and computations of one experimenter with those of another more objective experimenter. That is, most of these errors are honest mistakes that are quite possibly the product of an experimenter's nonconscious desire to get positive results. If his work is checked by someone who is not as involved in the research, these errors can be detected and corrected.

The second group of experimenter effects are those that do affect subjects' performance in the experiment. The most troublesome of these effects is *experimenter expectancies*—the unintentional communication of desired behavior from the experimenter to the subject. It is best illustrated by the following three examples.

Rosenthal and Fode (1963) recruited twelve undergraduates as experimenters. They were told to show a series of pictures of people's faces to a group of subjects and have the subjects rate them as a success or a filure on a +5.00 to −5.00 scale. What the "experimenters" did not know was that: (1) the pictures had already been judged to be neutral on success and failure; (2) half the experimenters were told to expect a +5.00 rating and the other half a −5.00 rating; and (3) the experimenters themselves were the real subjects. Thus, the experimental manipulation was the experimenters' expectancies as to how people would rate the pictures.

Each experimenter-subject presented the pictures to other undergraduates. Those experimenter-subjects who expected a +5.00 rating elicited an average rating of +2.27. On the other hand, the experimenters who expected a −5.00 rating obtained an average rating of +0.48. These results were significantly different from each other. Bear in mind that the pictures had previously been rated neutral (i.e., 0.00) and that the same pictures were used by both groups of experimenters. How do we explain the results? Before trying to do so, bear in mind that it is reasonably certain that the experimenter-subjects did not cheat. Perhaps another example will provide the answer.

In the late 1800's, a number of entertainers on the vaudeville circuit made their living by performing with animals that could supposedly read and/or do simple mathematical problems. (One of the more notable of these was a pig that could read.) A school teacher named von Osten had a horse (later named Clever Hans) that could perform similar feats. The difference between von Osten and the others was that he did not profit from Clever Hans's talents and, more importantly, did not know how Clever Hans performed these acts. A man named Pfungst was asked to determine this. Pfungst soon found the asnwer. While keeping you in suspense for the moment, let us give you the following clues. First, Clever Hans was a rather ordinary horse if the person who asked him the question was not visible to him as he was working out an answer. (A typical question might have been, "How much is three times five?") Secondly, if the questioner did not know the answer, neither would Hans. If you have been able to figure out the explanation of Hans's ability, try to apply the same rationale to the previous study. Got it? Not yet? Read on!

As the final example of experimenter bias, consider this study by Rosenthal and Jacobson (1968). They gave an intelligence test to a number of grammar school students. Afterward, they told the teachers that some of the children were late bloomers; that is, the test indicated that these children would show a dramatic increase in I.Q. during the school year. Actually, there is no such classification as a "late bloomer"; more importantly, the children identified as late bloomers were chosen randomly. In other words, there were

no actual differences in potential between the supposed late bloomers and the rest of the students.

The most dramatic effect was observed in the first-grade children. In a retest of their I.Q., it was found that those children identified as late bloomers scored 15.4 points higher (on the average) than did other children.

You probably have a fairly good idea concerning the explanation of the three findings reported above. In the first case, the results were due to the subtle cues emitted by the experimenter-subjects, which were determined by their expectations as to how the pictures would be rated. Perhaps they smiled if the rating was in accordance with their expectations or grimaced if it was not. People respond to such cues and modify their behavior accordingly. Similarly, Clever Hans noticed the subtle cues emitted by the person asking him the question. (Pfungst found that people tilted their head forward when asking the question and straightened it when Clever Hans gave the correct answer.) The teachers' behavior is harder to specify. Rubovitz and Maehr (1971) suggest that the "late bloomers'" improved performance was due to the increased attention paid to them by their teachers.

What is the point of all this? It is, simply, that in all three examples, the "true" independent variable (i.e., the variable that caused the effect) was the experimenters' behavior. The experimenters' expectations caused subjects to act in a certain way and produced the observed behavior. Experimenter effects are a source of internal invalidity. This is because the observed effect is due not to the variable being manipulated but to an extraneous, uncontrolled variable—the experimenter's behavior.

While there is some question as to the importance of experimenter effects (cf. Barber & Silver, 1968), they are usually considered a serious problem in social psychology. It is commonly accepted that experimenters form hypotheses about their expected results and will unintentionally communicate these biases to their subjects. This problem can be solved by removing the opportunities for the experimenter to communicate his biases. This can be done in two ways: (1) automating the experimental procedures so that the experimenter never confronts his subjects or minimizes such contacts, and (2) using "blind experimenters." A blind experimenter is someone who does not know either the hypothesis of the study or which subjects are part of the experimental or control groups. An example of this procedure is provided by Orne and Evan's (1965) study, mentioned earlier, in which subjects were asked to pick a coin out of acid, throw acid at another person, and pick up a poisonous snake. The original purpose of this study was to determine if people would perform the same acts hypnotized as they would if awake. If the experimenter knew which subjects were hypnotized and which were not, his expectations about how

each type would act might affect the subjects' behavior. Therefore, the researchers either instructed subjects in how to feign hypnosis or actually hypnotized the subjects and then had the study itself conducted by a second experimenter. This second experimenter did not know who was faking and who was really hypnotized, and was also "blind" as to the true purpose of the study. Thus, the hypnotized–non-hypnotized differences, if any, could not be attributed to experimenter bias.

This is only a partial listing of the factors that threaten internal validity. If you understand these, however, you will have some idea of the problems a social psychologist must overcome in conducting his research.

A final comment about these factors. Most of them have been treated as problems the researcher should attempt to eliminate from an experiment. However, some of them might be interesting to study in themselves (McGuire, 1969b). For example, is it possible that demand characteristics can explain the success of some "faith healers" in curing people? That

---

"It runs in the family"

One of the more interesting real-world examinations of expectancy effects was carried out by Seaver (1973). He was interested in whether a teacher's experiences with a student would affect his expectations about the abilities of the student's younger brother or sister.

His subjects were two groups of first graders. The first group had a teacher who had taught their older brother or sister within the last three years. The other group also had older siblings in the same school, but they had had a different first-grade teacher.

Seaver looked at the relationship between older and younger siblings' performances in the first grade. Among the children who had the same teacher as their older sibling, he found that first graders whose brothers or sisters had done well also did well; those whose brothers and sisters had done poorly also did poorly. This was usually not the case for children who had different teachers than their older brothers or sisters.

Evidently, the older children's performance in first grade influenced a teacher's expectations about the abilities of their younger siblings. This expectation, in turn, affected the actual performance of the younger children.

is, could these peoples' expectations about a faith healer's miraculous powers contribute to the cures he produces? Evaluation apprehension might explain partially why minority group members often do poorly on I.Q. tests. And experimenter effects could possibly account for the apparent ability of some people to communicate their thoughts to others. (Also, see the box "It Runs in the Family.")

External validity

This chapter began with some examples of social behavior which occur in the real world. But most of the research described later was conducted in laboratory settings with college students as subjects. Does this research really tell us anything about real-world social phenomena?

Consider, for example, the typical study of human aggression. White male college students are used as subjects. They are brought into a laboratory and assured that nothing terrible will happen to them. They are made angry by a stranger insulting them. After this, their willingness to aggress against the stranger is measured by how many electric shocks they give him. The subject and the "victim" never really talk to one another, and after the shocks are given, the whole episode is over.

Now consider the following incident. In a suburb of Chicago, a jealous fifty-year-old woman shot her husband while he slept. The shot was not fatal, and several hours later he took the gun and shot her. For the next twenty hours, they took turns shooting each other. At one point, they sat in the bathtub, handing the gun back and forth, each taking a turn shooting the other (Tampa *Tribune*, Sept. 9, 1977).

Do the laboratory experiments on aggression really tell us anything about the reasons

for this bizarre episode? This is the issue of external validity. A study is *externally valid* if its findings can be generalized to: (1) people other than the original subjects used in it, (2) settings other than the one it was conducted in, and (3) independent and dependent variables which are similar to the ones measured in it (Campbell & Stanley, 1966).

One of the most persistent criticisms of social psychological research is that most of it is not externally valid. Some people claim that social psychologists construct situations in which subjects cannot act like real human beings. Some critics have argued that we make people behave not only like rats but like *solitary* rats (Argyle, 1969; Bannister, 1966).

In part, these claims are valid. Much social psychological research is conducted in highly structured, artificial settings. However, this environment is often needed so that we can isolate and identify the important causes of some social behavior. Also, society needs science for science's sake. That is, scientists must be allowed to examine phenomena that are not obviously relevant to today's problems.

But, we also strongly believe that much more attention must be paid to the generalizability of social psychological research. The phenomena we want to understand occur in the real world, not in the laboratory. For example, most of the real-world incidents of aggression do not consist of one stranger giving another stranger a limited number of electric shocks. In the real world, people most commonly attack friends, relatives, and lovers with any means available. Some attempt must be made to approximate these real-world conditions in the research on aggression.

Also, while society must let scientists work freely, it does have the right to demand that science help to solve its problems. This will require that social psychologists leave their laboratory, and theories of social behavior that work only in the laboratory, to examine the external validity of their research.

What factors interfere with external validity? The biggest single danger is the lack of internal validity. A study which is not internally valid cannot be externally valid. A researcher can't generalize from findings that are not due to the independent variables he believes caused them. For example, if history rather than the independent variable is the reason for some finding, and the researcher is unaware of this, then he will fail when he attempts to generalize his effect to other, similar independent variables. On the other hand, if a study *is* internally valid, one must consider other things that could jeopardize its external validity.

Unrepresentative subjects and selective sampling

It is fall 1980 and you are in charge of Jimmy Carter's reelection campaign. You believe that Carter's policies in the Middle East may have alienated a lot of voters. You contact a public opinion polling firm and ask them to conduct a survey for you. Obviously, the firm cannot ask every American over eighteen years of age how he or she feels about this matter. It would cost too much; besides, it's not necessary. The responses of less than 1 percent of the registered voters in the United States will be sufficient to give you the data you need. How is this possible? How can we estimate the opinions of more than 60 million people by asking only 1,500? The answer lies in the concept of sampling.

The first task in sampling is to identify your population. In the previous example, all registered voters in the United States served as the subject population. A *population* is the group to which you wish to generalize your results. It should be clearly identified before the research project begins. After you have identified your population, you randomly (by chance) sample (select) individuals from it. In its simplest form, *random sampling* means that every individual in the population to which you wish to generalize has an equal chance of being selected for use in your experiment. At this point, you may conduct your research on the sample only. Sampling theory says that if you truly sample randomly, you will be able to estimate accurately the behavior of the entire population in the same situation. Psychologists use samples and make inferences about populations because it is impossible to test every single member of most populations.

Are the people social psychologists study really a representative sample of the general population? An informal survey conducted by us and a study by Smart (1966) indicates that over 70 percent of social psychological research is conducted on college students.

According to McNemar (1946) "the existing science of human behavior is largely the science of (college) sophomores" (p. 333). McNemar's comment described the fact that most psychological research and the theoretical statements that come from it are based on the responses of a relatively unrepresentative group of subjects. The subjects are usually white, quite intelligent, and better educated than the vast majority of the general population. Oakes (1972) argues that college students are not "real people." While we would not go that far, it is true that they are not average citizens. Why do social psychologists (indeed, all psychologists) use these unusual subjects in their research? At the risk of insulting the readers of this text, the answer is probably that they are available and willing to work for free. Most social psychologists do not have the time to engage in a truly random selection procedure, and even if the necessary time were made available, the cost would be prohibitive. Therefore, the absence of money and/or time forces psychologists to conduct experiments on their students.

Now, this fact does not automatically create a problem. If you are investigating some phenomenon that is basic and common to all humans, the type of subject you use won't make much difference. For example, if you were studying how fast a nerve responds to some stimulus, the differences between college students and the general population are probably not important. Also, if your subjects differ from the general population in a way that could not possibly be related to the independent and dependent variables you are studying, there is no problem. For example, you are studying attitudes toward the exploration of Mars. You find that while 40 percent of the people in the world are left-handed, 80 percent of your subjects are. Common sense suggests that handedness is probably not related to attitudes on this topic, so there is no reason to be concerned.

Unfortunately, situations like these are relatively rare in social psychological research. Subjects often differ from the general population on the dependent variable the researcher wants to study. Consider the research on attitudes. College students, as a group, differ from non-college students in their political attitudes. For example, in the 1972 presidential election there was much greater support for Senator George McGovern on college campuses than for Richard Nixon. Now, no one seriously generalized from this finding to the non-college population. But if you pick up a current issue of one of the journals in social psychology, you will find articles about attitudes and attitude change which suggest that the results obtained are not just applicable to college students. That is, no attempt is made to qualify the generalizability of the findings. We are not suggesting that all research on attitude change is externally invalid simply because students' attitudes are not representative of the general population's. We are merely questioning whether it is appropriate to generalize from attitude studies conducted with college students to non-college populations without qualification.

A second kind of problem exists when a researcher's subjects might differ from the general population in how they react to the independent variable. For example, one major theory of attitude change assumes that attitudes change mainly because people want to be logical and consistent (Festinger, 1957). Most of the support for this premise comes from research conducted on college students. College students are (hopefully) continually asked to be logical and consistent. Would this theory have a different premise if it had been tested on a non-college population?

What is the solution to this problem? One possible solution to selective sampling is random sampling—that is, choosing subjects by chance from the general population. However, it is not easy to pick people at random and get them to sit in a laboratory for thirty to sixty minutes. Therefore, you must solicit volunteers, perhaps via an advertisement in a local newspaper. Even though you may obtain a *more* representative sample of subjects using this method, you will probably not obtain a random sample of the general population. That is, volunteering is not a random act. Volunteers differ from non-volunteers in some systematic ways.

The typical volunteer in an experiment is more likely to be a first-born child, younger, better educated, and from a higher socioeconomic class than non-volunteers. Further, he tends to be more sociable, less conventional, and more intelligent and to have more of a need for approval from others than the population in general (Altus, 1966; Leipold & James, 1962; McDavid, 1965; Marmer, 1967; Martin & Marcuse, 1958; Robins, 1963; Rosenthal & Rosnow, 1969: Suedfeld, 1964). In other words, the typical volunteer is a bright person who tends to want to please others. This may create some serious problems when one attempts to generalize about the influence process.

Note that the possibility of volunteers being more compliant than non-volunteers does not really jeopardize internal validity. The independent variable is responsible for the observed effect, but this variable may be effective only with a certain type of subject. Campbell and Stanley (1966) called this the interaction between selection biases and the experimental (independent) variable—a factor that jeopardizes external validity.

As an example of this self-selection process and the dangers it presents, consider the following example. A recent newspaper headline proclaimed, "American women unhappy with their marriages." The article described a study conducted by a prominent women's magazine on marriage as an institution. Questionnaires were sent to a large number of the magazine's readers on the topic of marriage. Less than 50 percent of the questionnaires were returned, but the vast majority of those women responding indicated that they were dissatisfied with marriage, particularly their own. On the basis of these data, the surveyors concluded that *most* women have unhappy marriages and that this explains the recent increase in the divorce rate in America. Although it's probably true that an unhappy marriage is a contributing factor in divorce, this survey does not allow us to conclude that most women are unhappy with their marriages. It seems at least reasonable to suspect that the majority of the women who returned the questionnaire were already unhappy in their marriages and desired to vent their feelings (anonymously, of course). One cannot generalize from these data to all other women.

Is there any way to overcome this problem? One solution is to study people in their natural environment without making them aware that they are being investigated. A researcher might conduct a field experiment, such as the one on guilt and helping described earlier. Or he might simply observe people's behavior and make no attempt to change it. For example, Nisbett and Kanouse (1969) were interested in the food-buying habits of normal and obese people. Therefore, they stationed observers in a supermarket and recorded the kinds and amounts of food normal and obese shoppers bought. (This technique is called a *field study* because no attempt is made to change the subjects' behavior.)

Field experiments and field studies are, unfortunately, very costly and time-consuming. Further, they do not give the researcher the precision and control he often needs. More importantly, there may be some ethical problems in these studies. In general, it is considered unethical to study a person without his being aware of it (Ethical Principles in the Conduct of Research with Human Participants, American Psychological Association, 1973). One of the results of the Watergate years was to increase the public's sensitivity to the invasion of their privacy. Psychologists have no more right to spy on people than the CIA, FBI, or any other government agency. For this reason, most of the research covered in this book was conducted in laboratory settings, with volunteers who were aware that they were in an experiment. What factors might jeopardize external validity in these circumstances?

Artificial experimental situations

The typical experiment is artificial in two ways. First, it examines a person's behavior in a setting in which he knows that some aspect of his behavior is being measured. Certainly, a person who knows he is being tested will react differently from someone who is not aware that he is being observed. This subject awareness may either increase or decrease the effectiveness of the independent variable; there is no general rule. But in either case, a person's behavior will probably be different if he knows he is being tested than if he does not know. This must be considered when making statements about the generalizability of research results.

The second way in which an experiment is artificial concerns the manner in which the independent variable(s) is administered. As has been pointed out, one of the primary goals of a social psychological experiment is to make it real—to create experimental realism (Aronson & Carlsmith, 1968). *Experimental realism* means that the subjects take the independent variable seriously; it has an impact on them. Experimental realism usually requires that only the independent variable(s) be presented to the subjects. If experimental realism is achieved, the experimenter can more easily determine the effects of the independent variable. But in achieving experimental realism, the experimenter may sacrifice mundane realism. *Mundane realism* refers to an event that occurs not only in the laboratory but in the real world as well. Contrived conditions in which the independent variable is designed to make a strong impression on the subject may result in the creation of a situation that has no real-life analogue. For example, as part of a study on obedience, subjects were asked (or instructed) to administer a large enough shock to another person (actually a confederate) to injure if not kill that person (Milgram, 1963). Obviously, this situation does not occur often in everyday life. The reactions of Milgram's subjects suggested that a good deal of experimental realism was created. But there was little mundane realism in this study.

Does this mean that Milgram's research tells us nothing about obedience in the real world? Absolutely not. It means only that his procedure must be repeated (psychologists use the word *replicate*) with other kinds of subjects and in other settings. This will enable social psychologists to determine if what Milgram learned about obedience in the laboratory explains obedience in a non-laboratory setting. In other words, one cannot state if a single study is externally valid or invalid. Replications of the study are needed to determine this.

Effectiveness of the independent variable

Before generalizing from an experiment, a researcher must consider any factors which might have influenced the effectiveness of his independent variable(s). First, he must consider who administers the independent variable to the subjects. In the typical laboratory it is the experimenter, an individual who usually has considerable prestige and credibility in the eyes of the subjects. Thus, an independent variable which is given by him may have more of an impact on the subjects than the same independent variable administered by an "ordinary" person in the real world (Hovland, 1959). Next, the researcher must examine the behavior of interest in a laboratory study. Typically, this behavior is of less importance to the subjects than a comparable behavior in the real world. Hovland has suggested that this may explain why attitude change is fairly easy to produce in a laboratory but difficult to produce in the field. Hovland argued that the attitudes which researchers try to change in the laboratory are usually less "ego involving" than those which people try to change in the real world.

Also, in the typical laboratory experiment, a relatively short period of time elapses between the administration of the independent variable and the posttest. In the real-life situation to which one is trying to generalize, a much longer period of time may elapse. For example, in the laboratory, frustration has been repeatedly shown to lead to aggression (Berkowitz, 1965). But in almost every study of this relationship, aggression has been measured shortly after frustration was created. Would the effect of frustration persist over time? The time interval must be specified if we are to make a statement about the external validity of this finding.

Finally, to what extent is there an interaction beween the taking of some pretest and the effectiveness of the experimental manipulation? The problem is not simply one of internal validity (cf. the section on the sensitizing effect of a pretest) but also of generalizing from a pretested group of subjects to a non-pretested population. It may turn out that a particular independent variable is effective only in conjunction with a pretest. Before a researcher generalizes to a non-pretested population, he must take this possibility into account.

Generalizing from the dependent variable

In the typical experiment, the experimenter attempts to determine if the effect observed was due to the independent variable (internal validity). Additionally, the experimenter may want to determine if the procedures used would produce similar effects in different settings with different groups of subjects (external validity). There is, however, a third question the experimenter may ask: with what other behaviors is this dependent measure correlated? This question will often be asked when the dependent variable is measured by a written test. For example, what is the relationship between subjects' responses to a written questionnaire on racial prejudice and their behavior when confronted by a black person? What is the correlation between one's self-reported feelings of anger and actual physical aggression? If the above relationship is strong (high), then the ability to generalize from the results is greatly enhanced. However, in actuality, these rela-

tionships have been consistently low; that is, the dependent measures have not correlated with other behaviors. For example, Wicker (1969) pointed out that written tests of attitudes do not correlate particularly well with actual behavior. (The reason for these findings will be discussed in Chapter Six.) A researcher must be able to demonstrate empirically that his dependent measure correlates with other similar dependent measures. If it does not, the external validity of a study is severely limited.

Conclusion

In the second half of this chapter, some of the problems encountered by social psychologists in their research were discussed. Basically, all such problems are related to two questions. The first is: was the independent variable(s) alone responsible for the observed change in an experiment? If the answer is yes, then the experiment is internally valid. If the answer is no, then the experiment is internally invalid and essentially worthless. A number of factors may jeopardize internal validity (e.g., history, reactive testing, demand characteristics, evaluation apprehension). All these factors are similar because they provide rival or alternative explanations of the results a researcher obtains in an experiment. Also, because of the nature of the phenomena social psychologists investigate, their research is especially susceptible to these factors.

The second question a researcher must be concerned with is: to what extent can I generalize my results? This question concerns the external validity of an experiment. A researcher can never be completely sure that the data from a study is completely generalizable—that is, that the results apply to all people in all settings. But he can increase the external validity of a study by the way in which he selects his subjects. The subjects should be randomly selected from the population to which he wishes to generalize. If they are not, the subjects should not differ from the population on any characteristics which could be related to the variable of interest. Further, external validity is aided by conducting experiments which are as realistic and lifelike as possible. The difficulty here, however, is that researchers cannot use subjects without telling them at some point that they are in an experiment. Such information, by itself, often makes an experiment artificial. Thus, a researcher must be very cautious in drawing conclusions about the external validity of his findings.

REVIEW QUESTIONS

(Twelve out of fifteen is passing)

1. The question of whether the independent variable is responsible for the observed effect concerns the concept of _____ _____ . (p. 15)
2. In an imaginary study on the effectiveness of some technique to convince people that there are supernatural events, an earthquake occurs between the pretest and the posttest. The obtained result may be due to _____ . (p. 16)
3. Changes in the subject as the result of the passage of time are said to introduce the variable of _____ into the experimental design. (p. 17)
4. A study which finds more attitude change with a group of subjects who received a pretest than with a group of subjects who did not receive a pretest demonstrates the _____ effect of a pretest. (p. 18)
5. Measuring a subject without his awareness is intended to solve the problem of _____ measures. (p. 18)
6. When a subject picks up cues from the experimental procedure, forms hypotheses on the basis of these cues, and then acts in accordance with these hypotheses, the results obtained may be due to the _____ _____ of the experiment. (p. 19)
7. The subject's fears that the experimenter may view him unfavorably are referred to as the problem of _____ _____ . (p. 21)
8. The unintentional cuing of a subject as to the desired behavior by an experimenter is called _____ _____ . (p. 22)
9. External validity is concerned with the researcher's ability to _____ his results. (p. 25)
10. One problem with using college students in social psychological experiments is that they may not be representative of the population to which the experimenter wishes to generalize. One possible means of solving this problem is for the experimenter to use the technique of _____ sampling. (p. 27)
11. The problem with using subjects in an experiment without their consent is that this procedure may be _____ . (p. 28)
12. An independent variable that has an impact on the subject is said to be _____ real (p. 29), but the fact that the experimental situation rarely occurs in the real world means that the experiment lacks _____ realism. (p. 29)

13. A researcher must consider: (1) who is the administrator of the experimental manipulation; (2) the time interval between the experimental manipulation and the posttest; (3) the behavior being manipulated; and (4) the pretest-experimental manipulation interaction before making any statements about the generalizability of the _____ variable. (p. 29)

14. In a study of attitudes, a psychologist finds that his dependent variable (a written questionnaire of attitudes toward Watergate) correlates quite highly with donations to the Republican Party. This measure of attitudes can be said to be _____ . (p. 30)

15. A study cannot be externally valid without first being _____ . (p. 26)

ANSWERS

1. internal validity 2. history 3. maturation 4. sensitizing 5. reactive
6. demand characteristic 7. evaluation apprehension 8. experimenter expectancy 9. generalize
10. random 11. unethical 12. experimentally/mundane 13. independent 14. externally valid
15. internally valid

SUGGESTED READINGS

There are a number of good books concerned with the basics of psychological research. Since this chapter only scratches the surface of how social psychological research is conducted, you may want to look at them.

Textbooks

The Human Subject, by John Adair. In this brief overview of the social psychology experiment, many of the problems I have described are developed in more detail.

The Psychology Experiment, by Barry Anderson. If you haven't had a previous course in experimental research, you might profit from reading this short book.

Experimental and Quasi-Experimental Designs for Research, by Donald Campbell and Julian Stanley. If social psychologists have a "bible," this fifty-page book is it. It is difficult.

Principles of Research in Social Psychology, by William Crano and Marilyn Brewer. This book is a little tougher than the first two, but it provides an excellent introduction to research in social psychology.

The Game of Science, by Garvin McCain and Erwin Segal. This is a well-written and even entertaining book on how scientists do research and the philosophy underlying scientific inquiry.

Popular literature

At the end of each chapter is a list of popular books that cover topics related to the subject matter of the chapter. Obviously, thrilling books about scientists in their laboratory are hard to find, but here are some we enjoyed.

Einstein: The Life and Times, by Ronald Clarke. This is probably the definitive book on Albert Einstein. It isn't easy reading, but if you stick with it you'll learn a lot about the scientific enterprise in general and physics in particular.

The History of Psychology in *Autobiography,* edited by Wayne Dennis. This is a series of books in which famous psychologists describe their lives and their research. It's enlightening and entertaining.

The Return of Sherlock Holmes, by Arthur Conan Doyle, or the *Seven Percent Solution,* by Nicholas Meyer. Both books describe the exploits of Sherlock Holmes, the world's foremost consulting detective. Holme's approach to the solution of crimes provides an excellent illustration of objective scientific inquiry.

Walden Two, by B. F. Skinner. We recommend this book over Skinner's more recent *Beyond Freedom and Dignity. Walden Two* is a more interesting and readable presentation of Skinner's views.

The Double Helix: A Personal Account of the Discovery of the Structure of DNA, by James Watson. Watson and his colleagues won the Nobel Prize for their work on DNA. In this informal account of their research, Watson describes the good and bad aspects of scientific investigation.

2 PERSONALITY VARIABLES AND SOCIAL BEHAVIOR

Arthur Schwartz

This chapter looks at the part personality variables play in the determination of social behavior. First, the chapter discusses the general question, are personality variables needed to understand and explain social behavior? Then three personality variables and their effect on people's behavior are described.

WHAT IS PERSONALITY

The first task in this chapter is to come up with a working definition of the word "personality." This is not easy. Think of all the different ways the word is used. Johnny Carson is a "personality," meaning that he is a well-known public figure. Your roommate tells you about someone who has a "terrific personality." In this case, she is probably talking about someone whom everyone likes and who is socially skilled. Freud used the term to describe the combination of the id, ego, and superego. Newspapers in New York City ran stories about the "sick personality" of "Son of Sam," a psychotic murderer who in 1977 claimed that he received his orders to kill from a labrador retriever. A best-selling book and a popular television movie were based on the sixteen "personalities" of a woman named Sybil.

None of these usages of the word "personality" are appropriate for this chapter. Instead, *personality* is defined as the ways in which a person typically reacts to the world around her. These typical reactions are called personality traits (or variables).[1] A *trait* is a way of thinking and/or acting which a person consistently displays across time and across situations. Consider Mohandas Ghandi, the father of modern India. Ghandi believed in simplicity, humility, and nonviolence. He acted in a simple, humble, nonviolent manner regardless of the situation he was in. When he lived among the poverty-stricken, miserable "untouchables" in the Black Hole of Calcutta, he wore a simple homemade cotton robe and cooked his own meals. When he stayed in the residences of kings and presidents, he wore a simple homemade cotton robe and cooked his own meals. He preached nonviolence when

the British ruled India and his fellow Hindus had no power. And he preached nonviolence to his fellow Hindus when they gained control of India and wanted to slaughter the Moslem minority.

It is important to point out that, in general, all people possess the same traits. People differ, however, in the extent to which they display these traits (Mischel, 1976). For example, consider the trait "charitable" and two fictional characters, Ebenezer Scrooge and Robin Hood. Robin was a kind of medieval socialist who, despite being born into a noble family, attempted to redistribute the wealth by stealing from the rich and giving to the poor. Scrooge, however, was someone who (until his experience with the three ghosts) viewed charity as something engaged in by the feeble-minded. Figure 2-1 shows Robin Hood and Scrooge as they might fall on the trait, charitable. Note that charitable is a continuous variable that has a *normal distribution*. What this means is that most people are moderately charitable; few are as uncharitable as Scrooge or as charitable as Robin.

Gordon Allport (1937), an early personality theorist, believed that people possess certain basic, or *cardinal,* traits which are at the core of their personality and change little throughout their lives. However, most contemporary personality theorists and social psychologists believe that people's traits can and often do change over the course of their lives. For example, one personality trait or variable is authoritarianism—the tendency to be closed-minded and submit uncritically to the orders of some authority figure (this personality variable will be discussed in Chapter Seven). It has been found that most students become considerably less authoritarian as they progress through college.

The trait approach assumes that all people possess the same traits, but in varying degrees. This differs from the *type approach,* which says that there are classes of people

---

[1]Contemporary social psychologists use the terms *personality variables* and *personality traits* interchangeably. I will do this also.

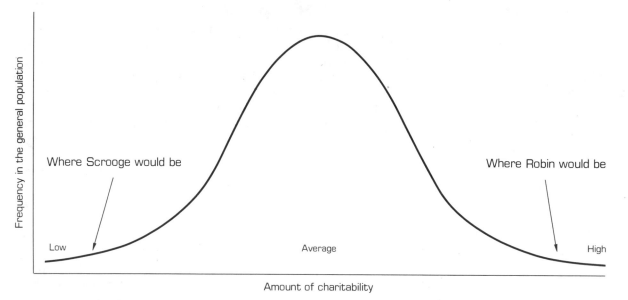

Figure 2-1. The distribution of the trait "charitable" in the general population.

who act one way and classes of people who act another way. In other words, some people possess a certain characteristic and others do not. Thus, whereas the trait approach assumes a continuity among people in terms of characteristics they possess, the type approach assumes discontinuity. A contemporary example of a type approach is astrology. Astrology proposes that if you are an Aquarius you will act one way, but if you are a Libra you will act another. Despite its popularity, astrology does not seem to be of much value in the prediction of behavior.

Measuring personality traits

A trait is a hypothetical construct. It doesn't really exist, and thus, it cannot be directly observed and measured. Therefore, traits are measured by asking people certain questions; these are contained in personality scales or questionnaires. Sometimes, these scales ask a person how well certain statements describe

her. For example, Spielberger, Gorsuch, and Lushene (1970) devised a scale to measure how anxious a person is. In this scale, the person is presented with statements such as: "I feel calm, cool, and collected" and asked to indicate whether she always, usually, sometimes, or never feels this way.

Other personality scales look more like attitude surveys. For example, Milton Rokeach (1960) devised a scale to measure dogmatism—the tendency to be closed-minded and reject ideas different from one's own. People who are tested on this scale are presented with statements such as "The United States and Russia have nothing in common" and asked to indicate whether they agree or disagree.

The crucial aspect of a personality scale is not the types of questions it asks but whether it has *construct validity*. A scale has construct validity if it really measures the personality variable it is supposed to measure. For example, Rokeach claimed that his scale validly measured dogmatism. For the scale to be of any value, he must be able to show that his scale does discriminate between people who have been *independently* judged to differ in their level of dogmatism. There are two basic ways of determining construct validity.

The known group technique

This means of establishing construct validity requires that the researcher identify groups of people who should differ on the personality variable in question. The scale is given to different groups. If they score differently on the scale and in the predicted direction, the scale has at least some construct validity.

Let us take the personality variable, need for approval, as an example of the known group technique. Crowne and Marlowe (1964) proposed that people differ in their need for approval—that is, the need to be socially accepted and to do and say socially desirable things. They devised a thirty-three-item, true-false questionnaire to measure this trait. The items in it were self-descriptive statements which, while socially desirable, were "untrue of virtually all people" (p. 22). For example, "I have never intensely disliked anyone" or "I always practice what I preach." According to Crowne and Marlowe, a person who agreed with these and other similar statements was giving a socially desirable but inaccurate description of herself and thus had

---

"I see a tall, dark, attractive stranger in your future (or perhaps an ugly, fair-haired, midget)"

Do you read your horoscope in the morning paper? Many people do. Recent surveys show that about half of all Americans put some faith in these descriptions of their personality and life. If astrology isn't really valid, why do so many people believe in it?

Some psychologists have proposed that the popularity of astrology is due to the generality of astrological predictions and descriptions of people born under certain signs. That is, astrologers give a person a description of her personality which is so general that it contains characteristics that every human being possesses. Thus, anyone who reads it believes that it describes her quite well (Snyder & Shenkel, 1975). This is called the "P. T. Barnum effect" because Barnum believed that his circus was successful because it contained something for everybody. Snyder and Shenkel studied how the P. T. Barnum effect is related to people's beliefs about astrology.

In one study, they wrote a general, flattering description of a person and gave it to a large number of people. Even though all the people received the same description, most people strongly believed that it had been written expressly for them.

A psychologist in France advertised himself as an astrologer in a newspaper and invited people to write in for their horoscopes. He sent the same description to everyone who requested it. Despite this, more than 200 people wrote back to tell him how accurate his description had been.

Finally, Snyder and Shenkel gave the same horoscope to a large number of people. Some were told that it was a general description of people. Others were told that it was based on the year, month, and day they were born. People who believed that this description was written especially for them saw it as much more accurate than did those who believed it was a general description.

a high need for approval. The known group technique of construct-validating this scale would be to identify some group whose members should have a high need for approval—say, sorority members—and another group who should have less of a need for approval—such as a group of nonsorority students. If the sorority members scored higher on the scale than the independents, this would suggest that the scale is measuring what it is supposed to measure.

Or would it? There are a number of reasons why some people join social organizations and others do not. A student's parents' income, her physical appearance, pleasantness or personality, and grades are related to membership in a sorority. People from different income levels could score differently on the scale for reasons that have nothing to do with need for approval. In general, the problem with the known group technique is a lack of control over those other variables which may be responsible for the obtained differences. In other words, it lacks internal validity (cf. Chapter One).

The extreme group technique

This is a more popular way to determine a personality scale's construct validity. People are given the scale and divided into high and low scorers on it. Then they are presented with a situation which should produce different reactions from people who differ in their scores on the scale. The advantage of this technique is that the researcher can pre-select her subjects and carefully devise a situation which should elicit only the personality variable in question. Crowne and Marlowe used such a technique with their social desirability scale.

They hypothesized that a person high in need for approval would be more likely than a person low in need for approval to indicate that a boring experiment conducted by a prestigious experimenter was enjoyable. There-

fore, they gave their scale to a group of students, divided them into high and low scorers, and conducted the experiment. It consisted of a subject taking twelve thread spools, putting them into a box, taking them out, and repeating this for twenty-five minutes. This task is incredibly boring. During the experiment, the experimenter acted in an aloof and professional manner. After the twenty-five minutes were up, subjects rated the study on interest level, scientific value, and their willingness to participate again. They made these ratings in front of the experimenter. Subjects who scored high on the personality scale given earlier (that is, indicated a high need for approval) said they found the study more interesting and valuable, and were more willing to participate in future similar studies than low scorers. Thus, the scale had predicted responses in a situation where need for approval should be relevant. Of course, Crowne and Marlowe conducted many more studies to further establish their scale's construct validity. But this study provides a good example of how a researcher construct-validates a personality scale by using the extreme group technique.

THE PERSON VERSUS THE SITUATION AS CAUSES OF SOCIAL BEHAVIOR

The killings began without warning. Harry Stanley told the C.I.D.[2] that one young member of Calley's platoon took a civilian into custody and then "pushed the man to where we were standing and then stabbed the man in the back with his bayonet . . . . The man fell to the ground and was gasping for breath." The GI then "killed him with another bayonet thrust or by shooting him with a rifle . . . . There was so many people killed that day it is hard for me to recall exactly how some of the people died." The youth next "turned to where some soldiers were holding another forty- or fifty-

[2]The C.I.D. is the Army's investigative unit.

(Ron Haeberle, *Life Magazine* © Time Inc.)

year-old man in custody." He "picked this man up and threw him down a well. Then [he] pulled the pin from an M26 grenade and threw it in after the man." Moments later Stanley saw "some old women and some little children—fifteen or twenty of them—in a group around a temple where some incense was burning. They were kneeling and crying and praying, and various soldiers . . . walked by and executed these women and children by shooting them in the head with their rifles. The soldiers killed all fifteen or twenty of them . . . ."

There were few physical protests from the people; about eighty of them were taken quietly from their homes and herded together in the plaza area. A few hollered out, "No VC. No VC" But that was hardly unexpected. Calley left Meadlo, Boyce and a few others with the responsibility of guarding the group. "You know what I want you to do with

them," he told Meadlo. Ten minutes later—about 8:15 A.M.—he returned and asked, "Haven't you got rid of them yet? I want them dead." Radioman Sledge, who was trailing Calley, heard the officer tell Meadlo to "waste them." Meadlo followed orders: "We stood about ten to fiteen feet away from them and then he [Calley] started shooting them. Then he told me to start shooting them. I started to shoot them. So we went ahead and killed them. I used more than a whole clip—used four or five clips." There are seventeen M16 bullets in each clip. Boyce slipped away to the northern side of the hamlet, glad he hadn't been asked to shoot. Women were huddled against their children, vainly trying to save them. Some continued to chant, "No VC." Others simply said, "No. No. No."

Haeberle noticed a man and two small children walking toward a group of GIs: "They just kept walking toward us . . . you could hear the little girl saying, "No, no . . . ." All of a sudden the GIs opened up and cut them down." Later he watched a machine gunner suddenly open fire on a group of civilians—women, children and babies—who had been collected in a big circle: "They were trying to run. I don't know how many got out." He saw a GI with an M16 rifle fire at two young boys walking along a road. The older of the two—about seven or eight years old—fell over the first to protect him. The GI kept firing until both were dead. (Hersh, 1970, pp. 49–50)

This passage is not from some gruesome novel. It is a summary of eye-witness accounts of the slaughter of more than 100 Vietnamese women, children, and old men by United States soldiers. It occurred in the village of My Lai on March 16, 1968. It resulted in the court-martial of the platoon's leader, Lt. William J. Calley, and a number of other officers.

Calley never denied that the massacre took place. His defense was basically that he was not personally to blame but was merely following orders under very difficult circumstances. The prosecution argued that Calley was an evil, vicious killer who should be punished. These two points of view can be rephrased into the following theoretical question. Was it the situation he was in, or was it his personality, that was responsible for Calley's actions? Although few if any social psychologists would condone Calley's actions, some might argue that the situation was to blame.

The situationists

The *situationists* are those psychologists who argue that the prime determinant of social behavior is the situation a person is in (Bowers, 1973). According to them, what people bring to a social situation (i.e., personality traits) is not as important as the characteristics of the situation itself (Harré & Secord, 1972).

The situationists' philosophical father is B. F. Skinner. Skinner and many others rebelled against the idea, prominent in psychology forty years ago, that all behavior could be explained by traits. He argued that if psychology bases its explanations of behavior on hypothetical constructs (e.g., traits), it will offer no real explanation of behavior; a trait approach stands in the way of adequately analyzing human behavior (Skinner, 1963).

Walter Mischel was, for a long time, the most outspoken advocate of the situationist position (Mischel, 1968, 1969). In 1968, he conducted an extensive review of the research on personality variables and found that, on the average, the correlation between personality variables and social behavior was only .30. If you square a correlation, it tells you what percentage of the difference between people on one variable can be explained by the other variable (cf. Chapter One). Squaring a .30 correlation produces the figure 9 percent. Thus, Mischel proposed that only 9 or 10 percent of people's social behavior could be explained by differences in their personality traits.

If personality variables are not an important cause of behavior, what is? Two findings from the research literature impressed Mischel. First, if the situation a person is in changes, her behavior will change. Also, understanding the characteristics of the situation produces a much more accurate prediction of her behavior than knowing about her personality traits. Thus, it seemed to Mischel that situational variables were the prime determinants of social behavior. Note that Mischel never claimed that people do not differ in their personality traits, and he did acknowledge that there is some consistency in people's behavior across time and situations. But (and this is an important "but") these personality differences are much less important in determining social behavior than are situational factors.

How might a pure situationist explain My Lai? She might first point to the attitudes of many of the American soldiers toward the Vietnamese. These people were considered by many G.I.'s to be subhuman. Someone who is a "gook" or a "slope" or a "slant" is not a human being. Second, the men were "shaped" in the same way rats are shaped to press a bar. At first, they were humane in their treatment of the Vietnamese, but as they spent more time in the field, they became increasingly brutal. One member of Calley's platoon described the process of change:

"It was like going from one step to another, worse one," he said. "First, you'd stop the people, question them, and let them go. Second, you'd stop the people, beat up an old man and let them go. Third, you stop the people, beat up an old man, and then shoot him. Fourth, you go in and wipe out a village." (Hersch, 1970, p. 43)

Next, there was the fact that the men had been in the field for weeks, were tired and with low morale, and had suffered numerous casualties. Three weeks before My Lai, six men in the company had been killed in a mine field. Two days before My Lai, a booby trap had killed one soldier and blinded another. It was the prevalent belief among the soldiers that these mines and booby traps were set by women and children, such as those they confronted at My Lai.

And finally, there was the pep talk given the night before My Lai by the company commander, Capt. Ernest Medina. In this talk, he seemed to have *ordered* the men to kill civilians in My Lai. From Hersch's account:

Harry Stanley told the C.I.D. that Medina "ordered us to 'kill everything in the village.' The men in my squad talked about this among ourselves that night," Stanley said, "because the order . . . was so unusual. We all agreed that Medina meant for us to kill every man, woman and child in the village." Charles West remembered hearing the captain say that when Charlie Company left the area "nothing would be walking, growing, or crawling." He also recalled the captain's saying that the women and children would be out of the area. Herbert Carter told the C.I.D. he thought Medina had been explicit. "Well, boys," he said the captain told them, "this is your chance to get revenge on these people. When we go into My Lai, it's open season. When we leave, nothing will be living. Everything's going to go." Sergeant Cowen testified that Medina "told us to destroy everything with life." He was asked if he took that to mean he was supposed to kill civilians. "Yes, sir," Cowen said. Charles Hall remembered Medina's saying, "Don't take any prisoners." Robert Maples recalled that Medina "told us everything in the village was the enemy. The way I think he said it—and the way they took it—was that anything in the village was VC." According to Michael Bernhardt, Medina said, "They're all VCs, now go in and get them. We owe them something . . . ." Then Bernhardt added, "He didn't have to specifically say women and kids." (Hersch, 1970, pp. 40–41)

Thus, the pure situationist would argue that the pattern of violence, the casualties suffered by the men, and Medina's orders resulted in ordinary soldiers acting like beasts. These men were in the wrong place at the wrong time, and this was the primary cause of their behavior. Slaughtering more than 100 people was something that almost anyone in a comparable situation might have done.

The trait theorists

The line of reasoning just presented would be hotly disputed by the *trait theorists*. They believe that behavior is determined primarily by a person's general tendencies, or dispositions, which she will display more or less independently of the situation she is in (Mischel, 1968). In other words, personality traits are the prime determinant of social behavior. How would the pure trait theorist explain My Lai? First, she might point out that despite being in a similar situation, not all the men in the platoon responded the same way. Some did not take part in the massacre. One even went so far as to shoot himself in the foot to avoid having to kill. Further, the trait theorist might observe that although My Lai was not the only atrocity committed in Vietnam, other soldiers in comparable situations did not do what Calley and his men did. Then the trait theorist would probably consider what type of person William Calley was. She might note that he was a relatively inept officer who kept getting his men lost and had been somewhat of a failure in civilian life. If the trait theorist accepted the accuracy of the description of Captain Medina's pep talk, she might argue that something about Calley's personality "caused" him to obey an order that was clearly illegal.

In the example just given, you can see the practical implications of the person-versus-situation controversy. Calley's defense at his court-martial was, in essence, a situationist explanation of his behavior. The prosecution, on the other hand, argued that Calley, rather than the situation, was responsible. How do you see it? In Figure 2-2 the reactions of a representative group of Americans are given.

The theoretical implications of this controversy are also important. The explanation of social phenomena that social psychologists propose will depend heavily on what they believe the causes to be. My position is that while personality variables are not as important as the trait theorists believe, they do play a significant role in determining social behavior. This point of view is based on two arguments. The first questions the notion that a .30 correlation accurately reflects the true relationship between personality variables and social behavior.

Is a .30 correlation the limit?

The nomothetic fallacy. Almost from the beginning of research on personality, psychologists have disagreed on how it might best be understood. In one camp are those who

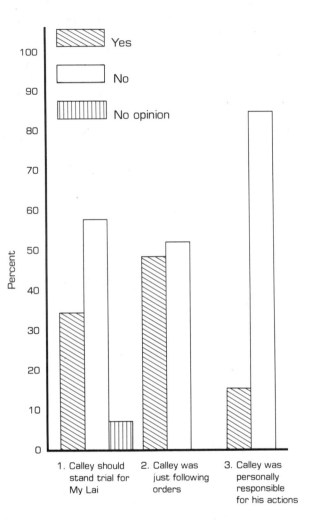

Figure 2-2. The attitudes of a random sample of Americans toward the trial of Lt. William Calley. (Adapted from Kelman & Lawrence, 1972)

have an *idiographic approach.* The leader of this group was Gordon Allport (1937, 1940, 1946). Allport believed that every human being is unique. Different people possess different traits, and traits which are relevant for one person's behavior may not be relevant for another's. Thus, in order to understand personality, a researcher must concentrate on why a particular individual acts in a particular way. Allport's idiographic approach eventually gave way to the *nomothetic approach.* According to the nomothetists, all people have certain traits in common; people differ only in terms of where they fall on the continuum. Thus, psychologists can formulate general, universal (i.e., nomothetic) laws of behavior which transcend specific traits, particular situations, and individual differences between people. (Note that the idiographic approach leads to a type view of personality; the nomothetic approach leads to a trait view.)

Daryl Bem and Andrea Allen (1974) generally accepted the nomothetic approach (as do most psychologists). But they also believed that errors in the application of nomothetic laws may, in part, be responsible for the conclusion that personality variables are only weakly related to social behavior. They identified three fallacies in the nomothetic approach. First, it assumes that all traits are relevant in all situations. This is probably incorrect. For example, it is unlikely that Muhammad Ali's feelings of compassion were relevant to his behavior in a boxing ring. Second, it assumes that traits will be manifested regardless of the situation. This, too, is probably an incorrect assumption. If I put a gun to your head and tell you to punch someone, you will probably do it, no matter how nonviolent you normally are. And finally, it is probably an error to believe that all people display the same trait in the same way or with the same consistency. For example, both my wife and I have strong feelings of love for our son. We would score identically on a scale which measured this. Yet my wife shows her feelings with physical affection toward our son, and I tend to show my love via games and joking with him.

According to Bem and Allen, if we lump traits, situations, and people together, the correlation between personality variables and social behavior will be low. But if we pick situations where certain traits are relevant and identify people who consistently show these traits in these situations, the relationship between personality variables and social behavior will be rather strong. Note that Bem and Allen have put an idiographic qualification on the nomothetic approach. That is, they say that one will only be able to accurately "predict certain behaviors across certain situations for certain people" (p. 511).

As part of a test of this proposal, Bem and Allen asked college students to indicate how friendly they were. Then the students were asked, "How much do you vary from one situation to another in how friendly and outgoing you are?" This question was used to classify the subjects into two groups: those who were consistently friendly and those who were not. Both groups were rated on how friendly they were across a wide variety of situations (e.g., their interactions with parents, friends, and strangers). Then the ratings were correlated for both the consistent and the inconsistent subjects. The average correlation between inconsistent subjects' friendliness across situations was no better than the .30 Mischel had reported earlier. But among the consistent subjects, this correlation was almost twice as large. The .30 "barrier" had been broken by the consistent subjects. For them, the trait of friendliness was an important cause of their behavior.

Other researchers (Campus, 1974; Snyder & Monson, 1975) have also found that people differ in how consistent they are across situations, and that it is much easier to predict the behavior of consistent than inconsistent people. Thus, the weak relationship between personality variables and social behavior may, in part, be due to the failure to recognize the fallacy of a purely nomothetic approach.

The multivariate critiques. Over the last ten to fifteen years, high school students' scores on the Scholastic Aptitude Test have fallen dramatically. What is the reason for this?

There is no one reason for the decline. An increased number of disadvantaged students taking the test, a movement away from the fundamentals in high schools, the increased amount of time spent watching television, and a host of other factors have, *in combination,* contributed to poorer performance on the test. The point of this brief example is this: relatively few phenomena can be explained by only one variable. Usually several interacting variables are responsible.

How have social psychologists investigated the relationship between personality variables and social behavior? Typically, they have used the *single variable correlational* approach. A researcher who uses this technique correlates *one* personality variable with some behavior. Kenneth Gergen and his associates have argued that this research strategy is inadequate and often produces misleading results (Gergen, Gergen & Meter, 1972; Marlowe & Gergen, 1969, 1970; Staub, 1974). It is quite unlikely that social behavior is the product of any one personality variable. It is determined instead by the simultaneous effects of many different personality traits. To examine these simultaneous, joint effects, Gergen and others have advocated the use of multivariate statistics.

Here is one illustration of the value of a multivariate approach to personality variables. A simple research question is: What personality and situational variables affect a person's decision to return or keep a lost item of value that she has found? I and several of my colleagues asked this question (Penner, Summers, Brookmire, & Dertke, 1976). We gave our subjects a number of personality scales. A few weeks later, each of them "happened upon" a dollar bill which we had planted in a room where they were taking a test. The dollar appeared to have been lost by the person who had used the room before them.

There were two ways we could have attempted to answer the above question. One

would be to use the single variable approach—that is, to correlate separately each personality scale with our dependent measure (returning or taking the dollar). When we did this, we found that none of the personality variables had much of an effect on the subjects' behavior. Then we used the second approach, a multivariate statistic, to determine the joint effect of all the personality variables we had measured on the subjects' reactions to the lost dollar. These personality variables, in combination, had a significant effect on our subjects' behavior.

Why? Probably because the decision to take or keep something that belongs to someone else is not determined by only one personality trait; it depends on a number of personality traits. Thus, another reason for the low correlation between personality variables and social behavior may be the use of the single variable correlational approach. Multivariate approaches may well show a much stronger relationship.

The interactionist viewpoint

The second criticism of pure situationism has come from the *interactionists.* Their basic premise is that social behavior results from the interaction between the person and the situation she is in. *Both* personality traits and situational variables determine social behavior (Endler & Magnusson, 1976).

The interactionists think it is inappropriate to pit personality variables against situational variables as the cause of behavior (Endler, 1973; Phares, 1973). There are several reasons for this belief.

First, personality and situational variables together can explain more of people's behavior than either class of variable considered alone. This point is seen in the lost dollar study described above. In addition to the personality variables, we examined the effect of the supposed owner of the lost money. (The dollar was owned either by an individual or an institution, or had no identifiable owner.) This situational variable, in combination with the personality variables, produced a more accurate prediction of our subjects' responses than either the situational or the personality variables alone.

Second, situational variables are not always more important than personality variables. When situational cues as to behavior are clear, they will determine behavior. But when they are ambiguous, personality traits will be the primary cause of how the person acts (Phares, 1973). An example will make this point.

Imagine you are Noah and you know a massive flood is coming. In one instance, the Lord gives you specific instructions to build an ark, with its size and the number and type of animals with which to stock it. In this instance, the situational cues clearly dictate your behavior. Most people would probably build an ark like Noah's and take two of each kind of animal. In other words, the existence of strong, explicit situational cues diminishes the effect of individual differences. But imagine another possibility. In this case the Lord tells you about the coming flood and stops. Could a psychologist predict your behavior? I don't think so. You might build an ark or you might simply build a boat big enough for your family. Further, if you were not instructed to do so, would you bring two of every animal aboard? Speaking personally, the prospect of sailing for years with a boatload of animals does not sound very appealing. Therefore, it would seem reasonable that in the second case your behavior could not be accurately predicted. The situational cue (a coming flood) does not give us enough information. One would need to know a great deal more about Noah—the man and his personality, for personality variables will determine much of his behavior.

The person and the situation cannot be treated as two separate and independent entities (Bowers, 1973). Just as the situation influences a person's behavior, the person influences the situation. One's personality, attitudes, values, etc., will affect her view of the situation and thus how she acts in it. People don't see the world around them in the same way a camera does (i.e., as a perfect reflection of reality). A dramatic example of this was provided by David Rosenhan (1973).

He trained eight normal individuals to act as if they were schizophrenics and sent them to various mental hospitals around the country. During intake interviews at these hospitals, Rosenhan's cohorts displayed schizophrenic symptoms and were admitted as patients. Once they were in the hospital, they started acting normally. One of them was reclassified as a "schizophrenic in remission" (meaning that he was still schizophrenic, but wasn't showing it). The remaining seven people's diagnoses never changed! The staff of these hospitals never noticed that these people were acting in a sane manner. We know that they were because their fellow patients recognized this and questioned them about it. How in the world could the hospitals' staffs have missed this? Rosenhan did not attribute it to gross incompetence. Rather, he believed that the staff's "set," or expectation, that everyone in their institution was emotionally disturbed was the reason. The inability of trained professionals to spot normal behavior was due to how they saw the situation they were in.

Bowers also pointed out that the person determines the situations she goes into. People do not randomly select the situations they enter. Instead, they choose situations which tend to have objectively similar characteristics. For example, Ronald Reagan does not talk with a conservative business group one night and go to a pot party thrown by a rock group the next. The people Reagan chooses to associate with and the situations he selects are much more consistent than that.

The interactionist position is becoming the prevalent point of view among personality theorists and social psychologists. Indeed, even Walter Mischel, once the chief advocate of situationism, is now considered to be an interactionist (Mischel, 1973, 1977). A research strategy which combines the multivariate approach with the interactionist point of view will demonstrate that personality variables do play an important role in social behavior.

Conclusion

We have been interested in how personality variables affect social behavior. The chapter began by pointing out that many social psychologists do not consider personality vari-

ables when explaining social behavior (Sarason, Smith, & Diener, 1975). This is partly because scores obtained from personality scales do not correlate very well with people's behavior.

Two questions were asked about this low correlation: What are the reasons for it? And, does it mean that social psychologists should not include personality variables in their explanations of social behavior? In answer to the first question, I argued that the low correlation may be the result of inadequate means of studying personality variables and how they affect behavior. The answer to the second question was a definite no. It is incorrect to ask whether personality variables or situational variables are more important causes of behavior. The most fruitful approach to understanding social behavior is to consider both types of variables together.

REVIEW QUESTIONS

(Eight out of ten is passing)

1. A _____ _____ is a hypothetical construct which is proposed as an explanation of the consistency in people's behavior across situations. (p. 37)
2. The notion that what differentiates people in terms of personality variables is how much of the variable they possess represents a _____ approach to personality. (p. 37)
3. Imagine you have constructed a personality scale which you believe measures tubomania (a need to watch television). You give it to a group of people and identify high and low scorers on the scale. You then place these two groups in a room with a stereo and a television set and record how much time they use each one. This is called the _____ group technique of construct validation. (p. 40)
4. If you were a lawyer who was defending a guilty client, you would hope the jury took a(n) _____ view of human behavior. If you were the prosecuting attorney, you would hope that the jurors believed that _____ were the causes of people's behavior. (p. 44)
5. The position that all people share certain traits in common is called the _____ approach to the study of behavior. (p. 45)

6. Bem and Allen's proposal that we identify subgroups of people for whom a certain trait is relevant to their behavior across situations represents an _____ approach to nomothetic laws. (p. 45)

7. Examining the correlation between scores on a scale of social desirability and membership in the Junior Chamber of Commerce represents a _____ _____ _____ approach to the study of the relationship between personality variables and social behavior. (p. 46)

8. If one looked at a number of personality variables simultaneously as they affect social behavior, a _____ approach would be used. (p. 46)

9. Theorists who believe that social behavior can be best understood by considering both personality and situational variables are called _____ . (p. 46)

10. The study which showed that staffs at mental hospitals had difficulty identifying normals supports the interactionist argument that people's _____ of a situation influences their behavior in it. (p. 47)

ANSWERS

1. Personality variable (or trait)   2. trait   3. extreme   4. situationists, trait   5. nomothetic (or trait)   6. idiographic   7. single variable correlational   8. multivariate   9. interactionists   10. perception (views, expectations about)

THREE PERSONALITY VARIABLES

I have selected three personality variables which social psychologists have studied extensively. Space does not permit me to discuss the origins of individual differences in them. Therefore I'll ask you to accept the following general statement on faith. Individual differences in personality traits are the result of different learning experiences people have had. The way we are treated by our parents, friends, and teachers, and our other day-to-day experiences with our environment, all contribute to the development of our personality traits.

As you read the research on these three variables, two things may strike you. First, most of the studies have used the single variable correlational approach that was criticized in the first half of the chapter. This is unfortunate. Single variable studies provide some information on the relationship between personality variables and social behavior, but not a full explanation of the behavior being investigated. I would much prefer to see studies that investigate the joint effect of a number of personality variables on behavior.

Also, you will see that the interactionist point of view is not reflected in this research. This, too, is unfortunate. Certainly, you would have a much better understanding of how personality variables are related to social behavior if their interaction with situational variables was considered.

Locus of control:
Who or what controls you?

Here's a puzzler for you aspiring clinical psychologists. In the early 1950's a man named Karl S. was referred to a clinical psychologist for psychotherapy. Karl was not really neurotic, but he was extremely unhappy and distressed. After several interviews, his therapist concluded that Karl was uncomfortable because he possessed almost no social skills. He didn't know how to talk to people and as a result had no job, no friends, and no female companions. The therapist did not attempt a Freudian solution to Karl's problems. Rather, he decided that if he could teach Karl how to talk to people and thus make friends and get a job, Karl's problem would be solved. One of the things Karl was taught was how to talk to a woman and ask her for a date. He used this training to meet and date several women. But Karl wasn't any happier. Karl also learned how to talk to a potential employer and eventually got a job, but he was still distressed.

According to learning theory, Karl should have improved. A behavior which is rewarded should be repeated in the future and should raise a person's expectations about future successes. But this wasn't happening. Should Karl's therapist have turned to Freud?

E. Jerry Phares, the clinical psychologist who treated Karl, found another explanation for his behavior. Although Karl was having several successful experiences, he did not believe that he was really responsible for them. For example, he explained his ability to get a job by proposing that the employer was partial to veterans (Karl was a vet), or happened to feel good that day, or perhaps there were no other applicants for the job. In short, Karl believed that what happened to him was determined by factors he could not control. As a result, he derived no satisfaction from the things he achieved (Phares, 1976).

Experiences such as this caused Phares and Julian Rotter to question a purely Skinnerian explanation of human behavior. The Skinnerian proposes that people respond to stimuli in their environment and if this response is rewarded, they will perform the behavior again. Thus, if you know a person's reinforcement history, you can predict her behavior. Rotter (1954) believed that more was needed to understand human behavior.

Rotter (1975) argued that the probability that a person will engage in a certain behavior is affected by two factors. The first is the person's perceptions as to whether this behavior will produce some reinforcer for her. This is called the person's *expectancy*. The second factor is the *value* of the reinforcer. If a person expects a behavior to lead to a certain reinforcer and values this reinforcer, she will probably perform this behavior. Although Rotter was interested in the factors which influence one's perceptions of both expectancy and value, I'll concentrate on the factors which influence expectancies. This is because of a key concept that grew out of Rotter's interest in expectancies.

Rotter proposed that two classes of variables determine a person's expectancies. First, there are cues about the specific situation the person is in. For example, people who are 4 feet 10 inches tall would probably not try out for a basketball team, no matter how badly they wanted to play. They know from previous experience that people under five feet do not do very well in basketball games. They would also notice that the players are considerably taller than they are.

The second factor in determining expectancy is the person's general estimate about how successful she will be in achieving certain goals. One such estimate concerns whether the person believes her reinforcers are controlled by her own behavior or factors beyond her control. This particular expectancy Rotter called *locus of control* (1966). According to Rotter, some people tend to have an *internal* orientation, while others are *externally* oriented. Lefcourt (1966) described the difference in these orientations. People with an internal orientation tend to see the things that happen to them as being due to their own actions; that is, they are responsible for what happens to them. People with an external orientation tend to see the things that happen to them as being unrelated to their own actions; they are due to factors beyond their control. It is important to note that I used the word "tend." The difference between people with regard to locus of control is one of degree. Further, the amount of influence this generalized expectancy will have on a person's behavior will depend on how clear the situational cues are and how much previous experience the person has had with the situation. If the cues are explicit and/or the person has had a great deal of experience in the situation, this generalized expectancy should have little effect on her behavior. In a new situation without any definite cues, this generalized expectancy will have considerable effect.

Race and sex differences

As a group, blacks tend to be more external than whites (Joe, 1971; Lefcourt, 1972; Phares, 1976). Why? There are two possible explanations. First, black children are brought up in an environment that keeps reinforcing externally oriented views of the world. The black child who believes that she is "the master of her fate" is soon told by her parents and peers that this is not the case. As a result, the child comes to believe that the world around her is beyond her control (Phares, 1976). The second, and probably better, explanation is that blacks actually do have less control over their environment.

The locus of control scale

The actual Locus of Control Scale (Rotter, 1966) consists of twenty-three items. A person is given two statements per item and asked to indicate which ones she agrees with. The four items given below are from an early version of the scale. Your answers to them won't really tell how internal or external you are. They should, however, give you some idea of how this personality variable is measured.

Choose one from each pair.

1a.* I am the master of my fate.
1b. A great deal that happens to me is probably a matter of chance.
2a.* Promotions are earned through hard work and persistence.

2b. Making a lot of money is largely a matter of getting the right breaks.
3a.* People like me can change the course of world affairs if we make ourselves heard.
3b. It is only wishful thinking to believe that one can really influence what happens in society at large.
4a.* In my case, the grades I make are the results of my own efforts, luck has little or nothing to do with it.
4b. Sometimes I feel that I have little to do with the grades I get.

*Asterisked statements represent an internal orientation.

Consider a young black person living in an urban ghetto. She is poorer than her white counterpart. She is more than twice as likely to be unemployed, and her family is probably receiving financial assistance from the government. Her neighborhood may be razed because some bureaucrat decides that urban renewal (which many black people call "black removal") is needed. Even if she gets a job, she may be told that it's because "The government says that we gotta hire your kind." Thus, a black person with an external orientation may simply be a realist. Her external orientation is a fairly accurate assessment of the way society operates. In a study which examined these two explanations, it was found that blacks are not external because they believe that luck controls what happens to them. Rather, their externality was based on the belief that *society* limits their control over their own lives (Gurin, Gurin, Lao, & Beattie, 1969).

Women, as a group, tend to be more externally oriented than men (Maccoby & Jacklin, 1974a). Two factors seem to be operating to produce this. First, there is the way women are socialized—that is, how their parents raise them. Girls are not encouraged to be as independent or competent in dealing with their environment as boys are (Maccoby & Jacklin, 1974a; Piacente, 1975). Independence and mastery over the environment as a child seem to lead to an internal orientation as an adult (Chance, 1965; Katkovsky, Crandall, & Good, 1967). In addition to socialization differences, the actual degree of control a woman has over her life is objectively less than a man's. For example, in many states women cannot hold property in their own name or sign legal contracts. Despite a good deal of political activity by women's groups, sex discrimination in the job market still exists. Many states are attempting to pass laws which will prevent a woman from getting an abortion even if she was raped or the

victim of incest.[3] Thus, women may be more external than men for the same reason that blacks are more external than whites. They do not, in fact, have as much control over their lives as men.

Carlos Garcia-Lozano

Locus of control and social behavior

People with an internal orientation have a different view of the world from people with an external orientation. This difference should be reflected in the two groups' social behavior.

[3]One female newspaper columnist suggested that these laws are based on the notion that it's all right to save the fetus and throw away the mother.

Externally oriented people should be more fatalistic about life than internally oriented people. This prediction follows from the statement that "externals" believe that their life is ruled by factors beyond their control. Thus, an external should make less of an attempt to cope with the environment than an "internal." The external should tend to accept passively what the environment brings. Sims and Baumann (1972) provided an interesting test of this proposition.

They had noted that the death rate from tornadoes in the American South was five times greater than in the North. The first and most obvious set of explanations of this difference would be that tornadoes in the South occur more frequently and/or are more severe, and/or the tornado warning system in the South is less efficient than the system in the North. It turns out, however, that no appreciable differences exist between the North and the South on these or other related factors. Sims and Baumann proposed that the higher death rate in the South may be due to Southerners' locus of control orientation. To test this, they compared an area of Alabama with an area of Illinois. Although tornadoes in the two areas struck just about as often, and with comparable intensity, the death rate in Alabama was twice that of Illinois. Residents of both areas were given a modified version of Rotter's locus of control scale.

The Alabama respondents were much more external than those from Illinois. For example, they stressed "God" and "luck" as the prime determinants of what happened to them far more than did the people in Illinois. Further, even when the Alabamians knew a tornado was coming, they were much less likely to take any action than were the people from Illinois. Sims and Baumann summarized the differences between the two samples in the following manner: "Persons like the respondents in Illinois, who believe they direct their own lives . . . use their heads and

the technology of society and they take action . . . the respondents from Alabama, who believe that God (or fate or luck) controls their lives, have less confidence in their own ability to have an impact on reality . . . await the fateful onslaught, watchful but *passive*" (p. 1391, italics added). Although, to be sure, other factors are also responsible for the difference in the death rates, this study does demonstrate the relationship between people's locus of control orientation and their response to the environment.

Internally oriented people should be more active in their attempts to master and change their environment than externally oriented ones. Internals should believe that they can change their environment and should also be more interested in doing so if the environment does not seem responsive to their needs. This tendency should take the form of political activism. I say this because political activists seem to be people who believe that they can change their environment and that they should have more control over their lives. Thus, we would expect political activists to have an internal orientation. It turns out, however, that the relationship is not this simple.

Let's first look at the evidence in favor of greater activism among internals. A number of researchers (e.g., Gore & Rotter, 1963; Sank & Strickland, 1973; Strickland, 1965) found that black civil rights activists were more internally oriented than nonactivists. Similar results were initially found for women involved in the women's liberation movement. But there is much more evidence which shows the opposite relationship—that externals are more likely to engage in active protests (Sanger & Alker, 1972). Indeed, Rotter (1970) found that at the same time political activism was increasing on college campuses (from 1960 through 1970), students were becoming more external in their scores on his scale. How can these conflicting data be explained?

First of all, there is reason to believe that political conservatives are more receptive to the internally oriented items on Rotter's scale (Thomas, 1970). Since conservatives are less likely to engage in picketing, protest marches, etc., this explains partly why externals are more likely to be activists. But this finding still does not clarify why externals engage in protest and political activism. To answer this question, we must examine more closely what Rotter's scale really measures. Mirels (1970) used a technique known as factor analysis and showed that Rotters' scale may measure two aspects of general locus of control—personal control and system control. *Personal control* refers to the extent to which a person believes that she controls her own life. *System control* refers to a belief concerning an individual's impact on institutions (Sanger & Alker, 1972). Mirels pointed out that a person may be internal with respect to her own life but external with respect to institutions. Most observers agree that one of the factors in political activism is the belief that the government is unresponsive to the people (Kenniston, 1968). Thus, the unexpected finding becomes explainable.

A political activist scores in an external direction on Rotter's scale because many of the items deal with *system control*. Activists believe they lack system control and are motivated to obtain it. Nonactivists believe they already have that control, score internally, and see no reason to protest. Thus, if one looks only at the total score on Rotter's scale rather than at the score on personal control and system control items, one reaches the oversimplified conclusion that political activists are externally oriented.

A more appropriate characterization of the political activist seems to be provided by Sanger and Alker's (1972) study of women involved in the women's liberation movement. They found that these women were internal on items that measure personal control but external on those that measure system control. More recent and detailed studies of militant blacks suggest a similar pattern. Caplan (1970) described the typical black militant as internal on personal control but external on system control. That is, they view the "system" as responsible for black Americans' plight. The slogan "All power to the people" thus seems to be a demand that system control move from institutions to individuals.

Externally oriented people should attribute other people's behavior to the environment to a greater extent than should internally oriented people. Rotter's scale not only measures a person's belief about what controls her own behavior but also about what controls people's behavior in general. As an example of this, let us return to the My Lai incident. Hochreich (1972) administered the locus of control scale, asking her subjects to assign blame for what happened. External males (but not females) placed more of the blame on the government and the military, and tended to downgrade the personal responsibility of Lieutenant Calley and his men. A similar result was found by Sosis (1974). Internals and externals read a description of an auto accident and were asked to indicate the driver's responsibility as opposed to bad luck. Internals found the driver more responsible than did externals. Probably as a result of this, they recommended more severe punishment for the driver than did externals.

Changes in locus of control

From what we have said so far, you might get the impression that if you are born black, female, or with the "wrong" set of parents, you are destined to spend the rest of your life wondering what the fates will do to you next. This is not the case. A person's orientation with regard to internal or external locus of control can be changed. Herbert Lefcourt

(1976), one of the leading theorists on this subject, vigorously argues that events in a person's life can change her orientation. For example, McArthur (1970) examined the effect of luck. At the time of his study, the Selective Service conducted a lottery to decide who would be drafted into the armed forces. Balls with each day of the year on them were placed in a bin and drawn randomly. If a man's birthdate was drawn early, there was a good chance he would have to serve. If it was drawn late, he would probably not have to serve. Thus, a truly chance event determined whether or not a person would be drafted. A group of college males filled out the locus of control scale before and after the lottery. Although there was no difference in the scores before the lottery, after the lottery those men who "lucked out" were significantly more external in their scores than were those who were likely to be drafted.

A more systematic attempt to change locus of control was reported by deCharms (1972). In this study, an attempt was made to move the locus of control orientation among black school children from an external toward an internal one. As already noted, blacks are more external than whites. It has also been found that externals have lower academic achievment than internals (Coleman et al., 1966). With this in mind, deCharms trained the children's teachers (who were also black) in exercises designed to change their students' locus of control. The instruction of the teachers, and later that of their students, lasted a year. These children were compared to a matched group of children who had not received locus of control instruction. It was found that the experimental children had become more internal.

The effects of this training on academic achievement were impressive. Normally, black children are only slightly behind white children academically until about the fifth grade. At this point, however, white children

continue to move ahead, while black children begin to slow down. This "normal" pattern occurred for those black children who did not receive the locus of control training. Those who *did* receive the training, in contrast, did not fall further behind their white counterparts. If these results can be repeated, they are extremely important and quite exciting.

Educational Resources, University of South Florida

Need for achievement

The concept of need of achievement grew out of Henry Murray's theory of needs (1938). According to Murray, a *need* is a force which moves a person to find a means to change an unsatisfactory situation. For example, hunger is a need. When a person gets the "munchies," she looks for food. She is deprived and seeks to end her deprivation. Murray proposed that there are two types of needs: (1) primary or unlearned needs, such as the need for food, water, sex, etc., and (2) secondary or learned needs. These secondary needs differ from primary needs in having no direct connection with physical satisfaction. They do not arise out of some physiological deficiency, such as lack of food or sleep. But like the more basic needs, the secondary needs motivate the person to act. To paraphrase an old adage: Man (or woman) does not live by bread alone.

Murray proposed a number of secondary needs. Among them were a need for power, a need for affiliation, and, most important for the present discussion, a need for achievement. He defined the *need for achievement* as the need "to accomplish something difficult . . . to overcome obstacles and obtain a high standard. To excel oneself. To rival and surpass others" (Hall & Lindzey, 1957, p. 173). This learned need to excel, to achieve, to be successful, motivates people just as the need for food motivates them. David McClelland and his associates' work on need for achievement (usually referred to as *n Ach*) demonstrated its importance in human behavior.

McClelland measured people's need to achieve by administering the Thematic Apperception Test (T.A.T.)(Murray, 1943). A picture from this test is presented on page 57. If you were taking this test, the interviewer would ask you to tell a story about the picture. What is going on? What has happened? This is a projective test—that is, it is based on the assumption that people will project their needs into the story they tell. McClelland found that people will project their need to achieve in the stories they tell about certain T.A.T. pictures.

There have been numerous attempts to devise more objective means of measuring n Ach. But the most commonly used technique is still the T.A.T. and the scoring of the achievement imagery in the stories the respondents tell. This technique has several drawbacks. First, the stories are not easy to score; people must be trained in the scoring system. Second, the test-retest reliability of this measure of n Ach is not very high.[4] Finally, the pictures themselves may influence how much n Ach is expressed in the story a subject tells. For example, if the people in the picture are facing one another, subjects will express a higher level of n Ach than if the people are not facing each other (Alper & Greenberg, 1967). Pictures of women elicit lower n Ach than pictures of men (Lesser, 1973). Despite these difficulties, there has been a great deal of research on n Ach. To begin the review of this research, let's examine race and sex differences.

Race and sex differences

There are two serious problems in writing about differences in n Ach between blacks and whites and men and women. The need to achieve is considered a positive characteristic in our society. As one oil company puts it in its advertisements: "The spirit of achievement is the spirit of America!" Therefore, it is difficult for a white, male psychologist to talk about need for achievement in blacks and women without sounding racist or sexist. The aim here is to give you an accurate review of the literature. This literature dicloses differences in n Ach between the races and the sexes. It is my hope that you will not react like the Ancient Greeks and kill the bearer of bad tidings.

The second problem is more serious. This chapter is being written in 1977; it is based on research which in many cases was conducted before 1970 (in psychology there is often a

[4]*Test-retest reliability* refers to the extent to which a person obtains the same scores on the test each time she takes it. The low test-retest reliability of the T.A.T. creates a serious problem for the researcher. She does not know which of the two scores she has obtained is an accurate indiciation of a person's need to achieve.

A picture from the Thematic Apperception Test (Murray, 1943).

two- to three-year lag between the collection of data and the publication of an article based on thosc data). By the time you read this book, much of the data presented in it will be at least ten years old. The status of and opportunities for women and blacks in America have changed dramatically over this period and will probably continue to change.

Need for achievement is a learned motive. As changes in the environment of blacks and women occur, their learning experiences will also change. Thus, what was true in 1970 may not be true in 1980. Therefore, much of what follows is unavoidably dated. Readers who are interested in n Ach in women and blacks should consult more recent references.

Women and achievement. It has commonly been assumed that a woman will inevitably have a lower need for achievement than a man. Part of the reason for this assumption is that the way parents treat their children affects a child's level of N ach. And we know that parents treat boys and girls quite differently. For example, parents who encourage their children to display independence and competence at an early age will probably produce children with a stronger need for achievement than parents who discourage these behaviors (Rosen & D'Andrade, 1959; Winterbottom, 1958). It has been found that girls are encouraged to show independence and competence at a later age than boys (Collard, 1964). Further, girls are more likely to be overhelped and overprotected by their parents. This should discourage independence and competence among girls and result in a lower need for achievement among women.

Thus, it may surprise you that women show as strong a need for achievement as men do when they respond to a T.A.T. picture (McClelland et al, 1953). But unfortunately, there is more to the story than a general need to achieve. When the specific goals a person wants to achieve are examined, men and women differ. For men, achievement means the attainment of intellectual and occupational goals—to be doctors and company presidents. Women aspire to be socially accepted and good homemakers, and if they desire occupational success, it is in such traditionally female occupations as teaching and nursing. In other words, men may want to be Harry Reasoner, but women don't want to be Barbara Walters (Mednick & Weissman, 1975; Stein & Bailey, 1973).

Further, as men and women grow older, the difference in a need for educational and occupational achievement seems to increase. While a man's need for achievement increases after he leaves college, a women's decreases (Baruch, 1967). What are some possible reasons for this sex difference?

Bonanza Jellybean, a character in Tom Robbins' brilliant novel, *Even Cowgirls Get the Blues,* provides us with the first explanation. She is explaining why she and her "sisters" have taken control of the dude ranch they work at.

"Little boys may be discouraged from adventurous yearning by parents and teachers, but their dreams are indulged, nevertheless, and the possibilities of fulfilling their childhood expectations do exist. But little girls? Podner, you know that story as well as me. Give 'em doll babies, tea sets and toy stoves. And if they show a hankering for more bodacious playthings, call 'em tomboy, humor 'em for a few years and then slip 'em the bad news. If you've got a girl who persists in fantasizing a more exciting future for herself than housewifery, desk-jobbing or motherhood, better hustle her off to a child psychologist. Force her to face up to reality. And the reality is, we got about as much chance of growing up to be cowgirls as Eskimos have got being vegetarians. I'll tell you." (Robbins, 1976, p. 130).

Ms. Jellybean's analysis is supported by several studies. For example, some data suggest that a woman's parents, friends, and teachers reinforce the idea that she should strive only for very limited achievement goals and should concentrate instead on winning social approval (Ellis & Bentler, 1973; Hoffman, 1972).

Another explanation is based on Atkinson's (1964) view of need for achievement. According to Atkinson, a person's level of n Ach is made up of her hope for success and fear of failure. People with a high N ach have a greater hope for success than fear of failure. Women, as a group, do not have much confidence in their abilities. For example, even though women's grades are usually better than men's, they *estimate* their academic performance to be inferior to that of men (Crandall, 1975). Thus, women may display less need for achievement because they fear they will fail if they try to excel in something.

Matina Horner (1972) proposed that it's not failure that women fear; rather, it is success. Horner believed that intellectual and occupational achievement places a woman in conflict. A woman is expected to do well in school, but at the same time, she knows that it is "unfeminine" to do better than men. Thus, a lower need for achievement in women is not due to a fear of failure but rather a *fear of success*. A woman fears that if she does well intellectually or occupationally, she will pay for this success by being rejected by the men (and women) in her environment. To demonstrate this, Horner (1968) asked male and female college students to tell stories about members of their own sex who were successful in a male-oriented occupation. The stories were scored in terms of the consequences of success for the people in the stories. About 65 percent of the women believed that success would result in negative outcomes for the woman. In contrast, less than 10 percent of the men believed that a successful man would be hurt. Horner's explanation of lower need for achievement among women is intuitively appealing, but is it correct? Subsequent research (e.g., Alper, 1973; Condry & Dyer, 1976; Monahan, Kuhn & Shaver, 1974) suggests that it may not be. For example, Monahan et al. found both males and females believed that a woman who is successful in a male-dominated occupation will have negative experiences. Thus, Horner's results may have simply reflected general societal stereotypes about nontraditional women. At present, there is no strong evidence for a fear of success in women.

Will these sex differences continue? Women are moving into the job market in ever increasing numbers. Further, women are entering occupations which were once the exclusive domain of men. Research has shown that women who are intellectually and professionally successful display as much n Ach as do their male counterparts (Block, von Der Lippe, & Block, 1973). Thus, the increasing rejection of traditional sex roles by women may eventually result in the disappearance of sex differences in the need to achieve.

Blacks and achievement. The interest in black people's need to achieve was based on the following facts. The need to achieve is rather strongly related to success in school and business. In the 1960's blacks, as a group, had the lowest n Ach level of any ethnic group in America (McClelland, 1960; Rosen, 1959; Veroff & Peele, 1969). And finally, the level of academic and economic achievement among black Americans was significantly lower than among white Americans. For example, the average black had two years less education than the average white. Almost 50 percent of black people did not have more than eight years of school (Fein, 1966). Blacks in school, on the average, scored lower on tests of academic performance than their white classmates (Epps, 1969). In the area of employment, the picture was equally distressing. The unemployment rate among blacks was twice that of whites. Black Americans comprised 10 percent of the experienced labor force but less than 3 percent of professionals (doctors, lawyers, engineers). Blacks, if they worked, were employed primarily in low-level jobs, such as laborers or domestic helpers.

Social psychologists recognized that racism was probably a major cause of these differences. But some also felt that the fact that blacks were low in n Ach might also be important. The first goal these researchers set was to try to understand why blacks, as a group, had such a low level of need for achievement.

One explanation proposed that blacks have a low need to achieve simply because they are poor. In general, it has been found that people from the lowest socioeconomic class will have the lowest levels of n Ach (Crockett, 1962). Thus, the problem was poverty rather than race. In support of this view was the finding that among black Americans, high levels of education and income are associated with a strong need to achieve (Nuttall, 1964).

Other researchers believed that there were certain unique things about the black experience in America that are responsible for their low n Ach. For example, David McClelland believed that slavery was an important factor. It resulted in black parents teaching their children that there was no reason to strive for excellence, because the white slave master controlled their lives. This message continued to be transmitted in the black culture even after slavery was abolished. McClelland also believed that the absence of a continuously present male figure in the homes of lower-class blacks contributes to a low need for achievement. This explanation is based on McClelland's rather chauvinistic assumption that only males are involved in truly achievement-oriented activities. Thus, a black boy who sees only his mother and has no achievement-oriented male to learn from will not have a strong desire to achieve.

This second explanation is quite offensive to many blacks (and women). It suggests that the basic black family structure is somehow deficient or sick. It probably also overstates the extent to which males are, in fact, absent from the typical black family. As the book *Roots* and other more scholarly studies have shown, slaves went to extraordinary lengths to keep their families intact. Among contemporary American blacks, the number of households without males has probably been overestimated. One reason for this is our welfare laws. A black woman on welfare will receive more money for her children if she claims she has been abandoned than will a woman who lives with her unemployed husband.

Is the gap between blacks' and whites' need to achieve narrowing? I'm not sure. In fall 1977, the unemployment rate among blacks was the highest in thirty years. This would argue against an increase in the need to achieve for blacks. Two factors might, however, be causing an increase in n Ach among blacks.

One is the increased number of desegregated schools in Northern and Southern cities. Veroff and Peele (1969) examined the effect of school desegregation in a "small midwestern city." A group of black children who had been transferred to a predominantly white school were compared to black children who remained in their almost entirely black school. A significant increase in the achievement motivation of the transferred boys (but not the girls) was found. This suggests that if the current trend toward full integration continues, one result might be increased n Ach among black school children.

The second factor is the emergence of a large number of black adult figures with whom black children can identify and who display high levels of n Ach. Prior research (Block et al., 1973) has shown that children who see adults with high levels of n Ach will tend to have a stronger need for achievement themselves. The black models who are high in n Ach come from two sources. One is the greater percentage of black Americans in the middle socioeconomic class. The other is the appearance in the media of successful blacks. Blacks are no longer portrayed on television and in the movies only as servants and maids. These successful, middle-class black models *may* produce higher levels of n Ach in black children. Subsequent research will determine this.

Need for achievement and social behavior

Researchers interested in need for achievement have examined how differences in people's need to achieve are related to academic, economic, and occupational success.

Need for achievement should be related to

academic success. However, the relationship between n Ach and grades is not as simple as you might suppose. In fact, it is *curvilinear.* People with very low and very high levels of n Ach do not perform as well in school as do people with moderately high levels of n Ach (McKeachie, 1961). The relationship at the low end seems to imply that these people are not motivated to perform well in school. In contrast, those who are extremely high in n Ach seem to have unrealistically high goals. That is, their actual ability does not match their estimate of their ability.

If, however, we eliminate the extremes, we do find a positive correlation between n Ach and grades (Bendig, 1958; Reiter, 1964). But the correlation is not overwhelming. The reason for this is probably that grades, like any other behavior, have multiple determinants. Factors such as intelligence, anxiety related to tests, and other competing motives, like a need to be socially accepted, probably serve to lower the correlation. Thus, the simple, obvious relationship between grades and n Ach is neither simple nor obvious, but it is in the predicted direction.

Need for achievement should be related to economic and professional success. There does, indeed, seem to be a positive relationship between these two factors. McClelland (1965) conducted a long term study of the relationship between n Ach and status of occupation. He assessed n Ach in a group of male college students. Fourteen years later, he contacted these men and determined the jobs they now held. He found that those men who were originally high in n Ach held jobs of greater status than those whose n Ach had been low. On the basis of this and other studies, it seems safe to conclude that n Ach is correlated with occupational success. Thus, we see that individual differences in n Ach can affect an individual's behavior.

Need for achievement should be related to economic growth. We know that people differ in n Ach and that this difference will show itself in differing occupational success. It is possible that entire countries differ in their need to achieve and that this difference is, in part, responsible for differences in their rate of economic growth.

How do we measure an entire culture's n Ach? What measure of economic growth do we use? How do we take factors such as war and the lack of natural resources into account? Difficulties of this type would scare off most researchers, but not David McClelland (1960).

McClelland believed that a society's collective need to achieve is reflected in what it teaches its children. Thus, he decided to use the stories contained in children's books to measure the need to achieve. A wide variety of children's stories were read and scored for achievement-related themes. It was much more difficult to decide on a valid measure of economic growth. After much trial and error, McClelland decided to use increases in per capita income and the amount of electricity a country consumed. He then collected data on need for achievement and economic growth in thirty countries over a twenty-five-year period. He believed that a country's collective need to achieve had a significant effect on its economic growth.

McClelland found what he had expected. His study showed that periods of economic growth were preceded by high levels of achievement-oriented stories in children's books. Economic decline followed periods in which achievement was not stressed.

Davies (1969) attempted an even more intriguing way to determine the relationship between a society's need to achieve and economic growth. To understand what he did, we need a little background. Eliot Aronson (1958) had found that people high and low in n Ach "doodle" in different ways. For example, a person with a strong n Ach will draw discrete, unattached lines, while people low in n Ach will draw blotchy, connected lines. Davies wondered if these achievement differences could be detected in the designs on the pottery from ancient cultures. He chose the Minoan society, which had existed on the island of Crete about 4,000 years ago. The Minoan culture flourished in its early stages but declined dramatically over the next 1,000 years and eventually disappeared. Davies used Aronson's doodle-scoring procedure on recovered Minoan pottery. He found that the designs on the pottery showed a decline in need for achievement that exactly paralleled the decline and eventual destruction of the Minoan culture.

These results may cause you to run out and investigate the books children are reading or examine that piece of pottery you received for Christmas. Therefore, let's put McClelland's findings in perspective. First, differences in the achievement-related themes in children's books could explain only about 20 percent of the differences in countries' rate of economic growth. Also, many people have questioned his measures of economic growth and whether he adequately controlled for wars and natural disasters in the countries he studied. Certainly, the fact that no war has been fought on American soil in more than 100 years has contributed to America's economic growth. Thus, while McClelland's research is innovative and his boldness to be admired, it seems unlikely that need for achievement can *totally* explain the rate of a country's economic growth.

Changes in need for achievement

If n Ach is partly responsible for economic growth, is it possible to systematically change a person's or a country's level of n Ach and thus increase their economic success? McClelland and Winter (1969) reported on a series of training programs conducted first in India and later in the United States that attempted to do this. The Indian program was designed for people who were already in business, but who were rather unsuccessful. They received about three weeks of workshop training designed to make them aware of the concept of need for achievement and its relationship to business success. They were trained in achievement-related business activities and given exercises to make them examine their own need to achieve. A few months after the program was completed, these men were compared to a group of businessmen who had not received it. On almost all measures of business success, the trained group was far superior. Of more interest to us here are the training programs conducted with black participants in America. As previously noted, blacks score lower on n Ach than whites (Rosen, 1959) and, as a group, have had less business success than whites.

A group of sixteen black men from a Boston ghetto took part in the training program. They were in their early thirties. Few had graduated from high school, and many had criminal records. Although they were not the hard-core unemployed, they were by no means successful businessmen. Although there was no control group (a group that did not receive the training), the results were so impressive that it seems unreasonable to attribute them to natural changes among these men. McClelland's description of these men two years after the program speaks for itself.

[One] man brought two income properties and went into business for himself as a building contractor. Another entered night school to take a business degree at a nearby university and obtained a much better job. A third bought a car and no longer works exclusively as a construction foreman for another man, but now operates his own apartment renovating business. A fourth expanded his photographic business, began a program series for the local educational television station, and helped form a new organization called the Massachusetts Achievement Trainers, Inc. (MAT).

Several graduates of the courses felt that the type of training they had received would be valuable for other men in their situation. With . . . help, several of them were given enough further training to become trainers themselves. The resulting company, MAT, has already successfully undertaken a number of motivation training jobs to prepare Negroes and other disadvantaged groups for employment and economic advancement. The organization began with seven part-time members and a capital investment of $350.00. During its first year of operation, 1966, the Roxbury area of Boston provided four small, short-term contracts. In two short years, MAT has grown into a non-profit corporation with nine board members, four provisional members, a full-time secretary, executive director and business manager, and numerous technical consultants. Training contracts are long-range and national in scope, and the financial worth of the organization has multiplied itself many times. (McClelland & Winter, 1969, p. 352)

Machiavellianism

In 1532 Nicolò Machiavelli wrote *The Prince,* dealing with the ways of obtaining power. Historians disagree as to whether Machiavelli intended the book as satire or as actual advice to the various noble families struggling for power in sixteenth-century Italy. Whatever his intent, Machiavelli's name has come to mean a *tactic of manipulating people in order to attain power and the belief that the end justifies the means.*

In the early 1950's Richard Christie became interested in whether or not certain people were more inclined to use such tactics than others. That is, were there people who basically agreed with Machiavelli's advice and who used these tactics in their day-to-day lives? Christie and some associates held long informal discussions on what such a person would be like. On the basis of these discussions and their observations of people who had been successful in attaining power, they arrived at four attributes which seemed to characterize these people.

First, to be an effective manipulator, *one must have a relative lack of emotion when dealing with other people.* That is, a good Machiavellian would probably not get emotionally involved with others in her environment. Why? because to attain power she might have to manipulate other people, and it would be hard to hurt someone she likes very much or form an allegiance with someone she hates. Yet these are the very things she may have to do in order to get what she wants. Therefore, a good manipulator will avoid emotional entanglements. A good example of a Machiavellian is H. R. "Bob" Haldeman, an advisor to former President Richard Nixon. Consider this example of lack of concern for a dying senator who had been a strong supporter of the President. (This passage is from *The Palace Guard,* by Dan Rather and Gary Gates [1975].)

[Once] a request came up through White House staff channels urging Nixon to telephone a mortally ill Republican Senator. When it reached Haldeman's desk, the super efficiency expert decided that since the Senator was in that bad a shape he probably wouldn't be able to talk very well over the phone anyway, and thus it would make more sense to hold off and place a call to his widow later. So, instead of passing the request on to Nixon, he sent it back down through the channels with the memorable command: "Wait until he dies."

The idea of two telephone calls for one dying Senator apparently offended his sense of efficiency. (Rather & Gates, p. 277)

Christie also proposed that *a good manipulator is not strongly committed to a political ideology.* Idealism brings with it a certain amount of inflexibility which might stand in the way of achieving power. Rather and Gates described Haldeman as follows:

Faced with a choice, he would bend or relax his supposed conservative principles if, by doing so, it would serve Nixon's purposes . . . . Other conservatives [may have been distressed by Nixon] . . .

courting the Soviets and mainland Chinese . . . . But no such concerns touched Haldeman's conscience (p. 291).

Haldeman said about himself in the 1968 presidential campaign:

I've never concerned myself with the issues. I'm a political mechanic. I work programs, not issues. . . . Dick [Nixon] says there has to be a few sons of bitches in any organization and I'm his (cited in White, 1975, p. 105).

Next, Christie proposed that a good manipulator would have *a lack of concern with conventional morality*. This is not because the manipulator is necessarily amoral or immoral. Rather, it is because the pursuit of power usually produces conflicts between conventional morality and the attainment of some goal. The effective manipulator is one who puts the attainment of the goal first. Thus, a good manipulator can be quite ethical and moral in some aspects of her life. Haldeman, for example, was a devoutly religious man. Yet at the same time, he condoned burglaries, wiretapping, political sabotage, and attempts to destroy political "enemies." Further, a good manipulator does not lie or cheat "for the hell of it." It is only when such behavior will lead to the attainment of some goal that she is more willing to do so and less remorseful after the act than a nonmanipulator.

Finally, Christie proposed that a good manipulator would *lack any gross psychopathology*. Christie did not believe that a Machiavellian is the picture of mental health. He was merely suggesting that to be a good manipulator, one must be able to make rational, unbiased judgments about other people. A person who is highly neurotic would have a hard time doing this since her inner needs might bias her perception of other people.

Before turning to a brief review of Machiavellianism and social behavior, some impor-

tant qualifications of the above statements are in order. First, do not conclude that a Machiavellian is a cold, unloving, unprincipled person. Bob Haldeman, for example, while almost robot-like in his role as Nixon's advisor, was warm and affectionate toward his family. Theodore White (1975), the noted political historian, described Haldeman as having an "almost puritanical morality" about certain matters, such as sex, obligations to one's family, and money. Thus, to characterize Haldeman as unloving or unprincipled would be grossly inaccurate. More generally, Machiavellianism does not exist in pure form in any individual. This is an important point, not only in considering Machiavellianism but the previous personality variables as well. These variables are abstractions; they do not exist exactly as described by psychologists in any real person. Finally, although the above example was drawn from a conservative Republican administration, the leaders of *most* political movements tend to be Machiavellian in their tactics. Anti-war activists, for example, used to place women in the front of their marches so that if the police attacked the demonstrators, the evening news would show the police beating women. (The cry was, "Chicks up front"!) In general, studies on Machiavellianism suggest that it is not peculiar to any racial or ideological group (Christie & Geiss, 1970).

Machiavellianism and social behavior

Manipulative tendencies can be measured at a relatively young age, and these differences result in relatively reliable differences in behavior. Dorthea Braginsky (1966) devised a scale to measure Machiavellianism in children. She gave this scale, called the "Kiddie Mach," to a group of ten-year-olds. On the basis of the children's scores, she classified them as high, low, or medium in Machiavellianism. The high and low children were introduced to an experimenter posing as a home economist who wanted them to taste a new type of cracker which was supposedly quite nutritious. In fact, it was an ordinary cracker soaked in quinine, which, as you might imagine, made it taste terrible. After the child tasted the cracker, winced, and was given some water and candy, the experimenter said that it was important to get other children's reactions to the cracker. She offered a nickel for every cracker the child could get another child to eat. Then each high Machiavellian and each low Machiavellian was paired with a middle scorer. To make a long story short, the high Machiavellians talked their partners into eating more than 6 crackers on the average, whereas the low group enticed their partners into eating an average of 2.79 crackers. This was true for both boys and girls.

A Machiavellian should have less of a concern with conventional morality that a non-Machiavellian. This proposal was tested by Exline, Thibaut, Hickey, and Gumpert (1970). They proposed that if they were correct, Machiavellians should be able to lie more effectively following an unethical act. One way this could be measured was by examining the amount of eye contact dis-

played by a person who has been accused of cheating. People who have Machiavellian tendencies should spend more time looking at their accuser (i.e., be more effective liars) than non-Machiavellians. Subjects who had been classified as either high or low Machiavellians on the basis of their responses to the Machiavellian scale (see "The Machiavellian Scale") were talked into cheating on an experimental task by the experimenter's confederate. Afterward, the experimenter questioned the subjects about how they managed to do so well on the task. After about ten minutes of innocuous questioning, the experimenter accused the team of cheating. Observers hidden behind a one-way mirror recorded the amount of time subjects looked into the experimenter's eyes before and after the accusation. Before the accusation, the two groups did not differ in the amount of eye contact displayed. After the accusation, however, the high Machiavellians continued to maintain eye contact, but the low Machiavellians looked away. Exline et al. proposed that this difference demonstrated that people with Machiavellian tendencies were less concerned with their cheating and subsequent lying and thus were better liars.

Machiavellians should be better manipula-

The Machiavellianism scale

Richard Christie and his colleagues used the sentiments expressed in *The Prince* and other similar sources to create items for their scale. Here are some items from an early version of the Machiavellianism scale. They will give you an idea of how this personality variable is measured. They will not tell you if you have a future as a White House aide.

Answer *true* or *false*.

1. Most people don't know what is best for them.
2. It is safer to be feared than to be loved.
3. There is no point in keeping your promise if it is to your advantage to break it.
4. It is wise to flatter important people.
5. Never tell anyone the real reason you did something unless it is useful to do so.

(On all questions, the answer *true* indicates Machiavellian tendencies.)

tors than non-Machiavellians. This statement has to be made less general. It will be true only when (1) the manipulation attempt occurs in a face-to-face interaction, (2) the situation allows for improvization (that is, it is not too highly structured), and (3) the situation involves issues which are important to the participants. This third point is the most important. According to Christie and Geiss, Machiavellians are not always more effective at manipulation than other people. It is only when a Machiavellian's stand on some issue might affect her effectiveness in making a deal that she should be more successful. Why? Because Machiavellians have a low ideological commitment.

This proposal was tested by Geiss, Weinheimer, and Berger (1970). They compared the ability of high- and low-Machiavellian male college students to convince other students to vote a certain way on bills in a mock legislature. If the other members of the "legislature" supported the sponsor of the bill, he was awarded "votes" which were exchanged for money at the end of the experiment. Members of this legislature considered two general types of bills: (1) those dealing with *neutral* or trivial issues, such as the issuance of a new postage stamp, and (2) those dealing with *emotional* issues, such as getting out of the United Nations. The rules of the legislature allowed a member to engage in informal bargaining in order to get his bill passed.

Now recall that what supposedly differentiates high and low Machiavellians is not their general manipulational skill. Rather, it is the high Machiavellian's ability not to let her own feelings on the issue get in her way (low ideological commitment). Therefore, Geiss et al. predicted that high and low Machiavellians would do equally well on the neutral issues, but *high Machiavellians would do much better than low Machiavellians on the emotional issues.* Why? Because passage of a bill sometimes required the sponsor to argue

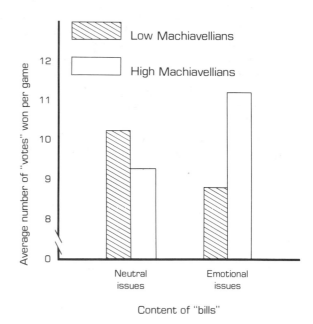

Figure 2-3. The relative effectiveness of high and low Machiavellians when arguing for neutral and emotional issues. (Adapted from Geiss et al., 1970; cited in Christie & Geiss, 1970)

against his own private opinion on an issue. For example, both a high and a low Machiavellian who favored United States membership in the United Nations might have to get a bill opposing this through the mock legislature. This, Geiss et al. conjectured, would interfere with the low Machiavellian's bargaining, but not the high Machiavellian's. Figure 2-3 presents the results of the experiment. As this figure shows quite clearly, high Machiavellians *were more successful only on the emotional issues.* The high Machiavellians' bargaining effectiveness was less influenced by how they felt about the issue than that of the low Machiavellians. The goal of winning votes (money) superseded their position on the emotional issues.

Thus, it seems that some people enjoy and are good at manipulating others. Can this tendency be changed? We are not aware of any research on this question. Society seems to be demanding that something be done about the Machiavellianism of its politicians. Unfortunately, it is not clear whether our political leaders have in fact become less Machiavellian. After all, what could be a better manipulative ploy than to claim you are not a manipulator? It would certainly be interesting to determine if, in fact, Watergate has reduced the Machiavellian tendencies among politicians in particular and among Americans in general.

Conclusion

The second half of this chapter described three personality variables and their effects on social behavior. It must be reemphasized that these variables do not exist independently of situational variables. As noted in the conclusion to the first half of the chapter, social behavior is determined by personality and situational variables acting together.

Rotter's concept of locus of control is concerned with generalized beliefs as to the factors responsible for what happens to us. People with an internal orientation tend to believe that they are personally responsible for the rewards and punishments they receive. People with an external orientation tend to believe that their reinforcers are due to factors beyond their control. As a result of this difference, internals tend to be more active in trying to master their environment than externals. Externals are more fatalistic about their lives than internals and are more likely to explain other people's behavior in terms of situational variables. Locus of control orientation is an acquired (learned) characteristic; thus, it can be changed by new learning experiences.

The concept of need for achievement (N ach) describes the desire to be successful and achieve excellence. Many studies suggest that educational, occupational, and economic suc-

cess may all be related to differences in need for achievement. Further, differences in economic development between entire societies may be related to the differences in these societies' need to achieve. Certain training programs have been designed to increase a person's level of N ach. Many of the participants have shown increased economic and occupational success as the result of these programs.

The final personality variable presented was Machiavellianism, the tendency to manipulate other people in order to obtain some goal. Research concerned with Machiavellianism has concentrated on identifying the characteristics of a successful manipulator and determining how these are manifested in interpersonal behavior. Researchers believe that four characteristics enable a person to be an effective manipulator. These are: (1) a lack of concern with conventional morality, (2) the absence of a strong commitment to a particular political ideology, (3) a relative lack of emotion in dealing with other people, and (4) the absence of any gross psychopathology.

REVIEW QUESTIONS

(Twelve out of fifteen is passing)

1. The personality variable, _____ _____ _____ , refers to people's generalized expectancies about the source of the reinforcers they receive. (p. 50)
2. Two students are talking about the A's they received in their courses. The first says, "I received an A because I stayed up three nights studying." The second says, "I received an A because my instructor got a raise the day grades were given out." The first statement represents a(n) _____ orientation. The second represents a(n) _____ orientation. (p. 51)
3. Although the reason for the difference is not clear, women and blacks tend to be more _____ in their beliefs about where the source of their reinforcers lies. (p. 52)
4. One line from the song "I am Woman" is, "I am woman, I can do anything." This represents an internal _____ control orientation. The phrase "You can't fight city hall" represents an external _____ control orientation. (p. 54)
5. People who have an external locus of control orientation tend to attribute other people's behavior to _____ factors. (p. 54)
6. A _____ is a force which activates a person and directs her to find a means of alleviating a presently unsatisfactory situation. (p. 55)
7. People who desire to excel in their chosen field have a high _____ _____ _____ . (p. 56)
8. The projective test which involves giving a person a picture and having her tell a story about it is called the _____ _____ _____ . (p. 56)
9. The correlation between people's scores on the same test at two points in time is called _____ _____ . (p. 56)
10. Atkinson has proposed that people low in n Ach should have little hope of _____ and a great fear of _____ . (p. 58)
11. Women who are not socialized in the traditional manner tend to have _____ levels of n Ach. (p. 59)
12. A person who manipulates people in order to attain power and who believes that the end justifies the means is called a(n) _____ . (p. 63)
13. A lie detector test essentially measures a person's emotional reaction if the person lies. A person who is _____ in Machiavellianism should be better able to "fool" a lie detector than someone who is _____ in Machiavellianism. (p. 65)
14. The study conducted by Geiss et al. on the relationship between Machiavellianism and the passage of bills in a mock legislature showed that people high in Machiavellianism were more effective than people low in Machiavellianism only when the bills dealt with _____ issues. (p. 66)
15. The general position taken in this chapter is that social behavior can be best understood by considering both _____ and _____ variables. (p. 67)

ANSWERS

15. personality, situational
10. success, failure   11. high   12. Machiavellian   13. high, low   14. emotional
6. need   7. need for achievement   8. Thematic Apperception Test   9. test-retest reliability
1. locus of control   2. internal, external   3. situational   4. personal, system   5. situational

SUGGESTED READINGS

If you want to learn more about personality research in general and the specific personality variables we have covered, you might consider these books.

Textbooks

Interactional Psychology and Personality, edited by Norman Endler and David Magnusson. This book is long and, in places, very technical. However, Endler and Magnussen have managed to gather together most of the important articles on the person-versus-the-situation controversy.

Personality and Social Behavior, edited by Kenneth Gergen and David Marlowe. While all the chapters in this book are interesting, the first one (by Marlowe and Gergen) provides an excellent review of how social psychologists view the role of personality variables in social behavior.

Studies in Machiavellianism, edited by Richard Christie and Florence Geiss. This book is a collection of a number of separate studies on Machiavellianism and how it affects people's behavior. You don't need to read the entire book, just the introduction and those studies which appeal to you.

The Achieving Society, by David McClelland. In this fascinating book, McClelland presents data to support his thesis that a society's collective need to achieve affects its rate of economic growth.

Human Motivation: A Book of Readings, edited by David McClelland and Robert Steele. This book contains chapters written by various researchers on the need to achieve and other needs. Although some of the chapters on n Ach are dated, they do present the basic research in this area.

Either Locus of Control in Personality, by E. Jerry Phares, or *Locus of Control,* by Herbert Lefcourt. Both of these books are well written. Phares and Lefcourt are two of the leading researchers on locus of control.

Popular literature

Any good biography or autobiography of some public figure will give you a better understanding of the role of personality variables in social behavior. Here are some books which impressed me.

Becoming, by Gordon Allport. This isn't really popular literature, but it is so beautifully written that it can be read like a novel.

The Best and the Brightest, by David Halberstam. In this Pulitzer Prize-winning book, Halberstam describes the personalities of the people who shaped America's foreign policy during the Kennedy and Johnson administrations.

Catch-22, by Joseph Heller. Heller's hilarious description of the life of a pilot during World War II embodies many of the concepts discussed in this chapter. If you've read it already, read it again. I've read this book four times, and each time I get more from it.

Mother Night, by Kurt Vonnegut, Jr. Vonnegut provides a beautiful fictionalized account of the person versus the situation as determinants of social behavior.

3 INTERPERSONAL BEHAVIOR

This chapter examines interpersonal behavior. Strictly speaking, this term describes a situation in which two people interact and their behaviors jointly determine what happens to them. However, in order to really understand interpersonal behavior, you must know something about the earliest stages of the relationship between two people. Therefore, the chapter begins with a discussion of how people form their initial impressions of each other. It then turns to the variables which influence the formation of friendships and love relationships. Finally, the factors which influence people's behavior in face-to-face interactions will be discussed.

PERSON PERCEPTION

Consider these two characterizations of the same man. According to Harry S. Truman:

He not only doesn't give a damn about the people; he doesn't know how to tell the truth. I don't think the son of a bitch knows the difference between telling the truth and lying. (Miller, 1974, p. 139)

Theodore White, the noted political historian, saw the man this way:

I had observed him by this time for many months, and he had persisted as a puzzle to my mind and understanding from my first glimpse and sound of him. Now I decided that rather than being the hard, cruel, and vengeful man as constantly described in the liberal press, [he] was above all a friend seeker, almost pathetic in his eagerness to be liked. He wanted to identify with people and have a connection with them. (White, 1961, p. 359)

The person they were discussing is Richard M. Nixon. Both statements were made thirteen years before the Watergate scandal and Nixon's resignation. Truman, drawing on his political activities, and White on his historical research, both knew Nixon fairly well. Neither statement can be dismissed as political rhetoric. White was a historian with no

axe to grind. Truman spoke at a time when it seemed that Nixon would never again seek public office. Their political views played no role. Yet, to Truman, Nixon was a man who "doesn't give a damn about the people." To White, he was a man who wanted people to like him. Why were their views so different?

One obvious explanation is that Truman disliked Nixon and White did not. But why did Truman feel this way? Part of the answer lies in the way each man formed his impressions of Nixon. Another part of the answer concerns the process they used to explain Nixon's behavior. The former is called *impression formation;* the latter, *attribution processes.* Research in these two areas deals with the processes we use to judge other people. Whether the judgments are right or wrong does not matter.

Impression formation

We often prejudge people on the basis of hearsay evidence. For example, you and your roommate are looking for a third person to share the rent. Your roommate announces that he has found someone and gives you a brief biography: school, home town, major, possibly religion or race, and physical appearance. He may then add a personal description: smart, introverted, funny, thoughtful, and hard-working. You have now been given a lot of information. Research on impression formation tries to explain how you would process it to arrive at your first impression of this person.

Solomon Asch

Asch (1946) was the first social psychologist to study impression formation. He believed two things. First, your goal in forming an impression about another person is to arrive at a consistent, unified picture of him. Second, you do not consider each trait individually and then add them all up. The total picture you form is qualitatively different from the sum of the parts.

One important factor in producing this unique total picture, said Asch, is *central traits*. These are key descriptive terms which color your reactions to the other terms presented. As a result, central traits are extremely important in impression formation. To show this, Asch gave two groups of subjects a description of a hypothetical person. The first group was told that he was intelligent, skillful, hard-working, warm, determined, and practical. The second group was given the same description, except that the word *warm* was changed to *cold*. After hearing the description, both groups were asked to state other characteristics the person would have. Of the subjects told he was warm, 90 percent thought he would be good-natured. This was true of only 34 percent of the subjects who were told he was cold. Asch also tried changing other terms (e.g., *intelligent–stupid*). These terms had far less impact on the subjects' evaluation than did *warm–cold*. Thus, *warm–cold* is a central trait.

Later research (Wishner, 1960) may explain why certain traits are more important than others. A trait's importance (or centrality) depends on the situation in which a judgment is made. For example, if you are thinking of a person as a possible date, the fact that this person is warm (or cold) will be far more important to you than the fact that the person is strong. A person's warmth will not, however, exert much of an influence on your judgment when you are looking for someone to help you move an old sofa out of your apartment.

Order effects

You are given three pieces of information about someone you have never met. How will the order affect your first impression? Some researchers believe that the first terms are the most important—the *primacy effect* (Asch, 1946). Others stress the last terms—the *recency effect*. Consider the following problem. You have been asked to write a letter of recommendation for a friend who has applied for a public relations job. She has the training and personal attributes for the job, but when she gets nervous, she clears her throat loudly and bites her nails. You feel obligated to mention this, but where do you put it? Do you place it up front and get it out of the way, or do you wait until you have noted her many strong points and tuck it in at the end?

The primacy effect. Researchers who stress the primacy effect believe it can operate in three ways. The first is when the early description changes the meaning of the later one. For example, if I described a young medical student, first, as money hungry, this would probably affect your evaluation of later information: he is studious, hard-working, and conscientious. You would probably see these traits as geared to making money. In the same way, if your letter of recommendation began with your friend's nervous habits, the reader might worry about her performance under stress.

Second, primacy can occur if the later terms do not "match up" with the earlier ones (Anderson & Jacobson, 1965). For example, if I told you that Adolf Hitler was responsible for the murder of millions of innocent people but was also capable of great pity, wouldn't you tend to discount his kindness? You would see it as a less accurate description than the first statement.

Finally, primacy can occur when the person believes that the first terms are the most important and the last terms much less so. This can happen if the person is not told to disregard the order in which the terms are given (Hastorf, Schneider, & Polefka, 1970). Suppose your letter of recommendation mentioned your friend's nervous habits first, without stating that her other qualifications were so good that this hardly mattered. The reader might take the order literally, believing the nervousness was so important that you had to mention it first.

The recency effect. If a person is first described to you positively and then negatively, this may result in a *contrast effect.* This effect causes you to see the later characteristics as extremely important and to give them greater weight in your overall impression (Jones & Goethals, 1971). For example, you move into a new neighborhood and a neighbor is describing a woman on the block. She is married, with three children, is active in local politics, quite amusing, *and* she is having a torrid love affair with the milkman. The fact that this married mother of three is openly unfaithful makes her infidelity even worse.

Another situation in which the recency effect occurs is when the information given clearly describes a process of change in a person (Jones & Goethals, 1971). The biblical story of the prodigal son (Luke, 15:11) illustrates this. The son took his inheritance, left his father, and squandered his money on a life of debauchery. When the son returned, his father took him back "because this son of mine was dead and has come back to life, he was lost [and now he is] found." (Luke 16:24). The father focused on the change in his son.

Additive theories

Another explanation of how people form impressions is provided by the additive theories. These theories propose models of how people combine the information they receive to form an overall impression. These models are not intended to describe the actual processes involved in impression formation. Rather, they provide a way of conceptualizing these processes. The additive theories propose that you can predict an overall impression by examining how a person evaluates each term and how he combines these terms. Note that this premise is different from Solomon Asch's. Asch argued that the descriptive terms, in combination, produce an overall impression that could *not* be predicted by considering them one at a time.

To introduce these theories, consider this hypothetical example and examine the predictions each theory would make. In most criminal trials the sentence a convicted person must serve is determined separately from the person's guilt or innocence. One way the length of the sentence is decided is by conducting a pre-sentencing investigation. That is, the judge appoints someone to investigate the convicted person's background and prior criminal record, interview his friends, employers, and relatives, and then report the findings. On the basis of this information the judge can decide whether to give the person the maximum or minimum sentence, or one part way in between. In our hypothetical situation a young white male has been found guilty of armed robbery. In most states the punishment for such an offense can range from probation to twenty or twenty-five years (Katzenbach, 1967). So you can see that the judge's decision is almost as important as the jury's determination of guilt or innocence. The pre-sentencing investigation tells the judge that this is the man's first conviction as an adult. He is well educated and a talented musician who has had five different jobs in the last year and was arrested when he was sixteen years old for car theft. In terms of personal characteristics, he is well groomed and pleasant. On the basis of this limited information, the judge must form an overall impression of the young man and pass sentence. How does the judge reach his decision?

Summation. The summation theory or model proposes that the first step involves mentally rating each characteristic in terms of how positive or negative it is. For example, the judge might evaluate the fact that the man is married very positively and the fact that he has had five jobs in one year very negatively. Then the judge would add up all his positive and negative evaluations to arrive at an overall impression. In other words, the *summation theory* proposes that the overall impression will be the sum of the evaluations given to each term.

Averaging. The *averaging theory* also proposes that the judge will mentally rate each term. But it predicts that the judge's overall impression will not be the sum of these evaluations. Rather, it will reflect the average evaluation he has given each term.

To clarify the important difference between the summation and averaging models, imagine that the man's lawyer was given a chance to reply to the pre-sentencing investigation. The summation model would advise the lawyer to find as many additional positive things about his client as possible and tell these to the judge. This is because the new information would change the sum of the individual evaluations. The averaging model would call this effort a waste of time, unless the new information was evaluated more favorably than the information the judge already has. That is, the lawyer would need to change the average evaluation of the individual terms.

Weighted Averaging. This theory proposes that in addition to evaluating each term, the judge would also consider the relative importance of each one. For example, he might consider the man's arrest at the age of sixteen to be a more important aspect of his character than the fact that he is well groomed. The previous arrest will influence the judge's overall impression more strongly than the man's grooming habits. The *weighted averaging theory* predicts that the judge's overall impression will reflect the average of the weighted evaluations of the terms.

The relative importance a person places on different descriptive terms reflects his biases and sometimes his own self-interest. For example, the prodigal son, mentioned earlier, had a brother. The brother had stayed at home and been a loyal child. He was infuriated by his father's treatment of his prodigal sibling: ". . . you never offered me so much as a kid [a baby goat] to celebrate with your friends. But for this son of yours when he comes back after swallowing your property— he and his women—you kill the calf we had been fattening [to celebrate his return]" (Luke, 16:29–30). Note that while the father gave the greatest weight to the prodigal son's return, the brother stressed the fact that he had left and squandered the inheritance.

All three of these theories assume that a person's overall impression of someone can be predicted by combining the terms in some manner. The final theory covered suggests that in some instances this may not be true.

A variant of weighted averaging

I've looked on a lot of women with lust. I've committed adultery in my heart many times . . . . I [don't] condemn someone who not only looks on a woman with lust but who leaves his wife and shacks up with someone. . . . Christ says don't consider yourself better than someone else because [he] screws a whole bunch of women while [you] are loyal to your wife.

These remarks were made by Jimmy Carter during the 1976 presidential campaign in an interview with *Playboy* magazine. If we consider the interview as data for impression formation, then we have the following information about Carter. He is a Southern Baptist and born-again Christian who lusts after women and uses words such as "screw" and "shacking up." The public reaction to the Carter interview was far more negative than any of the additive models would have predicted. How can this be explained?

Rokeach and Rothman (1965) proposed that there are times when the combination of certain characteristics will totally determine the overall impression. In other words, the combination of the terms receives a 100 percent weighting. One of these is when someone or something that is generally considered positive is linked with a negative characteristic. For example, the combination "irresponsible father" will be evaluated much more negatively than the sum, average, or weighted average of these terms.

Now the adverse reaction to Carter becomes explainable. Being a devout Christian is considered by most people to be a positive characteristic. Using mild obscenities in public is viewed by most people as bad but not terrible. But when a born-again Southern Baptist talks about "shacking up" . . .! The combination of these characteristics produced a configuration which was evaluated much more negatively than would be predicted by considering them individually.

You now have four theories of impression formation. Which one makes the most accurate prediction of how people form impressions? Overall, the weighted averaging theory seems to be best (Kaplan & Kemmerick, 1974). But it must be strongly emphasized that in certain instances the other theories produce more accurate predictions (Hastorf et al., 1970). In other words, these theories are not competitors for the one best explanation of impression formation.

Your first impressions of people affect interpersonal behavior in three important ways. The first is fairly obvious. If the information you receive about someone turns you off, you may never even bother to meet him. Second, if you do meet him, your first impressions will influence how you act toward him. Bond (1972) asked women to take part in a three-person conversation and then to rate their partners on a number of traits. In each of the groups, two of the women were given information about the third. She was presented as a cold person to one of them and as a warm person to the other. Then all three of them talked for a while, while observers rated them on how they acted toward one another. Surprisingly, the woman who was told that the third woman was cold acted friendlier toward her than did the woman who was told she was warm. Bond could not explain this, but the direction of the difference is not important here. What is important is that these first impressions influenced the behavior of two people toward a person they hardly knew. Finally, the initial information you receive about a person leads you to make further inferences about his personality. This will be seen in the next section.

Implicit personality theory

Why do people often assume that because someone is fat he is also jolly? The answer seems to be that people often assume that certain traits or characteristics are correlated. This is called *implicit personality theory* (Rosenberg & Sedlak, 1972)—the belief that if a person possesses one characteristic, he must also possess certain others. For example, it has been found that people who are told someone is intelligent will assume he is also friendly. This occurs even though no information about the person's friendliness was ever given (Rosenberg & Sedlak, 1972).

Besides showing the importance of first impressions, implicit personality theory has a more practical application. Stop and think about these examples: John is black; he must have great rhythm. Paul is Polish; he must be dumb. Betty, because she is a woman, must be flighty. What are these? They are stereotypes. The assumption behind a stereotype is that certain behavior patterns or personal characteristics correlate with certain demographic characteristics (e.g., sex, age, race). A *stereotype* is the belief that all members of a certain group possess the same characteristic.

Consider the stereotype that blacks are thieves. In one sense, this stereotype has some basis in fact (most stereotypes do); the proportion of blacks arrested for crimes is greater than the proportion of whites (Reckless, 1973). But what about the individual black person you meet—is he likely to be a criminal? Probably not, since less than 5 percent of blacks in America have ever been

---

"Don't get me wrong. It's a nice name, but I don't think the Romans will surrender to someone named Percy the Hun"

It's 11:30 Friday night and three old movies are playing on television. They star Norma Jean Baker, Marion Morrison, and Bernie Schwartz, respectively. Which one would you watch? Which comedian do you think is funnier, Melvin Kaminsky or Joseph Levitch? What, you've never heard of these people? Well, maybe if I asked you about Marilyn Monroe, John Wayne, and Tony Curtis, you could make a choice. And you may think that Mel Brooks is funnier than Jerry Lewis. Why did these celebrities change their names? Jerry Lewis gave his reason in a recent interview: "Would you pay forty bucks to see a guy named Joseph Levitch?" Do our names really influence other people's impressions of us?

First, let's consider social popularity. John McDavid and Herb Harari (1966) asked ten- and eleven-year-old children to rate how much they liked a number of first names. Then, another group of children were asked to identify three other children they like the most and three they liked the least. It was found that children with popular names were much better liked by their peers than children with unpopular names.

In another study, teachers were asked to grade essays written by fifth graders (Harari & McDavid, 1973). These essays were all the same, but the names of the students who had allegedly written them were varied. Some essays were "written" by children with popular names (e.g., Karen, Lisa, David) while the others were attributed to children with unpopular names (e.g., Elmer, Adele, Bertha). On the average, essays "written" by children with uncommon and unpopular names received lower grades than those by children with popular names.

More generally, children with names that teachers like (e.g., Craig, James, Richard) are better adjusted and do better in school than children with names that teachers dislike (e.g., Horace, Maurice, Roderick)(Marcus, 1976).

convicted of a felony (Reckless, 1973). The error made in stereotyping is twofold. First, it assumes that the characteristics of one member of a group are possessed by all the members. Second, it assumes that if the majority of the group possesses some characteristic, so does every member of the group.

The effect of physical appearance

Most people do not really believe that beauty is only skin deep. In fact, our judgments of people are influenced by how physically attractive they are. For example, college students were given pictures of attractive and unattractive college-age men and women and asked to rate them on a number of traits. The attractive people were seen as kinder, stronger, more poised, more interesting, and generally of "better character" than the unattractive people (Dion, Berscheid, & Walster, 1972).

This bias is not peculiar to college students. Children as young as four years old assign positive traits to attractive people and negative traits to unattractive ones (Dion, 1973b; Dion & Berscheid, 1974). A study done in Canada revealed that the better looking a political candidate was, the more likely he was to be elected (Efran & Patterson, 1974).

There are, however, certain circumstances where beauty is not an asset. College students, playing the role of jurors, read about two women who had been found guilty of either burglary or a swindle. Half the subjects in each type of case saw a picture of an attractive defendant, the other half an unattractive defendant (Sigall & Ostrove, 1975).

When the crime was burglary, the attractive defendant received a lighter sentence than the unattractive one. But when the crime was a swindle, the attractive defendant received a heavier sentence. Why? Subjects may have believed the swindle was aided by the attractive woman's appearance; she used her beauty for illegal purposes. This resulted in a more negative evaluation of her than of the unattractive woman. In terms of evaluation, this is an interesting interaction between physical appearance and behavior. But remember that in the absence of specific information about someone's behavior, people seem to believe that what is beautiful is also good.

Attribution processes

In summer 1976 a group of terrorists hijacked an airplane carrying many Israeli citizens. The terrorists ordered the plane flown to Entebbe airport in Uganda. One of the things which made this episode stand out was the role of Idi Amin, President of Uganda. Amin claimed that he was not an ally of the hijackers, but rather an impartial third party, whose airport had been chosen by the terrorists. Most observers, however, believed that Amin was a willing and active partner. How did they reach this conclusion?

Questions of this type have been addressed by social psychologists interested in the *attribution process,* the process whereby people draw conclusions about the causes of a person's actions and his character based on their observations of his behavior.

Heider's theory

Fritz Heider, the father of attribution theory, believed that people need to impose order on the world around them and be able to make predictions about future events which might affect them. The belief that you understand and can explain another person's actions serves this need. Heider focused largely on how people reach conclusions as to the cause of someone's behavior.

The person who sees the behavior and draws conclusions is called the *observer.* The person who performs the behavior is called the *actor.* People can attribute behavior to a *personal cause,* which means that the actor knowingly and willingly engaged in the behavior. Or the behavior can have an *external cause,* meaning that the actor was forced into the behavior or did it accidentally. According to Heider, observers base their judgments on the actor's ability to perform the behavior and his efforts in doing so. The greater an actor's ability and effort, the more likely observers are to attribute his behavior to a personal cause. Now let's apply this theory to explanations of Idi Amin's behavior.

Observers considered Amin's ability to control events and the effort he made while the passengers were held at the airport. Amin was the absolute dictator of Uganda and could control anything that happened there. Yet when the plane landed, other terrorists were waiting for it. They had large amounts of arms and medical supplies with them. Observers felt that Amin could have prevented these careful preparations if he had wanted to do so. Second, people looked at Amin's own efforts. He had the airport prepared for the plane's arrival, personally greeeted the terrorists, visited them and their hostages almost daily, provided them with help to guard the passengers, negotiated on their behalf, and ordered Ugandan soldiers to fight the Israeli commandos who rescued the passengers. Amin's ability to control events at Entebbe airport, together with his efforts during the time the hostages were there, led most observers to conclude that Amin was an active accomplice of the terrorists.

Kelley's theory

Another theory or model of how observers judge the cause of an action has been proposed by Harold Kelley (1967, 1973). Kelley's theory does not compete with Heider's; it extends and elaborates on it. Kelley believed that when an observer sees a single act he uses a *discounting principle* in making attributions.

He will decide that an act has a certain, specific cause only if he can discount all other possible causes. If an actor engages in some behavior in the absence of any external pressure, then the observer will attribute this act to a personal cause. But if there are external pressures on the actor, the observer cannot discount these as the cause of the behavior.

For example, you see a Boy Scout help an old woman across a busy street. Was this action voluntary—that is, was it performed in the absence of any external pressure? As an observer, you will look for external forces which could have been responsible for the Scout's action. If you see his Scoutmaster standing across the street, you are unsure about why the Scout helped the woman. He may have done it because he is a good Scout (personal cause) or because his Scoutmaster was watching him (external cause). You cannot be sure. People will attribute an actor's behavior to personal causes only when they can discount or eliminate external factors as explanations of the behavior.

Kelley proposed that when an actor's behavior is observed over time people operate on a *covariation principle.* They look for unique sets of circumstances (e.g., some person or entity) which are present when an actor behaves in a certain way and absent when he does not—that is, conditions which *covary* with the actor's behavior. Let us look at how this covariation principle operates.

Imagine you and a friend have a class at 8:00 Monday morning (an unpleasant premise). For the last six weeks, he has been depressed when he comes to class. There are a number of possible reasons for this. The end of the weekend could depress him, or having to get up at 7:00 Monday morning. Or it could be the fact that his favorite professional football team lost its last six games. The following week, your friend seems to be fine Monday morning, but on Tuesday he looks as if his dog had died. You check the newspaper and find that his favorite football team played a game on Monday night and lost 49–9. The following Monday morning, he acts happy and carefree. You look up the football scores and discover that his team has finally won a game. The covariation of the team's performance with your friend's mood leads you to a conclusion about the cause of his behavior. It is due to your friend's avid devotion to the team.

Now if an observer decides a behavior has an environmental or external cause, the attribution process is over. But if the observer believes a personal cause is involved, the observer moves to the final stage of the attribution process. This is called *dispositional attributions*—the predictions an observer makes about how the actor will behave in the future. An observer could decide that a behavior, while personally caused, is due to temporary factors and will never be repeated. Or he could decide that the behavior is due to some enduring personality characteristic of the actor and is likely to recur. How do people make dispositional attributions? Edward Jones and Keith Davis have proposed one theory.

Theory of correspondent inferences

Jones and Davis (1965) were interested in two aspects of dispositional attributions: (1) the types of behaviors which lead to the conclusion that an act was due to the actor's personality and (2) the factors which affect the observer's confidence in this conclusion. Their theory is called *correspondent inferences*. It attempts to specify the conditions under which an observer *infers* that the actions he has seen *correspond* to the actor's personality characteristics.

Jones and Davis believed that one important aspect of an actor's behavior was whether it has *common effects*. If an actor engages in a series of actions over a period of time; if all these actions have a common effect; and if this effect could not be produced by other actions

(i.e., it is unique), an observer will tend to attribute these actions to the actor's personality. For example, imagine you are at a local newstand, and you see a casual acquaintance looking at a number of magazines. He chooses *Playboy*. Now, he could have chosen *Playboy* because he wants to read an interview with some celebrity or because he enjoys looking at pictures of nude women. At this point, you cannot really make any inferences about his behavior. A few days later, however, you see him coming out of a theater featuring a pornographic movie. Finally, you hear that he was seen at a topless bar. All these behaviors seem to have one thing in common—an interest in nude and semi-nude females. Thus, you may well decide that these behaviors are part of his basic personality.

Sometimes an observer makes a dispositional attribution based on a single act. If an actor is faced with a choice between two actions and their effects are similar in every way but one, he may use this single *unique effect* to make a dispositional attribution. For example, imagine that you see the above hypothetical person in front of a movie theater where two films are being shown. The films start at the same time, cost the same, last the same amount of time, and have both received good reviews. The first film is entitled *The Nordic Skiers of Norway,* while the other is *The Nude Skiers of Norway.* The movies are identical in every respect except one. The latter shows nude women on skis. If the person chooses this film, you may well infer that his choice reflected his basic personality. Why? Because it produced a unique effect (seeing nudes).

But wait, you say. There are behaviors I engage in consistently. These behaviors all produce the same effect, and this effect is unique to them. For example, I shower and brush my teeth every morning. Do people make inferences about my personality on the basis of *these* behaviors? No, they do not.

According to Jones and Davis, a behavior which is socially desirable and/or expected of the actor will not cause this behavior to be attributed to the actor's personality. It is socially desirable and expected that you brush your teeth and shower. It is only when a behavior: (1) produces common effects over time *and* (2) is considered socially undesirable or unexpected that the behavior will be attributed to the actor's personality.

For example, imagine that you learned that the person we have been discussing was majoring in criminal justice and enrolled in a course on pornography in America. In this case, you might conclude that his behavior was expected and thus did not reflect his enduring personality. If, on the other hand, you learned that this person was a deacon of a local church, you would probably attribute his behavior to his personality. Why? Because it is not considered socially desirable for church deacons to spend their time looking at nude women.

According to Jones and Davis, an observer's confidence in his attributions is affected by two factors. The first is *hedonic relevance*. This concept concerns the importance of the act to the observer. As a rule, the more important a behavior is to an observer, the surer he will be that this behavior is due to the actor's personality. For example, if you are strongly offended by nudity, you would be more likely to attribute this person's behavior to his personality than would someone who is not offended by nudity.

Jones and Davis also believed that the more personally affected an observer is by the actor's actions, the more likely he is to attribute these actions to the actor's personality. They called this the factor of *personalism*. Imagine you had planned to meet the person in our example for lunch, but he went to see a sex film instead. According to the concept of personalism, this will increase your confidence in the conclusion that the actor's behavior was part of his personality and thus is likely to be repeated in the future.

Actors versus observers: Differing explanations of behavior

Adam and Eve are discussing the circumstances surrounding their banishment from the Garden of Eden.

ADAM: You need a good psychiatrist. We had a perfect deal going, and you had to screw it up. Why was it so damn important that I eat that apple?

EVE: It wasn't my fault. That serpent talked me into it. He tricked me.

Obviously, they have been discussing Adam's eating of the "forbidden fruit" at Eve's urging. Note that Adam (the observer) has attributed Eve's behavior to a personal cause, while Eve (the actor) has indicated an external cause. This conflict between the first actor and the first observer on earth is typical of the difference between actors and observers in general. Actors tend to attribute their behavior to an external cause, observers to a personal cause (Jones & Nisbett, 1971).

One of the more interesting experimental demonstrations of this phenomenon was performed by West, Gunn, and Chernicky (1975). College students were approached by an experimenter posing as a private investigator. They were asked to help him break into the offices of a small business firm, either to photograph its records or to steal some of its plans. In exchange, they would receive $2,000. After hearing this, the students were asked to decide whether they would help in the break-in and to explain their reasons. Then West et al. described this situation to another group of students and asked them to explain why a person would agree or refuse to help. The actors (i.e., the people actually asked to take part in the break-in) tended to attribute their behavior to external factors, such as the safety of the plan or the reward offered. The observers (i.e., the people who had the situation described to them) tended to attribute the actors' behavior to personality characteristics, such as honesty.

Why do actors and observers tend to arrive at different explanations? One possibility is that they have different information about the behavior in question. For example, Adam had only Eve's word about the conversation with the serpent. But interestingly, there will be differences in attributions even when actors and observers have the same information. In a study conducted by Jones, Rock, Shaver, Goethals, and Ward (1968), subjects watched a person solve the first few reasoning problems in a test and then fail the later ones. The subjects attributed this to the actor's intellect. Then the subjects were given the same problems and the same feedback on their own performance. They explained their own scores by saying that the later problems were harder than the earlier ones. Jones and his associates (Jones, Worchel, Goethals, & Grumet, 1971) also found that even when an observer is told that an actor had no choice, he will still tend to explain his behavior with a personal cause.

Although actors generally tend to attribute their behavior to the environment, there are exceptions. If a person does quite well on a task, he is likely to credit his own ability (Miller, 1976). However, if he fails, he will attribute it to the environment (Harvey, Harris, & Barnes, 1975). If you don't believe this, find two friends, one who has received an A in a course and another a F. If you ask the first person his grade, he will probably answer, "I got (i.e., earned) an A." The second person will probably tell you, "The stupid bastard flunked me."

Conclusion

This section introduced the topic of person perception as related to interpersonal behavior. There are certain important points to remember. First, people do not perceive their environment as a camera does. They actively process the information they receive about others. Their goal is to arrive at accurate judgments about another person and the reasons for his behavior. The discussion of impression formation and attribution processes showed that given the same data, two observers may reach radically different conclusions about the person they have observed.

The judgments a person reaches have two effects on interpersonal behavior. First, they influence his present and future reactions to the other person. Second, these first judgments will lead him to make further assumptions about the other person. Research on implicit personality theory confirms this. Thus, first impressions have an important effect on a relationship.

Research on impression formation is concerned with how we use information about another person to form impressions of him. The review of central traits, order effects, and the additive models of impression formation showed that the way information is presented, its content, and the values and biases of the receiver all influence the impression he forms.

Theories of attribution processes are concerned with how we explain the behavior of an actor. Basically there are two types of explanations: (1) the behavior did not indicate a personality characteristic of the actor and is not likely to recur or (2) the behavior observed was due to a personality characteristic of the actor, and, as such, will probably recur. These attributions depend upon the behavior itself, the context in which it was committed, whether it is the actor or the observer making the attributions, and the personal involvement of the observer with the effects of the behavior.

An understanding of impression formation and attribution processes should enable you to understand more fully the nature of interpersonal behavior.

REVIEW QUESTIONS

(Twelve out of fifteen is passing)

1. A descriptive term which colors or influences a person's reactions to other descriptive terms in impression formation is called a(n) _____ . (p. 74)

2. A person is speaking on behalf of a candidate for public office. He describes Senator Claghorn as a distinguished public servant, a man of vision, a friend of the worker, a fighter for individual freedom, and someone who will not be deterred by the three years he served in jail for embezzlement of public funds. Since the speaker feels he is helping the Senator, he evidently believes that _____ effects determine the impressions we form. (p. 74)

3. The _____ model of impression formation holds that additional descriptive terms which are positive will produce a more positive overall evaluation. The _____ model holds that these additional terms will improve the evaluation only if they are more positive than the previous terms. (p. 76)

4. The model of impression formation which proposes that people weight the descriptive information they receive about someone in different ways is called the _____ _____ model. (p. 76)

5. In the early days of his presidency, Gerald Ford kept bumping his head. Many people assumed that since Ford was clumsy, he was also stupid. This illustrates _____ _____ theory. (p. 78)

6. The assumption that all members of a group possess the same characteristic is called a(n) _____ . (p. 78)

7. In general, people believe that someone who is attractive will have a _____ character than someone who is unattractive. (p. 79)

8. Theories of _____ _____ are concerned with how a person explains the behavior of other people. (p. 79)

9. A behavior which is perceived as accidental or as being forced is attributed to a(n) _____ cause. (p. 80)

10. According to Heider, observers focus on the _____ and the _____ of an actor when they make causal attributions. (p. 80)

11. Every time Jacques Cousteau sees a shark he breaks into a cold sweat and his teeth begin to chatter. The _____ principle would enable an observer to attribute Cousteau's behavior to a specific cause. (p. 80)

12. The stage in attributions in which the observer decides if an actor's behavior is (or is not) due to the actor's personality is called _____ _____ . (p. 81)

13. People will attribute a behavior to the actor's personality if the effects of the behavior are _____ and _____ . (p. 82)

14. An observer's attributions are influenced by how personally affected he is by the behavior he observes. This is called the effect of _____ . (p. 82)

15. Generally, the observer will attribute a behavior to a(n) _____ cause; the actor will attribute the same act to a(n) _____ cause. (p. 82).

ANSWERS

Michael Minardi

INTERPERSONAL ATTRACTION

Stop reading for a moment and think about your best friend. Why did you two become friends? What is it about this person that makes you like him so much? Questions of this type have been investigated by social psychologists interested in interpersonal attraction. The research conducted in this area can provide some answers.

Factors which lead to friendship

Propinquity

First, you and your friend either presently or at one time probably lived or worked very close to each other. The closer two people are geographically, the more likely it is that they will like each other (Berscheid & Walster, 1969). This is known as the effect of *propin-*

quity (degree of physical closeness) on friendship. Why do we tend to like those who are physically close to us?

There are two basic theories. The first was proposed by Fritz Heider (1958), mentioned earlier. Heider believed that the key to understanding interpersonal attraction was to consider how a person viewed his relationship with another person rather than the objective characteristics of the relationship. Heider proposed that what a person looks for in a relationship is *balance,* "a harmonious state in which a person's feeling about another person fit together without stress" (Heider, 1958, p. 180). In Heider's view, balance explains the effect of propinquity.

A person who spends a good deal of time with someone else comes to see himself and the other person as a *unit* belonging together. And because of his need for balance, this will lead to liking. If this is confusing, an example may clarify it. Imagine that I am observing you and your friend. You two are together constantly; you room together, study together, go to concerts together, etc. One day I ask you, "Why do you spend so much time with him?" It is much more likely that you will answer "Because I like him" than "Because I dislike him." This second answer is illogical—or, to put it in Heider's terms, it describes an unbalanced relationship. The first answer, in contrast, describes a balanced relationship in which your feelings and behavior "fit together without stress."

Does the belief that you belong with someone really lead to liking? Darley and Berscheid (1967) gave women virtually identical descriptions of two people. The women were told that they would meet and work with one of the other persons. Then they were asked to indicate how much they liked each of the persons they had read about. Just as Heider would predict, the women liked the person they believed would be their partner signifi-

cantly more than the person they thought they would never meet.

The other major theory regarding the effect of propinquity is based on reinforcement theory. According to reinforcement theory, the primary factor in whether a friendship will develop is the ratio of rewards to costs involved in the relationship (Homans, 1961). A reward is some sort of positive payoff from a relationship, such as being loved, praised, or respected. A cost is a negative payoff. Costs can be tangible things, such as the time and money expended in a relationship. Or they can be less concrete things, such as rejection, ridicule, or social disapproval. People prefer to be in relationships that provide more rewards than costs. Now let's apply this simple idea to the effect of propinquity on interpersonal attraction. It usually costs less (in terms of time, money, and effort) to interact with someone who is physically close than with someone who is physically distant, Thus, you are more likely to be friends with someone who lives close to you than with someone who lives far away.

Reinforcement theorists also propose that propinquity produces liking indirectly. Physical closeness provides the opportunity for people to talk to one another. If the people find this conversation rewarding, they will come to like each other (Newcomb, 1961). Segal (1974) has demonstrated how powerful an effect this opportunity for interaction can have on the formation of friendships.

She found a police academy where new recruits were assigned roommates and seats in their classes on the basis of alphabetical order. Thus, two people whose last names began with "A" would spend more time with one another than would two people whose last names began with "A" and "Z." After they had been at the academy for a while, the recruits were asked to name their friends. Segal found that the closer two recruits' names were in the alphabet, the more likely they were to be friends. The physical closeness that the alphabetical order produced led to liking.

It is quite reasonable to assume that the men Segal studied held similar attitudes, were from similar backgrounds, and had similar interests. Thus, it is not surprising that when they were brought into close contact, they became friends. But what would happen if people with nothing in common were brought together?

Consider the situation at the armistice line in Korea. The American and North Korean representatives have been sitting across a table from one another for almost thirty years. If we can believe the press reports, their relationship has gone from one of hatred and insults to one of insults and hatred. Their behavior does not seem to be for propaganda purposes. Rather, the two groups seem to have a deep and abiding loathing for one another. What propinquity has done in this instance is to provide each side with enough information about the other to enable each to conclude clearly that the other side's representatives are monsters. This example shows that although propinquity is necessary for interpersonal attraction, it is not enough. Some similarity in terms of beliefs, attitudes, and values is also needed.

Similarity

For the lion and lamb shall lie down together, but the lamb won't get much sleep. (Woody Allen)

A second prediction about you and your best friend is that, unlike the lion and the lamb, you two have common interests and attitudes. People tend to like those who hold similar attitudes (Berscheid & Walster, 1969; Byrne, 1969).

Fritz Heider explained this well-documented fact in terms of people's need for balance in their interpersonal relationships.

According to Heider, people strive to keep their feelings about important issues and important people in their lives in balance, or consistent with one another. For example, if you feel that strong gun control laws are needed, you are likely to have friends who feel the same way.

The basic assumption underlying Heider's proposal is that people prefer balanced relationships to unbalanced ones. To test this, Jordan (1953) gave college students descriptions of situations where a person's attitudes either agreed or disagreed with a friend's. He asked the students to tell him which of the two types of relationships they preferred. In accord with Heider's theory, the students chose the balanced relationship over the unbalanced one.

Reinforcement theory's explanation of the effect of similarity is more straightforward. It proposes that similar attitudes lead to liking because having someone agree with you is rewarding, and we like those who reward us. In support of this proposal, Golightly and Byrne (1964) found that people react to agreement with their attitudes just as they react to any other positive reinforcer.

Not only do we like people who have beliefs, attitudes and values similar to our own, but in addition, *if we like someone we will see that person's beliefs, attitudes, and values as similar to our own.* That is, people will perceive the attitudes of people they like as more similar to their own than they really are. For example, Byrne and Blalock (1963) had married couples fill out attitude scales and a personality scale, first for themselves and then as they believed their mate would. The assumed similarity (i.e., the correlation between one spouse's own responses and his or her estimate of the other's) was much greater than the actual similarity. Theodore Newcomb (1961) examined the formation of friendships over an extended period of time and found a comparable result. As the males he observed became closer friends, their estimates of the similarity of their attitudes became greater. Newcomb called this a *strain toward symmetry*. People try to keep the amount of similarity between themselves and their friend equivalent with how much they like the other person (Newcomb, 1956, 1961). Thus, we see that although similarity is necessary for liking, the relationship is not static. As liking grows, so does perceived similarity of attitudes.

Not only does similarity in terms of attitudes and values lead to liking, but there is also evidence to suggest that similarity in terms of personality and physical appearance leads to interpersonal attraction. Cattell and Nesselroade (1967) found that happily married couples had more similar personalities than did unhappily married couples. Perhaps more interesting is the research on dating choices and similarity of physical attractiveness.

Numerous studies of physical attractiveness as a variable in interpersonal attraction found (as you would expect) that attractive men and women are preferred as dates over unattractive people (remember what was said about beauty in the previous section; Berscheid & Walster, 1974). But within this general trend, people prefer dates who are similar to themselves in attractiveness. Beautiful men and women choose each other, while their less attractive counterparts also match up. Silverman (1971) tested this matching process in a natural setting. Observers stationed in bars, theaters, and other dating places independently rated each member of a dating pair on a scale of physical attractiveness. Eighty-five percent of the dating pairs were rated within one point on the five-point scale used. Other studies (e.g., Murstein, 1972) have produced similar results. Berscheid and Walster (1974) proposed that this matching reflects people's realistic level of aspiration. That is, people ask out individuals whom they *believe* will go out with them. Little is to be gained by being turned down by the most attractive person on campus.

Being liked

Finally, your friend probably likes you. If we find out that someone likes us, we will like

---

"Wealthy nobleman with strong interest in hematology wants to meet woman with a desire for the ultimate hickey. Call Transylvania 6–5000 after dark"

One of the more popular features of tabloids such as the *National Enquirer* and the *Midnight Tattler* is the "pen pals" section. People write in, giving their assets and describing the characteristics they seek in a pen pal. Albert Harrison and Laila Saeed (1977) used these personal advertisements to investigate what people offer to and desire from potential "friends."

Men were more likely to seek attractive companions and offer financial security than were women. Conveniently, women tended to offer attractiveness and seek financial security. Of special interest was Harrison and Saeed's test of the *matching hypothesis* of interpersonal attractiveness. This hypothesis proposes that people desire companions who are as attractive as they are. It was indeed found that men who described themselves as attractive sought attractive women as pen pals, and attractive women desired attractive men.

them (Berscheid & Walster, 1969). Backman and Secord (1959) gave students evaluations which either flattered or criticized them. Then the students were asked to indicate how much they liked the person who had evaluated them. As you would expect, the students liked the favorable evaluators more than the unfavorable ones.

Balance theory would explain this finding as follows. People have attitudes toward themselves as well as toward objects in their environment. Since most people think well of themselves, someone who likes you is expressing an opinion similar to yours on an important issue. Thus, the relationship is balanced. Reinforcement theorists would say that being liked produces the rewards of self-esteem and social approval (Homans, 1961). And we like those who reward us.

It also seems that the way we communicate our feelings will affect the other person's reaction. For example, Aronson and his associates (Aronson & Linder, 1965; Sigall & Aronson, 1969) had subjects listen to evaluations of themselves. These evaluations were either always positive, always negative, first positive then negative, or first negative then positive. Then the subjects were asked to indicate how much they liked the person who evaluated them. Somewhat surprisingly, subjects liked the person who evaluated them first negatively and then positively more than any of the other evaluators. The reason is not really clear. One possible explanation is that the shift from negative to positive produced a gain in self-esteem for people which, in turn, created increased liking for their evaluator.

There are circumstances, however, in which people do not like those who say they like them. One is called the *ingratiation exception* (Jones, 1964). It describes a situation in which a person believes that someone is being nice to him because of some ulterior motive. For example, I do not like students who tell me that I am a credit to my race and

teach the best course they have ever taken—twenty minutes before the final examination.

This concludes the review of the variables which seem to be responsible for the formation of friendships. Although these studies are important, they provide a somewhat incomplete picture of interpersonal attraction. They do not deal with continuing interactions. With the exception of Theodore Newcomb's examination of how friendships are formed, most research on interpersonal attraction has studied one person's initial reactions to another person. Certainly interpersonal attraction involves more than that. Gergen (1975) and Levinger and Snoek (1972) suggested that to fully understand interpersonal attraction, social psychologists should turn from an examination of brief interactions between people who are basically strangers to long-term, continuing relationships. One such continuing relationship is romantic love.

Love

"Hey dum whap ah, dum whap ah, dum whap ah. Ooh wah, ooh wah, oo-h wah, ooh wah, Why do fools fa-ll in love?" (Frankie Lymon and the Teenagers, 1957)

Ironically, song writers and poets have appeared to show more interest in this question than have social psychologists. Part of the reason is that society has frowned on scientific investigations of it. Recently, two distinguished social psychologists were publicly ridiculed and attacked by a United States Senator because they dared to investigate why people fall in and out of love. Thus, our knowledge of why people fall in love is somewhat limited. But love is such an important part of people's daily lives that the research on it should be presented.

What is love? This simple question has

Lynne Gardner

generated considerable disagreement among those social psychologists who have studied it. Heider (1958) and Berscheid and Walster (1969) have proposed that love is merely an intense form of liking. Zick Rubin (1973) has argued that three things differentiate our feelings toward our lovers from our feelings toward our friends. (1) We feel dependent on the person we love and want to be with him or her. (2) We want to help our lover. (3) We feel that our lover is the only one we love—a total absorption with this person. To test this idea, Rubin (1970) asked college students who were either same-sex friends or were dating to fill out a liking scale and a loving scale on each other (the love scale measured the factors mentioned above). He found that friends and couples who were dating liked each other very much. Among the couples who were dating, the love scale scores correlated much better with their intention to marry than did scores on the liking scale. Also, the love scale pre-

dicted how much time these couples would spend gazing into each other's eyes better than did the liking scale. Thus, if would seem that although people like those they love, liking and loving are not the same thing.

Why do we fall in love with a particular person? Certainly, propinquity, similarity, and being liked are all important, but the research on romantic love suggests that other variables are involved as well.

One interesting finding is that if a person is physiologically aroused in the presence of someone he could reasonably fall in love with, this arousal itself may increase his attraction to the other person. Dutton and Aron (1974) conducted an unusual test of this proposal. Men were approached by a female interviewer as they crossed either a shaky wooden suspension bridge 250 feet above a raging river or a sturdy wooden bridge 10 feet over a small stream. The men were asked to respond to a picture from the Thematic Apperception Test (cf. Chapter Two). Following this, the woman gave both groups of men her phone number and invited them to call her. The men on the shaky suspension bridge gave responses to the picture which contained significantly more sexual themes and were significantly more likely to call the woman than the men who crossed the sturdy bridge. These differences were not found when men were interviewed by men.[1]

The most popular explanation of this finding is based on Stanley Schachter's (1964) *two-factor theory of emotion*. Schachter's theory is an extremely important contribution to social psychological theory and research. It will be used many times throughout this book. Therefore, a brief digression to explain it is needed.

---

[1] Only psychologists would think of conducting an experiment while some poor man hung on for his life 250 feet over a raging river.

Schachter's theory is concerned with the way people come to label or identify their emotions. Some early theorists (e.g., James, 1890) believed that different types of physiological arousal accompany different emotions, and a person uses these differences to label his emotions. But Schachter argued that the accompanying physiological arousal is usually general rather than emotion-specific. Thus, a person cannot identify the emotion he experiences solely on the basis of arousal. For example, there is no one set of physiological responses for love and another for hate. How, then, do people label their emotions? Schachter proposed they will often use cues from their environment to help identify their emotions.

Thus, Schachter would explain the reactions of the men on the shaky bridge by proposing that they mislabeled or misattributed the emotional arousal they felt. Rather than attributing it to the fear they felt while on the bridge, they linked it to sexual attraction toward the woman.

Another variable which is believed to increase feelings of love is the "Romeo and Juliet" effect (Driscoll, Davis, & Lipitz, 1972). Driscoll et al. proposed that parents who interfere with their children's dates may create increased feelings of love. This prediction is based on Brehm's (1966) *reactance theory*. According to Brehm, people value their freedom of choice. If someone attempts to restrict that freedom, the person will react unfavorably and desire the thing he had chosen even more. For example, if your parents tell you that Mr. or Ms. Right looks like a junkie and you must never, ever see him or her again, this may make you want the person all the more. Driscoll et al. found that the couples with disapproving parents reported being more in love than did couples with neutral parents.

Although these two theories of romantic love are interesting, they obviously do not totally explain it. As Kenrick and Cialdini (1977) have argued, some attention must be paid to the rewards one's lover provides. It seems quite likely that just as being rewarded leads to friendship, it also leads to love.

Conclusion

This section focused on the formation of friendships and love relationships. Three factors seem to be involved in friendship: physical closeness, perceived similarity, and being liked. It must be reemphasized that no one of these factors, in itself, will result in interpersonal attraction. All three are needed for people to become friends.

Although there has been a good deal of research on friendship, there has been relatively little on love. Further, the research on love has taken a rather narrow view of its causes. Most of it has focused on the mislabeling of emotions as an important variable in love. This mislabeling probably contributes to some love affairs. But common sense tells us that it can't totally explain love. Future research should address the positive factors related to falling in love.

If there is one major shortcoming in the research on interpersonal attraction, it is the scarcity of studies examining long-term, continuing relationships. Propinquity, perceived similarity, and being liked are all related to the formation of friendships. We do not know, however, if they are important in an ongoing relationship. Most of the time people spend in dyadic behavior is with individuals they have known for a long time. Thus, it is important to move from the study of how strangers become friends to the study of why some friendships and marriages last and others fail. The "social psychology of the stranger" provides an incomplete view of interpersonal attraction.

REVIEW QUESTIONS

(Eight out of ten is passing)

1. The study of _____ _____ is concerned with the variables related to the formation of friendships. (p. 85)
2. Heider (1958) proposed that physical closeness (propinquity) leads to interpersonal attraction because the people perceive themselves as a unit. This explanation is based on the concept of _____ . (p. 86)
3. _____ theory bases its explanation of the effect of propinquity on interpersonal attraction on the rewards and costs involved in the relationship. (p. 86)
4. The old adage "Birds of a feather flock together" illustrates the effect of perceived _____ on interpersonal attraction. (p. 87)
5. Happily married couples perceive their attitudes as more similar than they really are. This illustrates Newcomb's concept of _____ _____ _____ . (p. 88)
6. The research on physical attractiveness and dating suggests that people tend to choose dates who are of _____ attractiveness to themselves. (p. 88)
7. An acquaintance tells you that you are his closest friend and a fine human being and then tries to borrow $100 from you. The fact that you probably won't like this person is explained by the _____ exception. (p. 89)
8. Rubin said that _____ is composed of feelings of dependence on another person, a tendency to help another person, and absorption with another person. (p. 90)
9. Schachter's two-factor theory of emotion proposed that when a person is aroused and cannot identify the cause of the arousal, he will use environmental cues to _____ his emotions. (p. 91)
10. Parental interference in a romance may intensify a couple's feelings for one another (the "Romeo and Juliet" effect). This may be explained by the theory of _____ . (p. 91)

ANSWERS

1. interpersonal attraction   2. balance   3. reinforcement   4. similarity
5. strain toward symmetry   6. equal   7. ingratiation   8. love   9. label   10. reactance

Lynne Gardner

INTERPERSONAL BEHAVIOR

Dear Ann Landers: Yes, it's true, Hitler-like extermination is not only immoral but criminal. Yet, problems with the aged are so difficult. I am sick and tired of writing that check every month for my husband's 90-year-old mother who doesn't know anybody and can't even comb her own hair. She is a terrific burden to the family, yet the doctor says her heart is better than mine and she may outlive all of us. My children need financial help badly. We are not rich—barely making it, in fact. It gripes me to to see all this money being spent to keep a useless woman alive. Where does the point of justice lie—Anonymous, Of Course—What Else Could I Be?

I selected this letter to begin this section for several reasons. First, it describes a *dyadic relationship*—a relationship between two people in which what happens to one person affects the other. If "Anonymous" stopped supporting her mother-in-law, the woman would die. And the older woman's existence exacts a price from "Anonymous." Second, this letter is not from a monster, but from a frustrated, confused person who is expressing a universal desire for justice in a dyadic relationship. People desire relationships which produce fair and equitable payoffs for them. This woman feels she is being asked to pay an enormous emotional and financial cost while receiving no rewards. Finally, this letter shows that often what is justice for one person may be injustice for the other person in the relationship. As Ann Landers stated in her answer, we cannot kill people just because they are a burden on us.

The next few pages will examine dyadic relationships. First, the factors which influence a person's judgment as to what is a fair or unfair relationship will be identified. Following it will be a review of how people react when they believe that they are involved in an unfair relationship.

Equity theory

The basic premise of equity theory is that people desire a fair or equitable distribution of rewards and costs among the parties involved in a relationship (Berkowitz & Walster, 1976). This theory views the relationship between two or more people as consisting of inputs and outcomes. An *input* is, quite simply, what a person puts into a relationship. The inputs of "Anonymous" would be the time she spends caring for her mother-in-law and the money she sends her. An *outcome* is what the person gets out of the relationship. These outcomes can be rewards (e.g., money, love, praise) or costs (e.g., loss of money, rejection, ridicule). According to Homans (1976), a relationship can be considered *equitable* when all parties involved in it believe that their rewards equal their inputs.

If all people saw their relationships as equitable, the world would be a simple and pleasant place to live. But people often find themselves in inequitable relationships. A person can experience two kinds of inequity. First, he may believe that he is getting *more* out of a relationship than he is putting into it, a condition called *benign inequity*. Or he may believe that he is getting *less* out of a relationship than he is putting into it. This is called *malignant inequity* (Gergen, 1969).

It may surprise you to learn that most people are as bothered by benign inequity as they are by malignant inequity (Walster, Berscheid, & Walster, 1973). When a person receives a gift or favor from someone, he will usually be eager to repay it and will be upset if he cannot (Gergen, cited by Walster et al., 1973; Greenberg & Frisch, 1972). However, as you might guess, people are more likely to see malignant inequity than benign inequity (Weick, 1966). Therefore, we will concentrate on this type of inequity. What factors lead a person to believe that he is getting the "short end" of a relationship?

The perception of inequity

Equity, like beauty, is in the eye of the beholder, as the letter to Ann Landers shows. Many people might believe that after ninety years, "Anonymous's" mother-in-law deserved the care she was receiving and that there was nothing unfair about the relationship. "Anonymous" obviously did not feel this way. Why?

There seem to be two factors which lead people to judge a relationship equitable or inequitable. First, a person compares the ratio of his inputs and outcomes from the relationship to those of the other parties involved in it. If he does not see these ratios as equal, he will conclude that this relationship is inequitable (Adams, 1965). In addition, he will compare the payoff he is receiving to the payoffs he has received in past relationships. These past relationships provide a standard

which is used to judge the present situation. Thus, it is possible for a person to have the same input/output ratio as another person in the relationship and still see it as inequitable (Lane & Mess'e, 1971; Mess'e & Lane, 1974; Weick, 1966).

For example, imagine a child who is good and does everything his parents want. On Christmas morning he finds a lump of coal in the stocking he has hung over the fireplace. The fact that his equally good brothers and sisters also received a lump of coal will probably not matter; he will still see his relationship with his parents as inequitable.

A person who experiences malignant inequity will usually also feel tense and distressed—and, in general, in an unpleasant emotional state. Let us examine five common reactions to malignant inequity.

Reactions to inequity

Reducing inputs. If a person believes that his inputs are not equalled by his outcomes, he may reduce his inputs (Clark, 1958). Consider the case of a prostitute interviewed by Terkel (1974) in his book *Working.* This woman had once been a call girl who received $50 to $100 for her services; now she is a streetwalker receiving $10 at most for the same act. She sees this as inequitable and has reduced her inputs:

As a streetwalker, I didn't have to act. I let myself show the contempt I felt for the tricks. They weren't paying enough to make it worth performing for them. As a call girl, I pretended I enjoyed it sexually. You have to act as if you had an orgasm. As a streetwalker, I didn't. I used to lie there with my hands behind my head and do mathematics equations in my head or memorize the keyboard typewriter. (Terkel, 1974, p. 98).

Altering outcomes. Another way to reestablish equity in an interaction is to keep your inputs the same but demand a greater outcome (Homans, 1953). For example, consider the pro football strikes of 1974 and 1975. (Although some people found it hard to believe that men who earned up to $300,000 per year saw their situation as inequitable, the football players did.) In this case, the players could not reestablish equity by reducing their effort; this strategy would result in their being dropped from their team. Therefore, what they demanded was an increase in salary, better fringe benefits, and more freedom in deciding which team they played for—an increase in the outcome for the same input.

Rationalization of the inequity. A person may perceive their situation to be malignantly inequitable but still be unable to alter the inputs or outcomes. In such a situation, he may attempt to rationalize away the inequity. This process can take two forms. First, the person can attempt to justify the inequity (Walster et al., 1973). That is, he can derogate himself and thus conclude that, given his low status, he is indeed receiving an equitable payoff (Lerner & Matthews, 1967). Remember, equity is a comparative process. If a person sees himself as less deserving of a certain outcome than the other person in the relationship, then the objectively inequitable outcome may be perceived as equitable.

The second alternative is to reestablish equity by derogating the person who is receiving a better payoff. Consider this attendant in a men's washroom whose customers treat him in a rude or patronizing way. Here is how he sees them:

The man I hand the towel to is perfectly aware of my presence. Sometimes he wants it to appear that he is unaware of you. You have to be aware of him whether he's aware of you or not. A very common ploy is for two men to come in discussing a big business deal. I stand with the towels and they just walk right by, talking about thousands of dollars in transactions. I'm to assume they're so occupied with what they're doing that they don't have time

for me. They ignore me completely. They don't bother to wash their hands. (Laughs.) I laugh at them inside. The joke's on them as far as I'm concerned. Sometimes just for the hell of it, when they go back to the urinal, I'll have the water running: "Towel, sir?" "No, I gotta hurry and get back to eat." He's just come from the toilet. He hasn't bothered to wash his hands. (Chuckles.) (Terkel, 1974, pp. 156–157)

Note what this man has done; he has cognitively "put down" his customers. Thus he has reestablished equity in this interaction.

Retaliation. If the perception of inequity in an interaction is due to the other person's behavior, the "victim" may attempt to reestablish equity by retaliating (Ross, Thibaut, & Evenbeck, 1971). This method is as ancient as the Old Testament proposal of taking an "eye for an eye." In fact, according to Berscheid, Boye, and Walster (1968), the earliest legal codes (e.g., the Code of Hammurabi, established 5,000 years ago) saw retaliation as the only means of reestablishing equity. Note what retaliation does. It does not directly affect the injured party's inputs and outcomes. What it does is to bring the offending party's inputs and outcomes back into line with the victim's.

Leaving the field. If a person has tried all other means of reestablishing equity in an interaction and they have failed, he may simply discontinue the relationship (Patchen, 1961). For example, a marriage partner who perceives the relationship as inequitable and cannot put less into the marriage, get the spouse to put in more, rationalize the inequity or retaliate may resolve the inequity through divorce.

However, in certain instances, people may choose to remain in extremely inequitable relationships. Let me provide an example of this via an old story.

A man riding a bus is seated next to a man in a bright red suit. The first man quickly notices a pungent odor coming from his seat companion. The odor is so strong that he feels compelled to mention it.

"Excuse me, sir. I don't mean to be rude, but you stink!"

"Yeah, I know. It's my job. You see, I work in a circus, and when the elephants enter the arena, I follow them and clean up after them. Well, it's a messy job to begin with, and sometimes I follow the elephants too close, and . . . I get forty dollars a week. My clothes stink. I can't get rid of the smell. My wife left me. I have no friends. And strangers keep coming up to me and telling me how bad I smell."

The first man replies: "My God, that's awful. Why don't you quit this job."

The elephant attendant looks at the other man with disbelief and says: "What, and give up show business?"

To explain this apparently illogical reaction, we need to introduce the concept of comparison levels. Thibaut and Kelley (1959) proposed that on the basis of past experiences in other relationships, people develop internal standards as to the reward/cost ratio they should receive from a relationship. This internal standard is called a *comparison level*. If the actual reward cost ratio a person receives meets his comparison level, he will view the relationship as equitable or satisfactory.

If the reward/cost ratio is below the person's comparison level, he will then examine his *comparison level for alternatives*. This involves comparing one's present relationship to other, alternative relationships. If the person decides that these alternative relationships would provide an even worse reward cost ratio than the one he is in, he may remain in the present unsatisfactory relationship. Thus, people may stay unhappily married because they fear a divorce, and our elephant attendant continues on his messy but show business-related job.

The decision as to which of these five kinds of behaviors to use in order to reestablish equity is largely determined by the situation the person is in. For example, a person whose spouse is an unfaithful drunk would probably not feel that equity had been reestablished by his also becoming an unfaithful drunk. Similarly, retaliation does not seem to be practical for the washroom attendant described earlier. Thus, the situation determined that he reestablish equity by rationalizing away the inequity.

Equity is a simple concept to understand. In public opinion poll, most people would probably state that relationships should produce fair and equal payoffs for all parties concerned. Why is it, then, that so many relationships are inequitable? One reason is that the relationships often involve two people who desire the same payoff. And only one person can win. For example, "Anonymous" wants some peace, security, and comfort in her life, and so does her mother-in-law. However, she could achieve these reasonable goals only with her mother-in-law's death. Thus, in order to reach equity, there must be some attempt at cooperation. How does cooperation come about?

Cooperation in dyads

It is 10:00 on the night before your final examination in chemistry. You are in a panic. You bought the required textbook the first day of the term but never attended class. The test will be based on the book and lecture notes. As you frantically race around the dormitory, you find a classmate who attended class and took excellent notes but neglected to buy the textbook. The need for a cooperative arrangement is obvious. But how will you accomplish this?

The use of threat
"How did your father get him to sign the contract?"

"He made him an offer he couldn't refuse." "What was it?" "He put a gun to the guy's head and told him that either his brains or his signature were going to be on the contract."

Will threat be as effective a strategy for you as it was for Don Corleone (the Godfather)? Would it be effective for you to threaten to beat this person up if he refused to let you use his notes? The answer is probably no.

Deutsch and Krauss (1960) conducted an experiment where two women played the roles of owners of trucking companies. Each person could earn money if she could get her truck from one warehouse to another within a certain period of time. However, both companies had to use the same road and only one truck could use it at a time. Under these circumstances, the players alternated using the road, and both made money. Then each player was given the chance to threaten the other. This was done by giving each of them control over a gate which prevented the other person's truck from reaching its destination.

The effect of the introduction of threat is shown in Figure 3-1. As you can see from this figure, the "owners'" ability to threaten each other turned a profitable situation for both into a losing proposition. The reason is that both "owners" used their gates to threaten each other. The result was a standoff; neither would back down, and both lost money.

If we look at dyads in the real world, a similar finding is obtained. Marriage involves two people trying to control each other's behavior. The wife wants to rest while the husband wants her to make dinner. The husband wants to watch the football game while the wife wants him to take out the garbage. And so on. Birchler, Weiss, and Vincent (1975) examined how couples who were either happily or unhappily married attempted to achieve cooperation in these activities. They found that couples whose marriages were in trouble were much more likely to use threats,

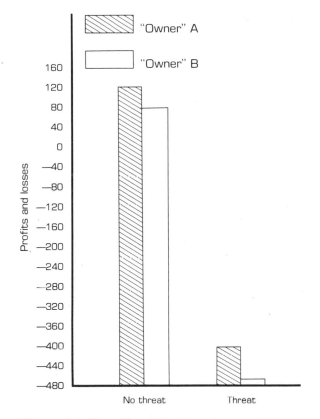

Figure 3-1. The effect of the introduction of threat on "owner's" profits and losses in the trucking game. (Adapted from Deutsch & Krauss, 1960)

complaints, and criticism than were couples with good marriages. Further, Birchler et al. found that unhappy couples used these tactics only with each other. When dealing with strangers, they used much more positive means to induce cooperation.

Why doesn't threat produce cooperation? Brehm's (1966) reactance theory provides one explanation. According to reactance theory, people do not like to have their freedom of choice restricted. This is exactly what threat does. It attempts to force a person to act a certain way. This may result in his being less inclined to cooperate with the person who has threatened him.

Total cooperation

A second possible strategy you might use is to totally cooperate with the other person. You could say, "I understand you need a textbook for the chemistry final. Here, use mine. Don't worry about me, I'll make out somehow." Your hope is that he will be so moved by your generosity that he will offer you his lecture notes. Unfortunately, this probably won't happen.

Instead, it is much more likely that he will either refuse your offer or take the book and give you nothing in return. In other words, people usually respond to total, unconditional cooperation with total and unconditional exploitation (Gallo & McClintock, 1965).

Why? One reason is that people do not like a martyr, especially when they feel responsible for his fate (Lerner, 1974; Leventhal, 1976). Instead of reacting positively, people will often derogate a martyr. That is, they will attempt to reestablish equity in the relationship by concluding that the martyr is a person who deserves his fate.

Also, a totally cooperative gesture is often misinterpreted. This violation of the equity principle is often seen as stupidity. Worse, it is seen as part of some "snow job." Thus, the recipient refuses to cooperate and instead attempts exploitation. Total cooperation will work only if the other person understands that it is an intentional act made by someone with no ulterior motives (Enzle, Hansen, & Lowe, 1975).

Matching

A third possible strategy for you to use would be to "feel out" the other person. Let him know that you have the book, but make no offer. If he asks for the book but does not offer you his notes, refuse. If he offers you his

---

The prisoner's dilemma

Because interpersonal behavior in the real world is so complex, many social psychologists have turned to games to study cooperation in dyads. One of the more popular games is the Prisoner's Dilemma. It is based on the following situation. Two people are suspected of committing a holdup, but the police don't have a very strong case. They are separated by the police, and the first suspect is asked to testify against his partner. If he does, he will get off while his partner will get a long term in jail. This sounds very appealing to him, at first. But suddenly he realizes that the police are probably making the same offer to his partner. The dilemma becomes apparent. If he stays loyal and his friend defects, he's been victimized. But if they both defect, they will both get long sentences. The dilemma can be diagrammed as follows:

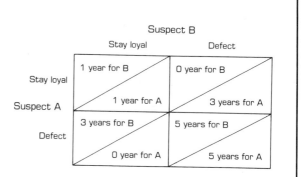

If you want to try the various strategies for inducing cooperation, get a friend two pieces of paper and pencils. Both of you look at this "payoff matrix" and write down your choice (defect or stay loyal) at the same time. Keep score and after a few trials try threat, or total cooperation, or matching.

notes, you can reciprocate by offering him the book. This strategy for inducing cooperation is called *matching* or *tit for tat*. A number of studies have shown that it will produce cooperation (e.g., McClintock, 1972). The reason for this is that you are rewarding cooperative behavior and punishing competitive behavior. If the other person realizes what you are doing, he will respond by cooperating.

Small concessions

A final strategy that seems to produce cooperation in a dyad is to make unilateral but very small concessions to the other person. These should be acts which show good faith on your part but do not seriously endanger your own position. For example, you might offer to let him use your book for a few minutes. If he reciprocates, you might make a larger concession, such as offering your book for a few hours. A number of studies have shown that this technique does produce cooperation (Hamner, 1974; Pilisuk & Skolnick, 1968).

One of the interesting things about this means of producing cooperation is that it was first offered as a way to reduce international tension between the United States and the Soviet Union (Osgood, 1959; 1962). According to Osgood, the level of conflict between two countries could be lowered by one country making small, unilateral conciliatory gestures toward the other. These gestures would be well publicized. The first country would invite the second country to reciprocate but would not demand it. Osgood called his proposal G.R.I.T. (Graduated Reciprocation in Tension Reduction). Does G.R.I.T. really work?

Etzioni (1969) looked at the relations between the United States and the Soviet Union in the period preceding the signing of a nuclear test ban treaty in August 1963. In June 1963, President John F. Kennedy had announced that the United States had halted nuclear testing in the atmosphere. A few days later, the Soviet Union dropped its objection to an American plan in the United Nations. America reciprocated by allowing the Hungarian delegation to the United Nations to be seated. The Soviets then announced they had stopped the production of strategic bombers. Note that each of these moves was unilateral and conciliatory but did not endanger the maker. The first bilateral agreement came on August 5, 1963, when the two countries signed a nuclear test ban treaty. In Etzioni's judgment, Kennedy's use of the G.R.I.T. strategy resulted in a dramatic decline in the tension between the United States and the Soviet Union.

Conclusion

The final section of this chapter examined interpersonal behavior—that is, behavior in a situation where what happens to one person depends on the joint actions of all the people involved in the relationship. This review began with a very simple premise. People desire just and fair payoffs from their relationships with others. This idea forms the core of equity theory. However, payoffs which are considered fair by all parties are often difficult to obtain. When a person feels that he has been treated inequitably, he will usually be motivated to reestablish equity. This can be attempted in a number of ways, and the choice a person makes will depend on the situation he is in and his personality.

Cooperation in dyads was discussed next. There are several strategies which can be used to produce cooperation. A matching strategy, in which one person responds in kind to the other, seems to produce the most cooperative dyad.

In concluding this chapter, I want to share one of my concerns with you. Some readers may dismiss the reward/cost theory of interpersonal behavior as too cold and sterile a view of how human beings interact. Certainly much of the research covered has this fault. But I believe that this view of interpersonal behavior may enable us to understand the incredibly complex phenomenon of dyadic behavior. In the hands of an intelligent researcher, a reward/cost conceptualization can provide as rich and full a picture of what two people are doing as a video tape of their behavior. More importantly, this view of interpersonal behavior may allow us to explain why these two people are acting as they are.

REVIEW QUESTIONS

(Eight out of ten is passing)

1. Most theories of dyadic behavior are based on the premise that a person in a dyad is motivated primarily by a desire for _____ . (p. 93)
2. In equity theory, the effort a person expends on a relationship is called a(n) _____ . (p. 93)
3. If a person feels he is getting more out of a relationship than he is putting in, he will experience _____ inequity. Alternatively, a person who feels he is getting less out of a relationship than he is putting in will experience _____ inequity. (p. 94)
4. Besides comparing one's own outcome from a relationship to that of other people, a person uses a(n) _____ _____ to determine if he is being treated equitably. (p. 94)
5. An opera singer who used to get $1,000 per performance now gets $100. Therefore, he sings softer. He is attempting to reestablish equity by _____ his _____ . (p. 94)
6. A person may use _____ to reestablish equity if he cannot physically alter the outcomes or inputs from a relationship. (p. 95)
7. The Old Testament statement, "An eye for an eye," suggests that equity can be reestablished via _____ . (p. 95)
8. A person may stay in an unsatisfactory relationship because his _____ _____ is judged worse than the present relationship. (p. 96)
9. The strategy which seems to yield the most cooperative behavior in a dyad is _____ . (p. 99)
10. The technique of reducing international tension by one country making a number of small, unilateral, conciliatory gestures toward another is called _____ . (p. 99)

ANSWERS

1. justice (profit would be acceptable)   2. input   3. benign, malignant   4. internal standard   5. reducing inputs   6. rationalization   7. retaliation   8. comparison level for alternatives   9. matching   10. G.R.I.T. (Graduated Reciprocation in Tension Reduction)

SUGGESTED READINGS

There are a number of excellent books on the topics covered in this chapter. Here are some you might consider.

Textbooks

Person perception

Person Perception, by Albert Hastorf, David Schneider, and Judith Polefka. This is a short but extremely comprehensive review of the basic principles of person perception.

An Introduction to Attribution Processes, by Kelly Shaver. This brief overview of the attribution process provides almost everything you need to know about how people make causal attributions.

Nobody Wanted War, by Ralph K. White. In this award-winning book, White applies many of the principles of person perception to international conflicts. He provides a highly creative approach to one of the causes of war.

Interpersonal attraction

Interpersonal Attraction, by Ellen Berscheid and Elaine Walster. These two social psychologists are among the foremost theorists and researchers in the area of interpersonal attraction. This book and their other articles provide a coherent, unified examination of the factors related to liking.

The Psychology of Interpersonal Relationships, by Fritz Heider. This is one of the most scholarly books I've ever read. It must be read slowly and carefully. But if you persevere, you will understand why Heider is such an important figure in social psychology.

Liking and Loving, by Zick Rubin. In this well-written, lively book, Rubin presents his theory of love and examines the nature of interpersonal relationships.

Interpersonal behavior

Equity Theory (Volume 9 of *Advances in Experimental Social Psychology*), by Leonard Berkowitz and Elaine Walster. This book brings together chapters by the leading equity theorists. It contains just about everything you ever wanted to know about the concept of equity.

Either The Psychology of Behavior Exchange or *Social Exchange Theory,* by Kenneth Gergen. The first book is short and easy to read. The second presents most of the major theorists of social exchange. You might read the short one first and decide if you want to tackle the more difficult second book.

Popular literature

There are so many novels and plays about interpersonal behavior that it's hard to say which are the best. However, here are some books I really enjoyed reading.

Who's Afraid of Virginia Woolf?, by Edward Albee. This is a play about two people who have created a hellish relationship for themselves.

Kinflicks, by Lisa Alther. Most of the concepts presented in this chapter are contained in this best-selling novel.

Stern, by Bruce Jay Friedman. Friedman is a very funny writer. This book describes a neurotic's view of the people around him.

Ordinary People, by Judith Guest. Guest's description of how a family deals with its problems may tell you more about interpersonal behavior than this chapter did.

4 INTERPERSONAL AGGRESSION

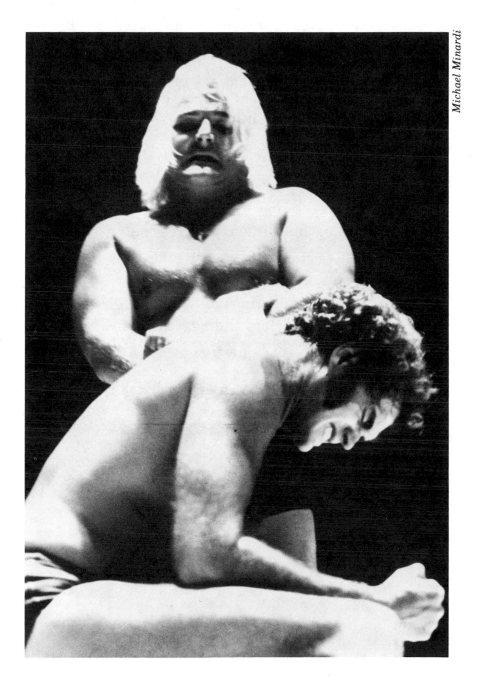

Michael Minardi

This chapter examines the causes of human aggression. Human beings aggress in many ways, and it is impossible to cover them all here. Thus, the discussion will be limited to interpersonal aggression. It will begin by considering the factors that cause one person to aggress against another. Then it will turn to some explanations of the reasons for different forms of aggression in different people. Finally, the control of aggression will be discussed.

WHAT IS AGGRESSION?

From the day Cain slew Abel, humans have been concerned about *aggression,* the intentional injury of another person (Berkowitz, 1975). They have condemned it and tried to control it. But at the same time, humans have shown an amazing ability to act aggressively. These acts come in a wide variety of forms.

First, there is the ultimate collective aggression, war. During the last 150 years, more than 70 million people have died in wars (Singer & Small, 1970).

The "controlled" violence of sports is an integral part of contemporary society. People such as Muhammad Ali have made millions of dollars by showing that they can beat another human being into submission. In the city where I live, 5,000 people turn out every week to watch professional wrestlers supposedly brutalize each other.

The most common type of aggression is probably *interpersonal aggression,* the injury of one person by another. Interpersonal aggression can be verbal, such as that of a child who makes fun of another child's speech impediment. Her words are doing injury to another person. Obviously, interpersonal aggression can also be physical. Physical aggression can range from two people shoving each other in order to get a seat on a bus to one person violently assaulting another with her hands or a weapon.

The statistics on extreme interpersonal aggression are frightening. During the last fifteen years, the number of reported murders has gone up by 120 percent. Beatings serious enough to require police action have increased by 150 percent in the same period (F.B.I. Uniform Crime Reports, 1977). Many people think that these increases are due to a greater number of criminals who prey on innocent, honest citizens. Thus, people buy handguns to protect themselves and their family. The tragedy is that if these people ever use their gun, it will probably be to shoot a friend or relative. No more than 30 percent of all murders committed occur as part of robbery or similar crimes. In the majority of cases, the victims are "relatives, lovers, or friends of the murderer." (Gillin & Ochberg, 1970, p. 253)

The same pattern is found in reported cases of aggravated assault (defined by the F.B.I. as an "unlawful attack by one person on another for the purpose of inflicting severe bodily injury"). Most of these attacks occur among family members, neighbors, and friends (Reckless, 1973). If all cases of aggravated assault were reported to the police, the percentage that occurred among relatives, friends, and neighbors would probably be overwhelming. This is true because a fight between two people in their home, no matter how severe, is less likely to be reported to the police than a mugging or a fight in a bar.

These examples and statistics illustrate the pervasiveness of aggression in the world around us. They also show the wide variety of behavior that could be discussed in a chapter on aggression. If this chapter is to have any focus, it must be limited to certain kinds of aggressive behavior.

We will be concerned almost exclusively with interpersonal aggression—aggressive acts carried out by one person against another. Collective aggression in the form of war and the reasons for the incredible popularity of violent sports are important issues. But a discussion of these topics is beyond the scope of a social psychology textbook.

Forms of interpersonal aggression

In discussing interpersonal aggression, we must distinguish between two types of aggression. Most social psychologists agree that

"You usually hurt the one you love"

Murder is the ultimate act of aggression. Donald Lunde (1976), a psychiatrist, conducted an exhaustive examination of murders in the United States. His findings are interesting . . . and frightening.

The Chances of Being Murdered

Over the course of a normal life span (about 70 years) 1 out of every 200 Americans will be murdered.

Who will Be murdered?

Murder victims do not make up a random cross section of the American population.

Black Americans are about seven times as likely to be murdered as are white Americans.

A person living in the South is twice as likely to be murdered as someone living in another part of the country.

Most murder victims are under thirty years of age.

The Conditions Surrounding a Murder

About 70 percent of all murders are impulsive, unplanned acts which produce no financial rewards for the murderer. Murders break down as follows:

Twenty-five percent occur among members of the same family. Half of these result from an argument between a husband and wife, usually over infidelity. (Husbands usually are killed in the kitchen, wives in the bedroom.)

Another six percent occur between more distant relatives.

Over thirty-three percent occur among friends or acquaintances as the result of a barroom brawl or an argument in the murderer's home.

In a substantial percentage of the murders studied, the victim had provoked the murderer, and the majority of these provokers had been drinking.

What is the Typical Murderer Like?

A murderer is about three times more likely to be a man than a woman. (although the percentage of female murderers has increased substantially in recent years).

A murderer will be young, probably less than twenty-five years old.

Less than four percent of all murderers are insane. Mentally ill people are no more dangerous than the general population.

The typical murderer will be someone with a long history of violent behavior. But a substantial percentage of murderers have no such history. On the contrary, they have never allowed themselves to engage in socially accepted forms of aggression. Megargee (1966, 1971) has speculated that these people's hostility builds until it reaches a breaking point, and then they commit the ultimate form of aggression.

aggressive behavior can be characterized as either hostile or instrumental (Berkowitz, 1965; Buss, 1971; Feshbach, 1970). *Hostile aggression* is aggression which results from some internal motive state (e.g., anger) with the intention of injuring another person.

Instrumental aggresion, in contrast, is behavior in which the aggressor is usually not angry with the victim. The victim's injury is simply the means by which the aggressor reaches some end. That is, the aggression is instrumental (useful) in attaining some reward. The difference between these two types of aggression may be clarified by two examples.

In the first example, two men are seated in a bar talking about politics. One man says that he is a lifelong Republican and believes all Democrats are traitors and communists. The second man objects strongly, saying he is a Democrat, and therefore, the other man is calling him a traitor and a communist. "Absolutely right," says the first man, and besides that, "anyone who is a Democrat is a moron." The Democrat, in the spirit of enlightened political debate, picks up a beer bottle and fractures the Republican's skull—hostile aggression. The Democrat was angered (internal motive state), and this caused him to behave aggressively. The object was the injury of the Republican.

The example of instrumental aggression comes from Vincent Teresa's factual account of his life in the Mafia. In his autobiography, Teresa told about the Mafia's "hit men," people who kill for money. Usually, they don't hate their victim; they are just "doing their job." Here is Teresa's description of one such person.

Today, every mob has its own assassination squads made up of men who get a regular weekly salary just to be ready for the day a hit is needed. The members of the squad are hand-picked by a boss. Their talents always include three things. They are experts with a variety of guns and other weapons. They are cool under pressure. They also have no emotion.

I remember there was one guy I heard about who worked for Anastasia's old Murder, Inc., who is typical of what I mean. They called him Ice Pick Barney. His technique was as cold and as calculating as they come. He and other men assigned on a hit would force their victim into a men's room. Then Ice Pick Barney would pull out his ice pick and, while the others held the guy, he'd put the ice pick through the guy's eardrum into his brain. The pick left a tiny hole and would cause very little bleeding. They'd wipe away the blood that trickled from the ear, but the bleeding in the brain would cause the guy to die. When a doctor examined him, he'd rule the guy died from a cerebral hemorrhage. They're a special breed, the assassins. (Teresa, 1973, p. 185)

The statistics on murder and assault presented earlier suggest that most interpersonal aggression is hostile rather than instrumental. Therefore, we will concentrate on hostile interpersonal aggression.

However, in the real world, hostile and instrumental aggression are often interrelated. For example, a child beats up another child in a schoolyard because she's been provoked by taunts and insults. But besides making the other child "pay" for the verbal abuse, the aggressor may use the fight to move up in the schoolyard hierarchy (Bandura, 1973). Acts which are initially hostile may acquire goals which go beyond the simple injury of another person.

A final comment, and then we can turn to the causes of aggression. Most of the research covered here is concerned with physical rather than verbal aggression. There are two reasons for this. First, social psychologists view physical aggression as a greater threat to society than verbal aggression. No one ever died as the *direct* result of being insulted. Second, physical aggression is easier to observe and measure than is verbal aggression. Scientific investigations of some phenomenon need clear measurements of it. Therefore, verbal aggression will be discussed only when it helps to explain physical aggression.

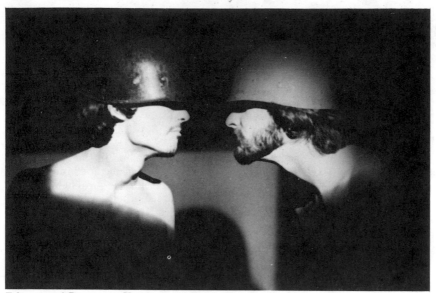

Educational Resources, University of South Florida

THE CAUSES OF AGGRESSIVE BEHAVIOR

Aggression can result from being physically attacked, verbally abused (i.e., insulted), or frustrated. It is no great surprise that if you hit another person or call her a moron, you will make her angry. Aggression as the result of frustration is a little less obvious.

Frustration and aggression

Frustration results from the interference with a goal-oriented activity. For example, I am writing this chapter on a Sunday afternoon. I use Sundays to write because I believe that my goal-oriented activity (i.e., writing this book) will not be interfered with by people interrupting me. So far today, eight of my colleagues have dropped in to chat. This is very frustrating.

One of the first attempts to specify the relationship between frustration and aggression was made in the *frustration-aggression* hypothesis (Dollard, Doob, Miller, Mowrer, & Sears, 1939). This hypothesis originally proposed that: (1) frustration will always lead to aggression and (2) frustration is the cause of all aggression. But in the forty years that have passed, this proposal has changed considerably.

Most social psychologists now recognize that aggression can occur in the absence of frustration and that frustration does not always lead to aggression. One important factor in whether frustration produces aggression is how a person interprets the frustrating act.

The deliberate, intentional interference with someone's attempt to reach a goal is called *arbitrary thwarting*. It is much more likely to result in aggression than is *nonarbitrary thwarting*—the accidental or unintentional interference with a person's attempt to reach some goal. An example may illustrate the difference between the two.

Imagine you are studying in your room one night for a difficult exam. You have your lecture notes and book spread out before you.

Your roommate comes in, slightly drunk, and as a "joke" pours ink all over your book and notes. She has deliberately interfered with your goal-oriented activity (studying for an exam). This is arbitrary thwarting and is more likely to lead to aggression than the following situation.

Again you are studying for an exam, but this time your roommate is quietly reading a book. In reaching for a cigarette on the table in front of you, she accidentally spills ink all over your lecture notes and book. Again a goal-oriented activity has been interfered with, but this time your roommate's behavior was accidental and unintentional. This non-arbitrary thwarting will usually not produce aggression (Burnstein & Worchel, 1962; Kregarman & Worchel, 1962).

Insults, physical attacks, and frustration are unpleasant experiences which cause emotional arousal. But they do not always result in aggression. An aggressive act depends upon: (1) how a person interprets the arousal she is experiencing, (2) the characteristics of the situation she is in, and (3) her general aggressive tendencies. We will examine how each of these factors affects aggression.

Arousal and aggression

A person who sees a snake and a person who is insulted will have almost exactly the same physiological reactions to these stimuli. Yet people usually run away from snakes and respond to insults with verbal or physical aggression. What is the reason for this difference?

Part of the answer may lie in Stanley Schachter's two-factor theory of how people label or identify their emotions (cf. Chapter Three). Schachter proposed that people will often use cues from their environment to label the emotions they experience. Thus, it is reasonable for a person who has seen a snake and is physiologically aroused to call her emotion fear and for a person who has been insulted to label her arousal as anger.

Let's apply this labeling process to a situation in which anger should occur but doesn't. You are in a large room with a group of other people. A short, bald man walks to the front of the room and begins to talk to the group. He looks at you and calls you a "hockey puck." He then tells the black person next to you that all blacks are stupid. He asks if there are any Italian-Americans in the audience, and when someone raises his hand, he says all Italians are Mafiosi. You feel yourself getting upset. Who does this guy think he is? You jump up and move toward the front of the room, intent on punching him in the face. As you storm toward him, you realize that the other people do not share your anger. In fact, they are laughing and seem to enjoy being insulted. Has the world gone mad?

By now, you may have realized that the man I have been describing is the comedian Don Rickles. Consider what happens in Rickles's night club act. He insults a person (verbal aggression), who usually turns red or starts to sweat (physiological arousal). The victim should aggress, but usually Rickles's victims do not. Why? Rickles is an entertainer. His insults are for the purpose of amusement. Therefore, people do not see his intent as hostile. Further, the laughter of others provides a framework for interpreting the physiological arousal which Rickles's insults produce. Thus, his audience does not label their physiological reactions as anger; they react with laughter instead.

The point of this example is that arousal will not lead to aggression unless it is labeled as anger or frustration. What would happen if a person's arousal was due to factors other than insults or physical attacks, but was labeled as anger?

It has been found that arousal, whatever its cause, which is labeled as anger will increase a person's willingness to aggress (Konečni, 1975). In one study, arousing tones which were followed by an insulting remark produced more aggression than just being insulted. The reason seems to be that the insult gave the subjects a label for the arousal, namely, anger.

Even sexual arousal can sometimes increase aggression (Yaffe, Malamuth, Feingold, & Feshbach, 1974; Zillman, 1971). In these studies, subjects were sexually aroused and then attacked by a confederate. This resulted in their aggressing against the confederate more than a group of subjects who were just attacked.[1] This was probably because the attack gave the subjects a label for the arousal they felt.

However, sexual arousal does not always increase aggression; in fact, it may often decrease it (Baron, 1974b; Baron & Bell, 1973; Donnerstein, Donnerstein, & Evans, 1975). Erotic material presented *after* a person has been angered will decrease the person's level of aggression. The reason is that the material diverts the person's attention from the anger he feels.[2] This *attentional shift* decreases the person's anger and results in a lessened tendency to aggress (Donnerstein et al., 1975).

To return to the main point, emotional arousal, whatever its cause, is an important part of aggression.

Situational factors and aggression

In the following situations, assume that a person has been angered or frustrated and has labeled her arousal correctly. Even in this case, aggression is still not a "sure thing." Furthermore, if the aggression does occur, its

P. Michael Smith

intensity will be affected by the situation the person is in. For example, a man is driving in a car with a woman. His attraction to her and the fact that they are headed to a motel has created considerable arousal. As he reaches an intersection, a car runs a stop sign and smashes into the front of his car, causing considerable damage and certainly spoiling an afternoon of fun and frolic. The driver of the other car screams "Why the hell don't you watch where you're going, you moron?" He has been aroused, frustrated, insulted, and physically attacked. He leaps from his car and apologizes profusely, says it was all his fault, and offers to pay all damages. What is going on here? All the preconditions for aggression are present. Why doesn't he actually attack the man? Well, in our fictional situation the man is Muhammad Ali and there is a distinct possibility that he will turn the driver into a

[1]In almost all studies of aggression, the "victim" is the experimenter's confederate and is never really hurt.
[2]The subjects in this study were males.

hood ornament. Ali's ability to retaliate is a situational variable that has inhibited his aggressive tendencies—at least temporarily (Baron, 1973).

No sane person is going to aggress against Muhammad Ali—hardly a startling insight. If this was all there was to the effect of situational factors on aggression, we could stop right here. However, there is evidence that more subtle aspects of the situation also affect aggressive behavior.

Cues for aggression

Leonard Berkowitz (1965, 1969) has proposed that the characteristics of situations may influence how aggressively a person acts. He called these characteristics *aggression-eliciting stimuli*. These are stimuli which increase the chances of aggression because they are (1) associated with the source of anger or frustration and/or (2) associated with aggression in general. They are *cues* for aggressive behavior.

To see how these cues may operate, consider a scene from an old movie starring Bud Abbott and Lou Costello. Costello is in a prison cell with a mentally deranged man. This man has killed his wife and her lover when he caught them together at Niagara Falls. Costello is told he is harmless *unless* someone says "Niagara Falls." If he hears these words, he will fly into a frenzy and attack whoever is nearby. If you have ever seen an Abbott and Costello movie, you can pretty well predict what happens next. The words "Niagara Falls" keep coming up. And every time this happens, Costello's cellmate goes into a trance. With vacant eyes he approaches Costello and says, "Slowly I turned, step by step, inch by inch, even closer. Until . . . I grabbed them and hit them, and knocked them down and crushed the life out of their bodies." Having said that, he grabs poor pudgy little Lou Costello and tosses him

about the cell. His assault continues until he almost recreates the original crime.

How would Berkowitz explain Costello's misfortune? First, he would note that the man was mentally deranged and ready to aggress. Situational cues will increase aggression only if a person is ready to aggress (i.e., is angry or frustrated). Given this state, the words "Niagara Falls" served as a cue which sent the man into a frenzy.

Berkowitz has tested his proposal more systematically than by analyzing a scene from an Abbott and Costello movie. Swart and Berkowitz (1976) recruited male college students for an experiment. The students believed that the experiment was designed to investigate the effects of stress on learning. A subject was told that he and two other people would each experience a different kind of stress in different parts of the experiment. Swart and Berkowitz arranged their procedure such that all the subjects experienced stress simultaneously. Subjects spent five minutes in a creative task—devising a promotional campaign for a local gas station. Their work was then evaluated by one of the two other people (who was really a confederate of the experimenters). The evaluation took the form of electric shock. Half the subjects received eight shocks, while the other half received one. This procedure made the members of the first group quite angry.

In the second part of the study, the confederate (the subjects' evaluator) engaged in a learning task. During this task, the experimenter supposedly created stress in the confederate by giving him different intensities of electric shock. The subjects were to help the experimenter by watching a white light in front of them. Every time the confederate experienced pain, this light would go on. The light was thus associated with pain in the confederate. Swart and Berkowitz reasoned that this association would make the light an aggressive cue for the angry subjects.

In the final phase of the study, the subjects were to administer electric shocks to the third person in order to distract him while he worked on a test.[3] The subjects could give shocks of whatever intensity and duration they desired. All subjects were asked to shock the third person forty times. Shortly before twenty of the shocks were given, the white light went on. Shortly before the other twenty shocks, a blue light went on. Swart and Berkowitz recorded the duration and intensity of the shocks when each light was lit. They hypothesized that angry subjects would give stronger shocks after seeing the white light than after seeing the blue light. Why? Because the white light was associated with pain in someone who had angered them. The results of this study are presented in Figure 4-1.

As this figure shows, the prediction was confirmed. The angry subjects aggressed more in the presence of the white light than the blue one. Also important is the fact that the white light did not have this effect on the nonangry subjects. It affected only the behavior of the angry subjects. Other studies (Berkowitz, 1965; Berkowitz & Geen, 1966) have produced similar results. Thus, it would seem that stimuli associated with specific events in a person's life can increase her aggression.

Weapons as aggressive cues. Berkowitz was also interested in whether the presence of a weapon might affect a person's willingness to aggress. He reasoned that since weapons are generally associated with aggression, they might serve as an aggressive cue. To test this idea, he and Le Page (1967) had subjects either angered or not angered by a confederate. Then, both groups were placed in a room where either guns or a badminton racquet had supposedly been left by another experimenter. When the subjects were given a

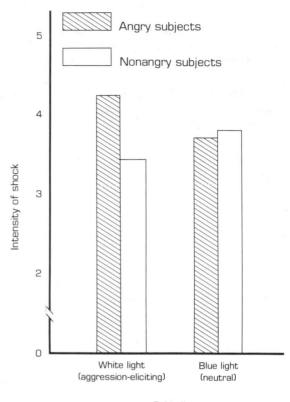

Figure 4-1. The amount of aggression displayed by subjects in response to aggression-eliciting and neutral stimuli. (Adapted from Swart & Berkowitz, 1976)

chance to shock the confederate, those who were angry and saw guns aggressed more than any other group. The guns had no effect on the nonangry subjects. This is consistent with Berkowitz's general theory. Aggressive cues will have an effect only when a person is ready to aggress.

Interesting as these results are, other researchers have had trouble replicating them. Buss, Booker, and Buss (1972) and Page and Scheidt (1971) have both failed to find that weapons are aggressive cues. Even Berkowitz (1971) acknowledged that the aggression-eliciting effect of weapons is, at best, weak and

[3]In fact, this person was never shocked.

that other factors in the situation may moderate or even wipe out this effect. Thus, we must view the generalizability of Berkowitz and Le Page's results with a great deal of caution.

Still, even though the simple presence of a gun may not heighten actual aggression, a gun is an extremely handy way to kill someone. Prosterman (1972) reported that in the United States most assaults are committed by people using knives or blunt objects, but 60 percent of the deaths caused by assaults result from gun shots. To put it another way, the attacker who uses a gun is five times as likely to kill her intended victim as the attacker who uses a knife.

Environmental stressors

One rapidly growing research area is concerned with the effects of the environment on social behavior. Some social psychologists have looked at *environmental stressors*. These are negative or unpleasant aspects of the environment (e.g., air pollution, crowding, excessive noise, extreme temperature) which might produce stress in a person. These factors can create both physiological and psychological stress reactions. Physiologically, people react to stress with alarm, then with resistance; if they can't cope with the stress, they may become ill or even die. This is called the *general adaptation syndrome* (Selye, 1956). This syndrome, as it relates to aggression, is important in that it includes physiological arousal.

A person reacts to stress psychologically first by feeling threatened and then by appraising the threat and attempting to cope with it. One of the best indicators of psychological stress is a "bad mood" (Lazarus, 1966). Physiological arousal and bad moods are emphasized because these two states often lead to aggression. Do environmental stressors affect aggression?

Temperature. During the summer of 1967, the urban ghettoes of America were racked by a series of violent and destructive riots. Goranson and King (1970) were interested in the relationship between changes in temperature and the onset and duration of these riots. First, they identified the seventeen cities that had experienced the worst riots and obtained their daily temperatures during the summer of 1967. They compared these to the average daily temperatures during previous summers. This comparison, presented in Figure 4-2, shows a clear-cut pattern.

The temperature in these cities was significantly higher than average on the days immediately before the riots began. Further, the longer the abnormally high temperatures persisted, the longer a riot continued. No one would seriously argue that high temperatures were the sole cause of the riots.[4] However, they may have increased the probability that a riot would occur. Laboratory studies on the effect of temperature on mood and aggression shed some light on the relationship.

We know that if you place people in a hot room, they will like each other less and be in a poorer mood than will people placed in a room with a normal temperature (Griffitt & Veitch, 1971). Thus, high temperatures might increase aggression by putting people in a state of mind where they are ready to aggress.

Baron and Lawton (1972) took a somewhat different approach from Goranson and King. They pointed out that a resident in the riot area saw large numbers of other people acting aggressively. These people may have served as *aggressive models*. Prior research has shown that observing an aggressive model will increase the tendency to aggress, and this

---

[4]The National Commission on Civil Disorders (1968) found the primary cause of the riots to be "white racism," which caused the deplorable conditions that existed (and still exist) in the black ghettoes of America's largest cities.

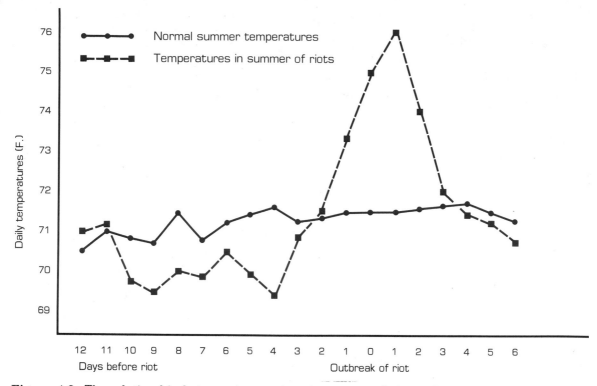

Figure 4-2. The relationship between temperature increases and the outbreak of riots. (Adapted from Goranson & King, 1970)

effect may be heightened if the observer is physiologically aroused[5] (Bandura, 1973). Since extreme temperatures produce arousal, Baron and Lawton proposed that the high temperature may have caused the ghetto residents to be more influenced by the actions of aggressive others.

To test this possibility, Baron and Lawton had subjects angered by a confederate in rooms which were either hot or comfortable. Then half the subjects in each temperature condition saw an aggressive model, and the other half a non-aggressive model. Following this, all subjects were allowed to aggress

against the confederate. Subjects in the hot room with an aggressive model were found to aggress more than any other group.

These two studies might make an air conditioner salesperson happy, but there is more to the story. Not all people become more aggressive as the result of high temperatures. Men from low socioeconomic classes, for example, were found to respond to high temperatures with increased verbal and physical aggression. Middle- and upper-class males did not (Rohles, 1967). The reason probably lies in cultural differences. Lower classes tend to be more aggressive than middle and upper classes (Bandura, 1973). This suggests that temperature may have its strongest effect on people who already have aggressive tendencies.

[5]The effects of models on learning to aggress and acting aggressively are discussed further on pages 120–127.

There is also evidence that under certain circumstances, high temperatures may serve to decrease aggression. Baron and Bell (1975, 1976) placed subjects in a hot, warm, or cool room. Then half the subjects in each setting were angered by a confederate. When they were allowed to aggress against the confederate, a surprising result was found. Among angry subjects, there was *less* aggression in the hot and warm rooms than in the cool room. Increased aggression as the result of higher temperatures occurred only with non-angry subjects.

Why did angry subjects aggress less in a hot room than in a cool one? Baron and Bell believed that the combination of being hot *and* angry created extremely unpleasant feelings among these subjects. Extreme aggression would not reduce this feeling. On the contrary, it could make the subjects feel even worse (because of guilt or seeing the confederate in pain). To reduce their discomfort, they minimized their aggression. On the other hand, the nonangry subjects did not feel as uncomfortable and reacted to high temperatures with high aggression.

Another experiment by Baron and Bell supported this explanation. They found that angry subjects in a hot room who were given a drink of water aggressed more than angry, hot subjects who received no drink. Evidently, the drink reduced the subjects' discomfort to a point where they were willing to aggress. This and the study by Rohles demonstrate that there is no automatic relationship between high temperature and aggression. A person's cultural background and the characteristics of the situation will also influence how she reacts to high temperatures.

Noise. Stop, hold your breath, and listen. What do you hear? If you are reading this book in an environment similar to the one in which it was written, you probably hear people talking, typewriters clacking, traffic, airplanes, and perhaps even a rock record played loud enough to wake the dead. If any of these sounds annoy you, this is called *noise* (Moos, 1976). It is difficult if not impossible to avoid these and even more dramatic sounds in your environment. "Noise pollution" is an inevitable by-product of an affluent, modern, industrialized society. Unless you opt for living in a crypt, you cannot avoid noise.

Noise is an environmental stressor. In 1973 the Environmental Protection Agency reported on a nationwide survey of people's reactions to excessive noise. The E.P.A. concluded that excessive noise causes bad moods and produces anxiety and irritability. This fits the description of psychological stress quite well. Does the stress caused by noise affect the tendency to aggress?

Ward and Suedfeld (1973) recorded sounds on a busy highway and then played them back, using a sound truck stationed outside a college dormitory. The unfortunate residents of this dorm were bombarded day and night for three days. Their behavior during this period was then compared with their behavior during a normal three-day period. During the noisy period, the residents became more tense, disagreed with each other more often during discussions, and in general showed a deterioration in their social relationships. They were so angry about the noise that on two occasions the power lines to the truck were cut, and some students threatened to destroy the sound equipment if it was not turned off.

Ward and Suedfeld's study showed that noise certainly puts people in a bad frame of mind. But does it actually cause people to aggress? Some of the studies on this topic have looked at the joint effects of noise and anger on aggression. These studies are based on the effects of arousal on aggression. Since noise itself creates arousal, this arousal, plus the arousal created by an insult or physical attack, might produce increased aggression.

To test this, subjects were either angered or treated neutrally by a confederate and then exposed to either high or low levels of noise. The results of this study are presented in Figure 4-3.

As you can see, high noise levels affected the aggressive tendencies of only the angry subjects. Noise and anger had a cumulative effect on aggression (Donnerstein & Wilson, 1976).

Noise may also affect a person's behavior even after the noise has stopped. This idea has been tested by exposing subjects to excessive noise, turning it off, and then seeing how they deal with other people. In comparison to subjects who have not heard the noise, these subjects show less willingness to help another person, less tolerance for frustration, and an increased tendency to respond to an insult with aggression. Noise had lingering effects on these subjects (Donnerstein & Wilson, 1976; Glass & Singer, 1972).

Thus, excessive noise seems to affect subsequent agressive behavior. Why? One explanation is that the arousal caused by the noise carries over to the anger felt and results in increased aggression. Another possibility is that excessive, uncontrollable noise is both annoying and frustrating. When this annoyance and frustration are added to the anger a person already feels, this increases the probability of aggression and the intensity of aggressive behavior. Both of these effects probably occur.

Does the laboratory research on temperature and noise have implications for aggression in the real world? It is true that most people do not like being hot and that the percentage of people who notice and are annoyed by excessive noise has more than doubled in the last twenty to thirty years (Moos, 1976). However, if every other aspect of the environment were "letter perfect," these stressors alone would probably not have much effect on aggressive tendencies.

But consider the environment in which many people are forced to live. Chicago's black ghetto provides an illustration. The apartments on 63d Street, in the heart of the ghetto, are old, run down, and extremely hot in the summer. For a stretch of five miles they are located less than 100 yards from the tracks of an ear-shattering elevated train. Further, 63d Street is a commercial street with a constant stream of cars. The noise from these cars echoes off the underside of the elevated tracks, and the tracks serve to trap the cars' exhaust. In such a hellish environment, these factors, in combination, may well have a dramatic effect on people's willingness to aggress. And 63d Street is, unfortunately, not an unusual situation.

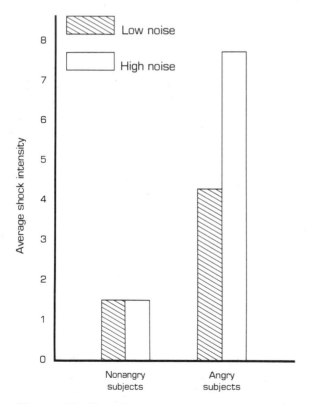

Figure 4-3. The relationship between noise intensity and physical aggression. (Adapted from Donnerstein & Wilson, 1976)

Conclusion

This chapter began by defining aggression. Aggression refers to such a wide variety of behaviors, but because of space limitations the focus was placed on interpersonal aggression. This form of aggression is due to some internal motive state (e.g., anger) and is called hostile aggression. It differs from instrumental aggression, in which a person is not angry and aggresses in order to gain some reward. That is, instrumental aggression is impersonal.

Hostile aggression is always preceded by emotional arousal. This arousal is usually caused by insults, physical attacks, or frustration. Arousal will not, however, always result in actual aggression. It must first be labeled as being due to anger or frustration. If this occurs, aggression is quite likely to take place. Also, arousal which is unrelated to anger will increase aggression if a person labels it as anger or frustration.

The effect of situational factors on aggression was then described. The situation a person is in may affect her. Aggression-eliciting stimuli and cues associated with aggressive acts will, in combination with anger or frustration, dramatically increase a person's willingness to aggress.

The other situational characteristics looked at were environmental stressors—such as excessive heat and noise, which arouse a person and put her in a bad mood. As a result, these stressors often increase the likelihood that a person will aggress. But it must be emphasized that arousal and situational factors do not totally explain aggression. The third factor is individual differences in aggressive tendencies. These will be discussed in the second half of the chapter.

REVIEW QUESTIONS

(Eight out of ten is passing)

1. In _____ aggression a person's goal is the injury of some other individual rather than the attainment of some reward. (p. 117)
2. _____ results from interference with a goal-oriented activity. (p. 108)
3. The intentional, deliberate prevention of someone from reaching a desired goal is called _____ _____ . (p. 108)
4. The finding that erotic material presented before a person is angered will increase aggressive behavior demonstrates the relationship between _____ and aggression. (p. 110)
5. Waving a cape at a bull in order to get it to charge could be viewed as an example of _____ _____ _____ . (p. 111)
6. Berkowitz believed that because they are generally associated with aggression, the presence of _____ will tend to increase the tendency to aggress. (p. 112)
7. Noxious environmental factors may indirectly affect aggression by generating _____ and _____ stress reactions in people. (p. 113)
8. These stress reactions tend to cause _____ _____ in people and put them in _____ _____ . (p. 113)

9. While high temperatures will generally _____ aggression, the combination of anger and heat may result in _____ aggression. (p. 115)

10. Any sound which a person finds unpleasant is called _____ . Such sounds tend to _____ a person's tendency to aggress. (p. 115)

ANSWERS

9. increase, decreased   10. noise, increase

7. physiological, psychological   8. physiological arousal, bad moods (make them feel unpleasant)

5. aggressive cues (or, aggression-eliciting stimuli)   6. weapons or guns

1. hostile   2. frustration   3. arbitrary thwarting   4. arousal

INDIVIDUAL DIFFERENCES IN AGGRESSIVE TENDENCIES

The review of this topic will deal mainly with the origins of individual differences in aggressive tendencies. More specifically, we'll examine how children acquire aggressive tendencies and the effect of television violence on aggression.

The origins of aggressive behavior

There are two general points of view on the origins of human aggressive behavior.

The instinctual explanation

The first position is that aggressive behavior is an instinct. An *instinct* is an inborn pattern of behavior which an animal displays whenever certain stimuli are present. For example, baby ducklings do not have to be taught to follow their mother; it is an unlearned, automatic response.

The instinctual explanation of human aggression was proposed by Freud more than fifty years ago (Freud, 1930). More recently, this view has been promoted by a branch of biology known as ethology. *Ethology* is concerned with the behavior of animals in their natural environment. Ethologists believe that most, if not all, of this behavior is due to instincts (Eibl-Eibesfelt, 1970). The ethologist most noted for his theory of human aggression is Konrad Lorenz (1966).

How does Lorenz explain aggression in humans? He believes that in *all* animals (including humans), aggression is an instinct. However, among those animals that possess the physical ability to kill each other easily (e.g., lions, tigers), built-in mechanisms have evolved which control their instinct to kill their own species. Human beings use their intelligence rather than their strength to kill. As a result, they have never developed innate mechanisms to control their aggressive instincts. Thus, aggression in humans results from their instincts and the absence of any inherited means of controlling them.

Lorenz is a gifted and acclaimed scientist (he was awarded the Nobel Prize), but few psychologists accept his explanation of aggression in humans. One reason is that there is little if any evidence to support his claim

World Wide Photos

that aggression is instinctive (Bandura, 1973; Lehrman, 1953; Montague, 1968; Scott, 1972). For example, Scott (1958) carefully reviewed the research on this topic and concluded that there is no physiological evidence "of any internal need or spontaneous driving force for fighting" (p. 98).

Social learning theory

Most social psychologists prefer a *social learning theory* explanation of human aggression. Social learning theory proposes that humans learn to be aggressive the same way they learn any other behavior. Thus, these theorists concentrate on how this learning occurs.

The learning process which they believe explains a good deal of human aggression is

called *operant conditioning*. It works as follows. A person engages in a behavior more or less by chance. This behavior is either rewarded or punished; if it is rewarded, it is likely to occur again. If it is punished, it is much less likely to be repeated. Let's apply this to aggression.

Two-year-old Mary has gotten up on the "wrong side" of her crib. Her morning cereal doesn't please her, and *Sesame Street* has been preempted by a show on the Alaskan elk. Her year-old brother takes one of her dolls, and Mark cracks him with a toy truck. How does Mary's mother react? If she smiles and says, "Atta girl, Mary. Show him who's boss," she is rewarding Mary's aggressive act. This should increase the probability that Mary will act aggressively in the future. If the mother punishes Mary (by spanking her or sending her to her room), Mary will be less likely to aggress in the future. Mary's level of aggressive tendencies in later life will depend largely upon whether she is rewarded or punished for aggressive acts by her parents and other significant people in her life (e.g., siblings, relatives, friends, teachers, etc.)[6]

If the learning of aggressive tendencies were this simple, understanding human aggression would be easy. But as you might imagine, in the real world, extremely complex patterns of rewards and punishments occur. Social learning theorists are interested in how these various patterns affect human aggression.

Schedules of reinforcement. A *reinforcement schedule* is the pattern of rewards and punishments a person receives for performing some act. She may be continuously rewarded, continuously punished, or rewarded and punished at certain regular or irregular intervals.

There has been a good deal of research in laboratory and field settings on the learning effect of reinforcment schedules. In the laboratory, children are given a situation in which they are likely to aggress. When they do, they are given a tangible reward (e.g., marbles or candy) or a verbal one (e.g., "That's a good girl/boy). After this period of reinforcement, (called the *acquisition* or *learning stage*), the rewards are stopped. The children's willingness to aggress in the absence of any rewards is then measured.

What do these studies tell us about the learning of aggressive behavior? Both verbal and tangible rewards will increase aggression even after the rewards are discontinued (Cowan & Walters, 1963; Patterson, Ludwig & Sonoda, 1963). If a child is rewarded for

---

[6]I have said "largely" because, as we will see shortly, social learning theorists also believe that humans learn to be aggressive by observing others.

verbal aggression, this carries over into physical aggression (Lovaas, 1961; Parke, Ewall, & Slaby, 1972). And finally, aggression which is rewarded irregularly will persist longer and generalize more than aggression which is rewarded continuously (Walters & Brown, 1963).

This last finding is of tremendous practical importance. Parents may want to be consistent in how they react to aggressive behavior, but often this is quite difficult. One parent may reward and encourage aggression while the other ignores or punishes it. Even more common is the practice of punishing aggression in one situation and rewarding it in another. These irregular or selective patterns of reinforcement may produce an aggressive child whose behavior is difficult to change.

This has been demonstrated in several studies done in the real world. For example, Bandura and Walters (1959) and Bandura (1960) compared the reinforcement patterns used by the parents of aggressive and nonaggressive teenage boys. In both studies, they found that the parents of the nonaggressive boys rarely, if ever, rewarded their sons for engaging in physical violence. The parents of the aggressive boys punished aggression directed at them but encouraged and rewarded it when it was directed at other children. While Bandura and Walters (1963) placed great importance on direct reinforcement, they believed that children learn to be aggressive by other processes as well.

Observational learning and aggression. A friend of mine came home one day and found that a reel of tape with some beautiful classical music on it had been destroyed. He called his two children in and asked which one had done it. Both denied any guilt. My friend then proceeded to beat both of them.

"Why both of them?" I asked. "Well," he explained, "one of them got punished for screwing up the tape and the other learned what would happen to him if he ever did." A good point, but could my friend have been doing something else as well? Could he have shown the innocent child how one reacts when one is angry? Could such an example affect the innocent child's aggressive tendencies?

Psychologists have long argued that humans learn a great deal by watching and imitating others (e.g., Lloyd-Morgan, 1896; McDougall, 1908; Tarde, 1903). However, Bandura and Walters (1963) did the most thorough examination of how observational learning and aggression are related. They believed that direct reinforcement is only a partial explanation. A large part of what humans learn results from observing the actions of others. These others are called models, and the learning is called modeling.

Modeling. Modeling is a process whereby a person learns some behavior by watching another person engage in it. Bandura (1973) identified two ways in which a child may *learn* aggression from models.[7] First, she can imitate the model's aggressive act. In this case, the model has provided her with a new pattern of aggressive behavior. A bizarre and admittedly extreme example of this is provided by an incident in Boston a few years ago. A movie entitled *Fuzz* had been shown on television one Sunday evening. Parts of its plot involved a group of adolescents who set sleeping derelicts on fire. A few days later, the Boston police arrested adolescents who had tried to do this. The boys admitted having gotten the idea from watching *Fuzz*. More commonly, imitation involves less extreme acts (e.g., seeing one's mother scream at one's father, seeing one's father punch the next-door-neighbor).

Second, a model can help the learning of aggression by providing information about the results of acting aggressively. These results, in turn, affect an observer's tendency to aggress. An observer who sees a model being rewarded will be more likely to overcome her own inhibitions against aggressing than an observer who sees a model being punished (Bandura, 1973).

In one laboratory study, Bandura, Ross, and Ross (1963) exposed nursery school children to one of five experimental conditions: (1) a live aggressive model, (2) a filmed aggressive model, (3) a cartoon aggressive model, (4) a nonaggressive model, and (5) no model. After this, the children in all five groups were mildly frustrated and then placed in a room with a number of toys. The amount of aggression displayed by the children is shown in Figure 4-4. As you can see, the three aggressive models produced more aggression than did a nonaggressive model or no model.

Modeling does not occur independently of other factors. A child who is frustrated or angry will be more likely to model an aggressive act than one who is not (Christy, Gelfand, & Hartmann, 1971). Further, what happens to the model after it acts aggressively will affect a child's behavior. A model who is rewarded is more likely to produce aggression in an observer than one who is punished.

The most important variable in whether modeling will have a long-term effect on a child is what happens to the child when she imitates the model. If she is not rewarded for the modeled aggression, it will not persist very long. For example, a child sees her father get dinner by threatening to beat up her mother. The next day, the child tries the same tactic in order to get lunch. The fact that the child ends up in her room with a sore rear end may decrease her tendency to model her father's aggressive behavior. If, however, the child is rewarded for her threats, they will probably increase later on.

---

[7]"Learn" is italicized because here the topic is how modeling is related to learning aggressive behaviors. The review of media violence will present another effect of models—the facilitation of an aggressive behavior which the observer already knows and is ready to engage in.

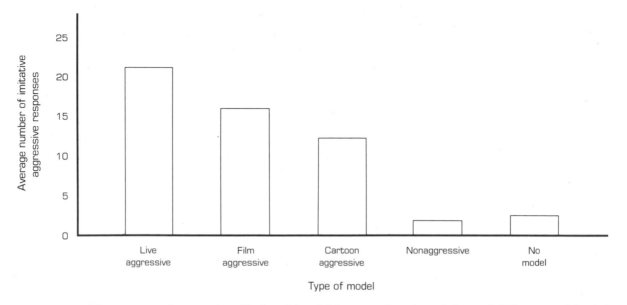

Figure 4-4. The amount of aggression displayed by children as a function of the model they saw. Adapted from Bandura, Ross, & Ross, 1963)

In the real world, aggressive models and the direct rewarding of aggressive behavior often go hand in hand. For example, Bandura and Walters (1959) and Bandura (1960) compared aggressive and nonaggressive boys from an upper-middle-class neighborhood. The aggressive boys' parents provided aggressive models and rewarded their sons for aggression. One father, for example, threatened to beat his son with a belt if he did not beat up two boys who had attacked him. It has also been found that mothers who were domineering and used physical and verbal punishment to control their children had offspring who used the same tactics with their friends (Hoffman, 1960).

Of course, parents are not the only models that influence a child's aggressive tendencies. The next section will look at the effects of other aspects of a child's environment.

Television violence and aggression

Violence on television often has been blamed for producing aggressive behavior in children, but now it is being charged with causing a murder. Ronald Zamora, 15, admitted that he shot and killed an elderly woman neighbor after looting her Miami Beach home last June. At his trial, scheduled for later this month, his lawyer plans to argue that the boy is not guilty by reason of insanity due to "prolonged, intense, involuntary subliminal television intoxication."

In order to prove that Zamora was unable to distinguish between right and wrong at the time of the murder, his lawyer, Ellis Rubin, plans to call on psychiatrists to testify that his client's reasoning ability was impaired by constant television viewing. Zamora watched at least five hours of television a day, tuning in violent crime programs like "Police Story," "Kojak," and a CBS special on the Manson murders, "Helter Skelter." He's watched thousands of shootings and in these shootings there have been no consequences," says psy-

John Perrachione

chiatrist Michael Gilbert, who has examined Zamora and will be called for the defense. "The implication is that death is just an incident in the total plot. He didn't know the consequence and nature of the act when he pulled the trigger." (*Newsweek*, September 12, 1977)

Did the lawyer have a valid case? Many people would believe that he did. That is, many people believe that one of the primary causes of aggression in children is the amount of violent television they watch.

Children spend more time watching television than any other activity except sleeping (Liebert, Neale, & Davidson, 1973). The television networks promised that beginning in fall 1977, the amount of violence shown on television would be dramatically reduced. It could hardly increase. It is estimated that over 75 percent of the dramatic shows seen on television contain violence. Other studies have found that children's programs presented a violent episode every two minutes (Gerbner, 1972). What are the effects on children?

Theoretical positions

The catharsis hypothesis. The *catharsis hypothesis* is based on the ethological explanation of human aggression. Specifically, the ethologists (e.g., Lorenz, 1966) believe that general aggressive energy builds up in humans more or less naturally. This aggressive energy must find some outlet or a person will aggress with little provocation; she may even aggress in the absence of any provocation.

How can this aggressive energy be released? Catharsis theorists propose as a solution the catharsis, or draining, of the aggressive energy. This can be done in many ways. Singer (1971) and Lorenz believed that observing violence on television may be one way. More specifically, the observation of violent television may allow an observer to engage in "fantasy aggression." That is, she identifies with the violent people she sees and vicariously expresses her aggression. This has a cathartic effect on her energy level and thus decreases the probability that she will actually aggress. If this position is valid, then television shows such as *Charlie's Angels*, *Kojak*, and *Police Woman* are performing a valuable public service. They are reducing aggression in their viewers.

The social learning hypothesis. The social learning theorists (e.g., Bandura, 1973; Bandura & Walters, 1963) base their position on the effects of violent television on the modeling research described earlier. They propose that violent television gives children *symbolic aggressive models*—people who are not real but who provide models of aggressive behavior. These models affect a child in three ways. They present aggressive behavior which can be imitated. They show that aggression is rewarded. And they reduce a child's reluctance to engage in aggressive behaviors it already knows (Bandura, 1973; Zillman, 1971).

This last effect is supposedly due to the arousing effect of violent television on the observer. This arousal, in turn, increases the chances that an observer will aggress when provoked. Thus, the social learning theorists believe that violent television causes increased aggressiveness in the children who watch it.

The "no effect" position. The final position on violent television is basically that there has been "much ado about nothing." That is, television does not reduce aggression in children, as the catharsis theorists have claimed. But neither does it increase aggression, as the social learning theorists have argued (Kaplan & Singer, 1976). According to the advocates of this position, the research on the effects of violent television has failed to show any positive or negative effects. What do the findings from this research look like?

Research on violent television. The study most often presented in support of the beneficial (i.e., aggression-reducing) effects of violent television was conducted by Feshbach and Singer (1971). They examined its effects on more than 600 boys who lived at the schools they attended. These schools ranged from private, exclusive boarding schools to state-run institutions for delinquent or abused children. These boys ranged from extremely aggressive to normal and from very wealthy to very poor.

Within each of these schools, half of the boys were allowed to watch only violent television shows (e.g., *Batman, Bonanza*) while the other half saw only nonviolent shows for six weeks. After this, adults in the schools rated all the boys on how physically and verbally aggressive they were.

It was predicted that the violent shows would have a cathartic effect on the boys. They would provide an outlet for the boys' aggressive tendencies and thus reduce their level of verbal and physical aggression. Boys who were deprived of violent television would show an increase in both forms of aggression.

These predictions were confirmed only for boys from poor families and who were quite aggressive to begin with. Among middle- and upper-class boys, no effects were found. Thus, the catharsis hypothesis was supported for some of the boys. Or was it?

There were several problems in this study. First, the boys shown the nonviolent shows complained bitterly when they found out that they couldn't watch *Batman*. The experimenters gave in and let the boys watch *The Caped Crusader*. Thus, the boys in the supposedly nonviolent condition were made angry, engaged in verbal aggression, and were rewarded for it. Certainly, this could partially explain their tendency to show increased verbal aggression.

Also, the boys who seemed to experience catharsis were so aggressive to begin with that if they changed they could only become less aggressive. Because of these and other problems, a number of researchers have attempted to repeat this study. Most of these studies have found an *increase* in aggression as the result of watching violent television (Parke, Berkowitz, Leyens, & Sebastian, 1977; Stein & Friedrich, 1971; Wells, 1973).

For example, Stein and Friedrich conducted a field experiment with children in a nursery school. These children were rated for aggression and then randomly assigned to three different television-watching conditions: (1) violent shows, (2) prosocial shows (e.g., *Sesame Street*), or (3) neutral shows. The children watched these shows for an hour and a half a week for four weeks and then were rated again on their aggressive behavior. Violent television shows increased aggressiveness only among the children who had been rated as extremely aggressive to begin with.

Other researchers have looked at the long-term effects of television. In one study, the amount of violent television watched by a group of eight- and nine-year-olds was recorded. Ten years later, the researchers asked friends of these children (who were now young adults) to rate how aggressive they were (Eron, Huesmann, Lefkowitz, & Walder, 1972). The relationship between violent television at age nine and aggressive tendencies at age nineteen for male subjects is shown in Figure 4-5. (No relationship was found for female subjects.) As you can see, the more violent television the males watched as boys, the more aggressive they were at age nineteen.

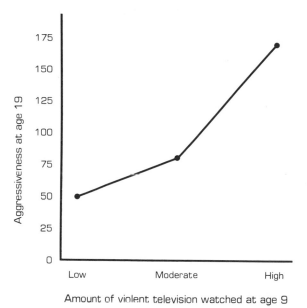

Figure 4-5. The relationship between violence on television and subsequent aggressiveness. (Adapted from Eron, Huesmann, Lefkowitz, & Walder, 1972)

What can we conclude about the effects of violent television? First, it is incorrect to totally blame television for a person's aggressive tendencies (as the lawyer mentioned earlier did). Children do not watch television twenty-four hours a day. The pattern of rewards and punishments a child receives for aggressive behavior, the models her parents and other provide, and her interactions with friends all affect her level of aggression. This fact was illustrated in the long-term study just presented. The relationship for males, while statistically significant, was not very powerful. Less than 10 percent of the difference in the aggressiveness of these men at age nineteen could be explained by the amount of violent television they had watched ten years earlier. Also, note that this relationship was not found for females. This is probably due to the fact that parents, friends, teachers, and society in general discourage and punish aggression in women.

"The story behind the Dirty Harry killing"

Social psychologists have primarily studied long-term effects of violent television. But sometimes a violent television program can have an immediate effect. In early fall 1977, NBC presented the movie *Dirty Harry*. Newspaper columnist Bob Greene tells what happened.

Saturday night, Dolphus and Micros had watched *Dirty Harry*. The movie, originally released in 1971, is a violence-soaked police drama in which [Clint] Eastwood portrays Harry Callahan, a San Francisco cop who doesn't mind taking the law into his own hands. Thus his nickname—Dirty Harry. The movie was such a box office success that it spawned several sequels.

Near the beginning of the movie, Dirty Harry approaches a criminal who is sprawled on the street. The criminal's gun has fallen out of his hand, but is within reaching distance. Dirty Harry pulls out his own gun and aims it at the criminal. There has been a shootout; it is not known whether Dirty Harry has any more bullets left in his gun. The question is, should the criminal reach for his gun?

Dirty Harry says approximately the following:

"Listen, punk, this here is a .44 caliber magnum revolver, the most powerful handgun ever made. Now you're probably thinking, 'Did he fire six shots or just five?' Well, to tell you the truth, in all the excitement I kinda lost count myself. It just depends. Do you feel lucky today?"

The criminal's hand trembles.

"Well, do you, punk?" Dirty Harry says.

The criminal looks up the barrel of Dirty Harry's magnum. He trembles and decides to give up and be arrested by uniformed officers. Dirty Harry walks away.

"Hey, mister," the criminal calls.

Dirty Harry turns around.

The criminal gestures towards Dirty Harry's gun.

"I gots to know," the criminal says.

Dirty Harry carefully takes aim at the criminal's head and squints his eyes. The man shrinks back in fear. Dirty Harry pulls the trigger. The gun clicks on an empty shell. Dirty Harry laughs.

Later in the movie the same scene is repeated, this time featuring a different criminal. This time the criminal feels lucky. He reaches for his own gun. This time Dirty Harry fires again. This time Dirty Harry's gun has a bullet in it. And this time the criminal is shot to death.

That is what Dolphus and Micros Thompson saw on television Saturday night.

According to Columbus Police Dept. homicide Sgt. Tom Aurentz, this is what happened Sunday morning:

Dolphus and Micros decided to play *Dirty Harry*.

Dolphus got a .22 caliber two-shot derringer from his father's nightstand.

The two boys went to Dolphus' bedroom, where a toy *Star Trek* ray gun was laying on a table near Micros.

Dolphus held the derringer in his hand and pointed it at Micros.

Dolphus said:

"In all the confusion, I bet you don't know if this gun is loaded." He then ordered his younger brother to reach for the toy gun. Micros Thompson did.

Dolphus Thompson shot him once in the chest. Micros took a few steps into the hallway, collapsed and died.

When Columbus police arrived at the scene, Dolphus told them, "We were just playing *Dirty Harry*."

Does this lead us to accept the "no effect" position? No. Violent television does appear to make already aggressive children even more aggressive. Also, there is a weaker but still positive relationship between violent television and aggressiveness among children in general (Liebert et al., 1973). It certainly wouldn't hurt if the amount of violence on television could somehow be reduced.

THE CONTROL OF AGGRESSION

What is the best or most efficient way to reduce or eliminate aggression? The next few pages will cover the control of physical rather than verbal aggression, since physical aggression presents a much greater danger to society. This doesn't mean that a high level of verbal aggression is desirable. Rather, the point is that someone who is only verbally aggressive will usually be less dangerous to herself, other people, and society in general than a physically aggressive person.

There are two general theoretical positions on how aggression can be controlled or eliminated. They are based on the two major theories of the origins of aggression—catharsis and social learning.

The catharsis hypothesis

Recall that hostile aggression is preceded by physiological arousal. Some theorists have interpreted this to mean that anger (or frustration) is a drive (e.g., Freud, 1959; Lorenz, 1966; Singer, 1971). A *drive* is a state of excitation that will not subside unless its cause is removed (Berkowitz, 1965). For example, hunger is a drive caused by the lack of food. If you starve a person, she will search for food and the excitation will continue until she is fed. If you punish the person for searching for food (for example, shock her every time

she gets near a hamburger), she may temporarily modify her behavior but her hunger drive will not subside. The hungry person must somehow satisfy her drive.

According to Konrad Lorenz (1966), a similar situation exists for aggression. If a person is angered, the drive will not subside unless she gets the anger out of her system. If she is prevented from doing this, the anger drive will not go away. Rather, at some later date, the person will aggress.

For example, a garage mechanic is accused of being an incompetent crook by a customer who is dissatisfied with the work done on her car. The mechanic's first response is to tell the customer what he thinks of her and use the tire iron he is holding to put a few well-placed dents in her car. However, the presence of the garage owner (his boss) prevents him from doing so. According to Lorenz, the mechanic's anger will not subside. He will either aggress against the customer at some later date (e.g., by removing the brake lining from her car) or displace his anger onto someone or something else (e.g., go home and beat up his wife). How can these acts of aggression be controlled?

The catharsis theorists believe that the reduction or elimination of aggression depends upon a person's ability to drain, or cathart, the aggressive energy from her system. They propose two ways in which this can be done. First, the person can directly aggress against the source of her anger.

Reducing aggression via direct aggression

The catharsis hypothesis proposes that aggressing against someone who has angered you will have two effects. First, it will reduce your level of subsequent aggression. Second, it will lower the level of aggressive energy within you (Hokanson, 1970).

Hokanson and Shetler (1961) provided some empirical support for this hypothesis.

Subjects were insulted and angered, and then either allowed to shock the perpetrator (a confederate) or restrained. For both groups of subjects, blood pressure and heart rate readings were taken. For those subjects who were allowed to shock the confederate, the readings returned to pre-insult levels. The readings of the subjects who were prevented from giving shocks remained high.

Reducing aggression via substitute aggression

A second, related means of getting rid of this aggressive energy is to displace it from the source of the anger or frustration. This can involve aggressing against another person or inanimate object, or engaging in an activity that will reduce the aggressive energy. This point of view is based on the premise that once aggressive energy exists, it will not simply go away.

Fritz Perls, the founder of gestalt psychotherapy, expressed this position quite clearly:

If a person suppresses aggression . . . if one bottles up his rage, we have to find him an outlet. We have to give him an outlet to let off steam. Punching a ball, chopping wood, or any kind of aggressive sport such as football will sometimes work wonders. (Perls, 1969, cited by Berkowitz, 1973, p. 26)

Perls's point of view is extremely popular among nonpsychologists as well as psychologists. Parents are encouraged to buy inflatable "Bo-Bo" dolls (which pop back up when hit) as a substitute for the pummelings that a child might give an irritating younger brother or sister. Workers in Japan are given dolls made up to look like their bosses and encouraged to hit them.

There is some experimental support for this point of view. Subjects were annoyed by a confederate and then either given the opportunity to shock someone else or prevented from shocking anyone. Then both groups were allowed to shock the confederate. Subjects who were given a substitute to shock aggressed significantly less against the confederate than did subjects with no substitute. Note that this result was not obtained for subjects who had not been angered (Konečni & Doob, 1972)

Catharsis theorists also believe that it is possible for an angry person to drain her aggressive energy vicariously by watching someone else punish the source of her anger.[8] Doob and Wood (1972) investigated this possibility. They had a confederate insult their subjects and exposed the subjects to one of two conditions: (1) the experimenter shocked the confederate or (2) the confederate received no shock. Then both groups of subjects were allowed to shock the confederate. Subjects who saw the confederate shocked by the experimenter aggressed against her significantly less than did subjects whose annoyer had not been previously shocked.

Social learning theory

Social learning theorists believe that aggression is primarily a learned response to certain stimuli (Bandura, 1973). There is no drive state associated with aggression. You can control it basically the same way you can control any other behavior, by rewards and punishments. For example, Zeilberger, Sumpen, and Sloane (1968) and Bostow and Bailey (1969) showed that punishing aggressive behavior and rewarding nonaggressive behavior can produce long-term declines in aggressiveness among chronically aggressive

---

[8]Note that this is quite similar to the catharsis theorists' position on the effects of television. The only difference is that here they are concerned with the aggressive energy created by a specific act. In their defense of violent television, they were concerned with a person's general level of aggressive energy.

individuals. Note what these results suggest. The frequency and intensity of aggressive behavior can be reduced *without* letting a person aggress.

The social learning theorists go even further. They argue that in certain instances an aggressive act may be arousing and rewarding. If a behavior is rewarding, it is likely to recur. Thus, social learning theorists believe that allowing a person to engage in direct and/or substitute aggression may *increase* her subsequent aggression. To show the difference between the social learning and catharsis positions, let's reexamine some of the basic premises of the catharsis theorists.

Reducing aggression via direct aggression

One finding that impresses catharsis theorists is the effect of aggression on physiological arousal. An angry person who aggresses will show a decrease in her arousal level. A catharsis theorist would say that this indicates a draining of aggressive energy and would predict that the person will be less likely to aggress in the future. Some social psychologists have questioned whether a lowered arousal level does, in fact, lead to less aggression (Geen, Stonner, & Shope, 1975).

In one study, two groups of subjects were angered by a confederate, but only one group was allowed to aggress against him. As we would expect, this group showed a decrease in arousal. The group that was prevented from aggressing remained aroused.

Usually studies of this type stop at this point. But Geen et al. continued. After a short period of time, they gave both groups a chance to shock the confederate. The results were quite damning to the catharsis hypothesis. The group that had been previously allowed to aggress showed a reduction in arousal, but they aggressed *more* than the group that was still aroused. How can this finding be explained?

Aggression may be rewarding. Many social learning theorists propose that people often find it rewarding to hurt someone who has angered them. A reward causes behavior to increase in frequency and intensity. Thus, the person may want to aggress even more.

Consider for example, Rubin "Hurricane" Carter. At one time, he was the leading contender for the middleweight boxing champion of the world. Today he is serving a life sentence for the murder of six people (a crime he claims he didn't commit). His brilliant autobiography, *The Sixteenth Round,* tells the story of an incredibly violent man and provides some excellent illustrations of the rewarding aspects of aggressive behavior.

As a child, Carter stuttered so badly that he was afraid to speak. When he did talk, he was ridiculed by his playmates. Angry and frustrated, young Carter found himself in a number of fist fights. In the passage that follows, he describes his first fights and how he felt afterward. His brother had been severely beaten by another boy called "Bully." Rubin, age five, decided to retaliate.

I hurled my body into him with all my might, and with a vengeance that shocked even me. I hadn't known I was capable of such feelings.

Bully tripped and went down. I crouched over him, whaling like mad, until he finally managed to fight his way back to his feet. We stood toe to toe, slugging it out, swinging for all we were worth. Then I landed a sizzling haymaker against his bullet head, and he started backing up, with me crowding him, firing on him. The fighting became easier then, and I found I liked it. The more we fought, the better I seemed to get.

A shiver of fierce pleasure ran through me. It was not spiritual, this thing that I felt, but a physical sensation in the pit of my stomach that kept shooting upward through every nerve until I could clamp my teeth on it. Every time Bully made a wrong turn, I was right there to plant my fist in his mouth. After a few minutes of this treatment, the cellar became too hot for Bully to handle, and he made it out the door, smoking.

This was my first experience in fist fighting, and

the fruits of my victory were sweet indeed. I could feel the pull of the little muscles interlinked and interchained from my fingertips to the small of my back. I felt the muscles in my legs too, from hip to toe, supporting me as I swayed, tired now. But dammit, I felt *good*. Even though I had come out with a busted lip, I had beaten the big bad block bully—and, man, I was hot-to-trot to fight some more. (Carter, 1975, pp. 21–22)

It seems obvious that Carter found this fight a rewarding experience. Learning theory would predict that Carter would aggress a great deal in later life, and he did. His high level of aggressiveness was due, at least in part, to the rewards of aggression. Wait a minute, you say, Carter is a man who has spent half his life in prison. Do "normal" people find aggression rewarding?

In one study, college students were angered by a confederate and then given a chance to aggress against him. Half of them were told that they were causing the confederate extreme pain. The other half received no information. The subjects who received the feedback aggressed *more* against the confederate than did those who didn't know if they were hurting him (Baron, 1974a). This did not occur for nonangry subjects. Why? Baron proposed that the confederate's supposed pain may have reinforced the angry subjects' aggression.

Reducing aggression via substitute aggression

The catharsis theorists strongly believe that a person's anger cannot be bottled up. This will only delay the inevitable explosion. Thus, they recommend that people aggress in substitute or indirect ways (e.g., by verbal aggression). Will this, in fact, reduce subsequent aggression?

College students were asked to describe how often their parents engaged in physical aggression. If couples who freely vented their

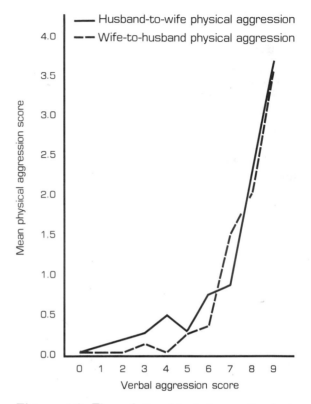

Figure 4-6. The relationship between the incidence of verbal and physical aggression among married couples. (From Straus, 1974)

emotions (by yelling at or insulting one another) were getting rid of their aggressive energy, then they should engage in less physical aggression than couples who were not verbally aggressive (Straus, 1974). Figure 4-6 shows the relationship for more than 350 couples.

The more verbal aggression a couple engaged in, the more physical aggression they displayed. These results don't mean that verbal aggression causes physical aggression (you can't infer cause and effect from such data). But they are exactly opposite to what catharsis theory would predict.

On the basis of these and a number of other studies, the social learning theorists strongly reject the catharsis approach to the control of aggression. Instead, they propose that there is nothing unique about aggression. Like any other behavior, it can be controlled by the intelligent use of rewards and punishments.

Note the word "intelligent." It is not intelligent to reward or punish while ignoring the reason why a person is aggressing. People aggress because they are angry or frustrated. If the cause of the anger or frustration is not dealt with, reward and punishments will only delay the eventual aggression.

One currently popular approach to dealing with the causes of aggression is assertiveness training. Assertiveness training is intended to teach people how to stand up for their rights in a nonaggressive manner. Theoretically, this should allow a person to deal effectively with the cause of her anger and frustration.

Another application of the notion that we must consider the cause of aggression is provided by a recent innovation in police officers' training. Bard (1971) and Driscoll, Meyer, and Shanie (1973) have attempted to train police officers as crisis intervention specialists. As noted earlier, family fights make up a significant percentage of the reported acts of violence in the United States. The police spend a good deal of their time intervening in these domestic quarrels. Their role has traditionally been to stop the violence and if necessary make arrests. According to Bard (1971), police officers find this work unpleasant and dangerous. Bard estimated that 40 percent of all the injuries sustained by police occur while they are intervening in family disputes.

Bard devised a crisis intervention program designed to help the police deal with the source of the violence. Police volunteers received extensive training on the role of the police in family disputes, the causes of violent behavior, family structure and interactions, and other similar topics. They engaged in simulated family disputes and received feedback on their behavior.

The performance of the trained officers was compared to that of officers who had not received training. The results in both Bard's and Driscoll et al.'s studies were impressive. In contrast to the 40 percent injury rate mentioned above, none of Bard's trainees were injured during the program. Their intervention resulted in 22 percent less arrests than the untrained police personnel. About 95 percent of the untrained officers referred family members to the courts; only 45 percent of the trained officers did. Instead, these families were referred to social welfare agencies designed to deal with the source of the problem.

The police trained by Driscoll et al. reported a decrease in the use of force and an increase in overall effectiveness. The families visited by the police in Driscoll et al.'s study "reported greater rapport between themselves and officers, greater involvement of officers, more satisfaction with the intervention and an increased regard for the police." (Driscoll et al., 1973, p. 62). It seems reasonable to suggest that at least part of this program's success was due to the fact that the police personnel dealt with the cause of the fight rather than merely stopping the fight.

Conclusion

This part of the chapter has been concerned with the development of aggressive tendencies and possible means to control aggression. There are two opposing theories on the origins of aggressive behavior. The catharsis theorists believe that aggression is an instinctual behavior. The social learning theorists argue that aggression is a learned behavior. As a result, they concentrate on the processes involved in learning aggression. Specifically, social learning theorists have been interested in operant conditioning and observational learning. The research on these two kinds of learning strongly suggests that they do explain a good deal of the differences between people in aggressive tendencies.

The disagreement between catharsis and social learning theorists also emerged in the discussion of the effects of television violence. The former group believes that violent television may reduce a viewer's aggressiveness. The latter group believes that violent television may increase it. The social learning position seems to be more valid. That is, there is considerable evidence that watching violent television does make some people more aggressive. But this effect is relatively weak. Further, television violence is probably less important a cause of a aggressive tendencies than the behavior of parents and peers. Even if all violence on television were eliminated, it is unlikely that the level of aggression in society would decline.

Finally, the control of aggression was considered. The catharsis theorists and social learning theorists disagree on this issue also. The catharsis theorists view aggression as due to a drive which must be satisfied. If the aggressive energy which builds up is not somehow discharged, a person will aggress more strongly later on. Thus, the catharists argue for letting angry people aggress in direct but mild ways toward the source of their anger or, preferably, letting them get rid of their aggressive energy by substitute forms of aggression. The social learning theorists believe that such free expressions of aggression may often increase the chances of subsequent physical aggression. They believe that aggression is a learned behavior. Reinforcement of this behavior (which may occur if you allow a person to aggress freely) will increase the likelihood that she will aggress again. I strongly support the social learning theorists. The control of aggression requires the same techniques as the control of any other learned behavior—the intelligent usage of reward and punishment. But I must quickly add that in attempting to control aggression, one must consider why a person is aggressing. If the sources of a person's anger or frustration are not eliminated or reduced any attempt to control her aggression over time is doomed.

REVIEW QUESTIONS

(Eight out of ten is passing)

1. Ethologists such as Konrad Lorenz see human aggression as being due to _____ . Most social psychologists, however, believe that aggression is a(n) _____ behavior. (p. 119)
2. _____ _____ proposes that if a behavior is reinforced, it is likely to recur. (p. 119)
3. Johnny watches his sister beat up a playmate in order to get a toy she wants. Johnny tries the same thing. This phenomenon is called _____ . (p. 121)
4. The premise that television violence provides an outlet for the buildup of aggressive energy in humans is held by the _____ _____ . (p. 124)
5. Characters on television who use aggression to achieve their goals may provide _____ _____ _____ for the viewer. (p. 124)
6. The research on violent television suggests that it will have its strongest effect on children who are _____ . (p. 127)

7. The _____ position on the control of aggression is that the aggressive energy which builds up when a person is angry must find some sort of release. (p. 127)

8. This point of view is based on their conceptualization of anger as a(n) _____ . (p. 127)

9. The social learning theorists base their position on the control of aggression on the premise that aggressive behaviors are _____ . (p. 128)

10. Therefore, the social learning theorists would generally argue _____ the free expression of angry feelings since people might find this aggression _____ . (p. 129)

ANSWERS

1. instincts, learned   2. operant conditioning   3. modeling   4. catharsis theorists
5. symbolic aggressive models   6. aggressive   7. catharsis   8. drive   9. learned
10. against, reinforcing

SUGGESTED READINGS

Human aggression is an interesting topic, and most of the books written on it reflect this.

Textbooks

Aggression: A Social Learning Analysis, by Albert Bandura. Even though Bandura is a dyed-in-the-wool social learning theorist, he does an excellent job of presenting most of the major theories of aggression.

Aggression: A Social Psychological Analysis, by Leonard Berkowitz. This book is somewhat dated, but Berkowitz is such an important figure in the research on human aggression that I am recommending this book. There are more recent short articles on aggression by Berkowitz.

The Early Window: Effects of Television on Children, by Robert Liebert, John Neale, and Emily Davidson. This book covers a number of aspects of the effects of television on children. The authors' review of the effects of violent television is well written and comprehensive.

The Dynamics of Aggression, edited by Edwin Megargee and Jack Hokanson. This is a collection of some of the most important essays and experiments on aggression.

The Control of Violence and Aggression, edited by Jerome Singer. This is a group of original articles concerned with what aggression is and how it can be controlled.

Popular literature

The Sixteenth Round, by Rubin "Hurricane" Carter. As already mentioned, Carter is a gifted and eloquent writer. His autobiography presents a vivid picture of aggression in the real world.

On Aggression, by Konrad Lorenz. Although I disagree with Lorenz's theory of human aggression, this is an excellent book. Lorenz is an entertaining and informative writer.

Out of Their League, by Dave Meggyesy, or *North Dallas Forty,* by Peter Gent. Both books were written by ex-professional football players. They describe the violent world of professional sports. Neither book has made the National Football League very happy.

5 PRO-SOCIAL BEHAVIOR

What factors affect our willingness to help another person? This chapter looks at three general determinants of helping. The first is the characteristics of the situation a person is in when his help is requested. Another is the attributes of the person in need of help, which affects his chances of receiving it. The third factor that influences helping is individual differences in pro-social tendencies. How these differences develop is discussed in the final part of the chapter.

PRO-SOCIAL BEHAVIOR

Unless you were raised by Attila the Hun, you were told that it is good to help others. Every major religion teaches the virtues of selflessness and the evils of selfishness. Thus, when the situation arises, human beings should rush to the aid of someone in need.

In March, 1964, a young woman named Kitty Genovese was returning home from her job. It was about 2 A.M. As she left her car, she was attacked by a knife-wielding man. Her screams woke up the people in the building next to the parking lot and temporarily scared off her attacker. He returned and stabbed Ms. Genovese again; her screams continued. It took the man over an hour and a half to kill her. She screamed and pleaded for help throughout most of this time. But not one of the estimated thirty-eight people who watched the murder came to her aid. No one even called the police.

So, despite all we are taught, we don't really care what happens to the other person. Or do we? Twelve years after Kitty Genovese was murdered, the actor Sal Mineo (he appeared in *Rebel without a Cause* and *Exodus*) was returning to his apartment about 1 A.M. As he left his car, he was set upon by a knife-wielding assailant. Wounded, Mineo screamed for help. Several neighbors called the police. One man ran into the alley where Mineo lay and attempted to save his life by means of mouth-to-mouth resuscitation. Although Mineo died, his neighbors did *not* idly stand by.

These two episodes illustrate the complexity of social behavior. Humans are capable of great compassion and concern for others. But they also often show a callous disregard for another person's well-being. Why do people sometimes respond to and sometimes ignore the plight of others? This chapter presents some of the answers discovered by social psychologists.

The first task is to define the type of behav-ior in question. Some people call it *altruistic behavior;* this consists of acts which involve tremendous sacrifice for the person who performs them and produces no rewards for him. This is a troublesome definition. It assumes that a person will engage in a behavior without any anticipation of reward. This violates what learning theory and common sense says about human behavior. Therefore, another definition is needed.

A much simpler and more satisfactory definition was proposed by Wispe (1972), who used the term *pro-social behavior*. This is behavior which "produces or maintains the physical and psychological well being and integrity of other persons" (p. 7). Note that Wispe makes no assumptions about the motives of the person who engages in this behavior. This is a much more useful definition because it avoids the sticky question of whether a helper did or did not expect a reward. Pro-social behavior is simply behavior in which one person helps another. It can range from a soldier throwing himself on a grenade to save his buddies, to someone giving two million dollars to a home for orphaned cats. What factors influence this kind of behavior?

CHARACTERISTICS OF THE SITUATION

A good deal of the research on helping has been concerned with *bystander intervention*. This describes the situation in which a person sees someone in trouble and must decide whether or not to intervene and help him. The first step in this process is the bystander's realization that his help is needed. Situational factors are important here.

Ambiguity

Imagine you are seated in a room with another person waiting to take part in a

psychology experiment. A maintenance man carrying a long ladder and a window blind enters the room. He goes into an adjacent room, evidently to repair or replace a blind. After about five minutes, you hear a loud crash. What has happened? Has the man (1) fallen and injured himself or (2) merely dropped the materials he was carrying? If he has hurt himself, then coming to his aid is appropriate and might even bring you a reward. If he has merely dropped something and you burst into the room like a movie hero, you may find youself in an embarrassing situation. There he is, swearing to himself for his clumsiness, when some college student comes dashing to his rescue. He may respond with something less than undying gratitude. Given this second possibility, it is not unreasonable to expect you to hesitate or perhaps never investigate at all. But what would happen if the man had screamed, "Oh, my back, I can't move," and groaned? Here, the ambiguity of the situation has been eliminated and intervention clearly is appropriate.

Clark and Word (1972) looked at how the ambiguity of the situation affects people's willingness to help. When there was ambiguity as to what had happened to the man, people were slow to come to his aid or did not help at all. But when there was little doubt as to the nature of the situation, little evidence of the apathetic, unresponsive bystander described earlier was found. When the maintenance man announced he was hurt, 100 percent of the subjects in the Clark and Word study intervened. Thus, we can conclude that one of the important variables in bystander intervention is how clear it is that help is needed.

This point may strike you as stupendously obvious and hardly worth the space given it. But in fact, many emergency situations *are* ambiguous. A scream in the night might be a person in trouble or a loud-mouthed drunk. Two people struggling at a distance from you may be a mugger and his victim or two teenagers fooling around. Many times it is hard to know.

One way people determine what is really going on is by the reactions of others to the same event. If another person who sees the same thing as you does not respond, you may define the situation as not requiring intervention and therefore not help. Latané and Darley (1968) have investigated the influence of other people's reaction on how a person responds to an ambiguous situation. A subject was seated in a waiting room alone and asked to fill out a series of questionnaires. As he worked on the questionnaires, smoke started to come out of a vent in the room. Within four minutes, a subject who had not left the room would have had his vision obscured, some difficulty breathing, and smelled a mildly acrid odor. Most (75 percent) of the subjects who encountered this smoke-filled room did not wait four minutes. Within two minutes, they had investigated the source of the smoke, hesitated slightly, and then left the room to find someone in authority and report it. Remember, this was when each subject was *alone* in the room.

In another condition of the experiment, each subject filled out the questionnaires in the presence of two confederates who were supposedly also subjects. When the smoke started billowing out the vent, these confederates looked at it, shrugged their shoulders, and continued to work on the questionnaires. In this condition, 90 percent of the true subjects never reported the smoke!

Latané and Darley's study clearly shows the impact of others' reactions to an emergency situation. These reactions provide a framework in which a person defines the situation, *and* they provide cues as to appropriate behavior. But let us return to the murder of Kitty Genovese. It may strike you as unreasonable to propose that all thirty-eight people were unclear as to what was going on. After all, Ms. Genovese was screaming for help. Might the presence of other observers have other influences on helping behavior?

Diffusion of responsibility

Imagine yourself to be a resident of the apartment building next to the parking lot where Ms. Genovese was murdered. You hear the screams. You go to your window and look out. You can see her bleeding, and she looks toward your window and pleads for help. No one else is around. Clearly, there is some danger in coming to her aid. But if you are her only hope, you could bear all the blame for not helping her.

But what if you are one of thirty-eight observers? You now bear only one thirty-eighth of the responsibility. Darley and Latané (1968) proposed that *diffusion of responsibility*—a person's belief that because there are other people present, he is less personally responsible for the fate of the person in trouble—may partially explain the nonintervention of people in an emergency.

To test this hypothesis, Darley and Latané conducted the following experiment. Subjects were asked to talk over an intercom about problems they were having in adjusting to college. During the discussion, they heard one of the other subjects supposedly have an epileptic seizure. Subjects heard this seizure in one of three conditions: (1) when they thought they were the only other person who had heard it, (2) when they thought one other person had heard it, and (3) when they thought four other people had heard it. If diffusion of responsibility affected bystander intervention, then subjects who heard the epileptic seizure in the presence of four other people should respond more slowly and/or less often than subjects who thought one other person heard the seizure. And subjects who

thought they were alone would seek help for the epileptic most quickly. The results of the study are presented in Figure 5-1. They show rather convincingly that the presence of other people at the time of the seizure resulted in fewer people intervening. Further, those people who did intervene took longer to do so.

Diffusion of responsibility provides a partial explanation of why people sometimes fail to help in an emergency. But it would be incorrect to conclude that it provides a complete explanation. There are other important

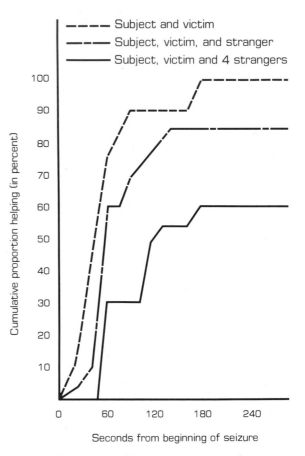

Figure 5-1. The effect of the presence of bystanders on willingness to help and the speed with which they helped. (From Latané & Darley, 1970)

variables which interact with diffusion of responsibility to influence whether one person comes to the aid of another.

Costs

Jane and Irving Piliavin (1976) have proposed one of the few general models of why people help. This model is based on a general premise which was presented in Chapter Three: namely, that humans are motivated by *profit* in their interactions with others. *Profit,* according to Thibaut and Kelley (1958), is a person's estimate of the reward/cost ratio that results from an interaction. Thibaut and Kelley believe that people are motivated to maximize their rewards and minimize their costs. As an introduction to the Piliavin model of bystander intervention, consider the following hypothetical emergency.

One day in a city called Metropolis, Clark Kent is leaving the *Daily Planet* after finishing a story for the paper's late edition. As he mild-manneredly strolls down the street, his super-hearing picks up a cry for help. Using his X-ray vision (Clark Kent is really Superman), he scans Metropolis and locates Lois Lane (also a reporter for the *Daily Planet* and a close personal friend) in an abandoned warehouse. She is tied to a chair with a time bomb set to go off in fifteen minutes.

According to the Piliavin model, the sight of Lois in distress would be physiologically arousing to Superman. As time passes and she receives no help, this arousal becomes physiologically and psychologically unpleasant. Therefore, Superman should be motivated to help Lois. He will dash into a phone booth, strip away his business suit, and emerge as Superman. Is this first proposal of the model valid?

We can examine this by looking at a study by Weiss, Boyer, Lombardo, and Stitch (1973). In this study, subjects watched another person (really a confederate) receive (supposedly) painful electric shocks while she performed a task. The subjects' job was to evaluate the confederate's performance on a series of dials in front of them at various points in the experiment. After an evaluation was made, a signal flashed on in front of the subjects. When they saw this, they were to press a button labeled "Record". Each subject made fifteen evaluations. For some subjects, the (supposed) shock to the confederate was terminated after they pressed the "Record" button. For other subjects, the length of the (supposed) shock was not affected by their pressing of the button. Weiss et al. measured how quickly both groups of subjects pressed the "Record" button. It was predicted that the subjects who could stop the shock would press the "Record" button more quickly over the fifteen evaluations. Why? Because the sight of the confederate in pain was aversive to them. Thus, they would learn to terminate this aversive stimulus as quickly as possible. This increase in speed should not occur for the subjects whose actions were unrelated to the confederate's receiving the shocks. The results of this study are presented in Figure 5-2.

As predicted, the subjects who could stop the shocks became faster over time; the other subjects did not. Evidently the former group of subjects did find the confederate's pain aversive and were motivated to reduce it. The results of this study support the Piliavins' contention that people find the sight of another person in distress unpleasant and are motivated to stop it.

If Superman's situation were similar to that faced by Weiss et al.'s subjects, he would leap into the air, fly to the warehouse, break down the door, and save Lois. In other words, when the cost of not helping is high (Lois might be blown to bits) and the cost of helping is low (breaking down doors is easy for Superman), people will help.

But let's make the situation Superman

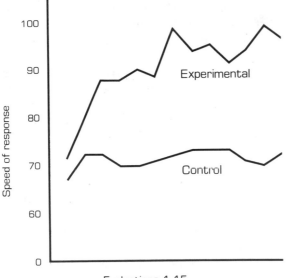

Figure 5-2. The reinforcing effects of being able to alleviate shock to another person. (From Weiss, Boyer, Lombardo & Stitch, 1973)

faces somewhat more complex. In this example, as Superman rushes to Lois's aid, she screams, "Superman, stop. My clothes have been sprayed with Kryptonite." Kryptonite, in sufficient quantities, is fatal to Superman. Now Superman faces a dilemma. He wants to help Lois, but this act may cost him his life. The Piliavin model proposes that when in a situation similar to Superman's, people will attempt to reduce the unpleasant arousal in a way that results in the fewest net costs (i.e., most profit).

One way in which Superman might avoid any costs is to simply say, "Tough luck, Lois," and leave. Thus, the cost of helping is totally eliminated. Superman expends no time or effort and is in no danger. But there are other important costs in the situation; the costs to Superman of *not* helping.

The consequences of not helping

If Superman does not help Lois, he might blame himself for her death. Others (e.g., Jimmy Olson and Perry White, friends of Lois) might criticize him for not helping. Further, if Superman does not help, he might forego rewards, such as "raised self-esteem, thanks, praise, honor, and glory" (Piliavin, Piliavin & Rodin, 1975).

What will Superman do? The costs of helping are high; the costs of not helping are high. Remember, according to the Piliavin model, the course of action a person chooses will be determined primarily by the person's belief about how he can get the most profit out of the situation. The model proposes two courses of action.

Indirect help

One way to resolve the dilemma is to help Lois indirectly. Superman could call the police or Jimmy Olsen. A number of studies (cf. Latané and Darley, 1970) have found that when the costs are high, people will chose indirect or *detour* means of helping. They will get someone else to aid the person in trouble.

Cognitive redefinition

It is also possible that Superman will cognitively redefine the situation. In *cognitive redefinition,* the potential helper changes his view of the dilemma. Rather than seeing it as a situation which demands that he take some immediate, direct action, he decides that either the other person doesn't really need help and/ or that someone else will probably help.

Cognitive redefinition is not simply a "cop-out" the nonhelper uses to explain his behavior. According to the Piliavin model, it will occur only under certain circumstances. First, the costs of both helping and not helping must be high. Second, the situation must be ambiguous enough to cause the bystander to wonder if his help is really needed, or if there are other people present who could conceivably help. Irwin Silverman (1974) describes the relationship between ambiguity and cognitive redefinition.

The man who happens across a dangerous crisis is confronted with a conflict of exceptional implications. Every fiber of his masculine image tells him he should plunge between the knife-wielding rapist or the muggers of the victim, but his more pragmatic instincts will give him great qualms, particularly if he is among the mass of us who are not as adept as Mannix or James Bond or the Lone Ranger, or the multitude of other models of masculinity referred to us by the media. He resolves the conflict . . . by distorting the event, by making it something other than an emergency requiring his intervention. Thus, a rape becomes a family quarrel, a mugging becomes a private dispute, and so on. (Silverman, 1974, p. 11)

Piliavin et al. tested whether high costs will lead to the diffusion of responsibility.

They varied the cost of helping by changing the physical appearance of the person in need of help. Prior research had shown that people dislike interacting with someone who is disfigured. So in one condition of their experiment, the person to be helped was made up with an ugly birthmark on his face. This man entered a car on the New York City subway carrying a cane. A short time later, he fell to the floor, apparently unconscious.

The possibility that people could diffuse the responsibility for helping him was created by sometimes having a person dressed as a medical intern in the car. As Piliavin et al. expected, the intern's presence resulted in less help only for the man with the birthmark. That is, diffusion of responsibility occurred only when the costs of helping were high.

The concept of cognitive redefinition helps to tie together the situational factors which influence helping. It shows that the ambi-

---

An explanation of the death of chivalry?

When Kitty Genovese's neighbors were asked to explain why they didn't help, several of them said that they thought it was just "a lover's quarrel." In 1973, twenty-five men stood and watched while a young woman was raped. They justified their inaction by saying that the rapist "might have been her boyfriend." Are these just after-the-fact "copouts"? Or do they illustrate the Piliavins' concept of cognitive redefinition in a high-cost situation? Lance Shotland and Margaret Shaw (1976) have tried to provide some answers.

They staged a fight between a man and woman in a campus building and obtained people's reactions to it. Almost 70 percent of the people who watched a film of the fight thought that the couple were either on a date, lovers, or married. Further, people assumed that a fight between individuals with a close relationship would result in less injury to the woman than a fight between strangers.

Do these beliefs influence a bystander's actual willingness to help? In another part of this study, subjects saw one of two kinds of fights. In the first, the woman screamed at her attacker, "I don't even know you." In the other fight, she said, "I don't know why I ever married you." A fight between two strangers resulted in three times as many interventions as a fight between a supposedly married couple.

guity of the situation and the presence of others are most likely to affect a bystander's behavior when the costs of helping/not helping are high.

The final situation identified by the Piliavin model is where the cost of helping is high and the cost of not helping is low. For example, Superman might survey the situation and decide that the kryptonite will kill him and Lois could, in fact, untie herself. If this were the case, Superman would probably yell, "Up, up, and away," and leave.

Social norms

The "economic" approach of the Piliavins bothers many social psychologists. They feel that it reduces helping to the bottom line in an accountant's books. People are motivated by factors other than profit. One alternative factor that has been proposed to explain helping is social norms.

A *social norm* is society's expectation about how a person should behave. Society communicates these norms to its members and may punish those who deviate from them. Two specific social norms may influence helping.

Social responsibility

We are our brother's (or sister's) keeper. Most societies tell their members that they are expected to help those people who need it. This is the norm of *social responsibility*. Does this social norm actually affect helping? This question has been asked in several studies. People are reminded of this social norm, and then the effect of this reminder on helping is examined. None of the studies that used this procedure have shown an increase in helping (Berkowitz, 1972; Darley & Batson, 1973; Krebs, 1970).

Schwartz (1973) has not, however, been willing to abandon this explanation. He suggested that a personal rather than a social norm of responsibility may be related to helping. A *personal norm* is a person's own expectation about how he should behave. A personal norm is derived from social norms, but it differs from them in the following manner. If a person violates a social norm, society is the punishing agent. If a person violates his personal norms, he himself is the punishing agent. That is, a person who violates his expectations about how he should behave will experience self-imposed guilt, a loss of self-esteem, and other negative feelings. Further, Schwartz believed that some people tend to accept responsibility for their own actions, while others reject such responsibility. Among those who accept it, violation of a personal norm will result in self-recrimination. Among those people who reject responsibility for their actions, violation of a personal norm will not have this effect. Thus, Schwartz predicted that people who: (1) had a strong personal norm about some specific act of helping and (2) tended to accept responsibility for their actions would help more than people who lacked either or both of these traits.

Schwartz tested this hypothesis by examining people's willingness to donate bone marrow. Subjects received a questionnaire in which they were asked how strong a moral obligation (personal norm) they felt to donate bone marrow to someone who needed it. Then subjects filled out a personality scale which measured their tendency to accept or reject responsibility for their actions.

About three months later, the subjects received a request from a doctor who specialized in transplants which asked them to join a bone marrow transplant pool. Subjects indicated how willing they were to donate. Schwartz found that people with a strong personal norm (a strong moral obligation to donate bone marrow) *and* a tendency to accept responsibility for their actions were significantly more willing to donate bone marrow than any other group of subjects.

Schwartz's research suggests that a normative explanation may be somewhat useful in explaining helping behavior. But it also points out that the value of the normative explanation may be limited to people with strong personal norms and a tendency to accept responsibility for their own behavior.

Reciprocity

Another social norm is *reciprocity,* the idea that if someone helps you, you should return the favor. The research on equity theory (presented in Chapter Three) strongly suggests that people do accept this norm. For example, Regan (1971) found that people would help someone who had done them a favor even when this person was a rather obnoxious character. Further, they were more willing to help this disagreeable person than a pleasant person who had not helped them.

Despite these findings, many social psychologists are not satisfied with a normative explanation of helping. It ignores the important variable of the costs involved. It fails to account for the fact that there are tremendous individual differences in helping tendencies. Finally, it is so general a concept that it doesn't really aid us in predicting behavior in a specific situation (Latané and Darley, 1970).

Temporary states of the helper

Situational variables may indirectly influence helping. They can cause feelings in a person which, in turn, affect his willingness to help.

Mood

You sleep through your alarm clock's ringing and awake fifteen minutes after your first class is over. In your hurry to get to campus, you grab a tube of shampoo rather than toothpaste and end up brushing your teeth with Prell. Your car takes five minutes to start, and when it does, there is a frightening sound from the engine. When you finally arrive on campus, you are approached by a blind student. He asks you to help him find his classroom. Will you help?

The research on mood and helping suggests that you probably will not. Or at least, you will not be as likely to help him as would someone who is in a good mood. For example, Isen and Levin (1972) arranged a situation in which half their subjects found a dime in a public phone booth, while the other half did not. Then both groups of subjects were asked by a confederate to help him pick up some papers he had dropped. The lucky subjects (i.e., those who found the dime) were more willing to help than the unlucky ones.

Guilt

Guilt can be defined as feelings of regret at and responsibility for one's actions (Freedman, 1970). A number of studies have shown that such feelings will increase a person's willingness to help his victim. For example, Carlsmith and Gross (1969) had subjects either: (1) shock another person when that person made an error or (2) sound a buzzer when an error was made.[1] Then both groups were asked by the person to do a favor. It was found that the shock group was much more likely to help.

There are several possible explanations for these results. Walster et al. (1973) based their's on equity theory (which was covered in Chapter Three). According to this explanation, hurting a person generates distress in the offender because he realizes that "his

---

[1]This study was also presented in Chapter One.

partner's relative outcomes are less than his own" (1973, p. 154). Thus, the harm doer worries about retaliation and attempts to restore equity before this occurs.

Cialdini, Darby, and Vincent (1973) proposed that hurting someone creates negative feelings in the harm doer. The harm doer acts pro-socially toward his victim simply to eliminate these feelings. In support of this position, Cialdini et al. showed that when one eliminates a harm doer's negative feelings (e.g., by giving him some money), his willingness to help his victim is reduced.

Finally, Krebs (1970) has argued that harming someone lowers the perpetrator's self-esteem. This causes him to engage in *reparate altruism*—a pro-social act which returns the a harm doer's self-esteem to an acceptable level.

Obviously no one theory of how situational factors influence helping will adequately explain all instances of pro-social behavior. You should view the explanations presented as pieces of a jigsaw puzzle. All contribute to its completion, but no one piece finishes it. Another important part of this puzzle is the characteristic of the person who needs help.

CHARACTERISTICS OF THE RECIPIENT

Helping obviously involves two people—the potential helper and the potential recipient of his aid. Thus, it is not surprising that the characteristics of the potential recipient influence pro-social behavior. Let's look at the effects of some recipient characteristics.

Need and dependency

One reason we help other people is because we believe they need our help. As a rule, the greater a person's known need for help, the more likely he is to receive it. For example,

the more pain a person is in, the quicker people will be to help him (Weiss et al., 1973). In another study, it was found that a family that needed money to fly to see a dying son was more likely to receive it than was a group of people who needed money for social activities (Wagner & Wheeler, 1969).

The dependency of the recipient has a similar effect. The less able a person is to help himself, the more likely he is to receive help. For example, college students saw a man drop a book as he walked across campus. Half of them saw the man on crutches, while the other half saw him walking normally. They were much more likely to help him when he was on crutches (Clark, 1975).

Probably none of these findings surprise you. Why even bother with the effects of need and dependency, when they're so obvious? Well, there are circumstances in which the relationship is not so simple and straightforward.

The reason for dependency

Imagine yourself in the following two situations. In the first, you are hurrying to a class when a man approaches you. He is staggering badly and is carrying a half-empty bottle of cheap red wine. As he passes you, he stumbles and falls unconscious to the ground. You are already five minutes late for your class. What do you do?

In the second situation, everything is the same except that the man is walking normally and without the wine. As he passes you, he stumbles and falls unconscious to the ground. What do you do? Research tells us that you are more likely to help the man in the second situation (Piliavin, Rodin, & Piliavin, 1969; Schopler & Matthews, 1965). Why?

One explanation of this finding is provided by Lerner's (1966) *just world hypothesis.* Lerner proposed that people see the world as a just or fair place. The good are rewarded and the bad are punished. If a good person is punished, this violates people's view of the world and they will act to restore justice. Thus, a person who is not the cause of his troubles will usually receive help. Someone who gets himself into trouble (e.g., a drunk) doesn't violate the just world hypothesis. As a result, people are not motivated to help him.

Costs and dependency

Another exception to the simple, positive relationship between dependency and helping is when the costs of giving help are extremely high. In this circumstance, the relationship may become reversed. The more dependent a person is, the *less* likely he is to receive help. The following study demonstrates this.

Schaps (1972) used unsuspecting salesmen in a shoe store as his subjects. The stores where these men worked paid on a commission basis and allowed them to wait on only one customer at a time. Confederates of Schaps entered the store either in a state of dependency—the heel on their shoe had broken and they could walk no farther—or in a nondependent state—their shoes were in perfect order. In both conditions, the confederates put the salesmen through a minor ordeal. They looked at several pairs of shoes and were never satisfied. Schaps reasoned that when there were few other customers, the cost to a salesman (in terms of lost commission) was low. But when the store was crowded, the salesman was paying a high price for staying with this difficult customer. Observers kept track of the number of people in the store when the confederates went into their act. They also recorded how many trips a salesman made to the stock room, how many pairs of shoes he brought out, and other general measures of the quality of the service the customer received. Figure 5-3 presents Schaps's results. Under low-cost conditions, the dependent customer received better service than the nondependent customer, but under conditions of high cost the pattern was reversed. The dependent customer received poorer service than the nondependent customer.

The final aspect of dependency to be discussed has to do with dependency as a perceived trait of the potential recipient. Are there classes of persons who are *perceived* as less able to help themselves and thus more likely to receive help? The answer seems to be yes. One group that seems to create this perception is women.

Recipients' gender and helping

Kay Deaux (1976) has pointed out that women are seen "as less competent, less cap-

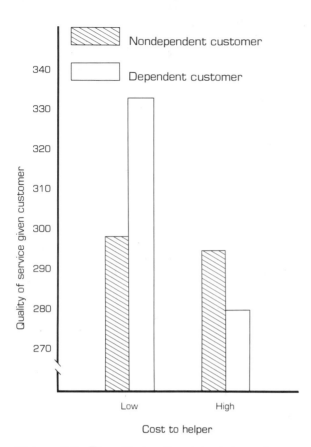

Figure 5-3. The effects of recipient dependency and cost to the helper on willingness to help. (Adapted from Schaps, 1972)

able of making decisions and more excitable in minor crises" (p. 73). This belief, regardless of its accuracy, should result in women being seen as more dependent and thus being helped more. Although no studies have directly measured men's perception of women's dependency, some studies suggest this is the case.

For example, Penner, Dertke, and Achenbach (1973) placed a supposedly disabled car along the side of a highway equipped with a "flash system." This system enabled a passing motorist to report the presence of a disabled vehicle to the Highway Patrol by merely flashing his car's headlights at signs placed along the side of the road. Thus, a passing motorist had the choice of helping indirectly, by flashing his lights, or directly, by stopping and offering assistance. The person standing alongside the car was either a man or a woman. In terms of total helping (i.e., flashing and stopping), men and women were helped equally. But when the types of help were examined, an interesting pattern emerged. About 80 percent of the help offered the male confederate was indirect; the motorists (all of whom were male) flashed their lights. But almost 60 percent of the help offered the female confederate was direct; the male motorists stopped and offered assistance. Why? A reasonable explanation is that the female confederate was perceived as less able to deal with a broken-down car (i.e., more dependent), and thus, direct intervention was required.

(It should be noted, however, that women will receive help more often than men only if their dependency is sex-linked. For example, Deaux (1976) reported that women who attempted to borrow money were no more likely to be successful than men.)

It seems that in general, women are more likely to receive help than men because of their perceived dependency. But wait, what about Kitty Genovese and Sal Mineo? His neighbors were more willing to help than hers. How can we explain this?

Here is one intriguing study on this question. Borofsky, Stollak, and Messé (1971) recruited subjects to watch a psychodrama—a play in which people are given roles and are asked to act in whatever way they feel is appropriate. Although Borofsky et al. used both male and female subjects, only the behavior of the male subjects will be presented. The psychodrama called for the two participants to work through an argument as they thought people actually would. The participants were, in fact, trained actors who staged a very convincing fight in which one actor was apparently badly beaten by the other. Borofsky et al. systematically varied the sex of the aggressor and the victim and recorded the percentage of the subjects who intervened to stop the fight. When a male was attacking another male, 80 percent of the male subjects intervened. But when a male was attacking a female, *none* of the male subjects intervened. Despite the implicitly greater dependency of a female victim, no one helped. Why?

Borofsky et al. proposed that the men might have experienced a vicarious sense of sexual or hostile gratification from seeing a woman being beaten up. There is, however, an alternative explanation of their results. Recall that Schaps (1972) found that when the cost of helping was high, shoe store salesmen were less likely to help a dependent recipient. In Borofsky's study, a woman who was being beaten may have been seen as more dependent than a man in a similar situation. Stopping a person who has assaulted someone is probably a high-cost act. It is thus possible that the more general interaction between cost and recipient dependency may provide a better explanation than one based on the vicarious enjoyment of seeing a woman being assaulted. Obviously, additional research is needed to determine the validity of either explanation. (The box entitled "An Explanation of the Death of Chivalry" may also be relevant here; see page 143.)

Similarity

The following episode took place in a Nazi concentration camp during World War II. An order was issued to execute a number of inmates. The guard responsible for carrying it out lined up a few hundred prisoners and began to count them off by tens. Every tenth person in the line was pulled out and sent to the gas ovens. This grotesque ritual continued until the guard was about halfway through the line. At this point, he chose the *eleventh* prisoner from a group and then returned to marking every tenth person for death. Later he was asked why he had temporarily deviated from his selection procedure. He explained that he knew the man he had skipped from his own village (Cohen, 1972).

This macabre incident illustrates the effect of similarity on helping. The more similar a recipient is to a potential helper in terms of his attitudes, background, personality, values, or even physical appearance, the more likely he is to receive help (Emswiller, Deaux, & Willets, 1971; Pandey & Griffitt, 1973). One reason is that similarity leads to liking and liking leads to helping (Baron, 1971; Gross, Wallston, & Piliavin, 1975). But there is another reason as well.

Empathy

Empathy is the phenomenon of one person's emotional state producing almost exactly the same emotional state in another person. For example, seeing another person crying causes you to cry, or another person's obvious happiness makes you happy. Note that in empathy you do not directly experience the cause of the happiness or sadness. Rather, you experience it indirectly as the result of the cues (e.g., facial expressions, words) the other person provides. Empathy is believed to produce helping behavior (Aronfreed, 1970; Krebs, 1970).

Now, let's relate this to similarity. Krebs (1975) proposed that the belief that you are similar to someone will increase your tendency to empathize with him. This, in turn, will increase your willingness to help him. To test this idea, he told half of his subjects they were similar and half that they were dissimilar to another person who was taking part in an experiment with them. Then all the subjects watched this person receive an electric shock. While they watched, Krebs measured their blood pressure, heart rate, and other physiological responses. As Figure 5-4 shows, subjects who believed they were similar to the other person showed a much stronger physiological response to the other person's distress than did those who believed they were dissimilar.

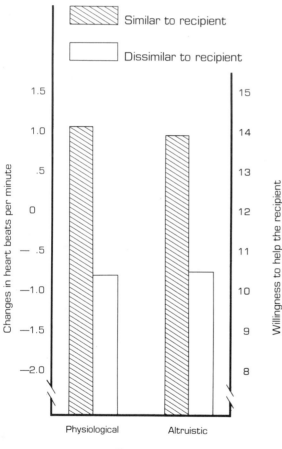

Figure 5-4. The effect of similarity to another person on empathy and willingness to help that person. (Adapted from Krebs, 1975)

Following this, the subjects had the choice of giving the other person money or keeping it for themselves. As predicted, the subjects in the similar condition (who had reacted more empathically) sacrificed more money than did the subjects in the dissimilar condition.

Race

In the absence of any other information, two people of the same race see themselves as more similar than two people of different races (Byrne & Wong, 1962). Perceived similarity leads to liking; liking leads to helping. Thus, we would predict that people of the same race will help each other more than would people of different races.

The actual research findings don't always support this very reasonable prediction. For example, in one study, whites and blacks living in New York City were called by a supposedly stranded motorist. The caller, who spoke with either a black or a white dialect, claimed that he was trying to reach a garage and had dialed the subject's number by mistake. Further, this wrong number had taken his last dime. He asked the subject to help by calling the garage for him. The number of subjects who made this call was used as the measure of helping. White subjects helped a white caller more than a black one. Black subjects helped callers of both races equally (Gaertner & Bickman, 1971).

In a study conducted two years later, subjects were approached by a black or a white person who wore a hearing aid. He asked them to help him make a phone call. The rates of cross-race and same-race helping were virtually identical (Thayer, 1973).

Finally, Wegner and Crano (1975) had black and white confederates drop computer cards in front of black or white subjects. White subjects were equally willing to help people of both races. But black subjects helped another black person more than they helped a white.

It is hard to come up with any simple explanation of these contradictory results. I suspect that it is not sufficient just to look at racial similarity and ignore the other factors that affect helping. That is, it is probably wrong to assume that race itself will solely determine a person's willingness to help. For example, the extreme dependency of a person with a hearing aid who had to make a phone call might have wiped out any racial effects.

A recent study (Gaertner & Dovidio, 1977) supports this conjecture. They found that when white subjects were presented with a clear emergency in which they couldn't diffuse responsibility, white and black victims were helped equally. However, when the situation was ambiguous and the bystanders could diffuse responsibility, white subjects were less likely to help black victim than a white one.

Conclusion

In the first few pages of this chapter, we saw that human beings are capable of callous disregard for the lives of others, *and* acts of heroism and selflessness. To understand why these extremes occur, we first had to define the phenomenon we were interested in. The term *pro-social behavior* was preferred over *altruism*. Altruism implies that an act has absolutely no rewards for the performer.

In fact, most, if not all, helping behaviors produce some sort of reward for the helper. This reward may be as tangible as the Congressional Medal of Honor or as intangible as feeling better after you've helped someone. Humans help because of some sort of reward.

Then, the relationship between situational characteristics and helping was examined. The ambiguity of the situation, the presence of other people, the costs of helping, social

Ripping off the campus bookstore

Many students view the bookstores on their campus as their natural enemy. They believe that bookstores overcharge them when they buy a book and underpay them when they sell it back. How would students react if they saw someone ripping off the campus bookstore?

The manager of a university-run bookstore gave Max Dertke and his associates permission to stage thefts in the paperback section of the store. A confederate waited until a student was standing alone looking at books and then blatantly proceeded to steal a book. Then an experimenter, dressed as an employee of the bookstore, approached the student. "May I help you?" he asked, and waited to see if the student reported the theft. If he didn't, the experimenter said, "Did you see that guy (girl) steal that book?"

Two hundred forty students clearly saw the theft, but fewer than twenty spontaneously reported it. Only slightly more than half confirmed that a theft had taken place when the employee asked them the second question.

Another interesting finding from this field experiment concerned the effects of the thief's race. A theft committed by black person was significantly more likely to be spontaneously reported and confirmed than was a theft committed by a white person (All the students were white.) (Dertke, Penner, & Ulrich, 1974).

norms, and situational influences on a person's state of mind are all related to a person's willingness to help. It is important to remember that helping is an extremely complex act. No one aspect of the situation will totally explain why helping does or does not take place.

The characteristics of the recipient are also an important determinant of pro-social behavior. There are two broad classes of characteristics: (1) the extent of a person's need and (2) the person's similarity to the potential helper. The greater a person's need and the more similar he is to a potential helper, the more likely he is to receive help. However, these recipient characteristics also interact with situational factors. For example, under conditions of high cost to the helper, highly dependent people are less likely to receive help than nondependent people. Thus, we cannot consider the situation and the characteristics of the recipient to be independent of each other.

REVIEW QUESTIONS

(Ten out of twelve is passing)

1. An act which benefits another person and produces absolutely no rewards for the actor is called _____ . The term _____ _____ makes no assumptions about the rewards involved in helping someone. (p. 137)

2. The finding that the more people who see someone in need of help, the less likely the person is to receive help, is possibly explained by _____ _____ . (p. 140)

3. According to the reward/cost model of pro-social behavior, people will generally act pro-socially only when such an action will produce a _____ for them. (p. 141)

4. Betty sees a house on fire and hears people yelling for help. Instead of rushing into the house, she runs to a phone booth and calls the fire department. This is _____ _____ . (p. 142)

5. Bobby hears a woman screaming, "Rape," but decides she is only kidding and does not help. In this instance, Bobby has kept his costs of not helping low by _____ _____ the situation. (p. 142)

6. A _____ norm differs from a (an) _____ norm in that violation of the former results in the person's punishing himself. (p. 144)

7. "If you scratch my back, I'll scratch yours" illustrates the norm of _____ . (p. 145)

8. If a person's dependency is due to a situation he himself has created, he is _____ likely to receive help than someone whose dependency is due to factors beyond his control. (p. 147)

9. One explanation of this finding is that people believe that the world is _____ . (p. 147)

10. Women are generally more likely to receive help than men because they are perceived to be more _____ than men. (p. 148)

11. Similarity seems to increase helping because it increases a bystander's ability to _____ with the person in need of help. (p. 149)

12. Feelings of regret and responsibility for the harm done to another person are called _____ . In general, these feelings will _____ a person's willingness to help. (p. 145)

CHARACTERISTICS OF THE HELPER

Just north of downtown Chicago, there is a large concentration of poor whites who have come north from Appalachia. In the midst of this urban ghetto lives Sister Evelyn, a nun. She is a twenty-six-year-old attractive, well-educated woman. She is asked why she has chosen to live here.

"We're here in this neighborhood because the Applachian people are here . . . to bring service where the church has not been able to provide it . . . we're here because Christ must be wherever mankind is. There is a special necessity for having [us] present in this neighborhood." Why has she chosen to be a nun, her questioner asks. " . . . if our commitment to remain single enables us to give more of our time, our energies, more of our concern to mankind—or that limited area of mankind in which we're concerned—then it is valid." (Terkel, 1967, pp. 142, 147)

Sister Evelyn's behavior can't be explained by situational factors or the characteristics of the person in need of help. Her helping doesn't involve a transitory response to some

Tampa Tribune

emergency situation. Rather, she has committed her life to others. What is the cause of her behavior?

Biological explanations

Recently some psychologists have become dissatisfied with a pure learning theory explanation of human social behavior (Campbell, 1975). They have been impressed with a sociobiological explanation. *Sociobiology* is a branch of biology which argues that many complex social behaviors are basically instinctual (Wilson, 1975).

Sociobiologists point to the fact that among lower animals there are totally altruistic, instinctual behaviors. For example, ants and bees will sacrifice themselves for the sake of their colonies and hives. The sociobiologist believes that humans may engage in comparable behaviors. That is, humans perform acts which involve sacrifice and produce absolutely no rewards for them. Since there are no rewards for these altruistic behaviors, they cannot be explained by learning processes. Rather, they are instinctual responses caused by our genetic structure.

The sociobiological explanation of pro-social behavior is intriguing and deserves more study. However, at present, most social psychologists do not believe that it is a valid explanation of helping behaviors. They acknowledge that lower animals do engage in truly altruistic behaviors, and these behaviors are instinctual. But they have difficulty identifying any comparable behaviors in humans. An even more important reason for their rejection is what geneticists say about the function of our genes. Genes give humans the potential to engage in complex behavior. But in humans, they do *not* determine the content of these behaviors (Wispe & Thompson, 1976). For example, our genes give us the *ability* to rush into a burning building to save

a child. They do not *cause* us to engage in this behavior. Most social psychologists believe that pro-social behavior is learned.

The learning of pro-social behavior

It is believed that three learning processes are involved in the development of pro-social tendencies in humans.

Classical conditioning

At the risk of boring you, let's briefly review the way classical conditioning works using Pavlov's research on salivation in dogs (1927). If you give a dog meat powder, it will salivate. The meat powder is called an *unconditioned stimulus,* and the salivation is called an *unconditioned response.* If you strike a tuning fork in front of the same dog, it will not salivate. The sound made by the tuning fork is called the *conditioned stimulus*—that is, one that initially has no effect on the person or animal you are trying to condition. Now, if you repeatedly present the sound of the tuning fork along with the meat powder, the dog will come to associate this sound with the powder. Eventually the dog will salivate in response to the sound of the tuning fork alone. This salivation is called a *conditioned response.* Thus, in classical conditioning, the animal (or person) learns to respond to a previously neutral stimulus. Since dogs are not well known for their altruistic tendencies (except perhaps Lassie and Rin Tin Tin), how is this conditioning related to the development of pro-social behavior in humans?

Recall the concept of empathy, introduced earlier. Empathy is the phenomenon whereby one person's emotional state produces almost exactly the same emotional state in another person. Remember that experiencing empathy will increase a person's willingness to help someone.

Aronfreed proposed that empathic responses to other people can be acquired by classical conditioning. More specifically, he believed that pairing positive feelings, in the recipient of a pro-social act with positive feelings in the helper would produce empathy. This empathy would, in turn, cause an increase in helping. Aronfreed and Paskal (1965) tested this idea in the following experiment.

Three groups of six- to eight-year-old girls were shown a machine with two levers on it. An adult demonstrated that if one of the levers was pulled, a red light would go on 60 percent of the time. If the other lever was pulled, the person working the machine would receive candy 60 percent of the time. In the demonstration presented to the first group of girls, every time the light went on, the adult broke into a big smile and said, "There's the light." For the second group, the adult said nothing when the light went on, but instead turned and hugged the girl sitting next to her. Finally, in the third group's demonstration, the adult paired these two reactions. That is, when the red light went on, she smiled, said, "There's the light," and hugged the girl sitting next to her. Note that in this third condition, positive feelings in the adult (smiling) were paired with positive feelings in the girl (as the result of being hugged). After this, the adult gave the girls in all three groups a chance to work the machine. Aronfreed and Paskal recorded the number of times girls in each of the groups chose to pull the lever which turned on the light, thus denying themselves the candy.

The girls who had experienced positive reactions in the adult paired with the hugs were more willing to pull the lever associated with the light than girls in the other two groups. Why? Presumably this act produced positive, but intangible, feelings in them as the result of the previous pairing of feelings. In other words, as a product of classical conditioning, the girls felt good when they helped the adult (by turning on the light). In another study, Midlarsky and Bryan (1967) repeated Aronfreed and Paskal's procedure but added an additional dependent variable—the anonymous donation of money to needy children. They found that girls in the pairing condition donated more money than did the girls in the other two conditions. Evidently the good feelings generated by this pairing generalized to other kinds of helping.

In addition to the effects of classical conditioning, the effects of operant conditioning on pro-social behavior have been studied. To no one's surprise, it was found that children who are reinforced for sharing are more likely to share in the future than children who are not reinforced (Bryan & London, 1970). Let's now turn to the effects of models on helping.

Modeling

In the discussion of the learning of aggressive behavior, it was shown that much of what a child may learn about aggression is due to the behavior of models. Are models also important in learning pro-social tendencies?

Unless you are the child of Ebenezer Scrooge (cf. Chapter Two), it is likely that your parents preached the goodness of sharing your toys with others and the general virtues of charity. But how did they *act*? Did your father drop old campaign buttons instead of money into the church collection plate? Did your mother sneer and turn the other way when she saw the sidewalk Santa Clauses collecting money for charity at Christmas time? More importantly, what would be the relative effect of your parents' words versus their actions on your pro-social tendencies? This question has been investigated in a number of studies.

For example, Bryan and Walbek (1970a, 1970b) varied the words and actions of an adult model a group of young children saw.

The models' actions (being charitable or uncharitable) were either consistent or inconsistent with their words (one should be charitable or one should be selfish). After the children saw the model, they were given the chance to make donations of money they had won to charity. Bryan and Walbek found that what the model did (i.e., its actions) had a much stronger impact on the children's willingness to make donations than what the model said. Thus, models can influence helping behavior. What are the processes which enable a model to do this?

We learned most of the answers to this question in the section on observational learning and aggression in the previous chapter. There is, however, one additional concept which is related to the influence of models. Recall that an observer will be affected by the consequences of an action to the model. A partial reason is that these consequences tell the observer what will happen to him if he performs the same action. But the consequences to the model may have an additional effect on the observer. They may produce vicarious reinforcement. According to Bandura (1971), *vicarious reinforcement* is a process whereby an observer who sees a model reinforced may experience the feelings associated with this reinforcement, even though the observer is not directly reinforced. The observer vicariously experiences the same feelings as the model. (Note the similarity between vicarious reinforcement and empathy.)

In a study which examined the effects of vicarious reinforcement on helping, children were shown one of three models. The first model had won money in a game, donated it to charity, and said how good his generosity made him feel. The second model won money, said how good winning made him feel, and then gave the money to charity. (Note that the first model was happy about giving money; the second was happy about winning.)

The third model was selfish; he won money and kept it. The children then played the game, won money, and were given the chance to give it to charity. The children who saw the generous models gave more money than those who saw the selfish model. Of more interest is the difference between the children who saw the two types of generous models. The model who expressed pleasure in giving produced more donations from the children than the model who expressed pleasure in winning. In other words, his description of how being charitable made him feel produced an increase in pro-social behavior (Midlarsky & Bryan, 1972).

Not only do the actions of the model affect children's pro-social tendencies; the characteristics of the model have an effect as well. For example, children are more likely to model the actions of a warm, friendly model than one who is cold to them (Staub, 1971).

Up to this point, no attempt has been made to tie these three types of learning (classical, operant, observational) together. The result is a rather artificial view of how parents can affect the pro-social tendencies of their children. Parents do not use classical conditioning *or* operant conditioning *or* provide models; they tend to do all these things simultaneously. How do these different forms of learning, in combination, affect the behavior of children?

Midlarsky, Bryan, and Brickman (1973) examined this question. Children saw a model who acted in either a charitable, neutral, or selfish manner. The children then had a chance to donate money (which they had won in a game), to charity. In all three conditions, the model verbally reinforced half the children for their charitable behavior (a typical verbal reinforcer was: "You're nice to give money away."). A comparison of the donations made by the children who were reinforced and not reinforced in each condition is presented in Figure 5-5.

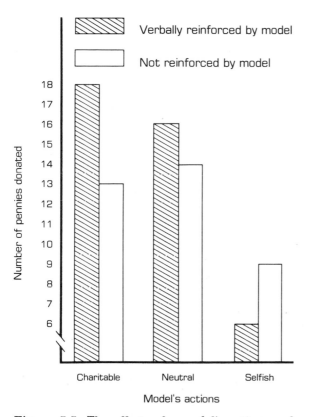

Figure 5-5. The effects of a model's actions and verbal reinforcement on children's willingness to donate money to charity. (Adapted from Midlarsky, Bryan, & Brickman, 1974)

This figure shows that the charitable model and the model who had acted neutrally were about equally effective in producing donations from the children. Further, verbal reinforcements from these models tended to increase the amount of money the children donated. But now, consider the results for the children who were verbally reinforced by the selfish model. These children donated less than any other group. Midlarsky et al. speculated that this occurred because approval from an inconsistent person (i.e., one who practiced selfishness but reinforced charity) was unpleasant to the children. This caused a decreased amount of charitable behavior.

Thus, parents who themselves act selfishly but who reward their children for acting charitably may actually reduce helping behavior in their children.

Parental behaviors and helping

Thus far, we have looked at laboratory studies of how children might learn pro-social tendencies. Now let's consider some field studies on the behaviors of parents of people with strong pro-social tendencies. These studies usually don't deal with the ways the parents' behaviors influenced their children. However, I believe that classical conditioning, operant conditioning, and modeling provide excellent explanations of why certain parental behaviors may produce strong pro-social tendencies in children.

In the late 1960's, David Rosenhan conducted a field study which attempted to differentiate between people who actively participated in the civil rights movement of the mid-1960's and those who only gave money to civil rights organizations. He found that one of the best discriminators between the two groups was the presence of at least one parent who had shown a long-term commitment to an altruistic endeavor (Rosenhan, 1970). London (1970) found a similar pattern in his examination of non-Jews who helped Jews to escape the Nazi concentration camps during World War II. According to London, these people strongly identified with a parent who held "very firm opinions on moral issues and serv(ed) as a model of moral conduct" (p. 247).

Hoffman (1975) attempted to determine the relationship between parental values and children's pro-social orientations in a more controlled environment. He obtained classmates' ratings of how pro-social a group of fifth graders were. Then he obtained information from the children's parents in three areas: (1) the extent to which they held altruistic values, (2) how much affection they showed toward their children, and (3) the extent to which they used victim-centered discipline. This third measure was obtained by giving parents a hypothetical situation in which a child hurts another child via an insult. Then the parent is asked how the offending child should be handled. A parent who used a *victim-centered discipline* technique would be one who encouraged the child to compensate the person it had offended. For example, a parent who used this technique would want a child who knocked down a playmate's doll house not only to apologize but also to help rebuild the house.

Hoffman's findings supported an explanation of the acquisition of pro-social tendencies which is based on learning. With regard to modeling, Hoffman found that pro-social children had parents who held altruistic values. This suggests that these parents were providing pro-social models for their children. Parents who used victim-centered discipline were more likely to have pro-social children than ·parents who did not. This finding may show the effect of direct reinforcement of pro-social acts by parents. Finally, Hoffman reported some trend toward pro-social children's having more affectionate parents. This finding was consistent with Staub's (1971) laboratory study on the relative ability of warm and cold models to produce pro-social behavior in children who watched them.

Let's leave the learning theories of the development of pro-social behavior now and turn to another extremely influential point of view. It is Jean Piaget's (1932) theory of moral development.

Developmental theories

Jean Piaget

Piaget's viewpoint about pro-social behavior, in particular, and social development, in general, is quite different from those presented so far. Piaget saw the crucial aspect of social development as being maturation. *Maturation* refers to changes which occur in a person as he grows up. These changes are genetically determined, occur in a fixed order, are usually irreversible, and are not greatly affected by learning (Harlow, McGaugh, & Thompson, 1971). The changes which occur in how humans move physically illustrate one maturational process.

All humans have the genetic potential to walk.[2] But they do not leave their mothers' womb, thank the doctor for a fine job, and stroll out of the delivery room. For the first few months, they do not move at all; then they move by pulling themselves with their arms; next, they crawl; and finally when their legs are ready they walk. A parent (or grandparent) can use instruction to speed up this process (Mussen, Conger, & Kagan, 1974), but the effect of this training is small. Children in a normal environment will begin to walk in the absence of instruction.

Piaget believed that humans' intellectual and social development follows a pattern which is similar to that of their physical development. Just as a child cannot walk before a certain age, he is incapable of certain ways of thinking before a certain age. And just as a child changes the way it moves physically as it grows older, so it changes its ways of thinking. It must be emphasized that Piaget did not totally discount the importance of parents and peers in a child's social development. However, he saw their effect as depending upon where a child is in the maturational process.

Now let's apply these general principles to Piaget's explanation of pro-social behavior. He believed that pro-social behavior was due

[2]This assumes that the person does not have a genetic defect and was not crippled by accidents or disease.

to the development of morals and values. In keeping with his maturational viewpoint, he proposed that children must mature to a certain stage of moral development before they are capable of true pro-social behavior.

According to Piaget, there are two sequential stages in moral development. The first he called the *heteronomous stage*. During this stage, a child's moral judgments would delight Archie Bunker. His judgment about the morality of his own and others' behavior is rigid and authoritarian. A behavior is good if it agrees with some hard and fast rule; it is bad if it violates this rule. And the child never questions these rules.

The child acts pro-socially only if some authority figure orders him to do so. Without these orders, the child acts in an egocentric manner. He is incapable of helping someone without being told to do so (Piaget & Inhelder, 1969). Piaget believed that this stage lasts until a child is seven or eight years old.

At about the age of eight, moral judgments become more flexible and less the product of authority figures. Piaget called this stage the stage of *autonomous morality*. By autonomous, Piaget meant that the child has become much more independent of others in making his moral judgments. When he judges the actions of another person, the child considers not only what a person did but also why the person did it. A well-intentioned act (e.g., trying to save someone from a speeding car) which produces a negative consequence (e.g., breaking that person's arm) will be seen as more positive than a negatively intentioned act with negative consequences. With regard to pro-social behavior, the child is more influenced by his peers, considers their needs, and possesses the ability to know how others feel. It is at this stage that the child is capable of true pro-social behavior.

Tests of Piaget's theory. Piaget collected his data in a different manner than the social learning theorists. Rather than conduct tightly controlled laboratory experiments, Piaget primarily observed children as they played in their natural environment. Indeed, a good portion of Piaget's theory was based on the conversations he had with small boys as they played marbles in the streets of Geneva, Switzerland. Despite this "unscientific" manner of data collection, many of the predictions generated by Piaget's theory have held up quite well when tested in the laboratory.

For example, Piaget's theory would lead to the prediction that pro-social behavior in children should increase with age. That is, as children move from the heteronomous to the autonomous stage, they should become more pro-social.

In one study, children of varying ages were asked to make moral judgments about the behavior of characters in stories they had read. Then the children's willingness to give money to charity was measured. In accord with Piaget's theory, older children were more flexible in their judgments of others and were more generous than the younger children (Rushton, 1975; similar results have been found by Emler & Rushton, 1974; Rubin & Schneider, 1973).

But wait, if Piaget is right, then aren't the learning theorists wrong? The answer to this question depends on what you mean by "right." These laboratory confirmations of Piaget's theory only show that he is a brilliant and gifted observer of the behavior of small children. These studies do not answer the crucial theoretical question of whether the changes Piaget correctly identified were due to maturation, learning, or some combination of the two. My personal view is that Piaget provides an extremely valuable description of the development of pro-social behavior. Were his maturational thesis to be proven entirely wrong, it would not greatly lessen his contribution to our understanding of social development.

Kohlberg's stages of moral development

Another influential theory of moral development has been proposed by Lawrence Kohlberg (1967, 1969). Kohlberg's theory, while more complex than Piaget's, is based on the same premises. An outline of Kohlberg's conceptualization of moral development is presented below.

A. Preconventional Level

Stage 1: *Punishment and Obedience Orientation.* The person's judgment as to whether his actions are good or bad is based on the consequences to him. An act which harms someone else but does not result in punishment to him is not considered bad by him.

Stage 2: *Self-centered or Hedonistic Orientation.* The person's judgment as to whether his actions are good or bad is based on whether the action satisfies his own needs. Acts which benefit others are performed only if there is some payoff for him.

B. Conventional Level

Stage 3: *Good Boy/Girl Orientation.* The person's judgment as to whether his actions are good or bad is based on whether other people approve of what he has done. Acts are judged, at least partially, on the intention behind them rather than solely on their consequences.

Stage 4: *Legalistic, Law-and-Order Orientation.* The goodness or badness of an action is determined by the extent to which the behavior follows established rules and supports the existing social order. The person is concerned with doing his duty and respect for authority.

C. Postconventional level

Stage 5: *Social contract orientation.* The person's judgment as to whether an act is good or bad is based on whether it violates the rights of others. While a person who operates at this level will try to obey democratically agreed upon rules of conduct, he will advocate changing these rules if he sees this change as benefiting society.

Stage 6: *Universal ethical principles orientation.* The person's moral judgments are not based on a particular society's laws and rules, but rather on his own ethical principles. These principles are not concrete moral rules but broad, abstract, universal principles. Among these are the ideas of justice and equal rights for all people and the dignity of a human being as an individual.

Kohlberg believed that the pattern he identified was universal, but that not all people reach stage six. Indeed, many people never get beyond stages three or four. Note that Kohlberg, like Piaget, sees a child's moral judgments as being quite concrete and based on hard and fast societal rules. People who reach the final stage make their moral judgments on abstract universal principles. One might consider Jesus and Ghandi as examples of people who reached this stage.

Personality variables and helping

Are there people who, across time and across situations, show a strong tendency to want to help others? Are there people who are generally selfish and unwilling to help? You would probably answer "yes" to both questions. Further, you probably believe that we can identify those characteristics which distinguish an Albert Schweitzer or Martin Luther King, Jr., from a person who steals candy from crippled children. Thus, it might surprise you to learn that most social psychologists don't share your view.

Generally, they believe that personality variables do not explain helping behavior. In support of this belief, they note that personality variables usually do not predict a person's helping behavior very well (Latané & Darley, 1970). Is this an accurate assessment of the importance of personality variables in determining helping? I don't think so. There appear to be several major causes of the weak relationship.

First, most of the research on helping has been conducted in highly structured laboratory settings where individual differences in pro-social tendencies will be "washed out" by strong situational factors. Second, most studies have looked at the effect of only one personality variable on helping. Staub (1974) and Gergen, Gergen, and Meter (1972) have both argued quite strongly that this single-variable correlational technique fails to test adequately for the personality correlates of pro-social behavior. Staub and others have proposed that the multivariate approach (described in Chapter Two) would provide a more valid means to investigate the relationship between personality variables and helping.

Staub used this approach in a 1974 study. Subjects filled out a number of personality scales and three weeks later were confronted with the following situation. While they were filling out a questionnaire, they heard a person moaning in an adjoining room. Staub deliberately had his confederate keep these distress cues mild because he did not want situational influences to wipe out the effect of personality variables. He recorded the subjects' willingness to help the person in distress.

Staub found a *cluster* of personality variables that were related to the subjects' willingness to help. Specifically, he found that those people who helped (1) were less Machiavellian, (2) believed they were personally responsible for others' welfare, (3) had a greater sense of social responsibility, and (4) considered the values of helpfulness and equality more important than the people reluctant to help.

As noted in Chapter Two, Penner et al. (1976) employed a similar approach in an attempt to predict how people would respond to a lost dollar. We found that the subjects' responses could be predicted by a cluster of personality characteristics similar to those found by Staub.

Hobfoll (1977) attempted to identify those personality characteristics which distinguished people who volunteered to spend twelve weeks helping disadvantaged children from nonvolunteers. In this field study, Hobfoll found the same pattern of differences between volunteers and nonvolunteers that Staub and Penner et al. found between helpers and nonhelpers in their laboratory studies.

The important thing about these three studies is not the personality variables themselves. Rather, it is that these studies illustrate the following points. First, the consistency of the results suggests that there may, indeed, be reliable individual differences in pro-social orientations which show up in many different situations. Second, these differences are most appropriately studied by looking at a number of personality variables acting together, not by examining one personality variable at a time. Third, although situational variables are important determinants of helping behavior, to understand it fully, we must consider how personality and situational variables interact.

This final point can be illustrated by looking at the personality variable, sociopathy. *Sociopathy* is the tendency to engage consistently in anti-social behaviors (APA Diagnostic and Statistical Manual, 1952). An extreme sociopath is "unsocialized . . . incapable of significant loyalty to individuals, groups, or social values . . . grossly selfish, callous and irresponsible" (APA Diagnostic and Statistical Manual, 1968). If one considers the characteristics of sociopathy, one might also wonder if sociopathic tendencies could be related to helping. These descriptions suggest that someone who is even moderately sociopathic might be less inclined to help than someone who is far less sociopathic.

Penner et al. (1976), Brookmire (1976), and Penner, Michael, and Brookmire (1978) gave a paper and pencil measure of sociopathy (Spielberger, O'Hagen, & Kling, 1977) to college students. Then they measured the students' willingness to return a lost item of value they had found. In all three studies, it was found that subjects who returned the lost item were significantly less sociopathic than those who had kept it.

Remember the Piliavin reward/cost model of helping? It proposes that the prime determinants of helping are the person's estimates of the rewards and costs involved. Are these cost estimates due entirely to situational variables? Penner et al. (1978) found that high sociopaths saw the taking of the item as: (1) causing less harm to the owner, (2) resulting in less punishment to the taker if he was caught, and (3) less indicative of a personality defect in the taker than did the low sociopaths. In other words, subjects with sociopathic *tendencies* (remember, these were college students) estimated the costs of their

behavior as less than did subjects without these tendencies.

As we saw earlier in the chapter, another variable related to helping is a person's ability to empathize with a victim (Aronfreed, 1970; Krebs, 1970). In some recent studies, the ability of high and low sociopaths to empathize was examined. It was found that high sociopaths were significantly less upset by the sight of another person being shocked than were low sociopaths (House & Milligan, 1976; Stone, 1977). In addition, Stone found that when high sociopaths were given the chance to help the person being shocked, they were significantly less likely to do so than were low sociopaths. Evidently, their inability to empathize made them less willing to help.

I would like to make my own position on the relationship between personality variables and pro-social behavior clear. First, in many instances, helping (or not helping) is determined by situational rather than personality variables. Second, no single variable or set of variables is related to pro-social behavior across all situations. As Gergen, Gergen, and Meter (1972) have pointed out, in different situations different personality variables may apply. But at the same time, I feel that social psychologists may have prematurely discounted the importance of personality variables. If one employs a multivariate approach in cases where there are no strong situational demands on the potential helper, one will probably find that some personality variables are reliably and significantly related to pro-social actions.

Conclusion

The second half of this chapter examined how personal characteristics affect helping. Thus, the primary focus was on the origins of pro-social tendencies.

As in the review of the origins of aggressive tendencies, an explanation of pro-social tendencies based solely on genetic factors was rejected. Instead, it was proposed that the pro-social tendencies of a person result from the learning experiences which make up the socialization process. The laboratory and field research on the development of pro-social tendencies provides a strong argument for the importance of classical conditioning, operant conditioning, and observational learning in the acquisition of pro-social behavior.

The learning theory explanation of pro-social behavior in children is not, however, the only accepted explanation. Many people believe that developmental theories such as Jean Piaget's explain the acquisition of pro-social tendencies. Piaget's ideas about moral development are creative and impressive, but they are hard to test by the procedures most social psychologists use. Thus, it is difficult to make any definitive statement on the validity of his theory.

Finally, the importance of personality variables in determining pro-social behavior was considered. Although I discussed some specific personality variables, my goal was not simply to list those variables which have been found to be related to helping. It was to provide data in support of the interactionist view of social behavior (presented in Chapter Two). Recall that the interactionists argue that social behavior is the product of both personality and situational variables. These two classes of variables, in combination, provide a better understanding of pro-social behavior than a consideration of just one of them.

REVIEW QUESTIONS

(Eight out of ten is passing)

1. The viewpoint that pro-social behavior in humans can be better explained by genetic factors than by learning is held by the _____ . (p. 154)
2. Aronfreed has proposed that classical conditioning may be related to the development of pro-social behavior because it accounts for the acquisition of _____ responses. (p. 154)
3. In the classical conditioning described above, the reactions of the recipient are called the _____ stimulus. (p. 155)
4. A child watches a model who acts pro-socially and is rewarded. The child experiences the feelings associated with being rewarded. This is called _____ _____ . (p. 156)
5. A parent of a child with pro-social tendencies sees the child break a playmate's toy. The parent will use _____ _____ discipline on the child. (p. 158)
6. The finding that parents of pro-social children tend to be affectionate toward their children is in accord with the laboratory finding that children will be more influenced by _____ models than by _____ models. (p. 158)
7. Piaget's theory of moral development stresses _____ rather than _____ processes. (p. 158)
8. According to Piaget's theory, a child is incapable of true pro-social behavior until it reaches the stage of moral development called the _____ _____ . (p. 159)

9. _____ is the tendency to engage in anti-social behaviors. It may be related to a person's ability to _____ with another person in need of help. (p. 162)
10. It is probably most reasonable to consider helping as the product of both _____ and _____ variables. (p. 162)

ANSWERS

10. personality, situational
6. warm, cold   7. maturational, learning   8. autonomous morality   9. sociopathy, empathize
1. sociobiologists   2. empathic   3. conditioned   4. vicarious reinforcement   5. victim centered

SUGGESTED READINGS

These three textbooks all provide a comprehensive examination of the theory and research on pro-social behavior.

Textbooks

Pro-social Behavior, by Daniel Bar-Tal. This is an extremely well written, comprehensive review of the theory and research on pro-social behavior. I highly recommend it.

The Unresponsive Bystander: Why Doesn't He Help, by Bibb Latané and John Darley. These two researchers were among the first to systematically study the factors which affect bystander intervention. The book is written in an informal and lively manner.

Altruism and Helping Behavior, edited by Jacqueline Macaulay and Leonard Berkowitz. This book contains chapters written by leading researchers in the area of pro-social behavior. Some of the chapters are quite good; others are almost impossible to understand.

Popular literature

As was observed in the first few pages of this chapter, we humans act both compassionately and cruelly. These books illustrate this fact quite well.

Either *A Night of Watching,* by Elliott Arnold, or *Voyage of the Damned,* by Gordon Thomas and Max Morgan Witts. Both of these books are exciting factual accounts of incidents which took place during World War II. They describe individual and collective acts of helping as well as "man's inhumanity to man."

Freedom at Midnight, by Larry Collins and Dominique La Pierre. These very talented authors describe the events surrounding India's independence from Great Britain. You will find descriptions of Ghandi, but you will also read about some of the most incredible acts of brutality ever to have taken place.

Anthem, by Ayn Rand. I find Ms. Rand's philosophy offensive. But if you want an exposure to an argument for the virtues of *selfishness,* try this book.

Tampa Tribune

No topic is more central to social psychology than attitudes. In fact, some people view interest in attitudes as the beginning of social psychology as we know it today. This chapter introduces contemporary theory and research on attitudes, beginning with what attitudes are and how they are acquired. Then the relationship between attitudes and behavior will be discussed. The second half of the chapter will examine some techniques to change attitudes and the relationship between attitudes and behavior change.

In 1975, a doctor on the staff of a large Boston hospital performed an abortion on a woman in the sixth month of pregnancy. The woman had requested the abortion and the U.S. Supreme Court in 1973 had declared that abortions under these conditions were legal. Thus, the doctor treated the operation as a routine affair. However, a few months later, the state of Massachusetts charged him with manslaughter. The basis of the state's case was that the fetus could have survived outside its mother's womb. The doctor's defense was that he was acting in accordance with the law. Since the facts in the case were never in dispute, the jury's decision rested solely on their attitudes toward abortion. The doctor was found guilty. (The judge called the verdict a travesty of justice, and it was overturned by a higher court.)

A social psychologist can ask three questions about the jury's decision. First, what variables produced their attitudes toward abortion before the trial began (the acquisition of attitudes)? Second, how did the arguments of the prosecution and defense lawyers affect the jurors' attitudes (how are attitudes changed)? Finally, what was the relationship between the jurors' attitudes and their voting for a manslaughter conviction (the relationship between attitudes and behavior)? To answer any of these questions, we must first know what an attitude is.

WHAT IS AN ATTITUDE?

An *attitude* is a person's tendency to respond favorably or unfavorably to the objects and situations she encounters (Allport, 1935; Fishbein & Ajzen, 1975; Rokeach, 1968). Another way of putting this is to view an attitude as a hypothetical construct—an entity that doesn't physically exist—which is believed to precede and cause a person's behavior when she encounters a particular object or is in a certain situation.

For example, consider singer Anita Bryant's campaign against equal rights for homosexuals. A social psychologist would explain Ms. Bryant's behavior by proposing that her negative attitude toward homosexuality caused her to act as she did. Further, her attitude was not a mass of disconnected ideas and beliefs; it had a definite structure. To fully understand what attitudes are, we must examine their structure in some detail.

The structure of attitudes

Social psychologists believe that an attitude has three interrelated components (Fishbein & Ajzen, 1975; Rokeach, 1968). Each of these components can be examined by presenting the views of a man who holds the same attitudes toward homosexuality as Anita Bryant. He writes a syndicated column in which he answers questions about moral issues of the day. A number of the questions deal with the rights of homosexuals and whether or not homosexuality should be tolerated. I must emphasize that while I disagree with the columnist's views, my intent is not to hold him up to ridicule; it is simply to present the components of an attitude.

The first part of an attitude is the *affective* component. It concerns how much a person likes or dislikes the object of the attitude. In answering a question about a company that refuses to hire known homosexuals, the columnist writes: "It [the company] recognizes, praise be, that the normal person reacts towards faggots somewhat as he does towards maggots" (Lester, 1975, p. 102). His reaction to homosexuality is obviously one of violent dislike.

Next, there is the *cognitive* component, which consists of beliefs about the attitude object. A belief, according to Rokeach (1968), is any statement that can be preceded by the phrase "I believe that." A person's beliefs can be statements of objective fact—for example, "Homosexuality involves sexual relations between members of the same sex." Or they can be statements which are somewhat more debatable, such as, "Homosexuality is a grave moral evil" (Lester, 1975, p. 95). More generally, a belief is a statement of the attributes the person believes the attitude object possesses.

One of the more important beliefs in the cognitive component is the belief about the attitude object's relationship to some important goal. Does the attitude object help or hinder the attainment of that goal? Rosenberg (1956) labeled a person's belief about this relationship the *perceived instrumentality* of the attitude object. What Rosenberg meant was: does a person perceive the attitude object as instrumental (causal or related) to the attainment of some important goal? For example, the columnist says that homosexuality "eats away at the strength of a nation" (Lester, p. 45). Thus, for him, the perceived instrumentality of homosexuality is that it will cause the decline or destruction of a country.

Finally, there is the *behavioral* component of an attitude.[1] This is a person's feelings about how she and others should act toward the attitude object and/or her actual behavior toward the object. The behavioral component is the component that links the attitude to behavior. For example, the columnist believes that homosexuality "ought to be suppressed" and that "the community should want to prevent as far as possible her citizens from stooping to acts of homosexuality" (Lester, p. 45). Note that he is now stating his beliefs

---

[1]Some social psychologists (e.g., Rosenberg, 1965a) believe that attitudes contain only two components: affect and cognition.

about what *action* should be taken toward the attitude object.

These three components, although presented separately, are obviously interconnected. In real life, the affective component will have elements of the cognitive component, and the behavioral component will have aspects of the affective component. Also, these three components will normally agree with each other (Rokeach, 1968; Rosenberg, 1956). That is, if someone likes an attitude object (affective component), she believes that it will lead to something good (cognitive component) and will be inclined to act positively toward it (behavioral component). At this point, this observation is fairly obvious. But the idea that attitudes are organized in a consistent or balanced manner will become crucial when theories of attitude change are discussed later on.

HOW ARE ATTITUDES ACQUIRED?

It is generally agreed that attitudes are learned. Three processes seem to be involved in this learning.

Classical conditioning

Some social psychologists believe that a person's attitude toward an object is, in part, the connotative meaning she attaches to it (Chein, 1948; Doob, 1947; Osgood, 1953; Staats, 1975). The *connotative meaning* of a word is what the word implies—its emotional coloring. This is different from the word's *denotative meaning*—its formal or dictionary definition. For example, the word "boy" would be formally defined as a young male. But if you think this is all the word means to a black person, try calling a black defensive end for the Oakland Raiders "boy." Your hospital stay will be

Wide World Photos

ample evidence of its connotative meaning to him. How do words and objects acquire connotative meanings?

If you repeatedly give someone a neutral word and immediately follow it with a word (or any stimulus) which produces a reaction from her, this will eventually cause her to react to the previously neutral word (Staats & Staats, 1958). This process is called *classical conditioning*. It is almost identical to the procedure Pavlov used to get his dogs to salivate when they heard a tuning fork (cf. Chapter Five).

A word or object can often acquire a connotative meaning simply by being followed by positive or negative words. To illustrate, consider this study by Staats and Staats (1958). Subjects looked at the names of various nationalities, such as Dutch, French, Italian, and Swedish. Every time they saw the word "Dutch," an experimenter said words with positive meanings (e.g., "happy," "gift"). When the subjects saw the word "Swedish," they heard words with negative meanings (e.g., "bitter," "ugly," "failure"). After a number of these pairings, the subjects were asked to evaluate the various nationalities. They evaluated the word "Dutch" much more positively than the word "Swedish." The nationalities had acquired connotative meanings via classical conditioning.

Comedian Gabriel Kaplan shows how children acquire attitudes toward people and things in their environment via classical conditioning. Kaplan's parents were worried about blacks moving into their building in Brooklyn. At dinner, they constantly talked about the "schwartzes" (a negative term in the Yiddish language for black people) moving in and how bad this would be. As a child, Kaplan shared their concern. There was one small problem, however: he had no idea what a "schwartze" was. He did know that whatever it was, it was bad, since his parents always paired it with words with negative connotations. One day while playing in the yard, Kaplan saw a black child whose family had just moved in. Kaplan approached him and told him that his (the black child's) parents had picked a bad place to live. "Why?" asked the black child. "Because," Kaplan replied, "schwartzes are moving in."

Once a person has started to react to a particular word or attitude object, another important process occurs. She begins to react in a similar way to words or objects that are comparable to the original term. For example, Zanna, Kiesler and Pilkonis (1970) used classical conditioning to make people dislike the word "dark." They found that a person who disliked "dark" also disliked the word "black." This process is called *stimulus generalization*. It explains why a person who is negative toward blacks may have a generalized dislike of all dark-skinned minority groups.

Operant conditioning

In addition to classical conditioning, people learn attitudes by operant conditioning. In classical conditioning, a neutral stimulus is paired with some stimulus which brings an automatic response from the learner. This differs from operant conditioning, in which the person *emits* a behavior in the absence of any obvious stimulus. This behavior "just happens." If it is reinforced, this increases the chance that it will occur again. If a behavior becomes more frequent as the result of reinforcement, operant conditioning has probably occurred.

Imagine that you and a four-year-old are talking. She has seen a television show which portrayed the police positively, and she says, "The police are our friends." She has just emitted a behavior. You smile and say, "That's right, the police are our friends." Your response has two effects. First, it rewards the child. Second, it increases the probability that she will make similar statements in the future. If other people react to her views on the police in the same way you have, she will probably grow up with positive attitudes toward them. The same process could have been used to make the child a "cop hater." Suppose she made a positive comment about the police and you had replied, "No, cops are pigs who beat up innocent people." If other people around her make similar statements, she is likely to develop negative attitudes toward the police. Thus, the rewards and punishments given to children when they express attitudes can have a strong impact on the attitudes they develop.

Observational learning

In reviewing how aggressive and pro-social tendencies are learned, the role of models was stressed. Recall that a model is someone a child observes and learns from. There has been relatively little research on how people acquire attitudes through observing models. But it seems reasonable that children acquire many of their attitudes via this process. A child who sees her parents smile and talk to a neighborhood police officer should like the police more than one who sees her parents sneer. Note, however, that not all models have the same impact on the observer's attitudes. For example, a model who is powerful and warm will have a greater impact than one who is weak and cold (Bryan, 1975).

In the early years of life, a person's attitudes are probably influenced primarily by the words and actions of her parents. Thus, it is not surprising that most people hold attitudes similar to their parents' (McGinnies, 1970). But as people grow up, their peers begin to influence them.

Peers provide the person with a *reference group*. This is a group of people she: (1) identifies with, (2) compares her attitudes to, and (3) uses as a means to evaluate her attitudes. Theodore Newcomb's classic Bennington College study (1943) showed how a reference group can influence one's attitudes. Newcomb measured the change in political attitudes among women at Bennington from their first term to their graduation. In their first year, most of these students held the same conservative political attitudes as did their parents. However, over the next three years, they gradually became more like their classmates—that is, more liberal. Further, when Newcomb and his colleagues (Newcomb, Koenig, Flacks, & Warwick, 1967) tested these women some twenty-five years later, they found that these liberal attitudes had persisted. For example, 60 percent of the women who had become more liberal in the 1930's voted for John Kennedy over Richard Nixon in the 1960 presidential election. This was true of only 30 percent of a control group who were similar to them in age and socioeconomic class.

A word of warning: although the basic principles of attitude acquisition are relatively simple, the actual process is incredibly complex. If you look at an adult's attitudes, it is often difficult, if not impossible, to trace them back to specific earlier events. Further-more, attitudes are not static. They may change rather dramatically throughout her life. It remains for future research to specify the relative importance of all these factors and determine how each is related to the acquisition and maintenance of attitudes.

THE RELATIONSHIP BETWEEN ATTITUDES AND BEHAVIOR

Why are social psychologists so interested in attitudes? The answer would appear to be obvious. Attitudes precede and cause behavior. But, obvious as this answer is, it would be hard to support it with actual evidence. Alan Wicker surveyed more than forty studies on the relationship between attitudes and behavior. The attitudes examined ranged from how people feel about their jobs to how mothers feel about breast feeding. Astoundingly, less than 10 percent of the difference in how people actually behave could be attributed to differences in their attitudes! In other words, the research evidence suggests that attitudes are at best "only slightly related to overt behaviors. . . ." (Wicker, 1969, p. 65).

Joseph Ferrandino

Three attitude scales

The Thurstone Scale

This attitude scale is named after its origina-tor, Louis Thurstone. The first step in using it is to write a large number of statements which express different points of view toward some attitude object or issue. Then "judges" are recruited to rate these statements. They are not rated in terms of how the judges personally feel about the issue. They are rated in terms of how favorable or unfavorable a sentiment they express toward the issue. The average rating given a statement is called its *scale value*. After the scale values for all statements have been determined, the researcher selects those statements which clearly express different points of view on the issue. These statements make up the actual attitude scale.

The person taking the scale is instructed to check only those statements she agrees with. Her attitude toward the issue is defined as the median or average scale value of the state-ments she has checked (Thurstone, 1928; Thurstone & Chave, 1929).

Usually there are ten to fifteen statements in a Thurstone Scale. I have devised a five-statement scale (with made up scale values) as a illustration. It deals with attitudes toward Laetrile, a controversial drug which some people believe cures cancer.

Scale value	*Statement*
10.5 _____	1. Laetrile can cure cancer.
1.5 _____	2. Laetrile is a totally worthless drug.
5.0 _____	3. More testing is needed on Laetrile before its value can be determined.
9.5 _____	4. Laetrile may cure some forms of cancer.
2.5 _____	5. Chemotherapy is a much better form of cancer treatment than Laetrile.

Someone who checked statements 1 and 4 (average scale value = 10.0) would be judged as having a positive attitude toward Laetrile. Someone who checked statements 2 and 5 (average scale value = 2.0) would be judged as having a negative attitude toward Laetrile.

The method of summated ratings

This technique, usually called a *Likert Scale,* is much simpler to use than the Thurstone Scale. The researcher writes a series of simple declarative statements on some attitude object or issue. These are presented in a question-naire, and people indicate whether they strongly agree, agree, disagree, or strongly disagree with each statement. Each of these responses is given a numerical value. A per-son's attitude toward the issue is defined as the sum of these numerical values (Likert, 1932).

Likert Scales usually contain twenty to twenty-five statements, but here is a three-statement scale on Laetrile.

1. Laetrile will cure cancer.

Strongly agree	(4)
Agree	(3)
Disagree	(2)
Strongly disagree	(1)

2. Laetrile is the wonder drug cancer victims have been waiting for.

Strongly agree	(4)
Agree	(3)
Disagree	(2)
Strongly disagree	(1)

3. Laetrile should be legalized.

Strongly agree	(4)
Agree	(3)
Disagree	(2)
Strongly disagree	(1)

A person who strongly agreed with all three statements would have a total score of 12. This would indicate a positive attitude toward Laetrile. A person who strongly disagreed with all three statements would have a total score of 3. This would indicate a negative attitude toward Laetrile.

The semantic differential

This final technique is interested in determining the connotative meaning of some attitude object or issue for a person. That is, it attempts to find out if a person sees some object as: (1) good or bad (the evaluative component), (2) active or passive (the activity component), and (3) strong or weak (the potency component) (Osgood, Suci, & Tannenbaum, 1957). The object is presented at the top of the page, and the person filling out the Semantic Differential rates it on a number of bipolar adjectives. These adjectives represent the evaluative, ac-

tivity, and potency components of the object's connotative meaning.

Here is how a Semantic Differential on the connotative meaning of Laetrile might look.

Laetrile

1. Good   – – – – – – – Bad
2. Passive   – – – – – – – Passive
3. Worthless – – – – – – – Valuable
4. Strong   – – – – – – – Weak
5. Harmful   – – – – – – – Helpful

A person filling out the Semantic Differential would indicate whether she thought Laetrile was entirely good, entirely bad, or somewhere in between by marking one of the seven dashes between these pairs of adjectives. Then she would do the same with the other four pairs. Her attitude toward Laetrile would be defined as its connotative meaning, as measured by the Semantic Differential.

Why is it so hard to find a strong relationship between attitudes and behavior? I don't think it is because attitudes are only slightly related to behavior. I believe it is because there are several practical and theoretical roadblocks to showing the true relationship. The next few pages will present some of these problems and describe how social psychologists have attempted to deal with them.

Problems in attitude measurement

As noted when defining *attitude,* it is a hypothetical construct. A person's attitude toward, say, the neutron bomb does not physically exist within her. Rather, it is a hypothetical entity which we believe causes her to act in a certain way. Since attitudes do not physically exist, we must infer them from her actions and responses. One way to do this is to give

her an attitude scale and estimate her attitudes based on her answers. The box "Three Attitude Scales" presents three of the scales most frequently used. While these paper and pencil attitude scales will often produce reliable and valid estimates of a person's attitudes, they are all subject to a common problem—*reactivity.*

Reactivity

Reactivity occurs when the means you use to measure something cause a change in the thing you are measuring. For example, if you attempted to determine the boiling point of mercury by using a thermometer that had been kept in a refrigerator, you would find that the temperature of the thermometer itself affected the measurement. Reactivity in this situation can be solved fairly easily by taking into account how much the thermometer's temperature affected that of the mercury. However, when attitudes are being measured, reactivity is often hard to spot and to eliminate. In certain instances, responses on an attitude scale or questionnaire are not accurate. They are biased or distorted by the questionnaire itself. Consider this extreme example of reactivity. It is based on an attempt by a former mayor of Cleveland, Ohio, to determine Clevelanders' attitudes toward pornography.

You awake one morning and find that the person who picks up your garbage has left you a questionnaire on pornography. Along with the questionnaire is a covering letter from the mayor. He wants you to fill out the questionnaire so that it reflects your true attitudes toward pornography. The mayor needs this information so that he "can have the ammunition to declare war on the degenerates who peddle this filth." With this kind of letter, it is quite unlikely that your responses will really reflect your attitudes toward pornography.

Although social psychologists use far better judgment than the mayor of Cleveland when they construct attitude scales, the same basic problem exists.[2] The topic of the questionnaire or the content of the questions themselves can cause people to slant their response. This, in turn, reduces the strength of the relationship between their attitudes (as measured by an attitude scale) and their actual behavior.

Social psychologists have attempted to solve the problem of reactivity by using nonreactive or unobtrusive measures of attitudes. These are techniques which measure attitudes in a way that does not affect the attitudes themselves (Webb, Campbell, Schwartz, & Sechrest, 1966). This has been done in two ways. The first is to select some aspect of a person's

behavior which reflects her true attitudes but which she is not aware of. In recent years, social psychologists have turned to nonverbal behavior—so called body language—as one means of doing this (Bateson, 1965; cited by Ekman).

Some of the nonverbal behaviors used to measure attitudes are: eye contact (looking at the eyes or facial region of another person), posture during a conversation, and the physical distance between two people in conversation (cf. Argyle & Dean, 1965; Hall, 1963; Mehrabian, 1969). To show the usefulness of nonverbal behavior as a nonreactive measure of attitudes, consider something that happened when I was doing my dissertation research (Penner, 1971).

I was interested in the relationship between white college students' attitudes toward civil rights for blacks and how they reacted to an individual black person they met. Therefore, I placed white subjects in a room with a black confederate and observed the subjects' eye contact, posture, and how far they sat from the confederate during a ten-minute conversation. I conducted a number of training sessions for the black confederates to show them how I wanted them to act during the actual experiment. During one of these sessions, a white student told the confederate that he planned to become a policeman when he graduated from college. Despite his instructions to respond neutrally, the black confederate told him that he was a racist, a fool, etc. During the ten-minute session, eye contact, posture, and distance from the confederate were recorded. Rather than giving you sterile statistics, let me try to describe how the student was sitting at the end of the session. He had turned in his chair so that his side faced the confederate; his head was down, and his arms and legs were tightly crossed. He looked like a nervous pretzel. When I entered the room to stop the session, he looked at me the way the settlers besieged by

[2]They also probably have better judgment in general. During an industrial safety demonstration a few years ago, this man managed to set his hair on fire.

Indians looked at the cavalry in the old cowboy movies.

After I separated the two, I had the student fill out a questionnaire on his reactions to the confederate. In response to the question "How much did you like your partner?" he answered, "Very much." Why? Probably because he did not want to appear to be anti-black. On a college campus in the late 1960's, it was not socially desirable to indicate that you disliked blacks. Thus, despite an extremely unpleasant ten minutes, the student evaluated the black confederate very favorably. The student's nonverbal behavior, which he was much less conscious of, suggested a different (and negative) reaction.

The other way to measure attitudes nonreactively is to not let the subjects know that they are being observed: Several techniques can be used in this approach; all involve the observation of behavior that should be related to some attitude. Here are three examples.

Milgram (1969) employed the "lost-letter technique" to measure political attitudes. Letters addressed to the offices of Democratic or Republican candidates were dropped on the streets of a large Northeastern city. Milgram recorded the percentage of letters which were found and mailed to each candidate's office. He believed that these percentages would provide a measure of people's attitudes toward the two candidates.

Wrightsman (1969) investigated the attitudes of supporters of Governor George Wallace toward one aspect of "law and order." In the area where Wrightsman conducted his study, all car owners were required by law to display a sticker which indicated that they had paid a local vehicle tax. Wrightsman recorded the percentage of cars which bore "Wallace for President" bumper stickers on them and also displayed the tax sticker. He compared this to the percentage of cars belonging to supporters of other candidates which also displayed the sticker.

Finally, Gaertner (1973) used the "wrong number technique" to test racial attitudes. White subjects received supposedly incorrectly dialed phone calls from black and white confederates who claimed they were stranded on a highway. After "learning" that the number he had called was not a garage, the confederate said that he had no more change and asked the subject to call the garage for him. As his measure of attitudes toward blacks and whites, Gaertner compared the number of subjects who called the garage for the white and black confederates.

This approach to measuring attitudes has a possible weakness. In the three studies presented above, the researchers assumed that the behavior they measured was due to a specific attitude or set of attitudes. But in this technique, there is no way to determine if this assumption is correct. That is, since these researchers never asked their subjects why they acted as they did, they made a potentially incorrect inferential leap from the behavior they had observed to the attitude which supposedly caused it.

The use of nonreactive techniques to measure attitudes will often strengthen the relationship between attitudes and behavior. But it is not a cure-all for the problem. Let's look at some other explanations of and solutions to the weak relationship.

The specificity of behavior

Every four years, Americans elect a President. A ritual that accompanies the election campaign is the public opinion poll. Over the past eight elections, these polls have been amazingly accurate. The winner and his margin of victory have been predicted within a few percentage points. Why is it that these polls make such a good prediction of behavior (voting) on the basis of attitudes while social psychologists have done so poorly with other behaviors?

I believe that at least a partial answer lies in the difference between the problems social psychologists study and those that interest the pollers. People such as George Gallup (of the Gallup Poll) are interested in predicting a *specific* behavior at a specific time. Thus, they measure the behavioral component of a particular attitude. Social psychologists are usually interested in the broader theoretical question of the relationship between attitudes and behavior. Therefore, they typically measure all three components of an attitude in a much more general way. This presents a more difficult task when one attempts to predict a specific behavior. There are two possible solutions to this problem.

Fishbein and Ajzen (1975) present the first. They argue that if there is a relationship between attitudes and behavior, it will be shown across situations. They propose that behaviors supposedly related to an attitude should be measured via a *multiple act criterion*. This involves measuring (1) the same behavior across time, (2) different, but related, behaviors at the same point in time, and (3) the combination of (1) and (2). A researcher who looks at only one behavior at one point in time may obtain an attitude-behavior relationship that is out of context and is an inaccurate estimate of the true relationship between the attitude and the behavior.

For example, a researcher is interested in whether born-again Christians show Christian attitudes in their behavior. According to Fishbein and Ajzen, it would not be adequate or appropriate simply to measure whether or not these people attend church one Sunday. Rather, the researcher should look at: (1) the same behavior across time (e.g., church attendance over the course of a year) and/or (2) the frequency of other behaviors which should be related to their religious attitudes (e.g., attending Bible class, giving "witness" to their faith, tithing part of their salary to the church). It is these behaviors which will provide a valid picture of the relationship between these people's attitudes and their behavior.

The second solution is to use a means of attitude measurement closer to that used by public opinion pollers—that is, to measure specific attitudes. A number of researchers (e.g., Cook & Sellitz, 1964; Crespi, 1971; Fishbein & Ajzen, 1975; Weigel, Vernon, & Tognaci, 1974) have argued that the low correlation between attitudes and behavior may be partly because in many studies, the attitude measured was general but the behavior predicted was specific. To demonstrate this, Weigel et al. conducted a field study of attitudes toward environmental problems. Residents of a medium-sized Midwestern town were given a questionnaire with three types of attitude questions: (1) those dealing with the Sierra Club, an organization concerned with ecology, (2) those dealing with the kinds of specific ecological issues that might interest the Sierra Club, and (3) those dealing with general environmental concerns. Scores on these three types of attitudes were then correlated with the subjects' willingness to join/work for the Sierra Club about five months later. There was no relationship between people's attitudes on general environmental issues and their willingness to work for the Sierra Club. The relationship between attitudes toward specific issues and behavior toward the club was not much stronger than the relationship which has caused social psychologists so much concern. But specific attitudes toward the Sierra Club predicted people's willingness to join it quite well. In fact, the size of the correlation was over twice that which social psychologists usually find.

Similarly, Fishbein (1966) found that while general attitudes toward premarital sex did not predict very well whether female college students would engage in sexual intercourse, their specific intention to engage in this activity did.

The specificity argument provides only a partial explanation of the weak relationship between attitudes and behavior. Even when specific attitudes are measured, they will often not correlate with actual behavior very well (Kelman, 1974; Wicker & Pomazal, 1971). Thus, we must turn to some other reasons for this troublesome finding.

Behavior does not exist in a vacuum. Author Merle Miller (1971) once described a "kike" as a "Jewish gentleman who has just left the room." Although intended as a put-down of racial and ethnic prejudice, Miller's definition provides an important explanation of why even specific attitudes often do not correlate very well with behavior. Miller's definition implies that the situation a person is in will have a dramatic effect on whether her attitude will be manifested in behavior. Even though the person described by Miller dislikes Jews, this behavior is not displayed until the Jew leaves the room. Why?

Triandis (1971) has pointed out that a person's behavior toward some attitude object is due to more than her attitudes. Social norms, expectations about the behavior's consequences (will it be rewarded or punished?), and personal habits will all affect her actions. Triandis's proposal seems quite reasonable. The bigot in Miller's example might not act in accord with her attitudes in front of the Jew because (1) it is not proper to insult someone to his face (social norms), and/or (2) he might strike her (consequences of the behavior), and/or (3) prejudiced though she may be, the bigot is not in the habit of insulting people.

More generally, Rokeach (1968) and Rokeach and Kliejunas (1972) have argued that to predict behavior, one must consider not only a person's attitude toward some object but also the situation in which the object is confronted. People not only have attitudes toward objects, but attitudes toward situations as well. A person's behavior in a given situation, Rokeach proposed, is determined by her attitude toward the object, her attitude toward the situation itself, and her feelings about how important these two attitudes are.

To test this proposal, Rokeach and Kliejunas attempted to predict the number of times students had cut a psychology class using: (1) just the students' attitudes toward the instructor (attitudes toward the object), (2) just the students' attitudes toward attending class (attitudes toward the situation), or (3) a value derived by measuring both these attitudes and their relative importance to the students. They found that measuring both attitudes and their importance provided by far the best predictors of actual class cuts. This study shows that attitudes do not exist in a vacuum. Even when specific attitudes are being measured, the person's attitude toward the situation in which she confronts the object should probably be measured as well.[3]

There is, however, another point of view on predicting behavior from attitudes. It is presented by Milton Rokeach in his theory of values (1968, 1973). Even though measuring a person's values will tell you something about her *general* orientation toward people and things, Rokeach believes that values may be a better predictor of behavior than attitudes. To understand the rationale behind this radical proposal, we must look at Rokeach's value theory.

Values and behavior

According to Rokeach (1973), a *value* is a person's enduring belief about how she should behave and the goals she should strive for. The accompanying box presents Rokeach's Value Survey, which measures the importance of a person's values.

---

[3]Readers interested in additional reasons why attitudes do not correlate very well with behavior should go back to the discussion of personality variables and social behavior in Chapter Two. Many of the arguments presented there are applicable to attitudes and behavior.

"East is east, west is west, and shall the twain ever meet?"

About three months before the North Vietnamese and National Liberation Front's victory in Vietnam, Tran Anh and I (Penner & Anh, 1977) gave a translated version of Rokeach's Value Survey to a randomly selected group of Vietnamese living about 250 miles north of Saigon. The values called *terminal values* are concerned with beliefs about end states of existence—ultimate goals in life. The Vietnamese ranked them in order of importance to themselves. Then they ranked the values called *instrumental values*. They concern beliefs about how a person should behave.[4] The numbers which follow each value represent the relative importance of that value to the people surveyed. Look at the rankings and think about how you would rank these values.

Terminal values

A comfortable life	5
An exciting life	17
A sense of accomplishment	12
A world at peace	1
A world of beauty	18
Equality	8

[4]In the actual value survey, each value is accompanied by a phrase which clearly defines it.

The Value Survey is copyrighted by Milton Rokeach (1967). Copies of the actual survey (Form D) can be obtained from Halgren Tests, 873 Persimmon Circle, Sunnyvale, California 94087.

Family security	2
Freedom	7
Happiness	4
Inner harmony	13
Mature love	15
National security	3
Pleasure	16
Salvation	11
Self-respect	9
Social recognition	14
True friendship	10
Wisdom	6

Instrumental values

Ambitious	17
Broad-minded	15
Capable	7
Cheerful	13
Clean	6
Courageous	5
Forgiving	3
Helpful	10
Honest	1
Imaginative	18
Independent	4
Intellectual	12
Logical	16
Loving	11
Obedient	2
Polite	9
Responsible	8
Self-controlled	14

Now, why does Rokeach propose using values rather than attitudes? First, he believed that a person's values will be less affected by specific objects and situations than will her attitudes. Second, values are more central to her personality makeup. Thus, the attitudes she holds, and the behavior she engages in, are determined by her values. Finally, people have many more attitudes than values—in fact (according to Rokeach), as many attitudes as the number of direct or indirect encounters she has had with specific objects and situations. But values are general standards about one's goals or how one should behave. These general standards are fewer in number than attitudes. If these proposals are valid, values should be as good as attitudes in predicting behavior, if not better. What data are there to support this?

The importance a person places on the value of equality has been found to be related to joining a black civil rights organization and taking part in a civil rights demonstration. Equality is also correlated with how much a white person likes an individual black person she meets (Penner, 1971; Rokeach, 1973).

During the Vietnam war, the Value Survey was given to people who both opposed and supported the war. Parrott and Bloom (1971) found that people who joined anti-war marches considered "a world at peace" very important and "national security" relatively unimportant. Members of the John Birch Society (a conservative group that favored escalation of the war) had almost exactly the opposite reaction.

These data are impressive because they show a strong relationship between general values and specific behaviors. This suggests that values may indeed provide a good alternative to the prediction of behavior. Note, however, that these studies do *not* show that values cause behavior. To show that they do, a researcher would have to prove that changes in values result in changes in behavior. This aspect of Rokeach's theory of values will be covered later in this chapter.

The above comment about values also applies to attitudes. The fact that something is strongly correlated with something else does not mean it causes it. Thus far, social psychologists have assumed that attitudes cause behavior. However, some believe that attitudes are not the cause of behavior but rather the result of it.

Does behavior cause attitudes?

The strongest believer that behavior causes attitudes is Daryl Bem (1967, 1972). His belief is contained in his self-perception theory.

Self-perception theory

Bem has attempted to apply B. F. Skinner's analysis of the relationship between thinking and behavior to the relationship between attitudes and behavior. As you may recall, Skinner believed that it is more appropriate to explain a person's behavior in terms of external stimuli than internal stimuli (e.g., thinking). Her thoughts are not the cause of her behavior. Similarly, Bem believed that, in most cases, attitudes (internal stimuli) do not cause people to act in a certain way. Rather, their behavior is due to external stimuli. Attitudes are *after-the-fact inferences* people make about the causes of their behavior. To illustrate, Bem gives the following example. If you ask him if he likes brown bread (i.e., his attitude toward brown bread), he will reply, "I suppose so, I'm always eating it." In other words, Bem has inferred his attitude from his behavior.

Note what Bem has proposed. We infer our attitudes basically by the same process observers use in making attributions about an actor's behavior. In other words, this inference is merely a special case of the general attribution process discussed in Chapter Three. In this special case, the observer and the actor are the same. Basic to Bem's position is the assumption that our attitudes are affected by external cues in our environment.

Is this a valid assumption? The answer is, it depends on the circumstances. People do not automatically infer their attitudes from their behavior. For example, you find yourself running down the street at breakneck speed Monday morning at 7:00. Do you automatically conclude, "I must love jogging"? If you are racing to catch a bus that will take you to your 8 o'clock class, you probably will not. In other words, one limit to Bem's theory is that it will apply only when there is some ambiguity about why a person is acting a certain way. To illustrate this, Snyder and Ebbesen

(1972) asked college students to write essays in favor of their having no control over the courses they took. Half the students were told that while writing the essay would help the experimenter, they had the option of not writing it. The other half were told that they had no choice. After the essays were written, attitudes of both groups toward this topic were measured. Significant attitude change was found in the choice group, but none in the forced group. The reason seems to be that the forced group had an explanation for its behavior and thus did not rely on its behavior to infer its attitude.

A second limitation concerns the importance of the attitude, involved. The more important an attitude is, the less likely we are to infer it automatically from our behavior. For example, Valins (1966) found that he could influence men's ratings of how attractive a woman was by giving them falsified feedback about changes in their heartbeat when they saw her. But Taylor (1975) showed that people who believed their rating would determine whom they dated were not influenced by such external cues about their attitudes toward the person.

The difference in these findings makes sense. Consider United Nations Ambassador Andrew Young, a man with a long history of involvement in the black civil rights movement. Imagine that President Jimmy Carter told him to give two speeches at the U.N. The first praised the glorious People's Republic of Outer Fredonia; the second praised the white supremacist government of South Africa. Since Ambassador Young knows little about Fredonia except that its government doesn't persecute blacks, he is considerably more likely to infer his own attitudes from this speech than from the speech on South Africa.

Perhaps a more important qualification of Bem's position has been provided by Kelman (1974). Kelman argued that even if Bem is correct, this does not mean that attitudes are useless in predicting behavior. If a person infers her attitudes from her behavior, this explains only one of the ways in which attitudes are acquired. It does not mean that once acquired, an attitude will have no effect on subsequent behavior.

Kelman used Bem's favorite example from self-perception theory to make his point. Recall that Bem says that if a person is asked if she likes brown bread, she might reply, "I suppose so. I'm always eating it." Bem's point was that the person inferred her attitude from her behavior. Kelman pointed out that this inferred attitude will affect her subsequent behavior. She will be likely to buy brown bread, serve it to her friends, and do whatever else a person who likes brown bread does. Thus, Kelman argued that people may infer some of their attitudes from their behavior, but this does not reduce the importance of the concept, attitude. Attitudes can determine subsequent behavior, just as behavior can determine attitudes.

Conclusion

The first half of this chapter dealt with three interrelated issues concerning attitudes and their relationship to behavior. Attitude was defined and its structure explained. An attitude is a hypothetical construct which influences a person's behavior when she confronts objects and situations related to that attitude. An attitude consists of three parts: (1) the affective component (how much a person likes or dislikes the attitude object), (2) the cognitive component (what a person believes about the attitude object), and (3) the behavioral component (how the person acts toward the attitude object).

Although attitudes seem to be acquired primarily by learning, other processes may also be involved. For example the chapter on ethnic prejudice will review the research on the authoritarian personality. This viewpoint argues that biased attitudes may be partially the result of one's personality characteristics. Also, consistency theory (presented in the second half of this chapter) provides some reasonable arguments as to how attitudes are acquired.

Do attitudes cause behavior? This question has two interrelated parts. First, how well do attitudes correlate with behavior? I believe that when attitudes are appropriately mea-sured, the relationship will be quite strong. Second, do attitudes cause behavior, or does behavior cause attitudes? In my opinion, we can't answer this question in an either-or fashion. In some instances, our attitudes may, in fact, be due to our behavior. But in other cases, these attitudes (no matter how acquired) will help cause our behavior. Either way, attitudes are an important determinant of social behavior.

REVIEW QUESTIONS

(Twelve out of fifteen is passing)

1. In a commercial for a popular mouthwash, an actor says, "I hate its taste, but it cures my bad breath." The first part of the sentence represents the _____ component of his attitude, the second the _____ component. (p. 167)
2. A person's belief about whether some attitude object will facilitate or hinder the attain-ment of some important goal is called the _____ _____ of that attitude object. (p. 168)
3. Every time Johnny hears about Polish-Americans, his mother says they are dumb. Johnny comes to dislike Poles because they are stupid. This is an example of attitude acquisition via _____ conditioning. (p. 169)
4. Every time Betty says she dislikes socialized medicine, her cousin, the doctor, tells her that she is very smart. This is an example of attitude acquisition via _____ conditioning. (p. 170)
5. When Mary starts college, she is a devout churchgoer, like her parents. But as she pro-ceeds through college, she stops attending church and adopts her classmates' atheistic views. This illustrates the power of _____ _____ in the acquisition of attitudes. (p. 171)
6. In a Thurstone Scale, the judge's rating of how favorable or unfavorable a statement is toward some attitude object is called the statement's _____ _____ . (p. 172)
7. In a Likert Scale, a respondent's attitude is defined as the _____ of her responses to the individual items (p. 172)
8. The _____ component of the Semantic Differential indicates how good or bad a person believes some attitude object is. (p. 173)
9. The Semantic Differential attempts to assess attitudes by determining the _____ _____ of the attitude object to the respondent. (p. 173)
10. Some researchers have turned to unobtrusive techniques of attitude measurement because of the problem of _____ in paper and pencil scales. (p. 174)

11. The technique of determining the relationship between attitudes and behavior by examining a person's behavior across time and across situations is called the _____
_____ _____ . (p. 176)

12. If I attempted to predict if you were going to get a flu vaccination on the basis of your attitudes toward public health, I might be criticized by those who believe that attitude measurements must be _____ if they are to predict behavior. (p. 176)

13. Your friend quits the school soccer team. You ask her why. She replies, "Well I love soccer, but I couldn't stand practicing at 6 A.M." This demonstrates the need to consider both the attitude toward the _____ and the attitude toward the _____ in predicting behavior. (p. 177)

14. A belief about an end state of existence is called a(n) _____ value. A belief about a mode of conduct is called a(n) _____ _____ valuc. (p. 178)

15. The idea that people may infer their attitudes from their behavior is put forth in Bem's _____ _____ theory. (p. 179)

ANSWERS

1. affective, cognitive   2. perceived instrumentality   3. classical   4. operant
5. reference groups   6. scale value   7. sum   8. evaluative   9. connotative meaning
10. reactivity   11. multiple act criterion   12. specific   13. object, situation
14. terminal, instrumental   15. self-perception

HOW ATTITUDES ARE CHANGED

Ronald Kovic, sergeant, United States Marine Corps (retired):

I was in Vietnam when I first heard about the thousands of people protesting the war in the streets of America. . . . We swore they would pay, the hippies and draftcard burners. They would pay if we ever ran into them. (Kovic, 1977, p. 134)

Ronald Kovic, sergeant, United States Marine Corps (retired):

I went totally into speaking out against the war. . . . I went into it the same way I'd gone into everything else I've wanted to do in my life—the way I'd gone into pole vaulting or baseball or the *marines*. . . . I think I honestly believed that if only I could speak to enough people I could stop the war myself. I honestly believed people would listen to me because of who I was, a wounded American veteran. (Kovic, 1977, pp. 149–150, italics added)

This section examines the two major theoretical positions on attitude change and some ways in which attitudes can be changed.

Theories of attitude change

Learning theory

To some social psychologists, traditional learning theory explains attitude change. They see attitude change essentially as a learning process which is best explained by the laws of learning. Consider the work of Carl Hovland and his associates at Yale University (e.g., Hovland, Janis, & Kelley, 1953). Their basic premise was quite simple. People change their attitudes because they think they will be rewarded for doing so. Therefore,

Wide World Photos

the greater the rewards offered, the greater the attitude change. Hovland et al. called these anticipated rewards *incentives;* thus, their theory was labeled *incentive theory.* While there are other learning theories of attitude change, incentive theory seems to have generated the most interest.

Consistency theory

The most prominent of many consistency theories was proposed by Leon Festinger (1957). It is called the theory of *cognitive dissonance.* According to this theory, people

have a need or are motivated to keep the relationship among their *cognitions* (i.e., their attitudes, beliefs, ideas, opinions) consistent. If this relationship becomes inconsistent, they feel distressed. This is known as being in *dissonance.* Most people find this state quite unpleasant and are motivated to change it. They will do this by changing their cognitions and/or a behavior which is responsible for the dissonance.

Consider Ron Kovic, the Vietnam war supporter turned antagonist. Kovic was wounded in Vietnam and, as a result, was paralyzed from the chest down for life. When he returned home, he was honored as a hero at a rally in support of the war. But his wound had changed him. Once a person who had saluted when "The Star-Spangled Banner" was played on television, he now saw the war as a senseless destroyer of young men. At the rally, he had the following two cognitions:

"I hate the war and what it did to me."

"I am at a rally in support of the war."

Kovic describes his reaction after the rally:

"[I] left the church feeling very sick and threw up in the parking lot" (p. 108).

Kovic stopped attending pro-war rallies and became a leader in the anti-war movement. He resolved his dissonance by making his actions consistent with his cognitions.

Now, not all dissonance-producing situations are this dramatic. The more important the behavior and attitudes involved in the inconsistent relationship, the greater the feelings of dissonance will be and the stronger will be the motivation to eliminate them. For example, Kovic would not experience nearly as much distress from these two cognitions:

"I hate pizza."

"I just bought a pizza."

as he would from his feelings at the rally. Also, people will not invariably change their attitudes and/or behavior as the result of dissonance. In fact, they often rationalize away the inconsistency. For example, Kovic could have done this by thinking, "It's just a dumb rally that really has no effect on the war." But if rationalizations don't work, people will change their attitudes and/or behavior to produce consistency.

One final point. Dissonance will not occur unless the person sees her cognitions as inconsistent. The fact that you and I think a person is inconsistent does not mean that she does. And as you might expect, a person can hold two ideas which seem incredibly inconsistent to an observer but perfectly consistent to her. Thus, two cognitions can be logically inconsistent to the observer but psychologically consistent to the person who holds them. It is only when *psychological inconsistency* is present that dissonance occurs and attitude change will take place.

Now, let's turn to some techniques of attitude change that incorporate these two theories.

Techniques of attitude change

According to McGuire (1969a, 1974), the two most popular ways of producing attitude change are: (1) presenting a person with a persuasive message and (2) actively involving the person in the attitude change attempt. To clarify the difference between these techniques, consider a person who keeps snakes as a hobby and is trying to get a friend to change her attitudes towards snakes. If she uses the first technique, she might talk about the wonders of snake life and the glories of owning snakes. If she uses the second technique, she might give the friend a snake to hold or have the friend help her take care of her snakes. Her hope would be that as the result of these behaviors, the friend's attitudes toward snakes might change. Both incentive and cognitive dissonance theorists agree that either of these techniques will produce attitude change.

Persuasive messages

It is hard to get through a day without being exposed to this technique of attitude change. Eve used it to get Adam to eat the apple. You probably have used it in making a date. Regardless of the attitude the message is concerned with, the components of this technique are the same. Following is a review of theory and research on these components.

The source. The first component is the source—the person or organization which presents the persuasive message. The characteristics of the source are extremely important in determining whether an attitude will be changed. To explain why, let's return to the basics of a learning (or incentive) theory view of attitude change.

According to the incentive theorists (e.g. Hovland et al., 1953), attitude change depends on three things. The first is that the person who receives the persuasive attempt (called the *recipient*), must listen to it. Next, the recipient must understand its content. Finally—and most important—the recipient must accept the position being advocated. Acceptance depends upon the recipient's belief that if she changes her attitude, she will receive certain rewards or incentives. The belief that attitude change will produce these rewards, in turn, depends upon source characteristics. This will become clearer as the relationship between the source characteristic, credibility, and the incentive of being correct is discussed.

For a persuasive message to produce attitude change, the recipient must believe that the position being advocated is correct. This is important because it causes the recipient to expect that if she accepts the message, she will be right. People find it rewarding to hold attitudes considered correct (Insko, 1967). This expectation will be produced by a *credible* source. This is a source that is perceived as being: (1) expert on the topic in question and (2) trustworthy. If a source possesses these characteristics, it will probably produce attitude change (Choo, 1964; Hovland & Weiss, 1951; Watts & McGuire, 1964).

As an example of these two characteristics, consider the following television commercial. In it, a well-known actor says, "If I told you (so and so) aspirin was the most effective aspirin, you probably wouldn't believe me. But what would you think if I told you that nine out of ten doctors say so?" The actor then presents the doctors' opinions. The doctors are both expert and trustworthy. *Trustworthy* means that doctors (unlike actors) are seen as truthful. Thus, the logic behind this commercial is that doctors are more credible than actors when it comes to aspirin and that a credible source will produce attitude change. Why? Because it will lead to the reward of using the "right" aspirin. This commercial is based on a reasonable premise: the more credible a source, the more attitude change is produced (Kiesler, Collins, & Miller, 1969). Some early research, however, indicated that the superiority of a credible source may be short-lived. For example, Hovland, Lumsdaine, and Sheffield (1949) reported that a few weeks after people heard messages from credible and noncredible sources, there was no difference in the amount of attitude change produced. In fact, Hovland et al. claimed that over time the people moved *closer* to the position advocated by the less credible source and *away* from the position of the more credible source.

Kelman and Hovland (1953) called the delayed effectiveness of the less credible source the *sleeper effect.* They stated that, over time, people forget the source of a message but remember its content. They showed that if the source is reconnected with the message at a later date, the credible source again proves superior in producing attitude change.

The sleeper effect is troubling. It suggests that over a few weeks, a statement made by Adolf Hitler would produce as much attitude change as one by John F. Kennedy. This speaks rather poorly of people's ability to evaluate propaganda intelligently. It is, thus, with some relief that I report on a more recent study by Gillig and Greenwald (1974).

They reviewed the literature on the sleeper effect and found no statistically significant *increase* in delayed attitude change as the result of hearing a noncredible source. The sleeper effect merely indicates that over time, the initial superiority of a credible over a less credible source disappears. Gillig and Greenwald repeated the basic procedure used in previous studies of the sleeper effect in a new series of experiments. They found no evidence for a sleeper effect, and concluded that "if the sleeper effect is alive, we do not know where it is living" (1974, p. 139). Thus, although it is true that a credible source's effectiveness decreases over time, the effectiveness of a noncredible source does not increase over time.

A second important aspect of source characteristics concerns the source's motivation. If a recipient believes that a source has some self-serving, ulterior motive, her attitude will probably not change. People generally don't like to be used or manipulated. In some instances, a credible source may be less effective than a noncredible source because the message seems to serve the former's self-interest. Consider the following study.

Walster, Aronson, and Abrahams (1966) had subjects read supposed interviews with either (1) a prosecutor (a credible source) or (2) a convicted criminal (a noncredible source). For half of the subjects in each source condition, the interview consisted of the source (i.e., either the prosecutor or the criminal) advocating greater powers for prosecutors and the police. For the other half of the subjects, the source advocated less power. To create the appearance of self-serving behavior on the part of the prosecutor, subjects were told that in the country where he lived (Portugal), prosecutors were paid according to whether or not they obtained a conviction and how severe a sentence was imposed.

Thus, Walster et al. created a conflict between the credibility of a source and his motives for advocacy. The results of this study are shown in Figure 6-1. Subjects were more affected by the less credible source who argued against his own self-interest than by the credible source who appeared to be self-serving.

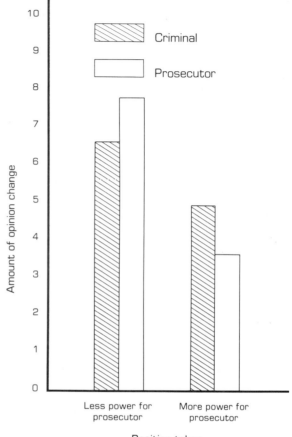

Figure 6-1. The effects of source credibility and position advocated (self-serving, not self-serving) on the effectiveness of a source. (Adapted from Walster, Aronson, & Abrahams, 1966)

What this study shows is that people do not like to be manipulated. They will usually resist such attempts. Thus, crucial to a source's effectiveness in persuasion is her ability to convince her audience that she has nothing to gain.

How does a source try to create a sense of credibility and impartiality in order to produce attitude change? Consider Richard Nixon's speech of April 29, 1974, in which he announced that he would give the Watergate tapes to the House of Representatives' impeachment committee. At the same time,

Nixon tried to convince the American people of his own innocence.

Nixon's techniques in this speech are not unusual for a politician. Lyndon Johnson's defense of his policy in Vietnam, Edward Kennedy's defense of his behavior at Chappaquidick, or even George Washington's defense against charges of padding his expense account while Commander of the Continental Army use the same methods.

To establish his credibility, Nixon first tried to create the impression that it was not Richard M. Nixon who was being attacked, but the *President*. The logic behind this tactic was apparently that a man named Nixon might not be an expert and might lie, but a *President* would not. Consider these two passages:

As far as what the President personally knew and did with regard to Watergate and the cover-up is concerned, these materials, together with those already made available, will tell it all. (The White House Transcripts)·

and

I want there to be no question remaining about the fact that the President has nothing to hide in this matter.

To conclude his speech, Nixon tried to further enhance his credibility by invoking Abraham Lincoln:

As for myself, I intend to go forward to the best of my ability with the work that you elected me to do. I shall do so in a spirit perhaps best summed up a century ago by another President when he was being subjected to unmerciful attack.

Abraham Lincoln said, "I do the very best I know how, the very best I can, and I mean to keep doing so until the end. If the end brings me out all right, what is said against me won't amount to anything. If the end brings me out wrong, ten angels swearing I was right would make no difference."

Nixon also tried to deal with the matter of his earlier refusals to release the tapes of conversations he had held with his subordi-

nates about Watergate. He attempted to convince his audience that he had nothing to gain from this behavior:

Many people assume that the tapes must incriminate the President, or that otherwise he wouldn't insist on their privacy. But the problem I confronted was this: Unless a President can protect the privacy of the advice he gets, he cannot get the advice he needs.

This principle is recognized in the constitutional doctrine of executive privilege, which has been defended and maintained by every President since Washington and which has been recognized by the courts whenever tested as inherent in the Presidency.

I consider it to be my constitutional responsibility to defend this principle.

Nixon expressed concern not only for this constitutional principle but also for the other persons involved in Watergate:

A second concern [which caused him not to release the tapes] was for the people who had been or might become involved in Watergate. Some were close advisers, valued friends, others whom I had trusted.

And I was also concerned about the human impact on others, especially some of the young people and their families who had come to Washington to work in my Administration, whose lives might be suddenly ruined by something they had done in an excess of loyalty or in a mistaken belief that it would serve the interests of the President.

Despite this rather skillful attempt to convince people of his innocence in Watergate, Nixon failed. His failure and his eventual resignation can, in part, be traced to his inability to prove that he was a credible source with no ulterior motives. His failure also shows that attitude change is not an automatic process. People evaluate the source of a message intelligently and critically. If the information they have about the source convinces them that she is not credible or is using them, their attitude will not change.

The final source characteristic related to attitude change is how similar the source is to the recipient (Insko, 1967). This is important because it leads the recipient to believe that the source's position would also be accepted by the recipient's peers. It is socially rewarding to hold the same attitudes as your peers.

Simons, Berkowitz, and Moyer (1970) reviewed the literature on source-recipient similarity and arrived at the following two conclusions. First, the more similar a source and her audience are in terms of attitudes related to the persuasive message, the more effective the source will be in changing attitudes. Second, a similar source who is also an expert in the area of concern will be more effective than a nonexpert. Similarity and credibility together produce an effective source.

The message. This review focuses on three aspects of the content of a persuasive message: the amount of change advocated, the advisability of presenting counter-arguments, and the use of fear.

How much change should a source advocate? Should the message present a position which is very different from the recipient's or one which is only slightly different? To clarify the difference between these two approaches, imagine that you have received a D in a course and you want the instructor to give you a higher grade. Which is a better strategy: (1) to argue for an A—that is, a large change in the instructor's attitude toward your work or (2) to argue for a C—a small change?

Advocates of the big-step position base their argument on a *linear operator model* (Anderson, 1959, Anderson & Hovland, 1957). This model proposes that the more attitude change you ask for, the more you will get. The small-step position is based on the assumption that if the message is too far removed from the recipient's own attitude, the message will be rejected. Although some studies support both positions, the majority of them suggest that the small-step approach

is more efficient in producing attitude change (Insko, 1967; Kiesler, Collins, & Miller, 1969).

Aronson, Turner, and Carlsmith (1963) examined the effects of (1) source credibility and (2) the distance between the message and the recipient's position on changing attitudes. They asked college students to read a stanza of poetry and give their opinion of it. Then half of the students were given an evaluation of the poetry supposedly written by a highly credible source—the noted poet T. S. Eliot. The other half read an evaluation supposedly written by a moderately credible source—a woman majoring in English at a Southern college. Aronson et al. arranged for the sources' opinion in both conditions to vary slightly, moderately, or considerably from the subjects' own opinions.

The researchers predicted that the highly credible source (T. S. Eliot) would be more effective in changing the subjects' opinions and could advocate a discrepant position more effectively than could the mildly credible source. But when Eliot's position became too different from the subjects' he, too, would lose effectiveness. The results of this study are presented in Figure 6-2.

As you can see, Aronson et al. were basically correct. The Southern English major caused the most opinion change when her position was moderately distant from the subjects' position. Her effectiveness dropped dramatically when her evaluation differed sharply from the subjects'. This did not occur for T. S. Eliot. His evaluation produced a change in the subjects' opinion even when it was quite different from theirs.

But note that even Eliot's persuasiveness leveled off when his judgment differed greatly from the subjects'. This highly credible source produced only slightly more opinion change with an extreme position than with a moderate one. If one examines this study, the following conclusion is reached: a moderately

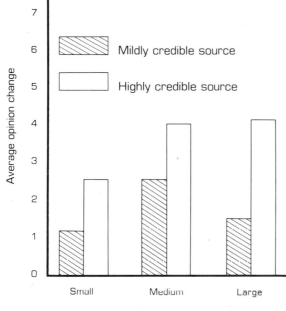

Figure 6-2. The effects of source credibility and discrepancy from recipient's own position on opinion change. (Adapted from Aronson, Turner, & Carlsmith, 1963)

discrepant persuasive message will produce the most attitude change.

The results of this and other similar studies have been put to practical use. For example, in 1970, Rosenberg, Verba, and Converse published a guide for anti-war activists who wanted to change people's attitudes toward the Vietnam war. Extreme rhetoric, they counseled, might be personally satisfying, but if one wanted to change people's attitudes toward the war, a moderate position would be most effective.

An illustration of what happens when a source's position is too far away from the recipient's is provided by Sherif, Sherif, and Nebergall (1965). Staunch Republicans and Democrats were given messages which contained positions diametrically opposed to their own. As a rule, subjects (1) saw the

message as *more* discrepant from their own position than it really was; (2) tended to put down the source of the message, and (3) (needless to say) did not change their attitudes.

This study demonstrates another important point. When a persuasive message concerns important, strongly held attitudes, these attitudes are extremely difficult to change. Partly for this reason, attitude change is easy in the laboratory but quite difficult in real life (Hovland, 1959). In laboratory studies, the attitudes involved are usually relatively unimportant and/or not strongly involving to the subjects. A real world attempt, (e.g., political campaigns), in contrast, concerns attitudes that are important and strongly held, and thus, difficult to change. The evidence (e.g., Hovland, 1959; Lazarsfeld, Berelson, & Gaudet, 1944; Rosenberg et al., 1970) suggests that despite the millions of dollars spent on advertising in presidential campaigns, for example, relatively little attitude change occurs among voters. In fact, the main goal of political ads and campaign activities is to identify people who already hold positive attitudes toward each candidate and strengthen these attitudes to ensure the vote. For example, consider the late Mayor Richard Daley of Chicago. He achieved his twenty-five years of political success simply by identifying those people who already favored him and making sure they went to the voting booths (Royko, 1971).

This is not to say that in the real world, attitudes are unchangeable. People do change their minds. The point is that it is hard to change important, strongly held attitudes and/or attitudes which are quite discrepant from the new position being advocated. Why? Cognitive dissonance theory provides an explanation.

Let's return to the study involving the evaluations of poetry. According to Aronson et al., subjects who read T. S. Eliot's evaluation which was quite different from their own were put in dissonance. More specifically, these two cognitions were psychologically inconsistent:

1. T. S. Eliot is a noted, respected poet.
2. He disagrees with my opinion of the poetry.

This psychological inconsistency could be resolved in one of two ways. The subjects could change either their opinion of the poetry or their opinion of Eliot. They tended to change their opinion of Eliot. Why? Quite simply, it was easier for them to change their opinion of Eliot than their estimate of their own ability to judge poetry. Thus, when people are faced with a discrepancy between their own attitude and that of another person, they will usually reject both the source and the message. This will occur unless the source is perfectly credible. About the only situation I can think of where a source had perfect credibility can be found in the Bible. When Moses came back from receiving the Ten Commandments, he found the Children of Israel worshiping the Golden Calf. Moses was, however, able to change their attitudes. After all, who could be a more credible source than the one Moses had just talked to?

One-sided versus two-sided messages. Is a persuasive message that presents only one point of view more effective than a message which presents opposing points of view? The research suggests that it depends largely on the characteristics of the recipient. If the recipient is opposed to the source's position and/or is well informed about the content of the message, a two-sided approach produces more attitude change. If she is in sympathy with the source's position and/or is not well informed, a one-sided message is more effective (Cohen, 1964; Insko, 1967; Kiesler, Collins & Miller, 1969).

Some people receive one-sided messages throughout their lives. Let's return to Ron Kovic. As far back as he could remember, Kovic wanted to be a Marine. As noted, he used to salute when the national anthem was played. His favorite movie was *The Sands of Iwo Jima*—a classic Hollywood story of the Marines during World War II, starring John Wayne. There was no more devout patriot than Ron Kovic. Yet the war in Vietnam and its harsh reality changed Kovic's attitudes rapidly and dramatically. Why?

William McGuire (1964) might explain this drastic change via his *innoculation theory*. According to McGuire, an attitude which has never been exposed to attack is like a person who has never been immunized against a disease. Further, our attitudes can receive innoculations in the same way our bodies can. A person's resistance to polio, for example, is increased by giving her a mild dose of the polio virus. Similarly, her resistance to attitude change can be increased by giving her a mild dose of the other point of view. It has been found that if a person receives weak counter-arguments to the attitudes she holds and is taught how to refute these counter-arguments, she will be more effective in resisting subsequent attempts to change her attitudes (McGuire & Papergeorgis, 1962; Papergeorgis & McGuire, 1961).

Fear-arousing appeals. As this is being written, I see two things in front of me: a burning cigarette and a statement on my cigarette pack: "Warning: The Surgeon General Has Determined That Cigarette Smoking is Dangerous to Your Health." By the time you read this, a cigarette pack may carry this message: "Warning: The Surgeon General Has Determined That Cigarette Smoking Will Cause Death." Will this much more direct statement affect my and other smokers' attitudes toward cigarettes? Initially, it was believed that the more fear a persuasive message generated, the more attitude change it would produce (Hovland, Janis, & Kelley, 1953). The reasoning was that fear is a negative reinforcer. If a persuasive message leads to a reduction in this fear, it should be accepted. Thus, a message which generates considerable fear and then presents a means to reduce that fear should produce attitude change. Is there any supporting evidence?

The answer is yes, but one must be *very* careful when using a fear-arousing appeal. For example, you would probably not change my attitude toward smoking by showing me pictures of rotting lungs and patients in an emphysema ward. This is because these pictures might so upset me that I will not listen to or understand what you are saying (Janis, 1967). Recall what was said earlier: a message which is not listened to, understood, and remembered will not produce attitude change.

Also, a persuasive message should avoid making me defensive about my present attitudes and behavior with regard to smoking. Insko, Arkoff, and Insko (1965) found that while nonsmokers were affected by a high-fear-arousing anti-smoking message, smokers were not. They reasoned that this was because the smokers felt defensive, while the nonsmokers did not.

Finally, it appears that fear alone will not produce attitude change (Leventhal, 1970; Rogers & Mewborn, 1976). The message must also contain concrete recommendations as to how these awful outcomes can be avoided.

If a person can do these three very difficult things, then fear-arousing messages would appear to produce attitude change (Evans, Rozelle, Lasater, Dembroski, & Allen, 1970; Leventhal, Watts, & Pagano, 1967).

Source characteristics and the content of the message are two components of attitude change via a persuasive message. There are three other components. The first is the *channel* over which the message is transmitted (e.g., face to face, print, television). Channel effectiveness will not be covered here, since it is a topic more appropriate for a text on communication. Next is the characteristics of the recipient. The relationship between recipient characteristics and persuasibility is covered in the chapter on social influence. The final component is the *destination,* or ultimate goal, of a persuasive message (McGuire, 1969a). This will be considered in the final section of this chapter. At this point, let's turn to the other major technique of attitude change.

Actively involving the recipient

In the attitude change technique just presented, the recipient passively receives a persuasive appeal. In the technique which follows, the key to attitude change is the recipient's active participation.

The value of this approach in attitude change was first observed in traditional psychotherapy (McGuire, 1969a). Sigmund Freud and Carl Rogers both reported that therapy which actively involved the client was more effective than one in which the client sat passively while the therapist tried to "persuade" her. One of the first demonstrations of the effectiveness of active participation was provided by Kurt Lewin (1947). Lewin was interested in the best way to get homemakers to serve their families certain unappetizing but nutritional parts of the cow (e.g., hearts, kidneys). The practical reason for Lewin's research interest was the meat shortage in America during the Second World War. Lewin used two approaches. Half of his subjects received a typical persuasive message which argued for the joys of eating a cow's heart (or kidney). The other half were actively involved in the attitude change process. They discussed how they could induce other homemakers to change their eating habits. Lewin then determined the percentage of people in each group who later served these organs to their families. Compared with only 3 percent of the persuasive message group, 32 percent of the discussion group served this type of meat in their homes.

Counter-attitudinal advocacy. It used to be hard to watch television news programs without seeing the following scene. Thousands of Chinese were gathered in the main square in Peking. In their hands was the "Little Red Book," which contains the thoughts of Chairman Mao; they were reading from the book aloud. This phenomenon is not unique to China. It has occurred in many countries that have undergone a radical change in government. What is the rationale behind this practice? For one thing, it gave loyal Chinese a chance to reaffirm their commitment to Chairman Mao. But it could also produce attitude change among the less loyal. That is, getting a person to publicly express an attitude or engage in a behavior which opposes her true attitude—called *counter-attitudinal advocacy*—will often produce attitude change. Both dissonance and incentive theorists agree that counter-attitudinal advocacy is a powerful attitude change technique. They disagree, however, as to why, and how it works.

Dissonance theorists propose that if one can get a person to advocate an opposing position for a *minimal* or *insufficient* reward, one can produce attitude change. In other words, *the less the reward for counter-attitudinal advocacy, the greater the attitude change.* The logic behind this proposal can be explained via the following example.

Imagine that you and a classmate are attending a psychologists' convention being held at your university. While talking to someone, you realize that he is none other than Professor Bonkers, the author of your abnormal psychology textbook. You are polite and don't tell him that the book was only slightly better written than the *Yellow Pages*. Professor Bonkers is very excited when he learns that you have used his book because with him is the head of the committee evaluating him for promotion to full professor. Bonkers believes that positive reactions from students will increase his chances for promotion.

He takes each of you aside and asks you to praise his text before the head of the commit-

tee. He offers you $1 for this endorsement and your classmate $50. Both of you agree. Now, each possesses the following cognitions:

1. I told someone that Bonkers' book was great.
2. I really thought it was awful.

You have both engaged in counter-attitudinal advocacy.

Will this form of advocacy cause either of you to change your own opinion toward Bonkers' book? In other words, are either of you experiencing dissonance which could lead to attitude change?

To answer this, we must first consider the importance of your behavior. According to the theory of cognitive dissonance, counter-attitudinal advocacy will not result in dissonance if the behavior is unimportant (Aronson, 1969; Festinger, 1957). Let's assume that Bonkers' evaluator is really impressed with your "unsolicited" testimonial. Thus, you view your behavior as important (i.e., it affects someone else).

Now for the second consideration: why did you engage in this behavior? Dissonance theorists propose that if you receive a sufficient reward for counter-attitudinal advocacy (Festinger, 1957) or feel that you have been coerced into it (Brehm & Cohen, 1962), you will not experience dissonance. Since neither you nor your classmate were coerced, you will both consider the size of the bribe. Your classmate has received $50, a fairly substantial payoff. This provides a rationale or justification for the attitude-behavior discrepancy, and she will not experience dissonance. But you have engaged in counter-attitudinal advocacy for only $1. In comparison to your classmate, you have received an *insufficient reward*. You cannot justify your behavior on the basis of the money. Therefore, you are in dissonance. How can you reduce or resolve it?

According to Festinger and his associates, you will probably do this by changing your private opinion to match your public behavior. You will decide that you really did like the book. If you change your attitude, you are no longer in dissonance. Thus, cognitive dissonance theory holds that the *smaller* the reward for counter-attitudinal advocacy, the *greater* the attitude change.

Next, consider how incentive theory would view the same episode. An incentive theorist would argue that the $50 bribe would produce greater attitude change. That is, the *greater* the reward offered for counter-attitudinal advocacy, the *greater* the attitude change. This prediction is based on the premise that a large reward will motivate a person to be a better advocate than a small reward. This increased effort will result in more self-persuasion than a slipshod job (in exchange for a small reward) and thus will produce more attitude change (Rosenberg, 1965b). The predictions of the two theoretical points of view are presented in Figure 6-3. As you can see, they lead

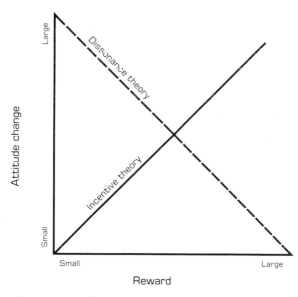

Figure 6-3. The theoretical positions of dissonance and incentive theories as to the effect of rewards for counter-attitudinal advocacy.

to exactly opposite predictions. Which one is correct? The answer is, each is correct under certain circumstances.

Carlsmith, Collins, and Helmreich (1966) believe that when the behavior is unimportant to the person who performs it, the larger the reward the greater the attitude change (incentive theory prediction); but when the behavior is important, the less the reward the greater the attitude change (dissonance theory prediction). Thus, the crucial variable is the *importance* of the discrepant behavior. This assumption was tested by Carlsmith et al.

High school students were given an extremely dull and repetitious task (crossing out certain digits from a series of numbers). They were told that they were a control group in a study on how a person's prior expectation would affect her accuracy on a task. Since they were the control group, their expectations would not be manipulated. After the subjects worked for an hour, the experimental manipulation was administered. Half of them were informed that the high school student who normally told people what to expect on the task was unavailable, and they were asked to fill in for him. Their job was to tell another student that the task was enjoyable, interesting, etc. The other half of the subjects were asked to help the experimenter write a new set of instructions for the experiment. Since he wanted these instructions to appeal to high school students, he needed sample essays from other students which described how interesting and enjoyable the study was. Only the experimenter would see these essays. Subjects in both conditions received either $0.50, $1.50, or $5.00 for their efforts. Later, supposedly as part of another study, all the students' attitudes toward the task (crossing out digits) were measured. Carlsmith et al. predicted that when the subjects had to talk to someone else, results consistent with cognitive dissonance theory would be obtained because the behavior had consequences for someone else and thus was important. In the essay-writing condition (where the behavior had less immediate effect on another person), incentive theory predictions would be confirmed. Why? In the former condition, dissonance had been created; in the latter condition, it had not. The prediction of Carlsmith et al. was confirmed. Their results are summarized in Figure 6-4.

Note that in the essay-writing condition, the greater the reward the greater the attitude change (which supports incentive the-

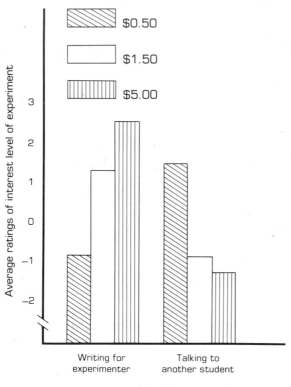

Figure 6-4. The effect of monetary rewards on attitudes toward a boring experiment under conditions of writing an essay and talking to another student. (Adapted from Carlsmith, Collins, & Helmreich, 1966)

ory). In the talking condition, the less the reward the greater the attitude change (which supports dissonance theory). These results have been replicated a number of times (e.g., Collins & Hoyt, 1972; Crano & Mess'e, 1970).

Thus, getting a recipient actively involved in the attitude change process does produce attitude change in her. Sometimes this attitude change can be best explained by incentive theory, other times by dissonance theory.

Before leaving the topic of attitude change via active participation, note that the dissonance theory explanation has encountered some criticism. Most important is that provided by Bem's (1965, 1967, 1972) *self-perception theory* (cf. page 179). Recall that Bem said that people make the same type of attributions about their own behavior as an observer would. Thus, Bem proposes, when a person says something publicly, she infers her attitude from her public statement: "I said it, so I must believe it." Bem did *not* say that the techniques used in counter-attitudinal advocacy studies are ineffective in producing attitude change. Rather, he questioned the reason for the change. Bem believed that an internal state, such as cognitive dissonance, does not explain the change. The reason for the change is the inference the person makes from her behavior. At this point, Bem's proposal cannot be definitively evaluated.

This concludes the review of techniques for producing attitude change. Now we must turn to a crucial question. Regardless of the particular technique used or theoretical explanation proposed, it is necessary to ask: what affect did the persuasive attempt have? Did it produce a meaningful change in the recipient? One way this question can be answered is to determine if the recipient's behavior changed. This question conveniently leads to the final problem in theory and research on attitude change.

Tampa Tribune

The relationship between attitude change and behavior change

You would think that a number of studies have been done on changes in behavior as the result of attempts to change attitudes. But, in fact, there are relatively few (Calder & Ross, 1972; Festinger, 1964; Rokeach, 1968). Further, the results of these studies have not been very encouraging. Sometimes attitude change produces behavior change, but just as often it does not. What is the problem?

Calder and Ross (1972) have proposed three complementary explanations. They point out that it is obviously easier to change attitudes than behavior. One reason is that the consequences of changing behavior may be much more serious than the consequences of changing attitudes. For example, you may decide that smoking marijuana is not dangerous after hearing a persuasive message from a group advocating its legalization. But the fact remains that in most parts of the United States, smoking marijuana is illegal. This may result in your not smoking marijuana (i.e., changing your behavior).

Calder and Ross also observed that attitude change may not last. Both incentive theorists and consistency theorists agree that attitudes will remain changed only if they are reinforced by others in the recipient's environment (Festinger, 1964; Hovland, Janis, & Kelley, 1953). Thus, attitude change may not produce behavior change because the recipient's attitudes may have reverted to their original state.

Finally, Calder and Ross argued that if a person has been engaged in behavior for a long time, she may be commited to the behavior and thus reluctant to change it. For example, a heavy smoker may agree that cigarettes are bad for her (after hearing an appeal from the American Cancer Society) but be unwilling or unable to stop smoking.

Another somewhat more radical explanation has been put forth by Rokeach (1968,

1971, 1973). Rokeach's theory of values, discussed earlier, proposed that a person's behavior and attitudes are determined by her values. If, Rokeach argued, only attitudes are changed, the underlying causal values are left intact. Thus, attitude change is temporary, and little or no behavior change will occur. Therefore, Rokeach believed that the best way to produce long-term behavioral change is to change values.

Rokeach (1968, 1971) has devised a technique to produce changes in the importance a person assigns to certain terminal values. It involves causing psychological inconsistency between the person's self-concept and the importance assigned certain values, and between values and attitudes. This is done by presenting people with interpretations of their value rankings. For example, in a 1971 study, Rokeach gave college students the value survey (cf. the box "East is east, west is west, and shall the twain ever meet?") and then interpreted the relative importance they gave to the values of equality and freedom. He suggested that people who considered freedom much more important than equality are very concerned about their own freedom but not that of others. The clear implication was that this is an inconsistent relationship. According to Rokeach, this psychological inconsistency should generate self-dissatisfaction among a sizeable percentage of people and thus produce attitude and behavior change.

Three to five months later, these students received a letter asking them to join the National Association for the Advancement of Colored People. Their willingness to join was compared to that of classmates who had not heard Rokeach's talk. Approximately three times as many of them joined the N.A.A.C.P. as did their classmates. A follow-up appeal fifteen to seventeen months later produced a similar difference between those who had heard Rokeach's interpretation of their value rankings and those who had not.

Rokeach continued to keep track of his subjects and found that two years later, significantly more of them had changed their academic major to one concerned with the problems of ethnic minorities than members of the control group.

At the end of two years, Rokeach told some of his subjects the purpose of the study and obtained their reactions to the value-change procedure. One woman provided a rather impressive account of how the thirty minute talk on values had affected her life.

She felt she was "a hypocrite, pretending to be a liberal when in fact I was quite self-centered." To seek out new answers she had left [her] natural science-oriented [major] for [a] social science-oriented [major] "to directly confront the issues of civil and human rights." She responded to the NAACP solicitation by joining the association, campaigned afterwards for Charles Evers in Mississippi, and "spent the summer in New York ghettoes working with teenage girls." She traced all these behaviors directly to the experimental session. (Rokeach, 1973, p. 302)

These findings have also been obtained by Rokeach and McClelland (1972) and Penner (1971).

Conroy, Katkin, and Barnette (1973) used Rokeach's value-change procedure to get people to stop smoking. Subjects received either a message designed to create psychological inconsistency between their values and their smoking or the more traditional fear-arousing appeal. Both techniques were initially effective, but Figure 6-5 shows what happened over time. After two weeks, the control group (fear technique) was almost back to its pretreatment level. Subjects who received the value-change procedure, however, were smoking fewer than two cigarettes per day.

The results of studies which have used Rokeach's value-change procedure are impressive and exciting. If they are repeatable, there is tremendous potential for this tech-

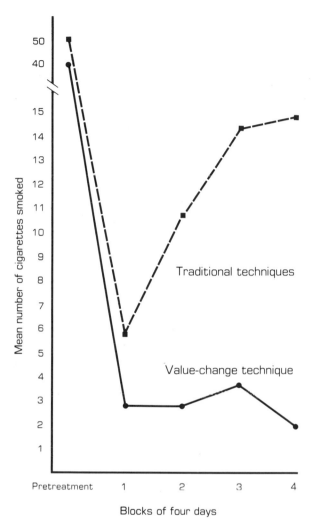

Figure 6-5. The relative effectiveness of the value-change procedure and traditional techniques on getting people to stop smoking. (From Conroy, Katkin, & Barnette, 1971)

nique in education and in producing large-scale attitude and behavior change in society. Lest this conjure up disturbing visions of *1984,* I will conclude this section by commenting on Rokeach's procedure in particular and attitude change in general.

There is nothing magical about the value-

change approach. It involves pointing out actual inconsistencies in a person. Many people will not accept the fact that certain relationships are inconsistent and will not change their values, attitudes, or behavior. People usually evaluate attempts to change their attitudes and values intelligently and critically. As noted before, attitude (or value) change is not easily done.

Value (or attitude) change will not automatically lead to behavior change. People evaluate their environment, determine the rewards and costs for changes in their behavior, and then make a decision. Rokeach's procedure will not make Jimmy Carter a communist or Fidel Castro a capitalist. Real attitude and behavior change is a slow, mild, and subtle process. In short, most people do not have to worry about having their values, attitudes, and behavior changed against their will.

Conclusion

The second half of this chapter has been primarily concerned with how attitudes are changed. There are two general theoretical positions. Learning or incentive theorists argue that for attitudes to change, rewards or incentives must be offered. Consistency theorists would agree that rewards are related to attitude change, but also propose that attitudes can be changed by generating psychological inconsistency or imbalance within a person.

Both learning and consistency theorists agree that the best techniques of inducing attitude change are (1) presenting a persuasive message, and (2) getting the recipient actively involved in the attitude change process. They disagree, however, on why and how these techniques work. This disagreement can be seen most clearly in their view of the effect of reward in changing attitudes when a person engages in counter-attitudinal advocacy. Incentive theorists propose that the greater the reward the greater the change; dissonance theorists propose that the less the reward the greater the attitude change. This conflict can be resolved by considering the nature of the counter-attitudinal advocacy. When it involves the public advocacy of an important attitude, dissonance theory predictions seem valid. But when it is advocated anonymously or is relatively unimportant, the incentive position seems to hold.

Both incentive and dissonance theorists have difficulty in determining whether attitude change results in behavior change. The few studies on this question have not found a strong relationship. This does not mean that attitude change is unrelated to behavior change. These previous failures may be due, at least in part, to the fact that other factors related to behavior change (e.g., habits, the situation a person is in) have not been considered. Further, someone who argues that attitude change does not produce behavior change must explain the impressive results obtained by Rokeach et al. on behavioral changes which seem to accompany value change.

Theory and research on attitude change is a vital and important aspect of social psychology. Further, the potential for attitude research to aid a society in solving its problems is boundless. Let us hope that this potential is realized someday.

REVIEW QUESTIONS

(Twelve out of fifteen is passing)

1. The basic premise of _____ theory is that attitude change is basically a learning process. The premise of _____ theory is that attitude change occurs as the result of imbalance and a desire to reestablish balance. (p. 183)
2. When a person simultaneously holds two or more cognitions which are psychologically inconsistent, she should be experiencing _____ _____ . (p. 183)
3. The statement "Everyone is out of step but me" illustrates the difference between _____ inconsistency and _____ consistency. (p. 184)
4. A source of a persuasive message who is seen as expert and trustworthy is said to be _____ . (p. 185)
5. Gillig and Greenwald questioned the existence of the _____ _____ which proposes that there will be delayed attitude change following a persuasive message delivered by a noncredible source. (p. 186)
6. An "overheard" conversation seems to be more effective in changing attitudes than a persuasive message designed to change attitudes. One possible reason is that in an overheard conversation, the source is perceived to be free of _____ _____ . (p. 186)
7. With regard to the position advocated in a persuasive message, the _____ _____ model predicts that the greater the change advocated the greater the change obtained. This model would work only when the source is perfectly _____ . (p. 190)

8. The idea of developing resistance to a counter-arguments by giving a person a weak "dose" of it is contained in McGuire's _____ theory. (p. 190)

9. Some say that a persuasive message which arouses fear will produce attitude change. The logic behind this proposal is that fear is a(n) _____ _____ and a message which shows how to alleviate that fear should be accepted. (p. 190)

10. The medium by which a persuasive message is transmitted is called the _____ . (p. 191)

11. A teacher tells a misbehaving student to write an essay on "Why I must not act up in class." In addition to punishing the child, the teacher may hope to achieve attitude and behavior change via _____ _____ _____ . (p. 192)

12. Dissonance theorists believe that when a person is publicly expressing an attitude she does not privately agree with, the _____ the reward the greater the attitude change. Incentive theorists hold that in the same situation, the _____ the reward the greater the attitude change. (p. 193)

13. The resolution of the disagreement presented in the previous question seems to lie in the _____ of the behavior. (p. 193)

14. Bem's self-perception theory proposes that people may _____ their attitudes from their _____ when they engage in counter-attitudinal advocacy. (p. 194)

15. Rokeach criticizes traditional attempts to change behavior via attitude change. He says that in order to produce behavior change, one must change more basic cognitions. According to Rokeach, these are a person's _____ . (p. 196)

ANSWERS

1. incentive, consistency 2. cognitive dissonance 3. logical, psychological 4. credible 5. sleeper effect 6. ulterior motives 7. linear operator, credible 8. innoculation 9. negative reinforcer 10. channel 11. counter-attitudinal advocacy 12. less, greater 13. importance 14. infer, behavior 15. values

SUGGESTED READINGS

If the topic of attitudes and attitude change interests you, you might consider these additional readings.

Textbooks

Belief, Attitude, Intention, and Behavior: An Introduction to Theory and Research, by Martin Fishbein and Isek Ajzen. This book is not easy reading, but it contains some extremely valuable theoretical perspectives on the relationship between attitudes and behavior.

Either *Theories of Attitude Change,* by Chester Insko, or *Attitude Change,* by Charles Kiesler, Barry Collins, and Norman Miller. Both of these books provide comprehensive reviews of the major theories of attitude change.

The Nature of Human Values, by Milton Rokeach. In this interesting book, Rokeach presents some intriguing findings about the relationship between values, attitudes, and behavior.

Influencing Attitudes and Changing Behavior, by Philip Zimbardo, Ebbe Ebbesen, and Christina Maslach. This relatively short book is quite readable and provides an excellent overview of current theory and research on attitude change.

Popular literature

World Without End, Amen, by Jimmy Breslin. This is a novel about an Irish Catholic policeman who becomes involved in the civil war in Northern Ireland. Breslin presents some excellent illustrations of why attitudes are often hard to change.

Born on the Fourth of July, by Ron Kovic. This decorated war hero eloquently describes how his attitudes toward the war in Vietnam and the American government underwent a dramatic change.

The Selling of the President, by Joe McGinniss. This is a hilarious factual account of the 1968 presidential campaign. It describes the art of attitude change in its purest form.

Fear and Loathing on the Campaign Trail, by Hunter Thompson. In 1972 *Rolling Stone* magazine hired Thompson to cover the presidential campaign. His description of what happened and why presents a view of American politics that you'll never get in a political science course.

The Making of the President, by Theodore H. White. White's books on presidential campaigns from 1960 to 1972 provide a comprehensive description of how Americans' attitudes are shaped and changed during an election.

7 PREJUDICE

In collaboration with Beth C. Stearns

This chapter examines prejudice. While there are many kinds of prejudice, the focus here is on ethnic and sexual prejudice. After prejudice and discrimination are defined, the causes of and possible cures for ethnic prejudice will be discussed. The second half of the chapter will deal with sexism. As with ethnic prejudice, we will first consider the causes of sexism and then some means for its reduction.

DEFINING THE PROBLEM

It is the Fourth of July. A crowd has assembled to hear a black activist speak on racism in America.

What to the American slave is your Fourth of July? I answer, a day that reveals to him more than all other days of the year, the gross injustice and cruelty to which he is the constant victim. To him your celebration is a sham; your boasted liberty an unholy license; your national greatness, swelling vanity; your sounds of rejoicing are empty and heartless; your denunciation of tyrants, brass-fronted impudence; your shouts of liberty and equality, hollow mockery; your prayers and hymns, your sermons and thanksgivings, with all your religious parade and solemnity, are to him mere bombast, fraud, deception, impiety, and hypocrisy—a thin veil to cover up crimes which would disgrace a nation of savages. There is not a nation of the earth guilty of practices more shocking and bloody than are the people of these United States at this very hour.

Go where you may, search where you will, roam through all the monarchies and despotisms of the Old World, travel through South America, search out every abuse and when you have found the last, lay your facts by the side of the everyday practices of this nation, and you will say with me that, for revolting barbarity and shameless hypocrisy, America reigns without a rival.

Four years earlier, a group of feminists held a convention on women's rights. In their closing statment, they described how the typical man treats the typical woman in America.

He has monopolized nearly all the profitable employments and from those she is permitted to follow, she received but scanty remuneration. He closes . . . all avenues to wealth and distinction which he considers most honorable to himself. As a teacher of theology, medicine and law, she is not known. He has endeavored in every way possible to destroy her confidence in her own powers, to lessen her self-respect and to make her willing to lead an abject and dependent life.

Do these two quotations sound a little strange? Was the wording a little stilted? The reason is that both were written more than 125 years ago. The condemnation of racism was made by Fredrick Douglas in 1852; the declaration on sexism was issued by the Seneca Falls Convention in 1848. Despite their age, these quotations describe phenomena which still exist today—ethnic and sexual prejudice. This chapter is concerned with their causes and possible cures.

Prejudice is a negative attitude toward a group and any member of that group. As an attitude, prejudice has three components: affective (how much the group is liked or disliked); cognitive (beliefs about the group); and behavioral (intentions toward the group). For example, imagine you are a personnel director on the Alaska pipeline. You dislike Eskimos (affective component), believing they are lazy, stupid drunkards (cognitive component). You would not want to hire Eskimos as part of your crew (behavioral component). Prejudice is an attitude. It is translated into behavior via *discrimination*. *Discrimination* is negative behavior toward a socially defined group and any member of that group. It can take many forms. It can be relatively subtle and nonviolent such as not wanting to sit next to a Mexican-American on a bus or refusing a Polish-American admittance to a country club. It can also be violent and dramatic.

An event which occurred in 1975 in Boston shows the violence possible in discriminatory behavior. A group of whites who had been protesting school busing were leaving City Hall, carrying an American flag on a long pole. As they left, they saw a black man. Evidently infuriated by the sight of a black face, they set upon him. As a symbol of patriotism, they used the pole (with the flag still attached) to break the man's nose and beat him unconscious.

ETHNIC PREJUDICE

Ethnic prejudice involves negative attitudes toward an *ethnic group*. This is a "group of people considered by both themselves and other people to have in common one or more of the following characteristics: (1) religion, (2) racial origin (as indicated by readily identifiable physical features), (3) national origin, or (4) language or cultural traditions" (Harding, Kutner, Proshansky, & Chein, 1969, p. 3).

Most of the research on ethnic prejudice has focused on anti-black and anti-Semitic attitudes. However, it should be emphasized that no ethnic group is immune from prejudice. For example, Protestants and Catholics in Northern Ireland hate each other. In Lebanon, a fratricidal civil war was fought between Christians and Moslems. The Arabs in Sudan oppress the blacks there. Light-skinned Jews in Israel discriminate against dark-skinned Jews (Garcia, 1975). On the southwest side of Chicago, people of Polish ancestry love to tell derogatory jokes about people of Bohemian ancestry. It is hard to identify an ethnic group which has not at

---

A sampler of racism and sexism

I thank thee, O Lord, that Thou hast not created me a woman.
ORTHODOX JEWISH PRAYER

How can he be clean that is born of woman?
JOB:4-4

Cowardly and cruel are those Blacks innate, Prone to Revenge, Imp of hate He that exasperates them soon espies, Mischief and Murder in their very eyes.
A PURITAN POEM (1697)

Why increase the sons of Africa by Planting them in America, where we have so fair an opportunity, by excluding all Blacks . . . of increasing the lovely White. . . .
BENJAMIN FRANKLIN

God created Adam, lord of all living creatures, but Eve spoiled it.
MARTIN LUTHER

Nature intended women to be our slaves . . . they are our property.
Napoleon Bonaparte

Comparing [blacks] by their faculties of memory, reason and imagination, it appears to me that in memory they are equal to the whites; in reason much inferior . . . scarcely capable of tracing and comprehending the investigations of Euclid; and that in imagination they are dull, tasteless and anomalous.
THOMAS JEFFERSON

And a woman is only a woman but a good cigar is a smoke.
RUDYARD KIPLING

I am not nor ever have been in favor of bringing about in any way the social and political equality of white and black races.
ABRAHAM LINCOLN

Coloreds only want three things: first [good sex], second, loose shoes, and third, a warm place to shit.
EARL BUTZ

The only position for women in S.N.C.C. [a black civil rights organization] is prone.
STOKELEY CARMICHAEL

some point been the object of prejudice and discrimination.

The causes of prejudice

Most social psychologists see ethnic prejudice as the result of certain experiences in a person's life.[1] These experiences can result in prejudice either directly or indirectly. For example, a person's parents or the culture he lives in can teach him that Italians are bad and should be hated (direct). Alternatively, his life experiences can result in personality characteristics which predispose him to hate Italians. Prejudice as the direct result of experience is viewed as a special case of social learning. Prejudice as the indirect result of experience is considered a symptom of some more basic psychological processes within a person.

Although these two views of the causes of ethnic prejudice overlap a great deal, for purposes of clarity they will be covered separately. Also, note that the explanations which follow are not competitors for the best or most correct explanation. Prejudice is the product of *all* these factors. Thus, these explanations complement rather than compete with each other.

Direct causes

There is little doubt that our parents' attitudes and behavior are important determinants of our ethnic attitudes (cf. Chapter Six). But parents are not the only agents that influence us. Friends, relatives, the media,

[1]Recently, some theorists (e.g., Freedman, 1974; McGuire, 1969a; Wilson, 1975) have suggested that there may be a genetic or inherited component to ethnic prejudice. At present, there is not enough data on this proposal to merit a review.

and our culture will also strongly affect how we feel and act toward an ethnic group.

Cultural norms From the mid-1950's to the late 1960's, it was hard to pick up a newspaper without reading about some act of racism in the American South. A fourteen-year-old black boy is mutilated and murdered because he smiled at a white woman. Three civil rights workers are murdered by a deputy sheriff in Mississippi. Alabama state troopers, mounted on horseback, charge into a crowd of peaceful marchers and beat them to the ground. And on, and on. What was the cause of the virulent racism in the South? Some theorists thought that Southerners were racist because of some deep-seated psychological pathology. The typical Southerner, they believed, was brought up to hate anyone who was not a white, native-born American. Pettigrew (1961), however, proposed a much simpler explanation based on social norms. A *social norm* is an expectation about what a person should believe and how he should act, which is agreed upon by members of his culture or society. A culture will put formal and informal pressure on its members to conform to these norms. Pettigrew believed that an anti-black social norm existed in the South. Anti-black attitudes and behavior among individual white Southerners were due, in part, to their conforming to this norm. Pettigrew based his argument on three areas of research.

First, although the average Southerner was quite prejudiced against blacks, he displayed little prejudice against other ethnic groups. For example, a number of studies had shown that Southerners were less anti-Semitic than the nation as a whole. Pettigrew concluded that anti-black feelings did not represent part of some general ethnic hatred among Southerners.

Second, Pettigrew looked at the Southern level of authoritarianism, a personality characteristic associated with broad-based ethnic prejudice[2] (Adorno et al., 1950). If authoritarianism was the cause of racism in the South, then Southerners should score higher on Adorno et al.'s measure of authoritarianism than Northerners. They did not.

Finally, Pettigrew hypothesized that if racism is associated with social conformity, then those people who showed the greatest general social conformity should be the most anti-black. People who showed the least general social conformity should be the least anti-black. This seems to be true. For example, [in the South] there is a strong social norm to attend church. Pettigrew reported that regular churchgoers (i.e., social conformists) were much more anti-black than people who did not attend church (i.e., nonconformists).

Although there is considerable merit to Pettigrew's position, it has a serious shortcoming. At the time he wrote, it was assumed that widespread anti-black prejudice existed only in the South. Some twenty years later, we know this was not true. The violence which has accompanied school and neighborhood integration in the North strongly suggests that racism may be no greater in the South than in the North. Dick Gregory, the black comedian and civil rights activist, has described the difference between Northern and Southern America as follows. Both areas are equally racist. But in the North, blacks could get big but not too close, while in the South, they could get close but not too big. In other words, Southerners fear blacks obtaining economic and political power; Northerners fear blacks living next door to them. The fact that school integration has encountered more resistance in the North during the 1970's than in the South supports Gregory's point. Thus, before we can totally accept Pettigrew's analysis, the relationship between cultural norms and racism in the North must be demonstrated.

The "kernel of truth." Even if Pettigrew's analysis explained racism in the North, it would still be deficient. It does not explain why prejudicial social norms develop in the first place. Some theorists argue that these norms may have their origin in fact. This is known as the *"kernel of truth"* explanation of prejudice. This concept proposes that prejudice is due, at least in part, to the fact that some members of the group actually possess negative characteristics (Campbell, 1967; Schuman, 1966). Is there any evidence to support this position? Brigham (1971) reported that different groups show substantial agreement in their views of what a target ethnic group "is like." Since different people perceive the same characteristics, these characteristics may actually exist in the target group. Also, members of many ethnic groups hold the same stereotypes about themselves as do outsiders. For example, Dewey and Humber (1966) found that Jewish high school students held the same stereotypes about themselves as did non-Jews. Finally, there is some evidence which speaks directly to the accuracy of stereotypes. Abate and Berrien (1967) found a high correlation between Japanese perceptions of Americans' personality characteristics and the actual responses of Americans on a personality questionnaire.

Despite these findings, there is even stronger evidence that many ethnic stereotypes are inaccurate. Further, they are due to factors other than actual ethnic characteristics (Brigham, 1971). Different people *do* see similar characteristics in a particular ethnic group, but this may point to the cultural transmission of prejudice rather than the actual existence of these characteristics. For example, we were once told by an anthropologist about an extremely anti-Semitic Indian

---

[2]The relationship between authoritarianism and ethnic prejudice is discussed on pages 209 to 212.

he had interviewed. Almost every other word out of the Indian's mouth contained a derogatory view of Jews. Closer questioning revealed that the Indian had never seen or talked to a Jew. He had learned these stereotypes from a trader he dealt with.

One should also be aware that a large percentage of stereotypes are simply inaccurate. For example, in the Abate and Berrien study presented above, Americans were asked to describe the characteristics of Japanese. The correlation between their perceptions and the actual responses of Japanese on a personality questionnaire was practically zero.

Finally, note that the vast majority of stereotypes are negative (e.g., Puerto Ricans are lazy, Irish are drunks). It seems unlikely that a disliked ethnic group possesses only negative traits. A more reasonable explanation is that these negative perceptions are after-the-fact justifications of prejudice.

The effect of similarity. When Penner was in college, a friend of his was in love with a woman from a different ethnic background. He wrote telling his parents that he wanted to marry her. This is an almost verbatim transcript of their reply.

What in God's name is the matter with you? Why would you want to marry one of them? They're not like us. They look different, smell different, they don't like the same food we enjoy. People like her are trying to kill us and you want to bring one into our home. Stop all this foolishness and come back to your own kind. We need you.

The woman was a white, Anglo-Saxon Protestant. The man was a Chinese exchange student whose family lived in Malaysia. His parent's letter (which he translated for Penner) provides another explanation of ethnic prejudice—the effect of similarity.

Ethnic groups often differ in terms of their physical appearance and cultural traditions. These variations may cause one group to believe that another group differs in more than outward appearances. The differences may also involve beliefs, attitudes, and values. Now, recall what you learned about interpersonal attraction in Chapter Three. We tend to like people who are similar to us, and to dislike people who differ from us. Could this fact contribute to ethnic prejudice?

Milton Rokeach proposed that perceived dissimilarity may be a more important cause of prejudice and discrimination than simple membership in a racial or ethnic group. In other words, the man's parents didn't dislike the woman simply because she was white but rather because whites seem to be so different from Chinese (Rokeach, 1960; Rokeach, Smith, & Evans, 1960).

There is a positive relationship between prejudice and the belief that members of a different group hold different beliefs. For example, whites who are prejudiced against blacks feel that blacks' beliefs are very different from their own. This is not true of unprejudiced whites (Byrne & Wong, 1962). This relationship does not tell us, however, if perceived dissimilarity *causes* prejudice. To answer this question, we must look at studies which have pitted belief similarity against ethnic similarity.

Black or white job applicants at a state institution talked with four other people while they waited for an interview. They did not know that these four people were experimental confederates (Rokeach & Mezei, 1966). Two of them were of the same race as the applicant, and two were of a different race. The conversation concerned problems which these people might confront on the job. In each of the conversations, two of the confederates took the same position as the applicant, while the other two confederates disagreed with him. Afterward, the applicants were asked which of the people they had talked to they would prefer as co-workers.

This situation was devised so that the person always had to choose between a confederate of the same race who had disagreed with him and a confederate of a different race who had agreed with him. Rokeach and Mezei had thus pitted racial similarity against belief similarity. They found that a clear majority of subjects of both races chose a co-worker on the basis of belief rather than race. Comparable results have been obtained in a number of other studies (e.g., Hendrick, Bixenstine, & Hawkins, 1971; Silverman & Cochrane, 1972; Stein, Hardyck, & Smith, 1965).

Although Triandis (1961) and Triandis and Davis (1965) have disputed the belief similarity (or congruence) approach, most of the evidence is in its favor. Some caution is needed, however, in weighing this explanation of ethnic prejudice.

It is hard to determine if perceived differences in beliefs are a cause or an effect of prejudice. Does a white person dislike blacks because he sees them as different, or does he see blacks as different because he dislikes them? As with the "kernel of truth," perceived dissimilarity may be an after-the-fact effect of prejudice. We simply do not know to what extent perceived dissimilarity *causes* ethnic prejudice (Harding et al., 1969).

Thus far, the explanations of prejudice have been based on the factors which would cause an *individual* to be prejudiced. Blalock (1967) calls this the *micro-approach*. He argues that we can also take a *macro-approach*—that is, we can ask why *groups* of people are prejudiced. Blalock believed that prejudice may have its roots not only in how an individual responds to his environment but in how an entire society responds as well. More specifically, Blalock proposed that prejudice might be originally due to economic factors.

Economic factors. According to Blalock and others, prejudice may not be the cause of discrimination but the result. That is, a domi-

nant ethnic group may choose to discriminate against a minority group out of economic self-interest. This may take two forms: (1) exploitation, to obtain cheap labor and/or (2) restriction of the minority group's freedom in order to win the competition for scarce resources.

Let's look at exploitation. Imagine that you, the relative of a Pharaoh in ancient Egypt, have been given 100,000 acres of fertile land along the Nile. Your livelihood depends on your ability to plant and harvest crops. This task, however, requires hundreds of workers. So you put an advertisement on a number of tablets and distribute them in the area:

"WANTED: 1,000 WORKERS TO HARVEST WHEAT. WILL PAY TOP DRACHMA"

You wait for the workers to apply, but not one shows up. There is so much fertile land along the Nile that everyone is busy growing and harvesting his own crops. You are in serious trouble. Then it occurs to you that there are large numbers of second-class citizens from countries the Pharaoh has conquered. Since they have no power, you can force them to work for you as slaves. You send your soldiers to bring back 1,000 of them. These minority-group people are exploited because they will not willingly help you. Therefore, you must *force* them to work for you.

Blalock proposed that when there is much free fertile land available, the dominant group may force a minority group to work it. A cross-cultural analysis of slavery conducted by Nieboer (1910) indeed confirms that slavery was most common in agricultural societies. Further, as land became less available, slavery decreased and the voluntary labor of minority groups increased.

Blalock's and Nieboer's analyses would explain why slavery existed in the Southern but not the Northern United States. The land in the South was exceptionally fertile and the climate conducive to widespread agriculture.

Further, large numbers of people were needed to plant and harvest the crops. There were simply not enough people willing to work for others. Therefore, it was necessary to use force. Ethnic prejudice—perceiving blacks as inferior or even subhuman—was rationale for this exploitation.

The preconditions for *competition* leading to discrimination are quite different from exploitation. Exploitation occurs when there is an abundance of resources, competition when there is a shortage. If there is a shortage of resources (e.g., raw materials, jobs), the dominant group may feel compelled to keep the minority group from competing. How can they do this? One way is to pass laws and engage in practices which favor the dominant group. In other words, the discriminatory behavior is designed to eliminate competition. Prejudice is an after-the-fact justification for this behavior.

But why do prejudice and discrimination continue long after there is an economic reason for them? Blalock gave two possible reasons. First, the group that has been discriminated against may eventually start to act and feel inferior. This, in turn, contributes a "kernel of truth" to the originally untrue stereotypes. Second, status or social superiority accrues to the dominant group, and its members may be reluctant to give it up. In fact, they may want to maintain it even when it *hurts* them economically to do so. For example, one reason white Southerners have been slow to unionize is that while unions would bring higher pay, they would also demand that blacks be hired for the same jobs as whites (Greer, 1959; Northrup, 1944).

Indirect causes

There is little question that many of our experiences and the things we are taught lead directly to prejudice. But some social psychologists believe that our experiences may also indirectly affect our feelings about an ethnic group. Disliking a group may be a symptom of more basic psychological processes within us.

Authoritarianism. In the late 1940's, the American Jewish Congress was concerned that a Nazi-style extermination campaign might be mounted against American Jews. Why were they so worried? After all, America was not Nazi Germany. To understand their concern, a little background is needed.

First, while anti-Semitism had a long history in Europe, pre-Hitler Germany was one of the least anti-Semitic countries. It was one of the first European countries to grant Jews citizenship. Jewish scholars and businessmen were well integrated into the larger society. Yet this enlightened, progressive country almost succeeded in exterminating the Jews. America in the late 1940's was not a totally open society for Jews. The level of public anti-Semitism was greater than it had been in Germany before Hitler started his campaign of genocide (Adorno, Frenkel-Brunswick, Levinson, & Sanford, 1950). American Jews were still prevented from entering certain professions and businesses. Thus, their concern was not as unreasonable or paranoid as it might appear.

The American Jewish Congress asked Adorno and his associates to determine if there was a certain personality type that would be responsive to a fascist ideology. In dealing with this question, Adorno et al. made a distinction between ideology and personality. *Ideology* is those beliefs, attitudes, and values one holds about some political point of view. *Personality* is those internal forces which would lead one to accept a certain political ideology. Adorno et al. attempted to identify people with certain personality characteristics by first looking at ideology.

They believed that three things comprised

a fascist ideology: (1) anti-Semitism—negative and hostile attitudes toward Jews; (2) *ethnocentrism*—a tendency to glorify and submit to one's own ethnic group, accompanied by rejection of and hostility toward outgroups; and (3) political and economic conservatism—for example, a belief in laissez-faire capitalism or opposition to social change. Adorno et al. gave scales which measured these three things to a large number of Americans.

They predicted that the scores on these scales would correlate highly with one another, and they did. There was a very high correlation between anti-Semitism and ethnocentrism. People who disliked Jews also disliked blacks, Mexican-Americans, Filipinos, and other ethnic minorities. Conservatism correlated positively with anti-Semitism and ethnocentrism. But this relationship was much weaker than the relationship between anti-Semitism and ethnocentrism. Thus, these three ideologies did cluster together. However, the lower correlation between conservatism and the two other scales should be emphasized. A person who is conservative need not be anti-Semitic or anti-black. Conservatism should not be equated with fascism. Ronald Reagan is a conservative; Adolf Hitler was a fascist.

The next step in this research project was to gain more information about the personalities of people who were both anti-Semitic and ethnocentric. Adorno et al. collected biographical information about these people, gave them projective tests, and conducted in-depth interviews with them. On the basis of these data, they arrived at a personality trait called authoritarianism. They believed that *authoritarianism* has nine characteristics, which are presented in the accompanying box. They are illustrated with either an item from the questionnaire designed to measure authoritarianism (usually called the F [for fascism] scale) or quotations from Archie

Bunker, the loveable (?) bigot on the television show *All in the Family*). In many ways, Archie is the essence of the authoritarian personality type.

Adorno et al. found that scores on the F scale were highly correlated with anti-Semitic and ethnocentric ideologies and moderately correlated with political-economic conservatism. Subsequent research has shown that people who score high on the F scale tend to be ethnically prejudiced (Harding et al., 1969). That is, they tend to dislike any person who belongs to a different ethnic group.

What factors produce high authoritarianism? Adorno et al. believed that parental behavior was very important. It has been found that an authoritarian's parents tend to be very strict people who tolerate no deviations from traditional conservative values. When the child does misbehave, the parents use physical punishment and ridicule to discipline him and continue to punish him for a long time (Block, 1955; Hart, 1957; Levinson & Huffman, 1955; Lyle & Levitt, 1955).

Another factor that may lead to authoritarian tendencies is the belief that the world is a threatening place (Adorno et al., 1950). If this is true, then authoritarianism should increase during periods of economic threat. One study tested this prediction by looking at authoritarian themes in American popular literature during threatening and nonthreatening periods (Sales, 1973). For example, authoritarians are concerned with power and toughness. Sales analyzed how powerful comic strip characters were during a period of economic prosperity (1920–1929) and a period of economic hardship (1930–1939). As predicted, the comic strip heroes were significantly more powerful in the 1930–1939 period than during the 1920's. Another indication of authoritarianism is an interest in astrology. Sales found that during the period of upheaval over civil rights and Vietnam in the 1960's, significantly more books were pub-

The nine characteristics of the authoritarian personality

1. *Conventionalism*—Rigid adherence to middle-class conventional values.

   From the F scale: Obedience and respect for authority are the most important virtues children should learn.

2. *Authoritarian submission*—A submissive, uncritical attitude toward the leaders of the ingroup and devotion or obedience to that group.

   From the F scale: What this country needs more than laws and political programs is a few tireless, courageous, and devoted leaders in whom the people can put their faith.

3. *Authoritarian aggression*—A tendency to be on the lookout for and to condemn, reject, and punish people who violate conventional values.

   From Archie Bunker: "Anyone who goes around bothering other people, the only decent thing to do is knock 'em off. If you can't do it yourself, bring back the old death penalty."

4. *Anti-intraception*—An opposition to the subjective, the imaginative, the tender minded.

   From the F scale: If people would talk less and work more, everybody would be better off.

5. *Superstition and stereotyping*—The belief in mystical determinants of one's fate and the disposition to think in rigid categories.

   From an argument between Archie Bunker and his son-in-law, Mike, over the existence of God:

   MIKE: Arch, there is no heaven, there is no hell, and there is no God.

   ARCHIE: There he goes again, God! Did you hear that, Lord?

   MIKE: Oh, Arch . . . (Begins choking on food and sputtering)

   GLORIA: Michael, What's the matter?

   MIKE: (Still choking) Food . . . went . . . down . . . wrong way.

   ARCHIE: That's God payin' him back. Shovin' them words down your throat.

   GLORIA: (Pounding him on the back) Raise your arms over your head, honey!

   ARCHIE: The hell with him. Let him struggle. Serves you right, Meathead! Nobody fools around with the Lord . . . Go get him, God! Give it to him good, God! Do your stuff, Lord.

6. *Power and toughness*—Being preoccupied with leader-follower relationships, identification with power figures, and an exaggerated assertion of strength and toughness.

   Archie on his idol, "Moose" Hansen:

   MIKE: What makes him so respected?

   ARCHIE: What makes him so respected! Well, I'll give you a for instance! One day he's standin' out in front of the bowlin' alley arguing with some jerk over politics or something, and this jerk makes his final remark and he thinks he has Moose put away. You know what Moose done?

   MIKE: What?

   ARCHIE: He went over and ripped the door off the guy's car.

   MIKE: An intelligent man.

   ARCHIE: You're damn right. Then another time in the bowling alley he was waiting to get the phone to call his wife. And there was this hippy weirdo on the phone, so Moose started tapping on the door but the weirdo won't get off. So finally, do you know what Moose did?

   MIKE: He ripped the door off of the phone booth.

   ARCHIE: I told you the story before.

7. *Destructiveness and cynicism*—Generalized hostility, a basic distrust of others.

   From a conversation between Archie and his wife, Edith:

ARCHIE: . . . Edit', you ain't human.

EDITH: I'm just as human as you are.

ARCHIE: Oh yeah . . . then prove you're just as human as me. Do something rotten.

8. *Projectivity*—The belief that wild and dangerous things are going on in the world. A projection outward of unconscious emotional impulses.

From the F scale: "Most people don't realize how much our lives are controlled by plots hatched in secret places."

9. *Sexual concerns*—An exaggerated concern with sexual "goings on."

From the F scale: "The wild sex life of the old Greeks and Romans was tame compared to some of the goings on in this country."

lished on astrology than during the tranquil 1950's.

Although Adorno et al.'s work is important in helping us to understand prejudice, it has some serious flaws. First, it assumes that intolerance and authoritarianism exist only among extreme political conservatives. Is this a valid assumption?

What about Archie's son-in-law, Mike? Since the F scale seems to measure only right-wing authoritarianism and intolerance, Mike would not score very high. But isn't he as rigid and closed-minded as Archie? People like Mike led Milton Rokeach (1960) to investigate the concept of *dogmatism*—a tendency to be closed-minded, authoritarian, and rigid which is independent of any particular political ideology.

The research on dogmatism shows that authoritarian tendencies and intolerance of ideas different from one's own exist at both ends of the political spectrum. For example, Rokeach found that radical left-wing students are as closed-minded and rigid in their ideas as extreme right-wing students. Thus, Adorno et al. were wrong in believing that only right wingers display authoritarian tendencies.

The other major problem in Adorno et al.'s profile of authoritarianism is the implicit assumption that a bigot is mentally ill. Certainly, there are some people whose bigotry indicates an underlying pathology. but there are many more well-adjusted persons who are also bigoted. It is incorrect to equate prejudice with psychological pathology.

Frustration. A second view of ethnic prejudice as a symptom is based on the frustration-aggression hypothesis (cf. Chapter Four). Recall that one of the things that can lead to aggression is frustration (the interference with some goal-oriented activity). If the source is available and is not too threatening, the frustrated person may retaliate against him.

But what will happen if the source is unavailable and/or is too powerful to retaliate against? Then, Dollard et al. (1939) and Williams (1947) proposed, the frustrated person may *displace* his aggression onto someone else. The object of the displaced aggression is called a *scapegoat*. How is a scapegoat chosen? According to Williams, scapegoats are individuals who are available for aggression, highly visible (readily identifiable), and vulnerable (unable to retaliate).

Consider the following situation. You are a skilled welder at a defense plant. You are making six dollars an hour and are saving money to buy that home you always wanted. One day, your supervisor tells you that the company has lost its contract with the Defense Department. As a result, you and half of your co-workers will be laid off next Monday. This news so frustrates you that you want to punch somebody. But whom can you punch? Your supervisor? The layoff is not really his fault. Besides, if you punch him, you will probably never be hired again. The company? It's pretty hard to hit a company—or, alternatively, to hit the cause of the contract's termination, the Pentagon. How do you get rid of your anger? Miller (1959) and Williams (1947) say that you may displace it onto someone or something else. For example, you could go home and pull all the feathers off the family parakeet.

A number of researchers (e.g., Hovland & Sears, 1940; Miller & Bugelski, 1948; Pettigrew & Cramer, 1959) have proposed that some people's dislike for and hostility toward other ethnic groups may be a form of displaced aggression. These emotions are caused by nothing the ethnic group has done but by the frustrations a person has experienced. A minority, especially an ethnic minority, will be chosen as a scapegoat because it is available, highly visible, and often unable to retaliate.

Some tests of this theory have involved looking at the relationship between ethnic hostility and economic frustration. Perhaps the best-known example is the study by Carl Hovland and Robert Sears (1940). They calculated the annual price of cotton in the South from 1882 to 1930 and the number of lynchings of blacks for the same period. They found that as the price of cotton went down, the number of lynchings went up. Hovland and Sears interpreted their results as follows. A drop in the price of cotton frustrated white Southerners, but they were unable to aggress against the source of their frustration (the Northern cotton traders). Therefore, they displaced their aggression onto blacks, who were available, visible, and vulnerable.

The following two studies also seem to support the frustration-based explanation of ethnic prejudice. Pettigrew and Cramer (1959) found that whites from the poorest areas of the South voted for the most pro-segregationist candidates. Ross, Vanneman, and Pettigrew (1976) analyzed the supporters of George Wallace in his bids for the presidency. They found that nationwide, Wallace supporters were poorer and less educated than non-Wallace supporters. Presumably these whites were frustrated by their economic and social status and manifested this in anti-black behavior.

But do these data really support the frustration-displaced aggression theory of prejudice? The whites in these last two studies may have voted for segregationist candidates not because they hated blacks but because they thought such politicians would give them an edge in a poor labor market. (Remember Blalock's economic explanation of prejudice.)

There are other problems with this explanation. First, it is based on a psychodynamic, or drive, view of aggression. That is, there is something called "aggressive energy" which must be released. As noted in the review of interpersonal aggression, we can't accept this premise. We do not believe that frustration and aggressive energy build up in a person like steam in a pressure cooker and find an outlet in prejudice and discrimination.

In support of this view are a series of studies by Epstein and Komorita (1965, 1966). They tested the hypothesis that children of punitive, authoritarian parents would display more prejudice than children of non-punitive parents. Why? Because the children had experienced frustration at the hands of their punitive parents. Epstein and Komorita found that children of punitive parents were *not* more prejudiced than other children.

Another problem with the frustration explanation is its implication that frustration itself causes prejudice. This is not the case. In fact, frustration appears to increase ethnic hostility only among people who are *already*

Joseph Ferrandino

prejudiced. For example, Berkowitz (1959) and Weatherly (1961) frustrated anti-Semitic and non-anti-Semitic individuals and then had them evaluate a person with a Jewish name. Frustration increased hostility toward the Jew only among those who were already anti-Semitic. Among nonprejudiced subjects, frustration actually *increased* liking.

The reduction of ethnic prejudice

A house divided against itself cannot stand. (Abraham Lincoln, 1858)

The nation is rapidly moving toward two increasingly separate Americas . . . a white society . . . and a Negro society . . . . Within two decades, this division could be so deep that it will be impossible to unite. . . . (Report of the National Advisory Commission on Civil Disorders, 1969)

Some means must be found to reduce the ethnic prejudice in our society. The next few pages will be concerned with certain ways this might be accomplished.

The effect of intergroup contact

Tom Wicker grew up in a small Southern town in the 1930's. He had little contact with blacks as a youth. While not a violent racist, Wicker certainly did not like black people. When he was in the Navy, he spent ten days on a train with a group of black sailors. Here is a description of what happened.

. . . that 10 days had been the time of his discovery that black people were just that—people, individuals, human as he was, hurting, laughing, loving, worrying in much the same fashion about much the same things, whatever the inexcusable and ineradicable differences in their experience.

The blacks still were preoccupied, as he was, with families, jobs, schooling, girls. No two of them were much alike in temperament or personality. Some he liked, some he did not. One was better read than he; another was mentally deficient, or so it seemed . . . . Others shared plans and memories as equals with young Tom Wicker. Since in 10 days all the men on the car got only one shower—at the St. Louis YMCA, to which they were marched from the city's magnificent old railroad station one blessed evening—it turned out that whites when dirty smelled as bad as blacks when dirty. In such close quarters, it became apparent that black penises were no bigger than white and no more thought about by their possessors, which was constantly. The only major difference, other than skin color, was that, with one or two exceptions, the blacks were not as well educated as the whites, although all had gone to school. (Wicker, 1975, pp. 209–210)

Note the effect of Wicker's prolonged contact with the blacks. It gave him first-hand information about what black people were like. This, in turn, influenced two of the factors related to ethnic prejudice. First, he discovered that many of the stereotypes he held about blacks were simply untrue. Second, he found out that blacks were really not very different from him. Thus, negative feelings toward blacks as the result of stereotypes and perceived dissimilarity were reduced. Do other people respond to intergroup contact as Wicker did? The answer is yes, but with some qualifications. (These will be covered shortly.)

In 1949, Stouffer, Suchman, De Vinney, Star, and Williams were commissioned by the U.S. Army to study the ethnic attitudes of American soldiers. At that time, almost all military units were racially segregated. (It was not until the Korean war that they were ordered to integrate.) Stouffer et al. examined the attitudes of the few white soldiers who were in integrated companies. Their answers were compared to those of white soldiers who had no blacks in their company. A majority of white soldiers in integrated companies expressed neutral or positive attitudes toward including blacks. A majority of whites from all-white companies were against this idea.

It has also been found that whites who live in the same building as blacks have more favorable attitudes toward them than whites who live in all-white buildings in the same neighborhood (Deutsch & Collins, 1951; Wilner, Walkley, & Cook, 1955).

Now to the qualifications. First, recall the effect of propinquity on interpersonal attraction (page 85). Propinquity is necessary for attraction, but it is not enough. Physical closeness will not, by itself, produce liking. In fact, if closeness produces an unpleasant interaction, it can lead to disliking rather than liking. For example, imagine a white American who thinks that all Indians are slow-witted drunks and an American Indian who believes that all whites are slow-witted racists. They end up bunking next to one another in the Army. In this case, their interaction may well lead to aggression rather than attraction.

A second qualification is based on Brehm's (1966) concept of reactance. *Reactance* is a person's belief that somehow his personal freedom is being restricted. This produces many negative reactions in him. One reaction is to strengthen his already existing attitudes. Thus, reactance theory predicts that if a person believes that intergroup contact is being forced on him, he may become more, not less, prejudiced. This analysis may explain, in part, why forced school busing has aroused such passion among some whites.

This is not to say that intergroup contact is therefore undesirable. There is little question that it can help to reduce prejudice. It should not, however, be viewed as an automatic cure-all. It will work when there is some reason to expect that the information exchange will be positive and the participants do not see their contact as forced.

The effect of role playing

School teacher Jane Eliot was discussing racial prejudice with her third graders. Prejudice is a fairly sophisticated concept for eight-year-olds, so Ms. Eliot decided to show her students how it felt to be discriminated against. She divided them into two groups: one with blue eyes and one with brown eyes. On the first day of her demonstration, the brown-eyed children were the targets. The class was told that blue-eyed children were smarter, learned faster, behaved better, and were cleaner than brown-eyed children. Ms. Eliot denied certain privileges to the brown-eyed children and criticized them whenever she could. The next day, the roles were reversed. Could this creative teaching technique reduce ethnic prejudice?

Weiner and Wright (1973) tested Ms. Eliot's demonstration. Children were given green and orange armbands and were discriminated against in the same way Ms. Eliot had used. Then their attitudes were compared to those of children who had not played the minority group role. The role players were found to have more positive attitudes toward blacks and were more willing to interact with them than the control group. Why did this procedure work?

One possible explanation is that role playing may have increased the ability to empathize with black children. As the review of pro-social behavior showed, empathy can increase positive feelings toward another person (Aronfreed, 1968).

Consider also the research on attitude change. You will recall that a person whose behavior is inconsistent with his attitudes will often change his attitudes to match his behavior. Several studies have shown that role playing of this type will decrease ethnic prejudice (e.g., Culbertson, 1957; Gray & Ashmore, 1975).

Would Ms. Eliot's technique work with adults? We are not sure it would. Attitudes are only one of many determinants of how a person feels and acts. An adult might be pressured by his friends not to act positively toward blacks; he might have strong habits which are hard to break; and other factors may override the empathy this experience has created.

Data from the real world support this final possibility. Poor, uneducated whites probably have had similar experiences to many blacks. However, surveys show that these whites are among the most anti-black groups in America (Pettigrew & Cramer, 1959; Rokeach, 1973). The reason for this finding may be provided by Blalock's economic theory of prejudice. Poor whites are usually the most direct competitors with poor blacks for decent jobs, homes, and other scarce resources. This competition may shape the whites' feelings more strongly than sharing similar experiences. This possibility leads us to another approach to reducing prejudice.

The establishment of joint goals

There is little question that competition is a major cause of ethnic prejudice (Ashmore, 1970; Blalock, 1967; Hamblin, 1962; Silverthorne, Chelune, & Imada, 1974). But what would happen if two groups had to *cooperate* in order to reach some goal? A classic study investigated this (Sherif, Harvey, White, Hood, & Sherif, 1961).

The setting was a summer camp for boys. The boys were divided into two groups, the Eagles and the Rattlers. Through some carefully constructed situations, Sherif et al. created considerable conflict and animosity between them. As one might expect, each group became more cohesive and tended to avoid any contact with the other. Food fights, name calling, petty acts of vandalism, and actual violence between them were quite common.

Sherif et al. then examined the effect of a superordinate goal on intergroup conflict. A *superordinate goal* is one that is unattainable by any one group alone and supersedes other goals which each group might have (Sherif & Sherif, 1969). They believed that such a goal would increase interactions between the two groups. This would eliminate negative attitudes and stereotypes and would reduce future conflicts between them.

Sherif et al. created three situations involving superordinate goals: (1) the camp's water system "broke down," and both groups had to work together if it was to be repaired; (2) a movie which both groups wanted to see could be shown only if they worked together to obtain it; and (3) a truck which was to take both groups to lunch broke down, and could be started only if both groups pulled it.

Then the researches examined changes in the attitudes and behaviors of both groups. Friendships developed between them. Fighting and name calling decreased dramatically. Eagles made contact with Rattlers, and vice versa. It is important to note that these effects were not immediate; they developed over several weeks.

There is evidence that similar situations can reduce prejudice. For example, Burstein and McRae (1962) found that an external threat reduced anti-black feeling among white Southern college students. However, this was not found for highly prejudiced students.

The passage of laws

Many people argue that we can't legislate morality or attitudes. But the changes in America over the past twenty years suggest that perhaps we can. In 1954, the Supreme Court declared school segregation unconstitutional. In 1964 and 1965, Congress passed laws prohibiting racial discrimination in the areas of voting, employment, and public accommodations (i.e., hotels, restaurants).

There is little question that these three events produced dramatic shifts in racial attitudes and behavior.

In the early 1960's, George Wallace stood at the entrance to the University of Alabama to prevent black students from enrolling. "Segregation now. Segregation forever!" he proclaimed. Ten years later, he crowned a black woman homecoming queen at the same university. In areas of the South where they were previously forbidden to vote, blacks now hold public office. A number of Northern and Southern cities now have black mayors. A white Southerner has been elected President partly by appealing to black voters.

There have been changes in whites' attitudes as well. Hero (1973) pointed out that most Americans opposed the Civil Rights Act of 1964. But, he also notes, today over 75 percent of the public favors integration in schools, public accommodations, and employment. The increased contact that resulted from government-ordered integration may be responsible for another change. Many of the negative stereotypes held by whites about blacks have declined (Karlins, Coffman, & Walters, 1969). Some studies now show that whites may sometimes act *more* positively toward blacks than they do toward other whites (Dutton, 1976).

But before we congratulate ourselves on eliminating racism in America, let's look at the other side. Blacks, Indians, Mexican-Americans, Puerto Ricans, and other minority groups are still living at a level far below that of the average white American. Many people feel that the main effect of the civil rights legislation has been to ensure that a middle-class black Ph.D. will be able to get an excellent job. This person's brothers and sisters in the ghetto are still oppressed. A few statistics support this view.

The unemployment rate among blacks is more than twice that of whites. In fall 1977, it was the highest in thirty years. Just over 50

Racist honkey? Who's a racist honkey?

Donald Dutton (1976) reported on a series of studies concerned with *reverse discrimination*. This happens when majority groups treat members of their own group worse than they treat members of a minority group.

The first study was conducted in restaurants that required men to wear ties. Black or white men without ties entered and tried to get a table. A tieless black man was more than twice as likely to succeed as a tieless white man who followed him. When a white man entered the restaurant first, both he and the black man who followed him were likely to be refused service.

In subsequent studies, Dutton found that whites were more willing to give money to blacks collecting for charity and black panhandlers than to whites making the same request.

But does this demonstrate reverse discrimination or tokenism? That is, will whites favor blacks only when trivial behaviors are involved? If someone performs a small favor, he will usually be more willing to do a larger favor later on (cf. Chapter Eight for the reasons why). Dutton used this phenomenon to determine if preferential behavior toward blacks represented tokenism rather than reverse discrimination.

White students were asked by a white or black panhandler for money for a meal. The black beggar, on the average, received twice as much money. Then the effect of this small favor on subsequent behavior was examined. Students who had been approached by the panhandler and another group of students who had not were asked to help in a "Brotherhood Week" on campus. Students who had given money to the white panhandler were the most willing to help. This is in accord with the phenomenon described above. But students who had given money to the black panhandler were *least* willing to help. Evidently, these people's worries about being seen as a racist had been taken care of, and they saw no need to go further. This is closer to tokenism than reverse discrimination.

percent of all black workers are unskilled or semi-skilled. About 33 percent of all black Americans have an average yearly income which is below the poverty level; this is true of less than 9 percent of whites. The median income of the average black family is 60 percent that of the white family (Staples, 1976).

Many schools in the North are still segregated. Attempts to desegregate them have met with violent opposition.

All this suggests that while we have come a long way in the last twenty-five years, we still have a long way to go. Ethnic prejudice is still a serious problem in America.

Conclusion

In this section, the causes of ethnic prejudice and possible means to reduce it were examined. Prejudice can be the direct or indirect result of previous life experiences. The direct causes were examined first. Obviously, the attitudes and behaviors of one's parents are important in shaping one's attitudes toward other groups. Also, however, norms, beliefs about a group's characteristics, and the idea that the group is different may all contribute to prejudice. Economic factors, such as the need for cheap labor or to restrict competition for scarce resources, may also lead to prejudice and discrimination. The mistreatment of a minority group may continue long after there is any economic reason for it.

Prejudice as the indirect result of life experiences centered on the research on authoritarianism and the frustration-aggression hypothesis. The former approach views prejudice as a sign of underlying personality variables; the latter sees prejudice and discrimination as displaced aggression due to frustration. In other words, both approaches view prejudice as symptomatic of basic processes within a person. There are data which support both explanations. However, there are some serious deficiencies in each of them. For example, the research on authoritarianism implies that bigotry and closed-mindedness are confined to "sick" people of the political right. This is simply not true. The drive view of aggression which underlies the frustration-displaced aggression explanation has not been supported by the research on aggression.

Can ethnic prejudice be reduced? We really don't know. The experiments presented seem to suggest that it can, but these were conducted mostly in isolated artificial environments. The evidence from the real world is mixed. American is clearly a much less racist country than it was twenty years ago. New laws have reduced prejudice and discrimination. However, minorities are still largely discriminated against. We don't think that ethnic prejudice is permanent. But its reduction will be very difficult.

REVIEW QUESTIONS

(Ten out of twelve is passing)

1. The basic difference between prejudice and discrimination is that prejudice refers to a(n) _____ and discrimination refers to a(n) _____ . (p. 203)
2. People who have religion, racial origins, national origin, or language and culture in common are referred to as a(n) _____ _____ . (p. 204)
3. The fact that white Southerners in the 1950's tended to be anti-black but not anti-Semitic suggested that their prejudice toward blacks may have been due to _____ _____ . (p. 205)
4. The statement that all Irishmen are drunks is a(n) _____ _____ . (p. 206)
5. The _____ _____ explanation of prejudice is based on the finding from interpersonal attraction research that people like other people who hold comparable beliefs, attitudes, and values. (p. 207)
6. Blalock's macro-analysis of prejudice proposed that when there is plenty of land and no one to cultivate it, _____ might be the reason for ethnic discrimination. (p. 208)
7. The research on authoritarianism and displaced aggression views prejudice as a(n) _____ . (p. 209)
8. The tendency to glorify one's own group and reject outgroups is called _____ . (p. 210)
9. While anti-Semitism refers to a person's _____ , authoritarianism refers to a person's _____ . (p. 209)
10. The object of displaced aggression is called the _____ . (p. 212)

11. One reason why forced intergroup contact may not reduce prejudice is that it may generate _____ . (p. 215)

12. The existence of superordinate goals may reduce prejudice by reducing _____ . (p. 217)

ANSWERS

1. attitude, behavior   2. ethnic group   3. cultural norm   4. ethnic stereotype
5. perceived dissimilarity   6. exploitation   7. symptom   8. ethnocentrism
9. ideology, personality   10. scapegoat   11. reactance   12. competition

SEXISM

Shelley says "man be free and woman a slave and idiot." Never, say I. (Anna Wheeler, 1825)

Woman is the nigger of the world. (Yoko Ono, 1970)

Sexism consists of two beliefs. First, men and women each have a distinctive makeup which determines their respective lives. Second, one sex is superior to the other and therefore has the right to rule it (Task Force on Sex Bias and Sex Role Stereotyping in Psychotherapeutic Practice, 1975). Sexism involves *sex role stereotypes*. These are certain characteristics which are assigned to one sex but not the other and the expectation that because a person is of a certain sex, he or she will act in a certain way.

For example, Rosenkrantz, Vogel, Bee, Broverman, and Broverman (1968) asked male and female college students to list adjectives which described the "average man" and the "average woman." A partial listing of these traits is presented in Figure 7-1. Note the dramatic differences simply as a function of sex.

When one refers to sexism, one can be talking about prejudice against either men or women.[3] This discussion focuses on women—not because men, too, may not be victims but because sexism directed toward women is far more widespread and deeply ingrained.

Illustrations of sexism

Job discrimination

The number of women who hold either full or part-time jobs in the United States has increased dramatically over the last twenty years. In 1974, 46 percent of all women over sixteen years of age worked, representing 39 percent of the labor force (*A Statistical Portrait of Women in the United States,* 1976). Meanwhile, the gap between men's and women's salary has continued to increase. For example, in 1960 the average woman earned $2,000 per year less than the average man; in 1975 (the most recent year on which there are

---

[3]For example, Cohen and Bunker (1975) reported that recruiters for large companies found a man who was interested in a traditionally female job as less acceptable for the job than a woman with the same credentials.

statistics), this difference had grown to $5,000 (United States Bureau of the Census). A woman with a college education was earning less than a man with a high school diploma (Deckard, 1975).

The immediate cause of these discrepancies is the types of jobs men and women hold. For example, the percentage of women in clerical positions (e.g., secretaries) increased from 59 percent to 75 percent between 1950 and 1972, while the percentage of female professionals and managers declined slightly over the same period (Parsons, Frieze, & Ruble, 1976).

The "business" of education illustrates what is going on. In the New York State, 59 percent of all teachers are women, but 86 percent of all principals are men (*New York Times,* November 14, 1976). At the college

level, the percentage of women holding full-time teaching jobs has gone from 19 percent in 1910 to 18 percent in 1970.

Why are women ending up in lower-level jobs? In a 1970 study, Fidell revealed sexism in academic hiring practices. She sent descriptions of people with Ph.D.'s in psychology to the directors of psychology programs across the country and asked them if they would hire the person described. The descriptions of female and male Ph.D's were identical. Despite this fact, only the men were offered full professorships; men received more offers leading to tenure than women; and men were given higher ratings on a scale of job desirability.

A study by Virginia Schein (1973) suggests that such discriminatory hiring practices are largely due to sex role stereotypes. Schein

Average man	Average woman
Very aggressive	Not at all aggressive
Very independent	Not at all independent
Not at all emotional	Very emotional
Very objective	Not at all objective
Very dominant	Very submissive
Likes math and science very much	Dislikes math and science
Very logical	Very illogical
Very self-confident	Not all all self-confident
Not at all aware of the feelings of others	Very aware of the feelings of others
Very little need for security	Strong need for security
Not at all talkative	Very talkative
Very blunt	Very tactful

Figure 7-1. College students' listing of the traits of the average man and the average woman. (Adapted from Rosenkrantz, Vogel, Bee, Broverman, & Broverman, 1968)

asked male industrial managers to describe the characteristics of successful managers and then to describe a typical man and a typical woman. Schein found that these managers saw successful managers as possessing more of the characteristics, attitudes, and temperament of men than of women. In 1975, Schein repeated this study, using female managers. She found that these women held the same views as their male counterparts. Also, the opinion that women lack the necessary traits to be a successful manager was held most strongly by the *younger* and less experienced female managers. Note how Schein's second study provides another explanation of why women are underutilized in the labor force. Her data suggest that in some cases, women may select themselves out of the managerial market. They do not believe they have the necessary skills for success.

Reinforcement of sex role stereotypes

In general, men and women are judged and reacted to in terms of sex role stereotypes. For example, when people are not given clear information about someone's competence, they will believe that men are more competent than women. Goldberg (1968) gave female college students identical scientific articles to read and rate on their merit but varied the sex of the supposed author. Articles were rated as much less valuable and the authors as less competent when the author was a female. Pheterson, Kiesler, & Goldberg (1971) found that identical paintings attributed to male artists were rated as better than those attributed to female artists. Piacente, Penner, Hawkins, & Cohen (1974) showed college students videotapes of male and female experimenters who acted either competently or incompetently. Females were rated slightly better than males in the competent condition, but the interesting data come from the incompetent condition.[4] Subjects did not change their ratings of a male experimenter very much when he acted incompetently. However, the woman was judged as much more feminine when she acted incompetently than when she acted competently. Piacente et al. concluded that their subjects (both males and females) evidently equated competence with masculinity and incompetence with femininity.

Both men and women are expected to act in accord with their sexual stereotypes. When they deviate from these "typical" behaviors, they may be punished. For example, it is "natural" for a man to act aggressively and a woman to act dependently. However, an aggressive woman and a dependent man (called *sex role incongruent behavior*) are evaluated quite negatively (Costrich, Feinstein, Kidder, Maracek, & Pascale, 1975). Further, people who deviate from their sex roles are seen as more emotionally disturbed than people who

---

[4]Similar findings about judgments of clearly competent men and women have been found by Taynor and Deaux (1975).

conform. A man who acts submissively (a "feminine" characteristic) is less popular than one who acts forcefully. Among women, submissiveness does not affect popularity.

These are all examples of sex role stereotyping. People are judged by their sex rather than by their individual personalities and abilities. Sex role stereotyping is probably the primary cause of sexism.

The causes of sexism

Sexism and sex role stereotypes are widespread. To understand why they are so pervasive, one must look at history (or herstory).

A historical perspective

Even when our ancestors lived in caves, *sex roles* existed. That is, labor was divided on the basis of sex (Deckard, 1975). The assignment of jobs was based on biological differences between the sexes and the economics of survival. Because men were physically more muscular and did not bear children, they became the hunters. Women became the artisans, farmers, caretakers of children, and guardians of the home territory. Although roles were assigned on the basis of sex, there was no status difference; the separate roles were equally valued. With the development of agriculture and the domestication of animals, women became the farmers and men the animal herders. These roles remained equally necessary, and similar status was accorded to each.

After the invention of the ox-drawn plow, men, as animal caretakers, began to take over agriculture, and women's role as a food provider diminished. The loss of economic power was accompanied by a loss in social status (Deckard, 1975).[5]

[5]Much of this historical review is based on Deckard's 1975 review of this topic.

In some parts of the world, this situation continued for many centuries. In Europe, wealth began to be determined by land ownership. Laws of inheritance were written to formalize who would receive this valuable resource after a person died. Inheritance was determined mainly by whether the person was the legitimate child of the dead owner. Since women produced the children, a wife became a valuable piece of property for her land-owning husband. This resulted in the further isolation of women from the economic mainstream and the pressure to keep women exclusively as wives and mothers. After all, a land owner didn't want his "property" to run away.

This economically motivated oppression of women was reinforced by the norms and mores of the time. For example, by the thirteenth century, the Catholic Church was a potent force in Europe. Church doctrine reflected the then current view of the personal worth of women. Thomas Acquinas, the most important Catholic theologian of the thirteenth century, described women as follows:

As regard the individual nature, woman is defective and misbegotten, for the male seed tends to the production of a perfect likeness in the masculine sex; while the production of woman comes from a defect in the active force. (Quoted by Deckard, 1975, p. 193)

In the period following the Protestant Reformation (which occurred in the sixteenth century), European society changed from one where wealth was based on land ownership to one based on capital (e.g., money, goods). Further, an increasing number of people made their living in trade (e.g., shoemakers, blacksmiths). These changes, and the Industrial Revolution which followed them, made the economic justification for women's inferior status less valid. And, indeed, as a class of tradespeople emerged, women's status improved slightly. This was primarily because of women's role in their husband's trade.

But by this time, the second-class status of women was such a ingrained part of society that the justifications for it continued. In the early 1800's, a number of essays were published on the proper roles for women. Hogeland (1974) has provided some illustrative quotations. Drawing heavily on Christian doctrine, one early nineteenth century author wrote:

God created women merely as an afterthought for the benefit of his *central* creation, man. Thus the function of women, aside from perpetuating the race, was to please man. (Cited by Hogeland, 1974, p. 22; italics added)

Some writers were more generous than this nineteenth century author of the "*Playboy* philosophy" and actually saw women as having an important, if limited, role in society. Some believed that as a product of their "God-given natures," women were competent to raise their children as Christians, provide a home for their husbands, and preserve the moral fabric of a nation (Hogeland, 1974). A worthwhile but hardly fulfilling life's work.

The Victorian age of the late nineteenth and early twentieth centuries furthered sex role stereotypes. Marriage manuals pictured women as the guardians of purity, modesty, and virtue.[6] Women were told to discourage any wakenings of "animal passions" in men, since it was believed that sexual involvement weakened men's "vital forces." The young bride was told that she should have no interest in sex since "careless and amative acts by the female destroyed the innate dignity of the wifely role and led to the misuse of the sexual function in irresponsible and immodest responses in the male" (Haller, 1974, p. 133).

[6]Of course, this description was intended for the upper-class Victorian "lady." While she was being put on a pedestal, her poorer sisters were working sixty or seventy hours a week under terrible conditions for minuscule wages.

Economic conditions, which were partly responsible for the initial status differences between men and women, also (as least temporarily) changed people's attitudes about the appropriate activities for women. By the mid 1930's, many American women were working out of necessity. Still, a poll taken in 1935 showed that 80 percent of all Americans thought it was wrong for a woman, especially one with a family, to work. Two men—Hitler and Tojo—indirectly changed this attitude. World War II removed men from the civilian work force and encouraged women to take over their jobs. Characters such as "Rosie the Riveter" were popularized, and by 1942 over 70 percent of all Americans thought women could and should work (Deckard, 1975).

When the war ended, sex role stereotypes returned. The mass media began to promote the home as the natural place for women so that the (male) veterans could be given jobs. America's post-war economy continued to expand, however, and as a result, increasing numbers of women joined the work force. But these women were discriminated against in terms of wages, admission to professional schools, and promotions to positions of power and authority. A bill introduced by U.S. Representative Helen Gahagan Douglas in 1945 to guarantee women equal pay for equal work was not passed by Congress until 1963.

The 1950's and early 1960's saw an increasing concern for civil rights for blacks, but the role of women in American society remained unchanged. Even in civil rights groups, women were secretaries and clerks. Friedan described the popular portrayal of women during this period as follows: "Women's magazines reflected the image of women . . . [as] young frivolous, almost childlike; fluffy and feminine, passive, gaily content in a world of bedroom and kitchen, sex, babies, and home" (Friedan, 1963, p. 30).

In the mid 1960's women began to react against such stereotypes. Betty Friedan

(1963) published *The Feminine Mystique*, which attacked the myths about women and the validity of role stereotypes for both sexes. Three years later, the National Organization of Women (N.O.W.) was formed. In seven years, its membership increased from 300 to 300,000.[7]

This brief historical review shows that sex role stereotypes and sexism are hardly recent. Indeed, according to the Old Testament book of Leviticus, Moses was told by the Lord that a woman was worth thirty shekels of silver while a man was worth fifty. This difference is roughly equivalent to the average difference in pay between men and women in America in 1976. But this review also suggests that the economic reasons for sex role stereotypes are no longer valid. Why have they continued?

Biological explanations

Recall the "kernel of truth" explanation of ethnic prejudice; it suggests that bias may not be entirely unreasonable. It may be due to the fact that some group is actually inferior or really does possess negative traits.

As we all learned at some point, men and women are biologically different. Some people have argued that women are treated as inferior because they are, in fact, biologically inferior to men.

"Anatomy is destiny." One of the most prominent advocates of this position was Sigmund Freud (1933). Freud believed that our adult personality is the result of our experiences as

we pass through a series of developmental stages. One of the most important of these is the *phallic* stage. It occurs at about age four and involves the discovery of one's genitals. A boy realizes that he has a penis and a girl realizes that she has clitoris. Let's first consider the effect of this realization on boys.

According to Freud, the boy is faced with a very threatening situation. He has sexual desires toward his mother, but he fears that these will be discovered by his father, who will castrate him.[8] To resolve this castration fear, the boy abandons his sexual desires toward his mother and identifies with his father. Part of this identification process involves internalizing his father's and society's mores and values. Thus, the traumatic shift which most boys experience causes them to develop a mature superego (conscience). Girls, on the other hand, experience no such fear of castration. Thus, they do not have to shift their desires for and identification with one parent to another. Since girls do not experience this trauma-induced shift, they develop a weaker superego. This results in adult women having less of a sense of justice and being less moral than men (Williams, 1977).

Freud believed that the discovery that she lacks a penis has two related effects on the girl. She envies males and blames her mother for her deficiency. This *penis envy* causes feelings of inferiority. To compensate for these feelings, she becomes vain and places more emphasis on her physical charms. This penis envy also causes contempt for other women, since they share her deficiency, as well as jealousy of men, feelings of shame, excessive emotionality, and dependence. Freud believed that a woman could resolve her penis envy by substituting a desire to

---

[7]The feminist movement in the United States dates back formally to 1848 and the Women's Convention at Seneca Falls, New York. Although small in number, early advocates of women's rights successfully lobbied for the right to vote in the early 1900's. Although feminists such as Emma Goldman were active in the 1920's, 1930's, and 1940's, the movement waned after women were granted the right to vote.

[8]This castration fear arises out of the boy's belief that females lack a penis because they have been castrated and his desire to avoid a similar fate.

have a baby. But because of the early rein-forcement of penis envy among women, these feelings of inferiority and jealousy exist to a greater extent in them than in men (Willi-ams, 1977).

Freud's theoretical position has been popu-larly called *"anatomy is destiny."* This is be-cause of its basic premise that anatomical differences between men and women cause the personality differences between them.

Freud's disciples have continued and ex-panded this theme. For example, Erik Erik-son (1964, 1968) believed that females not only suffer from penis envy but also spend their lives worrying about never filling their "inner space" (i.e., the uterus). Garai (1970) put forth a much less psychoanalytic argu-ment than Freud and Erikson, but one that was also based on biology. He believed that personality differences between men and women were due to biologically determined differences in their needs. Men have a basic need to achieve; women have a basic need to be accepted by others.

Others explain stereotypic behavior in terms of male and female hormones. For ex-ample, a doctor who once attended Hubert Humphrey said that no woman could ever be President. He claimed that she would be at the mercy of her "raging hormones."

The animal studies. Some theorists have used the concept of dimorphism among animals to support the biological explanation of sex roles. *Dimorphism* is the difference between males and females of a species in anatomy, physiology, and behavior (Ratner, 1977). These theorists argue that anatomical and behavioral differences between the sexes ex-ist in almost all other species and therefore must apply to humans. For example, male primates tend to be more aggressive than females (Money & Erhardt, 1972). Therefore, human males must be biologically more ag-gressive than human females.

The effect of size. The final argument suggests an indirect effect of biological differences. It states that since men are usually stronger and more muscular than women, they must be better suited for positions of power and authority (Tiger, 1969). Are these arguments valid?

Problems with the biological argument

Is anatomy really destiny? There do seem to be some biologically determined differences in male and female behavior. For example, it seems that greater aggressiveness in men is due, at least in part, to different hormonal secretions (Maccoby & Jacklin, 1974a). But other than this, there is not much evidence that Freud and his disciples were correct.

In lower animals, a good deal of behavior is controlled by hormones and instincts. But this influence decreases as we go up the phylogenetic scale (Beach, 1969; Ford & Beach, 1951). For humans, experiences *after* birth seem to be the primary cause of stereo-typic behavior.

Studies which have compared the importance of a person's assigned and biological sex in determining behavior illustrate this. A per-son's *assigned sex* is the gender the person is given at birth (Hampson & Hampson, 1961). *Biological sex* consists of several biological indicators of gender (e.g., chromosomes, gona-dal sex, hormonal sex). For most people, as-signed sex is the same as biological sex. There are, however, a very small number of excep-tions. One such group is hermaphrodites.

Hermaphroditism is a relatively rare biologi-cal phenomenon in which a person is born with the biological characteristics of both a male and a female (e.g., both ovaries and testes). Money, Hampson and Hampson (1957) studied 105 biological hermaphrodites. These were people who could grow up with a discrepancy between their biological sex and their assigned sex. If a person's biology (or anatomy) is as important as some have claimed, then a large percentage of these hermaphrodites should have displayed behavior which deviated from their assigned sex. In fact, this was true of only 5 of the 105 hermaphrodites studied. In other words, the parents' decision as to whether these people would be raised as a boy or a girl was much more powerful in shaping their behavior than was their biological sex. After twenty years of working with transsexuals and homosexuals, Money & Ehrhardt (1972) concluded that a person's assigned sex is much more important for behavior than biological sex.

Further weakening the biological argument are Margaret Mead's classic anthropological studies of various tribes in the South Pacific (Mead, 1935). If anatomy is destiny, then one should find similar sex-typed behaviors everywhere in the world. A *sex-typed* behavior is one that reflects a society's norms regarding appropriate behavior for men and women. Mead (1935), however, reported on one tribe where the women were the leaders and managers and men were seductive, docile, and trained to entertain the women. In two other tribes, Mead found no evidence of sex role differences. What her work shows is that sex role stereotypes are neither worldwide nor genetically determined. Stereotyped behavior seems to result from the cultures socialization practices.

Are animal behaviors really sex-role stereotyped? Claims that lower animals always behave in a stereotyped manner are somewhat overstated. There is a good deal of variability across species (Rosenberg, 1976). For example, the lion may be the king of the jungle, but it is the lioness who does most of the killing and hunting. Among marmoset monkeys, males are responsible for most of the child care. Male and female gibbons are indistinguishable in their behavior and appearance (Rosenberg, 1976).

Is bigger really better? Men do tend to be larger and stronger than women, but does this mean that they should be considered superior? Consider the following two hypothetical situations.

Imagine it is 25,000 years age and your tribe must pick a new leader. Bruce and Martha are running for the job. The major "campaign issues" are what to do about the saber-tooth tiger that is bothering the tribe and how to get access to the water hole controlled by a rival tribe. Bruce, while somewhat slow-witted, is 6 feet 9 inches tall, weighs 300 pounds, and entertains children by ripping oak trees from the ground. Martha is quite bright, but weighs 100 pounds and is less than 5 feet tall. Given the goals of your tribe, Bruce might be the logical choice.

Now, imagine it is 1984 and you have to choose a new president of your student government. Bruce and Martha's direct descendants are running for the job. They are carbon copies of the originals. The two main campaign issues are the new student constitution and the allocation of student funds. Is a 300-pound dullard really the best person for the job? No! This job requires intelligence, a characteristic which is uncorrelated with physical size. Thus, small but bright Martha is the person best suited for this position of power and authority. In other words, today size and strength are simply not valid criteria for leadership. Further, size has not always been the basis of power throughout history. For example, white slave owners tended to be smaller than their black slaves (Rosenberg, 1976).

If biology doesn't explain sex role stereotypes, what does? We believe the answer lies in how humans are socialized.

Socialization

Socialization is the process of teaching children the appropriate things to believe and ways to behave in society. The aspect of socialization that concerns us here is *sex role socialization*—the direct and indirect teaching of children that boys and girls are different and that one sex may be better than the other.

Parents as socializing agents. In the reviews of aggression, pro-social behavior, and attitudes, the importance of parents in the development of social behavior was stressed. Parental influence is of equal, if not greater, importance in sex role socialization.

Infancy. Almost from the moment of birth, parents react differently to boys and girls. One study (Rubin, Provenzano, & Luria, 1974) investigated parents' views of their male and female children during the first twenty-four hours after birth. There were no differences between the infants on birth weight, length, or general reflexes. However, girls were rated as softer, finer-featured, smaller, and more inattentive than boys. Boys were rated "as firmer, larger-featured, better coordinated, more alert, stronger, and hardier" (Rubin et al., 1974, pp. 183–184). There was also some indication that fathers were more extreme in these descriptions than mothers.

Not only are female and male infants viewed differently, but they may be treated differently as well. One study examined the behavior of mothers who played with an infant which was identified as a boy or a girl. Will et al. found that when the infant was identified as a girl (but was, in fact, a boy), mothers smiled at it more and were more likely to give it a doll to play with than when it was identified as a boy. Infants identified as boys were more likely to be given a toy train. Two mothers who were sure the baby was a girl because "she" was "sweet" and cried softer. They were quite surprised to learn that they had been playing with a boy (Will, Self, & Datan, 1976). Other studies with infants

have found that mothers handle and stimulate boys more than girls (Moss 1967), and that such handling stimulates exploration by the infant (Rubenstein, 1967).

During childhood, parents reinforce sex-role-appropriate behaviors in children. One of these behaviors is independence. Collard (1964) found that girls were encouraged to cross the street alone, use scissors, and play away from home without checking in with parents at later ages than boys. Hoffman (1972) explained this difference by proposing that parents believe girls are more fragile than boys and thus should be more sheltered and allowed less freedom. One possible effect is that boys and girls may soon come to believe this and act accordingly.

Costanzo (1974) asked children to evaluate the behavior of boys and girls who acted aggressively or dependently on the basis of good or bad intentions. For example, a child might accidentally break another child's arm while trying to save it from a speeding car. This is an aggressive act with good intentions. On the other hand, a child might accidentally break another's arm while trying to get a swing it was using. This is an aggressive act with bad intentions. Costanzo found that children noted intentions when they were evaluating aggressive boys and dependent girls. An aggressive boy with good intentions, for example, was seen as better than an aggressive boy with bad intentions. But when boys acted dependently and girls acted aggressively, they were seen as bad *regardless of their intentions*. That is, it was "bad" for boys to act dependently and girls to act aggressively, regardless of the reason.

Children not only engage in sex role stereotyping but also make value judgments about the worth of men and women. For example, Schlossberg and Goodman (1972) asked children in kindergarten what kinds of jobs men and women should hold. The children identified being a librarian, nurse, or waitress as appropriate for a woman, but put no such constraints on men. Sherman (1971) reported a much greater incidence of girls who wanted to be boys than boys who wanted to be girls.

What is the cause of these apparently sexist attitudes? Sherman (1971) notes that both mothers and fathers prefer sons and value masculine traits more highly than feminine traits. Lynn (1960) has proposed that because a boy's sex role is well delineated, he is rewarded for being masculine and punished for being feminine. A girl, on the other hand, receives little reinforcement, either negative or positive. "She is, in a sense, punished simply for being born female; whereas the boy is rewarded simply for being born a male" (p. 264). In childhood, girls are permitted a wide range of behavior from "tomboy" to "delicate," but for boys the demands are more specific (Bardwick & Douvan, 1972). Boys are not permitted to be "sissies" (McCandless, 1970); they are discouraged from showing emotion through crying by warnings to "Act like a man," "Big boys don't cry," or more specifically, "You're acting like a *girl*." These attitudes may contribute to a general lack of self-esteem and self-confidence in girls (Kirsch, 1974).

In Western cultures, adolescence is a stressful period regardless of sex. One reason is the pressures placed on teenagers to choose a direction for their future life. In general, girls are encouraged to become interested in boys, to take care of their physical appearance so that they will be attractive, and to judge themselves in terms of their social success. They are told not to excel in school and in sports (Bardwick & Douvan, 1972). They are discouraged from developing a "self" so that they will be able to mold themselves in the image of their husbands (Douvan, 1972; Erikson, 1964). These socialization practices may be responsible for the stereotypes that women are too interested in their appearance, uncompetitive, and uncomfortable when they act aggressively.

The picture for boys is quite different. They are expected to broaden their interests during adolescence so that they can begin preparing for a career. They are encouraged to value themselves, to work independently, and to be unemotional (Hartley, 1970). The adolescent male is admired and respected if he becomes the captain of the football team. The adolescent female is admired and respected if she becomes his girlfriend.

So it would seem that parents are an important agent in learning sex role stereotypes. However, they are not alone. As one becomes more aware of one's environment, outside forces become important.

Television as a socialization agent. The reviews of aggression and pro-social behavior noted that much learning takes place through the observation of models. Models are also believed to play an important role in developing sex role stereotypes (Mischel, 1966; Sternglanz & Serbin, 1976). Obviously, one's mother and father are important sex role models, but other objects in the house play a part as well. In America, the average preschool child spends more time watching television than any other activity except sleeping (Liebert et al., 1973). What sex role models does television provide?

Clark (1972) has proposed that the positive portrayal of some group in a medium depends upon: (1) how often that group appears in the medium; frequent appearance leads to *recognition* of that group, and (2) the portrayal of that group in a positive manner, which leads to *respect*. Women have fared badly in both areas. In a February 1976 study, the United Methodist Women's Television Monitoring Project analyzed over forty top television shows to determine how women were portrayed on television.[9] While women comprise

---

[9]This is the most recent survey of the content of television we could locate. We are grateful to Mary Ellen Brown for bringing it to our attention.

John Perrachione

51 percent of the U.S. population, they comprised only 32 percent of the characters on these programs and held only 27 percent of the major roles. Figure 7-2 compares the percentage of men and women who were presented on television as holding jobs and the actual percentages in the labor force. Note that while women comprise almost 40 percent of the labor force, they make up only 22 percent of workers on television. Further, women are shown not in occupational settings but in terms of their relationship to others, such as a lover or a mother (McArthur & Resko, 1975; Sternglanz & Serbin, 1976).

Perhaps an even worse offender than the programs are the commercials. There, it has been found that men appear about 70 percent of the time in positions of authority, compared to 14 percent for women (McArthur & Resko, 1975). The typical commercial shows a man telling a woman why she should use a certain product.

In commercials where the product is used by both sexes, the rewards for using it are different. Men are usually offered business or social advancement; women are offered the approval of their husband and children. One laundry soap commercial is typical. A husband and wife are out on the town when the woman is publicly humiliated by a stranger who notices that her husband's shirt has "ring around the collar!" The husband looks at the wife as if she has just crawled out from under a rock.[10] The point seems to be that if this woman is to avoid total rejection and humiliation, she must keep her husband's collar clean.

[10]Nancey Penner (1977) responds to this commercial by asking, "Why the hell doesn't someone tell the slob to wash his neck?"

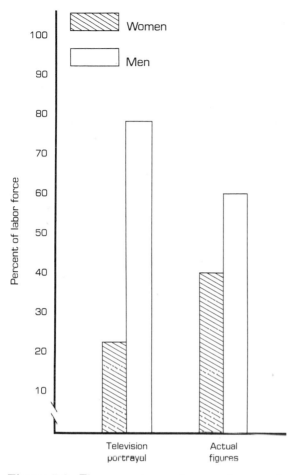

Figure 7-2. The percentages of men and women in the labor force as portrayed on television and as they actually are. (Adapted from United Methodist Women's Television Monitoring Project, 1976)

Sternglanz and Serbin (1976) examined popular children's television shows which regularly contained both female and male characters. They found that men were more active, aggressive, constructive, and helpful than women. Women deferred to men and were reacted to negatively when they were active. Further, women tended to have less impact on their environment than men. Fi-nally, women were more likely to be magical or unreal characters than men. Four out of the five shows starring women featured them as "witches of one kind or another" (Stern-glanz & Serbin, 1976, p. 237).

School as a socialization agent. There is con-siderable evidence that children's education reinforces sex role stereotypes both directly and indirectly. Consider the books that ele-mentary schools use. One study that analyzed 134 of these texts found that over twice as many of the stories were oriented toward boys as toward girls; six times as many male biographies were presented as female biogra-phies. In 2,760 stories, only 3 showed mothers working outside the home. Out of 67 stories in which one sex demeaned the other, girls were victims in 65. Girls were shown inside the house sewing, baking, and mopping, while boys were shown outside, building and being generally active (Weitzman, Eifler, Hokada, & Ross, 1972). Wirtenberg and Nakamura (1976) reported that similar sex biases were present in school books dealing with history, mathematics, and spelling.

Traditionally, schools have perpetuated sex role stereotyping by the way they prepare their students for future life. High school girls are encouraged to take home economics and typing courses, while boys interested in prac-tical skills are directed toward carpentry and auto repair courses (Wirtenberg & Nakam-ura, 1976). When students turn to their guid-ance counselors for advice, these counselors tend to channel them into "appropriate" courses or jobs and to discourage deviance from stereotyped occupations Schlossberg & Pietrofesa 1973; Thomas & Stewart, 1971).[11]

---

[11]Title IX of the 1972 Higher Education Act prohibits exclusion from a class on the basis of sex. It remains to be seen if this act will be vigorously enforced and what the effects will be.

THE REDUCTION OF SEXISM

Sexism pervades almost every aspect of our society. Further, it is such an ingrained part of our daily lives that in the long run, it may prove harder to eliminate than racism or other forms of ethnic prejudice. There has been little research on changing sexist attitudes and behavior. But a number of studies do provide some clues as to how we should proceed. One group of studies has tried to reexamine sex role stereotypes.

Richard Taylor

A reexamination of sex role stereotypes

Theory and research concerned with this issue has followed two lines. The first questions the validity of the data which show sex differences in personality and behavior. The second questions the traditional idea of a person's being either purely "masculine" or "feminine."

Are there really sex differences? Much of what is assumed to be true about stereotyped behavior is based on the psychological research on sex differences. But are these conclusions about sex-linked differences in personality, thinking, and behavior valid? Eleanor Maccoby (Maccoby, 1966; Maccoby & Jacklin, 1974a), reviewed studies on sex differences. The conclusions reached by her and Jacklin challenge many of the commonly held beliefs about sex differences in behavior and abilities.

For example, they found no evidence that girls are more sociable, more suggestible, less achievement-oriented, or less self-caring than boys. Similarly, there seems to be no differences between men and women in simple memory, intellectual, or analytic abilities. Maccoby and Jacklin did find that men are more aggressive than women, and do have better visual, spatial, and mathematical abilities. However, they have poorer verbal ability (Maccoby & Jacklin, 1974b).

Other researchers have not denied the existence of sex differences, but they have attempted to put them in perspective. For example, Freeman (1971) has observed that personality and behavior differences among members of the *same* sex are often greater than these differences *between* the sexes. This led Freeman to conclude that "Sex is just one of the many characteristics which define a human being" (1971, p. 126). Thus, its importance should not be overestimated.

Androgyny

Usually people are seen as either (1) feminine—possessing characteristics which are "typically" female (e.g., being gentle and dependent, and preferring cooking) or (2) masculine—possessing characteristics which are "typically" male (e.g., being aggressive and independent, liking sports). Further, it has been assumed that normal, healthy adjustment requires a woman to be feminine and a man masculine.

Recently, however, researchers (e.g., Bem, 1975; Spence, Helmreich, & Stapp, 1974) have proposed that femininity and masculinity are not mutually exclusive but instead two separate continua which are often positively related. Psychological health, they believe, may require us to have both feminine and masculine characteristics. A person who possesses both is called *androgynous*. (Androgyny is a term derived from two Greek words— *andros,* meaning "man," and *gyne,* meaning "woman.")

Is androgyny associated with good mental health? It has been found that extreme masculinity in men and extreme femininity in women is accompanied by high anxiety and low self-esteem and acceptance (Costentino & Heilbrun, 1964; Gall, 1969; Gray, 1957; Hartford, Willis, & Deabler, 1967; Mussen, 1962; Sears, 1970; Webb, 1963). Androgynous people, on the other hand, tend to have high self-esteem (Spence, Helmreich, & Stapp, 1974).

There is also reason to believe that androgynous people are more adaptable than nonandrogynous ones. For example, Bem (1975) classified people as androgynous, feminine or masculine using her Sex Role Inventory. (See "The Measurement of Androgyny.") These people were then exposed to two situations. The first required them to show "masculine" independence in the face of social pressure. The second required "feminine" playfulness in response to a small kitten. Androgynous individuals performed well in both situations. "Masculine" and "feminine"

The measurement of androgyny

Sandra Bem (1974) devised a means to determine whether people are strongly sex-typed or androgynous. It is called the *Bem Sex Role Inventory.* The person is presented with sixty adjectives which are either strongly masculine (i.e., characteristics that most people believe men possess), strongly feminine (i.e., characteristics that most believe women possess), or which are associated with either sex. He (or she) indicates how well each term describes him or her on a seven-point scale. A man who says that only masculine terms describe him well is a sex-typed male. A woman who says

that only feminine terms describe her is a sex-typed female. A person who says that both kinds of terms describe him (or her) quite well is androgynous. Here are some of the items used in the inventory.

Feminine	Masculine	Neutral
Shy	Aggressive	Happy
Soft-spoken	Dominant	Helpful
Tender	Forceful	Secretive
Warm	Individualistic	Solemn
Yielding	Self-sufficient	Truthful

people performed well only when the situation called for "male" and "female" behaviors, respectively. Lee (1977) studied women who held traditionally masculine jobs. She found that neither masculinity nor femininity was correlated with success. Androgynous women, however, were quite successful in their work.

These two lines of research suggest one avenue to the reduction of sexism. This is to reevaluate the inevitability and desirability of socializing people in accord with sex role stereotypes.

The enactment of laws

Although laws usually reflect existing attitudes, they can sometimes lead to attitude change. For example, it is generally agreed that the Civil Rights Act of 1963 was largely responsible for many of the dramatic changes in whites' attitudes toward the rights of blacks. If existing laws which prohibit discrimination on the basis of sex in education and employment (e.g., the 1964 Civil Rights Act, Title IX of the 1972 Higher Education Act) were rigorously enforced, a similar pattern might be found for sexism.[12]

Laws which increase educational and employment opportunities for women could reduce sexism in two interrelated ways. First, they would allow women to engage in traditionally male activities. This, in turn, might affect not only a woman's sense of self-worth but the attitudes of men around her as well. For example, Parelius (1975) found that the sons and husbands of working women favor sexual equality more strongly than those of traditional women. Second, these laws would make people behave in a nonsexist manner. Recall the research on attitude change. The

data show that a person whose behavior differs from his true attitudes will often change his attitudes to match his behavior (cf. Chapter Six). As an illustration, consider the effects of President Gerald Ford's decision in 1975 to allow women to enter the United States military academies. The superintendent of West Point expressed his feelings as follows: "I had grave misgivings [about the admission of women], but we are determined to make it work. My personal opinions are now irrelevant" (Lt. General Sidney B. Berry, *Newsweek,* December 1, 1975). It would be naïve to propose that anti-discrimination laws alone will eliminate sexism. However, they can help to reduce it.

Attitude change in women

Given the long, pervasive history of sexism, it is not surprising that many women themselves hold sexist attitudes. In the last few years, however, these attitudes have begun to change. For example, Milton Rokeach (1974) gave his Value Survey to a nationwide sample of Americans in 1968 and 1971. He found no change in the importance men placed on the value of equality, but this value had become significantly more important to women.

Among female college students, Parelius found a significant increase in feminist ideology and greater rejection of sex role stereotypes from 1969 to 1973. Mason, Szajka, and Arber (cited in Brown, 1976) reported that in 1964 only 50 percent of American women though that a woman could work and have a good relationship with her children. In 1974, this view was held by 75 percent of women.

There is even some recent evidence of chauvinism among women. For example, Levenson, Burford, Bonno, and Davis (1975) repeated the study in which women were asked to evaluate scientific articles supposedly written by men or women (Goldberg, 1968). The

---

[12]We are not suggesting that racism in the United States has been eliminated. It remains an extremely serious problem. The point is that racism seems to have decreased in the last twenty years.

women's work in this later study was not judged to be inferior, but rather superior. Another example of this trend is the finding that female school psychologists rated active girls as significantly more healthy than active or passive boys or passive girls. Male school psychologists rated all four groups as equal in health (Chasen & Weinberg, 1975).

Thus, women's attitudes about sexism and sex role stereotypes seem to have changed dramatically over the past few years. It is hard to pick out any single causal factor, but certainly the women's liberation movement has been important. This movement has attempted to change women's attitudes through self-help consciousness-raising groups, and society's sexist attitudes and behavior through political groups such as the National Women's Political Caucus. Mason et al. (1976) have described the relationship between the women's movement and changes in women's attitudes as follows: ". . . attitude change has probably been fairly general in the female population . . . and this change suggests that [American] women's outlooks are converging with those of the movement's leaders" (p. 5).

This is not to conclude, unfortunately, that sexism has been all but eliminated. Many of the most vocal opponents of the Equal Rights Amendment to the Constitution have been women. There has even been a counterrevolution to the feminist movement among some women. For example, Marabel Morgan (1973) in her book *The Total Woman* seems to have incorporated the stereotypes of male superiority and female submissiveness, advising female readers to accept, admire, adapt to, and appreciate their men. In the view of Kolson (1976), this philosophy would "turn women into submissive, subservient, sexpots" (p. 1k). Also, there are courses such as "Fascinating You," which teach women how to be seductive and use tears to get what they want from men.

Finally, men's attitudes have not kept pace with the changes in women's attitudes. Many men still disapprove of working women (Mason & Bumpass, 1973). Only 15 percent of men who classified themselves as liberal on sex roles actually shared the housekeeping and childrearing chores with their wives (Tavris, 1973). Although women comprise 51 percent of the American population, they hold less than 10 percent of the elected public offices (Goss, 1976). Finally, despite all the protests about the portrayal of women in the media, the most recent television survey (conducted in 1976), concluded that sexist stereotypes still predominate. Thus, sexism, like racism, is proving quite resistant to change.

Conclusion

This section examined sexism, a form of prejudice based on gender. The basic premise was that sexism is an ancient and pervasive form of prejudice which is due to sex role stereotypes. Thus, the discussion focused mainly on the causes of these stereotypes.

A brief historical review of sex roles, stereotyping, and sexism showed that sex roles were initially based on physiological and biological factors. They consisted of separate but equal functions in primitive societies. Sex roles could be explained partly by economic factors, but stereotyping and sexism continued long after there was any economic justification for them. The possibility that women are seen as inferior to men and are given lower status because of biological defects was explored. This point of view, while widely held, does not hold up well under examination. Men and women are obviously different, but the research literature strongly suggests that behavioral differences are due more to assigned sex than biological differences.

The effect of sex assignment is shown in the way men and women are socialized. Almost from birth, boys and girls are viewed and treated differently by their parents. Parental attitudes and behavior about which sex is more valuable, and the behavior expected from each, may cause children to accept stereotypes and sexist attitudes. But parents are not the only culprits. Television shows men and women in stereotyped roles and reinforces these stereotypes. The schools foster stereotypes in their books and curricula.

Finally, possible ways of eliminating or (more realistically) reducing sexism were considered. The first was to reexamine some of the basic assumptions about whether sex-linked behavioral differences exist and the value of socializing people into stereotypes. The research on these topics leads to the following tentative conclusions. (1) The existence of sex-linked behavioral differences may be somewhat overstated. (2) A person's psychological health might be improved by incorporating both female and male characteristics. The second means of reducing sexism concerned direct assaults on sexist attitudes. As the result of new laws and political activity, significant changes have already occurred. These changes could be furthered if nonsexist practices in business and education were enacted. While these possibilities do exist, society seems to have a long way to go.

REVIEW QUESTIONS

(Eight out of ten is passing)

1. Sexism is a form of _____ based on a person's _____ . (p. 220)
2. The belief that because someone is a man he will be aggressive and competitive is a(n) _____ _____ _____ . (p. 221)
3. The stage at which boys and girls supposedly discover their genitalia Freud called the _____ stage. (p. 225)
4. Freud's proposal that many aspects of a person's life are determined by biology and physiology is called _____ _____ _____ . (p. 225)
5. The existence of ovaries or testes is an indication of the person's _____ sex. (p. 226)
6. The work of Money on hermaphroditism suggests that _____ sex may be a more important determinant of behavior than _____ sex. (p. 226)
7. A woman becomes a nurse, while her brother becomes a doctor. This is an example of _____ _____ behavior. (p. 227)
8. Buying a three-week-old girl a doll and her three-week-old brother a truck is part of the _____ _____ _____ process. (p. 228)
9. On television, women are seen _____ frequently than men and in a(n) _____ favorable manner. (p. 230)
10. _____ refers to the ability to incorporate both masculine and feminine traits into one's personality. (p. 233)

ANSWERS

1. prejudice, gender (sex)   2. sex-role stereotype   3. phallic   4. anatomy is destiny   5. biological   6. assigned, biological   7. sex typed   8. sex-role socialization   9. less, less   10. androgyny

SUGGESTED READINGS

There are a number of excellent textbooks on prejudice, in general, and on racism and sexism, in particular. Here are some good ones.

Textbooks

Ethnic prejudice

The Nature of Prejudice, by Gordon Allport. This book is long and somewhat difficult, but it is considered a classic in the area.

Toward a Theory of Minority Group Relations, by Hubert Blalock. Only a small portion of Blalock's insightful and creative analysis of prejudice was covered in this chapter. If you want a scholarly approach to these topics, this is an excellent book.

Prejudice and Racism, by James Jones. This is a short, lively review of the history of racism, its causes, and some possible ways to eliminate it.

The American Dilemma, by Gunnar Myrdal. This is a massive book, but it is considered by many to be the definitive work on race relations in America.

Sexism

The Behavior of Men and Women, by Kay Deaux. This is a short but surprisingly comprehensive book about differences and similarities between men and women. It is one of the more readable books available.

The Psychology of Sex Differences, by Eleanor Maccoby and Carolyn Jacklin. This is an exhaustive review of the research of sex differences in personality and behavior.

The Psychology of Women, by Juanita Williams. This book explores the biological and social factors related to women and their role in society. It is scholarly without being overwhelming.

Popular literature

Little was said in this chapter about how a person reacts to racism and sexism. there are many fiction and nonfiction books on this topic. Don't limit yourself to these few.

Ethnic prejudice

Bury My Heart at Wounded Knee, by Dee Brown. Blacks and women have not been the only victims of prejudice and discrimination. This is an excellent history of how whites oppressed the Indians during the westward expansion of the 1800's.

Roots, by Arthur Haley. The book is better than the television show. Haley manages to combine fact and fiction in a most interesting fashion.

While Six Million Died, by Arthur Morse. An upsetting description of how America turned its back on Jews trying to escape from Nazi Germany.

Black Rage, by William Grier and Price Cobbs. Two black psychiatrists describe the psychological price of racism for black Americans.

Black Boy, by Richard Wright. This is an excellent novel from the 1940's about the experience of being black in America.

The Autobiography of Malcolm X. Malcolm X's life story and his view of the world makes this an important book. (Many people don't know that Arthur Haley was the collaborator.)

Sexism

I Know Why the Caged Bird Sings, by Maya Angelou. Angelou is a black woman, born in poverty, who had an illegitimate child while in her teens. This book describes her early life and her incredible ability to overcome the barriers society placed in her way.

The Feminine Mystique or *It Changed My Life,* by Betty Friedan. Friedan is one of the leaders of the feminist movement. These books illustrate how sexism works and women's reactions to it.

Norma Jean, by Frederick Lawrence Guiles. This biography of Marilyn Monroe describes how the ultimate female sex object was destroyed by the people around her.

Diary of a Mad Housewife, by Sue Kaufman. In this novel, the agony of one woman is eloquently described.

The Bell Jar, by Sylvia Plath. Plath committed suicide shortly after this book was written. This autobiographical novel describes some of the things that led to her death.[1]

---

[1] We would like to thank Colleen Clark, Marilyn Ferrandino, and Nancey Penner for their suggestions on the readings about sexism.

8 THE INFLUENCE PROCESS

This chapter is concerned with how people influence our attitudes and behavior. It begins with some definitions and then discusses why people conform to the judgments of others. There are different kinds of conformity and different reasons why people conform. The second half of the chapter presents some models of why people conform and discusses how personal characteristics might be related to our willingness to go along with others. Finally, a different aspect of social influence will be examined: anti-social action as the result of the presence of others.

THE INFLUENCE PROCESS

Once upon a time, there was a very rich and very famous rock star. He had been asked to sing at a huge concert and was offered $100,000 for his performance. He wanted to wear the finest clothes ever made for the event. So, he sent out his guitarist, drummer, and stage manager to find the best tailor in the world. Now, these three people weren't very bright and instead of finding the best tailor, they found the best "ripoff" artist ever.

She took hundreds of measurements and then went to work. From behind a locked door, she could be heard sewing and cutting. Several weeks later, the ultimate outfit was ready.

With great fanfare, the tailor entered the room. She carried a large box. "Before you try this on," she said, "there's something I have to tell you. I used a very rare kind of cloth. Only someone with the musical talent of a Peter Frampton or a Rod Stewart will be able to see your clothes." She then went through the motions of dressing him.

The rock star stood in front of a mirror naked. Elton John wouldn't be able to see the beauty of these clothes, but I can, he thought.

"Incredible, far out," said the guitarist, drummer, and stage manager in unison. "Stupendous," said the concert's promoter. And off they all went to the concert.

The news about the singer's new clothes had spread among the audience. Only those who really understood and appreciated rock music would be able to see them. As the singer walked onstage, the roars of approval erupted.

"Alice Cooper dresses like a milkman next to him," one fan proclaimed. " 'Kiss' looks like a group of accountants next to that dude," shouted another. And so, they all listened to his music and admired his beautiful clothes.

In the back of the crowd, a police officer stood directing fans to their seats. When he looked at the stage, he was shocked. "The stupid jerk doesn't have any clothes on," he screamed.

"What?" asked a few people nearby.

"That moron's naked as a jay bird," replied the officer.

"Hey, he is," they said in surprise.

The realization that the singer had been ripped off spread through the crowd like wildfire. And soon, the roars of approval turned to laughs and hoots. The concert was canceled, and the rock star served ninety days for indecent exposure.

This updated version of "The Emperor's New Clothes" illustrates the subject of this chapter, social influence. *Social influence* describes how a person or a group can modify another person's attitudes and behavior. The rock star was vain but was not in the habit of appearing nude in public. He performed naked in front of 100,000 people because of what the tailor had told him.

This fable also presents another important concept needed to understand social influence—norms. A *norm* is a group standard as to how a person should see the world and how she should behave (Kiesler & Kiesler, 1969). The fans' initial approval of the singer's style of dress was due to a norm which existed among them. The following discussion will be primarily concerned with how norms set by a group can change a person's attitudes and behavior. This process is called conformity.

CONFORMITY

Imagine that rather than attending a rock concert, you have gone to a football game. Prior to the start of the game, the announcer

asks the spectators to rise for the National Anthem. You are unhappy with America's foreign policy. As a symbol of your discontent, you remain seated and make funny faces as you hear "Oh, say, can you see?" As the third line of "The Star-Spangled Banner" is sung, you glance behind you and notice twelve U.S. Marines staring at you. You come to the conclusion that if you do not do something, your life may be in danger. Therefore, you jump to your feet, slap your hand over your heart, and sing in a manner that would make John Wayne proud. This is conformity.

Conformity is a change in behavior or belief toward another person's or group's behavior or belief as the result of real or imagined social pressure. In this case, the *social pressure*—the psychological force that causes a person to act in accordance with others' expectations—was the look on the faces of the Marines.

Note the phrase "real or imagined" social pressure. In this example, the Marines may not, in fact, want you to sing the National Anthem. Instead, they may be admiring you because you are willing to express your opinions publicly. But your belief is that the Marines want you to conform to their behavior.

This pressure can produce a change in public behavior without a change in private attitudes, as in the above example, or it can produce a change in private attitudes. The former is called *compliance,* the latter *private acceptance.* The basic difference between the two is that in private acceptance you have come to believe the group's position; in compliance, you do not. Since these are quite different outcomes, it is important to distinguish between them.

How can this be done? The basic technique is to determine if the change produced by social pressure will persist even when the pressure is removed (Deutsch & Gerard, 1955; Levy, 1960). For example, you and three other people share an apartment. You are a slob. Your clothes are strewn all over the apartment, your toothpaste is all over the bathroom, and the remnants of a peanut butter sandwich you made in August are still under your bed in November.

Your roommates decide they cannot take it any longer. They sit down and have a long talk with you about the problems your sloppiness creates and the virtues of neatness. Further, they use positive incentives (they give you a quarter every day your room is clean) and negative incentives (they refuse to speak to you when it is dirty) to modify your behavior.

As a result, you become Ms. Clean. You swear you are a changed person. "Cleanliness is next to godliness" becomes your motto. Your living area is as clean as the operating room in a hospital. Your roommates, however, are not sure you have reformed. They are afraid that if they stop their campaign, you will revert to your pig-like ways. Therefore, they decide to determine if your new behavior is due to compliance or private acceptance. They announce that they are going on a three-month trip. A week later, they sneak into the apartment and inspect it while you are out.

If the apartment looks like the Black Hole of Calcutta, their efforts have resulted in compliance. That is, when their pressure was removed, you reverted to your old ways. If, on the other hand, the apartment looks like an ad for *House Beautiful,* your roommates will conclude that they have produced private acceptance. You maintained the behavior in the absence of pressure.

The distinction between compliance and private acceptance is meaningful and impor-

tant. However, it is often difficult to determine which type of conformity a specific kind of social pressure has produced. Further, in some instances, the same factors that produce compliance also produce private acceptance. This review of comformity will try to distinguish between compliance and private acceptance. But it must be realized that in many instances, this is difficult if not impossible.

Historical background of conformity research

In 1935, Muzafer Sherif conducted a classic study in conformity research. He was interested in the effects of group judgments on the autokinetic phenomenon. If you place a person in a darkened room and project a spot of light on the wall, the light will appear to move. The light is actually stationary, and the apparent movement is due to the movement of the subject's eyes. This is the *autokinetic phenomenon.* Sherif found that individuals' judgments of how much the light moved were dramatically affected by the judgments of others. Group pressure seemed to cause private acceptance, since individual estimates of how much the light moved continued to agree with the group judgment even when the group was no longer present. In fact, Rohrer, Baron, Hoffman, and Swander (1954) found that the effect persisted as long as a year after exposure to the group.

Can group judgments also produce compliance? Some fifteen years after Sherif's study, Solomon Asch (1951) addressed this issue. He was interested in what would happen if a person were confronted with two conflicting answers to a simple question: (1) a person's own opinion and (2) the opinions of her peers.

To examine this, Asch showed subjects a series of cards similar to this one.

Standard   A   B   C

Which of the three lines is the closest to the standard line in length? This is easy. About 95 percent of the people asked this question choose B (Asch, 1956).

However, Asch made the situation somewhat more difficult. The subject was seated at a table with five or six other people and shown the lines. Before giving her answer, the subject heard four of the other people (who were really confederates) announce that the correct answer was C. Then it was the subject's turn. She was faced with two conflicting sources of information: (1) her own judgment and (2) the judgments of other people working on the same task. What did the typical subject do?

There were twelve trials on which the confederates unanimously gave an incorrect answer. Asch found that on the average, subjects agreed with this *unanimous majority* one-third of the time.

Although Asch's procedure was crude and cumbersome, his results are highly reliable. The finding that subjects generally conform about one third of the time to obviously incorrect judgments of a unanimous majority has been obtained in hundreds of studies. It is one of the most consistent findings in social psychology.

There is good reason to believe that what Asch generated was compliance. In a 1956 study, Asch showed subjects the same series of lines. But in this study, he had subjects give their answer either publicly or privately (by writing it down). Since the subjects' answers in the second condition were (supposedly) anonymous, there was no group pressure on them. In this private condition, agreement with the unanimous majority almost totally disappeared. This strongly suggests that the behavior displayed by subjects here represents compliance.

The findings of Sherif and Asch caused considerable interest in conformity among social psychologists. Sherif and Asch showed that people conform; later on, other researchers tried to determine why. One of the more popular explanations is based on social power.

Social power

Social power describes the ability of a person, group, or society to change the attitudes or behavior of an individual. French and Raven (1959) identified several different types of social power which allow the influencing agent to change the individual. Compliance seems due to two interrelated types of social power.

Reward social power

Reward social power is the ability to influence a person's behavior because the influencing agent controls the rewards the person can receive. The greater the control over rewards or the larger the rewards, the more power the influencing agent has.

You can see an example of reward social power in an old comedy sketch. An American tourist is sitting on a park bench in an Eastern European country. A woman, looking like everyone's stereotype of a spy, approaches her. Glancing around quickly, she says, "Here, take this package and give it to a man wearing a red carnation in his lapel. He will be under the town clock at midnight." The tourist resists this influence attempt. She explains she is only a visitor and has no desire to become involved in foreign intrigue. But the spy persists and employs reward social power. "If you do as I say, I'll give you twelve million zlotneys" (the unit of currency in this mythical country). "Twelve million zlotneys!" says the tourist, and agrees to help.

While waiting for midnight to arrive, she comes across a boy selling papers. "Paper, please," she says. "Yes, madam," says the boy. "That will be four million zlotneys, please."

The point of this example is the spy's use of reward social power to control or influence the tourist's behavior. Once the tourist discovered the true value of a zlotney, the spy's power was gone.

Not only can the group reward compliance, it also has the power to punish noncompliance.

Coercive social power

In *coercive social power,* a person's or group's ability to influence the individual's behavior depends on the agent's ability to control the punishments she receives. The agent can coerce her into saying or doing something. For example, the spy in the comedy sketch could have threatened to shoot the tourist if she did not comply.

At this point, you may be asking, what is the difference between reward and coercive social power? They seem to be different sides of the same coin. In fact, however, they have very different effects. Kipnis (1958) and Zipf (1960) have shown that when coercive social power is used, the influence attempt is resisted more strongly and the agent is liked significantly less than when reward social power is used. The most obvious reason for this is provided by Brehm's (1966) concept of reactance (cf. Chapter seven). Basically, Brehm proposed that people do not like to be forced into doing something and will react against it. One reaction will be to resist the influence attempt and dislike the agent.

In practice, groups use much more subtle forms of reward and coercive social power

than our imaginary spy. A group can reward a compliant member by praising her, giving her high status, or making her feel at home in the group. Using coercive social power, the group can punish noncompliance by ridiculing, ostracizing, or rejecting a deviant member (Schachter, 1951).

For example, Freedman and Doob (1968) convinced a group that one of its members had consistently deviated from its norm, while another had conformed. Then the group was asked to pick two members to take part in some experiments. In one a person would receive electric shocks; in the other a person would receive money. The group chose the deviant for the shock experiment and the conformer for the pleasant experiment.

Groups don't actually have to tell a deviant member that she will be punished. She already knows this. In one study, subjects were led to believe that either they had or had not deviated from their group's norm. Then both groups were asked whom they though their group would reject. Deviants were much more likely to identify themselves than were nondeviants (Allen, 1966).

Idiosyncracy credits. There are, however, certain circumstances in which a deviant will not be punished or rejected. This is when she has built up *idiosyncracy credits.* These are credits which a person can use to deviate from the group without being punished (Hollander, 1958). Three things enable a person to build up such credits: (1) she is seen as a valuable member of the group, (2) she is well liked by other members, and (3) in the past, she has conformed to the group.

Consider Jimmy Carter's mother, Lillian. In the mid 1950's, she attempted to get the congregation of the Plains Baptist Church to admit blacks as members. Although this idea was very unpopular among the other members of the all-white church, they did not reject or ostracize her. Probably in the past

she had been a valuable, well-liked, loyal member of the church. Because of this, she was allowed to deviate from its norm.

Note that these are credits, not privileges. This is an extremely important distinction. The term "credits" implies that if the person continues to deviate, eventually she will be rejected. The freedom to deviate has its limits.

It is generally agreed that reward and coercive social power will lead to compliance but not private acceptance (French & Raven, 1959; Kelman, 1961; Thibaut & Kelley, 1959). Further, Kelman pointed out that reward and/or coercive social power provides only short-lived control. If the influencing agent loses control over the rewards and punishments and/or is not watching the person's behavior, compliance will disappear.

This point is illustrated in the following experiment (Kelman, 1958). The subjects were students at all-black colleges in the period before the Supreme Court had ruled on the constitutionality of segregated schools. As a group, these students opposed the idea of all-black or all-white colleges.

They heard an interview with a person who was either the president of the "National Foundation for Negro Colleges" or an expert on black history. Both interviewees argued that even if the Supreme Court declared segregated schools unconstitutional, all-black colleges should be continued. The expert based his argument on concern for black students and his research on black history. The head of the National Foundation for Negro Colleges not only expressed his opinion but also made it clear that he had almost complete control over funds for black colleges and would not hesitate to use his power to achieve conformity.

Immediately after hearing the interview, the subjects filled out two similar questionnaires on whether all-black colleges should be continued. On the first questionnaire, they were asked to sign their names and were told that the interviewee would see their answers. The second questionnaire was presented as being solely for research purposes and was filled out anonymously (or so the subjects thought). About two weeks later, both groups of subjects filled out a questionnaire for a different experimenter. Embedded in it were questions related to the topic of the interview. Again, responses were supposedly anonymous.

Figure 8-1 shows the scores of the two groups of subjects on each of the three questionnaires. Note what happened. Initially, the students who heard the man with reward and/or coercive social power agreed with him. But when the questionnaire was filled out anonymously and his survelliance ability was removed, agreement declined. No comparable shift was found for those people who heard the expert.[1]

Thus, it seems that an influencing agent's ability to control rewards and punishments can change behavior, but only temporarily. The change will usually disappear as soon as the agent's power is lost. Are there forms of social power which will produce longer-lasting change, and change which does not depend on surveillance?

Referent social power

Referent social power is "a person or group's ability to control the behavior of an individual based on the individual's desire to identify with the influencing agent" (French & Raven, 1959). A person who likes another person or is strongly attracted to a group may comply in order to be accepted. She wants to become closer to the person or group.

How is referent social power different from

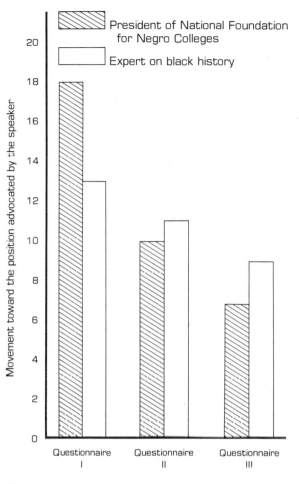

Figure 8-1. The relative long-term effectiveness of people with reward/coercive and expert social power. (Adapted from Kelman, 1958)

reward or coercive social power? After all, a group's ability to accept or reject a person seems to be the same thing as reward and coercive social power. There are, however, two important differents. First of all, referent social power depends on a person's own desire to avoid discomfort or gain satisfaction, not on the actions of the influencing agent. In referent social power, a person may conform to the wishes of the agent even when the agent has

---

[1]The attitude change was relatively permanent among students who heard the expert. This illustrates the effect of expert social power, which will be covered later.

no direct control over the person's rewards or punishments.

For example, consider a college student who joins a sorority. Initially her behavior will be influenced by the rewards and punishments set by the members. But when her pledging is over and she becomes an active member, she may continue to comform to the group's norms of speech and dress. Why? Because it makes her feel "like one of the sisters," not because the sorority insists on these standards.

A second important difference has been identified by Kelman (1958, 1961). Reward and/or coercive social power, as noted, depends on surveillance. When surveillance is lifted, control is lost. In referent social power, conformity will occur as long as the person sees it as relevant to the relationship with the influencing agent. It is only when the person is no longer attracted to the agent or does not see the behavior as relevant to identification with the agent that conformity will disappear. Let's return to the sorority member. Even when she is at home on vacation, she will probably dress and talk like her sorority sisters. It is only when she leaves college and no longer identifies with the sorority that this conformity will disappear.

In referent social power, the influencing agent can also be a person's role. A *role* is a pattern of behaviors which characterizes and is expected of a person who occupies a particular position in a group, culture, or society (Shaw & Costanzo, 1970). If a person believes that a behavior is expected of her because of her position, she will perform the behavior in the absence of surveillance or obvious rewards, or even in the face of punishment (Hunt, 1965). An extreme example of this is provided by the case of Frank Serpico.

Serpico was a young New York City police officer who discovered that a large percentage of his fellow officers were taking bribes. The corruption began with patrolmen walking beats and extended to police captains. In the precinct station where Serpico worked, for example, three officers were receiving over $250,000 in bribes per year.

Those officers who did not take bribes simply looked the other way. Frank Serpico was different; he embarked on a one-man campaign to clean up the New York City Police Department.

The campaign resulted in Serpico's becoming a social outcast. He was physically threatened by some of his peers and labeled a psychotic by his superiors. He was shot in the face in an episode which some people believe was arranged by fellow officers.

While recuperating, Serpico received the following "Get Well" card:

With Sincere Sympathy . . . That you didn't get your brains blown out, you rat bastard. Happy relapse. (Maas, 1973)

Yet for five years, Serpico persisted in his efforts to eliminate corruption. Why? Peter Maas, the author of Serpico's biography, explained Serpico's behavior in terms of his view of the role of the police. Maas describes the commencement ceremony when Serpico graduated from the police academy.

Serpico heard that he had received the best and most intensive police training in the world, that he had studied the law, the science of police work, police tactics, and "criminal *modus operandi,*" and that he was now fully prepared to engage in the war against crime, to put what he had learned into practice on the streets of the city. . . .

His role as a peace officer, he was told, had great moral, social, and political implications. His courteous, dignified, and impartial behavior both on and off duty was critically important in generating respect for law and government, since the number of contacts which the public had with the police was far greater than those with all other governmental agencies combined. . . . Serpico believed every word of it. (Maas, 1973, pp. 54–55)

At the end of five years, Serpico left the force and the country. Shortly before, he was asked if he thought things would change as a result of his efforts. Serpico replied:

I don't know. Its not up to me any more. *I only did what I had to do.* (Maas, 1973, 313; italics added)

The final sentence is stressed because Frank Serpico did not have to do what he did. His behavior was due largely to his own perceptions of the behavior expected of a policeman. He was conforming to those expectations.

Legitimate social power

This is the most complex form of social power. In *legitimate social power,* an individual obeys a person or group because she believes this agent has a legitimate right to control her behavior and because she is obligated to accept this control. For example, consider the legal battle between former President Richard Nixon and Leon Jaworski, the special prosecutor, over the tapes on the Watergate break-in and coverup. Jaworski had taken his demand for the tapes to the Supreme Court. But privately, he felt that even if the Court ruled against Nixon, there was no way Nixon could be made to give them up. In Jaworski's judgment, a President could not be charged with contempt of court (Woodward & Bernstein, 1976). Further, Nixon controlled the mightiest armed forces on earth. Certainly, a battalion of Marines could take care of the Court. Why, then, did Nixon give up the tapes when the Supreme Court ruled against him?

Part of the reason was public opinion, but an equally important factor was the behavior of his attorneys, Fred Buzhardt and James St. Clair. Both threatened to resign if Nixon refused to obey the Supreme Court's ruling. In their view, the Court had legitimate social power. It had the *right* to control the behavior of the President of the United States. Therefore, Buzhardt and St. Clair urged Nixon to comply. Their behavior was based on their internalized values about the power given the Supreme Court.

Legitimate social power appears to be necessary if a society is to function efficiently. A society cannot afford to watch over every member, and certain rules (laws) need to be obeyed. A society that could not generate legitimate social power would fall into anarchy. But can legitimate social power be carried too far? Stanley Milgram's (1963, 1964, 1965) research on obedience explores this question.

In the background is a smokestack for one of the gas ovens at Dachau concentration camp. The inscription on the statue reads, "To honor the dead. As a warning to the living."

Obedience. Two men taking part in an experiment on the effects of punishment on learning. One person is chosen as the learner. He is taken into a room, strapped into a chair, and has electrodes taped to his arm. As the other man listens, the learner's task is explained. He will hear a list of word pairs (e.g., blue-girl, fat-neck). After he has heard the entire list once, he will be given only the first word in each pair. His task is to give the correct second word.

The other man will be the teacher. He is placed in front of a generator capable of giving from 15 to 450 volts of electric shock. These voltage levels are clearly marked and described. For example, under 15 volts are the words "slight shock"; under 400 volts, "danger, severe shock." The first time the learner gives an incorrect answer, the teacher gives him 15 volts. The shock is increased by 15 volts for every subsequent mistake.

The learner performs quite poorly, and soon the shock is up to 200 volts. He begins to complain. "Let me out. I've got a heart condition." The teacher turns to the experimenter for guidance. "Go on," he is told. The complaints grow louder, and at 300 volts the learner refuses to answer any more.

"What do I do? I think that something's happened to that fellow in there," the teacher says.

The experimenter calmly tells him, "Continue. The experiment requires that you continue." Now the teacher is in a quandary. On the one hand, the learner may be seriously injured. But the experimenter has ordered him to continue. What will people do in such a situation?

Milgram (1963) believed that most Americans would disobey the experimenter very early in the sequence. Germans, however, are authoritarian and would comply. Thus, he planned to conduct this experiment in America, show that Americans would disobey, and then head for Germany.

Milgram never went to Germany. He is no longer interested in Germans; he is interested in Americans. Out of forty average, middle-class American males, twenty-six (65 percent) went all the way to 450 volts.[2] It can't be emphasized too strongly that they did not do this willingly or cheerfully. They protested, pleaded, sweated; some cried, and others giggled nervously. But 65 percent of them went all the way. No one broke off the shock before 300 volts. Why?

Milgram had demonstrated *obedience,* the act of complying with the orders of a legitimate authority. Further, he had shown that normal, nonsadistic people could be made to commit abnormal, sadistic acts.

Is there any way to reduce or eliminate this frightening obedience? Milgram conducted his original research at Yale University. Wondering if a less prestigious setting might reduce obedience, he moved his experiment to a run-down office building in another city. In this setting, 48 percent of the subjects obeyed. A decline, but not much. In subsequent studies, Milgram found that if the experimenter left the room or the learner was in the room with the teacher, willingness to give shock decreased significantly.

Subsequent research tells us more about the conditions which will lead to disobedience. A study conducted in Germany found that if the shock levels were left up to the teacher, only 7 percent of the subjects gave the maximum shock[3] (Mantell, 1971). The reason was probably that now, the responsibility for shocking the learner fell squarely on the teacher. In the original Milgram experiment, many subjects refused to shock the

---

[2]The learner was a confederate and never really got shocked.
[3]As Milgram had predicted, Germans were more obedient than Americans. Under conditions identical to those Milgram originally used, 85 percent of the German subjects obeyed.

learner unless the experiment accepted responsibility. In Mantell's study, this wasn't possible. The decision was the teacher's alone.

Another study attempted to reduce obedience by delegitimizing the experimenter. Experimenters were trained to act either competent and self-assured or incompetent and bumbling. The bumbling experimenter acted like someone in a slapstick comedy. He started the experiment late, dropped equipment, temporarily broke the shock apparatus, and explained his behavior by telling subjects that he had conducted the experiment only "twice before." Penner et al. measured how quickly subjects obeyed a command to administer shock. The bumbling experimenter produced significantly less obedience than the competent one (Penner, Hawkins, Dertke, Spector, & Stone, 1973).

These two studies tell us a little more about the reasons for obedience. But they don't provide much comfort. In both studies, rather extreme procedures were used to produce disobedience. In experiments where these procedures are not used, people seem incredibly and frighteningly obedient. Are these laboratory findings generalizable? Milgram (1974) believed that they are. And a man named Adolf Eichmann may support Milgram's position.

During the Nazi period in Germany, Eichmann had the responsibility of arranging the collection and deportation of hundreds of thousands of Jews to concentration camps. He escaped at the end of World War II but in 1960 was found by Israeli agents in Argentina. They brought him back to Israel to stand trial as a war criminal. At his trial, the following exchange took place between the prosecutor (Hausner) and Eichmann.

Hausner: Then you admit that you were an accomplice to the murder of millions of Jews? *Eichman:* That I cannot admit. I ask myself whether I am guilty as an accomplice from the human point of view. But I do not consider myself guilty from the legal point of view. I received orders and I executed orders. If the deportations which I carried out—the ones in which I had a part—led to death of some of these Jews, then the legal question must be examined as to whether I am guilty in terms of responsibility. (Pearlman, 1963, 467)

Was this merely the self-serving statement of a man on trial for his life? In the judgment of noted historian Hannah Arendt (1963), it was not. Arendt, herself a Jew, explained Eichmann's behavior as follows:

This was the way things were, this was the new law of the land, based on the Führer's order; whatever he did he did, as far as he could see, as a law-abiding citizen. He did his *duty,* as he told the police and the court over and over again; he not only obeyed *orders,* he also obeyed the *law.* (P. 120)

And just as the law in civilized countries assumes that the voice of conscience tells everybody "Thou shalt not kill," even though man's natural desires and inclinations may at times be murderous, so the law of Hitler's land demanded that the voice of conscience tell everybody: "Thou shalt kill." (P. 134).

While I would not go as far as Arendt in totally attributing Eichmann's behavior to legitimate social power, there is a good deal of validity in her explanation. Thus, perhaps Milgram was not being too extreme when he stated in a television interview that if he had to staff a Nazi-type concentration camp, he could find more than enough guards in any middle-sized American town. Milgram's statement was based not on his perception of latent anti-Semitism among Americans but rather on the strength of legitimate social power to produce obedience.

Expert social power

The final type of social power, French and Raven proposed, was expert social power. In *expert social power,* an agent's ability to influence another person's behavior depends on the agent's knowledge or expertise on the topic in question. If a person sees the agent as an expert, this will produce private acceptance (Allen, 1965). An expert has social power because she is perceived as correct, and it is rewarding to have the correct opinions and behavior[4] (Festinger, 1954; Kiesler, 1969).

One area in which expert social power is especially relevant is education. You accept what your instructor says because you want an A in the course, but also because she is an expert on the subject and it is rewarding to be correct about this material.

But suppose your perceptions of expertise are wrong? Consider this study of people's reactions to a visiting lecturer (Naftulin,

Ware, & Donelly, 1973). A group of psychologists, psychiatrists, educators, and college administrators listened to a lecture on "Mathematical Game Theory as Applied to Physical Education." The lecturer, a Dr. Fox, had impressive academic credentials. After the lecture and question-and-answer period, Dr. Fox's audience evaluated him and the quality of his presentation. Their evaluations were overwhelmingly positive. He was described as knowledgeable, articulate, and an astute analyzer of the subject.

Dr. Fox was a phoney. He was actually an actor, trained by Naftulin et al. to use double talk and nonsequiters and, in general, to make absolutely no sense. Naftulin et al. had shown that these highly educated listeners, instead of being "competent crap detectors," were "seduced by the style of Dr. Fox's presentation" (p. 633). Let the student beware!

[4]Note how similar expert social power is to the concept of credibility in attitude change (cf. Chapter Six).

"Listen, Adolf, no one's going to say 'Sieg Heil' to a guy dressed in cut-offs and a sweat shirt"

Most of us believe that our ability to influence people is due to our expertise. But it may be that how we dress is also quite important (Bickman, 1974).

A man dressed in a business suit or in work clothes entered a phone booth in a busy airport. When he finished using the phone, he left a dime on the shelf beneath it. He then waited until another person entered the booth. He approached it and tapped on the door.

"Excuse me, I think I might've left a dime in this phone booth a few minutes ago. Did you find it?"

People returned the dime to the well-dressed man about 77 percent of the time. The man dressed in work clothes got his dime back about half as often. When this procedure was repeated using well-dressed and poorly dressed women, exactly the same results were found.

In a later study, Bickman had a confederate dressed either in a police uniform or civilian clothes give pedestrians an order—for example, to give someone a dime for a parking meter. These people were twice as likely to obey the confederate in uniform. This was true even when the confederate left the scene immediately after giving the order. Evidently, the uniform itself created legitimate social power.

Social influence

Another way of viewing conformity is to see it as the product of social influence. Morton Deutsch and Harold Gerard (1955) proposed two kinds of social influence that may produce conformity. Their explanation should not be viewed as a rival to French and Raven's social power proposal. In fact, it could be seen as a way of classifying the various forms of social power. But social influence may have the added advantage of explaining why conformity occurs when an influencing agent's social power is hard to identify.

Normative social influence

In *Normative social influence,* a person complies or yields to the influencing agent not because she believes the agent is correct but because she sees a need to agree with the agent (Deutsch & Gerard, 1955).

What circumstances lead to this? Some of them have already been presented. If the group controls the member's rewards and/or punishments, she may comply. If she is highly attracted to the group and sees compliance as a means to gain entry, she may also comply. These are the effects of reward, coercive, and referent social power.

There is another condition under which compliance will occur. If a member of a group (1) wants the group to achieve some goal and (2) believes that her conformity will help accomplish this, she will probably be motivated to conform (Insko & Schopler, 1973). This is known as compliance to achieve *group locomotion.* The person complies to help the group move toward some goal.

The behavior of the Democratic and Republican parties illustrates how this works. As you know, a political candidate usually must go through two elections: a primary within her own party and then a general election

John Perrcchione

against an opponent from the other party. The primary is often more hard fought than the general election . But what usually happens after a primary? The process is described quite accurately in a children's book on the American political system.

Before people can become Senators and Representatives, they must run in two different races. The first is called the "primary"—which means "first." In the primary race, Democrats run against Democrats. Republicans run against Republicans. . . . When a primary race is over, the people who were running all shake hands, and pat one another on the back. All the Democrats are friends again, and the Democratic losers promise to help the Democratic winners in the next race. The Republican losers make the same promises to the Republican winners. (Addie, 1973, pp. 18–19, 22)

What is the reason for this apparently bizarre behavior? Has one candidate suddenly realized that her primary opponent is the better person? Probably not. Rather, the endorsement of her opponent is an act of compliance brought about by (1) the desire of a Democrat (for example) to see any Democrat elected over any Republican and (2) this Democrat's perception that party unity (compliance) is necessary to achieve this goal.

Although there are exceptions to this general pattern (e.g., the Republicans in the 1964 presidential campaign and the Democrats in the 1972 presidential campaign), compliance usually occurs after each party holds its primaries. In fact, this compliance is one of the major reasons why the Democrats and Republicans have had almost sole control over the American political system for the last 100 years. Smaller and more ideologically committed parties seem less able or willing to comply for the purpose of group locomotion. One's evaluation of the merits of these two types of behavior (i.e., compliance versus independence) depends on the value one puts on winning versus ideological purity.

In normative social influence, people con-

form because they want to be accepted by a group and/or because they want to help it reach some goal. They do not usually believe strongly in the position the group is advocating. As a result, normative social influence rarely leads to private acceptance (Allen, 1965; Campbell, 1961). Private acceptance can be explained by the second kind of social influence proposed by Deutsch and Gerard.

Informative social influence

Consider two people who are attending a Billy Graham crusade. Alice, a very serious young woman, is looking for some purpose in life. As she listens to Dr. Graham, she decides that, indeed, "Christ is the Answer." When it is time to come forward and make a "commitment," she goes to the pulpit.

Nora is also very serious—about how good looking the man sitting across the aisle is. She barely listens to Graham's sermon. When the time to make a "commitment" arrives, Nora remains seated until she sees the man move toward the pulpit. She follows him, probably hoping that he will be impressed with her acceptance of the same belief as his. This is conformity because of normative social influence.

Alice has gone forward because she believes in what Graham is saying. This is conformity because of *informational social influence*.

Some of the conditions which generate this form of influence are pretty obvious. If a person has a history of failure on the task she is performing or on similar tasks, she will look to others for help (Allen, 1965). For example, you are taking a multiple-choice final exam in physics. During the term, you have come to realize that physics is a mystery to you exceeded only by why the Mona Lisa is smiling. You have failed every exam with amazing consistency. In a moment of despair, you glance at the answer sheets of the persons on either side of you. Both have answered "B" to the third question. You have answered "A." In such a situation, it is not unreasonable to expect you will change your answer to "B." This is informational social influence.

It is important to realize that in this example, you have little or no real evidence about whether these two people know more about physics than you. The reason for conformity is the assumption that on a task where you know very little, your two classmates are probably right. In other words, the old axiom "Two heads are better than one" produces conformity.

Informational social influence also occurs when the task is extremely difficult or ambiguous. Campbell (1961) proposed that in this situation, a person will tend to weigh the judgments of others more heavily than her own and conform to the group decision.

Leon Festinger (1954) has proposed another characteristic which might lead to informational social influence. According to his theory of *social comparison processes,* people encounter two types of reality: physical and social.

When a person has to determine whether her view of physical reality is correct, she can make an objective judgment. For example, two friends are arguing about which new car gets better gas mileage. One says it is her new Alfa Italiano; the other says it is her new Volks Macher. The correct view can be determined objectively and concretely by comparing the mileage between them.

Judgments about social reality, in contrast, have no such objective right or wrong answers. For example, if these two people were arguing about which car has more prestige, there would be no definitive answer. It is really a matter of taste or preference. In this situation, Festinger proposed that a person will turn to other people. Their views will help her determine whose view of social reality is correct. These other people are similar to her in life-style, attitudes, etc. If they generally agree about a matter of social reality, she will tend to accept their opinion. Why? Because their opinions provide her with a socially defined correct view of the world.

Conclusion

This section has been concerned with the factors that cause people to conform. Some of the theoretical explanations of compliance and private acceptance were examined first. Compliance is a change in a person's behavior as the result of social pressure. However, while her behavior has changed, her underlying attitudes remain the same. Compliant behaviors will disappear when the social pressure that caused them is removed. In private acceptance, a person changes her attitudes in response to social pressure. In this case, her behavior will continue even in the absence of social pressure. This is because the person believes in what she is doing.

There are two closely related explanations of why people conform: social power and social influence. It must be re-emphasized that these explanations do not compete with but rather complement each other. In fact, Deutsch and Gerard's types of social influence can be viewed as a means of categorizing French and Raven's forms of social power.

Social power describes those characteristics which enable an influencing agent to control another person's actions. The five types of power an influencing agent can possess (reward, coercive, referent, legitimate, and expert) are not, in the real world, independent of one another. People usually conform because an agent has more than one form of social power. For example, you take notes in class because your instructor has reward social power, (giving you an A), coercive social power (giving you a F), expert social power (she is an expert on the subject), and perhaps even because you like and respect her (referent and legitimate social power).

The concepts of normative and informational social influence explain conformity in a way similar to that of social power. These two forms of social influence also expand our understanding of conformity by identifying some situational factors (e.g., ambiguity of the situation) which will lead to conformity.

There is one final point on the interrelationship between attitude change and conformity. Changing a person's attitudes via persuasion can be viewed as a special case of private acceptance. Thus, you should view much of the material presented in this chapter as additional explanations of how and why attitude change occurs.

REVIEW QUESTIONS

(Twelve out of fifteen is passing)

1. A speed limit of 55 miles (95 kilometers) per hour on a highway represents a(n) _____ as to the appropriate driving speed. (p. 241)
2. The primary cause of conformity is _____ . _____ . (p. 242)
3. Asch's experiment, which concerned the effect of a unanimous majority on a person's judgment on a simple task, demonstrated _____ as a result of group pressure. (p. 244)
4. In Sherif's study of group influence on the autokinetic effect, subjects were influenced by the group even when it was no longer present. This suggests that Sherif had created _____ _____ . (p. 243)
5. The influence of a person, group, role, or norm on another person's behavior or beliefs was called _____ _____ by French and Raven. (p. 244)
6. A large company in a small town is ordered to reduce the air pollution from its plant. The company tells the town mayor that if she enforces the order, the company will move. The company is attempting to control the major's behavior via _____ social power. (p. 245)
7. Another company in another town responds to the same type of order by offering the mayor a bribe. This represents _____ social power. (p. 244)
8. Both of these forms of social power are more likely to yield _____ than _____ _____ . (p. 247)
9. The leading salesperson for a large firm arrives at a sales meeting dressed in a sweat shirt, jeans, and badly in need of a bath. The president of the company and other members of the group (all of whom are formally dressed) just smile. This probably is because this person has _____ _____ . (p. 246)
10. Conformity due to liking or a desire to identify with another is said to be due to _____ social power. (p. 247)
11. When the President of the United States is sworn into office, he takes an oath to uphold the Constitution. This oath can be considered part of the _____ of the President. (p. 248)
12. Legitimate social power is based on a number of characteristics of the influencing agent. However, the one characteristic that distinguishes this form of social power from the others is that the agent has the _____ to control a person's behavior. (p. 249)

13. Many people believe that the Bible is without error. Therefore, they do what the Bible tells them because it has _____ social power. (p. 251)
14. A desire to conform to the positive expectations of another person even though she may not be correct is called _____ social influence. (p. 253)
15. Of the two types of social influence, _____ social influence is the closest to expert social power. (p. 254)

ANSWERS

1. norm 2. social pressure or social influence 3. compliance 4. private acceptance
5. social power. 6. coercive 7. reward 8. compliance, private acceptance
9. idiosyncrasy credits 10. referent 11. role 12. right 13. expert 14. normative
15. informational

REACTIONS TO SOCIAL PRESSURE

The material presented thus far might lead you to conclude that conformity in response to social pressure is automatic. Right? Wrong! People do not invariably conform. Further, some people may conform only slightly, others totally. Thus, it is important to understand how people react to social pressure.

One of the earliest models was put forth by Floyd Allport (1934). He proposed that responses to social pressure range from complete conformity to complete nonconformity; the difference is one of degree. To illustrate Allport's model and the one which follows, consider this example from American history.

It is 1836 at the Alamo. You are Davy Crockett. You and about 100 of your companions are surrounded by thousands of Mexican soldiers. Santa Anna, the Mexican general, has sent a message that anyone who wishes to surrender can do so. You are hopelessly outnumbered, and if you stay and fight, you will die. Your commanding officer, Colonel Travis, draws a line in the sand. Those who wish to surrender are to cross the line; those who

wish to stay and fight should remain where they are. You desperately want to get out. You are fifth in line. As the four men before you are called, they remain in place and tell why they are staying. It is now your turn. What do you do?

According to Allport's model, you could refuse to cross the line and totally agree with the people before you. You could deviate slightly (e.g., agree to stay only four days). Or you could announce that you are leaving (nonconformity).

Richard Willis (1963, 1965, 1972) has criticized this model and others like it on two counts. First, it tells what a person does but not why. Second, it is too simplistic. There are, Willis believes, at least four reactions to group pressure. His model is presented in Figure 8-2.

First, consider the horizontal axis of the diamond model: Self-anticonformity–independence. It is concerned with how much a person changes her position *in response to group pressure*. Both ends of this axis describe the absence of change, but the behaviors displayed at each end are quite different. At the *self-anticonformity* end is a rare and bizarre type of behavior (Willis, 1972). The person changes her position continually but never in response to group pressure. Rather, she acts one way at one point and exactly the opposite at another point. This person continually disagrees with her own previous position. In the above example, the self-anticonformist would cross the line, step back across it, cross it again, etc. *Independence* is a much more common (and less bizarre) response to group pressure. Here, the person does not change in response to group pressure. But unlike the self-anticonformist, the independent maintains her position. Independent behavior at the Alamo would mean deciding on your own to cross (or not cross) the line. You behavior may be the same as or different from those who preceded you, but the important point is that it was not affected by group pressure. And once you have made your decision, you stay with it.

The midpoint on the self-anticonformity-independence axis represents maximum movement in response to group pressure. But note that this axis does not indicate the direction of the movement. To determine this, one must look at the vertical axis, conformity-anticonformity.

In both conformity and anticonformity, the person changes her position in response to group pressure. But in conformity, she moves *toward* the group; in *anticonformity,* she moves *away* from it. Note that in both instances, she is equally affected by the group's judgment. The difference is in the *direction* this judgment causes her to move.

Let's return to conformity at the Alamo. Before the four people ahead of you had spoken, you were going to leave. But after you hear them, you decide to stay. Now, consider anticonformity. You had initially decided to

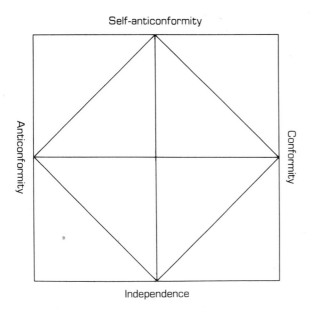

Figure 8-2. Willis's diamond model of reactions to social pressure. (From Willis & Levine, 1976)

stay. But as you listen to these four people, you decide that they sound like masochists with a strong death wish. This makes you decide to leave. In both instances, these people caused your position to change. But in conformity, you moved toward them; in anticonformity, you moved away from them.

While, in terms of behavior, anticonformity and independence may appear to be identical reactions, they are not. The independent has not changed her position. The anticonformist has moved away from the group.

This movement away from another's position is sometimes called the *boomerang effect*. Abelson and Miller (1967) have provided an interesting demonstration of how this works.

Interviewers approached people seated in a park and privately asked for their opinions on discrimination in employment. Then they were asked to state their opinions aloud. A confederate seated next to a subject reacted strongly, ridiculing and insulting the subject for holding such an opinion. The subjects were then asked their private opinion again. The typical subject did not move toward the confederate's position; rather, his opinion moved even further away. The confederate's behavior had a *negative* effect on the subject's opinions.

French and Raven's types of social power explain why you might fall at a certain point on the conformity-anticonformity continuum. For example, you might stay (i.e., conform) because you believe Colonel Travis wants this and it is your duty to obey him (conformity because of legitimate social power). Or you might feel that Colonel Travis and the men who preceded you are fools, incapable of making a correct decision (i.e., they lack expert social power). Therefore, you engage in anticonformity and decide to leave.

Further, if you conform, you may do so because of coercive social power (you are afraid that you may be shot if you leave). Or, conformity may represent private acceptance

due to referent social power. That is, you are attracted to the other men, identify with them, and as a result, accept their decision.

Willis's model is important because it explains *why* a person does or does not go along with the group. Failure to comply may reflect anticonformity or independence. As noted, these are quite different behaviors, and one must be able to discriminate between them.

One final point about Willis's model should be mentioned. People rarely react to social pressure with pure conformity or pure independence. These reactions are usually combined. For example, a person might go along with the group partially because of the group's judgment and partially because of her independent evaluation of the situation. You could decide to stay at the Alamo partially because of the other men's normative social influence and partially because you feel that despite the overwhelming odds, you have a chance of winning.

Characteristics of the conformer

Why do some people respond to social pressure by conforming, while others remain independent, and still others engage in anticonformity? Obviously, situational factors are important. But people may also differ as the result of variations in their personal characteristics. Let's examine some of the characteristics that seem to be related to a tendency to conform.

Sex

We all know that a woman is more likely to conform that a man. Right? Well, for a long time, this article of faith was accepted by social psychologists (e.g., Allen & Crutchfield, 1963; Endler, 1966; Nord, 1969). They attributed the greater conformity among women to sex role socialization, discussed in the previous chapter. The typical woman is brought up to be docile, compliant, and submissive. Her brother is taught to be strong and independent (Krech, Crutchfield, & Ballachey 1962). But in the early 1970's, some social psychologists began to question this widely held view.

Frank Sistrunk and John McDavid (1971) wondered if this finding might be due to factors other than socialization. They proposed that the tasks used in the typical conformity experiment may be partially responsible for the findings. Specifically, they questioned whether the material women had been asked to judge was as familiar and interesting to them as it was to men. If it was not, this might explain the consistent sex differences in studies of conformity.

Their first step was to give students a series of statements. Some of these statements concerned factual material, while others dealt with opinions. The students indicated whether a man or a woman would be more knowledgeable about and interested in each item. These judgments were used to create a set of male-oriented, female-oriented, and sex-neutral items. Men and women were given these items and were told how their peers had responded to them. The dependent measure was how often the subjects went along with their peers' judgments. Figure 8-3 presents the results of this study.

Note what Sistrunk and McDavid found. On masculine items, women conformed to their peers more often than men did, but on feminine items, men conformed more than women. On neutral items, women showed only a slightly greater tendency to conform then men.

This study is important in two respects. First, it demonstrates that sex differences in conformity are strongly related to the nature of the task. Second, it points out the dangers of making broad generalizations about group differences in compliant tendencies. Confor-

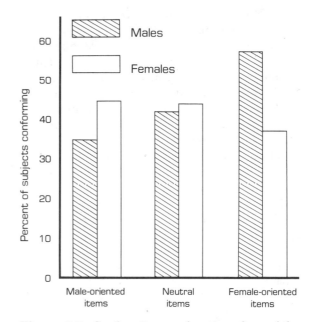

Figure 8-3. Conformity as a function of sex of the subjects and sex orientation of the items. (Adapted from Sistrunk & McDavid, 1971)

mity, like any other social behavior, is determined not only by personal characteristics but by the situation as well. Therefore, as we examine the personality correlates of compliant behavior, it is important to remember that individual differences as a result of personality variables can be changed or even eliminated by situational factors.

Personality variables

Authoritarianism. In the previous chapter, the concept of authoritarianism (Adorno et al., 1950) was introduced. An authoritarian person is greatly influenced by authority figures; she does what they tell her. It would thus seem reasonable to predict a positive relationship between authoritarianism and conformity. Richard Crutchfield (1955) measured authoritarianism and correlated it with the tendency to conform. As expected, he found that the more authoritarian people were, the more they conformed.

There should also be a positive relationship between authoritarianism and obedience to an experimenter in Milgram's study. Elms and Milgram (1966) gave the F scale (Adorno et al.'s measure of authoritarianism) to people who had displayed extreme obedience or extreme defiance in Milgram's original experiment. They found that the obedient group scored significantly higher on the F scale than the defiant subjects. Note that these were extreme groups. The obedient subjects, for example, agreed to force the learner's hand onto an electrical plate; the defiant subjects refused to shock the learner even when they could neither see him nor hear any sounds of pain and/or complaint. This point is important. For most people, obedience in the Milgram experiment is *not* associated with any personality variables.

Locus of control. As you may recall from Chapter Two, locus of control deals with people's beliefs as to how much control they have over the rewards and punishments they receive. People who believe that these are due to factors beyond their control are called externals. People who believe that they themselves are responsible are called internals (Rotter, 1966).

Since an external feels that factors beyond her control determine what happens to her, she should be more easily influenced by others than an internal (Phares, 1973). Research findings generally support this prediction. For example, it is easier to control the behavior of externals than internals by using social rewards. Also, a high-status communicator will produce more attitude change in an external than in an internal (Biondo & MacDonald, 1971; Doctor, 1971; Gore, 1962; Ritchie & Phares, 1969).

Under certain circumstances, however, this pattern is reversed. If you ask an internal to role-play (i.e., engage in a behavior she doesn't believe in), she will show more attitude change than an external. Why?

Put yourself in the place of an internal. You accept responsibility for your actions and tend to believe that you do things because you want to, not because outside factors have forced you. Thus, the inconsistency between your behavior and your true attitudes is likely to generate more dissonance for you than for an external. She can justify the inconsistency by viewing it as due to factors beyond her control. Thus, for her there is less cognitive dissonance and less attitude change.

Need for approval. Need for approval is a desire to win the approval of significant others (Crowne & Marlowe, 1964). Someone who is high in this need conforms more than someone who is low (Crowne & Liverant, 1963; Strickland & Crowne, 1962). One possible reason is that people with a high need for approval strongly want to be accepted by others. They may see conformity as a means to this end. Remember, groups tend to accept a person who conforms to their position and reject one who deviates from it.

But interestingly, people with a high need for approval are usually not very popular (Crowne & Marlowe, 1964; Jones, 1964). This may be because they try too hard and thus make other people uncomfortable. Or perhaps other people see their agreement as ingratiation. *Ingratiation* is a tactic some people use to enhance their image (Jones, 1964). Flattery, you may recall from the review of interpersonal attraction, is one form of ingratiation.

Jones proposed that people may conform as an ingratiation tactic. That is, they agree with another person in order to gain her acceptance and enhance their own position. The ingratiator doesn't conform because of social power. Rather, she knows that we like people who are similar to us. If she can get us to like her, she may derive some benefit for herself. Jones, Gergen, & Jones (1963) found that people do not like someone whom they believe is agreeing with them because of some ulterior motive.

I once had a graduate student who agreed with me no matter what I said. This annoyed me so much that sometimes I deliberately contradicted myself just to watch her change her position. I had written her off as an apple polisher until one day I noticed that she did this with everyone. She agreed with professors, other graduate students, secretaries, the person who ran the coffee shop, and the person who cleaned out the rat cages. I now believe that she wasn't a manipulative ingratiator, but rather a person with an incredible need to be accepted.

"Why don't you stick to your own kind?"

Most of the research on social influence is concerned with conformity. One way of looking at conformity is to consider it as a means of eliminating deviant behavior. But all of us are deviant in some way. How does deviance affect a person's behavior? Jonathan Freedman and Anthony Doob (1968) have investigated this question.

Since it's hard to turn a white Christian heterosexual into a black Jewish homosexual by giving her some independent variable, Freedman and Doob chose a less dramatic procedure to create the feeling of deviancy. Average college students were given information about their personalities which led them to believe that they were quite different from their classmates. This information had a dramatic effect on their behavior.

They tended to withdraw from "normal" society. When given a choice, they preferred to be with other deviants rather than with their nondeviant classmates. In another study, people who thought they were different selected another deviant for a pleasant experiment and nondeviants for an experiment that involved receiving electric shock. This is an extremely interesting finding. Even though their deviance was relatively mild, these students acted much like groups in the real world who deviate from society.

Minority group members may stick to their "own kind" because they believe they are deviant, not because they dislike the dominant group.

Freedman and Doob's research also showed that a deviant is often confused about her place in society. College students who believed that their "abnormality" was unknown to others preferred to keep it hidden. Further, they appeared to want to be accepted by normal people. For example, in one study, subjects who though they were deviant and subjects who thought they were normal were asked to help a nondeviant in a letter-writing campaign. A person who believed that she was different was generally willing to write twice as many letters as a person who believed she was normal.

These two findings seem to be related to the phenomenon of homosexuals who are torn between declaring their sexual preferences and their concern about being rejected by "straight" society. (If you're interested in a beautifully written account of this dilemma, read *On Being Different,* by Merle Miller.)

Comformity without social pressure

In the majority of cases, people conform because of social pressure. But under certain circumstances, compliance or even private acceptance may occur without social pressure.

The foot-in-the-door technique

This means of producing compliance is based on a technique which has been used for years by door-to-door salespersons. At some point in your life, someone has probably knocked on your door and tried to sell you a set of encyclopedias. These people believe that if they can avoid having the door slammed in their face (i.e., get a foot in the door), their chances of making a sale are greatly enhanced. Their reasoning is that if a person will agree to a small request (i.e., to talk with them), she is more likely to agree to a much larger request (i.e., to buy a $700 encyclopedia).

Jonathan Freedman and Scott Fraser (1966) showed that the foot-in-the-door technique does work. Imagine that you are at home and a well-dressed person knocks on your door. She explains that she is working on a safe-driving campaign and asks if she can put a "Drive Carefully" sign on your front lawn. You look at the sign; it is large and ugly. In such a situation, Freedman and Fraser found that very few people (17 percent) asked to do this will agree.

Now, imagine that the woman's request was to put a very small "Drive Carefully" sign in your yard, and you agree. A short time later, you are approached and asked if the large, ugly sign can be put up. Freedman and Fraser's data suggest that you will probably comply. In their experiment, this actually happened 76 percent of the time.

Subsequent research on the foot-in-the-door technique suggests that Bem's self-perception theory (cf. Chapter Six) may explain why it works. This theory proposes that as the result of agreeing to the first request, a person comes to see herself as compliant. This causes her to comply with the second larger request. In support of this interpretation is the fact that if a person *refuses* the first request, she will be *less* likely to comply with a subsequent request than someone who has not been previously approached (Cann, Sherman, & Elkes, 1975; Snyder & Cunningham, 1975).

Guilt

In Chapters One and Five, we saw that a person who feels guilty will show an increased willingness to help her victim. In addition, hurting someone will increase her tendency to comply with requests for help from other people (Carlsmith & Gross, 1969).

One explanation is that this willingness results from a person's desire to look good rather than from a guilty conscience. A study conducted by Wallace and Sadalla (1966) supports this explanation. Subjects were persuaded by a confederate to handle an expensive piece of equipment. As a result, the equipment exploded. When the experimenter entered the room and saw the damage, the confederate either told the experimenter what the subjects had done or covered up for them. The experimenter then asked both groups of subjects (i.e., those who had been caught and those who had not) to take part in an unpleasant alternative experiment. Subjects who had been caught were almost twice as likely to comply.

Cognitive dissonance

Thus far, I have discussed how compliance can occur in the absence of social pressure. Now, let's look at private acceptance. Chapter Six showed that a person who publicly supports an opinion she doesn't privately agree with will often change her opinion to match her behavior. The reason is believed to be the dissonance created by the inconsistency between her actions and her attitudes.

This technique of producing attitude change (i.e., private acceptance) is usually most effective when the reward for the behavior is quite small (Festinger & Carlsmith, 1959). It has been found that a person who is paid $1 for telling someone that a boring experiment is interesting will change her opinion more readily than a person who is paid $20. This finding demonstrates two very important points.

First, in this situation, the *less* the reward social power the *more* the attitude change. Second, the reason the subjects changed their opinions was not social pressure. Rather, it was to reestablish consistency between their opinions and their behavior.

DEINDIVIDUATION

One of the more interesting and frightening social phenomena is the apparently fragile hold we humans have on civilized behavior. For example, in summer 1977, a massive power blackout hit New York City. This was accompanied by an orgy of looting. At first, the looters were thought to be either habitual criminals and/or poverty-stricken people who saw a chance to get some free merchandise. But closer examination revealed that this description wasn't entirely accurate. Almost 40 percent of the looters had never been arrested, and many held full-time jobs. How can we explain their behavior? One possibility is that they were experiencing deindividuation.

Deindividuation is a psychological state in which a person feels a lessened sense of personal identity and a decreased concern with how people evaluate her. This feeling can cause her to act in an anti-social manner (Diener, 1976; Festinger, Pepitone, & New-

comb, 1952; Raven & Rubin, 1976; Singer, Brush, & Lublin, 1965; Zimbardo, 1970). Deindividuation seems to result from feelings of anonymity, lessened responsibility, and arousal (Zimbardo, 1970). There is reason to believe that simply being in a group can increase these feelings.

Group membership

It is Halloween, and the neighborhood children are out "trick or treating" in a large northwestern city." They knock on the door of one house and are shown into a room. In the room is a table with a bowl of candy at one end and a bowl of coins at the other. The children are told that they can have one piece of candy (the money isn't mentioned). Then the adult leaves the room. What these children do not know is that they are subjects in an experiment on the effects of a group on deindividuation (Diener, Fraser, Beamen, & Kelem, 1976).

Diener et al. compared the number of transgressions (i.e., taking more than one piece of candy or taking some money) committed by children who were alone and children who were in a group. Almost 60 percent of the children in the group either took an extra piece of candy or money. Slightly over 20 percent of the children who were alone did this. What is the reason for this difference?

There appear to be three interrelated answers. First, the presence of other people lessens an individual's feeling that she is personally responsible for an anti-social act. Note that this is really a case of diffusion of responsibility—the concept used by Darley and Latané to explain why people are more likely to help someone when they are alone than when they are with others (cf. Chapter Five).

Second, being a member of a group provides greater anonymity than being alone. The feel-

Educational Resources, University of South Florida

ing that you can't be identified will increase the chances of anti-social behavior (Dion, 1971).

Finally, a group may provide anti-social models for an individual. For example, Diener et al. found that 85 percent of the children in their study modeled the behavior of the first child who approached the table. If she took extra candy or money, so did they. If she did not, they did not.

Thus, the relationship between a group's presence and anti-social behavior may be circular. The group produces anonymity and diffusion of responsibility. This causes some members to act anti-socially. This behavior, in turn, provides anti-social models for other group members.

This is not to say that groups invariably increase anti-social behavior among their members (Diener, 1976), or that group membership is the only means of generating dein-

dividuation. There are other variables as well.

Anonymity

If a person feels that she cannot be identified (i.e., feels anonymous) her tendency toward anti-social behavior may be increased. This occurs presumably as the result of deindividuation. The feeling of anonymity can arise from some objective, identifiable aspect of the situation the person is in. Alternatively, it might be caused by subjective reactions to the general environment.

Diener et al.'s study of children's behavior on Halloween illustrates the first type of anonymity. A Halloween costume usually includes a mask and thus may provide anonymity. In this study, the number of transgressions committed by children who could and could not hide behind a mask was examined. When the children entered the homes, about half of them were asked their names and where they lived. These names and addresses were slowly repeated by the adult. No attempt was made to identify the other half of the masked children. Almost three times as many unidentified children took money or extra candy as did identified children. This was true of both children in groups and those who were alone.

Zimbardo (1973a) also believed that the general environment may create anonymity and thus deindividuation. He proposed that living in a large city may produce a feeling of anonymity and thus anti-social behavior. To test this premise, he placed apparently abandoned cars on streets in New York City and Palo Alto, California. The license plates had been removed and the hoods had been raised. Zimbardo and his associates hid themselves and watched people's reactions. In New York, ten minutes after the car had been placed on the street, it was approached by a man, a woman, and their nine-year-old son. While the woman stood acted as a lookout, the father and son deftly removed the radiator and battery. This family was not unique. Within twenty-four hours, the car had been stripped of every moveable part. Over the next two days, the tires were slashed, all the windows were broken, and stones and metal bars were used to smash the doors, fenders, and hood. Within seventy-two hours, the car had become a battered, unmoveable hulk. In contrast, the car in Palo Alto was untouched, except for one considerate person who lowered the hood when it rained.

One might think that the devastation of the car in New York was the work of street gangs. These gangs are much more common in New York than in Palo Alto. But, in fact, the overwhelming majority of the looters and vandals were well-dressed, white adults.

Zimbardo believed that this behavior was due largely to the greater sense of anonymity which exists in New York. As he put it:

It appeared to us that the greater sense of anonymity which exists in congested, metropolitan areas in part accounted for the observed difference. For many New Yorkers, their feeling of social anonymity is expressed as "they don't know who you are and don't care, and you don't know who they are and don't care." For the time being at least, there seems to be a greater prevailing sense of social consciousness, of social cohesion, of concern for property and people in the suburban locations. (Zimbardo, 1973, p. 411)

Zimbardo's explanation has a good deal of intuitive appeal. People in a city the size of New York are indeed more anonymous than people in Palo Alto. As Stanley Milgram (1970) has pointed out, a person who lives in a city with 8 million others personally knows a much smaller percentage of the total population than a resident of a city of 100,000 (the approximate population of Palo Alto). Thus, the probability of one New York vandal being identified by a passerby is much less than for a Palo Alto resident.

At the same time, it must be pointed out that Palo Alto is hardly a one-horse town. With a population of 100,000, there was a good deal of anonymity in Palo Alto also. Other characteristics of the two cities must have contributed to the differences obtained. For example, what was relative size of the police force in the two cities?

Milgram (1970) has proposed another aspect of big-city life which might explain part of the New Yorkers' behavior. He believed that because the population of New York is so highly concentrated, people cannot afford to get involved with other residents' affairs. To do so, he argued, would result in a continual disruption of one's own activities. To guard against this, New Yorkers have developed a norm of noninvolvement. It is possible that the New York vandals were aware of this norm. Therefore, they were less worried about passersby trying to stop them.

These alternative explanations are not meant to replace Zimbardo's anonymity explanation. The intent here is to underscore a theme recurrent throughout this book: It is extremely unlikely that any single variable can totally explain a complex social behavior.

Earlier, I presented the case of Frank Serpico as an example of how the role one assumes can produce positive behavior. Now let's look at a situation in which the opposite effect was produced.

Roles and deindividuation

Zimbardo and his associates (1973b) were interested in the psychological effects of being a prisoner or a prison guard. They recruited twenty-four normal, college-age males by advertising in a newspaper. These men were told about the experiment and offered $15 per day to participate.

After the men had agreed, a coin flip was used to decide who would be a prisoner or a guard. The "guards" were given a general briefing about the dangers inherent in being a prison guard but no specific instructions on how to act. It was left up to them to establish the prison's rules.

The experiment began with the "prisoners" being picked up unexpectedly at their homes. They were taken to a police station, fingerprinted, booked, and then taken to Zimbardo's mock jail. The prisoners were stripped, searched, deloused, and given a uniform with a number on it. Then they were shown to the cells where they were to spend the next two weeks.

Six days later, the experiment was terminated. This was considered necessary because many of the guards had become excessively brutal in their treatment of the prisoners. They took pleasure in acts of cruelty and

humiliation. The prisoners became "servile, dehumanized robots." They seemed to lose all sense of personal identity and social responsibility. Prisoners called each other by their numbers. On one occasion, they let another prisoner spend the night in a small closet rather than give up their blankets.

What would cause these people to act as they did? Zimbardo argued that labeling people as guards and prisoners and putting them in a situation where the labels are relevant (i.e., a prison) can produce pathological behavior of the type observed among his subjects.

The prison situation, as presently arranged, is guaranteed to generate severe enough pathological reactions in both guards and prisoners as to debase their humanity, lower their feelings of self-worth and make it difficult for them to be part of a society outside of their prison. (Zimbardo, 1973b, p. 164)

There is little question that in the case of prisoners, this dehumanization does occur. In the riot at Attica State Prison in 1971, the prisoners presented a list of demands which would have to be met before the riot would end. Consider the preamble to this list.

WE are MEN! We are not beasts and do not intend to be beaten or driven as such. The entire prison populace has set forth to change forever the ruthless brutalization and disregard for the lives of the prisoners here and throughout the United States. What has happened here is but the sound before the fury of those who are oppressed. (Quoted in Wicker, 1975)

This preamble strongly suggests that the prisoners believed that prison had turned them into something less than men (i.e., they had been dehumanized). At the same time, it may be simplistic to consider only the prison environment and the label "prisoner." A large percentage of prisoners are poor, uneducated, unskilled members of minority groups (63 percent of the prisoners at Attica were black or Puerto Rican) who have experienced dehumanization long before they enter prison. Further, most prisons are antiquated facilities with little or no recreational or training opportunities. If the environment of prisons were less oppressive, perhaps there would be less pathology among prisoners.

With regard to the guards, I agree that labeling a person as a prison guard may produce extreme behavior. A guard is required to carry out prison policy. According to Milgram (1974), people who carry out other people's orders may feel that they are merely agents. This produces *agentic behavior* in which the person feels that since she is simply carrying out orders, she is not personally responsible for the consequences. Feeling that you are only an agent may well produce feelings of deindividuation and thus increased anti-social behavior.

However, factors other than labeling are responsible for prison guards' behavior. Being a prison guard is not a prestigious job. The pay is terrible, the working conditions are atrocious, and most guards receive little or no training. Further, according to Wicker (1975), most guards are poorly educated, unskilled whites from small towns who are not psychologically prepared to deal with minority group members with vastly different values and life-styles. This clash of values further increases the animosity between guards and prisoners. Thus, guards' cruelty toward prisoners may be due as much to these factors as to the label "guard."

Conclusion

The second half of the chapter showed that conformity is a complex phenomenon. People do not always conform in response to social pressure. Some people stand fast while others yield. A person's reaction to social pressure seems to be determined mainly by situational factors. However, personality characteristics are probably also related to the nature of the response. Further, in certain instances (e.g., when one feels guilty or when one is in dissonance), conformity can occur in the absence of social pressure.

The review of deindividuation showed that social influence can also produce movement away from social norms. Further, deindividuation research suggests that even the environment can influence one's behavior. For example, the vandalizing of an abandoned car in New York City seems to have been due, at least partially, to the feeling of anonymity created by living in a large city.

The complexity of why and when people conform will, hopefully, caution you against making a simple value judgment about conformity. That is, conformity cannot be described simply as good or bad. The consequences of conformity for the conformer and for society in general depend on the situation. For example, democracy might be impossible if citizens did not accept the legitimate social power of the government. But legitimate social power does not always benefit humanity. Hitler's ability to carry out genocide was due, at least in part, to the German people's acceptance of his legitimate social power.

It seems fairly safe to propose that a society needs reward, coercive, referent, legitimate, and expert social power to function efficiently. But at the same time, too much conformity is a clear and present danger to a free society (Hollander, 1975). As Hollander has argued, ways must be found to encourage independence. If this cannot be done, we would become like the people in the fable who could not bring themselves to tell the emperor that he had no clothes.

REVIEW QUESTIONS

(Eight out of ten is passing)

1. A person who *deliberately* goes through red lights and exceeds the speed limit is displaying _____ . (p. 258)
2. A person who uses a group's judgment as one source of information about some decision she has to make, but essentially makes her own decision, is displaying _____ . (p. 258)
3. The foot-in-the-door technique suggests that you can get a person to comply by first getting that person to do a(n) _____ favor for you. (p. 261)
4. Agreeing with you instructor in a political argument because you believe this will lead to her giving you an A in the course is an example of _____ . (p. 261)
5. Cognitive dissonance theory proposes that one can produce private acceptance in the absence of social pressure if one gets a person to engage in counter-attitudinal advocacy for a(n) _____ reward. (p. 264)
6. Sistrunk and McDavid showed that sex differences in conformity may be due more to a person's _____ with the material being judged than to sex-linked general differences in conformity tendencies. (p. 260)
7. Since Milgram's research concerned obedience to an experimenter's orders, it is not surprising that the personality variable _____ is related to obedience to a command to shock someone. (p. 261)
8. A desire to be liked and accepted by others is called _____ _____ _____ . (p. 261)
9. The feeling of a loss of personal identity and a lessened concern for what others think of you is called _____ . It is manifested in _____ _____ behavior. (p. 264)
10. Someone who attempts to deny responsibility for his actions by saying "I was only following orders" is describing his behavior as _____ . (p. 268)

ANSWERS

1. anticonformity 2. independence 3. small 4. ingratiation 5. small, minimal, insufficient 6. familiarity or interest 7. authoritarianism 8. need for approval 9. deindividuation, anti-social 10. agentic

SUGGESTED READINGS

Somewhat surprisingly, there are only a few books devoted to social influence. Fortunately, the ones that do exist are quite good.

Textbooks

Conformity, by Charles Kiesler and Sara Kiesler. This is a short but very comprehensive review of conformity by two of the best reserchers in the area.

Obedience to Authority, by Stanley Milgram. This book is intended for the general public rather than for psychology students or teachers. It is an extremely interesting discussion of the research on obedience.

Interpersonal Influence, by Ladd Wheeler. This book covers basically the same material as the previous one. It has the advantage of being a little broader in orientation and being somewhat more readable than the Kieslers' book.

Popular literature

These fiction and nonfiction books and plays are all concerned with social influence as it operates in the real world.

Our Crowd, by Stephen Birmingham. This is a well-written description of the role of status in American culture. You'll also learn a great deal about what America was like in the early 1900's.

My Lai 4, by Seymour Hersh. A horrifying description of how deindividuation actually works in the real world.

Darkness at Noon, by Arthur Koestler, or *Eichmann in Jerusalem,* by Hannah Arendt. Both of these books provide excellent factual descriptions of how social power can be carried to a dangerous extreme.

The Crucible, by Arthur Miller. While this play takes place in the 1700's, it really was intended as a description of what America was like during the McCarthy era of the early 1950's.

Death of a Salesman, by Arthur Miller. This classic play is about a pathetic man who wants to be accepted by others but isn't.

1984, by George Orwell. In this classic novel, Orwell describes the attempts of a totalitarian state to completely control its citizens.

Even Cowgirls Get the Blues, by Thomas Robbins. The main character in this excellent novel differs from the norms of her society in a most unusual way. I think you'll enjoy reading about how she deals with the fact that she's different.

9 SMALL GROUPS

In collaboration with Stephen L. Cohen.

This chapter concerns behavior in small groups. To understand how people behave in this setting, you must first understand why people form groups, how they select a particular group to join, and how they organize the groups they belong to. After discussing these topics, we will turn to how people act when they are in a group. Finally, the reasons why groups perform well or badly will be discussed.

HUMAN BEHAVIOR AND SMALL GROUPS

I never cared for the sound of being alone.
                                    NEIL DIAMOND

We humans are incredibly social animals. We constantly seek out the company of others, and as the line from the song tells us, we dread being alone. Much of the time we spend with others is in a small group.

A *small group* is a small number of similar people who interact with one another. You have belonged to at least one small group from the day you were born—your family.

Your family has at least three members (mother, father, you) and probably no more than five or six. These people are similar biologically, culturally, and in terms of the experiences they have had. Most importantly, the members of your family interact. For example, you call your mother and tell her how you're doing in school. She tells your father the bad news. He calls you and says you can forget the new car. And so on. If there is one characteristic that defines a small group, it is that its members interact (Bonner, 1959). This interaction is what distinguishes a small group from an *aggregate,* a collection of people who are together in the same location but do not interact. For example, six people waiting for a bus is an aggregate. Six people who get together to organize a car pool (the bus is always late) is a small group.

Obviously, your family is not the only small group you belong to. Throughout your life, you have probably belonged to hundreds of small groups. The kids you played with after school; the athletic team you were on in high school; the people you share an apartment with in college; and your work team on the job you get after college are all small groups.

Your membership in these small groups differs from family membership in a very important respect. You did not choose to join your family. Your membership resulted from a decision made by your parents. In all the other small groups, you decided to join them. The groups you belong to because of factors beyond your control (e.g., birth) are called *ascribed groups*. The groups you choose to join are called *acquired groups*. We know how you came to be a member of your family, but how and why did you become a member of your acquired small groups?

Why do people join groups?

Needs

One of the most important reasons people form a group or join an existing one is that the group is seen as a way of satisfying some need.

Now, a person who has a need to fill will not automatically join a group. Before he joins, he has to be reasonably sure that the group will satisfy this need and not extract an unreasonable cost in doing so (Porter & Lawler, 1968; Vroom, 1964).

For example, imagine that you have a need to explore the great outdoors and are considering joining a mountain-climbing club. The first club you investigate has forty members, but only the five most experienced ones actually go on its mountain climbs. Since you have never climbed anything higher than a step ladder, you realize that you will probably not get to climb a mountain for a long time. Since the club doesn't satisfy your needs, you probably won't join it.

The second club you look into has all its members go on four climbs a year, but it has an extensive training program. Before a member climbs a mountain, he must run four miles with a sixty-pound pack on his back, descend the side of a sheer cliff with only a rope and a pick axe, and live for two weeks in the woods while equipped with only a compass and a hunting knife. These may all be reasonable requirements, but you decide that the reward of four climbs a year is not worth the costs involved. Thus, you will not join this club, either. It is only when you find a club that you expect will satisfy your need at an acceptable reward/cost ratio that you will join.

Shared goals

Each player is part of a whole team. A football team is a lot like a machine. It's made up of parts. I like to think of it as a Cadillac. A Cadillac's a pretty good car. All the refined parts working together make the team. If one part doesn't work, one player working against you . . . the whole machine fails. (George Allen, coach of the Los Angeles Rams)

What Coach Allen was describing is the fact that often there are goals which one person, working alone, cannot achieve. The joint efforts of a group are required. Thus, football coaches put eleven people on the field, and even someone like O. J. Simpson joins this group. This is because both realize that a group is needed to reach some shared goal (i.e., winning a game).

People also join and form groups because of shared activities and interests. People who engage in the same activities will band together to further them. For example, doctors join the American Medical Association, lawyers join the American Bar Association, and psychologists belong to the American Psychological Association. People will also form groups to pursue common interests. Model airplane builders get together to compare models, and bridge players get together to play bridge.

Shared threat

When people feel threatened or stressed, they show an increased tendency to band together. In one study, the behavior of a group of people who believed that they were going to receive electric shock was compared to the behavior of a control group. The threatened group members talked to one another more and liked each other more than did the nonthreatened group (Morris, Worchel, Bois, Pearson, Rountree, Samaha, Wachtler, & Wright, 1976).

Why do people come together in a time of threat? It is not simply because there's safety in numbers. Some theorists have proposed that when a person is frightened, he is unsure how to react. This uncertainty heightens his arousal and fear. To reduce these feelings, he will seek out other people who are in a similar threatening situation. These people give him the chance to compare his feelings and reactions to the threat with those of others. This *social comparison process* (Festinger, 1954) reduces his anxiety and fear. This seeking out of other people in similar situations (Schachter, 1959) has led Schachter to conclude that "Misery loves miserable company." Therefore, people who are facing the same threat will often coalesce into a group.

These three factors (needs, shared goals, and shared threat) are not independent of each other. People will often join a group for two or all three of these reasons. Also, it is often difficult to choose among these factors as reasons for joining. For example, do alcoholics form a discussion group because of their need to stop drinking, the shared goal of solving their problem, or the shared threat drinking presents to them?

How do people pick a group?

A person who desires to join a group doesn't choose the first one he finds. A number of factors influence his choice.

Needs

One important variable is needs. The person will often choose a group because it fills his unique needs. Perhaps the best known theory of how people differ in their needs is Abraham Maslow's (1943) *need hierarchy*. Maslow believed a person has a hierarchy of needs which are arranged in order of importance to his survival. The most basic needs are physiological, followed by needs for safety, belonging, self-esteem, and self-actualization. A person must feel that his lower needs have been met before he will try to satisfy his higher needs. For example, a person who has always been on the edge of starvation will not be concerned with safety. A person who feels isolated, insecure, and friendless will not be concerned with his self-esteem. These needs differ across individuals (and cultures) and thus will result in different behaviors.

The relationship between Maslow's need hierarchy and the selection of a group is illustrated by a field study conducted by Joel Aronoff (1967). Aronoff studied an island culture in the West Indies where people typically engaged in one of two occupations. They belonged either to a "gang" that cut cane in the sugar fields or a crew on a fishing boat. The cane cutter's job was a relatively secure one. There was always cane to be cut, and the men were paid on the basis of the entire group's effort. Being a member of a fishing crew was much riskier. The men were paid according to how much fish each one caught, and often a storm may destroyed a whole day's catch. However, fishing had two clear-cut advantages over cane cutting. First, if a fisherman was successful, he could make much more money than a cane cutter. Second, a fisherman was much more his own boss.

Aronoff proposed that the decision of which job to take was influenced by how well the men's needs had been satisfied. Cane cutters, he believed, had unfulfilled safety needs and thus chose a secure job. To support this, Aronoff found that cane cutters were far more likely to have lost a close relative when they were young than were fishermen (unfulfilled

safety need). Further, in responses to projective tests, fishermen showed a concern with self-esteem needs, while cane cutters showed a concern with physiological and safety needs.

Thus, part of the decision as to which work group to join was determined by where these men fell on Maslow's need hierarchy.

Similarity

The discussion of interpersonal attraction showed that perceived and actual similarity leads to friendship. Thus, it is not surprising to learn that similarity is also related to group membership.[1] Let's examine some of the research on this topic.

Biographic or demographic similarity. A *biographic* or *demographic* characteristic is one that we possess at birth and/or that describes a class of people. For example, race, sex, educational level, and age are all demographic characteristics. In general, people who are similar demographically are more likely to associate with each other than those who are not. For example, it has been found that religious similarity (Festinger, 1950; Goodnow & Tagiuri, 1952); similarity of occupation (French, 1951); and even the salary of one's father (Broxton, 1962) are all related to group membership.

There are three interrelated reasons. First, as already noted, people find those who are similar to themselves attractive. Second, people from similar backgrounds are more likely to meet than are people whose backgrounds vary. It is unlikely that the president of Standard Oil will find himself "rapping" with a resident of Harlem. Finally, demographic similarity often yields similarity in terms of attitudes and values, which leads to attraction.

---

[1]Propinquity and being liked, which also lead to attraction, also help a person decide which group to join.

Attitudes and values. There is good evidence that people join groups because of shared attitudes and values. For example, members of the Young Democrats are likely to hold the same views about political issues; the same is true of members of the Ku Klux Klan.

Although people will usually join groups who share their attitudes and values, there are certain exceptions. Situational factors, such as the cost of group membership, may keep a potential member from joining. Perhaps more importantly, personality characteristics of group members may deter someone even though he shares the group's attitudes and values. For example, a woman may support the feminist movement but may refrain from joining the National Organization for Women (N. O. W.) because she sees many of its members as part of the radical fringe.

Personality. The similarity, or at least perceived similarity, of personality may also attract people to a particular group. For example, Izard (1960a,b) found that friends were more similar in personality than were random pairs of people. Other studies have shown that if you ask a person to rate two individuals, one similar and one dissimilar to him in personality, he will usually give the former a much more favorable rating (Byrne, Griffitt, & Stefaniak, 1967; Griffitt, 1966).

These findings suggest that people will be attracted to others with similar personality characteristics. Winch (1952) however, has proposed that in certain instances a person will be attracted by *complementarity of needs;* that is, he seeks friends whose needs are different yet supportive of his own. For example, a masochist would seek a sadist for his mate. Although Rychlak (1965) has found support for this position, most social psycholo-

gists believe that similarity is more likely to lead to attraction than complementarity.

Skills and abilities. The relationship between skills and abilities and attraction to a group is not as straightforward as the relationship between the other types of similarity discussed. Some researchers (e.g., Gilchrist, 1952) have found that people begin by choosing groups whose members are much more successful than they. But eventually, people (even those who are unsuccessful) will choose groups with comparable abilities. Other researchers (Bramel, 1969; Stotland & Dunn, 1962) have found that attraction to another person increases with that person's ability; we prefer very capable friends.

Helmreich, Aronson, and Le Fans (1970) believed that the relationship between perceived ability and attraction may be affected by a person's self-esteem. A person low in self-esteem may prefer highly competent others so that they "can take care of him" (Helmreich et al., 1970, p. 260). A person high in self-esteem may also prefer others with high ability because he believes that he is like them. Finally, someone with average self-esteem prefers friends with comparable abilities and skills. To test this proposal, Helmreich et al. classified subjects by self-esteem and then introduced them to a competent person who either did or did not make a mistake (spilling a cup of coffee). Subjects then rated the this person on likability. The results of the study, shown in Figure 9-1, reveal that subjects high or low in self-esteem liked the competent person more when he did not spill the coffee than when he did. The opposite was true of subjects who were average in self-esteem.

Thus, in general, people seem prefer associating with others similar in ability. However, some people want to associate with others of lesser ability. It is reasonable that they want to be a "big fish in a small pond."

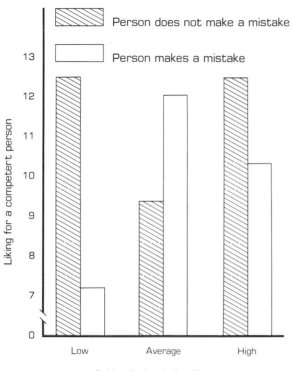

Figure 9-1. The effects of subjects' self-esteem and whether or not a competent person makes a mistake on liking for that person. (Adapted from Helmreich, Aronson, & Le Fans, 1970)

GROUP STRUCTURE

Once a group has formed, its first task is to get organized. This is done by formally or informally establishing a *group structure,* a pattern of interrelationships among group members (Shaw, 1971).

Groups, of course, can be organized in many different ways. Three things will influence the group's decision: (1) its beliefs about how to perform most efficiently, (2) its physical and social environment, and (3) the abilities, attitudes, needs, and motivations of its members (Cartwright & Zander, 1968).

Just as needs influence a person's decision as to which group to join, they also influence the group's structure. For example, a group of people with strong safety needs (Maslow's hierarchy) will establish a much more rigid, formal structure than a group concerned with self-esteem needs (Aronoff & Mess'e, 1971). The effect of attitudes and motivations on group structure can be seen in the following real-life example.

In the late 1960's and early 1970's, the leading radical student group was Students for a Democratic Society (S.D.S.). Its founders viewed rigid power hierarchies and established leaders as dangerous, undemocratic, and a major cause of America's problems. This view was reflected in the structure at S.D.S. meetings.

> . . . at group meetings their openness is apparent. They exhibit great tolerance, and no speaker is silenced, no matter how irrelevant or repetitious. And it is difficult to single out those who hold authority. Leaders, elected or *de facto,* hem and haw when they are called leaders, for traditional authority and arbitrary decision-making are incompatible with the values of the SDS staff. (Jacobs & Landau, 1966, pp. 30–31).

The almost nonexistent structure at S.D.S. meetings illustrates another important point. For a group to operate efficiently, it must have a structure. S.D.S.'s concept of participatory democracy may sound like a good idea, but in practice it did not work very well. The meetings tended to be four to six hours long and boring, and as a rule resulted in few, if any, concrete decisions as to what the group should do.

Roles

A group's primary purpose is to achieve some goal or goals. One way to do this is to give each group member certain duties. Sometimes these duties are assigned. Other times, they emerge as the group structures itself and/or redefines its purpose. This process can be illustrated in Piers Paul Read's (1974)

Carlos Garcia-Lozano

description of the behavior of a small group faced with a very specific and serious goal—to stay alive.

On October 12, 1972, a plane carrying a group of athletes and their friends left from Montevideo, Uruguay, headed for Santiago, Chile. The plane never arrived. It crashed in the Andes Mountains, and for the next ten weeks, the passengers endured starvation, illness, and constant sub-zero temperatures. Incredibly, sixteen of the forty-five passengers survived.

The overriding goal of these people was to be rescued. To accomplish this, positions within the group were established. A *position* is simply where a person falls in a group's hierarchy (McDavid & Harari, 1974). The behavior considered appropriate for a person holding a certain position is called a *role* (Sarbin & Allen, 1968).

In a group, two people who occupy the same position may play very different roles. There are three basic roles a person can take (Bales, 1958, 1970). They differ in the function they perform for the group.

The first is the *task-oriented role*. The person in this role is primarily concerned with the group reaching some specified goal. He initiates group discussions, seeks opinions and information from group members, and tries to direct and coordinate the activities of the group. Among the Andes survivors, this role was taken by a young man named Roberto Cannessa. He kept the others from starving to death by convincing them that in order to survive they would have to eat the bodies of their dead companions. He showed the group how to make blankets and hammocks to sleep in. He was in charge of medical supplies. Perhaps most importantly, Cannessa persuaded the group that they must organize expeditions to find help rather than wait to be rescued. He led the expedition that finally brought help.

The second possible role is the *maintenance role*. A person who takes on this role is concerned with group morale; he attempts to keep things harmonious and attends to the relationships between group members. While Cannessa played the task-oriented role quite well, he cared little about maintenance. He was short-tempered and abusive toward the other members. The maintenance role was played by Nando Parrado. Here is how his behavior was described:

> Parrado . . . who before the accident had been a gawky, timid, would-be playboy, was now a hero. His courage, strength, and unselfishness made him the best loved of them all. He was always the most determined to brave the mountains and the cold and set out for civilization; and for this reason those who were younger, weaker, or had less determination placed all their faith in him. He also comforted them when they cried and took on himself much of the humdrum work around the plane from which, as an expeditionary, he was officially excused. He would never suggest a course of action without rising at the same time to put it into effect. One night, when part of the wall blew down in a strong wind, it was Parrado who climbed out from under the blankets to build it up again. When he returned he was so cold that those sleeping on either side of him had to punch and massage his body to bring back the circulation; but when, half an hour later, the wall blew down again, Parrado once again rose to rebuild it. (Read, 1974, p. 127.)

Finally, there is the *individual* or *self-oriented role.* The person who takes this role basically cares about no one but himself. In fact, he will often attempt to undermine the efforts of the people playing the task and maintenance roles. Among the Andes survivors, people who played this role were called "parasites." They would sit in the sun trying to keep warm while complaining about their plight. They did nothing to help the group reach its goal or keep up group morale.

Factors which influence role behavior

People may differ greatly in the roles they play in a group. What factors influence the choice of roles?

Status. As already noted, group members assume different positions. These positions differ in *status,* the group's evaluation of a position—that is, how much prestige it has or where it falls in the group hierarchy. Those positions which contribute the most to the accomplishment of the group's goal will be given the highest status. This status, in turn, will affect the behavior (role) of a person occupying that position.

For example, the primary goal of the Uruguayans was to be rescued. Thus, those members who looked for help were given the highest status. They were treated like an elite warrior class. They were given the best food and places to sleep. They were excused from menial tasks and were deferred to by other group members. These people, in turn, became more and more arrogant and domineering toward the rest of the group (Read, 1974).

High-status members not only behave differently from low-status members but are reacted to differently as well. For example, they are allowed to deviate more (Hollander, 1958). Kelley (1951) found that high-status members are much more likely to receive communications than low-status members. Thus, it is not surprising to find that high-status positions usually bring a great deal of satisfaction for these members (Cohen, 1958).

Enacted and expected roles. The behavior displayed by a person in a certain position is called his *enacted role.* This role may or may not be in accord with the person's *expected role.* The latter refers to the expectations which he and the other group members have as to how he should behave.

In certain instances, role expectations may determine or at least influence role enactment. Consider, for example, the expectations associated with occupying the position of parent.

Most of us can recall our frustration at our parents' rules and regulations when we were children (e.g., eat with a knife and fork; don't play with your peas). If you are like us, you swore never to do that to your own children. Yet as we, in turn, (and most people), become adults and parents, we find ourselves acting the same way, perhaps with minor variations (e.g., don't play with your fondue fork; eat your granola). Why? Because of our expectations about the role of being a parent.

When a person's position changes, so will his role expectations. As a result, his attitudes and behavior will change as well. Lieberman (1956) demonstrated this in a classic study of foremen, union stewards, and workers in a medium-sized company. He examined the changes in attitudes among workers who went, for example, from the position of union steward to foreman. These changes were compared to those of workers whose position had not changed. Lieberman's major hypothesis—that people who changed positions would develop new role expectations and thus new attitudes—was substantially confirmed. Union stewards who became foremen became more pro-management, but workers who became union stewards became more anti-management. The control group—people who did not change positions—did not change their attitudes.

Lieberman kept track of his subjects for several years. Some of them remained in their new positions while others moved back to their original positions. Lieberman found that subjects who stayed in their new positions kept their new attitudes, but those who returned to their old positions returned to their old attitudes.

Role conflict. A group member who occupies two positions with incompatible role expectations—called *role conflict* (Sarbin & Allen, 1968)[2]—is motivated to change his behavior.

[2]Actually, Sarbin and Allen labeled this *interrole conflict.* They distinguished it from *intrarole conflict,* in which different people have contradictory expectations about the same role. However, here we are interested only in interrole conflict.

His goal is to eliminate the conflict. One way to do this is simply to make a choice between the two positions, abandoning the lower-priority one and the behavior associated with it.

As an illustration of role conflict, consider the problem faced by some members of the Boston Police Force during the school busing controversy. In the mid 1970's, a federal judge had ordered black students bused into the all-white South Boston High School. The residents of South Boston reacted violently. When they attacked the buses, the police were called in to protect the black students and enforce the ruling. However, many of the policemen were themselves residents of South Boston and believed that busing was "the worst thing that ever happened to this city" (Kifner, 1976, p. 36). Thus, they faced role conflict as the result of occupying two contradictory positions at the same time. As policemen, they had to enforce busing; as residents, they opposed it.

They resolved this role conflict by giving top priority to their position as law enforcement officers. They protected the black students, enforced busing, and punished those who used violence. To reduce the role conflict they felt, many of the policemen moved from South Boston (Kifner, 1976).

Conclusion

This section first examined the question of why people join or form groups. A person will join a group when one or more of the following three conditions exist. He has a need that he can't satisfy alone. He shares a common goal with other people. Or, he is threatened by the same thing as a group of other people.

While these three factors will cause a person to seek others, they will not determine which group he will join. This is determined primarily by the person's needs and characteristics. He will choose a group which satisfies his needs and whose members have characteristics which are similar to his.

The reasons for forming and/or for selecting a particular group also have a strong impact on the group's structure. One cannot understand why a group adopts a certain structure without knowing some of the factors that led to the group's formation and the members' reasons for joining it.

The discussion of group structure was concerned primarily with the roles people play. A role is the behavior a group member displays. It is influenced by his personal characteristics and the situation he is in. We concentrated on how situational factors influenced peoples' roles. The status associated with a person's position in the group, the expectations about how a person in his position should behave, and role conflicts will all affect his behavior (i.e., role enactment).

REVIEW QUESTIONS

(Ten out of twelve is passing)

1. The characteristic which distinguishes a group from an aggregate is the fact that group members _____ . (p. 273)
2. The basic difference between group membership by ascription and group membership by acquisition is that in the *latter* case, a person _____ to join the group. (p. 273)
3. Five explorers form an expedition to locate a primitive tribe in the Amazon jungle. The formation of this group is based on _____ _____ . If five explorers were working independently in the jungle and formed a group because they were attacked by the tribe, this would be group formation based on _____ _____ . (p. 274)
4. One of the things that other people many provide for a person who is threatened is a means to _____ his reactions to the situation with others. This, in turn, may _____ his fear. (p. 274)
5. The idea that people attempt to satisfy their needs in order of importance for survival is contained in Maslow's theory of a _____ _____ . (p. 275)
6. All other things being equal, a person will be more attracted to a group comprised of people who are _____ to her than a group comprised of people who are _____ to her. (p. 275)
7. The old nursery rhyme about Mr. and Ms. Sprat tells us that "Jack Sprat would eat no fat [meat]; his wife would eat no lean." Assuming the Sprats were happily married, this would support the _____ _____ _____ theory. (p. 276)
8. The behavior considered appropriate for a person occupying a certain position in a group is called a (an) _____ . (p. 278)
9. A group member who is primarily oriented toward getting the group to reach some goal is serving a (an) _____ _____ function. A group member who is concerned about group morale is serving a _____ function. (p. 278)
10. The _____ of a position is the amount of prestige associated with that position and is based on how much the occupant of the position contributes to the group's reaching its goal. (p. 279)

11. People's beliefs about how someone who occupies a certain position should behave is called a (an) _____ _____ . The actual behavior displayed by the person is called the _____ _____ . (p. 279)

12. When a person simultaneously occupies two positions which have incompatible role expectations, the person will experience _____ _____ . (p. 280)

ANSWERS

9. task-oriented, maintenance   10. status   11. expected role, enacted role   12. role conflict
5. need hierarchy   6. similar, dissimilar   7. complementarity of needs   8. role
1. interact   2. decides or chooses   3. shared goals, shared threat   4. compare, reduce

GROUP PROCESSES

Up to now, the concepts we presented could be applied to the behavior of individuals as well as to groups. For example, the discussion of roles overlapped a good deal with the discussion of roles in the chapter on social influence. Now, we turn to a topic which is unique to groups: group processes.

Group processes refer to the interactions between group members and the influence one member has on another. In the view of Marvin Shaw (1971), a group is defined not by its members' motivations or roles or by the group's structure, but rather by group processes.

Cohesiveness

It seems reasonable to begin the discussion of group processes by considering why a group stays together. One of the most important factors is how cohesive the group is. The *cohesiveness* of a group describes how attracted its members are to the group and how much they like each other. For a group to continue, its members must be more attracted to it than to another group. If not, it will disband. This point is illustrated in the old joke about the Lone Ranger and Tonto. The masked man and his "faithful Indian companion" are surrounded by 2,000 Sioux, 3,000 Apaches, and 4,000 Comanches.

The Lone Ranger asks: "What do you think they'll do to us, Tonto?"

Tonto replies: "What you mean 'us,' pale face?" Evidently, this two-person group was not cohesive enough to stay together.

Factors leading to cohesiveness

Cohesiveness is, in many respects, similar to attraction between two people. Thus, it is not surprising to find that similarity of attitudes, values, personality traits, and demographic characteristics all lead to a highly cohesive group (Festinger, Schachter, & Back, 1950). This is especially true when the goal of the group is essentially social (e.g., to provide companionship).

However, when a group's goal involves the completion of some task, this may be a more important determinant of cohesiveness than similarity. For example, Anderson (1975) found that when people were only required to

get acquainted, their perceived similarity influenced cohesiveness. But when these same people were asked to solve a problem, the group's ability to work together was much more important.

Another factor related to cohesiveness is how hard it is to enter the group. The more difficult it is to join, the more cohesive it is (Aronson & Mills, 1959; Gerard & Mathewson, 1966; Walker, 1968). For example, Walker found that fraternities with the hardest initiation rites (i.e., Hell Week) were the most cohesive.

Finally, it has been found that the presence of an external threat produces an extremely cohesive group (Bramel, 1969; Rabbie, Benoist, Oosterbaan, & Viser, 1974). This finding is consistent with a point made earlier: shared threat leads to group formation.

The effects of cohesiveness

Members of a highly cohesive group will talk to each other more, say more positive things to each other, cooperate more, and evaluate

each other more favorably than will members of a less cohesive group (Dion, 1973a; Lott & Lott, 1961; Shaw, 1971). Also, cohesiveness results in group members having a good deal of influence on each other and high conformity to the group's decisions (Back, 1951; Festinger, Schachter, & Back, 1950; Wyer, 1966). Finally, people in a highly cohesive group trust each other more and feel more secure than do members of a less cohesive group (Julian, Bishop, & Fiedler, 1966; Myers, 1962). This, in turn, makes the conversation among group members even more positive.

Communication patterns

Group process means interaction, and interaction is achieved via communication among group members. Although specific patterns of communication may be considered as part of group structure, they will be discussed here. This is because these patterns can either restrict or enhance interactions among members.

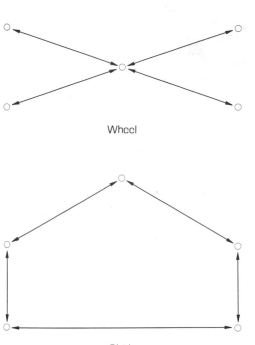

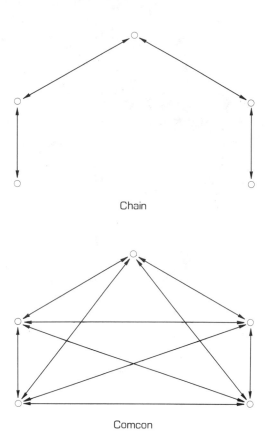

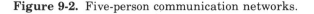

Figure 9-2. Five-person communication networks.

Communication networks

Figure 9-2 presents diagrams of four communication networks. In these diagrams, the small circles represent group members and the arrows indicate the channels of communication open to them. While the diagrams describe five-person groups, these communication patterns, or networks, could be drawn for groups of any size. Also, the exact pattern is not as important as its characteristics, which affect group interactions.

One important difference among these networks is how centralized they are. The *wheel* is the most centralized of the four. It has one person to whom all four other members can talk. This person is therefore the center of the network. Note that the four other people cannot communicate with one another. The least centralized network is the *comcon* network. Here, there is no central person. All the members of the group can talk to one another.

As an example of the comcon network, consider group psychotherapy. Typically, every member of the group can talk freely to every other member. A football team is an example of a wheel network. In general, players will direct their comments about what plays will be successful to the quarterback only. The quarterback, in turn, calls the play for the entire team. He is communicating with the other ten members of the group. Note that a football team uses a wheel network not because it is forced to but because this is believed to be the most efficient network. Similarly, people in group psychotherapy use a comcon network because they believe that allowing free and open communication is the best way to solve their problems.

Intermediate between the wheel and comcon networks in centrality and openness are the circle and chain networks. In the *circle,* every member can talk to two other members. Thus, there is no true central person, and communication is somewhat more open. As an illustration of a circle network, imagine a group of families who live around the lake where the Loch Ness monster (supposedly) lives. These people decide to form an association to help tourists who come to look for "Nessie." The depth of the lake and its size prevent people on one side of the lake from talking easily to people on the other side. Thus, the initial communication in this group will probably consist of people talking to their neighbors on either side of them.

A *chain* network differs from a circle in that the link between the two people at the end points is absent. Imagine you are in a small restaurant with one waiter and one cook. You order a hamburger. The waiter gives your order to the cook. The cook asks the waiter if you want the hamburger rare. The waiter asks you. This is a chain pattern.

The effect of communication networks. Interest in communication networks grew out of the work of Bavelas (1950) and Leavitt (1951), who studied their effect on group problem solving. Subsequent research has shown some quite consistent effects of communication networks.

In general, the networks that permit the greatest interaction rank highest in member satisfaction (Shaw, 1964). Further, those group members who interact the most are the most satisfied, and the isolates (people at the ends of the network) are the least satisfied (Shaw, 1964). Leavitt (1951) explained this in terms of *independence.* People have a need for recognition and achievement, and being an isolate frustrates these needs.

Despite the morale advantages of a decentralized or open network, it does not always produce the best performance. On tasks which involve simple problems, the centralized wheel network is most efficient (Collins & Raven, 1969). This is because the central person can direct the activities of the other group members without interruption.

However, when the problem is more complex and requires considerable information and thought, the wheel network is likely to be less effective. In this situation, the leader is often bombarded with too much and too complex information to solve the problem adequately by himself. He becomes *oversaturated* with information (Shaw, 1964). For complex problems, decentralized patterns like the circle and comcon are generally faster and make fewer errors than centralized patterns like the wheel and chain (Shaw, 1964).

These patterns also have different effects on the emergence of leaders. The wheel gives the central person the advantage of taking over as leader. In fact, this is usually the case. The central person obviously will have information unavailable to the other members and will be correctly perceived as the only link among them. On the other hand, in more decentralized groups, leaders are not as likely to emerge, and certainly not as quickly as those in centralized networks (Shaw, 1971).

Obviously, the emergence of a group leader is determined by factors other than where someone is in the network. The next section examines some of these other variables.

Leadership

A group rarely exists for long without a leader. This is true even of groups that are initially intended to be leaderless.

For example, George Orwell's classic satire of communism, *Animal Farm,* tells the story of a group of animals that overthrow the farmer who owns them. They set out to establish a truly classless society where pigs and chickens and horses and cows are all equal. But, soon the pigs issue the following statement:

"All animals are equal, but some are more equal than others." The "more equal" pigs became the leaders of the other animals. Among humans, the attainment of leadership is a little more involved.

Who becomes a leader?

It was once thought that leaders were born, not made. That is, certain people, so-called *Great men,* become leaders regardless of the specific group or situation they are in (Gibb, 1969). Considerable time and effort was spent identifying the personality traits these "natural" leaders possessed. The researchers finally concluded that great men do not exist. The more prevalent belief today is that leadership is primarily determined by the situation. A leader in one group is only slightly more likely than one of his followers to be a leader in another group (Bell & French, 1950; Gibb, 1969).

What, then, determines who becomes a leader? Bass (1960) has proposed that leadership consists of three behaviors: attempting, success, and effectiveness. A leader is someone who is efficient in all three of these behaviors.

Leadership attempting. Leadership attempting is the act of talking a great deal in the group and/or directing the activities of the other members. That is, a person engages in activities which may result in leadership. In a study to determine if such behaviors actually increase the likelihood of becoming a leader, Jaffe and Lucas (1969) found that the person who talked the most in a group was judged to have contributed the most. This was true even when what this person said was practically worthless!

This finding should not lead you to conclude that quality is irrelevant to leadership. For example, someone who talks a great deal but uses these occasions to tell other group members that their ideas are the "stupidest thing I've ever heard" is not likely to become a leader. The person who does become a leader is probably one who gives constructive suggestions, orients the group toward its goal, and is positive toward other group members.

Why do some group members attempt to lead and others do not? The answer does not seem to lie in personality differences. Leadership attempting seems to depend on the situation. A person who has relevant information about the task will attempt to lead. Also, a member who believes that what he is saying is correct will make more leadership attempts (Jaffe & Furr, 1968; Jaffe & Lucas, 1969; Levinger, 1969; Simkins & West, 1966).

A number of studies have demonstrated the second process. In these experiments, two group members are selected at random. One is told that what he is saying is really helping the group. The other is told that his contributions are trivial or unimportant. (This feedback has nothing to do with the actual quality of the two people's contributions.) The effect of this information is to increase the participation of the first person and decrease that of the second.

Leadership success. Leadership success is the ability to get group members to follow or listen to one's leadership attempts. Social power is strongly related to leadership success. As you may recall from Chapter Eight,

French and Raven (1959) defined *social power* as an influencing agent's ability to control a person. They identified five sources of social power: (1) *reward,* based on the agent's ability to give rewards, (2) *coercive,* based on the agent's ability to give punishments, (3) *expert,* based on the agent's expertise, (4) *referent,* based on the person's desire to identify with the agent and/or the person's liking for the agent, and (5) *legitimate,* based on the person's belief that the agent has a legal right to control the person.

In discussing power and leadership success, it is necessary to add a sixth type of power, charisma. *Charisma* is difficult to define. It is a person's magical or mystical ability to control others. Although it is difficult to define, people do differ in charisma. For example, most people agree that John F. Kennedy and Adolf Hitler had charisma, and Gerald Ford and Richard M. Nixon did not.

To clarify how these forms of power are related to leadership success, let's examine an infamous leader of a small group, Charles Manson. Presently, Manson is serving a life sentence (commuted from death) for the brutal murders of seven people. Manson was convicted by a jury that was told by the prosecuting attorney that Manson *did not* personally commit the killings. The basis of the jury's verdict was that while Manson was not physically present at the murders, they were the direct result of his orders. In a macabre sense, this is the ultimate in leadership. Manson was able to convince his followers to kill seven people they did not even know. How could he gain such control over them?

The answer is that he possessed all six forms of social power. With regard to reward social power, he told his female followers, most of whom were singularly unattractive, that they were beautiful. Further, in the view of Vincent Bugliosi, the prosecuting attorney, these young women had a strong need to belong which Manson satisfied. He also controlled the dispensing of drugs and sex within the group (Bugliosi & Gentry, 1975).

While Manson rewarded his followers with flattery, drugs, and sex, he also had considerable coercive social power. During the early stages of the murder investigation, a former follower was asked to testify against Manson; he refused. Was it because he feared Manson? the police officer asked. The man replied: "I'm scared shitless. I'm petrified of him. He wouldn't hesitate for a minute. If it takes him ten years, he'd find [my son] and carve him to pieces." (Bugliosi & Gentry, 1975, p. 152)

Manson's reward and coercive social power paled in comparison to his referent social power. His followers idolized him; they tried to identify with him and internalized his values. Why? Because many of them thought Manson was Jesus Christ. Susan Atkins, one of the actual murderers, believed that Manson was Christ and/or the Devil. The translation of this belief into Manson's power over his followers was expressed by Brooks Poston, another "family" member. When asked the basis of Manson's power over him, Poston replied: "I felt he was Jesus Christ. That is power enough for me" (Bugliosi & Gentry, 1975, p. 321). If "Jesus Christ" told his followers that killing was all right, it was.

Manson's legitimate social power also derived from his followers' belief that he was Jesus Christ (and therefore had the right to control them) and their bizarre interpretations of passages from the Bible and songs by the Beatles. For example, in this passage from the Bible, an angel is described: "And they had a king over them which is the angel from the bottomless pit." (Rev. 9:2). Manson's followers believed that this passage referred to him.

Manson's expert social power was based on the fact that he devised the group's "ideology" and was the prime interpreter of the Beatles and the Bible for his followers. Of equal if not greater importance was Manson's charisma. Susan Atkins said: "The words that would come from Charlie's mouth would not come from inside him [they] would come from what I call the infinite" (Bugliosi & Gentry, 1975, p. 235).

Even people outside the family found Manson charismatic. Jerry Rubin, the founder of the Yippies, considered him inspiring. Even Vincent Bugliosi, the prosecuting attorney, felt that Manson had certain strange powers. "Midway through the arraignment I looked at my watch. It had stopped. Odd. It was the first time I could remember that happening. Then I noticed Manson staring at me, a slight grin on his face. It was, I told myself, a coincidence" (Bugliosi & Gentry, 1975, p. 256).

Thus, we can see that Charles Manson's ability to dominate and control his followers grew out of his social power. He was a successful leader because he possessed social power. Despite the pathology of Manson and his followers, they provide a good illustration of the relationship between leadership success and social power.

Leadership effectiveness. Charles Manson was not only a successful leader, he was also (in a perverted sense) an effective leader. *Leadership effectiveness* describes a leader's ability to get his followers to move toward some goal and achieve it. (In Manson's case, it was the murder of seven people.) What kind of leader will be most effective?

Leadership style. One important determinant of a leader's effectiveness is his style. Leaders usually tend toward one of two styles. The first is called *task-oriented*. A task-oriented leader is one who is concerned primarily with moving the group toward some goal (Bales, 1950, 1970). This leader will define the group's activities and roles, assign tasks, and determine the most efficient way to get the job done. In other words, he will attempt to structure the group (Fleishman, 1953).

The other leadership style is the *person-oriented* style. A leader who adopts this style is concerned mainly with the individual needs of the members. He will attempt to generate trust, respect, and warmth among them and to encourage participation. He will be considerate (Fleishman & Harris, 1962; Halpin & Winer, 1952, 1957).

This is not to say that leadership style is an either/or proposition. Often leaders incorporate both styles. In fact, two of the leading researchers on leadership style, Robert Blake and Janet Mouton, believe that the best leadership style is one that is *both* task-oriented and person-oriented (1964, 1969). Other researchers believe that the relationship between style and effectiveness is more complex.

Fiedler's contingency model of leadership

Fiedler, (1964, 1967) like other researchers concerned with leadership, believed that leaders adopt either a person-oriented or a task-oriented style. He identified these types of leaders by giving them the *Least Preferred Co-Worker* (LPC) scale. A person who fills out this scale is asked to think of all the people he has ever worked with and to recall his least preferred co-worker. Then the respondent rates the co-worker. Someone who rates his least preferred co-worker relatively favorably is called a high LPC leader. This leader tends to adopt a person-oriented, democratic style. A person who rates his least preferred co-worker very unfavorably is called a low LPC leader and tends to adopt a task-oriented, autocratic style. Having identified these two types of leaders, Fiedler compared the performance of groups they led.

Fiedler expected that groups led by a high LPC leader would perform better than those led by a low LPC leader; he did not find this. Rather, he found that leader effectiveness (i.e., good group performance) depended, or was

contingent, on the interaction between the leader's style and three situational factors; task structure, the leader-member relationship, and the leader's power. When these three aspects were either very positive or very negative, a low LPC (autocratic, task-oriented) leader was most effective. When the situation was intermediate, a high LPC (democratic, person-oriented) leader was best. In other words, there was a curvilinear relationship between leadership style, situation, and leader effectiveness.

If you think about it, these findings are logical. For example, if the members know what they are supposed to do (good task structure), like their leader (good leader-member relationship), and the leader is in a strong position (good leader power), there is no need to be person-oriented. A leader who attends to the members would actually be wasting his time. On the other hand, on an unstructured task, where the members detest the leader, and the leader is not given clear-cut power, the best strategy is to be task-oriented. Attending to group members would be a waste of time here, too. The most effective leader would be one who takes charge, moves the group toward its goal, and does not worry about the members' feelings. This leader may not be well liked but he will be effective. A high LPC leader will be effective only when there is a chance to form good member-leader relations, to structure the task, and to establish power. In other words, when the situation is moderately favorable, a person with a democratic leadership style (high LPC leader) will be effective.

While there have been some recent criticisms of Fiedler's model (e.g., Ashour, 1973a, 1973b; Graen, Alvares, Orris, & Martello, 1970), it is widely accepted. Just as there are "different strokes for different folks," different situations seem to demand different styles if a leader is to be effective.

More recently, Victor Vroom (Vroom,

1974; Vroom & Yetton, 1973) has proposed a *normative model of leadership style.* Vroom believed that as a group proceeds on a task, the leader must decide at various points how much he should involve the members in decision making. His decision, Vroom argued, should be based not on an overall style but on the nature of the group's problem at each point. Effectiveness may depend on the leader's ability to choose the right style at those choice points. The important thing about Vroom's model is its proposal that a leader may have to change styles as a group continues. Sometimes the leader should involve the members in the decision making, other times not. This judgement should be based on the most effective way to get the group moving, rather than on a preference for a particular style. Vroom's model is quite new. But it appears to be a valid approach to understanding leadership effectiveness.

Conclusion

This section was concerned with group processes, or the interactions among group members. We discussed three variables that affect group interactions. The first was cohesiveness, the attraction of group members to each other and to the group as a whole. Cohesiveness results from a number of factors outside the group (e.g., similarity) and, it must be added, the nature of the group interaction itself. Thus, cohesiveness is both a cause and an effect of how a group interacts. Cohesiveness influences both the quantity and quality of group interactions. For example, members of a highly cohesive group will talk more and will say more positive things than members of a noncohesive group.

The second variable considered was the pattern of communication within a group. Research indicates that this pattern affects both how well a group performs and how satisfied its members are. While the review of communication patterns used examples in which patterns were imposed on the group, in practice most small groups freely choose their own pattern. What factors influence them? Generally, their choice will reflect the reasons the group was formed, the characteristics of its members, and the group's structure. The interdependence of these factors must be stressed.

Finally, we examined leadership, beginning with the question, who becomes a leader? The review showed that situational factors determine leadership. A leader is someone who effectively engages in three behaviors: leadership attempting, leadership success, and leadership effectiveness. Leadership attempting involves contributing to the group. It is influenced by a person's skills and abilities and, perhaps more importantly, by how the group reacts to him. Leadership success involves getting group members to follow one's leadership attempts. It depends mainly on the leader's social power. Note, by the way, that the leader's social power is often derived from what occurs during group interactions. Finally, the relationship between a leader's style and his effectiveness in getting the group to achieve some goal was discussed. The major conclusion is that there is no one "best" leadership style. Leadership effectiveness depends on group structure, group processes, and the task at hand. Further, effectiveness may even require a leader to change styles as a group proceeds on a task. Thus, while many people may see leadership and leadership effectiveness as independent of group processes, they, in fact, are highly interdependent.

REVIEW QUESTIONS

(Twelve out of fifteen is passing)

1. The study of group processes is the study of how members of a group _____ . (p. 282)
2. The cohesiveness of a group refers to how _____ group members are to one another and the group. (p. 282)
3. In highly cohesive groups, group members have _____ influence over each other than in less cohesive groups. (p. 283)
4. A late night "bull session" among a group of friends would probably have a communication pattern best described by a _____ network. (p. 284)
5. A wheel communication network tends to be inefficient on complex tasks because the person at the center of the wheel becomes _____ with information. (p. 285)
6. A group member who talks a great deal and makes a lot of suggestions is engaging in _____ _____ . (p. 286)
7. Leadership success depends on whether or not a person has _____ _____ . (p. 287)
8. A group democratically elects a leader. Even though one member did not vote for this leader, he follows the leader's orders. He does so because he believes that the election gave the leader the right to give orders. This right is called _____ _____ . (p. 287)
9. The almost magical or mystical ability to control other people is called _____ . (p. 287)
10. The ability to get a group moving toward and achieving a goal is called _____ _____ . (p. 288)
11. A leader who assumes a _____ _____ style will be most concerned with the needs of the group members. A leader who assumes a _____ style will be concerned with defining roles and other aspects of group structure. (p. 289)
12. According to Blake and Mouton, the best leader is both _____ and _____ oriented. (p. 289)
13. A person who has a low opinion of his least preferred co-worker will tend to adopt a(n) _____ style of leadership. (p. 289)
14. The idea that there is one best way to lead people would ignore the position that leadership effectiveness is _____ on the situation a leader is in. (p. 289)
15. Vroom's theory of leadership effectiveness proposes that an effective leader should _____ his style as the group works toward its goal. (p. 290)

ANSWERS

1. interacts   2. attracted   3. more   4. comncon   5. saturated   6. leadership attempting
7. social power   8. legitimate social power   9. charisma   10. leadership effectiveness
11. person-oriented, task-oriented   12. person, task (or product)   13. autocratic or task-oriented
14. contingent   15. change

GROUP PERFORMANCE

Groups form for a variety of reasons and interact in many different ways. But all groups have one thing in common: they produce some product. A *group product* is the result of a group's work on some goal or task (Davis, 1969). This product can range from something as intangible as how people "feel" after a group therapy session to the ability of a bomb squad to disarm a time bomb. This section will examine how groups work toward their goals, how they influence the performance of individual members, and whether groups perform better than individuals.

How groups work toward goals

Group tasks usually involve either decision making or problem solving. The basic distinction between the two activities is this. In *decision making,* the group's job is to choose between several alternatives. In *problem solving,* the job is to overcome some obstacle to the effective achievement of a goal. Of course, in many instances a group may do both. For example, when the Israeli cabinet had to decide what to do about the one-hundred and three people being held at Entebbe Airport in Uganda, they engaged in both decision making and problem solving. With regard to the former, the cabinet members had to decide whether to negotiate with the terrorists or attempt to free the passengers. Their decision to attempt a rescue was determined, in turn, by their ability to overcome the obstacle (or at least believe they could overcome it) of reaching heavily guarded civilians at an airport 2,000 miles away.

Stages in decision making and problem solving

Bales and Strodtbeck (1951) have identified three stages, or steps, in problem solving. The

Barry Kaufman

first is *orientation*. In this stage, the group receives the initial information about the problem. The members attempt to understand the problem and consider ways to organize themselves to solve it. The next stage is *evaluation,* in which the group judges which information is relevant to the problem and its solution. Finally, there is the *control* stage. Here, the group regulates its activities and environment in order to solve the problem.

The process in decision making is almost exactly the same, but the group's goal is different. Since decision making involves choosing among alternatives, the decision is based on the probability and utility of the various alternatives (Edwards, 1962).

The *probability* of an alternative refers to the likelihood that it will lead to a certain outcome. Estimates of an alternative's prob-

"The jury is instructed to disregard the statement that the defendant is a homosexual communist who pulls the wings off of small birds"

One type of small group that concerns social psychologists is the jury. Our legal system tries to guarantee a person a fair trial by selecting a jury of his peers to judge him. Ideally, personal attitudes, pre-trial publicity, and inadmissable evidence should not influence a jury's decision about the defendant's guilt or innocence. Does this actually happen?

In one study, two groups of people were given the same factual information about an alleged offense. One group was led to believe that the defendant's attitudes were similar to their's, while the other believed that his attitudes were different. Similar jurors were more lenient than dissimilar jurors. This was especially true when a juror had strong authoritarian tendencies (Mitchell & Byrne, 1973).

Stanley Sue and Ronald Smith (1974) conducted a series of studies on the effects of pre-trial publicity and inadmissable evidence. They found that people who had read a damaging newspaper article before the trial were almost twice as likely to convict the defendant as were people who had read a favorable article. This was true even though these people were told to ignore any information not presented during the trial.

Sue and Smith also conducted a study in which jurors received either inadmissable information about the defendant or no such information. If the prosecutor had a strong case, the inadmissable evidence had little effect on the jurors' decisions. If he had a weak case, over twenty-five percent of the jurors who received the inadmissable evidence found the defendant guilty. Among the jurors who did not receive this inadmissable information, no one found him guilty.

---

ability can be subjective or objective. The difference between these types of estimates can be illustrated in the following example.

In poker, a straight is five cards with consecutive numbers—for example, 3,4,5,6,7. A poker player who has the 3,4,5, and 7 cards, and who is to be dealt one more card, has a very small objective probability of "filling the straight" (i.e., being dealt a 6). Only four cards will fill the straight, and probably some of the other players already hold one or more of them. Therefore, the reasonable strategy in this situation is to drop out of the game. However, the confirmed gambler who has a hunch that "tonight's my lucky night" may stay in the game. This is because he has a high subjective estimate of the probability of getting a 6. A lot of people are washing dishes in Las Vegas because of subjective probability estimates.

The *utility* of an alternative is the value placed on the outcomes it would produce. An outcome's utility can be objective or subjective. For example, if we were watching the gambler, we might see his potential winnings (e.g., $10) as small. But to him, it may be a lot of money. The gambler places a much higher utility on the outcome than we do.

If we return to the Israeli cabinet's decision, we can see the interrelationship between probabilities and utilities. One of the first things the Israelis did was to have army officers estimate the probability of a successful rescue. Initially this estimate was quite low. However, as time passed and more and more information was gained about the situation at the airport, the estimate rose. Practice runs by Israeli commandoes convinced the cabinet that a rescue attempt was feasible.

At the same time, the Israelis considered the utility of this outcome. The successful rescue of the passengers would produce at least three valuable outcomes: (1) it would save 103 lives, (2) it would preserve the Israeli policy of refusing to negotiate with terrorists, and (3) it would increase morale among the citizens of Israel. This last outcome was considered especially important because prior to the raid on Entebbe there was a serious problem of national morale. After deciding that the probability of a successful rescue was high and the utility of a rescue was even higher, the Israeli cabinet opted to try to rescue the people at Entebbe.

Group influences on the individual

We spend much of our time in groups. For this reason, social psychologists are interested in how the experience of being in a group affects both the quantity and quality of an individual member's performance.

Social facilitation

One approach is to look at the effect of other people on an individual's performance. This grew out of some research done on bicycle racers eighty years ago (Triplett, 1897). Triplett timed bicycle riders who were either trying to break a record, following a faster rider, or competing with another rider in a race. He found that the fastest times occurred in the competitive situation and the slowest when the riders were trying to break a record. Later research has shown that the mere presence of other people will improve a person's performance on a wide variety of simple tasks.

This improvement as the result of the presence of others is called *social facilitation* (Allport, 1920). Allport believed that an audience will invariably improve a person's performance. However, subsequent work (e.g., Pessin, 1933; Wapner & Alper, 1952) has shown the opposite result.

Zajonc (1965) has attempted to reconcile this conflict. He believed that the main effect of onlookers is to increase a person's arousal level. One effect of being aroused is to increase the probability that a person will use a well-established or overlearned behavior. If a task is simple or a person has had a number of previous experiences with it, a well-learned or predominant response is likely to improve his performance. For example, consider a runner who has trained for three years for the Olympics. He might react to the cheers of 70,000 people as he makes the last turn in the 800-meter finals by running even faster and winning.

But what would happen if the task was novel or extremely complex? In this situation, a person's tendency to use an overlearned response might hurt his performance (Cottrell, Rittle, & Wack, 1967). For example, a chess master, playing for the world championship, might react to an audience's presence by making an overlearned, simple move which results in a checkmate. Thus, Zajonc proposed, the positive or negative effects of the presence of others will depend on both the person's level of arousal and the complexity of the task.

Risky shift

Another approach has been to study the *risky shift effect*—a person's willingness to take much greater risks if he has discussed a problem with a group than if he has to make a decision alone. Initially, this finding generated considerable excitement among social psychologists, because it ran contrary to their beliefs about group influence on members. It was assumed that being in a group made people more conservative in their decisions, but the early research on risky shift contradicted this belief (e.g., Bem, Wallach, & Kogan, 1965; Stoner, 1961; Wallach, Kogan, & Ben, 1962). This suggested that groups exert a powerful influence on their members.

Subsequent research, however, has caused social psychologists to "cool" on the risky shift effect. The primary reason is that it doesn't always occur. In general, people become more risk-prone only when hypothetical rather than real risk is involved (Cartwright, 1971; Goodman, 1972; McCauley, Stitt, Woods, &

Lipton, 1973). For example, group discussion produces a risky shift when subjects are asked to give a hypothetical person advice on whether to have heart surgery. But in a study where subjects were given money to bet at a race track, group discussion produced no risky shift.

Even in laboratory settings, where the subjects aren't really risking anything, the risky shift is not always obtained. Sometimes a conservative shift occurs. There seem to be two reasons for this. The first is contained in Roger Brown's (1965) *risk as a value* hypothesis. Brown proposed that the risky shift will occur only when risk is valued and people

---

"You bet your life"

The original experiment on risk taking asked subjects to make judgments about hypothetical situations. An item from the original risk taking questionnaire is given below (Stoner, 1961). A subject acting alone, chooses the lowest odds he would accept before he would advise the man to have the operation. Then he discusses the situation with three or four other people. They make a group decision, and then the subject makes a second choice by himself. A risky shift is defined as the selection of longer odds on the second choice (Wallach, Kogan, & Bem, 1962).

Mr. B, a forty-five-year-old accountant, has recently been informed by his physician that he has developed a severe heart ailment. The disease would be sufficiently serious to force Mr. B to change many of his strongest life habits—reducing his work load, drastically changing his diet, giving up favorite leisure-time pursuits. The physician suggests that a delicate medical operation could be attempted which, if successful, would completely cure the

heart condition. But its success could not be assured and might even prove fatal.

Imagine that you are advising Mr. B. Listed below are several probabilities or odds that the operation will prove successful.

Please check the lowest probability that you would consider acceptable for the operation to be performed.

____Place a check here if you think Mr. B should not have the operation regardless of the probabilities.

____The chances are 9 in 10 that the operation will be a success.

____The chances are 7 in 10 that the operation will be a success.

____The chances are 5 in 10 that the operation will be a success.

____The chances are 3 in 10 that the operation will be a success.

____The chances are 1 in 10 that the operation will be a success.

believe that they are riskier than their peers. In these situations, the discussion will show that the person is no riskier than the group. And because he values risk, he will move even further in this direction. But when the situation calls for caution, group discussion will produce a cautious shift. Studies on Brown's hypothesis have found it to be correct. People become more risky only when they believe, prior to group discussion, that they are riskier (Clark, Crockett, & Archer, 1971). And when caution is valued, group discussion produces a cautious shift (Fraser, Gouge, & Billig, 1971).

The second explanation is that risky shift is just a special case of the general *group polarization* phenomenon. That is, after group discussion, members' attitudes often become more extreme but are in the same direction as they were before (Fraser, 1971). For example, a group discussion among racists results in their expressing even more prejudicial attitudes in a group discussion with nonracists (Myers & Bishop, 1970).

Individual versus group performance

When a human being has a problem to solve or a goal to accomplish, he will usually puzzle over it for thirty seconds and then form a group to help him. Jesus had a *group* of disciples to help him spread his message. The founding fathers of the United States established a *group* to write the Declaration of Independence. Every President since George Washington has had a *group* of advisors to help him run the country. You will probably get a group of people together to study for the final examination in this course. Your instructor is probably not evaluated by one person, but by a *group* of other professors. And so on. Is this faith in the superiority of groups over individuals justified?

Situations which favor groups

On certain tasks, groups are superior to individuals. One of these tasks is where success requires abilities to be grouped together (Steiner, 1966). For example, a fifteen-person team in a tug of war will always beat an individual.

Further, on tasks which require a division of labor to attain a goal, groups will outperform individuals. This was the logic that led Henry Ford to establish an assembly line for the construction of his Model T. Ford correctly reasoned that if he broke the construction of a car into, say, fifteen steps and assigned one or two people to each step, he could produce cars faster than if each of the fifteen was responsible for building an entire car. This division of labor would enable each worker to concentrate on his specialty and would allow one worker to check on the quality of another's work. One person working on an entire car might be blind to his own errors.

Situations which favor individuals

On tasks which do not require the addition of abilities and/or the division of labor, evidence that groups are superior to individuals is harder to find. For example, consider the research on brainstorming. The goal of *brainstorming* is for a group to come up with as many new and creative ideas as possible. It was originally believed that a group whose members were encouraged to present their ideas without fear of criticism would produce better ideas than people working alone (Osborne, 1957). Contrary to this prediction, no evidence was found for the superiority of a brainstorming group (Lamm & Tromsdosff, 1973). Individuals performed better than the group in nine out of the twelve experiments on brainstorming which Lamm and Tromsdorff reviewed. On the other three studies, there were no differences. Although no one is

An exercise in group problem solving

The studies we've presented suggest that the advantages of a group approach to some problem depend largely on the problem itself. Here is a task on which groups usually do better than individuals.

In order to demonstrate this, you'll need to get two or three friends to help you.

Imagine that you, a space explorer, together with some friends, have escaped a dangerous enemy. You were supposed to meet some allies on the lighted side of Earth's moon. Unfortunately, your spaceship crash-lands, and you are 200 miles from their ship. You find an abandoned capsule and four spacesuits from the United States moon exploration program. Only the following items in the capsule are in usable condition.

A box of matches
Fifty feet of nylon rope
Five gallons of water
A first-aid kit with medicine and needles for injections
Food concentrate
A magnetic compass
One case of dehydrated milk
Parachute silk
Signal flares
A stellar map of the moon's constellation
A solar-powered FM receiver-transmitter
A solar-powered heater (portable)
Two .45-caliber pistols
Two 100-pound cannisters of oxygen
A self-inflating life raft

Your survival depends on reaching the other ship, so you must choose the items that will be most valuable on the 200-mile trip.

Now each of you rank these fifteen items in order of their importance. Do this individually; avoid any group discussion. Then get together and come up with a group decision. In reaching this decision, avoid simply arguing for your own individual rankings. Avoid getting stalemated on any one item, but at the same time, don't give in just to avoid conflict. Most impor-

tant, seek out differences of opinion; solicit information from all the group members.

We've presented the ranking of a group of scientists who worked on the Apollo program below. Add in the absolute differences between each of your individual rankings and those of the NASA scientists. Then do the same thing for the rankings arrived at by the group. The difference between the group decision and the scientists' rankings should be much smaller. That is, you should find that the group has done better than any individual member.

Why? Basically because the group discussion enabled people with different viewpoints and types of information to interact (Hall, 1971).

NASA Scientists' Rankings

1. Oxygen (without it, you'll never reach the ship)
2. Water (needed to replace the loss of body liquids on the lighted side of the moon)
3. Map (needed to navigate)
4. Food (to supply energy for you and others)
5. Receiver-transmitter (to communicate with the other ship; but works only within short ranges)
6. Nylon rope (can be used to scale cliffs)
7. First-aid kit (contains vitamins, medicines; NASA space suits have special opening for injections)
8. Parachute silk (protection from sun's rays)
9. Self-inflating life raft (the carbon monoxide bottle used to inflate the raft could be used for propulsion)
10. Signal flares (to send up a distress signal when you see the ship)
11. Pistols (possible means of propulsion)
12. Dehydrated milk (too bulky a form of food)
13. Heating unit (not needed unless you are on the moon's dark side)
14. Magnetic compass (totally worthless; the magnetic field on the moon isn't polarized)
15. Matches (there's no oxygen on the moon to sustain a flame)

sure why brainstorming does not work, the following explanations seem to be most plausible.

First, the presence of the group may produce one-track thinking as the result of pressures toward uniformity (Taylor, Berry & Block, 1958). Second, in brainstorming, the things which make a group effective—the summing of abilities and the division of labor—are not possible (Kleinhans & Taylor, 1976). That is, brainstorming calls for each member to generate his own ideas, not for the members to work together on the task.

Other studies of groups versus individuals have compared the two on so-called *Eureka* problems—that is, problems that have unique, nonobvious solutions (thus causing a solver to yell, "Eureka"). In early studies, it was found that groups of people reached a correct solution faster and more often than a single person working on the same problem (Shaw, 1932).

However, subsequent research has strongly suggested that the group's superiority may not be due to interaction among group members. Rather, it may be due to a "best-member effect" (Klienhans & Taylor, 1976). Remember, only one member of the group has to have the answer to a Eureka problem for the entire group to "solve" it. In these subsequent studies (e.g., Hoppe, 1962; Lorge & Solomon, 1955), it was found that five-person groups working on a Eureka problem performed no better than the best of the five people working alone. This has led researchers to conclude that the apparent superiority of groups on a Eureka problem is a *pseudogroup effect*. The superiority of the group is not due to group interactions.

Groupthink

One of the more interesting ideas on the topic of group performance to emerge in recent years is Irving Janis's concept of groupthink. Groupthink is a process which Janis believes can explain why a group which should be extremely effective actually performs very poorly.

Janis (1972) defined groupthink as follows: "I used the term '*groupthink*' as a quick and easy way to refer to a mode of thinking that people engage in when they are deeply involved in a cohesive in-group, when the members' strivings for unanimity override their motivation to realistically appraise alternative courses of action . . . groupthink refers to the deterioration of mental efficiency, reality testing, and moral judgment that results from in-group pressures" (p. 9, italics added).

Janis saw a feeling of extreme cohesiveness among a group's members as a primary cause of groupthink. But cohesiveness alone was not enough. Two other things were needed: (1) an insulation of the decision-making group from other, more unbiased information and (2) a strong endorsement of the group's decision by its leader.

Janis's initial interest in groupthink was apparently triggered by the Bay of Pigs disaster. In 1961, President Kennedy and his advisors had agreed to support an invasion of Cuba at the Bay of Pigs by a group of Cuban exiles. The invasion was a textbook case of terrible military and political planning. Most of the invaders were either killed or captured before they got off the beach.[3] The U.S. involvement immediately became known to the world. The fact that a country the size of the United States attempted to invade Cuba made it a laughingstock everywhere. What interested Janis was, how could Kennedy and his advisors have embarked on this fiasco? It certainly was not due to their lack of intellect or ability. These men were, in the words of

---

[3]Had the invaders gotten off the beach, they would have had to cross miles of snake-infested swamp.

David Halberstam (1972), the "best and the brightest" ever to be involved in American foreign policy decisions.

In looking at other similar decisions (e.g., American negligence at Pearl Harbor and the escalation of the war in Vietnam), Janis found that the people who made these decisions also had exceptional ability. But they were members of highly cohesive groups, insulated from unbiased sources of information, and with leaders who strongly endorsed their decisions. This factor, in Janis's view, produced groupthink. Groupthink was largely responsible for the incredibly poor decisions of these groups.

If Janis had published his work a few years later, we feel sure his examples of groupthink would have included the decisions made by President Nixon and his advisors on Watergate. People may argue about the seriousness of Nixon's crimes, whether he should have resigned, and a host of other matters, but one point seems clear. From the decision to break in to the days shortly before Nixon's resignation, the decisions made by him and his advisors consisted of one blunder after another. Further, even Nixon's most severe critics would not attribute the stupidity of these decisions to a lack of intelligence on the part of Nixon and his aides. The following material attempts to show how groupthink may explain the quality of the decisions made.

First, a brief background. On the night of June 17, 1972, James McCord, the director of security for President Nixon's re-election committee, and four other men were caught in the offices of the Democratic National Committee at the Watergate Hotel in Washington, D.C. This was the second time they had broken in and their third such attempt.

These men were not acting on their own; they were carrying out a plan. It is hard to identify the actual mastermind behind the decision to break in, since the responsibility for such actions was purposely diffused. The authorization came at a meeting attended by Attorney General John Mitchell, Gordon Liddy, and Jeb Stuart Magruder, among others. According to Magruder, it was Mitchell who was ultimately responsible. He describes what happened.

> We discussed the proposal for ten minutes or so, and all of us expressed doubts about it. We feared that it might be a waste of money, and also that it might be dangerous. "How do we know that these guys know what they're doing?" Mitchell asked once ... Mitchell, as we talked, scribbled on the paper Liddy had prepared, which listed the amount of money he wanted, and the number of men and types of equipment he'd need. Finally, Mitchell told me that he approved the plan, but that Liddy should receive only $250,000. We discussed the targets of the wiretapping program, and it was agreed that Liddy should go ahead with the wiretapping of the Demoratic National Chairman's office at the Watergate, then we'd see about other possible targets. (White, 1975, p. 158)

This decision-making group was, in turn, responsible to another group comprised of Mitchell, H.R. "Bob" Haldeman, John Ehrlichman, and President Nixon.[4] When Haldeman, Ehrlichman, and Mitchell resigned, their places were taken by people such as General Alexander Haig, Press Secretary Ron Ziegler, and James St. Clair. This latter group were Nixon's advisors in the final days of his Presidency.

Janis identified eight symptoms of groupthink. Let's see how each applies to Watergate. In groupthink group members share the illusion of *invulnerability*. They can succeed at anything. This feeling of immunity to failure, coupled with extraordinary optimism, is likely to encourage extreme risk taking, however illogical.

---

[4]We do not know if Nixon knew of the break-in plan, but it was certainly at least the indirect result of orders he gave and decisions he made. Further, there is no question that he was heavily involved in the decisions made after the break-in occurred (White, 1975).

There is little question that an illusion of invulnerability existed among the planners and actual participants in the break-in. After all, the President had at least indirectly authorized it, and $250,000 had been set aside for operations. The burglars, while aware of the risks involved, felt assured that they would receive legal aide (and they did). Evidence is found in the fact that one of the burglars, James McCord, had worked for President Nixon's re-election committee and the White House. In his book *Breach of Faith,* Theodore White offers this evaluation of the thoughts of those involved in Watergate.

There was probably little doubt in the minds of any of the culprits that their superiors, stretching up through the Committee to Re-Elect to the former Attorney General, who was now about to become executive director of the sprawling underground, could surely arrange for their release and, after appropriate explanation, cover up the episode. (1975, p. 160)

A second characteristic of groupthink is that group members will ignore or *rationalize* away clear signals about the dangers inherent in their actions.

Consider the break-in itself. It was a very poor job. The equipment used was cheap and unreliable. The techniques used would have been laughed at by any knowledgeable burglar. For example, it was necessary to tape door locks open so that the burglars could get out after they were done. Rather than taping these locks vertically so that the tape could not be seen, the burglars taped them horizontally. When a security guard spotted the locks and removed the tape, the burglars retaped them in the same conspicuous fashion. This led the guard to call the police. The break-in was so inept that some people initially thought it was an attempt by the Democrats to frame the Republicans.

The ability to rationalize away obvious dangers continued for two years. Consider, for

example, this description of a meeting which took place less than a month before President Nixon's resignation. One of his attorneys (Fred Buzhardt) had just heard the tape recording of June 23, 1972, in which Nixon told Haldeman to cover up the Watergate scandal.

Buzhardt was convinced that the June 23 tape completely undermined the President's position, but he couldn't get any support. Haig wasn't sure. The President disagreed categorically. And St. Clair had not only refused to listen but had remarked blandly that he was confident he had sufficient evidence to refute any allegation that the President had obstructed justice or abused his authority in the single act of sending Haldeman to talk to the CIA. (Woodward & Bernstein, 1976, p. 290)

In groupthink, group members are also likely to devise their own *morality* for the moral and ethical consequences of their actions. For example, two years before the break-in, Nixon approved the so-called Huston plan. This plan authorized wiretaps without court order, the opening of people's mail, and the power "to burglarize and enter private homes" (White, 1975, p. 135). Tom Huston, the author of this plan, had justified these flagrant violations of the Constitution on the basis of national security. White stated: "Of Tom Huston it can be said that he was true and loyal to what he felt was right, and a menace to the Republic" (1975, p. 136). Although this plan was later abandoned, it set the tone for the break-in and other actions: national security justified anything.

The group members also frequently *stereotyped* their opposition as evil, immoral, weak, and stupid. These misperceptions resulted in little attempt to reconcile differences with the "enemy."

Nixon and his aides seemed to classify people into two groups: those for and those against them. Those who were against Nixon were not seen as people who had a honest disagreement with the White House but as the enemy. Indeed, John Dean drew up an "enemies list" consisting of people whom the White House judged to be dangerous adversaries. It included such threatening individuals as actress Carol Channing and football player Joe Namath. The primary enemy, however, was the Eastern newspapers (e.g., the *New York Times,*, the *Washington Post*). It was Nixon's firm belief, and that of his aides, that the *Times* and the *Post* were out to get him. This was expressed in the White House's characterization of the articles about Watergate which appeared in these newspapers. They were part of a "careful coordinated strategy . . . to prosecute a case against the President in the press, using innuendo, distortion of fact, and outright falsehood" (*The White House Transcripts.* 1974, p. 854).

In groupthink, *pressures for conformity* are placed on any group member who doesn't express total agreement with the group's ideology, values, or decisions. Loyalty to the group is emphasized regardless of individual belief. For example, James McCord testified that he broke into Watergate to protect the President. Other people were asked to perjure themselves to protect the "team" (i.e., the White House). These pressures toward conformity are illustrated in the words of Nixon at a meeting in his office on March 22, 1973: "I want you all to stonewall it. Let them plead the Fifth Amendment, cover up or anything else which will save the plan. That's the whole point" (quoted in Woodward & Bernstein, 1976, p. 261).

Since pressures for conformity are so strong, individual members engage in *self-censorship,* which automatically minimizes any doubts or deviant thoughts. No one involved in the break-in openly expressed doubts about it at the time, and for the next two years a similar pattern of self-censorship existed. A reading of the *White House Transcripts, Breach of Faith,* and *The Final Days* discloses that until a few weeks before his

resignation no member of President Nixon's staff challenged any of his decisions regarding Watergate or even suggested to him that he resign. This was due not so much to fear of Nixon as to loyalty to him.

The fact that no one disagrees produces the *illusion of unanimity* among the group's members. That is, because no one protests the group's decision, each member assumes that all the others totally support it. Thus, in the case of Watergate, bright, sophisticated, and basically moral people engaged in illegal and stupid acts. Their belief in the rightness of what they did was, at least in part, based on their belief that other bright, sophisticated, basically moral men apparently saw nothing wrong.

Finally, in groupthink there are *self-appointed mind guards.* Their role is to head off any deviant information or information that may raise doubts about the effectiveness and morality of these decisions. This role fell mainly to Haldeman and Ehrlichman. Anyone who wanted to speak to Nixon had to tell one of these two men what they wanted to say. If Haldeman and/or Ehrlichman disliked what they heard, the person got no further (Rather & Gates, 1975).

When Haldeman and Ehrlichman resigned, Ronald Ziegler and Alexander Haig assumed the role of mind guards. When two of Nixon's lawyers suggested to other staff members that Nixon resign,

Ziegler became combative. The President was ill served by such comments and conclusions, he said. The lawyers were turning against the President. It wasn't their job to judge these matters. (Woodward & Bernstein, 1976, p. 30)

Woodward and Bernstein also describe how Haig put this suggestion to Nixon.

It was an awkward moment for Haig. He did not wish his own position to be misunderstood. He was merely conveying *their* judgment. He reassured the President that the lawyers were not doubting his innocence—only his chances to survive. (1976, p. 30)

Groupthink is important in two respects. First, it describes the process whereby intelligent people can make unintelligent decisions. Second, it illustrates the interdependence of the factors discussed in this chapter. For in groupthink, we see how the variables related to group formation, structure, and processes all play an important part in determining group performance.

Conclusion

The final segment of this chapter was concerned with group performance, the final product of a group. It began by considering the two types of group tasks—decision making and problem solving—how groups approach these tasks, and the factors related to group performance.

Group performance was discussed next. Two closely related questions were addressed. First, how can a group affect the performance of one of its members? Second, do groups outperform individuals who are working on the same task? The latter question is extremely important because it relates to why people form groups. Groups form primarily because people see them as more efficient than individuals. Is this a valid assumption? The review suggested that while belonging to a group will invariably affect a person's performance, the effect itself is not always positive. For example, on complex tasks, a group's presence can weaken one's performance. The question of whether groups outperform individuals working on the same task does not have a simple yes or no answer. Several factors must be considered.

First, while the group may be more accurate and faster than an individual, it consumes considerably more total person-hours. Thus, in terms of overall efficiency, a group of ten people that solves a problem in thirty minutes may be less efficient than one person who solves the same problem in sixty minutes.

Second, one must consider the nature of the task. On tasks which involve the summing of members' abilities (e.g., a tug of war) or division of labor, groups will be superior to individuals. But on tasks which involve creativity (e.g., brainstorming) or arriving at unique solutions to problems (e.g., Eureka problems), groups do no better than individuals and may actually do worse.

Finally, one must be aware that groupthink may occur. In groupthink, a group arrives at a decision which is much worse than the average abilities of its members would lead us to predict. It must be re-emphasized that no group is immune to groupthink.

Groupthink also demonstrates another extremely important point—the interdependence of group formation, structure, processes, and performance. That is, the reasons why a group forms, the nature of the people who join it, the positions assigned within the group, and group cohesiveness are all causal factors in groupthink. More generally, we cannot fully understand a group's performance without some knowledge of the group's formation, structure, and processes.

REVIEW QUESTIONS

(Eight out of ten is passing)

1. In _____ _____ the group's objective is to overcome the obstacles in the way of achieving its goal. In _____ _____ the group's objective is to choose from among several alternatives. (p. 292)
2. A group's choice of an alternative will depend on the likelihood that this alternative will lead to a certain outcome. This is called the outcome's _____ . The value the group places on that outcome is called its _____ . (p. 293)
3. Changes in a person's performance as a result of the presence of others is called _____ _____ . (p. 294)
4. On tasks which require the _____ _____ _____ groups will do better than individuals. (p. 296)
5. Laboratory studies have found that group discussions often produce decisions which are _____ risky than decisions people make on their own. One widely accepted explanation of this effect is that people _____ being risky. (p. 295)
6. The goal of _____ sessions is for group members to come up with new and creative ideas. On such tasks, groups tend to perform _____ than individuals. (p. 296)
7. The pseudo-group effect refers to those instances where the superiority of a group's performance over an individual's is not due to _____ . (p. 298)
8. Poor group performance as a result of a concern for unanimity rather than a realistic appraisal of alternatives is called _____ . (p. 298)
9. Self-censorship and self-appointed mind guards serve to foster the _____ _____ _____ in a group. (p. 301)
10. In groupthink, group members will tend to _____ estimate the dangers in the choices they make. (p. 300)

ANSWERS

1. problem solving, decision making   2. probability, utility   3. social facilitation
4. division of labor (or summing of abilities)   5. more, value   6. brainstorming, poorer
7. interaction   8. groupthink   9. illusion of unanimity   10. under.

SUGGESTED READINGS

These four textbooks should give you a good understanding of the processes involved in small group behavior.

Textbooks

Group Dynamics, edited by Dorwin Cartwright and Alvin Zander. This is a collection of the major research articles on small group processes. You may want to read selected articles after you have read the next book.

Group Performance, by James Davis. This is a short, well-written book about small groups by someone who has conducted extensive research in the area.

Victims of Groupthink, by Irving Janis. We have only skimmed the surface of Janis's concept of groupthink in this chapter. This readable, lively book provides a much more comprehensive examination.

Group Dynamics: The Psychology of Small Group Behavior, by Marvin Shaw. This is a fairly high-level book, but if you want to pursue small groups further, we highly recommend it.

Popular literature

There are many excellent books which describe small group processes in the real world. Here are some that we found to be especially good.

The Missile Crisis, by Elie Abel. In 1963, the United States almost became involved in a nuclear war with Russia. Abel's well-written account of how President Kennedy and his advisors avoided this describes the processes involved in group problem solving.

Helter Skelter, by Vincent Bugliosi and Curt Gentry. In 1969, followers of an ex-convict named Charles Manson brutally murdered seven people. Manson's ability to control these people illustrates the principles of leadership quite well.

Alive, by Piers Paul Read. This is a thrilling factual description of group processes. The behavior of the people who lived through ten weeks on a snow-covered Andes mountainside illustrates most of the concepts covered in this chapter.

Either *The Final Days,* by Bob Woodward and Carl Bernstein, or *Breach of Faith,* by Theodore H. White. We suggested in the chapter that groupthink may have been responsible for some of the blunders President Nixon and his advisors made before and after the Watergate break-in. These two books provide well-written descriptions of what went on in the White House during this period.

10 LARGE GROUPS

In collaboration with Stephen L. Cohen.

The topic of interest in this chapter is human behavior in large groups. We will be concerned, first, with organizational behavior, beginning with the different theories of what makes an effective organization. Then the effects of organizational characteristics on behavior will be examined. The second half of the chapter will look at collective behavior. Collective behavior differs from organizational behavior in that it is usually unplanned and spontaneous. Three aspects of collective behavior will be presented: crowding, crowd behavior, and social movements.

ORGANIZATIONAL AND COLLECTIVE BEHAVIOR

In May, 1972, a large group of anti-war protestors conducted the "Mayday Assault" on Washington, D.C. Their goal was to stop the U.S. government from functioning for at least one day. Standing in the way of the Mayday Coalition was another large group of people— the U.S. Department of Justice. A comparison of how these two groups behaved illustrates the two types of large-group behavior discussed in this chapter.

First, consider the protestors. They were supposed to "seize the government" but really had no plan for doing so. There was little, if any, coordination of the activities of the thousands who descended on Washington. It was hard to identify any person or group of people as the leaders. The typical protestor's behavior was unplanned, spontaneous, and with no real direction. These types of actions are usually called collective behavior.

The Justice Department, on the other hand, had a carefully worked out plan to stop the protestors. It had clearly identifiable leaders (e.g., the Attorney General) who coordinated the activities of its members. The Justice Department had a well established chain of command, and a member of this group acted only on the orders of her superiors. This pattern of group activities is usually called organizational behavior.

ORGANIZATIONAL BEHAVIOR

If this textbook had been written 200 or 300 years ago, there would have been little reason to include a section on organizations. Most people lived in rural areas and provided most of their own day-to-day necessities. The typical American family might go for weeks, months, or even years without ever coming into contact with a large organization. But over the last two or three centuries, there have been two changes in society. First, there has been a mass migration from the rural areas to the cities. Second, the production of goods has become industrialized. As a natural and inevitable by-product of these two changes, large organizations have emerged.

If you are a normal, active person, you cannot get through a day without being affected, either directly or indirectly, by large organizations. Consider this fairly typical day. Your radio alarm clock (which was made by a large organization) awakens you. You learn that the world is still in one piece (from the news provided by a large organization, e.g., ABC, CBS, or NBC), and no blizzards, hurricanes, or tornadoes are headed toward your city (from the Weather Bureau, another large organization). You leave your home and go to school, a large organization. After you finish classes, you go to a part-time job, which for most people involves working for a large organization. When you get home, you find your electricity is off, so you call another large organization, the power company. Then, you decide to see a movie. This movie was made by a large organization and is shown in a theater which is probably owned and operated by another large organization. And finally, before you turn in, you write a letter to your representative in the largest organization in the country, the federal government. You are concerned about how much income tax you have to pay.

What is an organization? According to Schein (1970), an *organization* "is the rational coordination of the activities of a (large) number of people for the achievement of some common explicit purpose, or goal, through division or labor and function and through a hierarchy of authority and responsibility" (p. 9). Less formally, an organization is a collection of groups. That is, it consists of a number

Educational Resources, University of South Florida

of small groups which each make a contribution to the organization's goal or purpose.

The most important single characteristic of an organization is its structure. *Organizational structure* is the relatively permanent pattern of relationships among the groups within an organization (Porter, Lawler, & Hackman, 1975). Without a structure, an organization would cease to exist. Why is structure so important?

Look at the second definition of an organization: a collection of groups. Each group carries out a *function*—some activities which, hopefully, serve the goals of the organization. How does the organization coordinate these more or less independent activities? The answer is, by its structure. Without structure, an organization would disintegrate into chaos and soon cease to exist.

For example, the school you attend is an organization with the overall goal of educating you. Imagine what would happen if the instructors did not coordinate their activities with those responsible for maintaining the building. Classes might be held in darkness or cleaning people might decide to scrub a classroom floor during a final examination.

All theorists and researchers interested in organizations agree that structure is the most important characteristic of an organization.

They disagree, however, as to what is the best structure and what aspects of the structure are most important. As a result, there are many different theories of how an organization functions and the most efficient way for it to operate.

Organizational theories

There are three major organizational theories. We will present them in the order they were proposed.

Classical theory

In the early 1900's, the United States and other countries experienced an urban migration and a phenomenal growth in industry. Where previously few people had lived in the same area and companies were usually small, now there were massive concentrations of people living and working together. At that time, little was known about how these large organizations worked and how they could be made to operate efficiently. Efficiency experts such as Fredrick W. Taylor were asked to describe the characteristics of an organization and to recommend the best way to run it. Taylor did this in his book, *Principles of Scientific Management,* published in 1911. To

"I don't give a damn what the registrar's office says. I didn't sign up for a course in the history of the Phillips screwdriver."

The classicists believed that an organization can operate in a perfectly logical and efficient manner. However, those of us who have to deal with a large organization (e.g., a college or university) on a day-to-day basis often encounter an illogical and inefficient organization. Why is this so?

In the late 1960's, Laurence J. Peter proposed a tongue-in-cheek explanation of organizational inefficiency. It was based on the Peter Principle:

"In a hierarchy [organization] every employee tends to rise to his level of incompetence." (Peter & Hull, 1969)

Peter's basic thesis was that a person who is competent in her job will eventually be promoted to a job she is unable to perform. For example, a psychology department will take its best researcher and make her the department chairperson—a job she is unequipped to handle. Since this person has now reached her level of incompetence, she will probably remain in it until she dies or retires. Why? Because she's performing too incompetently to move further up in the organization.

Peter proposed that a science be devoted to the study of this phenomenon. He called this science *hierarchiology*. Its objective would be to describe the process whereby people are invariably promoted to their level of incompetence and how people attempt to cover up this incompetence. Like any respectable science, hierarchiology has a jargon all its own. Here are a few of the more important terms.

Variables related to promotion

Success—an employee who finally reaches her level of incompetence.

Creative incompetence—feigned incompetence so that a person can avoid being promoted to her level of incompetence. This must be done very skillfully. If her superiors realize that she is, in fact, competent, they will immediately promote her to her level of incompetence.

Hierarchal exfoliation—firing a person who by some mistake is super-competent in her job. Such behavior consitutes a clear threat to the organization.

Lateral arabesque and *percussive sublimation*—apparent exceptions to the Peter Principle in which people who are already performing incompetently are promoted. Peter explains these paradoxes by noting that the person's job, responsibilities, and pay remain exactly the same. However, the job receives a more prestigious title. For example, an incompetent janitor is made vice president in charge of plant maintenance.

Peter's pretty pass—the inability of a person to rise to her level of incompetence because a super-incompetent already occupies the position.

Some indicators of incompetent performance

Papyromania—the compulsive accumulation of papers.

Papyrophobia—the abnormal desire for a clean desk.

Phonophilia—the abnormal desire for possession and use of voice transmission and recording equipment.

Professional automatism—the compulsive concern with rituals and a disregard for efficiency.

Rigor cartis—the abnormal interest in charts, accompanied by a lack of concern with the facts the charts represent.

Tabulatory gigantism—the obsession with large desks.

When you go through registration next term, remember the Peter Principle.

understand Taylor's view of what makes a good organization, we must examine his and other classical theorists' view of humans and organizations.

Human nature: Theory X. The classicists held the so-called *Theory X* view of human nature (McGregor, 1960). This theory is based on three premises about people. First, the average person dislikes work and will avoid it if possible. Second, because most people dislike work, they have to be coerced, tightly controlled, and threatened with punishment in order to get them to do their job. Finally, the average person has little ambition, wishes to avoid responsibility, desires to be directed by others, and values security above all else.

The organization as a machine. Some people have described this view of organizations as *machine theory* (Katz & Kahn, 1966). That is, an organization is seen as being identical to a machine. It is built according to a specified set of plans (i.e., a blueprint). It does not deviate from this blueprint, and anything that is not in the plans can't be important. Further, just as a machine can function perfectly and in a perfectly logical fashion, so can an organization. The "blueprint" that describes an organization is called the organizational chart.

The organizational chart. An *organizational chart* is a description of the chains of command and channels of communication within an organization. Figure 10-1 presents the organizational chart of a well-known mythical organization, the Star Fleet Armed Forces. As those of you who have watched *Star Trek* may recall, Star Fleet is the military branch of the United Federation of Planets. Its goal is "to maintain interplanetary peace and security" (Star Fleet Technical Order, TM 379260-0; *Star Fleet Technical Manual,* 1975).

The vertical lines in this figure are called *scalar processes.* They describe the hierarchy within an organization, the lines of authority and responsibility. For example, the vertical lines in Star Fleet's organizational chart tell us that the Operating Forces are lowest in this organization's hierarchy. The ultimate authority and responsibility in Star Fleet Command rest with the Federation Council.

The horizontal lines are called *functional processes.* They describe the channels of communication between various units at the same level within the organization. These units need these clearly specified channels so that they can coordinate their activities in order to reach the organization's overall goal.

A unit's place in a company's organizational chart will be primarily determined by whether the unit engages in a line or staff operation. A *line operation* is one which contributes directly to the organization's final product. A *staff operation* is one which contributes indirectly by advising or supporting the line operations (Bobbitt, Breinholt, Doktor, & McNaul, 1974; Landy & Trumbo, 1976). For example, the starships that actually patrol the galaxy are part of a line operation unit, Fleet Operations. The Logistics Support unit serves a staff function by keeping the starships well supplied.

The classicists believed that proper coordination of line and staff operations and their functions could produce a perfect system which operates in a totally logical manner. They advocated that companies operate on a *scalar principle* to achieve this (Bass, 1965). Authority and responsibility should start at the top of an organization and flow downward in a clear, unbroken line. Why? Because people will not perform unless they are told what to do and are responsible to someone if they don't do it.

Division of labor. The classicists believed that units should be assigned specific tasks and

Star Fleet Command

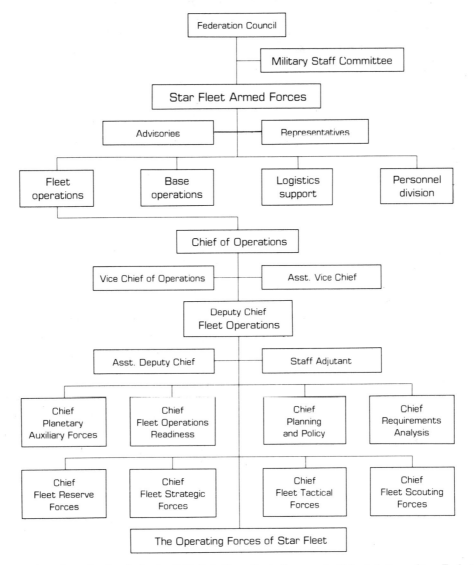

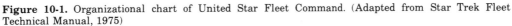

Figure 10-1. Organizational chart of United Star Fleet Command. (Adapted from Star Trek Fleet Technical Manual, 1975)

that large tasks should be divided into smaller components. This is known as *division of labor*. According to the classicists, it should result in workers who are experts in their specific part of the overall task. These experts would then put all these sub-parts together to make the final product. Here's how a classicist (e.g., Fayol, 1916; Gulick, 1937; Taylor, 1911; Weber, 1947) would organize Santa Claus's workshop.

The goal of this organization is to provide toys for all the good boys and girls. To accomplish this, a classicist would recommend that one elf design the toys, another carve them, still another elf sand them, and pass them to an elf who paints them. The final product is loaded into Santa's sack by other elves. The sleigh is pulled by reindeer and led by Rudolph.

Note that the classicist doesn't worry about the boredom division of labor might produce or the fact that the elves who design the toys never see the final product. The classicists believes that the average worker takes little pride in her work and is motivated only by the money she receives. This view of the average worker is also reflected in another important concept.

Span of control. Since workers are basically lazy and must be coerced into doing their job, supervisors must keep close watch over them. Classicists were quite concerned with a supervisor's *span of control,* the number of people she can effectively monitor. They believe that the number of people that could be effectively controlled was limited. For example, Fayol (1916) believed that at the executive level, a supervisor could efficiently supervise no more than five to seven subordinates, while a supervisor at a lower level could handle twenty to thirty.

Machine or classical theorists thus viewed an organization as capable of perfection. And that perfection can be achieved by a logical, rigid, well-defined organizational structure. Further, classical theorists saw workers as motivated solely by pleasure and money, and primarily as tenders of machines.

Neoclassical theory

The classicists did identify many important aspects of organizational structure, and their recommendations are still widely accepted today. However, their views of human nature and organizational efficiency have been seriously challenged by the neoclassicists (e.g., Likert, 1967; McGregor, 1960; Merton, 1957).

Human nature: Theory Y. The neoclassicists rejected the Theory X view of human nature and adopted *Theory Y* (McGregor, 1960). This theory proposes that people: (1) like to work, (2) can be motivated by rewards in their job and can show self-control and direction, (3) will accept and even seek responsibility, and (4) have the capacity for creativity, imagination, and ingenuity (McGregor, 1960; Porter, Lawler, & Hackman, 1975). This very different view of people led the neoclassicists to make different recommendations about how an organization should be run and its important characteristics. Let's examine the points of disagreement.

The blueprint. The neoclassicists admitted that a large company needs a pattern of organization. They agreed that scalar and functional processes specified in an organizational chart are important. But they disagreed with two aspects of the classicist position.

First, they didn't accept the idea that scalar and functional processes will automatically achieve perfection, are always without conflict, and invariably operate in a logical manner. When large numbers of people and different functions are involved, these processes are often imperfect, full of conflict, and often operate in an illogical manner.

Consider, for example, the following imaginary situation in an oil refinery. It produces 1,000,000 gallons of gasoline per day at a profit of ten cents per gallon. The company's stockholders complain about their dividends, so the comptroller tells the production people to cut costs and thus increase profits. Meanwhile, the legal department is facing several lawsuits brought by environmental groups for air pollution. As part of an out-of-court settlement, the lawyers agree to have air pollution control devices installed. The installation will cut production by 25 percent and profits by 50 percent. Finally, the personnel department is under pressure to comply with fair employment guidelines set by the federal government. It sends a memo to the engineer in charge of constructing the pollution controllers which states that the first fifty people hired for the job must be black or Mexican-American.

A neo-classicist would point out that in a situation such as this, there are overlapping lines of authority and conflicting areas of responsibility. Who does the production chief listen to, the lawyers or the accountants? Further, the neoclassicists would argue that these conflicts create human problems and may not be resolved in a logical manner. Differing individual needs and values among members of subunits may produce illogical responses. For example, the engineer may detest blacks and Mexican-Americans and refuse to hire them. Conflicting goals between the legal and financial departments may lead to internal friction between them. The production chief may disregard the comptroller's demands or at least delay in implementing them because of a dislike for "cold-blooded pencil pushers." People are not always as logical as the system in which they operate.

The second point of disagreement between the classicists and neoclassicists concerned the completeness of the organizational chart. The neoclassicists strongly believed that this formal blueprint did not describe everything of importance in a large organization.

Informal organizations. The neoclassicists placed tremendous importance on the informal organizations which exist within a company's formal structure. These *informal organizations* are the natural groupings of people at work. They resemble a small group much more than a formal organization does. As such, informal organizations are concerned with the needs of their members rather than the goals of the organization (Schein, 1970). People who take their coffee breaks together, work close to one another, or share common interests on or off the job are examples of informal organizations. Why did the neoclassicists consider informal organizations so important?

One reason was that the goals of an informal organization may sometimes conflict with those of the formal organization, and the norms of the two groups may be quite different[1] (Schein, 1970). For example, a company may expect a worker to produce ten widgets per hour. The worker's informal organization may have a norm of eight widgets per hour. To prevent a worker from being a "rate buster" (and thus make other people work harder), the informal organization may exert subtle pressure (e.g., not eating lunch with her) or direct pressure (e.g., ganging up on her) to make her conform to its norm.

An informal organization's leaders, status hierarchy, and means and channels of communication may be quite different from those of the formal organization. Status and leadership emerge in the informal organization as a result of a person's characteristics, not through appointment by the organization.

---

[1]Recall that the classicists believed that everything important about an organization was included in its formal structure or blueprint.

Units in the formal organization communicate along clearly specified lines, usually via a memo. The informal organization communicates via the "grapevine."

Finally, an informal organization will tend to resist change unless all its members agree to it. This is because an informal organization is like a small group. Thus, it derives its strength from unanimity and cohesiveness among its members, not from any particular structure.

The informal organization seems to have a strong influence on job performance. For example, Newcomb (1954) described the effect of informal group norms on a worker's productivity. This worker had decided to produce more than her group's norm of fifty units per day. The group pressure on her was so strong that her productivity dropped *below* this norm. However, when the group disbanded, she doubled her output (cited in Golembiewski, 1962,).

A study conducted among British coal miners (Trist & Bamforth, 1951) illustrated the effects of breaking up an informal group. These miners had worked in small (two-to eight-member), highly cohesive groups. However, a technological change caused these teams to be replaced by groups of forty to fifty men all working together in assembly-line fashion. The effect of this change was unexpected. Workers became alienated, indifferent and passive; the amount of coal mined decreased dramatically. As Schein (1970) has pointed out, the changeover was rational from an engineering standpoint. But the failure to consider the power of informal groups produced exactly the opposite effect.

Division of labor. The neoclassicists argued that dividing a task into its smallest parts might not always be the best strategy. Such specialization might isolate a person from other workers and make her feel that she had contributed little to the final product. Fur-

ther, the neoclassicists believed that the supervisor should be as concerned with coordinating and motivating the workers as she is with controlling them. To illustrate what the neoclassicists see as wrong, consider this interview with a "spot-welder" for a large automobile company.

I don't understand how come more guys don't flip. Because you're nothing more than a machine when you hit this type of thing. They give better care to that machine than they will to you. They'll have more respect, give more attention to that machine. And you *know* this. Somehow you get the feeling that the machine is better than you are. (Laughs.)

You really begin to wonder. What price do they put on me? Look at the price they put on the machine. If that machine breaks down, there's somebody out there to fix it right away. If I break down, I'm just pushed over to the other side till another man takes my place. The only thing they have on their mind is to keep that line running. (Terkel, 1974, p. 223)

Span of control. The neoclassicists also rejected the rigid approach to a supervisor's span of control. They believed that this approach ignores individual differences in people's abilities, a manager's style, the nature of different tasks, and other similar factors. These factors, the neoclassicists argued, determine the most effective span of control.

Modern organizational theory

The characteristics identified by both the classicists and neoclassicists are certainly important. But according to modern organizational theory, to understand how an organization functions, we must have more than a description of its parts.

The hallmark of modern organizational theory is the systems approach. A large organization is seen as a *system*—"a group of interacting, interrelated or interdependent elements [which form] a collective entity" (*American Heritage Dictionary of the English Language,* 1971, p. 1306). Note the words "interacting," "interrelated," and "interdependent." These aspects of an organization are the focus of the modern theorists' attention. Further, these theorists believe that we can't understand the parts of an organization without understanding the whole.

According to Katz and Kahn (1966), systems can be open or closed. Organizations are *open systems;* they take in energy, transform it into some product, and use this product to resupply the energy they need. Such an open system is the human body. We take in energy in the form of food and transform this food into the chemicals we need to function. This enables us to produce a product (e.g., work). We are paid for this work, which enables us to buy more food, and so on. Let's note certain other characteristics of this open system. One is the importance of the interdependence of its parts. Our brain, kidneys, and liver may all function perfectly, but if our heart stops, the system ceases to function. This system consists of a series of events (e.g., eating, metabolism, working) which renew themselves. One feature which distinguishes an open from a closed system is that an open system seeks to avoid entropy. *Entropy* is a "universal law of nature in which all organizations move toward disorganization or death" (Katz & Kahn, 1966, p. 21). A closed system cannot avoid entropy, but an open system attempts to avoid it by using negative feedback. *Negative feedback* is information from the environment which tells the system that it is heading for entropy. For example, a doctor tells you that you must quit smoking or you will develop cancer, so you quit smoking. You are using negative feedback to avoid entropy (i.e., death).

Let's see how this open system concept applies to organizations. Modern organizational theorists say that an organization is like a living body (Katz & Kahn 1966; Scott & Mitchell, 1976). To understand this "living system," it is not enough to study its components. For example, the modern theorists would agree with the classicists that the formal organization is important. They would also agree with the neoclassicists that it is important to be aware of individual workers' needs and motives. However, the modern theorists would be interested in how these two parts of an organization mesh or fuse (Bakke, 1953).

The modern theorists see an organization as a living system. Thus, they would not accept the classicists position that organizational success can be measured simply by efficiency. They would argue that the organization must also be healthy. This health depends on a smooth integration of the parts, signs of "vigor" and growth, and the ability of the organization to adapt itself to changes in its environment. When the modern theorists are called upon to treat a "sick" organization, they will attempt to treat it as a whole. They will not just consider some isolated part.

Individual behavior in an organization

These three theories provide the theoretical basis for predictions about how an organization's characteristics affect the people in it. This section examines how these characteristics actually affect behavior.

The shape of an organization

The *shape* of an organization refers to how many levels exist in the hierarchy. A company with many levels relative to its number of employees has a *tall* shape. A company with few levels is called *flat* (Porter et al., 1975). Figure 10-2 illustrates these two kinds of organizations.

A classicist would prefer a tall structure. It provides small spans of control and thus

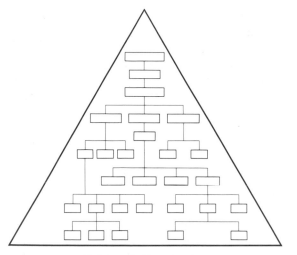

Tall organization structure

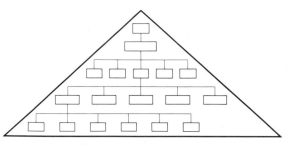

Flat organization structure

Figure 10-2. A tall and a flat organizationl structure.

should produce high worker productivity. (The classicist believes that workers must be closely supervised.) The neoclassicist would prefer a flat organization. This would give the workers more individual responsibility, and encourage the development of self-expression and creativity. The result would be satisfied workers and a more productive organization (Worthy, 1950). Which position is correct?

It turns out that neither shape is always best. Sometimes workers are more productive

and satisfied in a tall organization; sometimes the reverse is true. One factor which seems to influence a person's reaction to shape is the organization's size (Porter & Lawler, 1964). When a company is large (more than 5,000 employees), people seem to prefer a tall shape. If the company is small, they prefer a flat shape.

This relationship makes sense. Consider these two situations. In the first, you are working as a meat buyer for a restaurant chain the size of MacDonalds with, say, 5,000 employees in its main office. An organization this large contains a multitude of units with different functions (e.g., advertising, finance, marketing research). The interrelationships among the units will be quite complex, and it will be difficult to coordinate their activities and communications. If you are about to order 500,000 pounds of hamburgers, you would want know clearly which unit will be responsible for authorizing the purchase, which one will handle its delivery, etc. Further, you do not want to go through the unit responsible for Ronald MacDonald's costumes to get authorization for the purchase. A tall structure will provide these clear chains of command and communication patterns. As a result, your job goes smoothly and you are probably happier than a person working in a flat organization with 5,000 employees.

Now, imagine you are a meat buyer for a restaurant with fifty employees which has a tall structure. Before the owner approves the purchase of hamburgers, your request must pass through twenty-four levels. Such a shape would destroy the advantages of working for a small organization—namely, less managerial control, informality, and a feeling that one is contributing to the organization. Further, you might find this structure demeaning, frustrating, and unnecessary. Thus, a tall structure in a small organization may well produce negative attitudes.

The nature of one's job

Level in the organization. In general, the higher a person is in the hierarchy, the more interested and satisfied she is with her job (Porter, 1962; Stouffer, Suchman, Devinney, Star, & Williams, 1949). One reason is that upper-level workers have more control over their jobs than workers at lower levels do. The more control people have over their work, the more satisfied they are (Blauner, 1960; Porter, 1962).

Status. The higher a person is in the hierarchy, the more responsibility, respect, and recognition she will have. Further, she will probably be paid more and have better fringe benefits (e.g., stock options, longer vacations). All these things reflect the high status of her job. This, in turn, satisfies her self-esteem needs and make the job more pleasant (Porter, 1962).

A person with a low-status job may feel frustrated and pressured, and may show this distress in a variety of ways. One study recorded the number of times high- and low-level employees at a large company went to the infirmary. Excluding visits due to acci-

dents, it was found that lower-level employees visited the infirmary much more often. Even within different levels of the company, trips to the infirmary were correlated with job status. For example, among supervisors, the higher the level in the hierarchy, the less likely the person was to seek medical aid. When workers moved up in the hierarchy, their visits to the infirmary declined. If they moved down, visits increased (Kasl & French, 1962).

Tasks involved in the job. In general, a job which is monotonous, repetitive, and requires little thought or creativity will produce a dissatisfied worker. The reason seems to be that the person feels her skills are not being used (Garson, 1972; Guest, 1955; Walker & Guest, 1952).

Although boring, repetitive jobs are usually found in the lower levels of an organization, these lower-level jobs can sometimes be satisfying. For example, Morse (1953) found that clerical workers who used a wide variety of skills were quite satisfied with their jobs. This was true regardless of the salary they earned.

How people feel about their jobs

As a rule, the more status associated with a job, the more satisfied a person will be. Consider the following survey conducted with 3,000 Americans who held different jobs. They were asked, "If you had the chance to start your working life over again, would you choose the same kind of work as you are doing now?" (Blauner, 1964; Wilensky, 1964). The percentage of people in various jobs who answered "yes" to this question are presented below.

College professors	93%
Physicists	89%
Lawyers	84%
Journalists	82%
White-collar workers (secretaries, clerks)	43%
Skilled workers in a large plant	41%
Semi-skilled workers in a large plant	24%
Unskilled workers in a large plant	16%

These data seem to support the neoclassicist position. However, there are some arguments in favor of highly structured jobs. First, structured tasks with specific roles may reduce confusion and chaos (Hickson, 1966). This, in turn, may create less pressure and ambiguity for the worker. Further, Hickson noted that some people dislike unstructured jobs because they create anxiety as to what is expected of them. A worker's liking for a job will ultimately depend on her own abilities and needs, the job itself, the technology used, and many other factors. Not all people react the same way to highly structured jobs.

Organizational philosophy

In general, an organization's philosophy about how its employees should be treated will tend to reflect either a Theory X or a Theory Y view of human nature. How do these two philosophies affect morale and productivity?

Supervisory style. Theory X supervisors are task-oriented, watch their subordinates closely, and give them a good deal of training. Theory Y supervisors tend to be person-oriented, relaxed, and permissive, and give their subordinates a good deal of freedom. Several studies have compared the effects of these two styles.

In one laboratory experiment, women worked on assembly models while they received different types of supervision. Some women were exposed to Theory X supervisors, who gave a lot of instructions and were very sarcastic toward them. Other women were supervised by Theory Y people, who gave few instructions and were positive toward them. The women's attitudes toward their supervisor and productivity are presented in Figure 10-3.

As the figure shows, workers with Theory Y supervisors had better attitudes and were more productive than women directed by Theory X supervisors (Day & Hamblin, 1964). Field studies of worker productivity have found that productive workers feel they are treated like people rather than machines. Further, these people did not expect as much criticism from their supervisor as did less productive workers (Katz & Kahn, 1952, 1953; Katz, Maccoby, & Morse, 1950).

These studies strongly support a Theory Y supervisory style. But other research suggests that this style may not always be preferable. For example, Fiedler's (1971) work on leadership effectiveness (presented in the previous chapter) showed that under certain circumstances, an autocratic, Theory X style of leadership will produce better morale and productivity than a democratic Theory Y style. Further, different workers like different styles. Some prefer autocratic, highly structured supervision and perform better with it (Lewin, Lippitt, & White, 1939; Page & McGinnies, 1959; White & Lippitt, 1960).

In general, research has concluded that no one supervisory style is always best. The advantages of one style over another seem to depend on the situation the workers and supervisors are in (Korman, 1966; Porter et al., 1975; Sales, 1966).

Also, a subordinate's behavior rather than a supervisor's philosophy may sometimes determine the style a supervisor adopts (Farris & Lim, 1969; Lowin & Craig, 1968). The reason for this can be seen in the following example: Imagine you are called on to supervise three workers named Larry, Curly, and Moe (the Three Stooges). As you may recall from their movies, they spent most of their time punching each other, getting in each other's way, and in general "screwing up." Such behavior may cause you to adopt an autocratic, Theory X supervisory style even though you generally hold a Theory Y view of human nature.

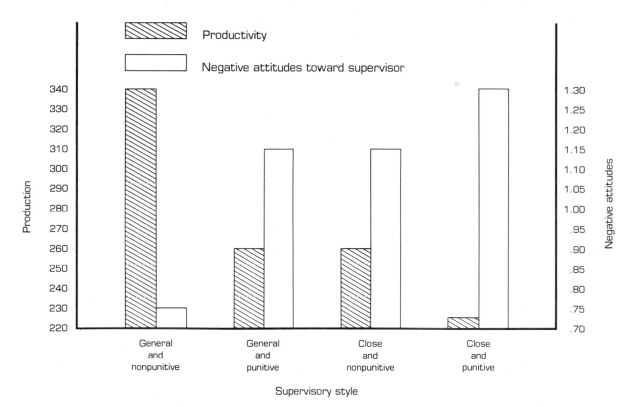

Figure 10-3. The effects of closeness of supervision and punitiveness of supervisor on productivity and on attitudes of workers. (Adapted from Day & Hamblin, 1964)

Decision making. Another way Theory X and Theory Y viewpoints are shown is in the extent of worker participation in decisions affecting their jobs. If you believe that people don't care about their work, can't think for themselves, and are concerned only with how much money they receive, you will probably not involve them in the decision-making process. But if you believe that people are creative, responsible, and interested, you will probably invite them to participate. Several studies have examined the effectiveness of these two strategies (e.g., Coch & French, 1948; Lawler & Hackman, 1969; Morse & Reimer, 1956).

Coch and French chose a company that made pajamas. Evidently, the pajama-buying public, at that time, was a fickle group whose tastes changed quite often. This called for frequent changes in production practices. The workers opposed these changes because they involved learning new techniques and earning less pay. Pay had dropped because workers were paid per unit produced, and new production techniques would reduce the number of units a worker could complete. As a result of these conflicts, many employees quit, efficiency dropped, and the remaining workers became more hostile with every change. Coch and French were asked to reduce the workers' resistance to these changes.

Coch and French established three conditions. The first served as a control. Workers in this condition received information in the usual fashion. They were told that the change in production would take place, what the new job would entail, and how much they would be paid for each new garment produced. In the second condition, workers were told the company's problem and were invited to discuss it. After the workers had agreed that a change was needed, they selected representatives to help design and learn the new jobs. Workers in the third condition were also told the problem and invited to discuss it. But instead of choosing representatives to take part in the design and training, everyone participated in it.

The total-participation group showed a dramatic increase in productivity. The group which had selected representatives took a little longer to adjust to the change. But after a month, it was producing more pajamas than ever before. The production rate of the noninvolved group dropped below its pre-change level and stayed there.

Further, among the workers who had been involved in the decision making, the number of quitters dropped and attitudes toward the company improved. Although there have been no studies of the long-range effects of participatory decision making, it is believed that this practice would produce relatively permanent benefits for both the company and its employees (cf. Argyris, 1964; Likert, 1967; Likert & Seashore, 1964; Porter et al., 1975).

Why does this technique work? There are probably two reasons. First, it increases workers' feelings of self-worth and the belief that the company really cares about them. Second, involving people in a decision which affects them is an extremely powerful way to change their attitudes (Lewin, 1947).

Despite all this positive evidence, we must caution you against seeing participatory decision making as a cure-all for a company's problems. Some people don't like it at all. For example, Vroom (1960) found that authoritarian people with little need for independence don't want to participate and are unhappy if they do. Different strokes for different folks.

Organizational climate. An *organization's climate* is the spirit, feeling, or atmosphere that pervades a company. It goes beyond the company's size, structure, or production techniques (Porter et al., 1975; Prien & Ronan, 1971).

A Theory X company will create a cold, authoritarian climate with little concern for its employees. A Theory Y company will generate a warm, supportive climate. Most people assume that the latter climate will result in productive, satisfied workers. Indeed, this premise is the sole reason for the rapid and widespread growth of the field of *organizational development.* Its goal is to improve a company's climate and the interpersonal style of its managers (Bennis, 1969; French & Bell, 1973).

While the idea of making big business warm and supportive sounds appealing, the value of this strategy has not yet been clearly demonstrated. Some studies find that people prefer a Theory Y climate (e.g., Blake, Mouton, Barnes, & Greiner, 1964; Schneider, 1972; Schneider & Hall, 1972). Others do not (e.g., Page & McGinnies, 1959). Some researchers even question whether there really is such a thing as organizational climate. They argue that measures of organizational climate may show nothing more than how satisfied workers are with their jobs (Guion, 1973; Johanneson, 1973). Thus, despite the extreme popularity of the field of organizational development, its basic premise (that workers want warm, supportive environments) has not yet been proven.

Conclusion

The first half of this chapter was concerned with organizational behavior. We began by differentiating between organizational and collective behavior and then described what an organization is.

The most important characteristic of an organization is its structure. All organizational theorists agree on this point. However, there is considerable disagreement about what the important characteristics of organizational structure are and what is the most efficient kind of structure. The classicists, who held a Theory X view of human nature, (i.e., that people are basically lazy, uncreative, and passive) argued for a rigid, formal structure in order to keep tight control over workers. Further, they believed that the most important thing about an organization is its formal structure. The neoclassicists took a much more positive view of human nature (Theory Y), which is reflected in their approach to organizations. They stressed the importance of informal groupings within the formal structure and noted workers' needs and motives. Finally, the modern organizational theorists take a systems approach. They agree that the characteristics identified by the classicists and neoclassicists are important, but they argue that these can be understood only in the context of the total system. Thus, the modern theorists study the total system and how its parts interrelate.

How do the characteristics of an organization affect the workers' attitudes and behavior? It is difficult and inadvisable to make any blanket statements about the effects of any particular organizational characteristic. Consider the nature of one's job and the supervisory style as an example. Most people dislike low-level, highly structured jobs with authoritarian, task-oriented supervisors. But sometimes, the opposite is true. We have to consider both the situation and the person in it. This is not to say that organizations which adopt a Theory X point of view are as effective as those with a Theory Y viewpoint. Indeed, in most cases the data favor Theory Y. The point is that no one approach to organizational behavior can adequately explain it. This is further evidence of the complexity of social behavior.

REVIEW QUESTIONS

(Ten out of twelve is passing)

1. The key to understanding an organization is its _____ which is the relatively stable pattern of relationships among group members. (p. 308)
2. Ebeneezer Scrooge worked his employees on Christmas Eve, distrusted them, and believed they were lazy. He probably adhered to a(n) _____ view of human nature. (p. 309)
3. The scalar and functional processes in an organization are usually described by a(n) _____ _____ . (p. 309)
4. Organization members who are directly responsible for the organization's product are engaged in _____ operations. Those members who contribute indirectly by offering support are engaging in _____ operations. (p. 309)
5. The number of workers a supervisor can effectively supervise is called the _____ _____ . (p. 312)
6. The classical organizational theorists thought the _____ organization was the most important characteristic of a large company. The neoclassicists, however, placed much emphasis on the _____ organization. (p. 313)

7. The modern organizational theorists view an organization as a(n) _____ and thus study the _____ of its parts or units. (p. 315)

8. In an open system, the goal is to avoid _____ . One of the ways an open system does this is by using _____ _____ . (p. 315)

9. The effect of organizational shape (i.e., tall or flat) on worker's attitudes seems to depend on the _____ of the organization. In a(n) _____ organization, members seem more satisfied with a tall rather than a flat organization. (p. 316)

10. Involving workers in production changes and other matters which affect their lives is called _____ _____ _____ . (p. 319)

11. The spirit or day-to-day feeling in a large organization is called the _____ _____ . (p. 320)

12. The goal of _____ _____ is to create a Theory Y type of atmosphere within an organization. (p. 320)

ANSWERS

1. structure   2. Theory X   3. organizational chart   4. line, staff   5. span of control
6. formal, informal   7. system, interdependence or interrelationships   8. entropy, negative feedback
9. size, large   10. participatory decision making   11. organizational climate
12. organizational development

COLLECTIVE BEHAVIOR

The second part of this chapter looks at collective behavior. According to Milgram and Toch (1969), *collective behavior* is group behavior "which originates spontaneously, is relatively unorganized, fairly unpredictable and planless in its course of development and which depends on interstimulation among participants" (p. 507).

This definition enables us to distinguish fairly easily between collective behavior and organizational behavior. The first important distinction concerns rules of procedure. Organizational behavior is group behavior which is governed by established rules of procedure (Turner & Killian, 1972). Any organization, whether General Motors or the Tuesday Morning Tulip Club, sees the establishment of these rules of procedure as one of its first goals. It attempts to make these rules fairly explicit and to codify them as soon as possible. The behavior within the organization and even who belongs is determined largely by these rules.

By contrast, collective behavior does not result from any established rules. It is spontaneous and unplanned. There is no organizational chart in a lynch mob. The members of the mob "are those who happen to be participating and the leaders are those who are being followed by the members" (Turner & Killian, 1972, p. 5).

A second important distinction concerns the effect of cultural norms on the behavior of the organization worker versus the person in a collective. In an organization, cultural norms have enormous influence on the organization's rules of procedure. Further, the members support these norms. Collective behavior shows a sharp contrast (Turner & Killian, 1972). Its norms may be peculiar to the group at that point in time and/or in opposition to the larger society.

Consider, for example, a riot which took place in Kent, Ohio, three days before the fatal shooting of four Kent State students by members of the Ohio National Guard.

It was a hot Friday night. Hundreds of student had filled the bars adjoining the campus when a spontaneous "street festival" began. Dancing and singing, people spilled out onto the street. Joe Eszterhas and Michael Roberts (1970) describe what happened.

> Sometime before midnight, as the festival continued without violence, a middle-aged man driving a new Oldsmobile refused to take the detour, rolled the car's windows up, and tried to drive through the crowd.
> "Get the pig!" someone yelled.
> The car was surrounded, its windows smashed, its body kicked in. The man backed up and fled. He was not hurt.
> "That changed the mood of the whole thing," a student said. "Here was this guy driving his new flashy chrome car through these Commie-faggot-long-haired-pimp-freaks and if any got in the way, it was too bad. It was a grim reminder of actualities."

The people on the main street began chanting obscenities; soon, they turned to violence:

> The group in the street surged south on Water Street toward Main Street. About twenty students began throwing rocks and bottles at windows. Most of the crowd stood on the sidewalk and watched.
> Steve Sharoff, who had organized the noon rally, was sitting in one of the bars. "I heard a crash and a guy came in and said, 'Guys are throwing bottles out there!' Wow, I thought, that's pretty far out." (Pp. 37–38)

This behavior is hardly consistent with the general norms of society. If any norms were responsible, they seem to be peculiar to the time and place in which this riot occurred.

We will examine three aspects of collective behavior: the effects of crowding, crowd behavior, and social movements.[2]

Crowding

The world's population is growing at an alarming rate (Ehrlich, 1968). From the beginning of human existence to 1650, it reached 500 million. From 1650 to 1850 this figure increased to 1 billion, a doubling time of 200 years. By 1930, this figure had increased to 2 billion people; the doubling time had dropped to 80 years. In 1970 the world's population was estimated at 4 billion people (Altman, 1975), a doubling time of 40 years. The pattern is clear: as the world's population increases, the doubling time decreases.

One obvious problem created by the population explosion is the possibility of a worldwide famine. This is a very serious concern. Most experts agree that the population is growing much faster than the food supply. Even if the food problem were solved, some scientists believe that the increased population itself might have negative effects on people.

Before we discuss the reason for this concern, one point should be clarified. The world is not running out of living space. If every man, woman, and child alive at this moment were distributed evenly across the available land on earth, each one would have almost ten acres (Freedman, 1975). Only the late Howard Hughes or a Himalayan hermit would perceive this as a dense population. What, then, is the concern about population density?

The answer is simple. People do not distribute themselves equally across the available land. Out of choice or necessity, they tend to

[2]Strictly speaking, crowding is not considered collective behavior. This is because the focus of interest is an *individual's* reactions to being crowded. Collective behavior research is usually concerned with the behavior of a *group*.

Mary Ellen Brown

concentrate in specific areas. For example, although there are ten acres of land available for every American, the density rate for the island of Manhattan is 70,000 per square mile! Seventy percent of all Americans live in large cities or their immediate suburbs (Kirk, 1974). The density of different neighborhoods in these urban centers varies, but someone who lives in them will spend part of her day in an incredibly crowded setting. For example, on the New York City subway, only two square feet are available for each passenger.

There has been a good deal of research on the effects of excessive density on animals. Crowding can produce extreme psychological and physiological pathologies even when their environment is normal in every other way (e.g., enough food and water). Elephants, fish, monkeys, rabbits, and rats all show pathological behavior as the result of crowding (Calhoun, 1962; Galle, Gove, & McPherson, 1972). For example, the rats in Calhoun's study became hyperaggressive and anti-social. Some died of thirst even though there

was an adequate supply of water. Female rats neglected their offspring. Monkeys who live in densely populated areas often show a breakdown in their social structure and sometimes kill their young.

Although there are explanations as to why being crowded has these negative effects, (cf. Freedman, 1975), there is little question that they do occur. The question is are these frightening effects generalizable to humans?

Density and crowding

The animal studies just presented dealt with the effects of population density. *Density* is a physical concept. It describes how many people (or animals) there are per unit of space (Altman, 1975; Stokols, 1972). *Crowding* is a psychological concept; it is the feeling that one does not have enough space (Altman, 1975; Stokols, 1972). Stokols has pointed out that density is needed for a person to feel crowded, but it does not automatically lead to that feeling.

What causes a person to feel crowded? One explanation concerns the concept of *personal space*. This is a small area with invisible boundaries that surround a person (Sommer, 1969). People do not like others to invade their personal space—that is, to cross this boundary. In one study, people were put in a small room under one of two conditions. Their chairs touched each other or were about two feet apart. People whose chairs were touching were much more likely to report feeling crowded (Worchel & Teddlie, 1976). Why? Apparently because their personal space had been violated.

Why does violation of personal space lead to the feeling of being crowded? Worchel and Teddlie explained this via Schachter's two-factor theory of emotion (cf. Chapter Three or Four). The invasion of our personal space, they said, is physiologically arousing. Since there is another person quite close we can label this arousal. We "feel crowded."

The effects of density on people can be studied in two ways. The first examines the correlation between density and social pathology in the real world. The second manipulates density in the laboratory.

The effects of density: Correlational studies

Galle, Gove, and McPherson (1972) conducted a carefully controlled field study on the effects of density. Based on the research done with animals, they predicted that high concentrations of people would increase the incidence of social pathology. To measure density, they used census estimates of the number of people living in a square mile in different communities. To determine social pathology, they used death rate and birth rate figures, inability of parents to care for their children, juvenile delinquency figures, and the number of admissions to mental hospitals.

On first inspection, the results of the animal studies seemed to be generalizable to humans. Densely populated areas did have much greater social pathology than less populated areas. Galle et al. realized, however, that density is highly correlated with income level and ethnic groupings. Poor people and minorities tend to live in densely populated areas—ghettos. Therefore, Galle et al. attempted to control for these factors. For example, they compared the social pathology of poor ghetto blacks with that of poor blacks in moderately populated areas. They found that social pathology was equal despite differences in density.

Similarly, Freedman, Heshka, and Levy (1975) looked at juvenile delinquency rates as a result of density and income level. They found that delinquency was correlated much more strongly with income than with density.

Inside density. There is another way of looking at density. Altman (1975) made a distinction between "inside" and "outside" density. *Outside density* refers to how many people live in a neighborhood or community of some specified size. *Inside density* refers to how many people live in a home or apartment. Inside and outside density are not necessarily correlated. For example, Jacqueline Kennedy Onassis lives in an apartment building with at least 100 other residents and thousands of people on her block (high outside density). But Ms. Onassis' apartment has at least fifteen rooms (low inside density). Conversely, an unemployed coal miner in West Virginia may live in the only house in some rural valley (low outside density), but this house may be a three-bedroom shack inhabited by twelve other people (high inside density). Altman correctly points out that many correlational studies consider only outside density.

If the feeling of being crowded results from invasion of one's personal space, then inside density might be a better predictor of social pathology than outside density. That is, there are probably many more violations of personal space in the coal miner's family than in Ms. Onassis's family.

Galle et al. looked at the relationship between inside density and social pathology. They found that areas with high inside densities had higher rates of all social pathologies (except admissions to mental hospitals) than low inside densities. This was true even when income and race were controlled for. However, Freedman et al. (1975) found no relationship between inside density and crime rates. In studies conducted in Hawaii (Winsborough, 1965) and Hong Kong (Schmitt, 1966), no relationships were found between population density and *any* forms of social pathology.

These correlational studies have one weakness: they don't tell us if the subjects actually felt crowded. Census data will tell you how many people live in a home, but not how they feel about their living arrangements. Thus, these studies do not really show how population density and social pathologies are related. Partially because of this problem, social psychologists have turned to laboratory studies.

The effects of density: Experimental studies

Most laboratory studies have found that men react to density by becoming more hostile, aggressive, competitive, and punitive. Women, however, become more cooperative and friendly[3] (Epstein & Karlin, 1975; Freed-

man, Levy, Buchanan, & Price, 1972; Stokols, Rall, Pinner, & Schopler, 1973).

Thus, most researchers conclude that, at least for men, crowding is stressful (Altman, 1975; Esser, 1972; Stokols, 1972; Worchel & Teddlie, 1976). However, one prominent researcher strongly disagrees.

Jonathan Freedman (1975) believes that the primary effect of crowding is to intensify a person's normal reaction to a situation. If she normally finds the situation pleasant, being crowded will make her feel more pleasant. The reverse is equally true. To test this, Freedman and his associates (Heshka and Levy, cited in Freedman, 1975) conducted the following experiment.

Subjects were placed in either crowded or uncrowded rooms. They then listened to and evaluated speeches each of them gave. Half the subjects in the crowded room were told to praise their peers' speeches, while the other half were told to criticize them. The same instructions were given in the uncrowded room. Then all subjects were asked how they felt about the situation they were in and the other people in the room. Some of the results are summarized in Figure 10-4. The most positive ratings were given by subjects in the crowded room who were praised by their peers. The most negative ratings were given by subjects who were also in the crowded room but whose speeches were criticized.

Freedman's position that crowding, per se, is not harmful is shared by other researchers (e.g., Jacobs, 1961; Moos, 1976). Indeed, Lawrence (1974) has reported that college students living in crowded dormitories enjoyed the experience. Now, we are not coming out in favor of fifteen people living in one room. The point is that there is no *hard* evidence to show that crowding in itself is harmful. Thus, despite the feeling that crowding is bad, the issue remains unresolved. What is the next step? The following factors might be considered.

---

[3]Epstein and Karlin proposed that this difference may be due to sex-linked norms for reactions to stress. They believed that both men and women find crowding stressful, but the norms which influence their reactions to it are quite different. A woman reacts to stress by sharing it with others and working with them to reduce it. Among men, the norm is to hide one's distress. This difference leads women to act more positively and men more negatively when crowded.

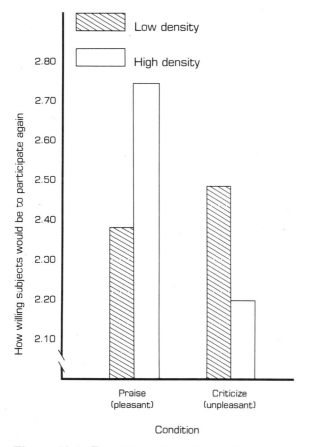

Figure 10-4. The effects of population density and pleasantness of the situation on subjects' willingness to be in the same study again. (Adapted from Freedman, Heshka, & Levy; cited in Freedman, 1975)

Some considerations in evaluating the effects of crowding

First, high density does not always lead to the feeling of being crowded. The social situation and the physical setting may be other important factors. For example, Desor (1972) found that people viewed a waiting room in an airport with a certain density as much more crowded than a cocktail party with the same density. Further, Desor found that the use of partitions in a room could reduce the feeling of crowding.

Second, people react to crowding in different ways. For example, women have smaller personal space zones than men, and Latin Americans have smaller zones than North Americans (Evans & Howard, 1973; Linder 1976). If violations of personal space are related to feelings of being crowded, then these social-cultural differences must be considered.

Third, high density must be considered along with other variables. Will a person in a hot, noisy high-density area feel worse than someone in an equally dense area that is cool and quiet? It would seem important to know the cumulative effects of crowding and such other environmental factors.

Finally, one must consider whether the crowding is long- or short-term. People may be able to cope with crowding for only a short time. Altman (1975) argues that over the long run, a person who must deal with crowding may suffer both physiological and psychological damage.

Human beings are remarkably adaptable. In parts of Hong Kong, they live day in and day out with only thirty-five square feet per person. But there is little evidence of any severe social disorders among them (Linder, 1976). Any theory of crowding will have to explain how people can function under such conditions.

Crowd behavior

Research on crowd behavior, like research on crowding is concerned with the behavior of large numbers of people in small spaces. But these two research areas differ in two important respects. First, crowding can be either long- or short-term; crowd behavior is short-term only. Second, crowding research focuses on the individual; crowd behavior research concerns the crowd as a whole.

People have been writing about crowd behavior for at least 400 years (e.g., Holinshed,

Too close for comfort

Personal space is different for different people (Hall, 1966). For example, people from a Latin culture have a much smaller personal space than do people from northern European cultures. If you've ever watched a conversation between a Latin and an Anglo, the effect of this difference is obvious. The Latin keeps trying to get close, while the Anglo keeps backpedaling to maintain her personal space.

Some researchers have wondered if the size of one's personal space is related to a tendency toward extreme violence (Kinzel, 1970; Lothstein, 1971). Kinzel worked with a group of violent and nonviolent inmates at a large prison. He placed these men in a large room one at a time and told them that he was going to approach them. When a man felt that Kinzel was getting too close, he was to say "Stop."

This procedure was repeated over several weeks.

The differences were dramatic. The size of a violent prisoners' personal space was almost four times larger than for nonviolent prisoners. Further, this difference was strongest when the men were approached from the rear. Two of the violent inmates would not let Kinzel approach them from the rear at all unless they could watch him. As a group, the violent prisoners were much more upset by being approached from the rear, even when they could see the person, than were the nonviolent prisoners.

These findings have led Kinzel and others to propose that some people who have a large personal space may react violently if it is violated.

1577). What is it about crowding that so intrigues people? Milgram and Toch (1969) believed that four aspects of crowd behavior are responsible.

First, there is the apparent irrationality of a crowd's actions. Often it seems to result from emotion rather than reason. Second, crowds seem more likely than individuals acting alone to become violent and destructive. Next, the course of action a crowd "chooses" is often extreme. For example, protestors at the 1968 Democratic convention tossed bags of excrement at passerbys. Meanwhile, the police indiscriminately beat people on the street and on more than one occasion threw people through windows. Finally, a crowd appears to act as a unified mass rather than as a collection of individuals. Early observers of crowd behavior (e.g., Le Bon, 1895) even compared members of a crowd to the parts of a body coordinated by a collective brain.

The crowd

According to Kinch (1973), a *crowd* has four characteristics. 1 It exists for only a short period; 2 its members are in close physical contact; 3 it lacks organizational rules; 4 its members interact spontaneously rather than logically.

A crowd can be active or passive (Brown, 1954). A passive crowd may be a group of people watching a movie or a sports event. They may cheer or laugh or boo, but unless they decide to actually "kill the umpire," they take no action.

By contrast, an active crowd engages in some sort of action, usually to reach some goal. Different crowd goals may be illustrated

Michael Minardi

via the slightly modified plot of an old horror film.

In the movie version of *Frankenstein,* a brilliant yet demented scientist creates a semi-human monster. One night, while the scientist, Count Frankenstein, is away from his castle, the monster breaks loose and strolls into the nearby village. With a sense of timing only a monster could have, it chooses a night when hundreds of villagers are celebrating at their yearly festival. The monster's presence causes a panic, and the goal of the crowd is to *escape.*

The next day, the villagers call a mass meeting to protest the monster's presence. Since Count Frankenstein is believed to be responsible, they march to his castle, waving their protest signs. The crowd's behavior is *expressive.* Their goal is to show their feelings on the issue of unleashed monsters. Count Frankenstein, however, is a smooth talker. He convinces the crowd that whatever they have seen, he knows nothing about it.

As the days pass, the villagers begin to notice that many of their cows, goats, and small children are disappearing. The trail leads to Frankenstein's castle. Now they are angry. They meet again and decide to kill the monster. Their goal is *destruction.* Most researchers describe an angry, destructive crowd as a *mob* (Milgram & Toch, 1969).

If the villagers had looted Frankenstein's castle, after destroying the monster, this would illustrate the final group goal—to *acquire* something.

While most researchers agree on the goals of crowds, there are a number of different views on why crowds act as they do.

Explanations of crowd behavior

The contagion theory. One of the earliest researchers on crowds was the French sociologist Gustave Le Bon (1895, 1903). Le Bon was interested specifically in mob actions. He saw a crowd as violence-prone, acting as a unified mass, and with the reasoning powers of a mentally retarded person. Crowds, according to Le Bon, shifted their attention rapidly, accepted extreme statements without evidence, and were capable of actions unthinkable to individuals.

Le Bon believed that crowd behavior is extreme for three reasons: (1) the anonymity a crowd gives its members, (2) increased suggestibility among the members, and (3) the mechanism of contagion. *Contagion* is the spread of a mood or feeling through a crowd; it is similar to the spread of an infectious disease. Although Le Bon considered suggestibility most important, later researchers seized on contagion. Blumer (1946) considered it the basic mechanism of crowd behavior.

Many researchers (e.g., Turner & Killian, 1972), however, have questioned whether contagion really explains crowd behavior. First, if a mood spreads through a crowd like a disease, then it should infect everyone. This does not occur. For example, the undercover agents who observed the anti-war demonstrations of the late 1960's were not caught up in the revolutionary fervor of the crowd.

Contagion also fails to explain why expressive crowds will often ignore the actions of the leader. Further, the actions of one person can sometimes stop an entire crowd bent on some course of action. To illustrate, consider this instance of crowd behavior involving Mahatma Gandhi. Gandhi had been viewed as a savior by his fellow Hindus, but shortly before India's independence, his defense of the Moslems in India had turned many Hindus against him. In the episode which follows, Gandhi has arrived at the Black Hole of Calcutta to try to keep peace between the two groups. He is confronted by a crowd of angry Hindus.

Faces contorted with rage and hate, they shouted "Go save the Hindus in Noakhali," "Save Hindus, not Moslems," and "Traitor to the Hindus." Then, as Gandhi's car stopped, they produced their welcome for the man half the world believed a saint. They showered the car with stones and bottles.

Slowly, one of its doors opened. The familiar figure emerged. Glasses slipping down his nose, one hand clutching his shawl, the other raised in a gesture of peace, the frail seventy-seven-year-old man walked alone into the mob's shower of stones.

"You wish to do me ill," Gandhi called, "and so I am coming to you."

At that sight, at his words, the demonstrators froze. . . .

"How can I, who am a Hindu by birth, a Hindu by deed, a Hindu of Hindus in my way of living, be an enemy of the Hindus?" he asked his angry countrymen. (Collins & Lapierre, 1975, pp. 270–271)

After saying this, Ghandi promised to talk with the people again and passed unmolested through the mob. If an infection existed among these people, it was a very mild one.

Penner and Dertke (1972) suggested that the major weakness of a contagion theory of crowd behavior is that it begs the "question of the initial sources of the behavior and emotions that supposedly spread through the crowd" (p. 349). In other words, what is the source of the infection? The next two theories attempt to answer question.

The convergence theory. Milgram and Toch (1969) contrast the contagion theory with the *convergence theory* as follows: "If the spread of an infectious disease serves as an analog for contagion models, the lukemia ward of a hospital can illustrate convergence" (p. 551). Convergence theory states that the members of a crowd share some common trait or purpose which causes them to join the crowd. The crowd's behavior is the release of its members' predispositions (Turner & Killian, 1972).

For example, Ransford (1968) found that not all residents of the Watts area of Los Angeles participated in the 1965 race riot. People who had felt alienated and powerless were most likely to join. Cantril (1941) reported that people in a small Southern town reacted to the news of a lynching plan in different ways. Although most of them knew of the lynching, only a few actually took part. These were presumably the most anti-black people.

However, convergence theory cannot explain why a crowd which forms for an expressive purpose (e.g., an anti-busing rally) may become aggressive (e.g., burning school buses). Penner and Dertke (1972) proposed that perhaps contagion and convergence theories can complement each other. Convergence theory might explain why the crowd forms. Contagion theory (with certain modifications) might explain the subsequent actions of the crowd.

The emergent norm theory. Turner and Killian (1972) did not believe that crowds are always made up of people who think or act alike. In its early stages, they said, a crowd is made up of people who have various reasons for being there and who are acting quite differently. For example, in the riot in Kent, Ohio (described on page 000), some of the rioters belonged to a motorcycle gang, some were anti-war activists, and some were apolitical college students looking for a good time. The illusion of crowd unanimity, said Turner and Killian, is due to the actions of a subgroup within the crowd. These people *are* unanimous in their actions; they draw the attention of onlookers and other members of the crowd. Further, onlookers and less involved crowd members are led to believe that the subgroup represents the feelings of the entire crowd (Turner & Killian, 1972).

This unanimous subgroup influences crowd behavior in another important way. It establishes the crowd's norms—its expectations or standards of behavior. Since these norms will be partly related to the situation the crowd is in, Turner and Killian call them *emergent norms.* They emerge from the circumstances surrounding the crowd.

To see how emergent norms operate, let's return to the riot in Kent, Ohio. When the people in the street turned violent and began tossing beer bottles and smashing the windows of a bank, the reaction of one college student was, "That's pretty far out." This reaction was an emergent norm, it was peculiar to the time and place in which the riot occurred. Here were predominantly middle-class college students "trashing" a town.

Unfortunately, the emergent norm theory fails to explain why some emergent norms take hold and others do not. Perhaps contagion theory is needed to explain this. A comprehensive theory of crowd behavior may need to draw on all three of these theoretical approaches.

The study of crowd behavior via broad theories is only one approach to this topic. Other researchers have focused on the physical characteristics of a crowd and the way the crowd operates.

Physical structure of crowds

A crowd begins when something of interest draws people to a specific location. This could be an accident, a scheduled speaker, or any other kind of event. The more people who initially gather, the easier it is to attract additional members (Milgram, Bickman, & Berkowitz, 1969).

At first, members of a crowd will mill about, exchanging information and rumors. As the focus of the crowd becomes clearer, the people will move closer together, forming a ring or semi-circle (depending on physical barriers) around the focus of interest (Milgram & Toch, 1969).

Members of a crowd are not distributed randomly. The most highly involved people position themselves at the center of the ring or front of the semi-circle. This positioning increases the probability that these people can establish emergent norms. You can learn a great deal about a crowd's ideology and commitment by looking at its characteristics once the ring or semi-circle has formed.

For example, you can examine the crowd's *boundary*. This boundary defines who can and cannot enter the crowd and how rigidly this is enforced (Milgram & Toch, 1969). A highly involved, ideologically commited crowd will have sharply defined boundaries and will be closed to outsiders. For example, a crowd of blacks discussing white racism would probably not allow a white person in a Ku Klux Klan uniform to enter. Similarly, a Klan meeting will probably not welcome a black person.

Polarization and density can also tell you something about a crowd. *Polarization* refers to how much attention people pay to the focus of interest. The more highly polarized a crowd is, the more highly involved are its members. *Density* seems to be related to the intensity of the crowd's feelings (Milgram & Toch, 1969). The more intense these feelings are, the closer together the members stand. It is impossible, however, to determine if closeness is due to intensity, or the reverse, as contagion theory might suggest.

These crowd characteristics apply to a stationary crowd. Depending on these and other factors (e.g., contagion, suggestibility, attitudes of the crowd members, emergent norms, rumors), the crowd may disperse, remain stationary, or become a moving crowd (i.e., a mob or a panic; Kinch, 1973).

Rumor

If you have ever been in a mass demonstration, you know the importance of rumor. It has a very strong influence on how the crowd will act. A *rumor* is an unverified statement of fact concerning the topic of interest to the crowd. Rumors are rarely the sole cause of how a crowd acts. However, they do contribute substantially to the crowd's behavior (Milgram & Toch, 1969).

The frequency of a rumor, how rapidly it spreads, and how widely it circulates depend on three things: (1) how much interest there is in the topic of the rumor, (2) how much ambiguity there is about the topic, and (3) how much tension this topic creates (Allport & Postman, 1947; Shibutani, 1966). As these three things increase, *rumor intensity* (incidence, speed, and coverage) also grows. As a rumor spreads, two things happen to its content. First, the content tends to become *leveled*—shorter, more concise, and more easily grasped. Second, it becomes *sharpened,* or focused, on a limited number of details.

Rumors seem to be connected most closely to riots. There is evidence that before a riot starts, rumor intensity is quite high (Norton, 1943; Smelser, 1963). Rumors probably do not cause riots, but they may strongly influence their scope and intensity.

This position receives some support from the National Advisory Commission on Civil Disorders, which was ordered to investigate the causes of the 1967 urban riots. The Commission (1968) saw white racism and rotting ghettos as the primary causes of the riots. But they also believed that rumors played an important role:

Rumors significantly aggravated tension and disorder in more than 65 percent of the disorders studied by the Commission. Sometimes, as in Tampa and New Haven, rumor served as the spark which turned an incident into a civil disorder. Elsewhere, notably Detroit and Newark, even where they were not precipating or motivating factors, inflaming rumors made the job of police and community leaders far more difficult. (Report of the National Advisory Commission on Civil Disorders, 1968, p. 326)

Many law enforcement officials believe that control and prevention of riots depends largely on getting facts rather than rumors to the people. To quote the International Association of Chiefs of Police: "The only antidote for poisonous rumor is fact. Get the facts out promptly and circulate them as widely as possible" (1961, p. 31).

This advice is well intentioned, but rumor

control alone will not prevent riots. As Milgram and Toch (1969) observed, this advice is based on the premise that actual conditions could never be bad enough to provoke a riot. Anyone who has ever been in an inner-city ghetto would realize that this premise is dangerously naive.

Social movements

A *social movement* is "an effort by a large number of people to solve collectively a problem which they feel they have in common" (Toch, 1965, p. 5). The goal of a social movement is to solve this problem by causing social change (McLaughlin, 1976). Unlike crowds, social movements have indefinite life spans. Some may exist for a few weeks. Others, like the black civil rights movement, may exist for more than 100 years.

Preconditions for social movements

Social movements are created when a group of people feel that there is a tremendous gap between their needs and society's ability to fulfil them. There is a problem which demands solution. Thus, grape pickers in California organize because they believe their working conditions and salary must be changed. Gay activists in New York organize because they see the current laws against homosexuality as unfair and repressive.

The existence of a problem alone will not lead to a social movement. Three other things are needed: First, the problem must be seen as serious enough to warrant action. This perception is determined largely by the relative deprivation of a group (Merton, 1957; Pettigrew, 1971). *Relative deprivation* is the belief that compared to other groups in society, your group is deprived. Thus, a comparison with other groups is needed. The concept of relative deprivation may explain why so many whites were bewildered by the black civil rights movement. To the whites, blacks in America were doing well. Blacks thought they were doing quite poorly relative to whites. Relative deprivation will be strongest when conditions for the society *as a whole* are improving. Thus, social movements tend to arise in periods of economic prosperity (McLaughlin, 1976).

Second, the founders of a social movement must believe that the problem can't be solved by the means now available (Toch, 1965). Members of the American Indian Movement may be impelled to action because they believe that the two major political parties and the federal government are either unable or unwilling to solve their problems.

The final and most important precondition for the emergence of a social movement is the belief that the problem can be solved by collective action (McLaughlin, 1976; Toch, 1965; Turner & Killian, 1972). Unless this occurs, a social movement will not begin.

To illustrate, let's compare the behavior of blacks in America and in South Africa. Despite their long history of racial oppression, conditions for black Americans are infinitely better than they are for black South Africans. In South Africa, blacks outnumber whites by twenty to one; yet, they have no say in the country's government. They are forced to live in certain specified regions and must carry "passports" when they travel in white areas. The money spent on black schools relative to white schools is miniscule. Blacks cannot own homes. Many jobs are closed to them, and on these jobs which are open, blacks earn half the pay of whites doing the same work (*New York Times,* August 30, 1976). Nevertheless, it is only in the last few years that blacks in South Africa have organized in large numbers to oppose the racist white government.

In contrast, black Americans have been engaged in widespread, well-organized civil rights activities for at least seventy-five years. What is the reason for the difference in the emergence of social movements?

It is difficult to identify a single overriding reason. However, one important fact is that, unlike South Africa, racial inequities in America were not total and absolute. South Africa's policy of racial separation (apartheid) rigidly enforces the second-class status of blacks. Although many parts of America had laws designed to suppress blacks, there were some opportunities for equal employment and equal education. Thus, blacks were led to have rising expectations and to believe that it was *possible* to remedy their problem.

Even when these three preconditions exist, not every member of the group joins a social movement. The next section discusses the characteristics of those who do join.

Characteristics of members of a social movement

There are many widespread beliefs about the type of people who join a social movement. Let's examine their validity.

One belief is that only members of disadvantaged or oppressed groups join social movements. This is only partly true. Some social movements attract upper-class people as well. For example, many of those involved in the anti-war movement of the 1960's and the women's liberation movement are from the "privileged" social classes (McLaughlin, 1976).

Further, even among the predominantly lower-class social movements, the leaders tend to come from the middle class. For example, Ghandi was a well-educated lawyer. Martin Luther King, Jr., came from a middle-class minister's family and was educated at prestigious schools (e.g., Boston College). Mao Tse Tung, the leader of the "peasant" revolt in China, described his father as a "rich" peasant (Snow, 1938); he was a relatively well-to-do businessman.

A second widely held belief is that social movements attract only political fanatics (cf. Hoffer, 1951). Among the lower classes, this is rarely true. Members of oppressed groups usually join a movement tentatively, with little commitment to its political philosophy (Milgram & Toch, 1969). They are usually attracted to the movement because they believe that it will satisfy some immediate, specific, simple need (Toch, 1965). Saul Alinsky, one of the most effective organizers of poor people in America, operated on this premise. When attempting to attract poor ghetto residents, Alinsky first showed them that he could satisfy their immediate needs (e.g., getting rid of rats). Only much later did he become concerned with political philosophy (Alinsky, 1971).

Liu Shao Chi, a leader of the Chinese Communist movement, complained that the first people who joined it had no understanding of communism. They joined because they saw the movement as a way to avoid unfair taxes and to feed their families. Similarly, one of the first issues Ghandi used in India to attract people was a tax the British rulers had put on salt (Collins & LaPiere, 1975). This is hardly a sophisticated political issue.

College-educated people who join social movements do seem to be primarily attracted by the movement's ideology. Why else do they join? Some people believe that college students may join in rebellion against their parents and society. Let's look at the data on this question.

A number of researchers examined the characteristics of students who joined the anti-war movement in the 1960's. The results don't support the rebellion explanation very well. Most anti-war activists held attitudes and values which were quite similar to their parents' (Haan, Smith, & Block, 1968). For example, Flacks (1967) reported that a majority of activists' fathers opposed the bombing of North Vietnam. In contrast, a majority of the nonactivists' fathers favored the bombing.

More generally, these students' involvement in the anti-war movement was consistent with their upbringing. McLaughlin (1976) described the typical family background: "[The anti-war activist was] from upper middle class, professional families, raised in (a) permissive environment where the political outlook was liberal, where children were socialized to be concerned with problems of social justice . . . academic values were [stressed]" (p. 447). Another study found that these middle-class activists were more independent and sociable than nonactivists. The two groups did not differ in emotional stability, intelligence, or sense of responsibility (Kerpelman, 1970).

Thus, it appears that not all joiners of social movements are motivated by political philosophy. And those who are seem to be manifesting the values they were socialized to hold.

If this is true, why do so many people believe that social movements consist of dogmatic fanatics and extremists? One reason is that some social movements do attract fanatics. And these people are much more likely to attract attention than the more rational members of the movement. Also, the actions of social movements are often quite extreme (e.g., mass marches, sit-ins). Attribution theory (cf. Chapter Three) tells us that observers will tend to attribute a person's behavior to his personality if the behavior is extreme, unexpected, or socially undesirable. Thus, participation in a demonstration which accidentally turns violent may cause observers to see the participants as violent.

At this point, you may find yourself becoming frustrated. What about the Ku Klux Klan or the Symbionese Liberation Army? Aren't members of these organizations dogmatic extremists? The answer is, yes. But as Milgram and Toch (1969) have pointed out, this fanaticism is probably the *result* of membership rather than the *cause*.

The effects of belonging to a social movement

Milgram and Toch identified several processes which may operate in social movements to produce fanaticism. First, some social movements see the changing of their members' personalities, attitudes, and values as their initial goal (McLaughlin, 1976). These movements believe that in order to change a society, it is necessary to change the personality of the people in it. When enough people change, so will the society. Certain aspects of the women's liberation movement illustrate this approach.

From the beginning of this movement, one of its integral components was the consciousness-raising group. The goal of this group was not to plan specific political actions but to change a woman's view of herself and the world. It was felt that when women took pride in themselves and stopped seeing themselves primarily as wives and mothers, the goals of the movement could be achieved.

Even if a movement does not set out to change its members, the change may occur. The beliefs that a person tentatively holds when she joins the movement are confirmed and reinforced by the leaders and the other members. Theories of attitude change and development tell us that this process will result in attitudes which are more extreme and more strongly held. Further, the members of the movement come to depend on their leaders and accept their viewpoints uncritically (Milgram & Toch, 1969). Thus, members may come to express their ideas by spouting the party line.

With increasing involvement in a social movement, a member may become emotionally as well as ideologically committed. This may produce "an increasingly dogmatic and irreversible attachment to membership [in the social movement]" (Milgram & Toch, 1969, p. 594).

As a result of these processes, a member of a social movement may come to see the world in a close-minded, dogmatic fashion. For example, in the 1950's America suffered a number of reversals in its foreign policy. Some members of the ultra-conservative John Birch Society explained these reversals by proposing that President Dwight D. Eisenhower was an agent of the Russian Communists. Such a simplistic view of the world makes it quite easy for an observer to conclude that all people who join social movements are close-minded dogmatists.

Conclusion

The second half of this chapter was concerned with collective behavior. Collective behavior, like organizational behavior, occurs in large groups but differs from it in several respects. Two of the more important differences are these: (1) Organizational behavior is governed by rules of procedure, while collective behavior is usually spontaneous and unplanned; (2) Organizational behavior is governed by and in accord with the norms of society; collective behavior is not.

The first topic examined was the effect of crowding on people's behavior. Strictly speaking, crowding is not collective behavior (because the unit of analysis is an individual rather than a group). However, we felt that crowding shared enough characteristics with other forms of collective behavior to justify its inclusion. Does being crowded have negative psychological effects on humans? The answer to that question is a *very* tentative yes. Being crowded generates arousal in a person, and the resultant feelings and behavior are often quite negative. But three important qualifications must be added. First, people differ greatly in their perceptions of crowding and their reaction to it. Humans are remarkably adaptive organisms, and some seem to thrive under crowded conditions. Second, there is evidence that the negative effects of crowding may depend upon other aspects of the environment. If these other aspects are negative, crowding may intensify a person's negative reactions. But in positive settings, crowding may increase positive feelings. Finally, the important effects of crowding probably occur over the long run. As yet, there is no hard evidence on whether people can adapt to being crowded or if crowding eventually takes its toll on people.

The review of crowd behavior and social movements presented theories on their behavior and descriptions of their important char-

acteristics. Note that these two topics generally do not involve laboratory studies. Such studies are difficult if not impossible to carry out. This is not necessarily bad. In fact, Gergen (1975) has eloquently argued for the superiority of observational research over the traditional laboratory approach. While we endorse Gergen's point of view, the research on crowds and social movements points up some of the perils in this approach. In the absence of controlled tests, one's conclusions about the causes of some phenomenon may be colored by one's own values and opinions. For example, crowd behavior has been assumed to be violent and irrational. There is no hard evidence of this (Milgram & Toch, 1969). Social movements were believed to be made up of hard-core crackpots. Subsequent research has challenged this idea. Thus, extreme caution and intelligence must be used when dealing with social phenomena in the real world. One must recognize the historical and situational limitations on the conclusions one draws (Gergen, 1973; 1975). More important, one must be sensitive to one's own biases. It is difficult to remove yourself from your treatment of crowds and social movements. If you disagree with some of the conclusions we have drawn, perhaps this is the reason.

REVIEW QUESTIONS

(Ten out of twelve is passing)

1. Whereas organizational behavior is usually _____ and in accord with society's _____ , collective behavior is usually _____ and may be in opposition to society's _____ . (p. 322)
2. _____ is a physical concept which refers to how many people are in a specified area. _____ is a psychological concept which refers to people's reactions to being with large numbers of other people. (p. 324)

3. Living in a room with nine other people (high inside density) is more likely to lead to invasions of a person's _____ _____ than living in a spacious apartment in a high-rise building (high outside density). (p. 325)

4. A group of citizens carrying protest signs in front of the White House is a crowd with a(n) _____ goal. If this crowd decides to sack and loot the White House to give vent to its feelings, it has become a(n) _____ . (p. 329)

5. The theory which proposes that a crowd's irrational behavior is due to a virus which spreads through the crowd is called the _____ theory of crowd behavior. (p. 330)

6. The theory of crowd behavior which proposes that a crowd's actions merely reflect the attitudes and values of its members is called the _____ theory. (p. 330)

7. One effect of a fiery speaker who incites a crowd to riot might be to establish a(n) _____ _____ for the crowd. (p. 331)

8. The extent to which members are attending to the focus of interest of the crowd (e.g., a speaker) is called the degree of _____ in the crowd. (p. 332)

9. The tendency of rumors to focus on a limited number of details is called _____ . (p. 332)

10. The effort by a large number of people to solve a problem they feel they share is called a(n) _____ _____ . (p. 333)

11. One of the preconditions for a social movement is the feeling that compared to other groups, your group is doing poorly. This is called _____ _____ . (p. 334)

12. One reason why some members of social movements are dogmatic and extreme in their beliefs is that social movements may _____ rather than _____ fanatics. (p. 336)

ANSWERS

1. planned, norms; unplanned, norms   2. density, crowding   3. personal space   4. expressive, mob   5. contagion   6. convergence   7. emergent norm   8. polarization   9. sharpening   10. social movement   11. relative deprivation   12. cause, attract

SUGGESTED READINGS

For some reason, books about people in large groups are exceptionally well written. Here are the ones we like.

Textbooks

Organizational Behavior

Organization Development: Its Nature, Origins and Prospects, by Warren Bennis. This book is intended for nonpsychologists. It presents an interesting and informative discussion of the field of organizational development.

Organizational Behavior, by Abraham Korman. This book takes an approach which is quite similar to ours. Korman integrates a number of social psychological concepts into his review of people's behavior in organizations.

Organizational Psychology, by Edgar Schein. Schein has provided a good deal of information about organizational theory and the behavior of people in organizations in this short, readable book.

Collective Behavior

The Environment and Social Behavior, by Irwin Altman, presents a thoughtful and scholarly discussion of how crowding and other environmental factors may affect our behavior.

Crowding and Behavior, by Jonathan Freedman. In this entertaining book, Freedman discusses the research on crowding and his view of how being crowded affects humans.

Collective Behavior and Social Movements, by Stanley Milgram and Hans Toch. (Volume 4 of *The Handbook of Social Psychology*). This is an excellent review of the theory and research on crowd behavior and social movements. We can't recommend it too highly.

The Social Psychology of Social Movements, by Hans Toch. Although this book is fifteen years old, the ideas it presents about social movements are still applicable today.

Popular literature

Many popular books have recently been written about people in large groups. They are enjoyable and informative.

Organizational Behavior

The Gamesman, by Michael Maccoby. Maccoby provides a very interesting description of the type of people who work in large organizations and the roles they play.

Working, by Studs Terkel. To find out how people see their jobs, Terkel spent two years interviewing people in a wide variety of occupations. They ranged from a prostitute to a corporation executive. This is an incredibly good book.

Up the Organization, by Peter Townsend. A former organization man presents a less than complimentary view of big business in America.

Piano Player, by Kurt Vonnegut, Jr. Before becoming a full-time author, Vonnegut worked for a large organization. This fictionalized account of life in a big company is amusing and informative.

Collective Behavior

Either *Confrontation at Kent State: 13 Seconds,* by Joe Eszterhas and Michael Roberts, or *Kent State,* by James Michener. Both books describe the events surrounding the shooting of four students at Kent State University in 1970. They provide excellent illustrations of collective behavior.

Sisterhood Is Powerful, edited by Robin Morgan. This collection of essays written by feminists provides an excellent illustration of the ideology of one social movement.

Miami and the Seige of Chicago, by Norman Mailer. Few authors are more talented than Mailer. This talent comes through in Mailer's description of the riots at the Democratic Convention in Chicago in 1968.

Red Star Over China, by Edgar Snow. Snow lived with Mao Tse Tung and the other leaders of the Chinese Communist revolution during the 1930's. His description of the early days of this social movement illustrates many of the concepts we've discussed.

REFERENCES

Abate, M., & Berrien, F. K. Validation of stereotypes: Japanese versus American students. *Journal of Personality and Social Psychology.* 1967, *7,* 435–438.

Abelson, R. P., & Miller, J. C. Negative persuasion via personal insult. *Journal of Experimental Social Psychology.* 1967, *3,* 321–333.

Adams, J. S. Inequity in social exchange. In L. Berkowitz (Ed.), *Advances in experimental social psychology* (Vol. 2). New York: Academic Press, 1965.

"Addie." *Christopher for president.* New York: Golden Press, 1973.

Adorno, T., Frenkel-Brunswik, E., Levinson, D., & Sanford, N. *The authoritarian personality.* New York: Harper, 1950.

Alinsky, S. D. *Rules for radicals.* New York: Vintage Books, 1971.

Allen, V. L. Situational factors in conformity. In L. Berkowitz (Ed.), *Advances in experimental social psychology* (Vol. 2). New York: Academic Press, 1965.

Allen, V. L. Effect of social support on fear of group sanction. Unpublished manuscript. University of Wisconsin, 1966. Cited by R. Willis and J. Levine. Interpersonal influence and conformity. In B. Seidenberg & A. Snadowsky (Eds.), *Social psychology.* New York: Free Press, 1976.

Allen, V. L., & Crutchfield, R. S. Generalization of experimentally reinforced conformity. *Journal of Abnormal and Social Psychology.* 1963, *67,* 326–333.

Allport, F. H. The influence of the group upon association and thought. *Journal of Experimental Psychology.* 1920, *3,* 159–182.

Allport, F. H. The J-curve hypothesis of conforming behavior. *Journal of Social Psychology.* 1934, *5,* 141–143.

Allport, G. W. Attitudes. In C. Murchison (Ed.), *Handbook of social psychology.* Worcester, Mass.: Clark University Press, 1935.

Allport, G. W. *Personality.* New York: Holt, 1937.

Allport, G. W. Motivation in personality: Reply to Mr. Bertocci. *Psychological Review.* 1940, *47,* 533–554.

Allport, G. W. Geneticism versus ego-structure in theories of personality. *British Journal of Educational Psychology.* 1946, *16,* 57–68.

Allport, G. W. The historical background of modern social psychology. In G. Lindzey & E. Aronson (Eds.), *The handbook of social psychology* (Vol. 1). Reading, Mass.: Addison-Wesley, 1968.

Allport, G. W., & Postman, L. *The psychology of rumor.* New York: Holt, 1947.

Alper, T. G. The relationship between role orientation and achievement motivation. *Journal of Personality.* 1973, *41,* 9–31.

Alper, T. G., & Greenberg, E. Relationship of picture structure to achievement motivation in college women. *Journal of Personality and Social Psychology.* 1967, *7,* 362–371.

Altman, I. *The environment and social behavior.* Monterey, Calif.: Brooks/Cole, 1975.

Altus, W. D. Birth order and its sequela. *Science.* 1966, *151,* 44–49.

The American Heritage Dictionary of the English Language. Boston, Mass.: Houghton Mifflin, 1971.

Anderson, A. B. Combined effects of interpersonal attraction and goal-path clarity on cohesiveness of task oriented groups. *Journal of Personality and Social Psychology.* 1975, *31,* 68–75.

Anderson, N. H. Test of a model of opinion change. *Journal of Abnormal and Social Psychology.* 1959, *59,* 371–381.

Anderson, N. H., & Hovland, C. I. The representation of order effects in communication research (Appendix A). In C. I. Hovland (Ed.), *The order of presentation in persuasion.* New Haven, Conn.: Yale University Press, 1957.

Anderson, N. H., & Jacobson, A. Effects of stimulus inconsistency and discounting instructions in personality impression formation. *Journal of Personality and Social Psychology.* 1965, *3,* 531–539.

Arendt, H. *Eichmann in Jerusalem.* New York: Viking, 1963.

Argyle, M. *Social interaction.* New York: Atherton, 1969.

Argyle, M., & Dean, J. Eye contact, distance and affiliation. *Sociometry.* 1965, *28,* 289–304.

Argyris, C. *Integrating the individual and the organization.* New York: Wiley, 1964.

Aronfreed, J. *Conduct and conscience.* New York: Academic Press, 1968.

Aronfreed, J. The socialization of altruistic and sympathetic behavior: Some theoretical and experimental analyses. In J. MacCauley & L. Berkowitz (Eds.), *Altruism and helping behavior.* New York: Academic Press, 1970.

Aronfreed, J., & Paskal, V. *Altruism, empathy, and the conditioning of positive affect.* Unpublished manuscript, University of Pennsylvania, 1965.

Aronoff, J. *Psychological needs and cultural systems.* Princeton, N.J.: Van Nostrand, 1967.

Aronoff, J., & Mess'e, L. A. Motivational determinants of small group structure. *Journal of Personality and Social Psychology.* 1971, *17,* 319–324.

Aronson, E. The need for achievement as measured by graphic expression. In J. W. Atkinson (Ed.), *Motives in fantasy, action and society.* Princeton, N.J.: Van Nostrand, 1958.

Aronson, E. The theory of cognitive dissonance: A current perspective. In L. Berkowitz (Ed.), *Advances in experimental social psychology* (Vol. 4). New York: Academic Press, 1969.

Aronson, E., & Carlsmith, J. M. Experimentation in social psychology. In G. Lindzey & E. Aronson (Eds.), *The handbook of social psychology* (Vol. 2). Reading, Mass.: Addison-Wesley, 1968.

Aronson, E., & Linder, D. Gain and loss of esteem as determinants of interpersonal attraction. *Journal of Experimental Social Psychology.* 1965, *1,* 156–171.

Aronson, E., & Mills, J. The effects of severity of initiation on liking for a group. *Journal of Abnormal and Social Psychology.* 1959, *59,* 177–181.

Aronson, E., Turner, J. A., & Carlsmith, J. M. Communicator credibility and communicator discrepancy as determinants of opinion change. *Journal of Abnormal and Social Psychology.* 1963, *67,* 31–36.

Asch, S. E. Forming impressions of personality. *Journal of Abnormal and Social Psychology.* 1946, *41,* 258–290.

Asch, S. E. Effects of group pressure upon the modification and distortion of judgments. In H. Guetzkow (Ed.), *Groups, leadership and men.* Pittsburgh, Pa.: Carnegie Press, 1951.

Asch, S. E. Studies of independence and conformity: A minority of one against a unanimous majority. *Psychological Monographs.* 1956, *70* (9), 177–190.

Ashour, A. S. The contingency model of leadership effectiveness: An evaluation. *Organizational Behavior and Human Performance.* 1973, *9,* 339–355(a).

Ashour, Λ. S. Further discussion of Fiedler's contingency model of leadership effectiveness. *Organizational Behavior and Human Performance.* 1973, *9,* 369–376(b).

Ashmore, R. D. The problem of intergroup prejudice. In *Social psychology* by Barry E. Collins. Reading, Mass.: Addison-Wesley, 1970.

Atkinson, J. W. *An introduction to motivation.* Princeton, N.J.: Van Nostrand, 1964.

Austin, W., & Susmilch, C. Comment on Lane and Mess'e's confusing clarification of equity theory. *Journal of Personality and Social Psychology.* 1974, *30,* 400–404.

Back, K. W. Influence through social communication. *Journal of Abnormal and Social Psychology.* 1951, *46,* 9–23.

Backman, C. W., & Secord, P. F. The effect of perceived liking on interpersonal attraction. *Human Relations.* 1959, *12,* 379–384.

Bakke, F. W. *The fusion process.* New Haven, Conn.: Labor and Management Center, Yale University, 1953.

Bales, R. F. *Interaction process analysis: A method for the study of small groups.* Cambridge, Mass.: Addison-Wesley, 1950.

Bales, R. F. Task roles and social roles in problem solving groups. In E. E. Maccoby, T. M. Newcomb, & E. L. Hartley (Eds.), *Readings in social psychology.* (3rd Ed.) New York: Holt, 1958.

Bales, R. F. *Personality and interpersonal behavior.* New York: Holt, 1970.

Bales, R. F., & Strodtbeck, F. L. Phases in group problem solving. *Journal of Abnormal and Social Psychology.* 1951, *46,* 485–495.

Bandura, A. *Social learning theory.* New York: General Learning Press, 1971.

Bandura, A. *Aggression: A social learning analysis.* Englewood Cliffs, N.J.: Prentice-Hall, 1973.

Bandura, A. The relationships of family patterns to child behavior disorders. Cited in A. Bandura, *Aggression: A social learning analysis.* Englewood Cliffs, N.J.: Prentice-Hall, 1973.

Bandura, A., Ross, D., & Ross, S. A. Imitation of film mediated aggressive models. *Journal of Abnormal and Social Psychology.* 1963, *66,* 3–11.

Bandura, A., & Walters, R. H. *Adolescent aggression.* New York: Ronald Press, 1959.

Bandura, A., & Walters, R. H. *Social learning and personality development.* New York: Holt, 1963.

Bannister, D. Psychology as an exercise in paradox. *Bulletin of the British Psychological Society.* 1966, *19,* 21–26.

Barber, T. X., & Silver, M. J. Fact, fiction, and the experimenter bias effect. *Psychological Bulletin Monograph Supplement.* 1968, *70,* 1–29.

Bard, M. The study and modification of intra-familial violence. In J. L. Singer (Ed.), *The control of aggression and violence.* New York: Academic Press, 1971.

Bardwick, J. M., & Douvan, E. Ambivalence: The socialization of women. In J. M. Bardwick (Ed.), *Readings on the psychology of women.* New York: Harper, 1972, 52–58.

Baron, R. A. Behavioral effects of interpersonal attraction: Compliance with requests from liked and disliked others. *Psychonomic Science.* 1971, *25,* 325–326.

Baron, R. A. *Threatened retaliation as an inhibitor of human aggression.* Paper presented at Midwestern Psychological Association. Chicago, Ill., May, 1973.

Baron, R. A. Aggression as a function of victim's pain cues, level of prior anger arousal and exposure to an aggressive model. *Journal of Personality and Social Psychology.* 1974, *29,* 117–124(a).

Baron, R. A. The aggression-inhibiting influence of heightened sexual arousal. *Journal of Personality and Social Psychology.* 1974, *30,* 318–322(b).

Baron, R. A., & Bell, P. A. Effects of heightened sexual arousal on physical aggression. *Proceedings of American Psychological Association,* 81st Annual Convention, 1973, 171–172.

Baron, R. A., & Bell, P. A. Aggression and heat: Mediating effects of prior provocation and exposure to an aggressive model. *Journal of Personality and Social Psychology.* 1975, *31,* 825–832.

Baron, R. A., & Bell, P. A. Aggression and heat: The effect of ambient temperature, negative affect and a cooling drink on physical aggression. *Journal of Personality and Social Psychology.* 1976, *33,* 245–255.

Baron, R. A., & Lawton, S. F. Environmental influences on aggression: The facilitation of modeling effects by high ambient temperatures. *Psychonomic Science.* 1972, *26,* 80–82.

Baruch, R. The achievement motive: Implications for career development. *Journal of Personality and Social Psychology.* 1967, *5,* 260–267.

Bass, B. M. *Leadership, psychology, and organizational behavior.* New York: Harper, 1960.

Bass, B. M. *Organizational psychology.* Boston, Mass.: Allyn and Bacon, 1965.

Bavelas, A. Communication patterns in task-oriented groups. *Journal of the Acoustical Society of America.* 1950, *22,* 725–730.

Beach, F. A. It's all in your mind. *Psychology Today.* 1969, *3,* 33–35.

Bell, G. B., & French, R. L. Consistency of individual leadership position in small groups of varying membership. *Journal of Abnormal and Social Psychology.* 1950, *47,* 49–56.

Bem, D. J. An experimental analysis of self-persuasion. *Journal of Experimental Social Psychology.* 1965, *1,* 199–218.

Bem, D. J. Self-perception: An alternative interpretation of cognitive dissonance phenomena. *Psychological Review.* 1967, *74,* 183–200.

Bem, D. J. Self-perception theory. In L. Berkowitz (Ed.), *Advances in experimental social psychology* (Vol. 6). New York: Academic Press, 1972.

Bem, D. J., & Allen, A. On predicting some of the people some of the time. The search for cross-situational consistencies in behavior. *Psychological Review.* 1974, *81,* 506–520.

Bem, D. J., Wallach, M. A., & Kogan, N. Group decision making under risk of aversive consequences. *Journal of Personality and Social Psychology.* 1965, *1,* 453–460.

Bem, S. L. The measurement of psychological androgyny. *Journal of Consulting and Clinical Psychology*. 1974, *42*, 155–162.

Bem, S. L. Sex role adaptability: One consequence of psychological androgyny. *Journal of Personality and Social Psychology*. 1975,*31*, 634–643.

Bendig, A. W. Predictive and postdictive validity of need achievement measures. *Journal of Educational Research*. 1958, *52*, 119–120.

Bennis, W. G. *Organizational development: Its nature, origins, and prospects*. Reading, Mass.: Addison-Wesley, 1969.

Berkowitz, L. Anti-semitism and the displacement of aggression. *Journal of Abnormal and Social Psychology*. 1959, *59*, 182–188.

Berkowitz, L. The concept of aggressive drive: Some additional considerations. In L. Berkowitz (Ed.), *Advances in experimental social psychology* (Vol. 2). New York: Academic Press, 1965.

Berkowitz, L. (Ed.) *The roots of aggression*. New York: Atherton, 1969.

Berkowitz, L. The "weapons effect" deviant characteristics, and the myth of the compliant subject. *Journal of Personality and Social Psychology*. 1971, *20*, 332–338.

Berkowitz, L. Social norms, feelings, and other factors affecting helping and altruism. In L. Berkowitz (Ed.), *Advances in experimental social psychology* (Vol. 6). New York: Academic Press, 1972.

Berkowitz, L. The case for bottling up rage. *Psychology Today*. 1973, *7*, 24–31.

Berkowitz, L. *A survey of social psychology*. Hinsdale, Ill.: Dryden Press, 1975.

Berkowitz, L., & Geen, R. C. Film violence and the cue properties of available targets. *Journal of Personality and Social Psychology*. 1966, *3*, 525–530.

Berkowitz, L., & Le Page, A. Weapons as aggression eliciting stimuli. *Journal of Personality and Social Psychology*. 1967, *7*, 202–207.

Berkowitz, L., & McCauley, J. *Altruism and helping behavior*. New York: Academic Press, 1970.

Berkowitz, L., & Walster, E. *Equity theory: Toward a general theory of social interaction: Advances in experimental social psychology*. (Vol. 9). New York: Academic Press, 1976.

Berscheid, E., Boye, D., & Walster, E. Retaliation as a means of restoring equity. *Journal of Personality and Social Psychology*. 1968, *10*, 370–376.

Berscheid, E., & Walster, E. H.*Interpersonal attraction*. Reading, Mass.: Addison-Wesley, 1969.

Berscheid, E., & Walster, E. H. Physical attractiveness. In L. Berkowitz (Ed.), *Advances in experimental social psychology* (Vol. 7). New York: Academic Press, 1974.

Bickman, L. Social roles and uniforms: Clothes make the person. *Psychology Today*. 1974, *7*, 48–51.

Biondo, J., & McDonald, A. P. Internal-external locus of control and response to influence attempts. *Journal of Personality*. 1971,*39*, 407–419.

Birchler, G. R., Weiss, R. L., & Vincent, J. P. Multimethod analysis of social reinforcement exchange between maritally distressed and nondistressed spouse and stranger dyads. *Journal of Personality and Social Psychology*. 1975, *31*, 349–360.

Blake, R. R., & Mouton, J. S. *The managerial grid*. Houston, Texas: Gulf Publishing, 1964.

Blake, R. R., & Mouton, J. *Building a dynamic corporation through grid organization development*. Reading, Mass.: Addison-Wesley, 1969.

Blake, R. R., Mouton, J. S., Barnes, L. B., & Greiner, L. E. Breakthrough in organizational development. *Harvard Business Review*. 1964, *42*(6), 133–155.

Blalock, H. M. *Toward a theory of minority group relations*. New York: Wiley, 1967.

Blauner, R. Work satisfaction and industrial trends in modern society. In W. Galenson & S. Lipset (Eds.), *Labor and trade unionism*. New York: Wiley, 1960.

Blauner, R. *Alienation and freedom: The factory worker and his industry*. Chicago: University of Chicago Press, 1965.

Block, J. Personality characteristics associated with father's attitudes toward child rearing. *Child Development*. 1955, *26*, 41–48.

Block, J., Von der Lippe, A., & Block, J. H. Sex role and socialization patterns: Some personality concomitants and environmental antecedents. *Journal of Consulting and Clinical Psychology*. 1973, *41*, 321–341.

Blumer, H. Collective behavior. In A. M. Lee (Ed.),

New outline of the principles of sociology. New York: Barnes & Noble, 1946, 165–220.

Bobbitt, H. R., Jr., Breinholt, R. H., Doktor, R. H., & McNaul, J. P. *Organizational behavior, understanding and prediction.* Englewood Cliffs, N.J.: Prentice-Hall, 1974.

Bond, M. H. Effect of impression set on subsequent behavior. *Journal of Personality and Social Psychology.* 1972, *24,* 301–305.

Bonner, H. *Group dynamics: Principles and applications.* New York: Ronald Press, 1959.

Borofsky, G. L., Stollak, G. E., & Mess'e, L. A. Sex differences in bystander reactions to physical assaults. *Journal of Experimental Social Psychology.* 1971, *7,* 313–318.

Bostow, D. E., & Bailey, J. S. Modification of severe disruptive and aggressive behavior using brief timeout and reinforcement procedures. *Journal of Applied Behavior Analysis.* 1969, *2,* 31–37.

Bowers, K. S. Situationism in psychology: An analysis and critique. *Psychological Review.* 1973, *80,* 307–336.

Braginsky, D. D. *Machiavellianism and manipulative interpersonal behavior in children.* Unpublished doctoral dissertation. University of Connecticut, 1966.

Bramel, D. Interpersonal attraction, hostility, and perception. In J. Mills (Ed.), *Experimental social psychology.* New York: Macmillan, 1969.

Brehm, J. W. *A theory of psychological reactance.* New York: Academic Press, 1966.

Brehm, J. W., & Cohen, A. R. *Explorations in cognitive dissonance.* New York: Wiley, 1962.

Brigham, J. C. Ethnic stereotypes. *Psychological Bulletin.* 1971, *76,* 15–38.

Brookmire, D. Pro and anti-social behavior as a function of personality and situational variables. Unpublished masters thesis. University of South Florida, 1976.

Brown, B. S. How women see their roles: A change in attitudes. *New Dimensions in Mental Health.* U.S. Dept. of Health, Education and Welfare, September, 1976.

Brown, R. W. Mass phenomena. In G. Lindzey (Ed.), *Handbook of social psychology* (Vol. 2). Reading, Mass.: Addison-Wesley, 1954.

Brown, R. *Social psychology.* New York: Free Press, 1965.

Broverman, I. K., Broverman, D. M., Clarkson, F. E., & Rosenkrantz, P. S. Sex role stereotypes: A current appraisal. *Journal of Social Issues.* 1972, *28,* 59–78.

Broxton, J. A method of predicting roommate compatibility for college freshmen. *Journal of the National Association of Women Deans and Counselors.* 1962, *25,* 169–174.

Bryan, J. H. Children's cooperation and helping behavior. *Review of Child Development Research* (Vol. 5). Chicago: University of Chicago Press, 1975.

Bryan, J. H., & London, P. Altruistic behavior by children. *Psychological Bulletin.* 1970, *73,* 200–211.

Bryan, J. H., & Walbek, N. H. The impact of words and deeds concerning altruism upon children. *Child Development.* 1970, *41,* 747–757. (a)

Bryan, J. H., & Walbek, N. H. Preaching and practicing generosity: Children's actions and reactions. *Child Development.* 1970, *41,* 329–353. (b)

Bugliosi, V., & Gentry, C. *Helter Skelter.* New York: Bantam Books, 1975.

Burnstein, E., & McRae, A. V. Some effects of shared threat and prejudice in racially mixed groups. *Journal of Abnormal and Social Psychology.* 1962, *64,* 257–263.

Burnstein, E., & Worchel, P. Arbitrariness of frustration and its consequences for aggression in a social situation. *Journal of Personality.* 1962, *30,* 528–554.

Buss, A. H. Aggression pays. In J. L. Singer (Ed.), *The control of aggression and violence.* New York: Academic Press, 1971.

Buss, A. H., Booker, A., & Buss, E. Firing a weapon and aggression. *Journal of Personality and Social Psychology.* 1972, *22,* 296–302.

Byrne, D. Interpersonal attraction and attitude similarity. *Journal of Abnormal and Social Psychology.* 1961, *62,* 713–715.

Byrne, D. Attitudes and attraction. In L. Berkowitz (Ed.), *Advances in experimental social psychology* (Vol. 4). New York: Academic Press, 1969.

Byrne, D., & Blalock, B. Similarity and assumed similarity of attitudes between husbands and wives. *Journal of Abnormal and Social Psychology.* 1963, *67,* 636–640.

Byrne, D., Griffitt, W., & Stefaniak, D. Attraction and similarity of personality characteristics. *Journal of Personality and Social Psychology.* 1967, *5,* 82–90.

Byrne, D., & Wong, J. Racial prejudice, interpersonal attraction, and assumed dissimilarity of attitudes. *Journal of Abnormal and Social Psychology.* 1962, *65,* 884–889.

Calder, B. J., & Ross, M. *Attitudes and behavior.* Morristown, N.J.: General Learning Press, 1972.

Calhoun, J. B. Population density and social pathology. *Scientific American.* 1962, *206,* 139–148.

Campbell, D. T. Conformity in psychology's theories of acquired behavioral dispositions. In I. A. Berg & B. M. Bass (Eds.), *Conformity and deviation.* New York: Harper, 1961.

Campbell, D. T. Stereotypes and the perception of group differences. *American Psychologist.* 1967, *22,* 817–829.

Campbell, D. T. On the conflicts between biological and social evolution and between psychology and moral tradition. *American Psychologist.* 1975, *30,* 1103–1116.

Campbell, D. T., Kruskal, W. H., & Wallace, W. P. Seating aggregation as an index of attitude. *Sociometry.* 1966, *29,* 1–5.

Campbell, D. T., & Stanley, J. C. *Experimental and quasi-experimental designs for research.* Chicago, Ill.: Rand McNally, 1966.

Campus, N. Transituational consistency as a dimension of personality. *Journal of Personality and Social Psychology.* 1974, *29,* 593–600.

Cann, A., Sherman, S. J., & Elkes, R. Effects of initial request size and timing of a second request on compliance: The foot in the door and the door in the face. *Journal of Personality and Social Psychology.* 1975, *32,* 774–782.

Cannell, C. F., & Kahn, R. L. Interviewing. In G. Lindzey & E. Aronson (Eds.), *The handbook of social psychology* (Vol. 2). Reading, Mass.: Addison-Wesley, 1968.

Cantril, H. *The psychology of social movements.* New York: Wiley, 1941.

Caplan, N. The new ghetto man: A review of recent empirical studies. *Journal of Social Issues.* 1970, *26,* 59–74.

Carlsmith, J. M., Collins, B. E., & Helmreich, R. L. Studies in forced compliance I: The effect of pressure for compliance on attitude change produced by face to face role playing and anonymous essay writing. *Journal of Personality and Social Psychology.* 1966, *4,* 1–13.

Carlsmith, J. M., & Gross, A. E. Some effects of guilt on compliance. *Journal of Personality and Social Psychology.* 1969, *11,* 232–239.

Carter, R. *The sixteenth round: From number 1 contender to #45472.* New York: Warner Books, 1975.

Cartwright, D. Risk taking by individuals and groups: An assessment of research employing choice dilemmas. *Journal of Personality and Social Psychology.* 1971, *29,* 361–378.

Cartwright, D., & Zander, A. The structural properties of groups: Introduction. In D. Cartwright and A. Zander (Eds.), *Group dynamics research and theory.* (3rd ed.) New York: Harper, 1968.

Cattell, R. B., & Nesselroade, J. R. Likeness and completeness theories examined by 16 personality factor measures on stably and unstably married couples. *Journal of Personality and Social Psychology.* 1967, *7,* 351–361.

Chance, J. E. Internal control of reinforcement and the school learning process. Paper presented at the meeting of the Society for Research in Child Development, Minneapolis, Minn. March 1965.

Chasen, B. G., & Weinberg, S. L. Diagnostic sex role bias: How can we measure it? *Journal of Personality Assessment.* 1975, *39,* 620–629.

Chein, I. Behavior theory and the behavior of attitudes: Some critical comments. *Psychological Review.* 1948, *3,* 175–188.

Choo, T. Communicator credibility and communication discrepancy as determinants of opinion change. *Journal of Social Psychology.* 1964, *64,* 1–20.

Christie, R., & Geis, F. L. *Studies in machiavellianism.* New York: Academic Press, 1970.

Christy, P. R., Gelfand, D. M., & Hartmann, D. P. Effects of competition-induced frustration on two classes of modeled behavior. *Developmental Psychology.* 1971, *5,* 104–111.

Cialdini, R. B., Darby, B. L., & Vincent, J. E. Transgression and altruism: A case for hedonism. *Journal of Experimental Social Psychology.* 1973, *9,* 502–516.

Clark, C. C. Communication, conflict and the portrayal of ethnic minorities. Unpublished manuscript, Stanford University, 1972.

Clark, J. V. A preliminary investigation of some unconscious assumptions affecting labor efficiency in eight supermarkets. Unpublished doctoral dissertation, Harvard University, 1958.

Clark, R. D. The effects of reinforcement, punishment, and dependency on helping behavior. *Personality and Social Psychology Bulletin*. 1975, *1*, 596–599.

Clark, R. D., Crockett, W. H., & Archer, R. L. Risk as a value hypothesis: The relationship between perception of self, others, and the risky shift. *Journal of Personality and Social Psychology*. 1971, *20*, 425–429.

Clark, R. D., & Word, L. E. Why don't bystanders help? Because of ambiguity. *Journal of Personality and Social Psychology*. 1972, *24*, 392–400.

Coch, L., & French, J. R. P., Jr. Overcoming resistance to change. *Human Relations*. 1948, *4*, 512–533.

Cohen, A. R. Upward communication in experimentally created hierarchies. *Human Relations*. 1958, *11*, 41–53.

Cohen, A. R. *Attitude change and social influence*. New York: Basic Books, 1964.

Cohen, R. Altruism: Human, cultural or what? *Journal of Social Issues*. 1972, *28*, 39–57.

Cohen, S. L., & Bunker, K. A. Subtle effects of sex role stereotypes on recruiter's hiring practices. *Journal of Applied Psychology*. 1975, *60*, 566–572.

Coleman, J. S., Campbell, E., McPartland, J., Mood, A., Weinfield, F., & York, R. *Equality of educational opportunity*. Washington, D.C.: U.S. Government Printing Office, 1966.

Collard, E. D. *Achievement motive in the four year old child and its relationship to achievement expectancies of the mother*. Unpublished doctoral dissertation, University of Michigan, 1964.

Collins, B. E., & Hoyt, M. F. Personal responsibility-for-consequences: An integration and extension of the forced compliance literature. *Journal of Experimental Social Psychology*. 1972, *8*, 558–593.

Collins, B. E., & Raven, B. Group structure: Attraction, coalition, communication and power. In G. Lindzey & E. Aronson (Eds.), *Handbook of social psychology* (Vol. 4). Reading, Mass.: Addison-Wesley, 1969.

Collins, L., & LaPiere, D. *Freedom at midnight*. New York: Avon, 1975.

Condry, J., & Dyer, S. Fear of success: Attribution of cause to the victim. *Journal of Social Issues*. 1976, *32*, 63–83.

Conroy, W. J., Katkin, E. S., & Barnette, W. L. *Modification of smoking behavior by the use of a self-confrontation technique*. Paper presented at meeting of Southeastern Psychological Association, New Orleans, La., 1973.

Cook, S. W., & Sellitz, C. A. A multiple indicator approach to attitude measurement. *Psychological Bulletin*. 1964, *62*, 36–55.

Cosentino, F., & Heilbrun, A. B. Anxiety correlates of sex role identity in college students. *Psychological Reports*. 1964, *14*, 729–730.

Costanzo, P. R. Unpublished manuscript. Duke University, Durham, N.C., 1974.

Costrich, N., Feinstein, J., Kidder, L., Maracek, J., & Pascale, L. When stereotypes hurt: Three studies of penalties for sex role reversals. *Journal of Experimental Social Psychology*. 1975, *11*, 520–530.

Cottrell, N. B. Performance in the presence of other human beings. In E. C. Simmel, R. A. Hoppe, & G. A. Milton (Eds.), *Social facilitation and imitative behavior*. Boston, Mass.: Allyn and Bacon, 1968.

Cottrell, N., Rittle, R., & Wack, D. The presence of an audience and list type (competitional or non-competitional) as joint determinants of performance in paired-associates learning. *Journal of Personality*. 1967, *35*, 425–437.

Cowan, P. A., & Walters, R. H. Studies of reinforcement of aggression: I effects of scheduling. *Child Development*. 1963, *34*, 543–551.

Crandall, V. C. Sex differences in expectancy of intellectual and academic reinforcement. In R. K. Unger & F. L. Denmark (Eds.), *Woman: Dependent or independent variable*. New York: Psychological Dimensions, Inc., 1975.

Crano, W. D., & Mess'e, L. A. When does dissonance fail: The time dimension in attitude measurement. *Journal of Personality*. 1970, *38*, 493–508.

Crespi, I. What kinds of attitude measures are predictive of behavior? *Public Opinion Quarterly.* 1971, *35,* 327–334.

Crime in the United States: Uniform crime reports—1976. Washington, D.C.: United States Department of Justice, 1977.

Crockett, H. J. The achievement motive and differential occupational mobility in the United States. *American Sociological Review.* 1962, *27,* 191–204.

Crowne, D. P., & Liverant, S. Conformity under varying conditions of personal commitment. *Journal of Abnormal and Social Psychology.* 1963, *66,* 547–555.

Crowne, D. P., & Marlowe, D. *The approval motive: Studies in evaluative dependence.* New York: Wiley, 1964.

Crutchfield, R. S. Conformity and character. *American Psychologist.* 1955, *10,* 191–198.

Culbertson, F. M. Modifications of an emotionally held attitude through role playing. *Journal of Abnormal and Social Psychology.* 1957, *54,* 230–233.

Darley, J. M., & Batson, C. D. "From Jerusalem to Jericho": A study of situational and dispositional variables in helping behavior. *Journal of Personality and Social Psychology.* 1973, *27,* 100–108.

Darley, J. M., & Berscheid, E. Increased liking as a result of the anticipation of personal contract. *Human Relations.* 1967, *20,* 29–40.

Darley, J. M., & Latané, B. Bystander intervention in emergencies: Diffusion of responsibility. *Journal of Personality and Social Psychology.* 1968, *8,* 377–383.

Davies, E. This is the way Crete went. *Psychology Today,* 1969, *3,* 42–47.

Davis, J. H. *Group performance.* Reading, Mass.: Addison-Wesley, 1969.

Davis, M., Seibert, R., & Breed, W. Interracial seating patterns on New Orleans Public Transit. *Social Problems.* 1966, *13,* 298–306.

Day, R., & Hamblin, R. Some effects of close and punitive styles of supervision. *American Journal of Sociology.* 1964, *69,* 499–510.

Deaux, K. *The behavior of men and women.* Monterey, Calif.: Brooks/Cole, 1976.

de Charms, R. Personal causation training in the schools. *Journal of Applied Social Psychology.* 1972, *2,* 95–113.

Deckard, B. S. *The women's movement: Political, socioeconomic, and psychological issues.* New York: Harper, 1975.

Dertke, M. C., Penner, L. A., & Ulrich, K. Observer's reporting of shoplifting as a function of thief's race and sex. *Journal of Social Psychology.* 1974, *94,* 213–221.

Desor, J. A. Toward a psychological theory of crowding. *Journal of Personality and Social Psychology.* 1972, *21,* 79–83.

Deutsch, M., & Collins, M. *Interracial housing: A psychological evaluation of a social experiment.* Minneapolis, Minn.: University of Minnesota Press, 1951.

Deutsch, M., & Gerard, H. A study of normative and informational social influences upon individual judgment. *Journal of Abnormal and Social Psychology.* 1955, *51,* 629–636.

Deutsch, M., & Krauss, R. M. The effect of threat upon interpersonal bargaining. *Journal of Abnormal and Social Psychology.* 1960, *61,* 181–189.

Dewey, R., & Humber, W. J. *An introduction to social psychology.* New York: Macmillan, 1966.

Diagnostic and statistical manual of mental disorders. Washington, D.C.: A.P.A. Publications, 1952.

Diagnostic and statistical manual of mental disorders II. Washington, D.C.: A.P.A. Publications, 1968.

Diener, E. Effects of prior destructive behavior, anonymity, and group presence on deindividuation and aggression. *Journal of Personality and Social Psychology.* 1976, *33,* 497–507.

Diener, E., Fraser, S. C., Beamen, A. L., & Kelem, R. T. Effects of deindividuation variables on stealing among Halloween trick or treaters. *Journal of Personality and Social Psychology.* 1976, *33,* 178–183.

Dion, K. *Determinants of unprovoked aggression.* Unpublished doctoral dissertation, University of Minnesota, 1971.

Dion, K. Cohesiveness as a determinant of ingroup-outgroup bias. *Journal of Personality and Social Psychology.* 1973, *28,* 163–171. (a)

Dion, K. Young children's stereotyping of facial attractiveness. *Developmental Psychology.* 1973, *9,* 183–188. (b)

Dion, K., & Berscheid, E. Physical attractiveness and social perception of peers in preschool children. Unpublished manuscript. Cited in E. Berscheid & E. Walster, *Physical attractiveness.* In L. Berkowitz (Ed.), *Advances in experimental social psychology* (Vol. 7). New York: Academic Press, 1974.

Dion, K., Berscheid, E., & Walster, E. What is beautiful is good. *Journal of Personality and Social Psychology.* 1972, *24,* 285–290.

Doctor, R. Locus of control of reinforcement and responsiveness to social influence. *Journal of Personality.* 1971, *39,* 542–551.

Dollard, J., Doob, L. W., Miller, N. E., Mowrer, O., & Sears, R. R. *Frustration and aggression.* New Haven, Conn.: Yale University Press, 1939.

Donnerstein, E., Donnerstein, M., & Evans, R. Erotic stimuli and aggression: Facilitation or inhibition? *Journal of Personality and Social Psychology.* 1975, *32,* 237–244.

Donnerstein, E., & Wilson, D. W. Effects of noise and perceived control on ongoing and subsequent aggression. *Journal of Personality and Social Psychology.* 1976, *34,* 774–781.

Doob, A. N., & Wood, L. Catharsis and aggression. The effects of annoyance and retaliation on aggressive behavior. *Journal of Personality and Social Psychology.* 1972, *22,* 156–162.

Doob, L. W. The behavior of attitudes. *Psychological Review.* 1947, *54,* 135–156.

Douvan, E. Sex differences in adolescent character processes. In J. M. Bardwick (Ed.), *Readings on the psychology of women.* New York: Harper, 1972, 44–48.

Driscoll, J. M., Meyer, R. G., & Shanie, C. F. Training police in family crisis intervention. *Journal of Applied Behavioral Science.* 1973, *9,* 62–81.

Driscoll, R., Davis, K. E., & Lipitz, M. E. Parental influence and romantic love: The Romeo and Juliet effect. *Journal of Personality and Social Psychology.* 1972, *24,* 1–10.

Dutton, D. G. Tokenism, reverse discrimination and egalitarianism in interracial behavior. *Journal of Social Issues.* 1976, *32,* 93–108.

Dutton, D. G., & Aron, A. P. Some evidence for heightened sexual attraction under conditions of high anxiety. *Journal of Personality and Social Psychology.* 1974, *30,* 510–517.

Edwards, W. Utility, subjective probability, their interaction and variance preferences. *Journal of Conflict Resolution.* 1962, *6,* 42–51.

Efran, M. G., & Patterson, E. W. J. Voters vote beautiful: The effect of physical appearance on a national election. *Canadian Journal of Behavioral Science.* 1974, *6,* 352–356.

Ehrlich, P. H. *The population bomb.* New York: Ballantine, 1968.

Eibl-Eibesfeldt, I. (Translated version.) *The biology of behavior.* New York: Holt, 1970.

Ekman, P. Communication through nonverbal behavior: A source of information about an interpersonal relationship. In S. Tomkins & C. Izard (Eds.), *Affect, cognition and personality.* New York: Springer, 1965.

Ellis, L. J., & Bentler, P. M. Traditional sex-determined role standards and sex stereotypes. *Journal of Personality and Social Psychology.* 1973, *25,* 28–34.

Elms, A. C., & Milgram, S. Personality characteristics associated with obedience and defiance toward authoritative command. *Journal of Experimental Research in Personality.* 1966, *1,* 282–289.

Emler, N. P., & Rushton, J. P. Cognitive-developmental factors in children's generosity. *British Journal of Social and Clinical Psychology.* 1974, *13,* 277–281.

Emswiller, T., Deaux, K. & Willets, J. E. Similarity, sex, and requests for small favors. *Journal of Applied Social Psychology.* 1971, *1,* 284–291.

Endler, N. S. Conformity as a function of different reinforcement schedules. *Journal of Personality and Social Psychology.* 1966, *4,* 175–180.

Endler, N. S. The person versus the situation—A Response to Alker. *Journal of Personality.* 1973, *41,* 287–303.

Endler, N. S., & Magnusson, D. *Interactional psychology and personality.* New York: Halsted Press, 1976.

Enzle, N. E., Hansen, R. D., & Lowe, C. A. Causal attribution in the mixed motive game: Effects of facilitory and inhibitory environmental forces. *Journal of Personality and Social Psychology.* 1975, *31,* 50–54.

Epps, E. G. Correlates of academic achievement among northern and southern urban negro students. *Journal of Social Issues.* 1969, *25,* 5–12.

Epstein, R., & Komorita, S. S. Parental discipline, stimulus characteristics of outgroups and social distance in children. *Journal of Personality and Social Psychology.* 1965, *2,* 416–420.

Epstein, R., & Komorita, S. S. Prejudice among Negro school children as related to parental ethnocentrism and punitiveness. *Journal of Personality and Social Psychology.* 1966, *4,* 643–647.

Epstein, Y. M., & Karlin, R. A. Effects of acute experimental crowding. *Journal of Applied Social Psychology.* 1975, *5,* 79–83.

Erikson, E. H. Inner and outer space: Reflections on womanhood, *Daedalus.* 1964, *93,* 582–606.

Erikson, E. H. *Identity, youth and crises.* New York: Norton, 1968.

Eron, L. D., Huesmann, L. R., Lefkowitz, M. M., & Walder, L. O. Does television violence cause aggression? *American Psychologist.* 1972, *27,* 253–263.

Esser, A. H. A biosocial perspective on crowding. In J. F. Wohlwill and D. H. Carron (Eds.), *Environment and the social sciences: Perspectives and applications.* Washington, D.C.: American Psychological Association, 1972.

Eszterhas, J., & Roberts, M. D. *Confrontation at Kent State: Thirteen Seconds.* New York: College Notes and Texts, 1970.

Ethical principles in the conduct of research with human participants. Washington, D.C.: American Psychological Association, 1973.

Etzioni, A. Social–psychological aspects of international relations. In G. Lindzey and E. Aronson (Eds.), *Handbook of social psychology* (Vol. 5). Reading, Mass.: Addison-Wesley, 1969.

Evans, G. W., & Howard, R. B. Personal space. *Psychological Bulletin.* 1973, *80,* 334–344.

Evans, R. I., Rozelle, R. M., Lasater, T. M., Dembroski, T. M., & Allen, B. P. Fear arousal, persuasion and actual versus implied behavior change: New perspective utilizing a real-life dental hygiene program. *Journal of Personality and Social Psychology.* 1970, *16,* 220–227.

Exline, R. V., Thibaut, J., Hickey, C. B., & Gumpert, P. Visual interaction in relation to an unethical act. In R. Christie and F. L. Geis (Eds.), *Studies in Machiavellianism,* New York: Academic Press, 1970.

Farris, G. F., & Lim, F. G., Jr. Effects of performance on leadership, cohesiveness, influence, satisfaction, and subsequent performance. *Journal of Applied Psychology.* 1969, *53,* 490–497.

Fayol, H. *Industrielle et Generale,* 1916 (English Version): *General and industrial administration.* London: Sir Isaac Pitman & Sons, 1949.

Fein, R. An economic and social profile of the negro American. In T. Parsons and K. B. Clark (Eds.), *The negro American.* Boston: Beacon Press, 1966.

Feshbach, S. Aggression. In P. H. Mussen (Ed.), *Carmichael's Manual of Child Psychology* (Vol. II). New York: Wiley, 1970.

Feshbach, S., & Singer, R. D. *Television and aggression: An experimental field study.* San Francisco: Jossey-Bass, 1971.

Festinger, L. Informal social communication. *Psychological Review.* 1950, 57, 271–282.

Festinger, L. A theory of social comparison processes. *Human Relations.* 1954, 7, 117–140.

Festinger, L. *A theory of cognitive dissonance.* Stanford, Calif.: Stanford University Press, 1957.

Festinger, L. Sampling and related problems in research methodology. *American Journal of Mental Deficiency.* 1959, *64,* 358–366.

Festinger, L. *Conflict, decision and dissonance.* Palo Alto, Calif.: Stanford University Press, 1964.

Festinger, L. & Carlsmith, J. M. Cognitive consequences of forced compliance. *Journal of Abnormal and Social Psychology.* 1959, *58,* 203–210.

Festinger, L., Pepitone, A., & Newcomb, T. Some consequences of deindividuation in a group. *Journal of Abnormal and Social Psychology.* 1952, *47,* 382–389.

Festinger, L., Schachter, S., & Back, K. *Social pressures in informal groups: A study of human factors in housing.* New York: Harper, 1950.

Fidell, L. S. Empirical verification of sex discrimination in hiring practices in psychology. *American Psychologist.* 1970, *25,* 1094–1098.

Fiedler, F. E. A contingency model of leadership effectiveness. In L. Berkowitz (Ed.), *Advances in experimental social psychology* (Vol. 1). New York: Academic Press, 1964.

Fiedler, F. E. *A theory of leadership effectiveness.* New York: McGraw-Hill, 1967.

Fiedler, F. E. *Leadership.* New York: General Learning Press, 1971.

Fishbein, M. Sexual behavior and propositional control. Paper presented at meeting of Psychonomic Society, 1966.

Fishbein, M., & Ajzen, I. *Belief, attitude, intention, and behavior.* Reading, Mass.: Addison-Wesley, 1975.

Flacks, R. The liberated generation: An exploration of the roots of student protest. *Journal of Social Issues.* 1967, *23,* 52–75.

Fleishman, E. A. Leadership, climate, human relations training, and supervisory training. *Personnel Psychology.* 1953, *6,* 205–222.

Fleishman, E. A., & Harris, E. F. Patterns of leadership behavior related to employee grievances and turnover. *Personnel Psychology.* 1962, *15,* 43–56.

Ford, C. S. & Beach, F. A. *Patterns of sexual behavior.* New York: Morrow, 1951.

Fraser, C. Group risk-taking and group polarization. *European Journal of Social Psychology.* 1971, *1,* 7–30.

Fraser, C., Gouge, G., & Billig, M. Risky shifts, cautious shifts and group polarization. *European Journal of Social Psychology.* 1971, *1,* 7–30.

Freedman, D. G. *Human infancy: An evolutionary perspective.* Hillsdale, N.J.: Laurence Erlbaum Associates, 1974.

Freedman, J. L. Transgression, compliance, and guilt. In J. MacCauley & L. Berkowitz (Eds.), *Altruism and helping behavior.* New York: Academic Press, 1970.

Freedman, J. L., & Doob, A. N. *Deviancy: The psychology of being different.* New York: Academic Press, 1968.

Freedman, J. L. *Crowding and behavior.* San Francisco: Freeman, 1975.

Freedman, J. L., & Fraser, S. G. Compliance without pressure: The foot-in-the-door technique. *Journal of Personality and Social Psychology.* 1966, *4,* 195–202.

Freedman, J. L., Heshka, S., & Levy, A. Population density and pathology: Is there a relationship? *Journal of Experimental Social Psychology,* 1975, *11,* 539–552.

Freedman, J. L., Heshka, S., & Levy, A. Crowding as an intensifier of pleasantness and unpleasantness. Cited in *Crowding and behavior* by J. L. Freedman. San Francisco: Freeman, 1975.

Freedman, J. L., Levy, A., Buchanan, R. W., & Price, J. Crowding and human agressiveness. *Journal of Experimental Social Psychology.* 1972, *8,* 528–548.

Freeman, J. L. The social construction of the second sex. In M. H. Garskof (Ed.), *Roles women play: Readings toward women's liberation.* Belmont, Calif.: Brooks/Cole, 1971, 123–141.

French, J. R. P., Jr., Group productivity. In H. Guetzkow (Ed.). *Groups, leadership, and men.* Pittsburgh: Carnegie Press, 1951.

French, J. R. P., Jr., & Raven, B. The bases of social power. In D. Cartwright (Ed.), *Studies in social power.* Ann Arbor, Mich.: University of Michigan Press, 1959, 150–167.

French, W. L., & Bell, C. A. *Organizational development.* Englewood Cliffs, N.J.: Prentice-Hall, 1973.

Freud, S. *Civilization and its discontents.* London: Hogarth, 1930.

Freud, S. *New introductory lectures on psychoanalysis.* New York: Norton, 1933.

Freud, S. Fragment of an analysis of a case of hysteria. *In Collected papers (Vol. 3).* New York: Basic Books, 1959.

Freidan, B. *The feminine mystique.* New York: Dell, 1963.

Gaertner, S. L. Helping behavior and racial discrimination among liberals and conservatives. *Journal of Personality and Social Psychology.* 1973, *25,* 335–341.

Gaertner, S. L., & Bickman, L. Effects of race on the elicitation of helping behavior: The wrong number technique. *Journal of Personality and Social Psychology.* 1971, *20,* 218–222.

Gaertner, S. L., & Dovidio, J. F. The subtlety of white racism, arousal, and helping behavior. *Journal of Personality and Social Psychology.* 1977, *35,* 691–707.

Gall, M. D. The relationship between masculinity-femininity and manifest anxiety. *Journal of Clinical Psychology.* 1969, *25,* 294–295.

Galle, O. R., Gove, W. R., and McPherson, J. M. Population density and pathology. What are the relations for man? *Science.* 1972, *176,* 23–30.

Gallo, P. S., & McClintock, C. G. Cooperative and competitive behavior in mixed motive games. *Journal of Conflict Resolution.* 1965, *9,* 68–78.

Garai, J. E. Sex differences in mental health. *Genetic Psychological Monographs.* 1970, *81,* 123–142.

Garcia, S. A. Color and culture in Israel. *Worldview,* October, 1975.

Garson, B. Luddites in Lordstown. *Harper's Magazine,* June 1972.

Garver, R. A. Polite propaganda: "USSR" and "America Illustrated." *Journalism Quarterly.* 1961, *38,* 480–484.

Geen, R. G., Stonner, D., & Shope, G. L. The facilitation of aggression: Evidence against the catharsis hypothesis. *Journal of Personality and Social Psychology.* 1975, *31,* 721–730.

Geiss, F. L., Weinheimer, S., & Berger, D. Machiavellianism in log-rolling. Paper presented at annual meeting of American Psychological Association, New York, 1966. Cited in R. Christie and F. Geiss (Eds.), *Studies in machiavellianism.* New York: Academic Press, 1970.

Gerard, H. B., & Mathewson, G. D. The effects of severity of initiation on liking for a group: A replication. *Journal of Experimental Social Psychology.* 1966, *2,* 278–287.

Gerbner, G. Violence in television drama: Trends and symbolic functions. In G. Comstock and E. Rubinstein (Eds.), *Television and social behavior* (Vol. I). Washington, D.C.: U.S. Government Printing Office, 1972.

Gergen, K. J. *The psychology of behavior exchange.* Reading, Mass.: Addison-Wesley, 1969.

Gergen, K. J. *Experimentation in social psychology: A reappraisal.* Paper presented at meeting of American Psychological Association, Chicago, Ill., 1975.

Gergen, K. J., Gergen, J. M., & Meter, K. Individual orientation to prosocial behavior. *Journal of Social Issues.* 1972, *28,* 105–130.

Gibb, C. Leadership. In G. Lindzey & E. Aronson (Eds.), *Handbook of social psychology* (Vol. 4). Reading, Mass.: Addison-Wesley, 1969.

Gilchrist, J. C. The formation of social groups under conditions of success and failure. *Journal of Abnormal and Social Psychology.* 1952, *47,* 174–187.

Gillig, P. M., & Greenwald, A. G. Is it time to lay the sleeper effect to rest? *Journal of Personality and Social Psychology.* 1974, *29,* 132–139.

Gillin, J. C., & Ochberg, F. M. Firearms control and violence. In D. Daniels, M. Gilula, & F. Ochberg (Eds.), *Violence and the struggle for existence.* Boston: Little, Brown, 1970.

Glass, D. C., & Singer, J. E. *Urban stress: Experiments on noise and social stressors.* New York: Academic Press, 1972.

Goldberg, P. Women prejudiced against women. *Transaction.* 1968, *5,* 28–30.

Golembiewski, R. T. *The small group.* Chicago: University of Chicago Press, 1962.

Golightly, C., & Byrne, D. Attitude statements as positive and negative reinforcers. *Science.* 1964, *146,* 798–799.

Goodman, B. C. Action selection and likelihood ratio estimation by individuals and groups. *Organizational Behavior and Human Performance.* 1972, *7,* 121–141.

Goodnow, R. E., & Taguiri, R. Religious ethnocentrism and its recognition among adolescent boys. *Journal of Abnormal and Social Psychology.* 1952, *47,* 316–320.

Goranson, R. E., & King, D. Rioting and daily temperature: Analysis of the U.S. riots in 1967. Unpublished manuscript, York University, 1970.

Gore, P. Individual differences in the prediction of subject compliance to experimenter bias. Unpublished doctoral dissertation, Ohio State University, 1962.

Gore, P., & Rotter, J. B. A personality correlate of social action. *Journal of Personality.* 1963, *31,* 58–64.

Goss, E. Women in politics: Not a vintage year. *The Philadelphia Inquirer.* October 31, 1976, 7-h.

Gough, H. G. *California Personality Inventory.* Palo Alto, Calif.: Consulting Psychologists Press, 1957.

Graen, G., Alvares, K., Orris, J. B., & Martello, J. A. Contingency model of leadership effectiveness: Antecedent and evidential results. *Psychological Bulletin.* 1970, *74,* 285–296.

Gray, S. W. Masculinity-femininity in relation to anxiety and social acceptance. *Child Development.* 1957, *28,* 203–214.

Gray, D. B., & Ashmore, R. D. Comparing the effects of informational role playing and value-discrepancy treatment on racial attitudes. *Journal of Applied Social Psychology.* 1975, *3,* 262–281.

Greenberg, M. S., & Frisch, D. M. Effect of intentionality on willingness to reciprocate a favor. *Journal of Experimental Social Psychology.* 1972, *8,* 99–111.

Greene, R. The story behind the "Dirty Harry" killing. *Chicago Sun Times.* September 16, 1977.

Greer, S. *Last man in.* Glencoe, Ill.: Free Press, 1959.

Griffitt, W. Interpersonal attraction as a function of self-concept, personality and similarity-dissimilarity. *Journal of Personality and Social Psychology.* 1966, *4,* 581–584.

Griffitt, W., & Veitch, R. Hot and crowded: Influences of population density and temperature on interpersonal affective behavior. *Journal of Personality and Social Psychology.* 1971, *17,* 92–98.

Gross, A. E., Wallston, B. S., & Piliavin, I. M. Beneficiary attractiveness and cost as determinants of responses to routine requests for help. *Sociometry.* 1975, 38, 131–140.

Guest, R. H. Men and machines: An assembly line worker looks at his job. *Personnel.* 1955, *31,* 496–503.

Guion, R. M. A note on organizational climate. *Organizational Behavior and Human Performance.* 1973, *9,* 120–125.

Gulick, L. Notes on the theory of organization. In L. Gulick & L. Urwick (Eds.), *Papers on the science of administration.* New York: The Institute of Public Administration, 1937.

Gurin P., Gurin, G., Lao, R. C., & Beattie, M. Internal-external control of motivational dynamics of Negro youth. *Journal of Social Issues.* 1969, *25,* 29–53.

Haan, N., Smith, M. B., & Block, J. Moral reasoning of young adults: Political-social behavior, family background and personality correlates. *Journal of Personality and Social Psychology.* 1968, *10,* 183–201.

Halberstam, D. *The best and the brightest.* Greenwich, Conn.: Fawcett, 1972.

Hall, C. S., & Lindzey, G. *Theories of personality.* New York: Wiley, 1957.

Hall, E. T. *The hidden dimension.* New York: Doubleday, 1966.

Hall, E. T. A system for notation of proxemic behavior. *American Anthropologist.* 1963, *65,* 1003–1026.

Hall, J. Decisions, decisions, decisions. *Psychology Today.* 1971, *5,* 51–54, 86–88.

Haller, J. S. From maidenhood to menopause: Sex education for women in Victorian America. In J. Williams (Ed.), *Interpretations of Woman: Readings in Psychology.* Lexington, Mass.: Xerox College Publishing, 1974, 129–143.

Halpin, A. W., & Winer, B. J. *The leadership behavior of the airplane commander.* Columbus, Ohio: Ohio State University Research Foundation, 1952.

Halpin, A. W., & Winer, B. J. A factorial study of the leader behavior descriptions. In R. M. Stogdill & A. C. Coons (Eds.), *Leader behavior: Its description and measurement.* Columbus, Ohio: Ohio State University, Bureau of Business Research, Research Monogr. No. 88, 1957, 39–51.

Hamblin, R. J. The dynamics of racial discrimination. *Social Problems.* 1962, *10,* 267–281.

Hamilton, T. Social optimism and pessimism in American Protestantism. *Public Opinion Quarterly.* 1942, *6,* 280–283.

Hamner, W. C. Effects of bargaining strategy and pressure to reach agreement in a stalemated negotiation. *Journal of Personality and Social Psychology.* 1974, *30,* 458–467.

Hampson, J. L., & Hampson, J. G. Ontogenesis of sexual behavior in man. In W. C. Young (Ed.), *Sex and internal secretions* (Vol. II). Baltimore: Williams and Wilkens, 1961.

Harari, H., & McDavid, J. W. Teacher's expectations and name stereotypes. *Journal of Educational Psychology.* 1973, *66,* 222–225.

Harding, J., Proshansky, H., Kutner, B., & Chein, I. Prejudice and ethnic relations. In G. Lindzey and E. Aronson, (Eds.), *Handbook of social psychology* (Vol. 5). Reading, Mass.: Addison-Wesley, 1969.

Hare, A. P. *Handbook of small group research.* New York: Free Press, 1962.

Hartford, T. L., Willis, C. H., & Deabler, H. L. Personality correlates of masculinity-femininity. *Psychological Reports.* 1967, *21,* 881–884.

Harlow, H. F., McGaugh, J. L., & Thompson, R. F. *Psychology.* San Francisco: Albion, 1971.

Harré, R., & Secord, P. F. *The Explanation of Social behavior.* Oxford: Basil, Blackwell, and Mott, 1972.

Harrison, A. A., & Saeed, L. Let's make a deal: An analysis of revelations and stipulations in lonely hearts advertisements. *Journal of Personality and Social Psychology.* 1977, *35,* 256–264.

Hart, I. Maternal child-rearing practices and authoritarian ideology. *Journal of Abnormal and Social Psychology.* 1957, *55,* 232–237.

Hartley, R. E. American core culture: Changes and continuities. In G. H. Seward & R. C. Williamson (Eds.), *Sex roles in a changing society.* New York: Random House, 1970, 126–149.

Harvey, J. H., Harris, B., & Barnes, R. D. Actor-observer differences in the perceptions of responsibility and freedom. *Journal of Personality and Social Psychology.* 1975, *32,* 22–28.

Hastorf, A. H., Schneider, D. J., & Polefka, J. *Person perception.* Reading, Mass.: Addison-Wesley, 1970.

Heider, F. *The psychology of interpersonal relations.* New York: Wiley, 1958.

Helmreich, R., Aronson, E., & LeFan, J. To err is humanizing—sometimes: Effects of self-esteem, competence and a pratfall on interpersonal attraction. *Journal of Personality and Social Psychology.* 1970, *16,* 259–264.

Hendrick, C., Bixenstine, V. E., & Hawkins, C. Race versus shared belief as determinants of attraction: A search for a fair test. *Journal of Personality and Social Psychology.* 1971, *17,* 250–258.

Hersch, S. *My Lai 4: A report on the massacre and its aftermath.* New York: Vintage, 1970.

Hero, A. Public reactions to government policy. In J. Robinson, J. Rusk, & K. Head (Eds.), *Measures of political attitudes.* Ann Arbor, Mich.: Institute for Social Research, 1973.

Hickson, D. J. A convergence in organization theory. *Administrative Science Quarterly,* 1966, *11,* 229–237.

Hobfoll, S. E. Volunteer vs. nonvolunteer mental health workers: Personality, value, and attitude change. Unpublished doctoral dissertation. University of South Florida, 1977.

Hochreich, D. J. Internal-external control and reaction to the My Lai courts-martial. *Journal of Applied Social Psychology.* 1972, *2,* 319–325.

Hoffer, E. *The true believer.* New York: Harper, 1951.

Hoffman, L. W. Early childhood experiences and women's achievement motive. *Journal of Social Issues.* 1972, *28,* 129–155.

Hoffman, M. L. Power assertion by the parent and its impact on the child. *Child Development.* 1960, *31,* 129–143.

Hoffman, M. L. Altruistic behavior and the parent-child relationship. *Journal of Personality and Social Psychology.* 1975, *31,* 937–943.

Hogeland, R. W. "The Female Appendage": Feminine life styles in America: 1820–1860. In J. Williams (Ed.), *Interpretations of woman: Readings in psychology.* Lexington, Mass.: College Publishing, 1974.

Hokanson, J. E. Psychophysiological evaluation of the catharsis hypothesis. In E. Megargee and J. W. Hokanson, (Eds.) *The dynamics of aggression.* New York: Harper and Row, 1970.

Hokanson, J. E., & Shetler, S. The effect of overt aggression on psychological processes. *Journal of Abnormal and Social Psychology.* 1961, *63,* 446–448.

Holinshed, J. R. *Chronicles of England, Scotland and Ireland.* London: Hume, 1577.

Hollander, E. P. Conformity, status and idiosyncracy credit. *Psychological Review.* 1958, *65,* 117–127.

Hollander, E. P. Independence, conformity and civil liberties: Some implications from social psychological research. *Journal of Social Issues.* 1975, *31,* 55–67.

Homans, G. C. Status among clerical workers. *Human Organization.* 1953, *12,* 5–10.

Homans, G. C. *Social behavior: Its elementary forms.* New York: Harcourt, 1961.

Homans, G. C. Commentary. In L. Berkowitz & E. Walster (Eds.), *Equity theory: Toward a gen-*

eral theory of social interaction. *Advances in experimental social psychology* (Vol. 9). New York: Academic Press, 1976.

Hoppe, R. A. Memorizing by individuals and groups: A test of the pooling of ability model. *Journal of Abnormal and Social Psychology*. 1962, *65*, 64–67.

Horner, M. S. Sex differences in achievement motivation and performance in competitive and noncompetitive situations. Unpublished doctoral dissertation, University of Michigan, 1968.

Horner, M. S. Toward an understanding of achievement related conflict in women. *Journal of Social Issues*. 1972, *28*, 157–175.

House, T. H., & Milligan, W. L. Autonomic responses to modeled distress in prison psychopaths. *Journal of Personality and Social Psychology*. 1976, *34*, 556–560.

Hovland, C. I. Reconciling conflicting results derived from experimental and survey studies of attitude change. *American Psychologist*. 1959, *14*, 8–17.

Hovland, C. I., Janis, I., & Kelley, H. H. *Communication and persuasion*. New Haven, Conn.: Yale University Press, 1953.

Hovland, C. I., Lumsdaine, A. A., & Sheffield, F. D. *Experiments on mass communication*. Princeton, N.J.: Princeton University Press, 1949.

Hovland, C. I., & Sears, R. Minor studies in aggression: VI: Correlation of lynchings with economic indices. *Journal of Psychology*. 1940, *9*, 301–310.

Hovland, C. I., & Weiss, W. The influence of source credibility on communication effectiveness. *Public Opinion Quarterly*. 1951, *15*, 635–650.

Hunt, R. G. Role and role conflict. In H. Hartley and G. E. Holloway (Eds.), *Focus on change and the school administrator*. Buffalo, N.Y.: State University of New York, School of Education, 1965.

Insko, C. A. *Theories of attitude change*. New York: Appleton-Century-Crofts, 1967.

Insko, C. A., Arkoff, A., & Insko, V. M. Effects of high and low fear arousing communication upon opinions toward smoking. *Journal of Experimental Social Psychology*. 1965, *1*, 256–260.

Insko, C. A., & Schopler, J. *Experimental social psychology*. New York: Academic Press, 1973.

International Association of Chiefs of Police. *With justice for all: A guide for law enforcement officers*. Washington, D.C., and New York: International Association of Chiefs of Police and the Anti-Defamation League of B'nai B'rith.

Isen, A. M., & Levin, P. F. The effects of feeling good on helping: Cookies and kindness. *Journal of Personality and Social Psychology*. 1972, *21*, 384–388.

Izard, L. E. Personality similarity and friendship. *Journal of Abnormal and Social Psychology*. 1960, *61*, 47–51. (a).

Izard, L. E. Personality, similarity, positive affect and interpersonal attraction. *Journal of Abnormal and Social Psychology*. 1960, *61*, 484–485. (b).

Jacobs, J. *Death and life of great American cities*. New York: Random House, 1961.

Jacobs, P., & Landau, S. *The new radicals*. New York: Vintage, 1966.

Jaffee, C. L., & Furr, R. M. The relationship of the number of reinforcements to extinction in a leadership conditioning situation. *Journal of Social Psychology*. 1968, *76*, 49–53.

Jaffee, C. L., & Lucas, R. L. Effects of rates of talking and correctness of decisions on leader choice in small groups. *Journal of Social Psychology*. 1969, *79*, 247–254.

James, W. *The principles of psychology*. New York: Holt, 1890.

Janis, I. L. Effects of fear arousal on attitude change: Recent developments in theory and experimental research. In L. Berkowitz (Ed.), *Advances in experimental social psychology* (Vol. 3). New York: Academic Press, 1967.

Janis, I. L. *Victims of groupthink*. Boston: Houghton Mifflin, 1972.

Janis, I. L., & Gilmore, J. B. The influence of incentive conditions on the success of role playing in modifying attitudes. *Journal of Personality and Social Psychology*. 1965, *1*, 17–27.

Janis, I. L., & Terwilliger, R. F. An experimental study of psychological resistances to fear arousing communications. *Journal of Abnormal and Social Psychology*. 1962, *65*, 403–410.

Joe, V. C. Review of the internal-external control construct as a personality variable. *Psychological Reports*. 1971, *28*, 619–640.

Johanneson, R. Some problems in the measurement of organizational climate. *Organizational Behavior and Human Performance.* 1973, *10,* 118–144.

Jones, E. E. *Ingratiation.* New York: Appelton-Century-Crofts, 1964.

Jones, E. E., & Davis, K. E. From acts to disposition: The attribution process in person perception. In L. Berkowitz (Ed.), *Advances in experimental social psychology* (Vol. 2). New York: Academic Press, 1965.

Jones, E. E., Gergen, K. J. & Jones, R. G. Tactics of ingratiation among leaders and subordinates in a status hierarchy. *Psychological Monographs,* 1963, *77,* (3, Whole No. 566).

Jones, E. E., & Goethals, G. R. Order effects in impression formation: *Attribution context and the nature of the entity.* Morristown, N.J.: General Learning Press, 1971.

Jones, E. E., & Nisbett, R. E. *The actor and the observer: Divergent perceptions of the causes of behavior.* Morristown, N.J.: General Learning Press, 1971.

Jones, E. E., Rock, L., Shaver, K., Goethals, G., & Ward, L. Pattern of performance and ability attribution: An unexpected primacy effect. *Journal of Personality and Social Psychology.* 1968, *10,* 317–340.

Jones, E. E., Worchel, S., Goethals, G., & Grumet, J. Prior expectancy and behavioral extremity as determinants of attitude attribution. *Journal of Experimental Social Psychology.* 1971, *7,* 59–80.

Jones, R. Cited in: *Works with Marijuana: I Effects,* S. S. Snyder. *Psychology Today.* 1971, *14,* 64.

Jordan, N. Behavioral forces that are a function of attitudes and cognitive organization. *Human Relations.* 1953, *6,* 273–287.

Joseph, F. *Star Trek Star Fleet technical manual.* New York: Ballantine Books, 1975.

Julian, J., Bishop, D., & Fiedler, F. Quasi-therapeutic effects of intergroup competition. *Journal of Personality and Social Psychology.* 1966, *3,* 321–327.

Kaplan, M. F., & Kemmerick, G. D. Juror judgment as information integration: Combining evidential and nonevidential information.

Journal of Personality and Social Psychology. 1974, *30,* 493–499.

Kaplan, R. M., & Singer, R. D. Television violence and viewer aggression: A reexamination of the evidence. *Journal of Social Issues.* 1976, *32,* 35–70.

Karlins, M., Coffman, T. L., & Walters, G. On the fading of social stereotypes: Studies in three generations of college students. *Journal of Personality and Social Psychology.* 1969, *13,* 1–16.

Kasl, S. V., & French, J. R. P., Jr. The effects of occupational status on physical and mental health. *Journal of Social Issues.* 1962, *17,* 67–89.

Katkovsky, W., Crandall, V. C., & Good, S. Parental antecedents of children's beliefs in internal-external control of reinforcements in intellectual achievement situations. *Child Development.* 1967, *38,* 765–776.

Katz, D., & Kahn, R. L. Some recent findings in human relations research in industry. In G. Swanson, T. T. Newcomb, & E. Hartley (Eds.), *Readings in social psychology.* (2nd ed.) New York: Holt, 1952.

Katz, D., & Kahn, R. L. Leadership practices in relation to productivity and morale. In D. Cartwright & A. Zander (Eds.), *Group dynamics.* Evanston, Ill.: Row & Peterson, 1953.

Katz, D., & Kahn, R. L. *The Social psychology of organizations.* New York: Wiley, 1966.

Katz, D., Maccoby, E., & Morse, N. *Productivity, supervision, and morale in an office situation.* Ann Arbor, Mich.: Institute for Social Research, University of Michigan, 1950.

Katzenbach, N. de B. *The challenge of crime in a free society.* Washington, D.C.: U.S. Government Printing Office, 1967.

Kelley, H. H. Communication in experimentally created hierarchies. *Human Relations.* 1951, *4,* 39–56.

Kelley, H. H. Attribution theory in social psychology. In D. Levine (Ed.), *Nebraska symposium on motivation* (Vol. 15). Lincoln, Neb.: University of Nebraska Press, 1967.

Kelley, H. H. The process of causal attributions. *American Psychologist.* 1973, *28,* 107–128.

Kelman, H. C. Compliance, identification and internalization. *Journal of Conflict Resolution.* 1958, *2,* 51–60.

Kelman, H. C. Processes of opinion change. *Public Opinion Quarterly.* 1961, *25,* 57–78.

Kelman, H. C. Attitudes are alive and well and gainfully employed in the sphere of action. *American Psychologist.* 1974, *29,* 310–335.

Kelman, H. C., & Hovland, C. I. Reinstatement of the communication in delayed measurement of opinion change. *Journal of Abnormal and Social Psychology.* 1953, *48,* 327–335.

Kenniston, K. *Young radicals.* New York: Harcourt, 1968.

Kenrick, D. T., & Cialdini, R. B. Romantic attraction: Misattribution versus reinforcement explanations. *Journal of Personality and Social Psychology.* 1977, *35,* 381–391.

Kerpelman, L. *Student activism and ideology in higher education institutions.* Washington, D.C.: U.S. Department of Health, Education, and Welfare, Office of Education, 1970.

Kiesler, C. A. Group pressure and conformity. In J. Mills (Ed.), *Experimental social psychology.* New York: Macmillan, 1969.

Kiesler, C. A., Collins, B. E., & Miller, N. *Attitude Change: A critical analysis of theoretical approaches.* New York. Wiley, 1969.

Kiesler, C. A., and Kiesler, S. B. *Conformity.* Reading, Mass.: Addison-Wesley, 1969.

Kifner, J. The men in the middle. *New York Times Magazine.* September 12, 1976, 36–37, 101–112.

Kinch, J. W. *Social psychology.* New York: McGraw-Hill, 1973.

Kinsey, A. C., Pomeroy, W. B., & Martin, C. E. *Sexual behavior in the human male.* Philadelphia: Saunders, 1948.

Kinzel, A. Body buffer zone in violent prisoners. *American Journal of Psychiatry.* 1970, *127,* 59–64.

Kipnis, D. The effect of leadership style and leadership power upon the inducement of attitude change. *Journal of Abnormal and Social Psychology.* 1958, *57,* 178–180.

Kirk, D. The misunderstood challenge of population change. In C. Loo (Ed.), *Crowding and behavior.* New York: MSS Information Corporation, 1974.

Kirsch, B. Consciousness raising groups as therapy for women. In V. Franks & V. Burtle (Eds.), *Women in therapy.* New York: Bruner/Mazel, 1974.

Klienhans, B., & Taylor, D. A. Group processes, productivity, and leadership. In B. Seidenberg & A. Snadowsky (Eds.), *Social psychology: An introduction.* New York: Free Press, 1976.

Kohlberg, L. Moral and religious education in the public schools: A developmental view. In T. Sizer (Ed.), *Religion and public education.* Boston: Houghton Mifflin, 1967.

Kohlberg, L. Stage and sequence: The cognitive developmental approach to socialization. In D. Goslin (Ed.), *Handbook of socialization theory and research.* Chicago: Rand McNally, 1969.

Kolson, A. *"The Total Woman":* For the glory of the Lord and sex. *The Philadelphia Inquirer,* August, 15, 1976, 1k–2k.

Konečni, V. J. The mediation of aggressive behavior: Arousal level versus anger and cognitive labeling. *Journal of Personality and Social Psychology.* 1975, *32,* 706–712.

Konečni, V. J., & Doob, A. N. Catharsis through displacement of aggression. *Journal of Personality and Social Psychology.* 1972, *23,* 379–387.

Korman, A. K. "Consideration, initiating Structure," and organizational criteria: A review. *Personnel Psychology.* 1966, *19,* 349–361.

Kovic, R. *Born on the fourth of July.* New York: Pocket Books, 1977.

Krebs, D. L. Altruism—an examination of the concept and a review of the literature. *Psychological Bulletin.* 1970, *73,* 258–302.

Krebs, D. L. Empathy and altruism. *Journal of Personality and Social Psychology.* 1975, *32,* 1134–1146.

Krech, D., Crutchfield, R. S., & Ballachey, E. L. *Individual in society.* New York: McGraw-Hill, 1962.

Kregarman, J. J., & Worchel, P. Arbitrariness of frustration and aggression. *Journal of Personality.* 1962, *23,* 379–387.

Lamm, H., & Tromsdorff, G. Group versus individual performance on tasks requiring identical proficiency (brainstorming): A review. *European Journal of Social Psychology.* 1973, *3,* 361–388.

Landy, F. J., & Trumbo, D. A. *Psychology of work behavior.* Homewood, Ill.: Dorsey Press, 1976.

Lana, R. E. The influence of the pretest on order effects in persuasive communications. *Journal of Abnormal and Social Psychology.* 1964, *69,* 337–341.

Lana, R. E. Inhibiting effects of a pretest on opinion change. *Educational and Psychological Measurements.* 1966, *26,* 139–150.

Lana, R. E., & Rosnow, R. L. Subject awareness and order effects in persuasive communications. *Psychological Reports.* 1963, *12,* 523–529.

Lane, I. M., & Mess'e, L. A. Equity and the distribution of rewards. *Journal of Personality and Social Psychology.* 1971, *20,* 1–17.

Latané, B., & Darley, J. M. Group inhibitions of bystander intervention in emergencies. *Journal of Personality and Social Psychology.* 1968, *10,* 215–221.

Latané, B., & Darley, J. M. *The unresponsive bystander: Why doesn't he help?* New York: Appleton-Century-Crofts, 1970.

Lawler, E. E. III, & Hackman, J. R. The impact of employee participation in the development of pay initiative plans: A field experiment. *Journal of Applied Psychology.* 1969, *53,* 467–471.

Lawrence, J. E. Crowding and human behavior. *Psychological Bulletin.* 1974, *81,* 712–720.

Lazarsfeld, P. F., Berelson, B., & Gaudet, H. *The people's choice: How the voter makes up his mind in a presidential campaign.* New York: Columbia University Press, 1944.

Lazarus, R. S. *Psychological stress and the coping process.* New York: McGraw-Hill, 1966.

Leavitt, H. J. Some effects of certain communication patterns on group performance. *Journal of Abnormal and Social Psychology.* 1951, *46,* 38–50.

Le Bon, G. Psychologie des Foules (1895). English Version: *The crowd.* London: Urwin, 1903.

Lee, M. D. The influence of individual, situational, and organizational factors on the success of women in traditionally male jobs. Unpublished master's thesis, University of South Florida, 1977.

Lefcourt, H. M. Internal-external control of reinforcement: A review. *Psychological Bulletin.* 1966, *65,* 206–220.

Lefcourt, H. M. Recent developements in the study of locus of control. In B. A. Maher (Ed.), *Progress in experimental personality research* (Vol. 6). New York: Academic Press, 1972.

Lefcourt, H. M. *Locus of control: Current trends in theory and research.* Hillsdale, N.J.: Lawrence Erlbaum Associates, 1976.

Lehrman, D. S. A critique of Konrad Lorenz's theory of instinctive behavior. *Quarterly Review of Biology.* 1953, *28,* 337–363.

Liepold, W. D., & James, R. L. Characteristics of shows and no-shows in a psychological experiment. *Psychological Reports.* 1962, *11,* 171–174.

Lerner, M. J. The unjust consequences of the need to believe in a just world. Paper presented at meeting of the American Psychological Association, New York, September 1966.

Lerner, M. J. Social psychology of injustice and reactions to victims. In T. L. Huston (Ed.), *Foundations of interpersonal attraction.* New York: Academic Press, 1974.

Lerner, M. J., and Matthews, G. Reactions to sufferings of others under conditions of indirect responsibility. *Journal of Personality and Social Psychology.* 1967, *5,* 319–325.

Lesser, G. S. Achievement motivation in women. In D. C. McClelland & R. Steele (Eds.), *Human Motivation.* Morristown, N.J.: General Learning Press, 1973.

Lester, W. *Morality anyone?* New Rochelle, N.Y.: Arlington House, 1975.

Levenson, H., Burford, B., Bunno, B., & Davis, L. Are women still prejudiced against women: A replication and extension of the Goldberg study. *Journal of Psychology.* 1975, *89,* 67–71.

Leventhal, G. S. Fairness in social relationships. In J. Thibaut, J. T. Spence, & R. Carson (Eds.), *Contemporary topics in social psychology.* Morristown, N.J.: General Learning Press, 1976.

Leventhal, H. Findings and theory in the study of fear communications. In L. Berkowitz (Ed.), *Advances in experimental social psychology* (Vol. 5). New York: Academic Press, 1970.

Leventhal, H., Watts, J. C., & Pagano, F. Effects of fear and instructions on how to cope with danger. *Journal of Personality and Social Psychology.* 1967, *6,* 313–321.

Levinger, G. The development of perceptions and

behavior in newly formed social power relationships. In D. Cartwright (Ed.), *Studies in social power*. Ann Arbor, Mich.: University of Michigan, 1969.

Levinger, G., & Snoek, J. D. *Attraction in relationships: A new look at interpersonal attraction*. Morristown, N.J.: General Learning Press, 1972.

Levinson, D. J., & Huffman, P. E. Traditional family ideology and its relation to personality. *Journal of Personality*. 1955, *23*, 251–273.

Levy, L. Studies in conformity behavior: A methodological note. *Journal of Psychology*. 1960, *50*, 39–41.

Lewin, K. Group decision and social change. In T. M. Newcomb and E. L. Hartley (Eds.), *Readings in social psychology*. New York: Holt, 1947.

Lewin, K., Lippitt, R., & White, R. Patterns of aggressive behavior in experimentally created "Social climates." *Journal of Social Psychology*. 1939, *10*, 271–299.

Lieberman, S. The effects of changes in roles on the attitudes of role occupants. *Human Relations*. 1956, *9*, 385–402.

Liebert, R. M., Neale, J. M., & Davidson, E. S. *The early window: Effects of television on children and youth*. Elmsford, N.Y.: Pergamon, 1973.

Likert, R. A technique for the measurement of attitudes. *Archives of Psychology*. 1932, No. 140, 5–53.

Likert, R. *The human organization: Its management and value*. New York: McGraw-Hill, 1967.

Likert, R., & Seashore, S. E. Making cost control work. *Harvard Business Review*. 1964, *41*, 96–108.

Linder, D. E. Personal space. In J. W. Thiabaut, J. T. Spence, & R. C. Carson (Eds.), *Contemporary topics in social psychology*. Morristown, N.J.: General Learning Press, 1976.

Lloyd-Morgan, C. *Habit and instinct*. London: Arnold, 1896.

London, P. The rescuers: Motivational hypotheses about Christians who saved Jews from the Nazis. In J. Macauley & L. Berkowitz (Eds.), *Altruism and helping behavior*. New York: Academic Press, 1970.

Lorenz, K. *On aggression*. New York: Harcourt, 1966.

Lorge, I., & Solomon, H. Two models of group behavior in the solution of eureka-type problems. *Psychometrika*. 1955, *20*, 139–148.

Lothstein, L. M. Personal space in assault-prone male adolescent prisoners. Unpublished doctoral dissertation, Duke University, 1971.

Lott, A. J., & Lott, B. E. Group cohesiveness, communication level and conformity. *Journal of Abnormal and Social Psychology*. 1961, *62*, 408–412.

Lovaas, O. J. Effect of exposure to symbolic aggression on aggressive behavior. *Child Development*. 1961, *32*, 37–44.

Lowin, A., & Craig, J. R. The influence of level of performance on managerial style: An experimental object-lesson in the ambiguity of correlational data. *Organizational Behavior and Human Performance*. 1968, *3*, 440–458.

Lunde, D. T. *Murder and madness*. San Francisco: Freeman, 1976.

Lyle, W. H., & Levitt, E. E. Punitiveness, authoritarianism and parental discipline of grade school children. *Journal of Abnormal and Social Psychology*. 1955, *51*, 42–46.

Lynn, D. B. A note on sex differences in the development of masculine and feminine identification. In J. M. Seidman (Ed.), *The adolescent—A book of readings*. New York: Holt, 1960.

Maas, P. *Serpico*. New York: Bantam Books, 1973.

Maccoby, E. E. *The development of sex differences*. Stanford, Calif.: Stanford University Press, 1966.

Maccoby, E. E., & Jacklin, C. N. *The psychology of sex differences*. Stanford, Calif.: Stanford University Press, 1974. (a)

Maccoby, E. E., & Jacklin, C. N. What we know and don't know about sex differences. *Psychology Today*. 1974, *8*, 109–111. (b)

Mantell, D. M. The potential for violence in Germany. *Journal of Social Issues*. 1971, *27*, 101–112.

Marcus, M. G. The power of a name. *Psychology Today*. 1976, *10*, 75–76, 108.

Marlowe, D., & Gergen, K. J. Personality and social interaction. In G. Lindzey & E. Aronson (Eds.), *Handbook of social psychology* (Vol. 3). Reading, Mass.: Addison-Wesley, 1969.

Marlowe, D., & Gergen, K. J. Personality and

social behavior. In K. Gergen & D. Marlow (Eds.), *Personality and social behavior.* Reading, Mass.: Addison-Wesley, 1970.

Marmer, R. S. The effect of volunteer status on dissonance reduction. Unpublished masters thesis, Boston University, 1967.

Martin, R. M., & Marcuse, F. L. Characteristics of volunteers and nonvolunteers in psychological experimentation. *Journal of Consulting Psychology.* 1958, *22,* 475–479.

Maslow, A. H. A theory of human motivation. *Psychological Review.* 1943, *50,* 370–396.

Mason, K. O., & Bumpass, L. L. Women's sex-role attitudes in the United States, 1970. Paper presented at meeting of American Sociological Association, 1973.

McArthur, L. A. Luck is alive and well in New Haven. *Journal of Personality and Social Psychology.* 1970, *35,* 213–216.

McArthur, L. Z., & Resko, B. G. The portrayal of men and women in American television commercials. *Journal of Social Psychology.* 1975, *97,* 209–220.

McCandless, B. R. Schools, sex differences, and the disadvantaged male. Unpublished manuscript. Emory University, 1970.

McCauley, C., Stitt, C. L., Woods, K., & Lipton, D. Group shift to caution at the race track. *Journal of Experimental Social Psychology.* 1973, *9,* 80–86.

McClelland, D. C. *The achieving society.* Princeton, N.J.: Van Nostrand, 1960.

McClelland, D. C. Achievement and entrepreneurship: A longitudinal study. *Journal of Personality and Social Psychology.* 1965, *1,* 389–392.

McClelland, D. C., Atkinson, J. W., Clark, R. A., & Lowell, E. L. *The achievement motive.* New York: Appleton-Century-Crofts, 1953.

McClelland, D. C. & Winter, D. G. *Motivating economic achievement.* New York: Free Press, 1969.

McClintock, C. G. Game behavior and social motivation in interpersonal settings. In C. G. McClintock (Ed.), *Experimental social psychology.* New York: Holt, Rinehart, and Winston, 1972.

McConnell, J. Learning theory. In H. Katz, P. Warrick, & M. Greenberg (Eds.), *Introductory psychology through science fiction.* Chicago, Ill.: Rand McNally, 1974.

McDavid, J. W. Approval-seeking motivation and the volunteer subject. *Journal of Personality and Social Psychology.* 1965, *2,* 115–117.

McDavid, J. W., & Harari, H. Stereotyping of names and popularity in grade school children. *Child Development.* 1966, *37,* 453–454.

McDavid, J. W., & Harari, H. *Psychology and Social Behavior.* New York: Harper, 1974.

McDougall, W. *An introduction to social psychology.* London: Methuen, 1908.

McGinnies, E. *Social behavior: A functional analysis.* Boston: Houghton Mifflin, 1970.

McGregor, D. *The human side of enterprise.* New York: McGraw-Hill, 1960.

McGuire, W. J. Persistence of the resistance to persuasion induced by various types of prior belief defenses. *Journal of Abnormal and Social Psychology.* 1962, *64,* 241–248.

McGuire, W. J. Inducing resistance to persuasion: Some contemporary approaches. In L. Berkowitz (Ed.), *Advances in experimental social psychology* (Vol. 1). New York: Academic Press, 1964.

McGuire, W. J. The nature of attitudes and attitude change. In G. Lindzey & E. Aronson (Eds.), *Handbook of social psychology* (Vol. 2). Reading, Mass.: Addison-Wesley, 1969. (a)

McGuire, W. J. Suspiciousness of an experimentor's intent. In R. Rosenthal & R. Rosnow (Eds.), *Artifact in behavioral research.* New York: Academic Press, 1969. (b)

McGuire, W. J. Persuasion, resistance and attitude change. In I. de Sola Pool & W. Schramm (Eds.), *Handbook of communication.* Chicago: Rand McNally, 1974.

McGuire, W. J., & Papergeorgis, D. Effectiveness of forewarning in developing resistance to persuasion. *Public Opinion Quarterly.* 1962, *26,* 24–34.

McKeachie, W. J. Motivation, teaching methods and college learning. *Nebraska Symposium on Motivation.* 1961, *9,* 111–142.

McLaughlin, B. Social movements. In B. Seidenberg & A. Snadowsky (Eds.), *Social psychology: An introduction.* New York: Free Press Macmillan, 1976.

McNemar, Q. Opinion-attitude methodology. *Psychological Bulletin.* 1946, *43,* 289–374.

McNemar, Q. *Psychological statistics.* New York: Wiley, 1969.

Mead, M. *Sex and temperament in three primitive societies.* New York: Morrow, 1935.

Mednick, M. T., & Weissman, H. J. The psychology of women: Selected topics. *Annual Review of Psychology.* 1975, *26,* 1–18.

Megargee, E. I. Undercontrolled and overcontrolled personality types in extreme antisocial aggression. *Psychological Monographs.* 1966, *80,* No. 3. (Whole No. 611.)

Megargee, E. I. The role of inhibition in the assessment of and understanding of violence. In J. L. Singer (Ed.), *The control of aggression and violence.* New York: Academic Press, 1971.

Mehrabian, A. Significance of posture and position in the communication of attitude and status relationships. *Psychological Bulletin.* 1969, *71,* 359–373.

Merton, R. K. *Social theory and social structure.* New York: Free Press, 1957.

Mess'e, L. A., & Lane, I. M. Rediscovering the need for multiple operations: A reply to Austin and Susmilch. *Journal of Personality and Social Psychology.* 1974, *30,* 405–408.

Midlarsky, E. Aiding responses: An analysis and review. *Merrill-Palmer Quarterly.* 1968, *14,* 229–260.

Midlarsky, E., & Bryan, J. H. Training charity in children. *Journal of Personality and Social Psychology.* 1967, *5,* 408–415.

Midlarsky, E., & Bryan, J. H. Affect expressions and children's imitative altruism. *Journal of Experimental Research in Personality.* 1972, *6,* 195–203.

Midlarsky, E., Bryan, J. H., & Brickman, P. Aversive approval: Interactive effects of modeling and reinforcement on altruistic behavior. *Child Development.* 1973, *44,* 321–328.

Milgram, S. Behavioral study of obedience. *Journal of Abnormal and Social Psychology.* 1963, *67,* 371–378.

Milgram, S. Group pressure and action against a person. *Journal of Abnormal and Social Psychology.* 1964, *69,* 137–143.

Milgram, S. Some conditions of obedience and disobedience to authority. *Human Relations.* 1965, *18,* 57–75.

Milgram, S. The lost-letter technique. *Psychology Today.* 1969, *2,* 30–33.

Milgram, S. The experience of living in cities. *Science.* 1970, *167,* 1461–1468.

Milgram, S., *Obedience to authority.* New York: Harper, 1974.

Milgram, S., Bickman, L., & Berkowitz, L. Note on the drawing power of crowds of different size. *Journal of Personality and Social Psychology.* 1969, *13,* 79–82.

Milgram, S. & Toch, H. Collective behavior: Crowds and social movements. In G. Lindzey & E. Aronson (Eds.), *The handbook of social psychology* (Vol. 4). Reading, Mass.: Addison-Wesley, 1969.

Miller, D. T. Ego involvement and attributions for success and failure. *Journal of Personality and Social Psychology.* 1976, *34,* 901–906.

Miller, M. *On being different.* New York: Random House, 1971.

Miller, M. *Plain speaking: An oral biography of Harry S. Truman.* New York: Berkley, 1974.

Miller, N. E. Liberalization of basic S–R concepts. Extensions to conflict behavior, motivation, and social learning. In S. Koch (Ed.), *Psychology: A study of a science* (Vol. 2). New York: McGraw-Hill, 1959.

Miller, N. E., & Bugleski, R. Minor studies in aggression: The influence of frustrations imposed by the in-groups on attitudes expressed toward out-groups. *Journal of Psychology.* 1948, *25,* 437–442.

Mirels, H. L. Dimensions of internal versus external control. *Journal of Consulting and Clinical Psychology.* 1970, *34,* 226–228.

Mischel, W. A social learning view of sex differences. In E. Maccobby (Ed.), *The development of sex differences.* Stanford, Calif.: Stanford University Press, 1966.

Mischel, W. *Personality and assessment.* New York: Wiley, 1968.

Mischel, W. Continuity and change in personality. *American Psychologist.* 1969, *24,* 1012–1018.

Mischel, W. Toward a cognitive social learning reconceptualization of personality. *Psychological Review.* 1973, *80,* 252–283.

Mischel, W. *Introduction to personality.* New York: Holt, 1976.

Mischel, W. On the future of personality measurement. *American Psychologist.* 1977, *32,* 246–254.

Mitchell, H. E., & Byrne, D. The defendant's dilemma: Effects of jurors' attitudes on judicial decisions. *Journal of Personality and Social Psychology.* 1973, *25,* 123–129.

Monahan, L., Kuhn, D., & Shaver, P. Intrapsychic versus culture explanations of the motive to avoid success. *Journal of Personality and Social Psychology.* 1974, *29,* 60–64.

Money, J., & Ehrhardt, A. A. *Man and woman; boy and girl.* Baltimore, Md.: Johns Hopkins Press, 1972.

Money, J., Hampson, J. G., & Hampson, J. L. Imprinting and the establishment of gender role. *A.M.A. Archives of Neurological Psychiatry.* 1957, *77,* 333–336.

Montague, M. F. A. (Ed.). *Man and aggression.* New York: Oxford University Press, 1968.

Moos, R. H. *The human context: Environmental determination of behavior.* New York: Wiley, 1976.

Morgan, M. *The total woman.* Old Tappan. N.J.: Revell Publishing Co., 1973.

Morris, W. N., Worchel, S., Bois, J. L., Pearson, J., Rountree, C. A., Samaha, G. M., Wachtler, J., & Wright, S. L. Collective coping with stress: Group reactions to fear, anxiety and ambiguity. *Journal of Personality and Social Psychology.* 1976. *33,* 674–679.

Morse, N. *Satisfactions in the white collar job.* Ann Arbor, Mich.: Survey Research Center, University of Michigan, 1953.

Morse, N., & Reimer, E. The experimental change of a major organizational variable. *Journal of Abnormal and Social Psychology.* 1956, *52,* 120–129.

Moss, H. A. Sex, age, and state as determinants of mother infant interaction. *Merrill-Palmer Quarterly.* 1967, *13,* 19–36.

Murray, H. A. *Explorations in personality.* New York: Oxford University Press, 1938.

Murray, H. A. *Manual of thematic apperception test.* Cambridge, Mass.: Harvard University Press, 1943.

Murstein, B. I. Physical attractiveness and marital choice. *Journal of Personality and Social Psychology.* 1972, *22,* 8–12.

Mussen, P. H. Long range consequences of masculinity of interests in adolescence. *Journal of Consulting Psychology.* 1962, *26,* 435–440.

Mussen, P. H., Conger, J. J., & Kagan, J. *Child development and personality.* New York: Harper, 1974.

Myers, A. Team competition, success, and the adjustment of group members. *Journal of Abnormal and Social Psychology.* 1962, *65,* 325–332.

Myers, D. G., & Bishop, G. D. Discussion effects on racial attitudes. *Science.* 1970, *169,* 778–789.

Naftulin, D. H., Ware, J. E., & Donelly, F. A. The Doctor Fox lecture: A paradigm of educational seduction. *Journal of Medical Education.* 1973, *48,* 630–635.

National Advisory Commission on Civil Disorders. Report of the National Advisory Committee on Civil Disorders. New York: Bantam Books, 1968.

New York City reflected in its schools. *New York Times.* November 14, 1976.

Newcomb, T. M. *Personality and social change.* New York: Dryden Press, 1943.

Newcomb, T. M. The prediction of interpersonal attraction. *American Psychologist.* 1956, *11,* 575–586.

Newcomb, T. M. *The acquaintance process.* New York: Holt, 1961.

Newcomb, T. M., Koening, K., Flacks, R., & Warwick, D. *Persistence and change: Bennington College and its students after 25 years.* New York: Wiley, 1967.

Neiboer, H. J. *Slavery as an industrial system.* The Hague: Martinus, Nijhoff, 1910.

Nisbett, R. E., & Kanouse, D. E. Obesity, food deprivation and supermarket shopping behavior. *Journal of Personality and Social Psychology.* 1969, *12,* 289–294.

Nord, W. R. Social exchange theory: A integrative approach to social conformity. *Psychological Bulletin.* 1969, *71,* 174–208.

Northrup, H. R. *Organizational labor and the negro.* New York: Harper, 1944.

Norton, W. J. The Detroit riots—and after. *Survey Graphics.* 1943, *32,* 317.

Nuttall, R. L. Some correlates of high need for achievement among urban northern Negroes. *Journal of Abnormal and Social Psychology.* 1964, *68,* 593–600.

Oakes, W. External validity and the use of real people as subjects. *American Psychologist.* 1972, *27,* 959–963.

Orne, M. T. On the social psychology of the psychological experiment: With particular reference to demand characteristics and their implications. *American Psychologist.* 1962, *17,* 776–783.

Orne, M. T. Demand characteristics and quasi-controls. In R. Rosenthal & R. Rosnow (Eds.), *Artifact in behavioral research.* New York: Academic Press, 1969.

Orne, M. T., & Evans, F. J. Social control in the psychological experiment: Antisocial behavior and hypnosis. *Journal of Personality and Social Psychology.* 1965, *1,* 189–200.

Orne, M. T., & Schiebe, K. E. The contribution of non-deprivation factors in the production of sensory deprivation effects: The psychology of the panic button. *Journal of Abnormal and Social Psychology.* 1964, *68,* 3–12.

Osborne, A. F. *Applied imagination.* New York: Scribners, 1957.

Osgood, C. E. *Method and theory in experimental psychology.* New York: Oxford University Press, 1953.

Osgood, C. E. Suggestions for winning the real war with communism. *Journal of Conflict Resolution.* 1959, *3,* 295–325.

Osgood, C. E. *An alternative to war or surrender.* Urbana, Ill.: Univeristy of Illinois Press, 1962.

Osgood, C. E., Suci, G. J. & Tannenbaum, P. H. *The measurement of meaning.* Urbana, Ill.: University of Illinois Press, 1957.

Page, R. H., & McGinnies, E. Comparison of two styles of leadership in small group discussion. *Journal of Applied Psychology.* 1959, *43,* 240–245.

Page, M. M., & Scheidt, R. J. The elusive weapons effect: Demand awareness, evaluation apprehension, and slightly sophisticated subjects. *Journal of Personality and Social Psychology.* 1971, *20,* 304–318.

Pandey, J., & Griffitt W. *Attraction and helping.* Paper presented at meeting of Midwestern Psychological Association, Chicago, 1973.

Papergeorgis, D., & McGuire, W. J., The generality of immunity to persuasion produced by pre-exposure to weakened counterarguments. *Journal of Abnormal and Social Psychology.* 1961, *62,* 475–481.

Parelius, A. P. Emerging sex role attitudes, expectations, and strains among college women. *Journal of Marriage and the Family.* 1975, *37,* 146–153.

Parke, R. D. *Readings in social development.* New York: Holt, 1969.

Parke, R. D., Berkowitz, L., Leyens, J. P., & Sebastian, R. The effects of repeated exposure to movie violence on aggressive behavior in juvenile delinquent boys: Field experimental studies. In L. Berkowitz (Ed.), *Advances in experimental social psychology* (Vol. 10). New York: Academic Press, 1977.

Parke, R. D., Ewall, W., & Slaby, R. G. Hostile and helpful verbalizations as regulators of nonverbal aggression. *Journal of Personality and Social Psychology.* 1972, *23,* 243–248.

Parrott, G., & Bloom, R. Peace marchers, the silent majority and the John Birch Society. Unpublished manuscript, 1971. Cited by M. Rokeach, *The nature of human values.* New York: Free Press, 1973.

Parsons, J. E., Frieze, I. H., & Ruble, D. N. Introduction. *Journal of Social Issues.* 1976, *32,* 1–5.

Patchen, M. A. A conceptual framework and some empirical data regarding comparisons of social rewards. *Sociometry.* 1961, *24,* 136–156.

Patterson, G. R., Ludwig, M., & Sonoda, B. Reinforcement of aggression in children. Cited in W. Bandura and R. H. Walters, *Social learning and personality development.* New York: Holt, 1963.

Pavlov, I. P. *Conditioned Reflexes* (Translated by G. V. Anrep). London: Oxford University Press, 1927.

Pearlman, M. *The capture and trial of Adolph Eichmann.* New York: Simon & Schuster, 1963.

Penner, L. A. Interpersonal attraction toward a black person as a function of value importance. *Personality,* 1971, *2,* 175–187.

Penner, L. A., & Anh, T. A comparison of American and Vietnamese value systems. *Journal of Social Psychology.* 1977, *101,* 187–204.

Penner, L. A., & Dertke, M. C. *A student selected reader in social psychology.* Reading, Mass.: Addison-Wesley, 1972.

Penner, L. A., Dertke, M. C., & Achenbach, C. J. The "flash" system. A field study of altruism.

Journal of Applied Social Psychology. 1973, *3,* 362–370.

Penner, L. A., Hawkins, H. L., Dertkte, M. C., Spector, P., & Stone, A. Obedience as a function of experimenter competence. *Memory and Cognition.* 1973, *1,* 241–245.

Penner, L. A., Michael, D. E., & Brookmire, D. A. The commission of a pro or anti social behavior as a function of the estimates of the costs involved in the behavior. Paper presented at the Southeastern Psychological Association, Atlanta, Ga., 1978.

Penner, L. A., Summers, L., Brookmire, D. A., & Dertke, M. C. The lost dollar: Situational and personality determinants of a pro-and antisocial behavior. *Journal of Personality.* 1976, *44,* 274–293.

Perls, F. *Ego, hunger and aggression.* New York: Random House, 1969.

Pessin, J. The comparitive effects of social and mechanical stimulation on memorizing. *American Journal of Psychology.* 1933, *45,* 263–270.

Peter, L. J., & Hull, R. *The Peter principle.* New York: Morrow, 1969.

Pettigrew, T. F. Social psychology and desegregation research. *American Psychologist.* 1961, *16,* 105–112.

Pettigrew, T. F. *Racially separate or together?* New York: McGraw-Hill, 1971.

Pettigrew, T. L., & Cramer, M. R. The demography of desegregation. *Journal of Social Issues.* 1959, *15,* 61–71.

Phares, E. J. *Locus of control: A personality determinant of behavior.* Morristown, N.J.: General Learning Press, 1973.

Phares, E. J. *Locus of control in personality.* Morristown, N.J.: General Learning Press, 1976.

Pheterson, G. I., Kiesler, S. B., & Goldberg, P. A., Evaluations of the performance of women as a function of their sex, achievement and personal history. *Journal of Personality and Social Psychology.* 1971, *19,* 114–118.

Piacente, B. S. Penner, L. A., Hawkins, H. L., & Cohen, S. L. Evaluation of the performance of experimenters as a function of their sex and competence. *Journal of Applied Social Psychology.* 1974, *4,* 321–329.

Piacente, B. S. Sex role stereotypes as related to

women in psychotherapy. Unpublished manuscript, University of South Florida, 1975.

Piaget, J. *The moral judgment of the child.* London: Kegan Paul, Trech, Trubner & Company, 1932.

Piaget, J., & Inhelder, B. *The psychology of the child.* New York: Basic Books, 1969.

Piliavin, I. M., Rodin, J., & Piliavin, J. A. Good samaritanism: An underground phenomenon? *Journal of Personality and Social Psychology.* 1969, *13,* 289–299.

Piliavin, I. M., Piliavin, J. A., & Rodin, J. Costs, diffusion and the stigmatized victim. *Journal of Personality and Social Psychology.* 1975, *32,* 429–438.

Piliavin, J. A., & Piliavin, I. M. The good samaritan: Why does he help? In L. Wispe (Ed.), *Positive forms of social behavior.* Cambridge, Mass.: Harvard University Press, 1976.

Pilisuk, M., & Skolnick, P. Inducing trust: A test of the Osgood proposal. *Journal of Personality and Social Psychology.* 1968, *8,* 121–133.

Porter, L. W. Job attitudes in management: I: Perceived deficiencies in need fulfillment as a function of job level. *Journal of Applied Psychology.* 1962, *46,* 375–384.

Porter, L. W., & Lawler, E. E., III. The effects of flat and tall organizational structures on managerial job satisfaction. *Personnel Psychology.* 1964, *17,* 135–148.

Porter, L. W., & Lawler, E. E. *Managerial attitudes and performance.* Homewood, Ill.: Irwin-Dorsey, 1968.

Porter, L. W., Lawler, E. E. III, & Hackman, J. R. *Behavior in Organizations.* New York: McGraw-Hill, 1975.

Prien, E. P., & Ronan, W. W. An analysis of organization characteristics. *Organizational Behavior and Human Performance.* 1971, *6,* 215–234.

Prosterman, R. L. *Surviving to 3000: An introduction to the study of lethal conflict.* Belmont, Calif.: Duxbury Press, 1972.

Puzo, M. *The godfather.* Greenwich, Conn: Fawcett, 1969.

Rabbie, J. M., Benoist, F., Oosterbaan, H., & Viser, L. Differential power and effects of expected competitive and cooperative intergroup instructions on intragroup and outgroup attitudes. *Journal of Personality and Social Psychology.* 1974, *30,* 46–56.

Random House College Dictionary. New York: Random House, 1968.

Ransford, H. W. Isolation, powerlessness and violence: A study of attitudes and participation in the Watts riot. *American Journal of Sociology.* 1968, *73,* 581–591.

Rather, D., & Gates, G. P. *The palace guard.* New York: Warner Books, 1975.

Ratner, S. C. Gender through the animal world: The comparative view. In E. Donelson & J. Gullahorn (Eds.), *Women: A psychological perspective.* New York: Wiley, 1977.

Raven, B. H., & Rubin, J. Z. *Social Psychology: People in groups.* New York: Wiley, 1976.

Read, P. P. *Alive.* New York: Avon Books, 1974.

Reckless, W. C. *The crime problem.* Englewood Cliffs, N.J.: Prentice-Hall, 1973.

Regan, D. T. Effects of a favor and liking on compliance. *Journal of Experimental Social Psychology.* 1971, *7,* 627–639.

Regan, D. T., Williams, M., & Sparling, S. Voluntary expiation of guilt. A field experiment. *Journal of Personality and Social Psychology.* 1972, *24,* 42–46.

Reiter, H. H. Prediction of college success from measures of anxiety, achievement motivation, and scholastic aptitude. *Psychological Reports.* 1964. *15,* 23–26.

Ritchie, E., & Phares, E. J. Attitude change as a function of internal-external locus of control and communicator status. *Journal of Personality.* 1969, *37,* 429–443.

Robbins, T. *Even cowgirls get the blues.* Boston: Houghton Mifflin, 1976.

Robins, L. N. The reluctant respondent. *Public Opinion Quarterly.* 1963, *27,* 276–286.

Rogers, R. W., & Mewborn, R. Fear appeals and attitude change: The effects of a threat's noxiousness, probability of occurrence and the efficacy of coping responses. *Journal of Personality and Social Psychology.* 1976, *34,* 54–61.

Rohles, F. H. Environmental psychology: A bucket of worms. *Psychology Today.* 1967, *1,* 55–63.

Rohrer, J. H., Baron, S. H., Hoffman, E. L., & Swander, D. V. The stability of autokinetic judgments. *Journal of Abnormal and Social Psychology.* 1954, *49,* 595–597.

Rokeach, M. *The open and closed mind.* New York: Basic Books, 1960.

Rokeach, M. *Beliefs, attitudes and values* San Francisco; Jossey Bass, 1968.

Rokeach, M. Long-range experimental modification of values, attitudes and behavior. *American Psychologist.* 1971, *26,* 453–459.

Rokeach, M. *The nature of human values.* New York: Free Press, 1973.

Rokeach, M. Change and stability in American value system, 1968–1971. *Public Opinion Quarterly.* 1974, *38,* 222–238.

Rokeach, M., & Kliejunas, P. Behavior as a function of attitude-toward-object and attitude-toward-situation. *Journal of Personality and Social Psychology.* 1972, *22,* 194–201.

Rokeach, M., & McClelland, D. D. Feedback of information about the values and attitudes of self and others as determinants of long-term cognitive and behavioral change. *Journal of Applied Social Psychology.* 1972, *2,* 236–251.

Rokeach, M., & Mezei, L. Race and shared belief as factors in social choice. *Science.* 1966, *151,* 167–172.

Rokeach, M., & Rothman, G. The principle of belief congruence and the congruity principle as models of cognitive interaction. *Psychological Review.* 1965, *72,* 128–172.

Rokeach, M., Smith, P. W., & Evans, R. I. Two kinds of prejudice or one. In M. Rokeach, *The open and closed mind.* New York: Basic Books, 1960.

Rosen, B. C. Race, ethnicity and the achievement syndrome. *American Sociological Review.* 1959, *22,* 185–218.

Rosen, B. C., & D'Andrade, R. The psychological origins of achievement motivations. *Sociometry.* 1959, *22,* 185–218.

Rosenberg, M. *The logic of survey analysis.* New York: Basic Books, 1968.

Rosenberg, M. J. Cognitive structure and attitudinal affect. *Journal of Abnormal and Social Psychology.* 1956, *53,* 367–372.

Rosenberg, M. J. Inconsistency arousal and reduction in attitude change. In I. D. Steiner and M. Fishbein (Eds.), *Current studies in social psychology.* New York: Holt, 1965. (a)

Rosenberg, M. J. When dissonance fails: On eliminating evaluation apprehension from attitude measurement. *Journal of Personality and Social Psychology.* 1965, *1,* 28–42. (b)

Rosenberg, M. J. Conditioning and consequences of evaluation apprehension. In R. Rosenthal and R. Rosnow (Eds.), *Artifact in behavioral research.* New York: Academic Press, 1969.

Rosenberg, M. J., Verba, S., & Converse, P. E. *Vietnam and the silent majority: The dove's guide.* New York: Harper, 1970.

Rosenberg, N. The biological basis for sex role stereotypes. In A. Kaplan and J. Bean (Eds.), *Beyond sex role stereotypes: Readings toward a psychology of androgyny.* Boston: Little, Brown, 1976.

Rosenberg, S., & Sedlak. A. Structural representations of implicit personality theory. In L. Berkowitz (Ed.), *Advances in experimental social psychology* (Vol. 6). New York: Academic Press, 1972.

Rosenhan, D. L. The natural socialization of altruistic autonomy. In J. Macauley and L. Berkowitz (Eds.), *Altruism and helping behavior.* New York: Academic Press, 1970.

Rosenhan, D. L. On being sane in insane places. *Science.* 1973, *179,* 250–258.

Rosenkrantz, P., Vogel, S., Bee, H., Broverman, S., & Broverman, D. Sex role stereotypes and self-concepts in college students. *Journal of Consulting and Clinical Psychology.* 1968, *32,* 287–295.

Rosenthal, R. *Experimenter effects in behavioral research.* New York: Appleton-Century-Crofts, 1966.

Rosenthal, R. Interpersonal expectations: Effects of the experimenter's hypothesis. In R. Rosenthal and R. Rosnow. (Eds.), *Artifact in behavioral research.* New York: Academic Press, 1969.

Rosenthal, R., & Fode, K. L. Three experiments in experimenter bias. *Psychological Reports.* 1963, *12,* 491–511.

Rosenthal, R., & Jacobson, L. *Pygmalion in the Classroom:* Teacher's expectations and pupil's intellectual development. New York: Holt, 1968.

Rosenthal, R., & Rosnow, R. L. *Artifact in behavioral research.* New York: Academic Press, 1969.

Ross, E. A., Thibaut, J., & Evenbeck, S. Some determinants of the intensity of social protest. *Journal of Experimental Social Psychology.* 1971, *7,* 401–408.

Ross, J. M., Vanneman, R. D., & Pettigrew, T. F. Patterns of support for George Wallace: Implications for racial change. *Journal of Social Issues.* 1976, *36,* 69–91.

Rotter, J. B. *Social learning and clinical psychology.* Englewood Cliffs, N.J.: Prentice-Hall, 1954.

Rotter, J. B. Generalized expectancies of internal versus external control of reinforcement. *Psychological Mongraphs.* 1966, *80,* (1 Whole No. 609).

Rotter, J. B. External and internal control. *Psychology Today.* 1970, *5,* 37–42, 58–59.

Rotter, J. B. Some problems and misconceptions related to the construct of internal versus external control of reinforcement. *Journal of Consulting and Clinical Psychology.* 1975, *43,* 56–67.

Royko, M. *Boss: Richard J. Daley of Chicago.* New York: Signet, 1971.

Rubenstein, J. Maternal attentiveness and subsequent exploratory behavior in the infant. *Child Development.* 1967, *38,* 1089–1100.

Rubin, J. Z., Provenzano, F. J., & Luria, Z. The eye of the beholder: Parent's view on sex of newborns. *American Journal of Orthopsychiatry.* 1974, *44,* 512–519.

Rubin, K. H., & Schneider, F. W. The relationship between moral judgment, egocentrism and altruistic behavior. *Child Development,* 1973, *44,* 661–665.

Rubin, Z. Measurement of romantic love. *Journal of Personality and Social Psychology.* 1970, *16,* 265–273.

Rubin, Z. *Liking and loving: An invitation to social psychology.* New York: Holt, 1973.

Rubovitz, P. C., & Maehr, M. L. Pygmalion analyzed: Toward an explanation of the Rosenthal-Jacobson findings. *Journal of Personality and Social Psychology.* 1971, *19,* 197–203.

Rushton, J. P. Generosity in children: Immediate and long-term effects of modeling, preaching, and moral judgment. *Journal of Personality and Social Psychology.* 1975, *31,* 459–466.

Rychlak, J. K. The similarity, compatibility or incompatibility of needs in interpersonal selection. *Journal of Personality and Social Psychology.* 1965, *2,* 334–340.

Sales, S. M. Supervisory style and productivity: Review and theory. *Personnel Psychology.* 1966, *19,* 275–286.

Sales, S. M. Threat as a factor in authoritarianism: An analysis of archival data. *Journal of Personality and Social Psychology.* 1973, *28,* 44–57.

Sanger, S. P., & Alker, H. A. Dimensions of internal-external locus of control and the women's liberation movement. *Journal of Social Issues.* 1972, *28,* 115–129.

Sank, Z. B., & Strickland, B. R. Same attitudinal and behavioral correlates of belief in militant or moderate social action. *Journal of Social Psychology.* 1973, *90,* 337–338.

Sarason, J. G., Smith, R. E., & Diener, E. Personality research: Components of variance attributable to the person and situation. *Journal of Personality and Social Psychology.* 1975, *32,* 199–204.

Sarbin, T. P., & Allen, V. L. Role theory. In G. Lindzey & E. Aronson (Eds.), *Handbook of social psychology* (Vol. 2). Reading, Mass.: Addison-Wesley, 1968.

Sarnoff, I. Psychoanalytic theory and social attitudes. *Public Opinion Quarterly.* 1960, *24,* 251–279.

Schachter, S. Deviation, rejection, and communication. *Journal of Abnormal and Social Psychology.* 1951, *46,* 190–207.

Schachter, S. *The psychology of affiliation.* Stanford, Calif.: Stanford University Press, 1959.

Schacter, S. The interaction of cognitive and physiological determinants of emotional state. In L. Berkowitz (Ed:), *Advances in experimental social psychology* (Vol. 1). New York: Academic Press, 1964.

Schaps, E. Cost, dependency, and helping. *Journal of Personality and Social Psychology.* 1972, *21,* 74–78.

Schein, E. H. *Organizational Psychology.* (2nd ed.) Englewood Cliffs, N.J.: Prentice-Hall, 1970.

Schein, V. E. The relationship between sex role stereotypes and requisite management characteristics. *Journal of Applied Psychology.* 1973, *57,* 95–100.

Schein, V. E. Relationships between sex-role stereotypes and requisite management characteristics among female managers. *Journal of Applied Psychology.* 1975, *60,* 340–344.

Schlossberg, N. K., & Goodman, J. A woman's place: Children's sex stereotyping of occupations. *Vocational Guidance Quarterly.* 1972, *20,* 266–270.

Schlossberg, N. K., & Pietrofesa, J. J. Perspectives on counseling bias: Implications for counselor education. *The Counseling Psychologist.* 1973, *4,* 44–54.

Schmitt, R. C. Density, health and social disorganization. *Journal of American Institute of Planners.* 1966, *32,* 38–40.

Schneider, B. Organizational climate: Individual preferences and organizational realities. *Journal of Applied Psychology.* 1972, *56,* 211–217.

Schneider, B., & Hall, D. T. Toward specifying the concept of work climate: A study of Roman Catholic diocesan priests. *Journal of Applied Psychology.* 1972, *56,* 447–455.

Schopler, J., & Matthews, M. W. The influence of the perceived causal locus of partner's dependence on the use of interpersonal power. *Journal of Personality and Social Psychology.* 1965, *2,* 609–612.

Schuman, H. Social change and the validity of regional stereotypes in East Pakistan. *Sociometry.* 1966, *24,* 428–440.

Schwartz, S. H. Normative explanations of helping behavior: A critique, proposal, and empirical test. *Journal of Experimental Social Psychology.* 1973, *9,* 349–364.

Scott, J. P. *Aggression.* Chicago: University of Chicago Press, 1958.

Scott, J. P. Hostility and aggression. In B. Wolman (Ed.), *Handbook of genetic psychology.* Englewood Cliffs, N.J.: Prentice-Hall, 1972.

Scott, W. G., & Mitchell, T. R. Organization theory: *A structural and behavioral analysis.* (3rd ed.) Homewood, Ill.: Dorsey Press, 1976.

Sears, R. R. Relation of early socialization experiences to self-concepts and gender role in middle childhood. *Child Development.* 1970, *41,* 267–289.

Seaver, W. B. Effects of naturally induced teacher expectancies. *Journal of Personality and Social Psychology.* 1973, *28,* 333–342.

Segal, M. D. Alphabet and attraction: An unobtrusive measure of the effect of propinquity in a field setting. *Journal of Personality and Social Psychology.* 1974, *30,* 654–657.

Selye, H. *The stress of life.* New York: McGraw-Hill, 1956.

Shaver, K. G. *An introduction to the attribution process.* Cambridge, Mass.: Winthrop, 1975.

Shaw, M. A comparison of individuals and small groups in the rational solution of complex problems. *American Journal of Psychology.* 1932, *44,* 491–504.

Shaw, M. E. Communication networks. In L. Berkowitz (Ed.), *Advances in experimental social psychology* (Vol. 1). New York: Academic Press, 1964.

Shaw, M. E. Group dynamics: *The psychology of small group behavior.* New York: McGraw-Hill, 1971.

Shaw, M. E., & Costanzo, P. R. *Theories in social psychology.* New York: McGraw-Hill, 1970.

Sherif, C. W., Sherif, M., & Nebergall, R. E. *Attitude and attitude change: The social judgment-involvement approach.* Philadelphia: Saunders, 1965.

Sherif, M. A study of some social factors in perception. *Archives in Psychology.* 1935, *27,* No. 187.

Sherif, M., Harvey, O. J., White, B. J., Hood, W. E., & Sherif, C. W. *Intergroup conflict and cooperation: The robber's cave experiment.* Norman, Okla.: University of Oklahoma, Book Exchange, 1961.

Sherif, M., & Sherif, C. W. *Social psychology.* New York: Harper, 1969.

Sherman, J. A. *On the psychology of women: A survey of empirical studies.* Springfield, Ill.: Thomas, 1971.

Shibutani, T. *Improvised news.* Indianapolis, Ind.: Bobbs-Merrill, 1966.

Shotland, R. L., & Shaw, M. Bystander response to an assault: When a man attacks a woman. *Journal of Personality and Social Psychology.* 1976, *34,* 990–999.

Sigall, H., & Aronson, E. Liking for an evaluator as a function of her physical attractiveness and nature of the evaluations. *Journal of Experimental Social Psychology.* 1969, *5,* 93–100.

Sigall, H., & Ostrove, N. Beautiful but dangerous: Effects of offender characteristics and nature

of the crime on juridic judgment. *Journal of Personality and Social Psychology.* 1975, *31,* 410–414.

Silverman, B. I., & Cochrane, R. Effect of social context on the principle of belief congruence. *Journal of Personality and Social Psychology.* 1972, *22,* 259–268.

Silverman, I. Physical attractiveness and courtship. *Sexual Behavior.* September, 1971, 22–25.

Silverman, I. Hedonistic considerations concerning altruistic behavior. Paper presented as part of symposium on current perspectives in bystander invervention. Annual Meeting of Southeastern Psychological Association, Hollywood, Florida, 1974.

Silverthorne, C., Chelune, G., & Imada, A. The effects of competition and cooperation on level of prejudice. *Journal of Social Psychology.* 1974, *92,* 293–301.

Simkins, L., & West, J. Reinforcements of duration of talking in triad groups. *Psychological Reports.* 1966, *18,* 231–236.

Simons, H. W., Berkowitz, N. N., & Moyer, R. J. Similarity, credibility and attitude change: A review and a theory. *Psychological Bulletin.* 1970, *73,* 1–16.

Sims, J. H., & Baumann, D. D. The tornado threat: Coping styles of the North and South. *Science.* 1972, *176,* 1386–1392.

Singer, J. D., & Small, M. *The wages of war, 1816–1965: A statistical handbook.* New York: Wiley, 1970.

Singer, J. E., Brush, C. A., & Lublin, S. C. Some aspects of deindividuation, identification and conformity. *Journal of Experimental Social Psychology.* 1965, *1,* 95–100.

Singer, J. L. The influence of violence portrayed in television or motion pictures upon overt aggressive behavior. In J. L. Singer (Ed.), *The control of aggression and violence.* New York: Academic Press, 1971.

Sistrunk, F., & McDavid, J. W. Sex variables in conforming behavior. *Journal of Personality and Social Psychology.* 1971, *17,* 200–207.

Skinner, B. F. Behaviorism at fifty. *Science.* 1963, *140,* 951–958.

Skinner, B. F. *Beyond freedom and dignity.* New York: Knopf, 1971.

Smart, R. G. Subject selection bias in psychological research. *Canadian Psychologist.* 1966, *7,* 115–121.

Smelser, N. J. *Theory of collective behavior.* New York: Free Press, 1963.

Snow, E. *Red star over China.* New York: Grove Press, 1938.

Snyder, C. R., & Shenkel, R. J. The P. T. Barnum effect. *Psychology Today.* 1975, *8,* 52–55.

Snyder, M., & Cunningham, M. R. To comply or not comply: Testing the self-perception explanation of the "foot in the door" phenomenon. *Journal of Personality and Social Psychology.* 1975, *31,* 64–67.

Snyder, M., & Ebbesen, E. B. Dissonance awareness: A test of dissonance theory versus self perception theory. *Journal of Experimental Social Psychology.* 1972, *8,* 502–517.

Snyder, M., & Monson, T. C. Persons, situations, and the control of social behavior. *Journal of Personality and Social Psychology.* 1975, *32,* 637–644.

Solomon, R. L. An extension of control group design. *Psychological Bulletin.* 1949, *46,* 137–150.

Sommer, R. *Personal space.* Englewood Cliffs, N.J.: Prentice-Hall, 1969.

Sosis, R. H. Internal-external control and the perception of responsibility of another for an accident. *Journal of Personality and Social Psychology.* 1974, *30,* 393–399.

Spence, J. T., Helmreich, R., & Stapp, J. The personal attributes questionnaire: A measure of sex role stereotypes, and masculinity and femininity. *Journal Supplement Abstract Service Catalog of Selected Documents in Psychology.* 1974, *4,* 43.

Spielberger, C. D., Gorsuch, R. L., & Lushene, R. E. *Manual for the State-Trait Anxiety Inventory.* Palo Alto, Calif.: Consulting Psychologists Press, 1970.

Spielberger, C. D., O'Hagen, S. E. J., & Kling, J. K. Dimensions of psychopathic personality: Anxiety and sociopathy, In R. Hare & D. Schalling (Eds.), *Psychopathy and behavior.* New York: Wiley, 1977.

Staats, A. W. *Social behaviorism.* Homewood, Ill.: Dorsey Press, 1975.

Staats, A. W., & Staats, C. K. Attitudes estab-

lished by classical conditioning. *Journal of Abnormal and Social Psychology.* 1958, *57,* 37–40.

Staples, R. *Introduction to black sociology.* New York: McGraw-Hill, 1976.

A statistical portrait of women in the United States. Washington, D.C.: U.S. Bureau of the Census, 1976.

Staub, E. A. A child in distress: The influence of nurturance and modeling on children's attempt to help. *Developmental Psychology.* 1971, *5,* 124–132.

Staub, E. A. Helping a distressed person: Social, personality, and stimulus determinants. In L. Berkowitz (Ed.), *Advances in experimental social psychology* (Vol. 7). New York: Academic Press, 1974.

Stein, A. H., & Bailey, M. M. The socialization of achievement in females. *Psychological Bulletin.* 1973, *80,* 345–366.

Stein, A. H., & Friedrich, L. K. Television content and young children's behavior. In J. P. Murray, E. A. Rubinstein, & G. A. Comstock (Eds.), *Television and social behavior (A technical report to the Surgeon General's Advisory Committee on Television and Social Behavior).* Rockville, Md.: National Institute of Health, 1971.

Stein, D. D., Hardyck, J. A., & Smith. M. B. Race and beliefs: An open and shut case. *Journal of Personality and Social Psychology.* 1965, *1,* 281–289.

Steiner, I. D. Models for inferring relationships between groups size and potential group productivity. *Behavioral Science.* 1966, *11,* 273–283.

Sternglanz, S. H., & Serbin, L. A. Sex role stereotyping in children's television programs. In A. Kaplan & J. Bean (Eds.), *Beyond sex role stereotypes: Readings toward a psychology of androgyny.* Boston: Little, Brown, 1976.

Stokols, D. On the distinction between density and crowding: Some implications for future research. *Psychological Review.* 1972, *79,* 275–278.

Stokols, D., Rall, M., Pinner, B., & Schopler, J. Physical, social and personal determinants of the perception of crowding. *Environment and Behavior.* 1973, *5,* 87–115.

Stone, A. V. Vicarious anxiety and altruism in high and low sociopathy individuals. Unpublished doctoral dissertation, University of South Florida, 1977.

Stoner, A. F. A comparison of individual and group decisions involving risk. Unpublished masters thesis, Massachusetts Institute of Technology, 1961.

Stotland, E., & Dunn, R. E. Identification, "oppositeness," authoritarianism, self-esteem and birth order. *Psychological Monographs*. 1962, *76*, No. 528.

Stouffer, S., Suchman, E. A., DeVinney, L. C., Star, S. A., & Williams, R. M., Jr. *Studies in social psychology in World War II. Vol. II, The American soldier: Adjustment during army life*. Princeton, N.J.: Princeton University Press, 1949.

Straus, M. A. Leveling, civility and violence in the family. *Journal of Marriage and the Family*. 1974, *36*, 13–29.

Strickland, B. R. The prediction of social action from a dimension of internal-external control. *Journal of Social Psychology*. 1965, *66*, 353–358.

Strickland, B. R., & Crowne, D. P. Conformity under conditions of simulated group pressure as a function of need for approval. *Journal of Social Psychology*. 1962, *58*, 171–181.

Sue, S., & Smith, R. E. How not to get a fair trial. *Psychology Today*. 1974, *7*, 86–90.

Suedfeld, P. Birth order of volunteers for sensory deprivation. *Journal of Abnormal and Social Psychology*. 1964, *68*, 195–196.

Swart, C., & Berkowitz, L. Effects of a stimulus associated with a victim's pain on later aggression. *Journal of Personality and Social Psychology*. 1976, *33*, 623–631.

Tampa Tribune, October 25, 1975.

Tarde, G. *The laws of imitation*. New York: Holt, 1903.

Task force on sex bias and sex role stereotyping in psychotherapeutic practice. Report. *American Psychologist*. 1975, *30*, 1169–1175.

Taylor, D. W., Berry, P. C., & Block, C. Does group participation when using brainstorming facilitate or inhibit creative thinking? *Administrative Science Quarterly*. 1958, *3*, 23–47.

Taylor, F. W. *The principles of scientific management*. New York: Harper, 1911.

Taylor, S. E. On inferring one's attitudes from one's behavior: Some delimiting conditions. *Journal of Personality and Social Psychology*. 1975, *31*, 126–131.

Tavris, C. Who likes women's liberation—and why: The case of the unliberated liberals. *Journal of Social Issues*. 1973, *29*, 175–198.

Taynor, J., & Deaux, K. Equity and perceived sex differences: Role behavior as defined by the tasks, the mode and the actor. *Journal of Personality and Social Psychology*. 1975, *32*, 381–390.

Teresa, V. *My life in the Mafia*. Greenwich, Conn.: Fawcett, 1973.

Terkel, S. *Division Street: America*. New York: Avon Books, 1967.

Terkel, S. *Working,* New York: Pantheon Books, 1974.

Thayer, S. Lend my your ears: Racial and sexual factors in helping the deaf. *Journal of Personality and Social Psychology*. 1973, *28*, 8–11.

The new gray line. *Newsweek*. December 1, 1975.

Thibaut, J. W., & Kelley, H. H. *The social psychology of groups*. New York: Wiley, 1959.

Thomas, A. H., & Stewart, N. R. Counselor response to female clients with deviate and conforming career goals. *Journal of Counseling Psychology*. 1971, *18*, 352–357.

Thomas, L. E. The I–E Scale, ideological bias, and political participation. *Journal of Personality*. 1970, *38*, 273–286.

Thorndike, E. L. *Animal Intelligence*. New York: Macmillan, 1911.

Thurstone, L. L. Attitudes can be measured. *American Journal of Sociology*. 1928, *33*, 529–554.

Thurstone, L. L., & Chave, E. J. *The measurement of attitude*. Chicago: University of Chicago Press, 1929.

Tiger, L. *Men in groups*. New York: Random House, 1969.

Toch, H. *The social psychology of social movements*. New York: Bobbs-Merrill, 1965.

Triandis, H. C. A note on Rokeach's theory of prejudice. *Journal of Abnormal and Social Psychology*. 1961, *62*, 184–186.

Triandis, H. C. *Attitude and attitude change*. New York: Wiley, 1971.

Triandis, H. C., & Davis, E. Race and belief as determinants of behavioral intentions. *Jour-*

nal of Personality and Social Psychology. 1965, *2,* 715–725.

Triplett, N. The dynamogenic factors in pacemaking and competition. *American Journal of Psychology.* 1897, *9,* 507–533.

Trist, E. L., & Bamforth, K. W. Some social and psychological consequences of the long wall method of coalgetting. *Human Relations.* 1951, *4,* 1–38.

Turner, R. H., & Killian, L. M. *Collective behavior.* Englewood-Cliffs, N.J.: Prentice-Hall, 1972.

T. V. on trial. *Newsweek,* September 12, 1977.

United Methodist women's television monitoring project. Reported at Meeting of Women's Division of the Board of Global Ministries, Chicago, Illinois, March 1976.

Valins, S. Cognitive effects of false heart-rate feedback. *Journal of Personality and Social Psychology.* 1966, *4,* 400–408.

Veroff, J., & Peele, S. Initial effects of desegregation on the achievement motivation of Negro elementary school children. *Journal of Social Issues.* 1969, *25,* 71–91.

Vroom, V. H. *Some personality determinants of the effects of participation.* Englewood Cliffs, N.J.: Prentice-Hall, 1960.

Vroom, V. H. *Work and motivation.* New York: Wiley, 1964.

Vroom, V. H. Decision making and the leadership process. *Journal of Contemporary Business.* Autumn, 1974, 47–64.

Vroom, V. H., & Yetton, P. W. *Leadership and decision-making.* Pittsburgh: University of Pittsburgh Press, 1973.

Wagner, C., & Wheeler, L. Model, need and cost effects in helping behavior. *Journal of Personality and Social Psychology.* 1969, *12,* 111–116.

Walker, C. R., & Guest, R. H. The man on the assembly line. *Harvard Business Review.* 1952, *30,* 71–83.

Walker, M. Organization type, rites of incorporation and group solidarity: A study of fraternity hell week. *Dissertation Abstracts.* 1968, *29* (2-A), 689–690.

Wallace, J., & Sadalla, E. Behavioral consequences of transgression I: The effects of social recognition. *Journal of Experimental Research in Personality.* 1966, *1,* 187–194.

Wallach, M. A., Kogan, N., & Bem, D. J. Group

influence on individual risk taking. *Journal of Abnormal and Social Psychology.* 1962, *65,* 75–86.

Wallach, M. A., Kogan, N., & Bem, D. J., Diffusion of responsibility and level of risk taking in groups. *Journal of Abnormal and Social Psychology.* 1964, *68,* 263–274.

Walster, E., Aronson, E., & Abrahams, D. On increasing the persuasiveness of a low prestige communicator. *Journal of Experimental Social Psychology.* 1966, *4,* 508–516.

Walster, E., Berscheid, E., & Walster, G. W. New directions in equity research. *Journal of Personality and Social Psychology.* 1973, *25,* 151–176.

Walters, R. H., & Brown, M. Studies of reinforcement of aggression III: Transfer of responses to an interpersonal situation. *Child Development.* 1963, *34,* 563–571.

Wapner, S., & Alper, J. G. The effect on an audience on behavior in a choice situation. *Journal of Abnormal and Social Psychology.* 1952, *47,* 222–229.

Ward, L. M., & Suedfeld, P. Human responses to highway noise. *Environmental Research.* 1973, *6,* 306–316.

Watts, W. A., & McGuire, W. J. Persistence of induced opinion change and retention of the inducing message contents. *Journal of Abnormal and Social Psychology.* 1964, *68,* 233–241.

Weatherly, D. Anti-semitism and the expression of fantasy aggression. *Journal of Abnormal and Social Psychology.* 1961, *62,* 454–457.

Webb, A. P. Sex role preferences and adjustment in early adolescents. *Child Development.* 1963, *34,* 609–618.

Webb, E. J., Campbell, D. T., Schwartz, R. D., & Sechrest, L. *Unobtrusive measures: Nonreactive research in the social sciences.* Chicago, Ill.: Rand-McNally, 1966.

Weber, M. *The theory of social and economic organization* (Translated by A. M. Henderson & T. Parsons). T. Parsons (Ed.). New York: Free Press, 1947.

Weber, S. J., & Cook, T. D. Subject effects in laboratory research: An examination of subject roles, demand characteristics, and valid inference. *Psychological Bulletin.* 1972, *77,* 273–295.

Webster's New World Dictionary of the American Language. New York: World Publishing, 1953.

Wegner, D. M., & Crano, W. D. Racial factors in helping behavior: An unobtrusive measure. *Journal of Personality and Social Psychology.* 1975, *32,* 901–905.

Weick, K. E. The concept of equity in the perception of pay. *Administrative Science Quarterly.* 1966, *11,* 414–439.

Weigel, R. H., Vernon, D. T. A., & Tognaci, L. N. Specificity of attitude as a determinant of attitude behavior consequences. *Journal of Personality and Social Psychology.* 1974, *30,* 724–728.

Weiner, M. J., & Wright, F. E. Effects of undergoing arbitrary discrimination upon subsequent attitudes toward a minority group. *Journal of Applied Social Psychology.* 1973, *3,* 94–102.

Weiss, R. F., Boyer, J. L., Lombardo, J. P., & Stitch, M. H. Altruistic drive and altruistic reinforcement. *Journal of Personality and Social Psychology.* 1973, *25,* 390–400.

Weitzman, L., Eifler, D., Hokada, E., & Ross, C. Sex role socialization in picture books for preschool children. *American Journal of Sociology.* 1972, *77,* 1125–1150.

Wells, W. D. Television and aggression: Replication of an experimental field study. Unpublished manuscript, University of Chicago, 1973.

West, S. G., Gunn, S. P., & Chernicky, P. Ubiquitous Watergate: An attributional analysis. *Journal of Personality and Social Psychology.* 1975, *32,* 55–65.

The White House transcripts. New York: Bantam Books, 1974.

White, R. K. *Nobody wanted war.* New York: Doubleday, 1970.

White, R. K. Misperception in the Arab-Israeli conflict. *Journal of Social Issues.* 1977, *33,* 190–221.

White, R., & Lippitt, R. *Autocracy and democracy: An experimental inquiry.* New York: Harper, 1960.

White, T. H. *The making of the president, 1960.* New York: Atheneum, 1961.

White, T. H. *Breach of faith: The fall of Richard Nixon.* New York: Atheneum, 1975.

Wicker, A. W. Attitudes vs. actions: The relation-ship of verbal and overt behavioral responses to attitude objects. *Journal of Social Issues.* 1969, *25,* 41–78.

Wicker, A. W. & Pomazal, R. J. The relationship between attitudes and behavior as a function of specificity of attitude object and presence of a significant person during assessment conditions. *Representative Research in Social Psychology.* 1971, *2,* 26–31.

Wilensky, H. Varieties of work experience. In H. Borow (Ed.), *Man in a world at work.* Boston, Mass.: Houghton Mifflin, 1964.

Wicker, T. *A time to die.* New York: Ballantine, 1975.

Will, J. A., Self, P. A., & Datan, N. Maternal behavior and perceived sex of infant. *American Journal of Orthopsychiatry.* 1976, *46,* 135–139.

Williams, J. H. *Psychology of women: Behavior in a biosocial context.* New York: Norton, 1977.

Williams, R. M. *The reduction of intergroup tensions.* Social science research council bulletin. No. 57. New York: Social Science Research Council, 1947.

Willis, R. H. Two dimensions of conformity-nonconformity. *Sociometry.* 1963, *26,* 499–513.

Willis, R. H. Conformity, independence, and anticonformity. *Human Relations.* 1965, *18,* 373–389.

Willis, R. H. Diamond model of social response. In W. Sahakian (Ed.), *Social psychology: Experimentation, theory, research.* Scranton, Pa.: Intext Educational Publishers, 1972.

Wilner, D. M., Walkley, R., & Cook, S. W. *Human relations in interracial housing: A study of the contact hypothesis.* Minneapolis, Minn.: University of Minnesota Press, 1955.

Wilson, E. *Sociobiology: The new synthesis.* Cambridge, Mass.: Harvard University Press, 1975.

Winch, R. F. *The modern family.* New York: Holt, 1952.

Winsborough, H. H. The social consequences of high population density. *Law and Contemporary Problems.* 1965, *30,* 120–126.

Winterbottom, M. R. The relation of need for achievement to learning experiences in independence and mastery. In J. W. Atkinson (Ed.), *Motives in fantasy, action and society.* Princeton, N.J.: Van Nostrand, 1958.

Wirtenberg, T. J., & Nakamura, C. Y. Education: Barrier or boon to changing occupational roles of women? *Journal of Social Issues*. 1976, *32*, 165–179.

Wishner, J. Reanalysis of "impressions of personality." *Psychological Review*. 1960, *67*, 96–112.

Wispe, L. G. Positive forms of social behavior: An overview. *Journal of Social Issues*. 1972, *28*, 1–19.

Wispe, L. G., & Thompson, J. N. The war between the words: Biological versus social evolution and some related issues. *American Psychologist*. 1976, *31*, 341–348.

Wood, D., Pilisuk, M., & Uren, E. The martyr's personality: An experimental investigation. *Journal of Personality and Social Psychology*. 1973, *25*, 177–186.

Woodward, J. *Management and technology*. London: H. M. Stationary Office, 1958.

Woodward, R., & Bernstein, C. *The final days*. New York: Simon & Shuster, 1976.

Worchel, S., & Teddlie, C. The experience of crowding: A two factor theory. *Journal of Personality and Social Psychology*. 1976, *34*, 30–40.

Worthy, J. C. Organizational structure and employee morale. *American Sociological Review*. 1950, *15*, 169–179.

Wrightsman, L. S. Wallace supporters and adherence to law and order. *Journal of Personality and Social Psychology*. 1969, *13*, 17–22.

Wyer, R. S., Jr. Effects of incentive to perform well, group attraction, and group acceptance on conformity in a judgmental task. *Journal of Personality and Social Psychology*. 1966, *4*, 21–26.

Yaffe, Y., Malamuth, N., Feingold, J., & Feshbach, S. Sexual arousal and behavioral aggression. *Journal of Personality and Social Psychology*. 1974, *30*, 759–765.

Yarrow, M. R., Waxler, C. Z., & Scott, P. M., Child affects on adult behavior. *Developmental Psychology*. 1971, *5*, 300–311.

Zajonc, R. B. The concepts of balance, congruity, and dissonance. *Public Opinion Quarterly*. 1960, *24*, 280–296.

Zajonc, R. B. Social facilitation. *Science*. 1965, *149*, 269–274.

Zanna, M. P., Kiesler, C. A., & Pilkonis, P. A. Positive and negative attitudinal affect established by classical conditioning. *Journal of Personality and Social Psychology*. 1970, *14*, 321–328.

Zeilberger, J., Sampen, S. E., & Sloane, H. N. Modification of a child's problem behaviors in the home with the mother as therapist. *Journal of Applied Behavior Analysis*. 1968, *1*, 47–53.

Zillman, D. Excitation transfer in communication-mediated aggressive behavior. *Journal of Experimental Social Psychology*. 1971, *7*, 419–434.

Zimbardo, P. G. The human choice: Individuation, reason and order versus deindividuation, impulse and chaos. In W. J. Arnold & D. Levine (Eds.), *Nebraska symposium on motivation, 1969*. Lincoln, Neb.: University of Nebraska Press, 1970.

Zimbardo, P. G. Vandalism: An act in search of a cause. In P. Zimbardo & C. Maslach, (Eds.), *Psychology for our times*. Glenview, Ill.: Scott, Foresman, 1973. (a)

Zimbardo, P. G. The psychological power and pathology of imprisonment. In E. Aronson & R. Helmreich (Eds.), *Social psychology*. New York: Van Nostrand, 1973. (b)

Zipf, S. G. Resistance and conformity under reward and punishment. *Journal of Abnormal and Social Psychology*. 1960, *61*, 102–109.

NAME INDEX

SUBJECT INDEX